ALCOHOL & ALCOHOLISM

PAPERS PRESENTED AT THE INTERNATIONAL SYMPOSIUM IN
MEMORY OF E. M. JELLINEK, SANTIAGO, CHILE

Alcohol &
Alcoholism

EDITED BY
ROBERT E. POPHAM

PUBLISHED FOR
THE ADDICTION RESEARCH FOUNDATION BY
UNIVERSITY OF TORONTO PRESS

Published in Spanish under the editorship of
Jorge Mardones and Aníbal Varela by the Cen-
tro de Publicaciones Biológicas de la Universidad de Chile, Santiago, as Supplement No. 3
of the Archivos de Biológia y Medicina
Experimental

Preface

The editor's willingness to accept responsibility, on behalf of himself and the Addiction Research Foundation, for the English edition of these proceedings stemmed from three considerations. First, the International Symposium was held in honour of the late Dr. E. M. Jellinek and, as noted in the tribute address by Mr. David Archibald, the program of the Foundation owes much to Jellinek's ideas and personal involvement. Publication of the proceedings under Foundation auspices therefore seemed an appropriate and tangible way to mark our particular indebtedness to him.

Secondly, and partly as a consequence of Jellinek's influence, we have long been concerned to encourage greater interest among North American scholars in the experiences and researches of their colleagues in other countries. That an international perspective is of crucial importance to the understanding of alcohol problems is now well established. But while the work of European students has become much better known on this continent in recent years, that of our Latin American *confrères* is still comparatively neglected. Since many distinguished Central and South American specialists participated in the Symposium, publication of their contributions in English offered the means to help remedy this deficiency.

A third consideration was the potential of the proceedings as the basis of a supplementary reading text for use in schools of alcohol studies and in university courses dealing in part with alcohol problems. A few such texts exist but are concerned mainly with social and psychological aspects. Without neglecting these points, the International Symposium stressed the areas of pharmacology, pathology, and psychiatry. Its proceedings are therefore better suited to the needs of those with a prospective medical interest in the field, whether from the standpoint of research, treatment, education, or the development of comprehensive programs embracing all these activities.

With this educative potential in mind, efforts were made to standardize the presentation of tabular, graphic, and bibliographic data; to check the accuracy of references and bring them up to date where necessary; and to compile a more than usually comprehensive subject index as well as a separate author listing.

It may be objected that conference papers are unsuitable for teaching purposes because the papers are too highly specialized and largely unselected: each author decides what to present and reports on a single piece of original work. However, in the present instance the organizers of the Symposium decided beforehand which topics should be covered and invited an appropriate authority to deal with each one. Contributors were free to report original work if relevant, and many did so. But they were also asked to review the current status of knowledge in their subject areas. Consequently, most papers are suitably general in character and comprise, on the whole, a logical series covering the field within the broad limits previously indicated.

It may be feared that the papers will now be somewhat out of date, since the Symposium was held in August 1966. This is more likely to be a concern of the experimentalist than of the clinician or behavioural scientist. It must be remembered that, since the study of alcohol problems is a multidisciplinary effort, what is standard knowledge to one's immediate colleagues may take a very long time to reach others in different parts of the field. In any event, each paper was returned to its author after editing, and although authors were requested to avoid major changes if possible, updating through the addition of new references and footnotes was invited. Since this process was concluded during the winter of 1969, the editor has some confidence in the current applicability of the material.

On behalf of the Organizing Committee, its president Professor Jorge Mardones, and all the participants, it is a pleasure to acknowledge indebtedness to the sponsors of the Symposium. These were: the Panamerican Health Organization, the Government of Chile through the University of Chile and the National Health Service, the International Council on Alcohol and Alcoholism, the International Union of Pharmacology, the Latin American Association of Physiological Sciences, the Medical College of Chile, the Medical Society of Santiago, the Biological Society of Chile, the Chilean Society of Neurology, Psychiatry, and Neurosurgery, and the Chilean Public Health Society. Without the support, financial and otherwise, of these organizations the Symposium could not have been held.

Lastly, the editor wishes to express his personal gratitude to a number of persons who assisted in the preparation of this volume of the proceedings. Professor Mardones obtained copies of the papers as presented, and provided translations of those given in Spanish or French. The staff of the Addiction Research Foundation checked and revised most of the bibliographies (Mr. R. K. Young), and redrew many of the figures (Mrs. J. A. E. Moreau). Dr. Harold Kalant responded with characteristic patience and helpfulness to frequent requests for advice on pharmacological and medical points. Mr. Gerald Brougham prepared the indexes, and the laborious task of retyping the edited manuscript was executed very competently by Mrs. Jean Zwingli and Mrs. Sylvia Jaychuk. I also wish to offer my sincere thanks to Mr. Jan Schreiber and his colleagues on the editorial staff of the University of Toronto Press. Their painstaking and skilful preparation of the manuscript for the typesetter caught many errors, inconsistencies, and unclear statements which otherwise might have been overlooked.

R.E.P.
August 1969

Contents

Tributes to E. M. Jellinek

The inaugural session of the Symposium constituted a memorial to the late Dr. E. M. Jellinek and was held in the Aula Magna of the University of Chile. Presiding were the Minister of Education of Chile, Mr. Juan Gómez Millas, and the Minister of Public Health, Dr. Ramon Valdivieso. Dr. Amador Neghme, Dean of the Faculty of Medicine of the University of Chile, represented the Rector of the University, and Mrs. Joy Moser represented the Director of the World Health Organization. Also presiding were Dr. Abraham Horwitz, Director of the Pan American Sanitary Bureau, Mr. Archer Tongue, Director of the International Council on Alcohol and Alcoholism, Dr. Francisco Mardones, Director of the National Health Service of Chile, and Dr. Emilio Villarroel, President of the Medical College of Chile. The following tributes to the life and work of E. M. Jellinek were presented on this occasion.

On behalf of the Chilean institutions sponsoring this Symposium, and of the Organizing Committee, it is with the greatest pleasure that I extend a sincere welcome to our distinguished visitors. Many have come great distances to this city, one of the most remote in the Occidental world, to contribute their knowledge and experience to the success of the symposium. I should like to express to all our best wishes for a pleasant stay in this country and for an intellectually fruitful meeting.

The thought that a symposium on alcohol and alcoholism might be a fitting memorial to the late Dr. E. M. Jellinek has been in the mind of many of his friends since the sad news of his death. This is because we considered that the best homage we could pay to his memory would be a collective contribution to knowledge of the problems of alcohol, following the paths he himself opened.

If one thing could be said to characterize the work of Jellinek, it would be his keen analytic ability, which allowed him not only to discover new facts, but to establish order among the known ones and to differentiate clearly between a valid judgment and a misinterpretation of the evidence.

When he focussed on the problems of alcohol and the variations in the character of alcoholism in different cultures, he enlightened the field in such a way that new avenues for research were opened and

E.M. Jellinek, 1890–1963

the relative importance of different areas appeared clear.

Subsequent speakers will analyse different aspects of Jellinek's personality and the importance of his contribution to the problem of alcoholism. But his Chilean friends want to emphasize the influence that his knowledge, his research ability, his co-operative mind, and his fine personality had upon those who worked with him in the study of alcoholism.

During his brief stay in Chile he gave us useful orientations for the better understanding of our alcohol problems. More than that, he encouraged us to continue our research work by showing how much still remained to be known, and by teaching us how the efficiency of the procedures for the prevention and treatment of alcoholism could be considerably improved when the main unknowns were resolved.

Following Jellinek's example, which was not to disdain the study of any aspect of the problems of alcohol, the program of this symposium has been developed to bring together persons with widely differing interests. These range from the metabolism and cellular actions of ethanol to the sociological and epidemiological problems of alcoholism. We hope that the conjunction of varying points of view will result in the emergence of new ideas and new lines of research.

We are aware that we Chileans will receive the greatest benefit from this symposium. Without it few of us would ever have the opportunity to listen to the teachings of the prominent scientists who honoured us by accepting our invitation to attend, and few would be able to participate in discussions which are sources of new ideas and new views and are therefore an inspiration for the researcher.

For this reason in particular I should like to acknowledge with gratitude all those persons and organizations who, through their financial and other support, have made the symposium possible, and to thank most warmly those participants who, moved by a spirit of international co-operation, are bringing to us their special knowledge of the problems of common interest.

JORGE MARDONES
Institute of Studies on Alcoholism
University of Chile, Santiago, Chile

It is a very great honour for me to have been selected by Dr. Mardones to take part in this splendidly convened symposium in memory of E. M. Jellinek. It is equally an exquisite pleasure to have the opportunity, through my special assignment in the program, to speak about E. M. Jellinek. It was my good fortune to be associated with him, as colleague and as friend, for nearly 25 years – memorable years, when history was made in the field of alcohol problems. Since others too will speak of Jellinek and of those times, I shall not try to detail that entire history. I propose rather to try to place the contributions of E. M. Jellinek in historical perspective: not just his own original and brilliant studies but also those which he initiated for others to carry out and those which he inspired, stimulated, and influenced. I hope to do more than merely name the parts and praise the maker of much scientific and scholarly progress in this field. I should like, if possible, to suggest the integral meaning in this remarkable career.

Picture the situation in which Jellinek found himself in the late 1930s. We might think of it as a United States of America situation, but actually the whole Western world was involved. During about a century a powerful anti-alcohol movement had gained a position of such dominance that with respect to alcohol hardly any word was heard in public and official life except that it was an unmitigated evil, the source of every trouble which burdened mankind, and that the only decent resolution for civilized people was to fight it and abolish it. If there was a tendency in the nineteenth century for science and religion to move apart, at least with respect to the damnation of alcohol they could still make common cause. In this atmosphere responsive politicians in many countries besides the United States attempted the solution proposed by the organized anti-alcohol movement: prohibition. This solution, as you know, failed repeatedly. In the United States, to which I revert now in order to come back to Jellinek, a crushing failure ultimately resulted in the dramatic reamendment of the Constitution in 1933 to repeal national prohibition and substitute a modified control under a variety of state and more localized systems.

Great was the concern of many thoughtful citizens lest the old evils which prohibition had hardly remedied would now flourish. Many of them realized that in fact society lacked the knowledge for coping with the problems of alcohol; for the one thing which had not been done, which had indeed been inhibited by the anti-alcohol movement, was to try to learn about alcohol. In the mid-1930s, therefore, a group of foresighted citizens, especially scientists from a variety of disciplines, organized the Research Council on Problems of Alcohol. (I may note that its usefulness became impaired in the late 1940s – I think through short-sightedness and lack of statesmanship in the alcoholic beverage industry – and it was then disbanded.)

In the meantime, in a special medical service of what was then called the Bellevue Psychiatric Hospital in New York (operated by the New York University College of Medicine) the young physician in charge, Norman Jolliffe, had launched an ambitious and fruitful series of researches on the diseases of the thousands of alcoholic patients who were admitted each year to that hospital. It was in this connection that I came into the picture: as an editor of early reports on the research, as an organizer of the growing mass of data which was becoming difficult to manage, and as a documenter of the relevant literature. But as Jolliffe and his staff helped to unravel the nutritional nature of some of the so-called alcoholic diseases, he came to realize that the fundamental disease of his patients was alcoholism itself – their inability to resist trying to drink, and their inability then to control the drinking. At this time we designed a grand interdisciplinary research into the etiology of alcoholism. We did not succeed in getting the money to carry it out, but the scientific advisory committee that was formed to sponsor it became the backbone of the Scientific Advisory Committee of the Research Council on Problems of Alcohol.

This Advisory Committee sponsored a project – dearly desired by Norman Jolliffe – to review the knowledge about alcohol and alcoholism, especially the biological knowledge, as it existed in the scientific literature. With a $25,000 grant from the Carnegie Corporation to the New York University College of Medicine, and with Jolliffe as medical director, supported by Dr. Karl M. Bowman as psychiatric director, by 1939 we were ready to begin the grand review. But we needed more help. And this is how it happened that E. M. Jellinek was brought into the field. Jolliffe went to the Worcester State Hospital in Massachusetts and lured E. M. Jellinek

away from Hoskins and his research on neuroendocrine aspects of schizophrenia. So Jellinek was switched to the medical-psychiatric aspects of alcoholism.

It could have happened that our staff would examine more than 5,000 articles, abstract about half of them, write a series of reviews, and then close up shop. In fact it nearly happened that way in spite of Jellinek's awareness of the potentials for a different and remarkable development. For there was no provision in our grant for continuity – and I remember that as our funds were expiring, Jellinek discussed with me the possibility of our going into business together as research consultants. But here Dr. Howard W. Haggard stepped into the picture and offered Jellinek the opportunity to come to Yale. Thus was laid the foundation of what was to become the Yale Center of Alcohol Studies.

What was it that Jellinek had started, which was to become a world-embracing achievement of scholarship and scientific progress?

First, when it became evident that existing knowledge about alcohol was scattered in all the books and periodicals of all the scientific disciplines in all languages throughout the world, he immediately began to devise a system for its management and control. This system was to become the Classified Abstract Archive of the Alcohol Literature. We subsequently modified this considerably so that we could establish Depositories of the Archive – now there are more than 50 in some 15 countries – but the essential idea was devised by Jellinek in 1939. It consists of a topical code which is notched around the edges of the card (on which we now also print the informative abstract); thus references and abstracts on any topic can be obtained very quickly. His next decision was to begin to compile a sort of universal bibliography (I informally named it the Master Bibliography), and actually its first volume was published in 1966, 27 years after we started it, as the *International Bibliography of Studies on Alcohol*.

The immediate outcome of the year and a half spent in that first grand literature review was a series of chapters published in the newly founded *Quarterly Journal of Studies on Alcohol*. One of these was the brilliant and now classical review of psychological experiments written by Jellinek and Ross McFarland. The other six reviews, including chapters on alcohol addiction and its treatment, alcoholic mental disorders, vitamin deficiencies in alcoholism, and cirrhosis of the liver, with Jellinek as coauthor of three of them, were then gathered into a book – *Effects of Alcohol on the Individual: Volume I. Alcohol Addiction and Chronic Alcoholism* – which was to become the fountainhead of knowledge in the field for the next generation. This book was published at Yale in 1942.

In the meantime we were building up the *Quarterly Journal of Studies on Alcohol* as a repository of new knowledge, and laying the foundations for what was to become the total documentation system in the field of alcohol problems. I pause to put emphasis on this because it was Jellinek's uncommon foresight to recognize the value of an indexed collection of abstracts, of a systematic control of bibliography, and of interdisciplinary publication, as indispensable tools for progress in the accumulation, dissemination, and application of scientific knowledge. The enormous value of this system has proved itself a thousand times in recent years when the burgeoning activity in this field, as in others, has threatened to swamp success by excess. But the control which a systematic documentation allows removes the imagined danger of too much knowledge. In fact, there is no such thing as too much knowledge; only confusion is too much.

What was it that Jellinek perceived which was to be so vital for this field, and which led him to work to establish these foundations? It was the history which I mentioned previously – the unfortunate dead-weight influence of the rigid anti-alcohol movement. Jellinek realized that if civilized society were ever to become able to cope successfully with the problems of alcohol, then science must replace sheer emotion as the basic means of coping. And that was what he adopted as his special cause: to replace the headless emotionalism of the century-old anti-alcohol movement with what was to be called the scientific approach.

How skillfully, learnedly, wittily he conducted this campaign! If I had several hours I could hardly detail and analyse each succeeding step, so I shall only be able to touch on some outstanding examples. In 1943 he started and conducted a Summer School of Alcohol Studies. Just last month it held its twenty-fourth annual session at Rutgers University with some 300 students in attendance, mostly professionals, and including 40 physicians. In the second year of the School its students included representatives of the anti-alcohol movement and of the liquor industry, and Jellinek succeeded in keeping both sides happy together – an achievement in statesmanship which gained nationwide notice. He was soon involved in founding the first American national volunteer health association concerned with alcoholism (now the National Council on Alcoholism), and then in initiating the model public clinics for the treatment of alcoholics – the famed Yale Plan Clinics. Later he had an important role in founding the North American Association of Alcoholism Programs – the organization of state and Canadian provincial agencies which has a major responsibility in the preparations for the next International Congress on Alcoholism to be held in Washington.

But while he was an active adviser and leader in all these steps, Jellinek was also working as scientist and protagonist of science. His bibliography, counting unduplicated publications, and limited to the alcohol field, consists of more than 90 items.* Some are popular essays, including a charming version of Doctor Masserman's experiments with neurotic cats, and a group of popular pamphlets. In addition there are a number of lectures which summarize, analyse, and interpret scientific knowledge with a critical insight and skill which was exquisitely convincing. I might cite, for example, his lecture on the heredity of alcoholism. There is also a series of commentaries on what he called Classics of the Alcohol Literature, in which he demonstrated his vast classical scholarship. As examples one may cite his notes on Seneca, Sebastian Franck, Montaigne, Immanuel Kant, and Erasmus Darwin.

Most important of all are the reports of his original researches: the interpretation of alcohol consumption rates; an analysis of death from alcoholism; trends in alcoholism and in alcohol consumption; distribution of alcohol consumption and of calories derived from alcohol in various populations. This group of statistical studies, published between 1942 and 1955, together with the first great analysis of liver cirrhosis statistics with Norman Jolliffe, mentioned previously, constitute one type of study in which he excelled. He taught us all how to handle alcohol statistics sensibly and how to interpret them rationally. But of course, in this realm, it will seem that his outstanding contribution was

*A bibliography of Jellinek's publications on alcohol and alcoholism is provided at the end of this book.

the famous Jellinek Estimation Formula. He did not think so, and I agreed with him, and I always thought it was rather a pity that his name and fame should be hinged on this device. Indeed, it was a clever invention, and it worked. But I think that the profounder analysis of his works will prove that his other statistical and biometrical productions were enormously more important, and that we can still learn a great deal from them. If you want to read painless reasoning on statistical information, read any of E. M. Jellinek's leading statistical analyses.

Another, quite different, class of Jellinek scientific contributions consists of his writings on alcoholism. These began with the two articles he co-authored with K. M. Bowman out of the first great review made in 1939–40: "Alcohol Addiction and Its Treatment" and "Alcoholic Mental Disorders." I can demonstrate what a remarkable man this was, what a brilliant student, by revealing a little-known fact. When Jolliffe brought Jellinek to New York in 1939, Jellinek did not know even the A-B-C-D of alcoholism. He had vaguely heard something about it, but his knowledge was on the level of a poorly informed layman. He proceeded to read everything the psychiatrists, psychologists, and others had written about it – here his familiarity with most of the common languages stood him in good stead – and a year later, lo and behold! Jellinek was telling the psychiatrists about alcoholism, and they were listening, for whether or not they chose to agree, it was obvious that he knew what he was talking about; he was a fountainhead of knowledge.

So he proceeded to collaborate in what was to be called the Bowman-Jellinek classification. But he was content to leave the mental disorders of alcoholics to the psychiatrists. He too was convinced that the important issue was alcoholism, and a whole series of researches and writings reflects this interest: it may be that the greatest of them – perhaps it is too soon to make a final evaluation – is his *Phases in the Drinking History of Alcoholics*. This brilliant analysis of responses of Alcoholics Anonymous members to a questionnaire which he had not designed, and which was barely suitable for its purpose, shows Jellinek seizing upon a smidgin of crude information and shaping it into a golden instrument of incalculable value. In this work he laid the basis for a systematic understanding of alcoholism as a process, into which a man enters and more or less gradually progresses through stages or phases of involvement. How fruitful and useful this

intellectual *tour de force* was to be is evident from the many doctoral dissertations in numerous universities which it inspired, and from the whole new trend in thinking about alcoholism which it evoked.

His later contributions to the understanding of alcoholism included "The Craving for Alcohol," "The Withdrawal Syndrome in Alcoholism," "Alcoholism, a Genus and Some of Its Species," and, of course, *The Disease Concept of Alcoholism*. I find it amusing to think that the man who in 1939 did not know the A-B-C-D of alcoholism had by 1959 invented the alpha-beta-gamma-delta alcoholisms. The world has a way of seizing on the dramatically named, and just as it overvalued the Jellinek Estimation Formula, so I think the Greek-letter alcoholisms are overvalued, and that the profounder Jellinek contributions lie elsewhere. But there is no question that Jellinek's ideas tended to be so interesting, and his personal style so persuasive, that whatever he said stimulated thinking and work.

This brings me to the next area of his contributions. As much as we admire the productions which are signed by Jellinek's name, whether in the statistical, psychiatric, psychological, or other realms, and those which bear the imprint of his espousal, such as the foundation of organizations, schools, lecture courses, and seminars, there are other achievements of monumental proportions which could easily be overlooked and forgotten. It is to these that I now wish to pay particular attention.

The calling of Jellinek to New York grew somewhat indirectly out of Norman Jolliffe's recognition of the need for an interdisciplinary approach to alcohol problems. Jellinek was the right man for this sort of conception: you could hardly say what he was, and if he sometimes called himself a biometrician it was because he happened to know how to be one. But that did not set a boundary to his abilities, as is evident from the stupendous range of his learning and interests in linguistics, psychology, anthropology, education, classical literature, and other fields. Now Howard W. Haggard at Yale had come independently to the conclusion that interdisciplinary work was needed, so it was natural for him to recruit E. M. Jellinek. And what a brilliant, effective, and fruitful decision that was! Within a few years of Jellinek's coming to Yale, what was to be the Center of Alcohol Studies had taken shape as a flourishing institution, outgrowing the parent institution, the Yale Laboratory of Applied Physiology. And the secret of this success was Jellinek's boundless imagination and vision in recognizing what needed to be done and inspiring and guiding capable people in doing it.

A young member of the Yale sociology faculty came along to ask whether there was any help for a task in which he was involved, having to do with persons arrested for intoxication. Jellinek did not let this young sociologist go, and thus was enlisted Selden D. Bacon, who in time became a permanent member of the staff and succeeded to the director-ship of the Center of Alcohol Studies, now at Rut-gers University. But most important from the scien-tific viewpoint – having nothing to do with adminis-tration – is that within a year or two this young sociologist had written *Sociology and the Problems of Alcohol: Foundations for a Sociological Study of Drinking Behavior*. Jellinek wrote the introduc-tion to this document in 1944 and over the years it did, in fact, become the foundation for sociological study of drinking by a growing group of social scientists. Indeed, only now, more than 20 years later, is the real achievement of this foundation be-ginning to emerge.

Jellinek had realized that the education of youth about alcohol was unrealistic, backward, sometimes hypocritical, and in any case ineffective as far as preventing either drinking, excessive drinking, or alcoholism was concerned. He inspired and directed Anne Roe to prepare a formal study of the mate-rials used in alcohol education in the schools of the United States, and even of the laws requiring such education. The effect, when we published *A Survey of Alcohol Education*, was nearly revolutionary. Educators became aware and some of them became ashamed. A great reform started, and it is still under-way.

Jellinek sought to apply the same remedy, the application of objective scholarship, to two other realms of painful misdirection of social effort: law and economics. He brought in a legal scholar to ex-plore and analyse the foundations of the alcohol control laws, and an economist to lay foundations for the study of economic aspects and effects of the alcoholic beverage industry. It must be said that in these cases there was neither great outcome nor sufficient later development. Yet from both these endeavours we published articles which resulted in considerable ferment, and in no inconsiderable effect.

The problem of heredity in alcoholism was still in a state of uncertainty, and old beliefs in the here-ditability of the condition sometimes discouraged efforts to tackle it. Jellinek directed Anne Roe in a study of the fate of children of alcoholic parents who had been raised in foster homes. The resulting monograph had a significant influence in putting to rest at least the crude notions about this subject.

I have cited this role in some detail – and yet in-completely – because actually I believe that this activity, which could easily go unrecognized since his name did not appear on most of these re-searches, was actually Jellinek's greatest contribu-tion and achievement. In this role we see him as the teacher of researchers, the inspirer of scientific in-vestigation, and the layer of foundations for the acquisition of new knowledge. In each of these in-stances he not only helped to design the study, but also critically reviewed the analysis and report of the results. In the latter task he was magnificent, and it was my special privilege to share in this work.

All of these activities were continued in various forms by Jellinek after 1950 when he left Yale to go to the World Health Organization. I shall not de-tail his later career, since this will be covered in subsequent addresses. I want rather to conclude by summing up my conception of what Jellinek wanted to do and did.

E. M. Jellinek was essentially a universal scholar. He never really earned a doctorate, although along the way he acquired a couple of honorary degrees, and he allowed himself to be referred to as Dr. Jel-linek because it was too inconvenient to correct everybody all the time. Of course he was a doctor of doctors in the truest sense. He knew that man was a creature of emotions and likely to be moved by feelings. But he understood that it was the capa-city for rational behaviour that needed the utmost cultivation in man if his ultimate civilization was to be achieved. So he sought, essentially, to lay the foundations upon which rational behaviour could be projected: systematic study and objective ana-lysis, or in a word, science. What was to become known as "the scientific approach" to alcohol prob-lems is indelibly associated with his name. I think the names of Jolliffe and Haggard and Bacon – and mine, too, I hope – are also associated with the his-tory of this particular ideology. But without ques-tion it was Jellinek who imaginatively created the tools, projected the researches, stimulated the studies, guided the analyses, enriched the reporting, which made the scientific approach a reality. For him this achievement was possible because his inexhaustible good will toward man, combined with a scintillating intellect and a limitless store of learning, captivated both the hearts and minds of all who came within his sphere of influence.

In this career I perceive a moral of profound significance to us who have to build on the foundations he laid. E. M. Jellinek knew that the best learning occurs when the student is emotionally involved. He was the ablest teacher I ever knew. But if anyone had suggested to him that the essential job of a teacher is to involve the student emotionally, as I recently heard a college professor say, he would have felt only contempt for such a half-baked notion. The job of a teacher is to have knowledge and to impart it. To involve the student's emotions in the desire for knowledge and in its acquisition is a first-rate educational technique. But to activate the student's emotions around a morass of ignorance and misinformation is to betray the purpose of education. It was with this philosophy that E. M. Jellinek fought to create knowledge – by the method of science – to replace the absence of knowledge which had prevailed in the realm of alcohol problems and which had allowed crude emotional reaction to govern. In this task he succeeded magnificently, and this learned symposium is therefore truly an appropriate memorial to him. He was the man most acutely responsible for turning the whole world from ignorance and emotionality, in dealing with problems of alcohol, to science and rationality. We do well to honour the name and reverence the memory of a true teacher, E. M. Jellinek.

MARK KELLER
Center of Alcohol Studies, Rutgers University
State University of New Jersey
New Brunswick, New Jersey, USA*

We are here to honour the memory of Dr. E. M. Jellinek and to acknowledge the affection we had for him. It is fitting that a conference of this kind, one that is both scientific and of international scope, be dedicated to the memory of our great friend and colleague. It is particularly fitting that this conference be held in this country, in this city, and at this

*Preparation of this tribute was aided by a grant (USPHS-NIMH-05655) from the National Institute of Mental Health, US Public Health Service, to the Rutgers Center of Alcohol Studies.

university, where he felt so much at home. It is here that he was honoured with the degree of Doctor of Surgery, a degree that meant more to him than any other academic honour he had received. As he told me, he valued the degree not only for its academic stature but as a symbol of the esteem his colleagues in Chile felt for him. This he treasured greatly.

Dr. Jellinek was a world scholar of international renown, to whom students (and we were all his students) turned automatically to seek inspiration and to tap his store of wisdom. All countries and peoples concerned about the problems of alcohol and man revered him. His many great contributions to the field of alcohol studies have been enumerated many times. I will not detail them here. His work at Yale University, his influence in the World Health Organization, his many books and scientific articles are widely known. His penetrating concepts are likely to dominate work in our field for many decades to come. Every program in alcoholism in the world today has been influenced – some very profoundly – by Jellinek's thoughts and writings.

In Canada, and in particular in the Addiction Research Foundation of Ontario, his influence was immeasurable. More than those of any other outside person, his ideas and concepts influenced the development of the Foundation. In 1949, when we were formulating our plans in Ontario, I spent two weeks with him. It was natural to turn to him first for advice and guidance. During this period we worked together, setting out the general structure of the Foundation, its major responsibilities, its major lines of investigation and study, and the kind of people required to develop and work in the organization. All during our growth and development we were in regular contact with him, both by visit and by letter. His counsel and interest in our work continued, and when he retired from the World Health Organization in 1958, he came to Canada to join us as a research consultant. He remained with us for more than three years, serving on both the faculty of the University of Toronto in the Department of Psychiatry, and the faculty of the University of Alberta. Some of the data that he had collected in his international surveys have been deposited with our Foundation. We are now preparing for publication an international survey of drinking habits, one of his last great contributions.

The impact on our Foundation of Jellinek the scientist is inextricably linked for us with the impact of the man. His enthusiasm for constructive thought was matched by the warmth he felt for people and the warmth he inspired in them. We remember, fondly, his parodies of ancient mythologies and his light-hearted verse. He made us feel that the straight-forward pursuit of knowledge was one of the greatest opportunities of man, against which the temptations of easy compromise and status paled into nothing.

Yet Jellinek's interests were so vast and varied that he could easily switch his language and thoughts from the world of learning to that of little children, for whom he had a vast storehouse of tales. Children easily recognized him as one of their own kind in the freshness and vitality of his spirit. His greatness owed much to his having kept throughout his life the fresh curiosity of the child. In his scientific pursuits he retained the child's zest for play. Like the child, too, he despised pomposity and falseness.

He had a singular talent for evoking tolerance among clashing viewpoints. He was beloved by people with sharply conflicting ideas about drinking and he was always ready to help those whose lives had been damaged by alcohol. One of his often quoted sayings was, "Alcoholism may be the source of much human misery – but fundamentally, human misery is a source of alcoholism."

We miss Jellinek. We miss his intellectual inspiration. We miss his delightful personality. Our sense of loss, however, is tempered by a deep sense of gratitude that we had the experience of knowing him, of working closely with him, and of being able to count him as one of our truly great friends and colleagues. We will ever be inspired by his example and, above all, by our love for him.

H. DAVID ARCHIBALD
Addiction Research Foundation
Toronto, Ontario, Canada

In devoting a few words to the memory of our friend Dr. E. M. Jellinek, it is possible to combine the sentimental with the lofty phrase in praise of his qualities. Anyone who had the privilege of knowing him can understand this, for he could speak of simple human things as well as of highly specialized scientific matters, but always in an idiom which was peculiarly his own and which brought him close to his fellow man's thoughts and feelings.

He was capable of establishing contact at any level, ranging from the strictly formal to the warmly and deeply human. He could discuss man and matter in terms of banter and relativity, but his tone always approached the ironic – never the sarcastic. He claimed no praise for himself, but knew well how to praise indirectly and without ostentation; and it was plain that he valued friendship and affection more highly than honour and praise.

His criticisms, like his praise, stimulated others to fulfil requirements. His marginal notes annotating written texts invariably started, as I know from experience, with a kind "Suggest that you ...," and never stated directly that something was wrong (although it might be wrong).

He was conscious of the temporal, but equally of the timeless when he said that the benefit of an old age pension does not end a man's possibilities and abilities. He knew fatigue, but he also knew how to make fatigue bearable by his effort and concentration on work. He was capable of joking about himself without ever making himself a caricature. He also knew the sorrow and anxiety inherent in life, could recognize it and bear it with serenity. The difficulties of others always seemed greater to him than his own. To those to whom he opened his heart and who learned to understand him, he was the very epitome of an intensely alive and charming man.

A citizen of the United States, he was nevertheless above all a citizen of the world, not only because of his broad knowledge of various conditions of life and his work in various parts of the world, but also by virtue of his broad vision and great powers of adjustment and understanding. Our first meeting occurred many years ago, at the reception counter of the League of Nations Palace in Geneva. Small and frail, with his unusually searching glance, he made an immediate and deep impression because what he said showed that he was entirely familiar with the data and reports on the care of alcoholics in the Netherlands. Besides his appreciation for the experimentally developed work in the fields of care and treatment, he expressed his hopes that research would not be forgotten. And almost in the same breath he said that research must not be regarded as a panacea; that the man in the street has an exceptionally good sense of proportion and feeling for the healthy and the unhealthy, so that one ought to look and listen in many directions. In a few broad sentences spoken during lunch, he outlined a program of work, analysis, and field investigation which was certainly not limited to the scope of activities in the Netherlands.

How vivid are my memories of the hours we spent sitting in the sun on the stairs leading to a church, discussing the problem of supplying useful information to groups of professionals likely to have initial contacts with alcoholics; discussing alcohol problems and an effective approach to alcoholism (a problem, by the way, which has not yet been solved).

His requests for participation in an investigation and for information were always formulated so that it was impossible to refuse, for he always managed to convey his understanding of the additional work and effort required. To fulfil his request was invariably to benefit, for much was to be learned from the questions to which he wanted answers.

Many in the Netherlands remember his magisterial addresses and talks at the WHO Seminar on Alcoholism in Noordwijk (1954) and the International Summer Institute on Prevention and Treatment of Alcoholism in Amsterdam (1961). In the course of the Summer Institute, a reception given in his honour saw a highly diversified gathering of officials, therapists, and patients who, understanding the importance of this man, came to greet him and give him their heartfelt compliments.

Through his personality and his stimulating activities, he has been of great importance to our work in the Netherlands. Indeed, the research centre – the Foundation for Study and Documentation on Alcohol and Alcoholism – was established in order to fulfil his expressed hopes. And it is no coincidence that the Amsterdam Clinic for Alcoholics was given the name "Jellinek Kliniek." The name is to give some expression to our friendship and admiration, and to honour his memory.

As I say these words, I realize once again how contacts with Jellinek, the duration of which can be measured in hours or at best days, have been and will continue to be of enormous significance. Let us be grateful, then, for having been allowed to live and work with him. Let us continue to give expression to the good that we have experienced through him – that he may live.

H. J. KRAUWEEL
Medical Consultation Bureau for Alcoholism
Amsterdam, Netherlands

On behalf of the Board of Directors of the National Council on Alcoholism and of the Christopher D. Smithers Foundation, I am honoured by this opportunity to pay once more our respects to the memory of "Bunky" Jellinek, who was the father of the modern concept that alcoholism is a treatable disease.

Dr. Jellinek is universally recognized as "the foremost protagonist of progress" in the scientific study of drinking and alcohol problems. Much of what the world knows today about the nature of these problems is due to his astoundingly rich work. The latter includes his discoveries of the species and phases of alcoholism, and his surveys of drinking patterns and attitudes in almost every country of the world. But in his monumental enlargements of our knowledge, his attention was forever fixed on the human problems and the human suffering caused by alcohol. He strove incessantly to make the lay and the professional public understand that the alcoholic is not a hopeless misfit, but a human being afflicted with an illness to which an end can be put if it is treated in an appropriate manner. It is in this spirit that he established the Yale Plan Clinic which was to serve as a model for treatment centres everywhere.

His scientific and practical activities are too numerous to detail here. They include his research directorship at Yale, his editorship of the *Quarterly Journal of Studies on Alcohol*, his long work with the World Health Organization in Switzerland, his chairmanship of the board of directors of the National Council on Alcoholism, his association with the Co-operative Commission on the Study of Alcoholism, and the two years that he spent as a consultant to the Christopher D. Smithers Foundation. During the latter period, he wrote his last book entitled *The Disease Concept of Alcoholism*, which is now well known throughout the world.

Dr. Jellinek not only had an unequalled fund of knowledge but a singular talent for evoking tolerance among clashing viewpoints. He was beloved by people with sharply conflicting philosophies about drinking and he was always ready to counsel those whose lives had been adversely affected by alcohol.

Dr. Jellinek came to give major attention to the problems of alcohol only in the last 25 years of his life. Before that he was engaged in far-flung researches in physiology, biology, botany, statistics, and psychiatry. These researches carried him to the four corners of the earth and at times were undertaken at great personal deprivation. We have all shared Jellinek's bright memories of his long student years in Europe during which there was no province of human knowledge that was alien to his curiosity. This background enabled him to bring to his studies of alcohol problems his knowledge of ancient and modern philosophy and literature as well as of modern science. Dr. Jellinek at any time could have occupied a professorship of classics and history with the same brilliance and grace as he exhibited in his work in psychiatry. He was equally at home in Grenoble, Leipzig, Budapest, and the jungle. It was during his biological researches in Africa that his attention was first directed to alcohol when associates of his with drinking problems came to him for counsel.

He made us feel that the straight-forward pursuit of knowledge was one of the greatest joys of man against which the temptation of the marketplace and of status were as nothing. His enthusiasm for thinking was matched by the warmth he felt for people and the warmth he inspired in them for him. People took to him on first sight and he almost instantly asked us to call him "Bunky," the name his father had given him when he was a little boy. His whimsical humour, which included poking fun at himself, were daily gifts. In the last three years we have missed him greatly, and the pain of his sudden death is still with us; but our sorrow mingles with our gratitude for having had the privilege of working and living close to him.

H. BRINKLEY SMITHERS
Christopher D. Smithers Foundation
New York, New York, USA

It is with very great pleasure that, after an absence of many years, I have returned to Chile and can once again enjoy the beauty, friendship, and warm hospitality of this wonderful country. As a native of California, and particularly of San Francisco, the charm of your Pacific shores – so much like our Pacific shores – and the splendour of your Andes – so much like our Sierra Nevada – make me feel that I have come home again.

It is also with great pleasure that I participate in this symposium to pay my own personal tribute to the memory of Dr. Jellinek. For many years he was to me a remarkable scientist, a fascinating teacher, a citizen of all countries. I am especially pleased that during the last years of his life, in California, he was my neighbour and friend.

Of Dr. Jellinek I have warm and pleasant memories. Perhaps the most important of these involves the statement he made to us repeatedly during his last years: "The time for talking has passed. At first it was necessary to talk, to convince the world that we must do something to control alcoholism. But now the time has passed for merely talking. Now is the time for doing."

Today we are following his precepts. Today the United States under the direction of President Johnson has embarked on a nationwide campaign to control alcoholism by mobilizing its full powers of research, treatment, training, education, and particularly of preventive techniques. Never before in our history has our country organized such an attack against a single disease.

The opening of this campaign was signalled by the President in 1966, when he presented a special message on health to the Congress of the United States. In that message, he emphasized that the alcoholic suffers from a disease which will yield eventually to scientific research and adequate treatment. Someday there may well be a specific treatment – perhaps a true cure – for alcoholism which will come from a research laboratory in our country, or in South America, or in Europe. But we cannot wait for that day, and we need not wait for it.

"Even with the present limited state of our knowledge," President Johnson said, "much can be done to reduce the untold suffering and uncounted waste caused by this affliction." He directed that a new national centre should be established within the United States Public Health Service to institute research on the cause, prevention, control, and treatment of alcoholism. That centre has been already established. He directed that a nationwide education program should be created in order to foster public understanding based not on fear, not on mythology, not on moral judgments, but on scientific fact. That program is now being developed to reach not merely the general public, but such special groups as very young school children, teenagers, college students, medical students, nursing students, law students, teachers, students in religious schools, labour groups, employer groups, hospital groups, social welfare workers, vocational rehabilitation workers, law enforcement groups, and the press, radio, and television.

In addition, the President directed that the new federal alcoholism program should be co-ordinated with the work of governmental and non-governmental agencies in the states and cities. This coordination is now being developed rapidly. The role of the federal government here is not to control or to dominate, but to provide all possible assistance, support, and stimulation; to work as a partner. Necessarily, some of this support will be provided in the form of finances. Money is required to build clinics, to operate laboratories, to provide for hospital care, and to help in the training of the men and women who will work in the clinics and laboratories and hospitals. It is my firm belief that we will provide the financial support commensurate with the gravity of the alcoholism problem. It is also my firm belief that a substantial portion of this financial support and of our overall efforts in the field of alcoholism will be devoted not to treatment of those who are already addicted to alcohol but to prevention.

Ten or fifteen years ago few of us were bold enough to talk openly about alcoholism prevention. If the treatment of alcoholism seemed remote, its prevention appeared to be even more remote – about as remote as sending a man to the moon. But today we are talking logically and reasonably about landing a man on the moon – and bringing him back again – and many of us confidently expect to live to see this accomplished. And today, many of us confidently expect to live long enough to see the development of practical, effective means of alcoholism prevention.

All of us, I am sure, recognize that our major goal must be prevention. Of course, it is essential that the best possible treatment techniques be provided for those who are already suffering from alcoholism. It is essential that the best techniques available today in a few treatment centres be made available in all. It is essential that we seek better and more effective techniques. It is logical, it is economically sound, it is only humane that we do this. But, as with nearly all public health problems, it is more logical, more economically sound, and even more humane that we set prevention rather than treatment as our major objective.

Today there seem to be no valid reasons why

effective, practical, and acceptable methods of prevention cannot be developed. The recent scientific literature is teeming with clues from new research in epidemiology, in sociology, in educational psychology. There is evidence that certain groups, certain cultures, certain segments of the population in almost every country have somehow learned to live without demonstrating any significant problems of excessive drinking, intoxication, or alcoholism. Some of these groups have apparently found a satisfactory solution through abstention. Others have apparently found a satisfactory solution through the development of safe drinking customs and attitudes. According to all available evidence, these effective techniques do not depend on genetic differences. Instead, they are learned. And if they can be learned by one cultural group, perhaps they can be learned by others.

To many thoughtful workers in this field, there is a close relationship between drinking and automobile driving. Even in this civilization of ours, it is not truly essential to do either one. One can live a happy and comfortable life without drinking or driving. Perhaps our children can learn this. And perhaps they can also learn that if one drinks or if one drives, then it is necessary to learn how to do so with maximum safety for himself and for others.

Finally, in the new alcoholism program being inaugurated in the United States, it is clearly understood that all activities will be co-ordinated as effectively as possible. No matter how much money is made available, there will never be enough to provide all the services and undertake all the research which might be desirable. There will never be enough money or skilled manpower to excuse needless duplication or needless overlapping. It is vital, therefore, that there be co-ordination of all alcoholism activities within the federal government. It is equally vital that federal activities be co-ordinated with those in states and local communities, with those in hospitals, clinics, research centres, and teaching institutions, and with those of the voluntary agencies. And since some of the most exciting and important research on alcohol and alcoholism is being conducted in such centres as Santiago, Mexico City, Stockholm, Helsinki, Paris, Rome, and Prague, it is essential that our work be co-ordinated with that in other nations. It is vital that the research findings in all centres, wherever they are located, be communicated as rapidly, accurately, and effectively as possible to health workers, educators, government officials, and the public.

What we may well be creating is a new and challenging partnership which will cross rigid departmental, regional, and even national boundaries. It must also cross the equally rigid boundaries between academic and professional disciplines. Alcoholism respects no boundaries. In the battle we are now waging against alcoholism, we cannot allow boundaries of any kind to limit our efforts. To Dr. Jellinek, who displayed during his lifetime a magnificent disregard for boundaries of every kind, such an approach would be the only obvious one. I think he would approve.

MILTON SILVERMAN
US *Department of Health, Education, and Welfare Washington* DC, USA

On behalf of the International Council on Alcohol and Alcoholism I should like first to express sincere thanks to our friends in Chile for making possible this international symposium in memory of the late Dr. E. M. Jellinek. Furthermore I should like to say how fitting it is that this meeting takes place in Santiago. I recall, as do others, with what warmth and appreciation Dr. Jellinek used to speak of his visits here and how this country and its people had a special place in his affections. On the last occasion when I met him in Geneva, he recounted some of his experiences and told me how much at home he felt among friends and colleagues in Chile.

In associating the International Council with the various tributes paid to E. M. Jellinek today, I first wish to record our gratitude for his advice and counsel, which influenced the development and growth of our organization to a high degree. He fully understood the pressures and stresses to which a body seeking to develop international co-operation is subjected. These are particularly acute in a field where scientific and professional activity cannot be completely divorced from political, economic, and religious considerations or from the diverse consequences of emotional and traditional attitudes in society. In this connection I recall a lecture given by him at our first international meeting in Geneva in 1955. His theme was the relationship between the men of science, the organizations com-

bating alcoholism, and Alcoholics Anonymous. His appraisal of the potential areas and conditions of co-operation was to be a valuable guide in the future.

He was always well aware of the complex situation regarding the organization and furtherance of research, treatment, and education existing in many countries. This awareness enabled him to formulate national policies in various areas of alcohol and alcoholism problems, ranging from legislative and economic action to the provision of treatment facilities. His comprehensive knowledge and analytic approach can be seen for example in the detailed international evidence which he presented to the Manitoba Liquor Enquiry Commission in 1955.

This leads me to refer to his influence on organizational structure and planning in many countries. The creation of state programs on alcoholism, begun in the 1940s in the United States and Canada, became a significant phenomenon internationally in the following decade when Jellinek was consultant on alcoholism to the World Health Organization. It will be recalled that in 1954 France and the Soviet Union set up national programs, that later state programs emerged in Australia, Central America, and elsewhere, and that the trend has continued with emerging programs in countries such as Britain, Italy, and Spain, where Jellinek prophesied they would be needed eventually. If any of these programs did not publicly acknowledge inspiration received from him, they nevertheless all reflected some of his ideas and concepts.

His emphasis on an interdisciplinary approach to the problems of alcohol and alcoholism will be mentioned by others. I would like to allude to one facet of his work which was particularly revealing of the wide and profound culture of the man. If one peruses the early numbers of the *Quarterly Journal of Studies on Alcohol* one finds a number of delightful and stimulating papers on literary, philosophical, and historical themes. An example is Jellinek's essay on Immanuel Kant, where we have, incidentally, a reminder of another of his international qualifications – his interest in philological questions and his facility in language. Here he translated from Kant's *Anthropologie* (a work apparently not hitherto translated into English) some reflections of the philosopher on the function of alcoholism in human life. There have been comparatively few, I imagine, who while expert in the scientific and medical aspects of the subject have devoted time and study to the philosophical and literary works which are relevant to an understanding of the problems involved in alcoholism.

It was this deep culture and aesthetic taste which made it possible for him to produce the first and perhaps only really satisfactory international film on alcohol and alcoholism. I believe that of all the World Health Organization films on any subject it is the one which has gone through the most language editions. Such an artistic but also truly scientific documentary film could only be the product of an intellect and culture such as he possessed.

All those who knew him will have felt the genuine warmth of his personality, his enquiring mind, his penetrating assessment of problems, and his friendliness. We shall all remember him with gratitude, and generations of workers in the field of alcohol and alcoholism will benefit from his great contribution. Certainly any further international activity in this field must build on the foundation he has laid.

ARCHER TONGUE
International Council on Alcohol and Alcoholism
Lausanne, Switzerland

We remember E. M. Jellinek as a man of science, of that science which, in his *En Torno a Galileo*, Ortega y Gasset symbolized as construction and judged, in relation to matters corporal or spiritual, as much a product of imagination as of observation: the latter not being possible without the former. Ortega y Gasset added, "This characteristic, in part at least, the imaginative element of science, makes of her a sister of poetry."

The ideal of science that tries to present a model of nature as a closed system of laws or axioms in order to explain the phenomena of the real world does not appear possible of realization. Those who are especially endowed with an inquisitive mind and great imagination seek to penetrate to the very essence of each process. The object is to interpret those forces which reveal the existence of new relationships requiring other principles and laws. Of this process of rational thinking, and in turn, of imaginative explanation, Jellinek gave constant demonstration in his extraordinary voyage in search of what he called "synthesis for obtaining the unity of science." His explorations in biology, in bio-

metrics, in psychiatry, and especially in alcoholism appear guided by this universal proposition.

In his *Function of Biometric Methodology in Psychiatric Research*, Jellinek declared: "I believe that the solution of the problem of synthesis in psychiatry, as well as that of 'unity of science' lies ultimately in some postulational method, in some logistic system. Such a system will lead to transcending concepts, but there must be initially a few clear-cut concepts to which the logistic system can be applied, and from which others can be derived. At present the specific logistic system is but a vague dream, and even the initial concepts have not taken final shape. Whether such concepts and systems can be achieved by an organized effort or only by a master mind is debatable. There is, however, little doubt that if organized psychiatric research embraces this problem, the solution will not be retarded; rather the prospective individual discoverer will be stimulated."

Those who have followed his work in detail recognize in these expressions the character of thinking and action which inspired all of his contributions, and are most evident in his studies in the field of alcoholism. Jellinek was, without doubt, a superior intelligence capable of finding and formulating basic concepts, and of developing a logical system which permits an understanding not only of the illness and its consequences, but also of its dynamic effect on society.

I do not believe it is possible to dissociate from his total intellectual product any of the elements, because these are guided by only one superior thought. Nevertheless, being interested in health as a function of society, I wish to highlight his contribution to the epidemiology of mental illnesses, which is derived from his work on alcoholism. By describing the pathogenesis and sequence of factors in alcoholism, he created a language which has been the basis for measuring its prevalence, for the exchange of ideas and experiences among researchers, for the interpretation of its natural and cultural history, and for the establishment of principles for its prevention and control.

It is hoped that an approach similar to that employed by Jellinek in the study of alcoholism may be followed in other mental illnesses. I believe that the empiricism attributed to modern psychiatry is due in large measure to the absence of consensus as to the nature of observations, the manner of recording and presenting them, and the definition and classification of what is deemed to be pathological. While experimentation establishes bases for identifying morbid processes, the epidemiological method has come to be a valuable instrument of which there are outstanding proofs in the history of medicine. When there are "operational definitions" about a certain disease entity, it will be possible to undertake transcultural studies which may shed light on the similarities and differences in the patterns associated with the worsening or improving of mental processes. In this manner the logistic system which will produce the "transcending concepts" referred to by Jellinek may be created in psychiatry.

His work impresses us, furthermore, because it establishes for research a functional relationship with the structures, tendencies, and paths of societal action. He penetrates into attitudes and conduct which are well referred to as the normal and pathological habits of drinking, and which permitted him to reveal the characteristics of social groups, the standards governing them, and the condition of indissociable entities. Furthermore, he analysed them in a culture-historical sense, as revealed in his series of Classics of the Alcohol Literature. It is sufficient to note the articles: "Seneca's Epistle LXXXIII: On Drunkenness," "Montaigne's Essay on Drunkenness," "Old Russian Church Views on Inebriety," and "The Ocean Cruise of the Viennese," among many others. The comments of Jellinek in each case show the breadth of his knowledge of philosophy, the rationality of his thought, and the ingenuousness of his spirit. These are writings of profound significance for the study of the evolution of the concepts relating to the habit of drinking in various cultures. They represent a true method of sociological investigation of a historical character that Jellinek extended to various literary sources.

In doing honour to Jellinek today, we must emphasize his permanent contribution to science and to the analysis of the social order. Our purpose is one of continuity, because we identify ourselves with his ideas and share in the essentially humanitarian intentions which he inspired. We honour him, furthermore, because we consider him a distinguished exponent of the modern concept of health that goes beyond the biological content and which makes of health a service to individual well-being and social progress. We find a fitting interpretation of the full measure of Jellinek's thinking in these words of Robert Oppenheimer from *Science and the Common Understanding*: "The wealth and variety of physics itself, the greater wealth and variety of the natural sciences taken as a whole, the more familiar, yet still strange and far wider wealth of the life of the human spirit, enriched by complementarity, not at once compatible ways, irreducible one to the other, have a greater harmony. They are the elements of man's sorrow and his splendor, his frailty and his power, his death, his passing, and his undying deeds."

ABRAHAM HORWITZ
Pan American Sanitary Bureau
Regional Office for the Americas of the
World Health Organization
Washington DC, USA

ALCOHOL & ALCOHOLISM

Biochemical and Pharmacological Aspects

The study of a drug liable to produce dependence must include pharmacological investigation as a fundamental part, since dependence is a consequence of the pharmacological action of the drug in question. In the case of ethanol, the metabolism of which is similar in part to that of the principle nutriments, the biochemistry of the drug is a very important part of its pharmacology.

In recent years pharmacological studies have been increasingly aimed at cellular and subcellular levels, and the study of alcohol is no exception. As a result of this trend, knowledge about the effects and metabolism of alcohol is increasing rapidly. To render this progress in basic knowledge useful for the interpretation of the human problems of alcohol, periodic review is mandatory.

Doubtless most psychiatrists, sociologists, and public health specialists are dissatisfied with the efficiency of the methods now employed for the prevention and treatment of alcoholism. Everyone is waiting for new and better methods. Experience shows that, in general, progress in the applied sciences arises from progress in the basic sciences supporting them. With reference to alcoholism, I believe that greater knowledge of the mechanisms involved in the acute and chronic effects of alcohol on the body – on the cells of different organs and even on enzymatic systems in each cell – will help to explain the characteristic features of dependence on alcohol.

These basic aspects are the subject of this section of the Symposium. The various topics are reviewed by persons who are specially qualified because of the important contribution each has made to the problem with which he deals.

The origin of the appetite for a drug liable to produce dependence is a problem which deserves the most careful study. Thus, an abnormal appetite is presumably always the starting point of the chain of events leading to the development of dependence. Biological factors influencing the desire for ethanol will also be reviewed in this section.

I am sure that all readers – including scholars who focus on the problem of alcoholism from the most diverse points of view – will find in every paper something relevant to their own special interests. Without the light shed by basic research, progress in methods for the prevention and treatment of alcoholism would be deprived of a major source of new ideas and largely restricted to a sterile pragmatism.

JORGE MARDONES
Institute of Studies on Alcoholism
University of Chile, Santiago, Chile

W. W. WESTERFELD

ROBERT J. BLOOM

Department of Biochemistry
State University of New York
Upstate Medical Center
Syracuse, NY, USA

1

Metabolic Pathways of Ethanol

Most of the alcohol a person consumes is metabolized via acetaldehyde (AcH) to acetic acid, and it enters the usual metabolic pathways as acetyl CoA. The liver is responsible for metabolizing most of the AcH (6) as well as the alcohol, although much of the acetic acid which is formed by these oxidations appears to be metabolized in other tissues. Hence alcohol and AcH are the only metabolites which are unique to alcohol metabolism unless small amounts of AcH are diverted into other pathways. The enzymes present in liver convert AcH primarily to acetic acid (Figure 1-1), but there are other enzymes abundant in muscle which can convert AcH to other products (Figure 1-2). None of these by-products of acetaldehyde metabolism appear to be formed in large amounts from administered acetaldehyde or alcohol, but we know relatively little about their significance, if any, in alcohol metabolism. Such by-products could have important pharmacological or pathological effects, or their formation could interfere with normal metabolic pathways even though they were produced in relatively small amounts.

This paper will describe another by-product of alcohol metabolism which has recently been identified in our laboratories as 5-hydroxy-4-ketohexanoic acid (HKH) (Figure 1-3). This substance has not been described previously in either the chemical or biological literature; it is formed by an enzymatic reaction which has not been recognized heretofore. The details of these studies are published or in press (1, 2, 3, 9), but will be summarized briefly here. Some additional studies on the formation of HKH *in vivo* will also be presented for the first time.

This new metabolite was detected originally (9) during a comparison of C^{14}-ethanol and C^{14}-acetate metabolism in rat liver homogenates. The products formed from each of these substrates were separated by column chromatography and followed by their radioactivities. Both substrates contributed C^{14} to the usual citric acid cycle intermediates, but alcohol also gave rise to an unidentified peak which later

The original studies reported herein were aided by grant M-1947 from the National Institute of Mental Health, US Public Health Service.

Xanthine oxidase

$$CH_3CHO \xrightarrow{\text{Mo, } B_2O_2} CH_3COOH$$

Aldehyde oxidase

$$CH_3CHO \xrightarrow{\text{Mo, } B_2O_2} CH_3COOH$$

Aldehyde dehydrogenase (Mutase)

$$CH_3CHO \xrightarrow{\text{DPN}} CH_3COOH$$

$$CH_3CHO + CH_3CHO \xrightarrow[\text{+alc. dehyd.}]{\text{DPN}} CH_3COOH + CH_3CH_2OH$$

$$CH_3CHO + CH_3COCOOH \xrightarrow[\text{+lact. dehyd.}]{\text{DPN}} CH_3COOH + CH_3CHOHCOOH$$

Figure 1-1
Enzymes capable of using acetaldehyde (abundant in liver).

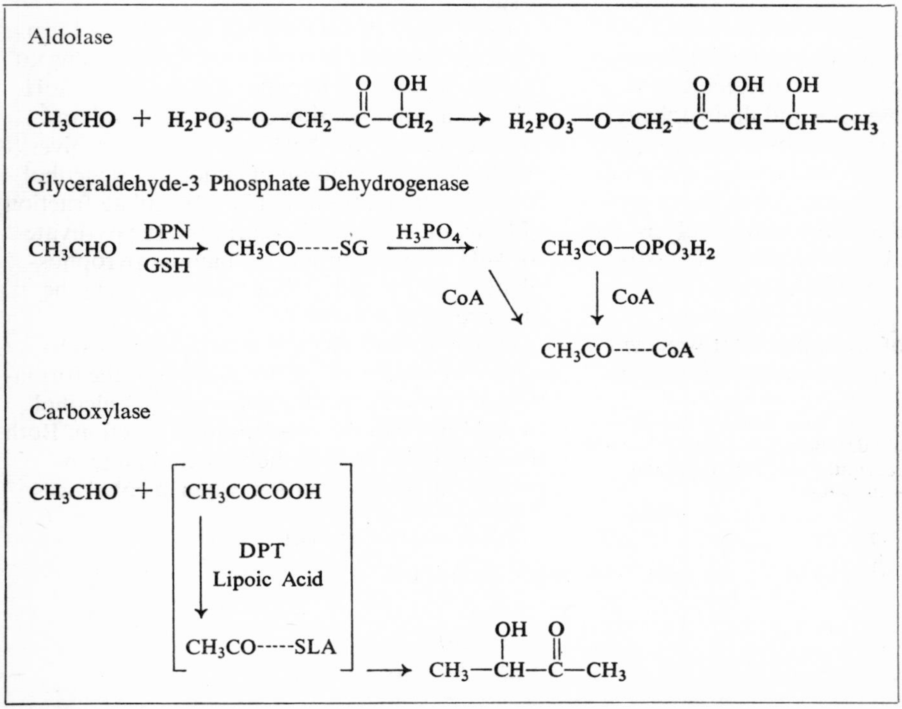

Aldolase

$$CH_3CHO + H_2PO_3-O-CH_2-\overset{O}{\overset{\|}{C}}-\overset{OH}{\overset{|}{CH_2}} \rightarrow H_2PO_3-O-CH_2-\overset{O}{\overset{\|}{C}}-\overset{OH}{\overset{|}{CH}}-\overset{OH}{\overset{|}{CH}}-CH_3$$

Glyceraldehyde-3 Phosphate Dehydrogenase

$$CH_3CHO \xrightarrow[\text{GSH}]{\text{DPN}} CH_3CO\text{-----}SG \xrightarrow{H_3PO_4} CH_3CO-OPO_3H_2$$

$$CH_3CO\text{-----}CoA$$

Carboxylase

$$CH_3CHO + \left[\begin{array}{c} CH_3COCOOH \\ \downarrow \begin{array}{c} DPT \\ \text{Lipoic Acid} \end{array} \\ CH_3CO\text{-----}SLA \end{array}\right] \longrightarrow CH_3-\overset{OH}{\overset{|}{CH}}-\overset{O}{\overset{\|}{C}}-CH_3$$

Figure 1-2
Enzyme capable of using acetaldehyde (abundant in muscle).

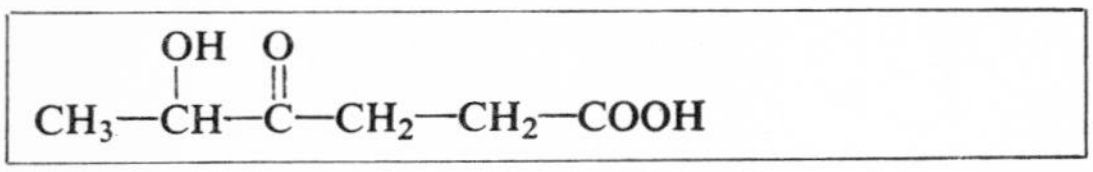

$$\begin{array}{c} \text{OH} \quad \text{O} \\ | \quad\quad || \\ \text{CH}_3\text{—CH—C—CH}_2\text{—CH}_2\text{—COOH} \end{array}$$

Figure 1-3
5-Hydroxy-4-ketohexanoic acid (HKH).

proved to be HKH.* When this material was oxidized with periodate, the split products were identified as AcH and succinic acid; nearly all of the radioactivity was present in carbon #1 of the acetaldehyde (carbon #5 of the HKH) when the HKH was obtained from ethanol-1-C^{14}. This provided a tentative structure for the metabolite, as well as the probable mechanism by which it was formed.

HKH is formed by a decarboxylation-condensation reaction between α-ketoglutarate (KG) and AcH, and is analogous to the formation of acetoin from pyruvate plus AcH (Figure 1-4). Relatively large amounts of unlabeled HKH have been prepared by incubating heart, kidney, or liver homogenates with KG plus AcH. The product was purified by column chromatography and was followed by the Voges Proskauer colour reaction. The isolated HKH was a levorotatory oil that gave a crystalline dehydroabietyl amine salt. The ketol grouping in the molecule gave a crystalline phenylosazone and dinitrophenylosazone derivative. The carboxyl group had a pK of approximately 4.6, and formed a crystalline p-phenylphenacyl ester. All of these products were subjected to elementary analysis, infrared spectrum, and nuclear magnetic resonance spectrum, and all of the data were in agreement with the postulated structure (3).

As a final proof of structure, HKH was synthesized by a malonic ester condensation with

*The following abbreviations have been used in this article: AcH, acetaldehyde; HKH, 5-hydroxy-4-keto-hexanoic acid; KG, α-ketoglutarate; TPP, thiamine pyrophosphate; BW, body weight.

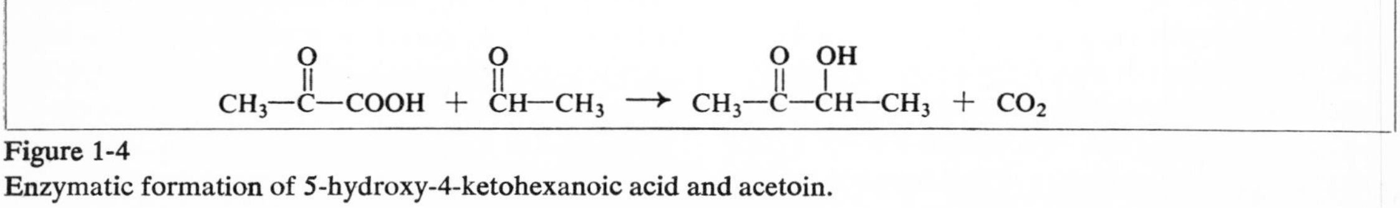

brominated acetoin (Figure 1-5). Acid hydrolysis and subsequent purification by the same column chromatography procedures used for the natural product gave an oil which formed the same derivatives as the natural product (3).

A colorimetric procedure for the determination of HKH (1) was based upon the Voges Proskauer colour reaction with creatine and α-naphthol in alkali. Acetoin was separated from HKH prior to the application of the colour reaction by adsorbing the HKH on a Dowex Column (formate form) and subsequently eluting it with formic acid. Acetoin ran through such a column freely and could be determined in the initial effluent (8). All rat tissue homogenates formed relatively large amounts of HKH when both KG plus AcH were supplied as substrates; heart and kidney were especially active (Figure 1-6). The yield of HKH in heart homogenate was almost a quantitative conversion of the AcH. The enzyme responsible for the condensation of KG plus AcH to form HKH was located primarily, if not exclusively, in the mitochondria of all tissues (1).

Heart homogenate was also capable of forming large amounts of HKH from pyruvate plus KG because it was able to convert pyruvate to AcH prior to a condensation of the latter with KG. This formation of AcH from pyruvate gives rise to the small amount of endogenous alcohol found in animal tissues. The particulate fraction of heart muscle can also carry out the pyruvate to AcH conversion when thiamine pyrophosphate (TPP) is added, but cannot do so in the absence of added TPP (1).

When KG and alcohol were added as substrates to various tissue homogenates, the formation of HKH reflected the conversion of alcohol to AcH prior to the condensation reaction. Both liver and kidneys gave the expected large increases in HKH formation when alcohol was

$$\begin{array}{c} \text{O} \quad\quad\quad\quad\quad \text{O} \quad\quad\quad\quad\quad\quad\quad\quad\quad\quad\quad \text{O} \quad \text{OH} \\ || \quad\quad\quad\quad\quad || \quad\quad\quad\quad\quad\quad\quad\quad\quad\quad\quad || \quad | \\ \text{HOOC—CH}_2\text{—CH}_2\text{—C—COOH} \;+\; \text{CH—CH}_3 \;\rightarrow\; \text{HOOC—CH}_2\text{—CH}_2\text{—C—CH—CH}_3 \;+\; \text{CO}_2 \end{array}$$

$$\begin{array}{c} \text{O} \quad\quad\quad\quad\quad \text{O} \quad\quad\quad\quad\quad\quad\quad \text{O} \quad \text{OH} \\ || \quad\quad\quad\quad\quad || \quad\quad\quad\quad\quad\quad\quad || \quad | \\ \text{CH}_3\text{—C—COOH} \;+\; \text{CH—CH}_3 \;\rightarrow\; \text{CH}_3\text{—C—CH—CH}_3 \;+\; \text{CO}_2 \end{array}$$

Figure 1-4
Enzymatic formation of 5-hydroxy-4-ketohexanoic acid and acetoin.

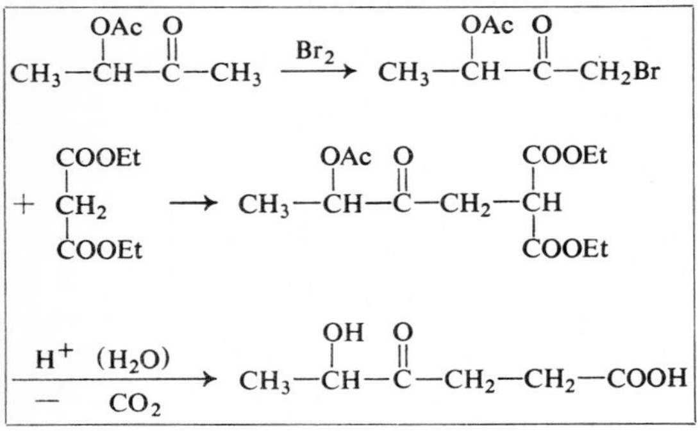

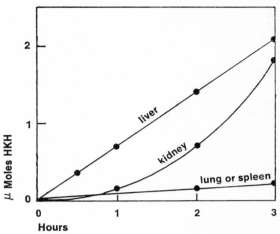

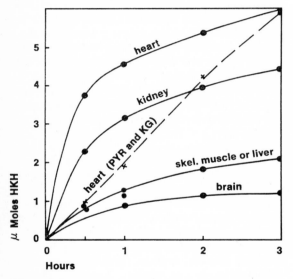

Figure 1-5
Synthesis of 5-hydroxy-4-ketohexanoic acid.

Figure 1-6
The formation of 5-hydroxy-4-ketohexanoic acid (HKH) from α-ketoglutarate plus acetaldehyde by rat tissue homogenates: 250 mg tissue, 0.05 M potassium phosphate buffer pH 7.1, 33 μM α-ketoglutarate, 7 μM acetaldehyde, total volume 3.2 ml incubated in closed vessels at 38° for indicated times. The dashed line shows the formation of HKH by heart homogenate when pyruvate (Pyr) plus α-ketoglutarate (KG) replaced AcH plus KG as the substrates.

added along with the KG (Figure 1-7). However, the amount of HKH formed by lung and spleen from KG was also increased to a small extent when alcohol was added with the KG. These tissues apparently have a small alcohol-oxidiz-

Figure 1-7
The formation of 5-hydroxy-4-ketohexanoic acid (HKH) from α-ketoglutarate plus alcohol by rat tissue homogenates. The values represent the net increase in HKH above that formed by KH alone when alcohol was added (200 mg/100 ml final concentration). Other details are the same as for Figure 1-6 except that the alcohol replaced the AcH.

ing capability. Similar experiments with brain were completely negative (1).

The enzyme which condenses pyruvate and AcH to form acetoin requires thiamine pyrophosphate as a co-factor. By analogy the HKH-forming enzyme would also be expected to be a thiamine enzyme. A defect in the HKH-forming system was observed in thiamine deficient rat liver and heart, but the defect was not reversed substantially by the addition of thiamine pyrophosphate *in vitro*. The formation of HKH from KG plus AcH was not seriously affected in other tissues by thiamine deficiency (1).

FORMATION OF HKH IN VIVO

Heart and kidney were the most active tissues in forming HKH from AcH plus KG *in vitro*, and they had the highest concentration of HKH (160–170 μg/gm) five minutes after the intraperitoneal administration of 30 mg/100 gm BW acetaldehyde to intact rats. Smaller doses of AcH gave correspondingly lower concentrations of HKH in all tissues, and repeated doses of AcH at ten-minute intervals gave correspondingly higher concentrations. The concentration of HKH in heart and kidney was 20 to 50 per cent higher when KG or pyruvate (but not glutamic acid or glutamine) was administered simultaneously with the AcH. Acetoin formation *in vivo* from administered AcH tended to parallel the HKH. There was no correlation betwen the AcH concentration found in the various tissues after AcH administration and the amount of HKH or acetoin formed by the tissue. Such studies showed that HKH could be formed from AcH in the intact rat, and except for the relatively poor formation of HKH by liver *in vivo*, the results of the *in vivo* studies were consistent with the relative activities of the various tissues *in vitro* (1).

ALCOHOL

The intraperitoneal injection of 300 mg/100 gm BW of alcohol to a normal rat gave only traces of HKH (12–15 μg/gm) in the heart five minutes later; no acetoin or HKH could be detected in any other tissue, and the 26-hour urine contained only small amounts of acetoin and HKH (30 μg HKH). Other studies have shown that approximately 70 per cent of administered HKH was excreted in the urine unchanged. When AcH was administered, only 1 per cent was recovered in the urine as HKH. Clearly, HKH formation was not a major metabolic pathway for alcohol or acetaldehyde. Prefeeding antabuse for three weeks did not alter the results obtained with alcohol or acetaldehyde alone, and therefore did not divert any major portion of the AcH into the acetoin or HKH pathways.

FATTY LIVER

I have been asked to comment briefly on the metabolism of alcohol as it relates to the production of fatty livers. Since I have not worked in this area I can only pass on what others have reported, together with some personal evaluations and comments.

The increase in liver lipids which is associated with the consumption of alcohol is believed to be the forerunner of liver cirrhosis. However, the mechanism by which alcohol increases liver fat is by no means clear. Fifty years ago it was attributed to an ill-defined hepatotoxic effect (of the CCl$_4$ variety). Between 1930 and 1940 alcoholic polyneuritis and pellagra were shown to be simple nutritional deficiencies that could be corrected by thiamine and niacin in spite of a continued intake of large amounts of alcohol. It then seemed probable that the alcoholic fatty liver was also nutritional in origin, and was due to a choline-lipotropic deficiency, since a lack of these factors was known to produce a fatty liver. Klatskin obtained evidence that alcohol does increase the choline requirement, but the alcoholic fatty liver does not respond to choline therapy, and does respond to a simple removal of alcohol from the diet. Hence the nutritional etiology of the alcoholic fatty liver has lost favour. In the meantime, a good deal of the basic biochemistry concerned with lipid metabolism has been worked out, and Isselbacher's laboratory, among others, is currently determining the effect of alcohol on the individual reactions which might be involved in the production of a fatty liver.

Many of the studies dealing with this topic have used unusually large (almost lethal) doses of alcohol. This is convenient experimentally because such doses will produce an easily measured increase in liver fat in 12 to 18 hours. The overall mechanism in this case seems to be clearly established (4). The alcohol produces a stimulus which is mediated through the adrenal and which causes a transfer of free fatty acids from the adipose tissue to the liver; the process can be blocked by adrenalectomy or by ganglionic blocking agents. In the presence of high concentrations of alcohol, the liver is less able to oxidize fatty acids to CO$_2$, or to release triglycerides into the blood stream (as low density lipoproteins), and it preferentially shunts the fatty acids into triglycerides instead of phospholipids (4).

The major question concerning these studies is their pertinence to the problem of fatty liver and cirrhosis in the human alcoholic. It is possible that these acute observations in the rat simply telescope smaller, more chronic but otherwise comparable effects in man. Conversely it is possible that man seldom achieves a blood alcohol level that would bring this mechanism into play, and that these observations have relatively little to do with the human problem.

The alcohol itself does not give rise to large amounts of fatty acids since most of the alcohol carbons can be recovered as CO_2 by the time the alcohol has disappeared from the body fluids. This failure to convert alcohol carbons to fatty acids is a little surprising since the acetyl CoA which is formed from alcohol is the starting point for fatty acid synthesis, and alcohol should theoretically be as good a precursor of fatty acids as is carbohydrate. However, the feeding of large amounts of carbohydrate leads to an adaptive increase in pentose shunt activity, and this supplies the TPNH which is the other major "substrate" requirement for fatty acid synthesis. During alcohol metabolism there is no obvious source of additional TPNH, and this may be the reason why most of the acetyl CoA formed from alcohol is burned via the citric acid cycle rather than converted to fatty acids. Relatively few studies have been conducted with animals given alcohol chronically, and we know nothing about the metabolic adaptations which might occur in chronic alcoholism. It is possible that the metabolic aberration which gives rise to a fatty liver in the chronic alcoholic cannot be detected in a rat which has never received alcohol previously.

Lieber and Schmid (5) suggested that the hydrogens from alcohol (rather than the carbons) gave rise to increased fatty acid synthesis, since more acetate was converted to fatty acids by liver slices in the presence of alcohol. This was confirmed by Scheig and Isselbacher (7), but the latter authors do not believe this is an important factor in the genesis of fatty livers, since the same effect was not observed in the intact animal. It is also difficult to see how the hydrogens from DPNH (formed by the oxidation of alcohol) would be transferred to TPN to give the reducing substance which is specifically required for *de novo* fatty acid synthesis.

There is no evidence to suggest that any of the by-products of alcohol metabolism are responsible for the fatty liver in chronic alcoholism, but none have been studied in this connection. Such a possibility would be attractive, especially if the by-product were formed by a system that adapted to a chronic alcohol intake. Studies are underway in our laboratory at the present time to determine whether HKH will produce any of the pathological changes associated with chronic alcoholism.

REFERENCES

1
BLOOM, R.J., FULLER, P.B., WESTERFELD, J.G., & WESTERFELD, W.W.
The formation and determination of 5-hydroxy-4-ketohexanoic acid
Biochemistry, **5**: 3211, 1967
2
BLOOM, R.J. & WESTERFELD, W.W.
A comparison of alcohol and acetate metabolites and the detection of a new metabolite from alcohol
In Frontiers in biochemistry, edited by R. E. Olson
New York: Marcel Dekker (in press)
3
BLOOM, R.J. & WESTERFELD, W.W.
A new intermediate in the metabolism of ethanol
Biochemistry, **5**: 3204, 1967
4
ISSELBACHER, K.J. & GREENBERGER, N.J.
Metabolic effects of alcohol on the liver
New England J. Med., **270**: 351 & 402, 1964
5
LIEBER, C.S. & SCHMID, R.
Effect of ethanol on fatty acid metabolism: stimulation of hepatic fatty acid synthesis *in vitro*
J. Clin. Invest., **40**: 394, 1961
6
LUBIN, M. & WESTERFELD, W.W.
The metabolism of acetaldehyde
J. Biol. Chem. **161**: 503, 1945
7
SCHEIG, R. & ISSELBACHER, K.J.
Pathogenesis of ethanol-induced fatty liver: 3. *In vivo* and *vitro* effects of ethanol on hepatic fatty acid metabolism in rats
J. Lipid Res., **6**: 269, 1965
8
WESTERFELD, W.W.
A colorimetric determination of blood acetoin
J. Biol. Chem., **161**: 495, 1945
9
WESTERFELD, W.W. & BLOOM, R.J.
A new metabolite from alcohol
Psychosom. Med., **28** (pt. 2): 443, 1965

OLOF A. FORSANDER

Research Laboratories of the State Alcohol Monopoly
(Alko) Helsinki, Finland

2

Utilization of
Ethanol Energy

At the end of the last century increasing interest in the nutrient value of ethanol first became apparent. It was shown that the substance had a considerable caloric value and that the breakdown of carbohydrates and fat diminished during its oxidation. But protein metabolism was not influenced. In 1913 Krieger (6) studied the utilization of ethanol energy for muscular work. His experiments seemed to show that alcohol could be directly used for work, but later investigators have shown that he was only partly correct in this regard. In a long series of investigations Le Breton and Trémolières (7) observed that alcohol could be used to cover the basal metabolism but not for muscular work or heat production.

In experiments with rats Richter (13) reported that ethanol could replace isodynamic quantities of food and also that it could be used for growth just as efficiently as calories from normal food. On the other hand, Michell (11) and Morgan *et al.* (12) claimed that only about 75 per cent of the energy content of alcohol was physiologically available. Their work was done on the assumption that the growth of young rats was directly proportional to the caloric intake. However, using a fully balanced diet, Gillespie and Lucas (3) showed that *all* the energy of ethanol found by bomb calorimetry was available for the metabolism and growth of the rats used in their experiment.

In countries where wine is used as table drink, the total amount of alcohol calories in the diet can be considerable. It has often been pointed out that wine or alcohol is used socially mainly because of its intoxicating effect. But if a pharmacological effect is desired, alcohol has to be consumed in large quantities as compared, for example, to caffein or nicotine. The metabolic and nutritional influence of alcohol will thus be rather important as long as the alcohol is oxidized. Le Breton and Trémolières (7) have calculated that the average alcohol consumption of a man in France amounts to between 10 and 15 per cent of the daily caloric intake, and for some persons up to 30 per cent. Jolliffe *et al.* (5) reported that among alcoholics some patients had lived for years on a diet comprised of 40 to 60 per cent alcohol. In a recommendation of the Food and Agriculture Organization of the

United Nations it has been agreed that up to 10 per cent of food intake may be calculated as alcohol. Even if higher amounts are used they should not be taken into account because of the deficiency of essential compounds in alcoholic beverages.

How do these findings correspond to theoretical calculations? One gram of ethanol gives 7.1 calories when oxidized in a calorimetric bomb. On the average, an individual can oxidize 7 gm of alcohol per hour, which gives 1200 calories per day if alcohol is consumed in quantities large enough to allow a day-long metabolism. The basal metabolism of a human subject has been estimated at 1500 calories per 24 hours. Therefore, up to 80 per cent of the energy requirement of basal metabolism can be covered by calories from alcohol. The actual energy consumption is, however, much higher than the basal requirement and depends on the amount of muscular work and the heat production. A rough calculation indicates that alcohol can furnish some 30 to 40 per cent of the calories required by an average man. The high alcohol content of the alcoholic's diet cannot be explained by these calculations, and other factors have to be taken into consideration.

The metabolism of ethanol takes place mainly in the liver. Only a minor amount is eliminated as alcohol or oxidized extrahepatically. In this respect ethanol differs from most other caloric substrates. Alcohol does not combust completely in the liver to carbon dioxide and water, but is oxidized partially to acetic acid (10). The acetate produced is transported by the blood from the liver and oxidized in other tissues to carbon dioxide and water. Thus, we have two sites for the oxidation of the ethanol molecule: the liver and the extrahepatic tissues of which muscle seems to be the most important. The rate of ethanol oxidation is dependent on the capacity of the liver. The acetic acid produced is oxidized very rapidly and can be detected only in small amounts in the blood.

The liver has an intensive metabolism with a high oxygen consumption. Although the weight of the liver is only 2 or 3 per cent of total body weight, it utilizes 25 to 30 per cent of total oxygen consumption. Since alcohol is only oxidized to acetate in the liver, just one part of the caloric content of the molecule is liberated there. During alcohol oxidation the oxygen consumption of the liver is not noticeably influenced (9). It has been estimated that the liver on the average consumes about 75 ml of oxygen per minute. Calculated on this basis, the oxidation of ethanol to acetate utilizes about 75 per cent of the liver's oxygen consumption. The rest is utilized for oxidation of some of the acetate to carbon dioxide and for the breakdown of other substrates. Since the rate of oxidation of ethanol is constant down to very low concentrations, alcohol oxidation will monopolize the use of oxygen and mainly cover the liver's caloric utilization as long as alcohol is present in the body.

Acetate is normally found in the blood of man in small quantities only, but during ethanol metabolism the concentration rises. It has been calculated that 1.2 moles of acetate on the average are produced from ethanol per minute (9). The formed substance is readily metabolized in various tissues in the body (4). The acetate formed from fermented carbohydrates in the bovine rumen is known to be an excellent nutrient and to play a major role in the energy supply of the animal (1). As far as the present writer is aware, only one study has been done on the quantitative extrahepatic utilization of the acetate produced during ethanol oxidation. Lundquist's group in Denmark (8) has studied its role quantitatively in the metabolism of the heart. This investigation was done with a heart perfusion technique. A calculation from the results showed that during ethanol oxidation about one-fifth of the oxygen consumption of the heart was utilized for the oxidation of acetate; the rest was consumed in the oxidation of free fatty acids, lactate, and unknown compounds.

The rate at which acetate is broken down in muscular tissue is dependent on the acetate concentration and the functional state of the tissue (2). The higher the concentration and the more work the muscle performs, the more intensive is the acetate oxidation. Even at low concentrations the oxidation is high, as indicated by the fact that the concentration in the blood never increases.

All animals, including man, are born with a very effective system which is able to break down alcohol and utilize its chemically bound energy.

In the liver the first steps in the breakdown chain – oxidation of ethanol to acetate – seem to be catalysed mainly by two dehydrogenase enzymes, the alcohol dehydrogenase and the aldehyde dehydrogenase (9). The hydrogen liberated in these two reactions is oxidized by the normal mitochondrial respiratory chain to water. The oxidation of acetate takes place in the tricarboxylic acid cycle which is present in most types of tissues. In this cycle four hydrogen molecules are liberated and two molecules of water and two of carbon dioxide are formed. If the hydrogen atoms liberated through the first two dehydrogenase reactions are utilized as efficiently as those liberated in the tricarboxylic acid cycle, one-third of the bound energy of the ethanol molecule will be liberated in the liver and two-thirds extrahepatically.

Ethanol can be utilized for muscular work and heat production only indirectly. Even under basal conditions the amount of acetate formed from ethanol is too small to meet the demand, and additional substrates will always have to be metabolized. With higher energy requirements the possible contribution of alcohol will be still less.

REFERENCES

1
ANNISON, E.F. & LINDSAY, D.B.
Acetate utilization in sheep
Biochem. J., 78: 777, 1961
2
FRITZ, I.B.
Factors influencing the rates of long-chain fatty acid oxidation and synthesis in mammalian systems
Physiol. Rev., 41: 52, 1961
3
GILLESPIE, R.J.G. & LUCAS, C.C.
Metabolic availability of energy of ingested ethyl alcohol
Can. J. Biochem. Physiol., 36: 307, 1958
4
HENNES, A.R.
Abnormalities of acetate metabolism in adrenal insufficiency in man
Am. J. Med., 32: 343, 1962
5
JOLLIFFE, N., COLBERT, C.N., & JOFFE, P.M.
Observations on the etiologic relationship of vitamin B (B$_1$) to polyneuritis in the alcohol addict
Am. J. Med. Sc., 191: 515, 1936

6
KRIEGER, K.
Die Verwertung der Energie des Alkohols für die Muskelarbeit
Pflügers Arch. Ges. Physiol., 151: 479, 1913
7
LE BRETON, E. & TRÉMOLIÈRES, J.
Part de l'alcool dans la dépense calorique
Proc. Nutr. Soc., 14: 97, 1955
8
LINDENEG, O., MELLEMGAARD, K., FABRICIUS, J., & LUNDQUIST, F.
Myocardial utilization of acetate, lactate and free fatty acids after ingestion of ethanol
Clin. Sc., 27: 427, 1964
9
LUNDQUIST, F., TYGSTRUP, N., WINKLER, K., MELLEMGAARD, K., & MUNCK-PETERSEN, S.
Ethanol metabolism and production of free acetate in the human liver
J. Clin. Invest., 41: 955, 1962
10
LUNDSGAARD, E.
Alcohol oxidation as a function of the liver
Compt. Rend. Trav. Lab. Carlsberg Ser. Chim., 22: 333, 1938
11
MICHELL, H.H.
The food value of ethyl alcohol
J. Nutr., 10: 311, 1935
12
MORGAN, A.F., BRINNER, L., PLAA, C.B., & STONE, M.M.
Utilization of calories from alcohol and wines and their effects on cholesterol metabolism
Am. J. Physiol., 189: 290, 1957
13
RICHTER, C.P.
Alcohol, beer and wine as foods
Quart. J. Stud. Alc., 14: 525, 1953

J. P. VON WARTBURG

Institute of Medicine and Chemistry
Berne University
Berne, Switzerland

3

Alcohol Dehydrogenase Distribution in Tissues of Different Species

Alcohol dehydrogenase* is widely distributed in nature. The enzyme has been found in various tissues of humans, in numerous mammalians, vertebrates, and insects, as well as in microorganisms and plants. In animals the liver is the main localization of the enzyme, and hence the highly purified ADH-preparations were obtained from this organ of the horse (1,2,11), human (17), and rhesus monkey (8). Alcohol dehydrogenases are metalloenzymes containing zinc, which is partly located in the active centres of the molecule and is essential for its activity (9,14).

Isoenzymes have been known for several years for a number of dehydrogenases. Best known in this respect is the lactic dehydrogenase. For this enzyme the multiple molecular forms have been investigated intensively. The determination of the isoenzyme patterns is now used in medicine as an organ-specific diagnostic tool. Two years ago we obtained a first indication for the existence of isoenzymes of alcohol dehydrogenase in the liver of the rhesus monkey (8). Further investigations revealed that other species too were heterogenous in respect to alcohol dehydrogenase.

ISOENZYMES OF ALCOHOL DEHYDROGENASE

The isoenzyme patterns of ADH in the liver of various species are shown in Figure 3-1. Liver homogenates were subjected to electrophoresis on agar gel. The various bands represent ADH activity which is visualized by the formation of a coloured formazan in the presence of ethanol, NAD, phenazine metosulphate, and a tetrazolium salt. A heterogeneity of ADH exists in human, rhesus monkey, horse, beef, and frog livers. There are no indications for the occurrence of isoenzymes in the livers of the other species. The number of the bands depends on the species. This stands in contrast to the findings with lactic dehydrogenase, where five isoenzymes are found in most species. Human liver reveals three isoenzymes of ADH, and horse liver at least five fractions. Only two are found in the liver of the

*The following abbreviations are used: LADH for liver alcohol dehydrogenase; NAD and NADH$_2$ for oxidized and reduced nicotinamide adenine dinucleotide.

14 / J.P. von Wartburg

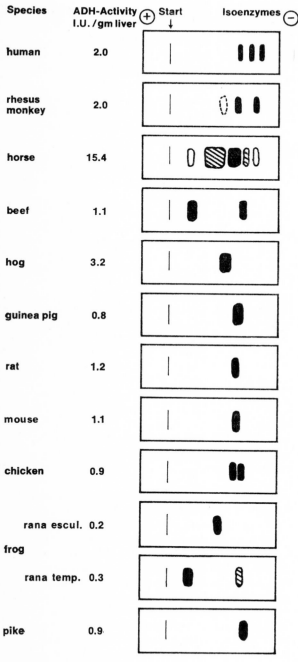

Species	ADH-Activity I.U./gm liver
human	2.0
rhesus monkey	2.0
horse	15.4
beef	1.1
hog	3.2
guinea pig	0.8
rat	1.2
mouse	1.1
chicken	0.9
rana escul.	0.2
frog rana temp.	0.3
pike	0.9

Figure 3-1

Isoenzymes of alcohol dehydrogenase in the liver of various species. Separation of the isoenzymes by agar gel electrophoresis. Activity in IU/gm fresh liver. For a detailed report on these studies see Moser *et al.* (6).

rhesus monkey and of the beef. There are also differences within the same species. The frog *rana esculenta*, for example, has only one band, but *rana temporaria* shows two.

Similar broad variations between the different species can be observed in the alcohol dehydrogenase activity. Most animals reveal activities between 1 and 2 IU/gm of fresh liver. Such activity in the horse seems to be exceptionally high, which is probably the reason why it was chosen by Bonnichsen and Wassen as the best source for the purification of ADH. Many commercial preparations of this enzyme are available today.

There is no obvious interpretation of these data and it seems that more species will be required to get some indication about the phylogenetic development of ADH. No reports are available which would permit the correlation of these results with the ability of these animals to detoxify ethanol. It is known that alcohol can be formed endogenously in the organism or by bacteria in the gastrointestinal tract.

To get some indications about the meaning and the implications of the isoenzymes of ADH it is necessary to isolate the purified isoenzymes and to characterize them. This was first done for the two isoenzymes of rhesus monkey liver. Both isoenzymes were purified by ammonium sulfate fractionation and subsequent chromatography on ion exchange celluloses (8). Table 3-1 summarizes some properties of the purified isoenzymes. The ratio of ethanol oxidation to acetaldehyde reduction under standard conditions is 8:1 for isoenzyme II and 25:1 for isoenzyme III. In contrast to the small differences in the pH optima for ethanol oxidation by both isoenzymes we find marked differences in the sensitivity toward effectors. The metal chelating agent ortho-phenanthroline inhibits isoenzyme III much more effectively than isoenzyme II. Similarly, the activation by thiourea is higher for isoenzyme III. Large variations are found in the substrate specificity. Isoenzyme II oxidizes butanol, cyclo-hexanol, and benzyl alcohol considerably faster than ethanol, whereas the situation is reversed for isoenzyme III. Finally, the two isoenzymes seem to have similar molecular weights as determined by gel filtration on Sephadex G-200.

It is of interest to note that the percentage of

TABLE 3–1

PROPERTIES OF ALCOHOL DEHYDROGENASE
ISOENZYMES FROM RHESUS MONKEY LIVER

Property	Isoenzyme II	Isoenzyme III
^{v}acetaldehyde/^{v}ethanol	8	25
pH optimum (ethanol)	10.85	10.15
I_{50} with o-phenanthroline (M)	1.5×10^{-3}	1.7×10^{-5}
effect of thiourea (0.66 M) (V_{Th}/V_C)	1.30	2.63
substrate specificity (per cent)		
1.6×10^{-2} M ethanol	100	100
3.3×10^{-4} M n-butanol	117	54
3.3×10^{-4} M cyclohexanol	133	23
3.3×10^{-4} M benzyl alcohol	150	40
molecular weight (Sephadex G-200)	80,000–90,000	

each of the two isoenzymes in the total activity
of the extract varies from 35 to 65 for isoenzyme
II and from 65 to 35 for isoenzyme III. Therefore,
we must expect that the overall kinetics of ADH
carried out on crude preparations can show a
considerable individual variation. This variability of course is superimposed on the large differences seen in the catalytic parameters between
various species. So far, broad variations have
been shown for the properties of purified human
ADH and the enzymes of the horse and rhesus
monkey. These circumstances make it impossible to extrapolate from *in vitro* kinetics for one
species to *in vivo* conditions in another one.

A separation of the five isoenzymes in horse
liver is achieved by chromatography on CM-
cellulose (16). The contribution of the single
isoenzymes to the total activity is about 45 to
50 per cent for isoenzyme III, 15 and 35 per cent
for II and IV respectively, and only a few per cent
for isoenzymes I and V. The commercial horse
liver ADH preparations contain the main fraction,
that is isoenzyme III. But several batches obtained from Boehringer (Mannheim) revealed
traces of isoenzymes II and IV. A steroid-active
alcohol dehydrogenase from horse liver has
recently been crystallized by Theorell *et al.* (12).
This enzyme seems to correspond to isoenzyme
IV described here.

In contrast to the remarkable differences in
the kinetic properties of both isoenzymes from
rhesus monkey, the five fractions in horse liver
differ less in their characteristics (see Table

TABLE 3–2

INHIBITION OF ALCOHOL
DEHYDROGENASE ISOENZYMES
FROM HORSE LIVER BY PYRAZOL
AND ORTHO-PHENANTHROLINE

Isoenzyme	Pyrazol	o-phenanthroline
I	0.4	170
II	0.7	260
III	35	310
IV	73	820
V	125	9000

Conditions: 1.6×10^{-2} M ethanol; 1.6×10^{-3} M
NAD; 3.3×10^{-2} M Na pyrophosphate buffer, pH
8.8. The figures represent the inhibitor concentration (in µM) for a 50 per cent inhibition of the
enzymatic activity.

3-2). So far we have found a decreasing sensitivity of the isoenzymes from I to V toward two
inhibitors. Pyrazol, as shown by Theorell and his
collaborators (10,13), inhibits ADH by compet-
ing with ethanol for the substrate site in the active
centre. At this time, this is the only known
specific inhibitor of ADH; o-phenanthroline, the
other inhibitor used here, chelates the zinc in the
enzyme, as was shown by Vallee and his coworkers (14). Furthermore, the relative velocities for the reduction of acetaldehyde and
butyraldehyde vary for the isoenzymes in a
systematic way. Additional differences between
the various isoenzymes are found in respect to
their activity with coenzyme analogues.

We still know very little about the physiological function of alcohol dehydrogenase. The

significance of isoenzymes in general and of ADH in particular lies even more in the dark. But we hope that the simultaneous investigation and correlation of the structural and functional features of ADH will prove illuminating. The number of isoenzymes, for instance, can give us indications about the substructure of the enzyme. It is known that lactic dehydrogenase is a tetrameric molecule, built from two different polypeptide chains in various proportions depending on the isoenzyme. By analogy to these findings we must expect three isoenzymes, if ADH is a dimeric molecule. This could be the case in human ADH. Two isoenzymes, as they are found in rhesus monkey liver, are hard to explain in this way. However, a third isoenzyme also occurs, located mainly in the gastrointestinal tract. The total tract contains approximately 10 per cent of the activity found in the liver. The lungs and the urinary bladder have even less enzyme.

So far we have discussed several factors leading to the broad variations between the species in respect to alcohol dehydrogenase: first, differences in the substructure and number of isoenzymes found in various species; second, differences in the percentage contribution of the single isoenzymes to the total activity within the same species; third, differences in the kinetic parameters of the isoenzymes of one species; and fourth, differences between the functional properties of the enzymes of different species. It is conceivable, of course, that the differences found between alcohol dehydrogenases of various species are partly brought about by the fact that different isoenzymes have been compared; that is, that isoenzyme III of man would have more similarity to isoenzyme III of the rhesus monkey or the horse than to the human isoenzymes I or II.

The investigation of the distribution and activity of extrahepatic ADH reveals further differences between the various species. Figure 3-2 shows the distribution pattern for ADH in four organs of eight species. It is apparent that all species show at least some activity in the gastrointestinal tract, the kidney, and the lung. But the patterns are quite different. In the rhesus monkey the extrahepatic activity ranges between 10 and 15 per cent of the hepatic ADH. In the chicken, on the other hand, there is no detectable activity in the gastrointestinal tract, but over 20 per cent of the hepatic activity is found in the kidney. This again is in contrast to the very low activities in the kidneys of other species such as the guinea pig. The horse has practically all its activity in the liver. The frog, on the other hand, has very little hepatic activity as compared with other species, but the extrahepatic activities are considerable. We can estimate that more alcohol is oxidized extrahepatically in this animal than is oxidized by the liver.

At this time it is rather difficult to interpret these data in a systematic way. It seems that for some species the order of magnitude of these activities corresponds to the one found for the extrahepatic ethanol metabolism. But even this correlation must be considered with caution, since it is known, for example, that the kidney of the rat can produce more acetaldehyde from ethanol by the catalase system than with alcohol dehydrogenase (15,18).

VARIANT ENZYME OF HUMAN LIVER ALCOHOL DEHYDROGENASE

Some years ago we were able to show that besides three isoenzymes, alcohol dehydrogenase in man also occurs in the form of an atypical variant (19). Table 3-3 compares and summarizes the properties of normal and atypical human ADH. Characteristic for the variant enzyme is its high specific activity. As a consequence, carriers of the atypical enzyme have a total ADH-activity in the liver which is four to five times higher than normal, when determined at a physiological pH and temperature. The pH optimum for the normal enzyme at pH 10.8 is shifted to pH 8.5 for the atypical ADH. Further differences are found in respect to the sensitivity toward o-penanthroline or the effect of thiourea.

Figure 3-2

Extrahepatic distribution of alcohol dehydrogenase in various species. The extrahepatic activity in the diagram is expressed as a percentage of the hepatic activity. The hepatic activity (numbers) is given in IU/gm fresh liver.

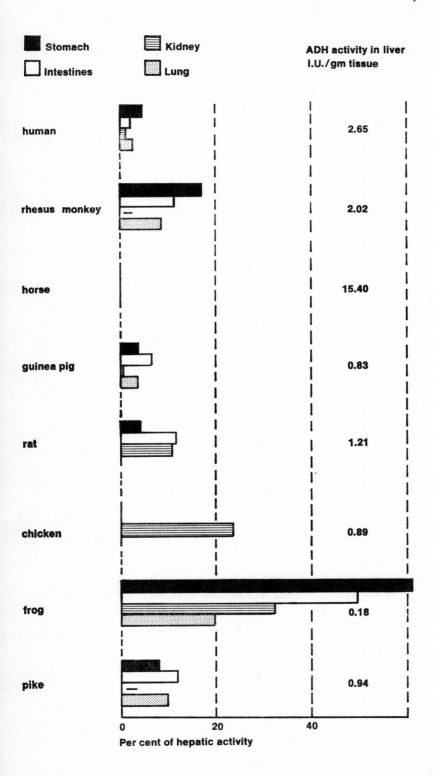

TABLE 3–3

PROPERTIES OF NORMAL AND ATYPICAL HUMAN
ALCOHOL DEHYDROGENASE

Property	Normal LADH	Atypical LADH
specific activity (I.U./mg protein)	ca. 3	ca. 10
total activity (I.U./liver)	ca. 3,600	ca. 17,000
pH optimum (ethanol oxidation)	10.8	8.5
I_{50} for o-phenanthroline (M)	6.7×10^{-5}	3.3×10^{-4}
effect of thiourea (0.66 M) (V_{Th}/V_C)	2.20	0.65
substrate specificity (per cent) 1.6×10^{-2} M ethanol 3.3×10^{-4} M butanol 3.3×10^{-4} M benzyl alcohol 3.3×10^{-4} M cyclohexanol	100 87 85 82	100 54 22 18

The activity of normal ADH is more than doubled
by thiourea, whereas the atypical enzyme is
strongly inhibited under identical conditions.
Furthermore, the substrate specificity is different
for both enzymes. The variant enzyme shows
less oxidation of butanol, cyclohexanol, and
benzyl alcohol. Finally, no differences were detected for the Michaelis constants for ethanol,
acetaldehyde, NAD, and NADH$_2$, or in the
molecular weights.

As a consequence of these findings we started
a screening program analysing biopsy material
obtained from a surgical department. In this way
we hoped to learn more about the frequency of
this enzyme anomaly and to find a living carrier
with the atypical enzyme. Altogether we have
tested 35 individuals, that is 18 livers and 17
stomachs. The mean activity of 13 normal livers
was 2.65 IU/gm of tissue, when determined at
pH 8.8. At pH 11.0 there was an increase in activity by a factor of 1.71, corresponding to the
pH rate profile of the normal enzyme. Five
atypical livers had much more activity at pH 8.8,
namely 11.3 IU/gm of tissue, and this activity
was decreased by ⅔ when determined at pH 11.0.
Analogous results were found for 16 normal
stomachs and one atypical one. In summary, six
individuals out of 35, or 17 per cent, were atypical. This figure, of course, can change with an
increase in number of individuals tested. But
it indicates that this anomaly is quite frequent

and that it would be desirable also to carry out
such screening tests in other countries and for
other races.*

These findings prompted an investigation of
the possible implications of the enzyme variant
for alcohol metabolism in humans. To test this
we first gave a dose of 0.7 gm of ethanol per kilogram of body weight to a normal person. This
dose leads to an initial blood alcohol concentration of about 0.1 per cent (see Figure 3-3).
The distribution factor *r* and the rate of alcohol
oxidation were calculated from the linear drop
of blood alcohol levels through time. A value of
90 mg of ethanol oxidized per kilogram of body
weight during one hour was obtained for the
normal individual (curve 1). It can be seen that
this drop was somewhat faster in the subject with
the atypical ADH (curve 2). The corresponding
value for the ethanol oxidation is higher, namely
141 mg/kg BW/hour. This figure is slightly
above the average value of approximately 100
mg/kg/hour found in the literature for ethanol
oxidation. But this enhancement by 40 to 50 per
cent does not correspond to the five- to seven-
fold increase in ADH as it is found in atypical

*Recent and more extended population studies on the
occurrence of the atypical ADH in Switzerland and
England have confirmed a high frequency of 20 per
cent in the Swiss population (20), and revealed a
lower frequency in England, i.e. 4 per cent in London
(20) and in Liverpool (3).

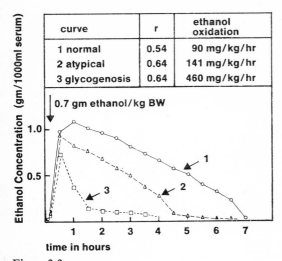

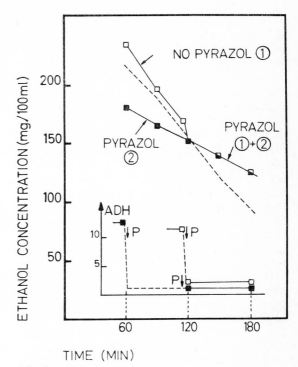

curve	r	ethanol oxidation
1 normal	0.54	90 mg/kg/hr
2 atypical	0.64	141 mg/kg/hr
3 glycogenosis	0.64	460 mg/kg/hr

0.7 gm ethanol/kg BW

Figure 3-3
Blood alcohol concentrations after a peroral administration of ethanol. 1. Normal individual. 2. Individual with the atypical human alcohol dehydrogenase. 3. Infant with glycogenosis (glucose-6-phosphate deficiency). Ethanol dose: 0.7 gm/kg BW. The blood alcohol concentration was determined enzymatically (ADH method).

Figure 3-4
Effect of pyrazol on the alcohol dehydrogenase activity and the alcohol oxidation in the isolated perfused rat liver. The alcohol concentration in the perfusing fluid is plotted as a function of the time. The dashed line represents the control experiment without pyrazol; the solid line between the squares represents the experiment with 3×10^{-3} M pyrazol. From Papenberg and von Wartburg (7).

livers.* Hence it is probable that another factor such as the reoxidation of $NADH_2$ formed in the alcohol dehydrogenase reaction becomes rate limiting. This interpretation is supported by analogous drinking experiments carried out with children suffering from glycogen storage disease (type I). They were performed in collaboration with Professor Rossi and his group in the Department of Pediatrics of the University of Berne. Curve 3 shows that these children are fully sober within one or two hours after an equal dose of ethanol. This is due to the manifold increase in alcohol oxidation, namely 460 mg/kg BW/hour. It is probable that this enhancement is correlated to an increase in $NADH_2$ reoxidation due to the high pyruvate concentration found in these patients (21).

These two aberrations of nature – that is, the occurrence of an atypical ADH with enhanced

activity on one hand, and the circumstances found in glycogen storage disease on the other – would indicate that the reoxidation of $NADH_2$ limits the rate of alcohol oxidation. On the other side, this does not mean that a decreased level of ADH activity is unable to limit the rate of ethanol oxidation. Such a decrease in ethanol oxidation by an inhibition of ADH in liver homogenates was demonstrated by Lundquist with o-phenanthroline (5). We have obtained analogous results using the more specific inhibitor pyrazol and the method of the isolated perfused rat liver (7). Similar results with this compound have been obtained by Goldberg *et al.* (4).

*This lack of an increased ethanol oxidation *in vivo* in carriers of the atypical ADH has been confirmed by Edwards and Evans (3).

In Figure 3-4 the effect of pyrazol on the oxidation of ethanol by the perfused rat liver is shown. The dose of 20 mg of pyrazol per 100 ml of perfusing liquid was recommended to us by Dr. Goldberg. The dotted line indicates a control experiment without inhibitor. We can see that after a control period of normal ethanol oxidation the addition of pyrazol leads to a sharp drop of ADH activity in the liver. This 85 per cent inhibition, determined by cutting off a small piece of liver tissue during the perfusion experiment, leads to a decrease in ethanol oxidation from 62 mg per liver per hour in the control period to 23 mg with pyrazol; that is, a reduction by 65 per cent (curve 2). An analogous inhibition is achieved over the whole period of experimentation when pyrazol is added at the beginning (curve 2).

These results, in conjunction with the fact that ADH activity *in vitro* is just sufficient to account for the whole ethanol oxidation *in vivo*, would suggest the following interpretation. In the normal state of living both the amount of alcohol dehydrogenase and the reoxidation of the coenzyme are equally rate limiting. An increase of each single parameter can only lead to an enhancement of ethanol oxidation when the reoxidation of the coenzyme occurs directly in the binary complex of ADH and coenzyme.

SUMMARY AND CONCLUSIONS

Alcohol dehydrogenase exists in multiple molecular forms in various species. The number of isoenzymes, their kinetic properties, and the activity in the liver and other organs depend on the species. Human liver ADH has three isoenzymes and also exists in an atypical form. The possible importance of the variability of the biochemical individuality for alcoholism has been stressed by R. Williams. Evidence for an important role of biological factors in the etiology of alcoholism has been found in recent years. They provide a stronger basis for the disease concept of alcoholism, although there is no doubt that social and cultural factors play a major role. The results reported here show that a considerable individuality occurs in respect to a specific enzyme involved in alcohol metabolism.

At this time it is still difficult to evaluate all possible implications of these findings for ethanol metabolism in normal individuals or for a possible hereditary predisposition to alcoholism.

REFERENCES

1
BONNICHSEN, R.K.
Crystalline animal alcohol dehydrogenase from horse liver
Arch. Biochem., **18**: 361, 1948
2
DALZIEL, K.
On the purification of liver alcohol dehydrogenase
Acta Chem. Scand., **12**: 459, 1958
3
EDWARDS, J.A. & EVANS, P.D.A.
Ethanol metabolism in subjects possessing typical and atypical liver alcohol dehydrogenase
Clin. Pharmacol. Therap., **8**: 824, 1967
4
GOLDBERG, L.
Personal communication
5
LUNDQUIST, F., SVENDSEN, I., & PETERSON, P.H.
The metabolism of ethanol–rat-liver suspensions
Biochem. J., **86**: 119, 1963
6
MOSER, K., PAPENBERG, J., & VON WARTBURG, J.P.
Heterogenität und Organverteilung der Alkoholdehydrogenase bei verschiedenen Spezies
Enzym. biol. clin., **9**: 447, 1968
7
PAPENBERG, J. & VON WARTBURG, J.P.
In preparation
8
PAPENBERG, J., VON WARTBURG, J.P., & AEBI, H.
Die Heterogenität der Alkoholdehydrogenase aus Rhesusaffenleber
Biochem. Z., **342**: 95, 1965
9
SUND, H. & THEORELL, H.
Alcohol dehydrogenases
In The enzymes, vol. 7, edited by P.D. Boyer, H. Lardy, & K. Myrbäck
New York: Academic Press, 1963
10
THEORELL, H.
The role of proteins in biological oxido-reduction
Bull. Soc. Chim. Biol., **46**: 1533, 1964
11
THEORELL, H. & BONNICHSEN, R.K.
Studies on liver alcohol dehydrogenase: I. Equilibria and initial reaction velocities
Acta Chem. Scandinav., **5**: 1105, 1951
12
THEORELL, H., TANIGUCHI, S., AKESON, A., & SKURSKY, L.
Crystallization of a separate steroid-active liver alcohol

dehydrogenase
Biochem. Biophys. Res. Comm., **24**: 603, 1966
13
THEORELL, H. & YONETANI, T.
Liver alcohol dehydrogenase-DPN-pyrazole complex:
a model of a ternary intermediate in the enzyme
reaction
Biochem. Z., **338**: 537, 1963
14
VALLEE, B.L.
Metal and enzyme interactions: correlation of
composition, function and structure
In The enzymes, vol. 3, edited by P.D. Boyer,
H. Lardy, K. Myrbäck
New York: Academic Press, 1960
15
VON WARTBURG, J.P.
Animal experimentation in the study of alcoholism
In Biochemical factors in alcoholism, ed. R.P. Maickel
Oxford: Pergamon Press, 1967
16
VON WARTBURG, J.P.
Isoenzymes of various alcohol dehydrogenases
3rd Meeting Fed. Europ. Biochem. Soc., Warsaw, 1966
Abstracts, F 180
17
VON WARTBURG, J.P., BETHUNE, J.L., & VALLEE, B.L.
Human liver alcohol dehydrogenase: kinetic and
physicochemical properties
Biochemistry, **3**: 1775, 1964
18
VON WARTBURG, J.P. & EPPENBERGER, H.M.
Vergleichende Untersuchungen über den oxydativen
Abbau von 1-C^{14} Aethanol und 1-C^{14}-Azetet in
Leber und Niere
Helv. Physiol. Pharmacol. Acta, **19**: 303, 1961
19
VON WARTBURG, J.P., PAPENBERG, J., & AEBI, H.
An atypical human alcohol dehydrogenase
Canad. J. Biochem., **43**: 889, 1965
20
VON WARTBURG, J.P. & SCHÜRCH, P.M.
Atypical human liver alcohol dehydrogenase
Ann. N.Y. Acad. Sci., **151**: 936, 1968
21
ZUPPINGER, K., PAPENBERG, J., SCHÜRCH, P.,
VON WARTBURG, J.P., COLOMBO, J.P., & ROSSI, E.
Vermehrte Alkoholoxydation bei der Glykogenose
Typ I. Schweiz. med. Wchnschr., **97**: 1110, 1967

H. KALANT

Department of Pharmacology
University of Toronto and
Addiction Research Foundation
Toronto, Ontario, Canada

4

Cellular Effects
of Alcohols

It has been known for many years that ethanol and other short-chain aliphatic alcohols, in suitable concentrations, are capable of influencing the metabolic and other functions of a wide range of living cells, from protozoa up to the tissue cells of the most complex organisms. The effects are typically depressant, and because of their generality and non-specificity the alcohols are usually classed as "narcotic agents" in the biological (though not the legal) sense. For example, ethanol, in concentrations ranging from less than 1 per cent to about 4 per cent, has been reported to inhibit such diverse processes as the motility of leukocytes (2), rat spermatozoa (22), and paramecia (44); the luminescence of bacteria (47); the contractility of isolated rat atrium (13) and guinea pig ileum (44, 46); the conduction of impulses by isolated peripheral nerves in frogs and mammals (6, 19, 52); and the release *in vitro* of histamine from lung tissue (44) and of acetylcholine from rat brain cortex slices (28).

However, it is equally clear that, like other "narcotics" such as barbiturates and volatile anesthetics, alcohols often produce an initial stimulation at low concentrations. Thus, in concentrations below 1 per cent, ethanol *increased* the motility of leukocytes (2) and spermatozoa (22). Numerous investigators have reported that similar concentrations of ethanol increase the excitability (i.e. lower the threshold for electrical stimulation) of frog sciatic nerve (6, 12, 19), cat cerebral cortex (15), and frog skeletal muscle (6).

The biphasic influence of ethanol – stimulation at low concentrations, inhibition at higher – is not seen with all types of test system studied, nor with all the other short-chain aliphatic alcohols. The question arises, therefore, whether we are dealing with many different actions of alcohols having different dose-response curves, or with a single fundamental action which gives different end results according to the balance of other factors acting upon the test systems. In an attempt to answer this question, I shall review in more detail the known cellular effects of ethanol in multicellular organisms, the quantitative relationships, and the possible mechanisms involved. Metabolic disturbances resulting from the metabolism of alcohols in the liver or other tissues will not be examined, nor indirect effects

TABLE 4–1

CONCENTRATION OF ETHANOL REQUIRED TO PRODUCE
50 PER CENT INHIBITION IN TISSUES FROM DIFFERENT
SPECIES

Tissue	Function	Species	ED_{50} (M)
erythrocytes	O_2 uptake	goose	1.6
skin	Na^+ transport	frog	.94
ileum	contraction	frog	.49
heart muscle	contraction	tortoise	.44
sympathetic ganglia	transmission	cat	.48
sympathetic fibres	conduction	cat	.24
lung	histamine release	guinea pig	.12

resulting from nausea, dehydration, acidosis, stress responses, or the like, but only the direct pharmacological effects of the alcohols themselves.

From an examination of the available data on thresholds and dose-response curves, it is evident that different tissues and organisms differ quite markedly in their sensitivity to alcohols. Table 4-1 illustrates the differences in concentration of ethanol required to produce 50 per cent inhibition of function in several tissues from different species (7, 23, 36, 44).

Even greater differences in sensitivity exist, as is evident from the fact that in man a concentration of about 0.13 M in body water causes death due to complete suppression of activity of the medullary respiratory centre. Differences in threshold also exist in relation to the functional state of the test issue. It has been shown repeatedly that nerve cells are more susceptible to inhibition by ethanol when they are active than when at rest.

Recognizing these differences in sensitivity to alcohols, related to species, tissue, and functional state, and recognizing that some of the possible cellular effects may not be important *in vivo* because the necessary alcohol concentrations *in vitro* are above the lethal level, it is none the less informative to examine the various known cellular effects to see what light may be shed on the possible mechanisms of action.

MEMBRANE RESTING POTENTIALS

The *in vivo* effects of alcohols upon the nervous system are extremely difficult to interpret because of the functional interrelationships between various parts of it. Direct and indirect effects are difficult, or sometimes impossible, to separate. Cellular effects must therefore be studied in isolated preparations which can be exposed to alcohols directly, which can be stimulated directly, and from which the responses can be recorded directly.

The earlier work cited above showed that alcohols modify the excitability of peripheral nerve axons, the lower alcohols biphasically, the higher alcohols causing depression only. Later workers (5, 12, 43, 52) have shown that these effects result from changes in the electrical potential of the cell membrane. As shown in Figure 4-1, the short-chain alcohols reduced the membrane potential (i.e., partly depolarized the cell), while the longer-chain alcohols increased the potential (i.e., hyperpolarized the cell). As a result, in the former case a smaller stimulus was adequate to complete the depolarization to the point necessary to trigger an action potential, while in the latter case a stronger stimulus was required.

Similar changes were found in frog skeletal muscle (6, 33) and in locally perfused cerebral cortical neurons in the cat (16); ethanol, in concentrations which produced a slow depolarization, reduced the threshold stimulus. Larger concentrations of all the alcohols produced a marked depolarization; the resting potential was so low that it could not undergo sufficient depolarization to initiate an action potential. Accordingly, the threshold stimulus first increased, and finally all response disappeared.

Attempts to explain these changes have been only partially successful. The resting potential of the cell membrane is a function of the difference in potassium (K^+) concentration inside and

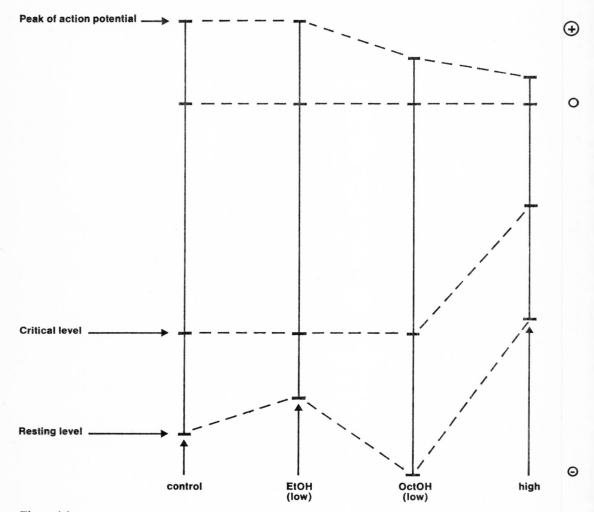

Figure 4-1

Effects of ethanol and octanol on membrane potentials in peripheral nerve. O = complete depolarization; + and − indicate positive and negative intracellular potentials respectively.

outside the cell, and a fall in resting potential normally indicates a decrease in intracellular K+. Normally K+ tends to diffuse out of the cell, and sodium (Na+) into the cell, because of their concentration gradients (see Figure 4-2); the diffusion is slow at rest, and rapid during the electrical phenomena of cell excitation ("action potentials"). Normally the concentrations are maintained by a cation transport system located in the cell membrane (Na, K, Mg-activated ATPase) which splits adenosine triphosphate

(ATP) into adenosine diphosphate (ADP) and inorganic phosphate, and uses the released energy to transport K+ back into the cell and Na+ out. The ADP so formed is known to stimulate mitochondrial respiration, accounting for the increased oxygen uptake by stimulated nerve cells both *in vivo* and *in vitro*.

As anticipated from the effects on resting potential, ethanol was found (24, 26, 27) to inhibit the action of this ATPase in a variety of tissues (see Figure 4-3), leading to a decrease in

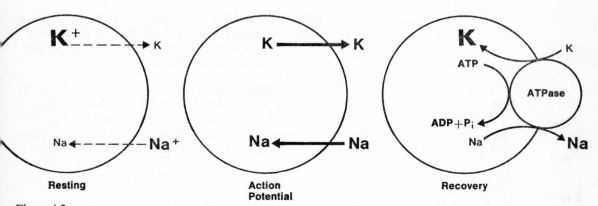

Figure 4-2
Schematic representation of directions and rates of Na and K movement across cell membrane in different states of activity of nerve cells.

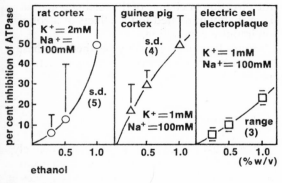

Figure 4-3
Effects of different concentrations of ethanol on NaKMg-stimulated ATPase activity of microsomal preparations from rat cerebral cortex, guinea pig cerebral cortex, and eel electroplaque. From Israel, Kalant, and Laufer (24).

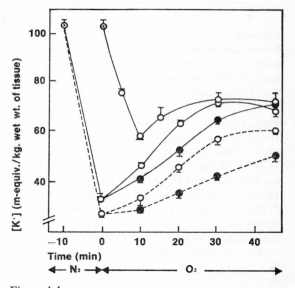

Figure 4-4
Effect of ethanol on K+ content of rat brain-cortex slices incubated in modified Krebs-Ringer bicarbonate media. Anaerobic preincubation, where used, took place between —10 and 0 min; aerobic incubation between 0 and 45 min. Continuous lines indicate the effect of incubation in a medium containing 6 mM K+; broken lines indicate effects in 3.6 mM K+. Mean initial value for 57 unincubated samples, ⊙; samples incubated without ethanol, ○; samples incubated in the presence of 108 mM ethanol, added at zero time, ●. Each vertical bar represents one standard deviation. From Israel, Kalant, and LeBlanc (25).

the active uptake of K+ (see Figure 4-4). This was true not only in excitable tissues but also in kidney (26), and presumably in other tissues as well, and a reduction in intracellular K+ was demonstrable in kidney and liver during ethanol intoxication (30).

Alcohol effects on the respiration of brain tissue could also be explained in terms of the reduction of ATPase activity. It has been shown repeatedly that concentrations of alcohol which do not affect the oxygen uptake of resting brain cortex slices, or which even increase it somewhat, cause a definite decrease in the extra

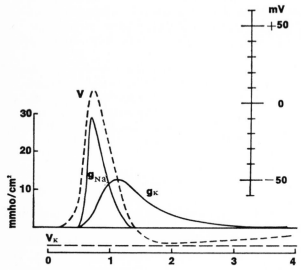

Figure 4-5
Ion movements and action potential. V = membrane
potential; g_{Na} = inward sodium conductance; g_K =
outward potassium conductance. Adapted from
A.F. Huxley. Science, **145**: 1154, 1964.

uptake which results from stimulation of the
tissue by a high-potassium medium (4). The
alcohol effect is even greater on slices which are
stimulated electrically (37, 50), probably because potassium stimulation has some additional effects which obscure the picture (11).
If alcohols reduce ATPase action, which is ordinarily increased by stimulation of the cell, they
will reduce the formation of ADP and hence
reduce the stimulus to mitochondrial respiration.
Since alcohols, in the concentrations relevant to
in vivo studies, do not appear to affect brain
mitochondrial respiration or oxidative phosphorylation either directly or through the formation of acetaldehyde (4, 31, 48, 49), it seems
most likely that their effects are indeed the result
of action on the ATPase system.

However, these findings raise some disturbing
points:
1
All of the alcohols tested have been found to inhibit ATPase activity and K^+ uptake (25), and
to inhibit the respiration of stimulated brain
slices (4, 37, 50). How can this be reconciled
with the finding that the longer-chain alcohols,

from butanol up, cause an initial hyperpolariza-
tion rather than depolarization? It implies that
some other effect of the longer alcohols must be
offsetting their action on the ATPase system.
2
Approximately 40 per cent of the oxygen uptake
by unstimulated brain slices is due to ATPase
activity associated with cation transport occurring even at rest. Why, then, do alcohol concentrations which inhibit the respiration of stimulated slices have no effect, or even a stimulatory
influence on the respiration of resting slices?
3
Application of an external hyperpolarizing current was found to restore membrane excitability and conductivity regardless of which alcohol was employed (12, 43). This indicates that
the direction of change of the resting potential
is probably unrelated to the effects of alcohols
on impulse conduction.

Some light may possibly be shed on these
matters by a study of alcohol effects on action
potentials.

ACTION POTENTIALS

When an excitable cell membrane is effectively
stimulated, the electrical changes which occur
are the result of rapid and short-lived changes in
permeability to Na^+ and K^+ (see Figure 4-5).
An initial change permits the rapid inflow of
Na^+ along its concentration gradient, and the
positive charge on the Na^+ neutralizes or even
reverses the normal resting potential (which is
negative inside the cell, positive outside). This
increased Na^+ conductance terminates, and is
followed by a temporary increase in outward
K^+ conductance, which restores the membrane
potential to its normal resting value. In the process, of course, the cell has gained Na^+ and
lost K^+, as already mentioned.

All of the alcohols up to n-octanol have been
found to decrease the height and duration of the
action potential in peripheral nerves (see Figure
4-6) and ultimately to block impulse conduction altogether. These changes, as already mentioned, could be abolished by application of an
external hyperpolarizing current; therefore the
alcohols do not block the conduction mechanism

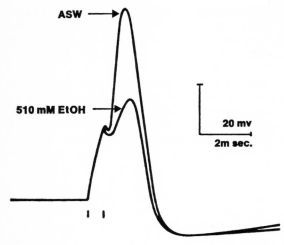

Figure 4-6
Action potentials of squid axon in artificial sea water (ASW) and in 510 mM ethanol (ETOH) solution. From Armstrong and Binstock (1).

itself, but only the changes leading to initiation of the impulse.

In recent studies on action potentials in the giant axon of the squid (1, 40) the principal and common effect of the alcohols was found to be a reduction in the maximum inward Na^+ conductance. The outward K^+ conductance was unaffected by the shorter alcohols, and was even increased by octanol (1). The combined result of these changes was that the loss of charge by outflow of K^+ overcame the gain of charge through inflow of Na^+ more quickly, resulting in a lower and shorter-lasting action potential, as already noted. Moreover, the increased outflow of K^+ under the influence of octanol would be in keeping with the hyperpolarizing effect of this alcohol. It is perhaps of interest that alcohols from n-butanol to n-octanol have been reported to increase diffusion of potassium through synthetic phospholipid membranes (3).

In contrast to the squid axon results, low concentrations of ethanol acting on the isolated atrium of the rat caused only a slight reduction in the height of the action potential, and did not alter the time to reach its peak, but shortened the overall duration by increasing the speed of repolarization (i.e., presumably increasing the rate of K^+ outflow). This suggests that differ-

ences in composition of cell membranes in different tissues modify the relative effects of the various alcohols on sodium and potassium conductances.

These findings help us considerably to understand the functional effects of alcohols on individual nerve and muscle cells, but they do not explain the effects on transmission between cells. It is necessary to examine separately the effects on synaptic transmission.

SYNAPTIC TRANSMISSION

While it is common to regard interneuronal synapses and nerve-muscle junctions as analogous structures, there is evidence that alcohols affect them in different ways. Earlier workers (6), studying the response of the isolated frog gastrocnemius to sciatic nerve stimulation, found that lower concentrations of ethanol were required to raise the threshold when the muscle was immersed than when the nerve was. This suggested to them that the nerve-muscle junction was particularly susceptible to block by alcohols. Apparently in keeping with this, polysynaptic reflexes in the intact animal were reported to be more susceptible than monosynaptic ones to inhibition by ethanol (39). Further, in the decapitated cat, in which inhibitory impulses descending from the brain to spinal synapses are eliminated, ethanol exerts only an inhibitory influence on spinal reflexes (34).

All of these findings suggested that alcohols inhibit synaptic transmission, presumably by inhibiting the release of acetylcholine. It was therefore not surprising that ethanol was reported to diminish the release acetylcholine from the perfused superior cervical sympathetic ganglion on preganglionic stimulation (35), and, as shown in Figure 4-7, from slices of rat and guinea-pig cerebral cortex *in vitro* (28).

Many observations, however, point to a directly opposite conclusion. Low concentrations of alcohols greatly increase the amplitude of contraction of the isolated frog gastrocnemius on sciatic stimulation (46), and the amplitude of end-plate potentials in the isolated rat diaphragm on phrenic nerve stimulation (10). This effect is very rapid in onset, and readily reversible by

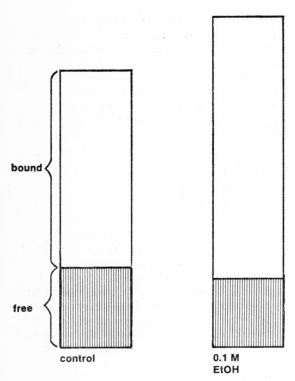

Figure 4-7
Acetylcholine in slices of brain cortex (bound) and released into medium (free) with and without ethanol. From data of Kalant, Israel, and Mahon (28).

washing with alcohol-free medium. This is not an eserine-like action, because acetylcholinesterase is not very sensitive to alcohols (32). The increased response is due in part to a greater sensitivity of the muscle sole plate to acetylcholine, as shown by the fact that alcohols, as well as other volatile "narcotics," greatly increase the contractile response of the frog rectus to exogenous acetylcholine even in the presence of eserine (8, 41 46). In part, however, the effect of the alcohols is claimed to result from an increased number of quanta of acetylcholine liberated from the nerve ending with each impulse (10).

To add to the confusion, a direct comparison of alcohol effects on conduction and transmission in the same preparation has shown different results with different alcohols (36). The myelinated preganglionic fibres entering the superior cervical ganglion of the cat follow two different courses: some synapse in the ganglion with unmyelinated fibres which continue in the sympathetic chain, while others pass through the ganglion without synapsing and enter the superior cardiac nerve. With preganglionic stimulation it is possible to record simultaneously the responses in both pathways. Higher alcohols, as well as barbiturates, ether, and chloroform, selectively depress synaptic transmission at concentrations which had little effect on conduction in non-synapsing fibres. Lower alcohols, on the other hand, have a relatively greater effect on the non-synaptic pathway. It is conceivable that these findings represent differential effects of the alcohols on the excitation thresholds of the two types of preganglionic fibre, rather than on synapses versus axons. This possibility, however, has not yet been explored. So far, therefore, there is no agreement concerning the effects of alcohols on various types of synaptic transmission, and no explanation for the apparently contradictory findings.

EFFECTS ON OTHER FUNCTIONS

The effects of alcohols upon membrane potentials, impulse conduction, and transmission have been considered; a logical next step is muscular contraction. The effects of alcohols upon the contractile mechanism itself appear to be much clearer: in all cases they depress it. When the sensitizing effect on acetylcholine receptors is ruled out by direct electrical stimulation, alcohols have no effect at moderate concentrations and are inhibitory at higher ones. This is true for skeletal muscle (10, 47), cardiac muscle (13), and intestinal smooth muscle (44, 46). The reversible block of gastric peristalsis by local application of 10 per cent ethanol (20) is in keeping with such a direct action. While the mechanism of alcohol effect has not been demonstrated, it is a reasonable guess, on the basis of current concepts of muscle contraction, that a reduction of sodium conductance during the action potential may reduce the inward displacement of calcium which triggers the contractile response.

Another apparently direct cellular effect of

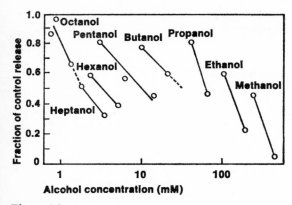

Figure 4-8
Concentration-action curves of alcohols on anaphylactic histamine release. Each point is the mean of all determinations at a particular alcohol concentration. From Rang (44).

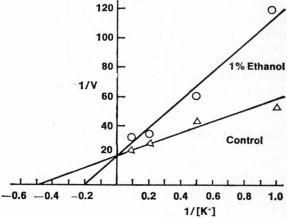

Figure 4-9
Lineweaver-Burk plot of reciprocals of NaKMg-stimulated ATPase activity (μ moles $P_{i/g}$ tissue/hr $\times$ 10^3) and K concentration (mM) for rat cerebral cortex microsomes. Each point represents the average of five different preparations. Na+ concentration was 100 mM and ethanol was 0.22 M. From Israel, Kalant, and Laufer (24).

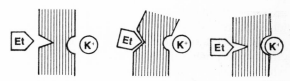

Figure 4-10
Concept of allosteric inhibition of K+ site on ATPase by alcohols.

alcohols, illustrated in Figure 4-8, is the inhibition of the antigen-stimulated release of histamine *in vitro* from lung tissue of sensitized guinea pigs (44). All of the short-chain alcohols were inhibitory, and ethanol caused a 50 per cent inhibition at a concentration of only a little over 0.1 M. If this is true of other histamine-containing tissues, it would argue against local release of histamine in the gastric mucosa as a factor in ethanol stimulation of gastric acid secretion. Indeed, the best evidence suggests that indirect vagal effects are involved (21, 51).

Alcohol effects have also been reported upon the release of other substances. It has been claimed or suggested that ethanol stimulates the release of catecholamines both centrally (17) and peripherally (42): 5-hydroxytryptamine (53), and gamma-aminobutyric acid (18). However, these effects have not been demonstrated convincingly under conditions in which indirect actions can be ruled out. In any case, we are quite ignorant of the mechanisms by which acetylcholine, histamine, catecholamines, and other possible chemical transmitter substances are normally secreted, other than that they involve some interaction between storage granules or vesicles and the cell membrane. Until more is known, it is useless to speculate about the mechanism of action of alcohols upon their release.

One final direct effect of alcohols is the stimu-lation of the active uptake of tetraethyl-ammonium ions by kidney cortex slices *in vitro* (9). This was seen at moderately high alcohol concentrations, but still higher concentrations depressed the uptake. The mechanism of this effect is, once more, unknown. Some speculation may be permissible, however. The inhibitory effect of alcohols upon cell membrane ATPase activity and ion transport is apparently competitive with potassium (24, 25), and can be reversed by raising the K+ concentration (see Figure 4-9). It seems probable that this is an allosteric effect, with alcohols and potassium interacting at different sites on the enzyme to produce mutually antagonistic changes in conformation (see Figure 4-10). The effect of the alcohols is more marked with K^+ than with other ions (29), and is dependent upon the ionic radius. It is conceivable that the effect of alcohols on the kidney tubules is to modify the carrier conformation in such a way as to improve the fit of the tetroethylammonium ion.

SUMMARY AND CONCLUSIONS

The foregoing review suggests that all of the direct cellular actions demonstrable at relatively low concentrations of alcohols are exerted upon functions of cell membranes: resting potential, action potentials, ciliary or pseudopodial movement, release of acetylcholine and histamine and other substances, and cation transport. So far no fully satisfactory explanation of the mechanisms of these actions has been offered, but many possibilities have been explored. The old concept of alcohols as non-specific "protoplasmic poisons" or protein precipitants is untenable in relation to *in vivo* actions, since non-specific lipid-solvent effects and inactivation of enzymes are seen only at concentrations far beyond the lethal range (14, 38).

It is difficult to conceive of any single alcohol effect on any one constituent of cell membranes which could account for all the observed functional changes. Proceeding further with the idea of allosteric interaction among alcohol, K^+, and ATPase, it seems reasonable to suggest that alcohols, and the other non-specific "narcotics" which they resemble, interact by hydrogen bonding and Van der Waals forces with a large variety of protein and lipid constituents of cell membranes to produce changes in molecular spacing and configuration that underlie the observed functional changes. It is noteworthy that brief treatment of the squid giant axon with cottonmouth moccasin venom, which contains a variety of phospholipases, markedly potentiates the inhibitory effect of ethanol on the action potential (45). If this concept of alcohol action is valid, then obviously a full understanding of differences in sensitivity among different species and different tissues, as well as of the cellular mechanisms of adaptation, acquired tolerance, and tissue dependence, will require much more knowledge of the chemistry of cell membranes than we now possess.

REFERENCES

1
ARMSTRONG, C.M. & BINSTOCK, L.
The effects of several alcohols on the properties of the squid giant axon
J. Gen. Physiol., **48**: 265, 1964

2
BAGLIONI, S.
Azione degli alcooli, della glicerina e della nicotina sui leucociti sopravviventi
Boll. Soc. Ital. Biol. Sper., **2**: 976, 1927

3
BANGHAM, A.D., STANDISH, M.M., & MILLER, N.
Cation permeability of phospholipid model membranes: effect of narcotics
Nature, **208**: 1295, 1965

4
BEER, C.T. & QUASTEL, J.H.
The effects of aliphatic alcohols on the respiration of rat brain cortex slices and rat brain mitochondria
Canad. J. Biochem. Physiol., **36**: 543, 1958

5
BISHOP, G.H.
Action of nerve depressants on potential
J. Cell. Comp. Physiol., **1**: 177, 1932

6
BLUME, W.
Comparative investigations on stimulating and paralyzing action of certain narcotics on peripheral nerve, striated muscle and motor nerve termination of frog
Arch. Exper. Pathol., **110**: 46, 1925

7
BRINK, F. & POSTERNAK, J.M.
Thermodynamic analysis of relative effectiveness of narcotics
J. Cell. Comp. Physiol., **32**: 211, 1948

8
ETTINGER, G.H., BROWN, A.B., & MEGILL, A.H.
Potentiation of acetylcholine by alcohol and ether
J. Pharmacol. Exper. Therap., **73**: 119, 1941

9
FARAH, A. & FRAZER, M.
The influence of some alcohols on the uptake of tetraethylammonium ion by renal slices of the dog
J. Pharmacol. Exper. Therap., **119**: 233, 1957

10
GAGE, P.W.
The effect of methyl, ethyl and n-propyl alcohol on neuromuscular transmission in the rat
J. Pharmacol. Exper. Therap., **150**: 236, 1965

11
GAGE, P.W. & QUASTEL, D.M.
Dual effect of potassium on transmitter release
Nature, **206**: 625, 1965

12
GALLEGO, A.
On the effect of ethylalcohol upon frog nerve
J. Cell. Comp. Physiol., 31: 97, 1948

13
GIMENO, A.L., GIMENO, M.F., & WEBB, J.L.
Effects of ethanol on cellular membrane potentials
and contractility of isolated rat atrium
Am. J. Physiol., 203: 194, 1962

14
GÖRES, E.
Einige pharmakologische Probleme der
Aethanolwirkung
Die Pharmazie 19, pt. 1: 433; pt. 2: 489, 1964

15
GRENELL, R.G.
Alcohols and activity of cerebral neurons
Quart. J. Stud. Alc., 20: 421, 1959

16
GRENELL, R.G. & O'NEILL, L.
Cerebral cell membranes and action of ethanol
Fed. Proc., 24: 327, 1965
Abstract

17
GURSEY, D. & OLSON, R.E.
Depression of serotonin and norepinephrine levels
in brain stem of rabbit by ethanol
Proc. Soc. Exper. Biol. Med., 104: 280, 1960

18
HÄKKINEN, H.M., KULONEN, E., & WALLGREN, H.
The effect of ethanol and electrical stimulation on the
amino acid metabolism of rat-brain-cortex slices
in vitro
Biochem. J., 88: 488, 1963

19
HANDOVSKY, H. & ZACHARIAS, R.
Notizen über die Wirkung einiger Substanzen auf die
Erregbarkeit des Nervus ischiadicus des Frosches
Arch. Exper. Pathol. Pharmakol., 100: 288, 1923–24

20
HARICHAUX, P. & MOLINE, J.
Influence d'un ingestion d'éthanol à 10 p 100 sur
l'évacuation gastrique chez le rat
C.R. Soc. Biol., 158: 1389, 1964

21
HIRSCHOWITZ, B.I., POLLARD, H.M.,
HARTWELL, S.W., JR., & LONDON, J.
Action of ethyl alcohol on gastric acid secretion
Gastroenterology, 30: 244, 1956

22
ISHIKAWA, Y.
Action of antiseptics and narcotics on spermatozoa
Progrès méd., 51: 187, 1923

23
ISRAEL, Y. & KALANT, H.
Effect of ethanol on the transport of sodium in frog skin
Nature, 200: 476, 1963

24
ISRAEL, Y., KALANT, H., & LAUFER, I.
Effects of ethanol on Na, K, Mg-stimulated
microsomal ATPase activity
Biochem. Pharmacol., 14: 1803, 1965

25
ISRAEL, Y., KALANT, H., & LEBLANC, A.E.
Effects of lower alcohols on potassium transport and
microsomal adenosine-triphosphatase activity of rat
cerebral cortex
Biochem. J., 100: 27, 1966

26
ISRAEL-JACARD, Y. & KALANT, H.
Effect of ethanol on electrolyte transport and
electrogenesis in animal tissues
J. Cell. Comp. Physiol., 65: 127, 1965

27
JÄRNEFELT, J.
Properties of sodium-stimulated adenosine-
triphosphatase in microsomes from rat brain
Exper. Cell. Res., 21: 214, 1960

28
KALANT, H., ISRAEL, Y., & MAHON, M.A.
The effect of ethanol on acetylcholine synthesis,
release and degradation in brain
Canad. J. Physiol. Pharmacol., 45: 172, 1967

29
KALANT, H., LAUFER, I., & ISRAEL, Y.
Unpublished results

30
KALANT, H., MONS, W., & MAHON, M.A.
Acute effects of ethanol on tissue electrolytes in the rat
Canad. J. Physiol. Pharmacol., 44: 1, 1966

31
KIESSLING, K.H.
The effect of acetaldehyde on rat brain mitochondria
and its occurrence in brain after alcohol injection
Exper. Cell. Res., 26: 432, 1962

32
KINARD, F.W. & HAY, M.G.
Effect of ethanol administration on brain and liver
enzyme activities
Am. J. Physiol., 198: 657, 1960

33
KNUTSSON, E.
Effects of ethanol on the membrane potential and
membrane resistance of frog muscle fibres
Acta Physiol. Scandinav., 52: 242, 1961

34
KOLMODIN, G.M.
Action of ethyl alcohol on monosynaptic extensor
reflex and multisynaptic reflex
Acta Physiol. Scandinav., 29 (Suppl. 106): 530, 1953

35
LARRABEE, M.G., GARCIA RAMOS, J., & BÜLBRING, E.
Effects of anesthetics on oxygen consumption and
on synaptic transmission in sympathetic ganglia
J. Cell. Comp. Physiol., 40: 461, 1952

36
LARRABEE, M.G. & POSTERNAK, J.M.
Selective action of anesthetics on synapses and axons
in mammalian sympathetic ganglia
J. Neurophysiol., 15: 91, 1952

37
LINDBOHM, R. & WALLGREN, H.

Changes in respiration of rat brain cortex slices
induced by some aliphatic alcohols
Acta Pharmacol. (Kobenhavn), 19: 53, 1962
38
MARDONES, J.
The alcohols
In W.S. Root & F.G. Hoffman
Physiological pharmacology, vol. 1
New York: Academic Press, 1963, p. 99
39
MEGIRIAN, D., VASEY, J., & POSTERNAK, J.M.
Action différentielle de quelques anesthésiques sur
de voies spinales monosynaptiques et polysynaptiques
chez le chat
Helv. Physiol. Pharmacol. Acta, 16: 241, 1958
40
MOORE, J.W., ULBRICHT, W., & TAKATA, M.
Effect of ethanol on the sodium and potassium
conductances of the squid axon membrane
J. Gen. Physiol., 48: 279, 1964
41
NELEMANS, F.A.
The influence of various substances on the acetylcholine
contracture of the frog's isolated abdominal muscle
Acta Physiol. Pharmacol. Neerlandica, 11: 76, 1962
42
PERMAN, E.S.
The effect of ethyl alcohol on the secretion from the
adrenal medulla of the cat
Acta Physiol. Scandinav., 48: 323, 1960
43
POSTERNAK, J.M. & MANGOLD, R.
Action de narcotiques sur la conduction par les fibres
nerveuses et sur leur potentiel de membrane
Helvet. Physiol. Pharmacol. Acta, 7: C55, 1949
44
RANG, H.P.
Unspecific drug addiction: the effects of a homologous
series of primary alcohols
Brit. J. Pharmacol., 15: 185, 1960
45
ROSENBERG, P. & PODLESKI, T.R.
Ability of venoms to render squid axons sensitive to
curare and acetylcholine
Biochim. Biophys. Acta, 75: 104, 1963
46
SACHDEV, K.S., PANJWANI, M.H., & JOSEPH, A.D.
Potentiation of the response to acetylcholine on the
frog's rectus abdominis by ethyl alcohol
Arch. Internat. Pharmacodyn., 145: 36, 1963
47
TAYLOR, G.W.
The effect of narcotics on respiration and luminescence
in bacteria with special reference to the relation
between the two processes
J. Cell. Comp. Physiol., 4: 329, 1934
48
THORE, A. & BALTSCHEFFSKY, A.
Inhibitory effects of lower aliphatic alcohols on
electron transport phosphorylation system:
I. Straight-chain, primary alcohols

Acta Chem. Scandinav., 19: 1591, 1965
49
TRUITT, E.B., JR., BELL, F.K., & KRANTZ, J.C.
Anesthesia: LIII. Effects of alcohols and acetaldehyde
on oxidative phosphorylation in brain
Quart. J. Stud. Alc., 17: 594, 1956
50
WALLGREN, H. & KULONEN, E.
Effect of ethanol on respiration of
rat-brain-cortex slices
Biochem. J., 75: 150, 1960
51
WEISE, R.E., SHAPIRO, M., & WOODWARD, E.R.
Effect of parenteral alcohol on gastric secretion
Surg. Forum, 12: 281, 1961
52
WRIGHT, E.B.
Effects of asphyxiation and narcosis on peripheral
nerve polarization and conduction
Am. J. Physiol., 148: 174, 1947
53
ZBINDEN, G. & PLETSCHER, A.
Experimentelle Untersuchungen über
5-Hydroxytryptamin-Gehalt und enterochromaffine
Zellen bei chronischer Reizung des
Magen-Darmtraktes durch Äthylalkohol
Schweiz. Ztschr. allg. Path., 21: 1137, 1958

FRANK LUNDQUIST

Department of Biochemistry
University of Copenhagen
Copenhagen, Denmark

5

The Effect of
Ethanol on
Liver Metabolism

The oxygen consumption of the liver as measured by conventional techniques is not changed by the presence of ethanol in small concentrations in the circulating blood. It is, however, evident that ethanol causes the whole metabolic pattern of the liver to be altered considerably. The fact that more than 70 per cent of the oxygen consumption is necessary to oxidize to acetate the ethanol removed from the blood clearly shows that other oxygen-consuming reactions, especially those connected with the tricarboxylic acid cycle, must be severely curtailed.

The most conspicuous primary changes in the liver during ethanol metabolism seem to be an increased cytoplasmic level of NADH relative to NAD, and the production of free acetate. A small part of the acetate is oxidized or used for synthetic processes in the splanchnic organs, but most of the acetate (70 to 100 per cent) is delivered to the hepatic venous blood and is utilized in peripheral organs, especially muscle. Acetaldehyde is present as an intermediate, but at a very small concentration. It is not believed to influence the general metabolism of the liver except in the case of fructose, which will be considered later.

The metabolism of all three major groups of nutrients is undoubtedly influenced by ethanol. I shall, however, limit myself to a consideration of carbohydrate metabolism, as the question of changes in fat metabolism will be treated in the section on Organic Complications of Alcoholism. The problems of protein and amino acid metabolism in connection with ethanol have not been sufficiently studied, but the fact that the tricarboxylic acid cycle is inhibited may well mean that availability of the carbon skeletons of the non-essential amino acids is significantly reduced.

Fructose is normally taken up by the human liver at a maximal rate of about 2 mM/min. The quantity of fructose metabolized is not significantly changed by the presence of ethanol, but the pathways and end products are strongly influenced.

Figure 5-1 shows the pathway believed to account for fructose metabolism in the liver: This scheme has been confirmed in experiments on human subjects given a continuous infusion of fructose. About half the fructose was

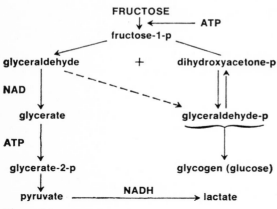

Figure 5-1
Pathway of fructose metabolism in the liver.

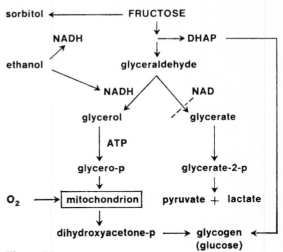

Figure 5-2
Influence of ethanol on the pathways of fructose metabolism in the liver.

(Polyol dehydrogenase)
sorbitol $+$ NAD$^+$ $\rightleftharpoons$ fructose $+$ NADH $+$ H$^+$

Figure 5-3
The initial step in sorbitol metabolism.

recovered as lactate and pyruvate in the hepatic venous blood, as would be expected if the glyceraldehyde formed were exclusively converted to phosphoglyceric acid. In the presence of ethanol, however, the amount of lactate and pyruvate is only 25 to 30 per cent of the control values as shown in Table 5-1. At the same time the glucose output from the liver is increased correspondingly and a small amount of sorbitol is also produced.

Our interpretation of these findings is based on the increased steady state concentration of NADH observed during alcohol metabolism as shown in Figure 5-2. This in itself will cause some reduction of fructose to sorbitol by means of the liver polyol dehydrogenase. Furthermore, the oxidation of glyceraldehyde to glyceric acid by aldehyde dehydrogenase will be inhibited in two ways: (*a*) through the presence of acetal-

dehyde which has an exceptionally high affinity for this enzyme, and (*b*) by the decreased ratio of NAD to NADH.

An alternative pathway for glyceraldehyde is reduction to glycerol by means of alcohol dehydrogenase, as suggested by Holzer and Schneider (2). In this way pyruvate formation is decreased and glycerol is formed instead. The glycerol is presumably converted via glycerophosphate and dihydroxyacetone phosphate to glucose, which explains the increased output of this substance. Apart from the changes in amount of various end products of fructose metabolism, the combination of fructose and ethanol also causes an increase of oxygen uptake in the liver by about 60 per cent, an effect for which we do not yet have a satisfactory explanation.

Sorbitol, the reduction product of fructose, is normally oxidized to fructose in the liver. Verron (7) has shown that during ethanol metabolism the rate of this conversion is reduced markedly, a finding which again may be interpreted as a direct consequence of the change in the NAD/NADH ratio (see Figure 5-3).

TABLE 5–1

UPTAKE AND OUTPUT OF METABOLITES IN THE SPLANCHNIC AREA IN HUMAN SUBJECTS GIVEN INTRAVENOUS INFUSIONS OF FRUCTOSE OR FRUCTOSE + ETHANOL (μM HEXOSE/MINUTE)

	Fructose	Ethanol + fructose
fructose	2.30	2.90
sorbitol	0.20	−0.62
glucose	−0.65	−1.94
lactate + pyruvate	−1.10	−0.33

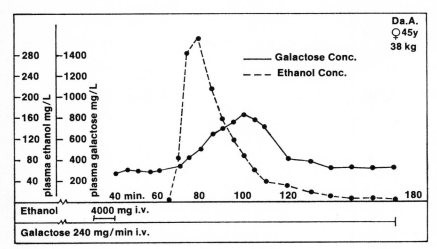

Figure 5-4
Influence of ethanol on galactose metabolism in a human subject given a constant
infusion of galactose. From N. Tygstrup & F.J. Lundquist. Lab. Clin. Med., **59**: 102,
1962, by permission of the C.V. Mosby Co., St. Louis, Missouri.

galactose $+$ ATP $\longrightarrow$ galactose—1—P

galactose—1—P $+$ UDPG $\rightleftarrows$ glucose—1—P $+$ UDP—GAL

UDP—GAL $\rightleftarrows$ UDPG

ethanol $+$ 2 NAD$^+$ $\longrightarrow$ acetate $+$ 2 NADH $+$ 2 H$^+$

Figure 5-5
Conversion of galactose to uridine diphosphate-glucose.
The mechanism of ethanol inhibition of the process is indicated.

Galactose is largely converted to glucose in
the liver. This reaction (or rather the uptake of
galactose) is considerably inhibited by ethanol,
as shown in Figure 5-4. Here galactose is infused
at a constant rate in a human subject until a
steady blood galactose concentration is obtained.
Infusion of ethanol causes the galactose concentration to increase, an indication that the
elimination rate is diminished. When the blood
ethanol concentration descends below the critical
level at which alcohol metabolizing enzymes are
saturated, galactose metabolism again returns
to normal.

An explanation of the influence of ethanol on
galactose metabolism was suggested by Isselbacher and Krane (3), as indicated in Figure
5-5. Maxwell observed that the enzyme uridine
diphosphategalactose-4-epimerase contains NAD
and is inhibited by NADH (4). This enzymatic
step is necessary for the conversion of galactose
to glucose. The increased NADH concentration
during alcohol metabolism should accordingly
inhibit the conversion of UDP-galactose to UDP-
glucose. The process which is actually measured
is, however, the first one, phosphorylation of
galactose. The recent finding that galactose-
1-phosphate inhibits the galactokinase reaction
seems to furnish an explanation of how the increased NADH concentration can inhibit galactose
uptake. When epimerase is inhibited, galactose-
1-phosphate piles up with the consequence that
galactokinase is also inhibited.

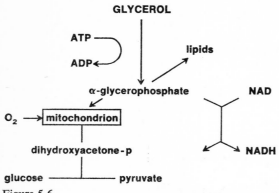

Figure 5-6
Possible metabolic pathways of glycerol in liver tissue.

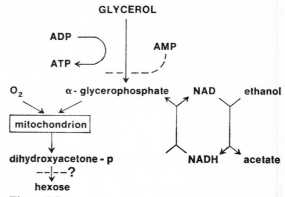

Figure 5-7
Suggested mechanism for the effect of ethanol on glycerol metabolism.

Glycerol, though not itself a carbohydrate, is easily converted to glucose in the liver. The metabolism of glycerol in initiated by a phosphorylation, as in the case of sugars. The alpha-glycerophosphate thus formed may be incorporated into phospholipids and triglycerides, or it may be oxidized by a mitochondrial enzyme to dihydroxy-acetone phosphate, which is a normal intermediate in glucose metabolism. In the cytoplasm another glycerophosphate dehydrogenase is present, but this is a NAD-requiring enzyme, which will reduce dihydroxy-acetone phosphate back to glycerophosphate when a high NADH concentration is present, as shown in Figure 5-6.

Glycerol infused in normal human subjects is removed by the liver at a rate of about 1mM/min. When ethanol is also given, the rate of hepatic glycerol uptake is reduced to about one-third of this figure. In experiments with liver slices, Thieden (6) in our laboratory has shown that large amounts of glycerophosphate accumulates in the presence of glycerol and ethanol, and at the same time there is a very strong inhibition of glycerol metabolism. The diagram in Figure 5-7 may explain this effect of ethanol on glycerol metabolism. Glycerophosphate is oxidized in the mitochondria and the dihydroxy-acetone phosphate formed is again partly reduced to glycerophosphate in the cytoplasm by the increased NADH concentration caused by ethanol oxidation. In this way an increased glycerophosphate concentration is built up in the liver.

Even when glycerol is not added the concentration of glycerophosphate is increased during ethanol metabolism, as is shown by Nikkilä and and Ojala (5). The inhibition of the first step in glycerol metabolism, the phosphorylation by glycerokinase, seems to occur by a mechanism different from that found in the case of galactose. Glycerophosphate does not inhibit the enzyme, but Grunnet and Lundquist (1) recently found that adenylic acid (AMP) inhibits this reaction strongly at physiological pH (see Table 5-2). When a considerable amount of glycerophosphate is formed, phosphate will be drained from ATP, and the AMP concentration will increase as adenylate kinase converts ADP to ATP and AMP. We believe that the increased AMP concentration is responsible for the inhibition of glycerol metabolism under these conditions.

The influence of ethanol on the metabolism of the most important carbohydrate, namely glucose, is not completely elucidated. The changes in input and output of glucose from the liver are

TABLE 5–2

INHIBITION OF RAT LIVER GLYCEROL KINASE BY 5′-AMP AT pH 7.2

Concentrations (mM)		Activity* per cent
ATP	5′-AMP	
1.8	0.09	88
1.8	0.30	54
1.8	0.60	36
1.8	0.90	26
1.0	0.90	17

*Per cent of control without AMP added. ADP is not present.

difficult to measure accurately, but so far no significant changes have been observed under the influence of ethanol. It is possible, however, that the amount of glucose which follows the different pathways changes, without much change in the quantity of glucose taken up or given off from the liver when alcohol is present in the circulating blood.

REFERENCES

1
GRUNNET, N. & LUNDQUIST, F.
Kinetic properties of glycerol kinase
Fourth FEBS Meeting, Oslo, 1967
Abstract no. 258
2
HOLZER, H. & SCHNEIDER, S.
Zum Mechanismus der Beeinflussung der
Alkoholoxydation in der Leber durch Fruktose
Klin. Wchnschr., **33**: 1006, 1955
3
ISSELBACHER, K.J. & KRANE, S.M.
Studies on the mechanism of the inhibition of
galactose oxidation by ethanol
J. Biol. Chem., **236**: 2394, 1961
4
MAXWELL, E.S.
The enzymatic interconversion of uridine diphospho-
galactose and uridine diphosphoglucose
J. Biol. Chem., **229**: 139, 1957
5
NIKKILÄ, E.A. & OJALA, K.
Role of hepatic α-glycerophosphate and triglyceride
synthesis in production of fatty liver by ethanol
Proc. Soc. Exper. Biol. Med., **113**: 803, 1963
6
THIEDEN, H.I.
Unpublished work
7
VERRON, G.
Vergleichende Untersuchungen über den
Sorbitstoffwechsel mit und ohne Alkoholzusatz
Zeitschr. ges. inn. Med. **20**: 278, 1965

V. ZAPATA-ORTÍZ

LUIS BATALLA

INÉS GONZÁLEZ

Department of Physiological Sciences
Cayetano Heredia Peruvian University
Lima, Peru

6

Metabolism of Alcohol at High Altitudes

It has been established that life at high altitudes requires some adaptive processes to compensate for the condition of permanent hypoxia due to the low partial pressure of oxygen in the inspired air. These compensatory mechanisms reach the highest degree of efficiency in the man who is born and raised in such an environment (1). There he develops a natural acclimatization, a condition that allows him to compensate for the chronic hypoxia.

We wish to determine if, in addition to such acclimatization, the inhabitants of high altitudes have a different reaction to drugs. We chose alcohol as one of the drugs to be studied because of the widespread claim among drinkers that its effects are less in the Andes than in the lowlands.

MATERIAL AND METHODS

We used two groups of sheep, with weights ranging from 12 to 45 kg. We would have preferred to use dogs but it is very difficult to obtain these animals in the Peruvian Andes, because their owners are opposed to their use in vivisectional experiments. On the other hand, it is very easy to obtain as many sheep as needed.

One of the groups comprised 16 animals born and raised at sea level, and the other, 15 descendants of animals born and raised for many generations in high altitudes. In each group, the experiments were carried out near the place of birth of the sheep, i.e., in Lima and in Cerro de Pasco at 150 and 4230 metres above sea level, respectively.

In both groups, the alcohol was administered intravenously at a concentration of 50 per cent in saline isotonic solution. The dosage, 6 ml of this dilution for each kilogram of body weight, was given in three subdoses of 2 ml/kg at five-minute intervals. In other words, each animal received a total of 3 ml of 95° alcohol per kg of weight.

At 15 and 30 minutes, and one, two, three, four, five, six, and seven hours after the last

This investigation was supported in part by Public Health Service Research Grant no. HE 08732-03 from the National Heart Institute, USA.

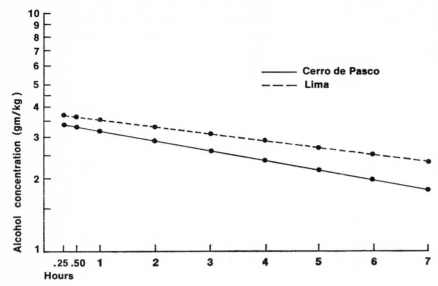

Figure 6-1
Alcohol concentrations in blood (time against logarithm of concentration) in sheep from Cerro de Pasco and from Lima.

injection, samples of blood were taken in order to determine the alcohol concentrations. The method of alcohol determination was that of Sheftel (4), which, as is known, is based on the oxidation of the alcohol by potassium bichromate in the presence of sulphuric acid.

To measure the blood volume we used the colorimetric method based on the intravenous injection of T 1824 (Evans' Blue). The statistical analysis of the experimental data was performed by means of an analysis of variance.

RESULTS

In Figure 6–1 is shown the curve of the blood alcohol concentration (time against the logarithm of concentration). As can be seen, we obtained two straight lines, which indicate that the data follow the exponential law. The mean blood volume in sheep at sea level was 70 ± 4.37 ml/kg BW, while in the high altitude animals it was 93 ± 2.47 ml/kg. This difference is statistically significant ($p < 0.001$).

The hypervolemia of the animals from the high altitudes is due mainly to the greater plasmatic volume, since in sheep from Lima it was 40 ± 2.42 ml/kg, while in sheep from Cerro de Pasco it was 54 ± 1.56 ml/kg. The difference is statistically significant ($p < 0.01$). The hematocrit values were very close: 39 ± 1.01 in Lima and 43 ± 1.34 in Cerro de Pasco. This difference does not reach statistical significance in our data ($0.20 > p > 0.10$).

In Table 6–1 the analysis of variance of the blood alcohol concentrations in the two groups of sheep is summarized. As can be seen, alcohol concentrations differ significantly between the two groups of animals ($p < 0.05$). Also, each time samples of blood were taken (interaction time and groups), the two groups reached different alcohol concentrations ($p < 0.01$).

No difference was found in the rate of alcohol disappearance from the blood of the two groups of sheep; the two regression curves remain almost parallel during the seven hours of observation. This is confirmed by a comparison of the slopes, whose values are -0.0005 and -0.0020 for sea level and high altitude, respectively. The difference is not significant ($p > 0.05$).

TABLE 6–1

ANALYSIS OF VARIANCE OF ALCOHOL CONCENTRATION IN BLOOD OF SHEEP
FROM CERRO DE PASCO AND LIMA

Source of variation	Degrees of freedom	Sum of squares	Mean square	F	p
times	8	3.4261	0.4282	F 8/8 = 57.093	<0.01
interaction time and groups	8	0.0600	0.0075	F 8/232 = 3.409	<0.01
sheep in each group	30	2.0260	0.0675		
between groups	1	0.3765	0.3765	F 1/30 = −5.577	<0.05
interaction time— sheep in each group	232	0.5199	0.0022		
total	279	6.4085			

DISCUSSION

In studies not yet published, we found that the effects on animals of some neurodepressor drugs were greater at high altitudes than at sea level. For example, the LD 50 of pentobarbital in guinea pigs was lower in Cerro de Pasco than in Lima; and using the same dosage of this barbiturate, guinea pigs from Cerro de Pasco developed a longer and deeper anesthesia than those at sea level. Safar and Tenicela (3) advise against using opiates as preanesthetic medication at altitudes above 3000 metres owing to the extreme cyanosis and tachycardia these drugs produced. Because of this, we were surprised at the statement that in high altitudes the effect of alcohol, which is also a neurodepressor, is less intense than at sea level.

In the literature available to us, we have not found any study on alcohol metabolism in persons adapted for generations to life in high altitudes. Nevertheless, there are some references to experiments performed under a condition of acute hypoxia. McFarland and Forbes (2), in experiments performed on persons at sea level and at altitudes above 2300 metres, found that at the latter alcohol, administered orally, reached higher blood concentrations in a shorter time than at sea level. These authors also mention comparable studies carried out by Bornstein and Loewy on three persons, with similar results. However, they refer to the studies of Biehler on rabbits in which the blood alcohol concentration reached the highest level more slowly as the altitude increased.

None of these papers contradict our results because we worked under different conditions. While other investigators have performed acute experiments on a small number of persons and animals from the lowlands, and after only a brief stay in high altitudes, we have worked on animals native to these places, and consequently perfectly adapted to chronic hypoxia. Furthermore, alcohol was administered orally in other studies, while we have administered it intravenously in order to eliminate any difference in the process of gastrointestinal absorption that could exist at high altitudes and at sea level.

The results we have obtained coincide with the statement that the effects of alcohol are less intense at high altitudes than at sea level. Our data suggest that this phenomenon is due not to more rapid metabolization, but mostly to the lower concentrations reached at high altitudes using the same doses. We also believe that this difference in concentration level is due to the hypervolemia of the high altitude sheep (and also of humans adapted to high altitudes). In other words, we think that the lower concentration reached by the alcohol in high altitudes is a consequence of its dilution in a greater blood volume.

Nevertheless, there still remains to be determined (and we are planning appropriate studies in human beings) the importance of other factors such as gastrointestinal absorption, urinary excretion, and particularly respiratory elimination, having in mind in the latter case that the inhabitant of the highlands hyperventilates as a compensatory mechanism for hypoxia (1).

Finally, we think that there exists one more reason for the inhabitant of the Andes to con-

sider himself more resistant to alcohol. This is
that he very often chews coca leaves (5) while
drinking alcoholic beverages. Accordingly, he
ingests a certain amount of cocaine, which
stimulates the central nervous system.

CONCLUSIONS

From the results obtained we deduce that: (*a*)
at equal doses per kilogram of body weight,
alcohol reaches lower concentrations in Cerro
de Pasco (4230 metres above sea level), than
in Lima (150 metres); (*b*) this difference is
maintained through seven hours of observation,
which indicates that the rate of metabolism is the
same at high altitudes and at sea level; (*c*) it is
probable that the less intense effect of alcohol at
high altitudes, referred to by many persons, is
due mostly to the dilution of the alcohol in a
greater blood volume.

REFERENCES

1
HURTADO, A.
Animals in high altitudes: resident man
In Handbook of physiology. Washington, DC:
Am. Physiol. Soc., 1964. Chap. 54, pp. 843–60
2
MCFARLAND, R.A. & FORBES, W.H.
The metabolism of alcohol in man at high altitudes
Human Biology, **8**: 387, 1936
3
SAFAR, P. & TENICELA, R.
High altitude physiology in relation to anesthesia
and inhalation therapy
Anesthesiology, **25**: 515, 1964
4
SHEFTEL, A.G.
A simple colorimetric method for determination of
alcohol concentration in urine and blood
J. Lab. Clin. Med., **23**: 234, 1938
5
ZAPATA-ORTIZ, V.
The problem of the chewing of the coca leaf in Peru
Bull. Narcotics, **4**: 26, 1952

LEONARD GOLDBERG

Department of Alcohol Research
Karolinska Institute
Stockholm, Sweden

7

Effects of Ethanol in the Central Nervous System

Behavioural effects of alcohol in man have been one of the objects of study in our laboratory. This communication will be devoted to subjective and objective effects of ethanol on the central nervous system, based on experiments in voluntary subjects under various conditions. Special reference will be given to subjective mood ratings and objective performance, including standing steadiness and certain ocular phenomena (PAN and ROM), the aim being to discuss the effects of ethanol in relation to blood alcohol levels, including the postalcohol ("hangover") phase, and the changes brought about by intake of different alcoholic beverages and by CNS-active drugs, in relation to phenomena of adaptation and tolerance.

METHODS

The work described in this paper comprised a total of 663 experiments in 211 healthy subjects.

Subjective mood estimates
Estimation of subjective mood ratings was carried out according to a magnitude estimation scale, using 10 as the reference standard. For subjective degree of intoxication the reference 10 denotes a subjective state of being "a little high" (5, 6, 12, 14).

Objective performance tests
A battery of psychological and psychotechnical tests, from arithmetic and word tests to reaction time and hand steadiness, were employed (7, 12, 14).

Statometry
For evaluating area of sway while standing, a device is currently being tested in our laboratory which comprises: (*a*) a transducer unit for transforming sway of centre of gravity into a varying voltage during a 60-second stay with open or closed eyes in a Romberg position, (*b*) a monitor for analog recording, (*c*) an analog-

The costs of these studies have been defrayed by grants from the Swedish Medical Research Council, the Swedish Institute for Malt Research, and the Department of Agriculture, California, USA.

to-digital converter and printer to obtain quantitative data, using a sample rate of one per second, i.e., 60 values per test, (*d*) a frequency analyser for possible pattern recognition and evaluation, and (*e*) a recorder permitting storage on magnetic tape and subsequent computer analysis.

Electro-oculography (EOG)
Ocular movements – positional alcohol nystagmus (PAN), alcohol gaze nystagmus (AGN), and roving ocular movements (ROM) – were evaluated from electrophysiological recordings (EOG) of displacements of cornea-retina potentials, vertically and horizontally, analysing direction, amplitude, frequency, and velocity of the slow component (1, 2, 3, 10).

EEG
Recordings were obtained from bipolar leads, monitored for analog reading and stored on magnetic tape for subsequent computer analysis for pattern recognition and evaluation of amplitude and frequency distribution.

Drugs
Ethanol was given as various alcoholic beverages, from distilled spirits to wines and beers, in single doses and in repeated doses (11). The drugs used ranged from antihistamines, CNS-depressant agents, and various phenothiazines, to tranquillizers, sedatives and stimulants (10, 11, 12).

Ethanol determination
Blood alcohol was determined in triplicate in micro samples by the Widmark micromethod (15) or by the enzymatic ADH method, adapted for Auto Analyser use (13).

Procedure
After one or two initial ("pre-drug") runs with the whole battery of tests to establish basal values, ethanol and/or a drug or a placebo were given under double-blind conditions. The tests and blood alcohol sampling were then repeated at 30–45-minute intervals for a total of five to seven hours, and in experiments to follow hangover at 10, 12, and 24 hours (11, 13).

Further references to pertinent literature regarding the methods used are given in Goldberg (12, 13).

RESULTS

A large number of CNS-functions affected by ethanol have been studied in our laboratory, from flicker fusion frequency, corneal sensitivity, standing steadiness, and hand co-ordination (8, 9), to attention, concentration, and subjective moods (5, 6, 14), ocular movements (2, 4, 10, 11, 12), and evoked pain and EEG changes. This communication will review some recent results with regard to subjective mood estimates, standing steadiness, and ocular phenomena (PAN and ROM), and then discuss the effects of different alcoholic beverages and CNS-active drugs, and the relation of hangover to blood levels.

Subjective mood estimates
Various subjective mood ratings, from absent-minded, calm, or hazy to tired and feeling "intoxicated," were studied in a series of experiments designed to compare time courses and intensities after the intake of alcohol or a placebo. Alcohol intake of even small amounts brought about a departure from normal, with a peak effect usually coinciding in time with that of the blood alcohol level, and a subsequent fall, the intensity as a rule being back to normal *before* blood alcohol had reached zero (see figures 7-1, 7-9, and 7-10).

Wide variations from this general course were observed in single individuals. In some subjects who were tired before the experiment, alcohol brought about an initial decrease in fatigue, followed by a subsequent increase over the initial level. Subjective working capacity was judged as increased by some individuals at a time when objective working capacity was reduced. These are two examples of the discrepancy between subjective and objective performance that may be noticed after alcohol intake.

With increasing doses of alcohol the intensity of subjective mood estimates increased, and individual variations tended to be more of a quantitative than qualitative nature (6, 12). The changes after different alcoholic beverages and after CNS-active drugs will be discussed later.

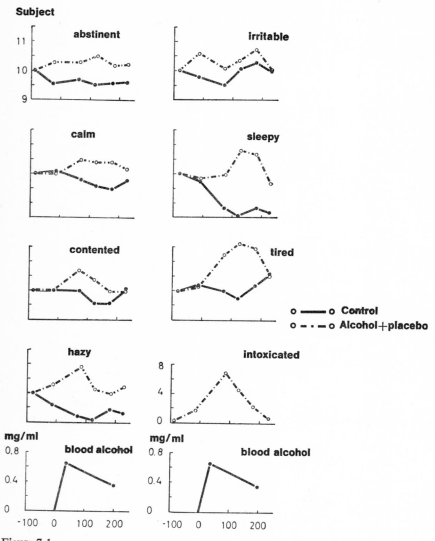

Figure 7-1

Time course of subjective mood estimates in a dry run and after alcohol plus placebo. *Ordinates*: Subjective mood estimates (subj.), starting point, changes according to subjective magnitude estimation (see Methods). Subjective intoxication estimate: starting point zero, reference point 10 = "a little high." Blood-alcohol: mg/ml. *Abscissa*: Time axis, from −100 to +200 minutes. 0 = time of alcohol intake.

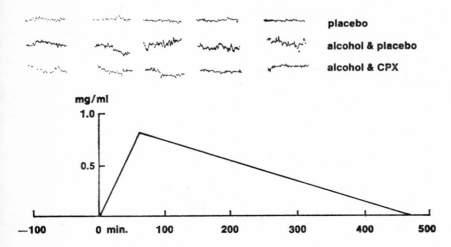

Figure 7-2
Variability in standing steadiness, measured by objective statometry. Upper three records: Area of sway while standing, recorded for 60 seconds. Time of recording, see time axis. *Lower graph*: Blood alcohol concentration. *Records of sway left of arrow*: Before administration of alcohol and drug. *Arrow*: Administration of alcohol (0.7 gm alcohol per kg) plus drug. *Record sof sway right of arrow*: Changes after alcohol plus drug. Plac = placebo. CPX = 20 mg chlordiazepoxide. After placebo no essential change in sway is seen for a total observation period of six to seven hours. After alcohol plus placebo an increase in sway (inco-ordination) appears; it does not return to normal within six to seven hours after the alcohol. After alcohol plus CPX most of the alcohol effect is counteracted, and less change in sway appears after alcohol plus CPX than after alcohol plus placebo.

Standing steadiness
Large variations in area of sway while standing were seen in one and the same individual from time to time, for example, during the day, and under various conditions, with open or closed eyes, on a fasting stomach or after a meal, as well as between different individuals under constant conditions. These variations comprised amplitude, frequency distribution, and variability in pattern (see Figure 7-2).

After alcohol intake, changes occurred in all parameters studied. Amplitudes and variability rose and the frequency distribution (i.e., the pattern of sway), was changed, the peak effects coinciding with blood alcohol maxima. After the peak the changes were reduced, parallel to the fall in blood alcohol, and reached the zero level before blood alcohol was zero. The frequencies recognized ranged from 0.1 to 2 periods per second.

The increase in *variability* (i.e., in the standard deviation of the series of subsequent measurements) rather than in amplitude, with increase in blood alcohol, was the most sensitive parameter, showing the closest correlation with changes in blood alcohol (see Figure 7-2).

This method when further developed should help to disclose the fundamental relationships between, for example, the effects of tiredness, and the intake of food or ethanol.

Ocular phenomena (PAN and ROM)
Detailed data on positional alcohol nystagmus (PAN) and roving ocular movements (ROM) have been presented earlier (2, 4, 10, 12).

PAN
The main findings can be summarized as follows: intake of *single* doses of alcohol brings about two phases of a horizontal positional

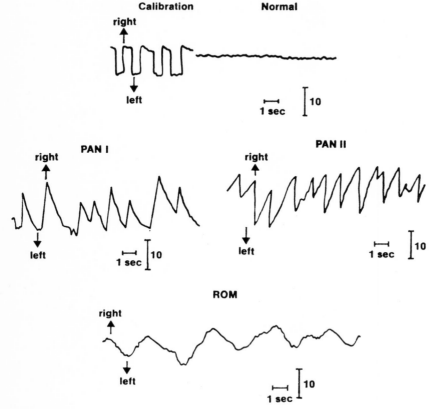

Figure 7-3
Electro-oculographic recordings (horizontal leads) with closed eyelids. *Upper*:
Calibration and normal electro-oculographic recording· *Middle right*: Positional
alcohol nystagmus phase II with head in right lateral position. *Middle left*: Positional
alcohol nystagmus phase I (PAN I) with head in right lateral position. *Lower*: Roving
ocular movements (ROM) in supine position.

alcohol nystagmus, beating mainly behind closed
eyelids, elicited in the vestibular system by the
combined effects of alcohol, its blood level and
gradient, and the position of the head; the two
phases show specific and uniform patterns of
appearance (see Figures 7-3 and 7-4).

Phase I (PAN I), appearing a half hour after
intake and lasting for three to four hours independent of dose, beats to the right in a right
lateral head position, changing to the opposite
direction in the left position.

Phase II (PAN II), first appearing after a

Figure 7-4
Positional alcohol nystagmus (PAN) after three different single doses of alcohol (exps. 7, 20, and 13). PAN phase
I (PAN I), PAN phase II (PAN II). At * the subject vomited. It is noted that the duration of PAN I and the beginning
of PAN II are independent of dose, whereas the intensities of PAN I and II and the duration of PAN II are correlated
with the blood alcohol level. Note that PAN II in every case lasts for hours after alcohol has left the blood.

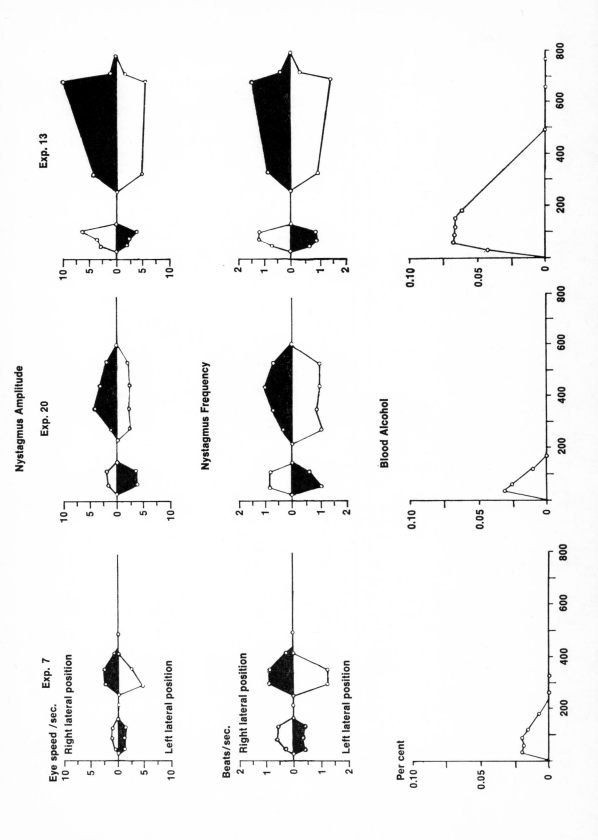

Nystagmus Amplitude

Exp. 7   Exp. 20   Exp. 13

Eye speed / sec.

Right lateral position   Left lateral position

Nystagmus Frequency

Beats / sec.

Right lateral position   Left lateral position

Blood Alcohol

Per cent

latency time of five to six hours, beats in the reverse direction to PAN I, i.e., to the left in the right lateral position, changing its direction in the left position. The duration and intensity of PAN II, depending on the dose of alcohol, range from five to ten hours and more; PAN II, however, always lasts for many hours *after* alcohol has disappeared from the blood. PAN II is thus a true, objective after effect and part of the "hangover" syndrome (see Figure 7-12).

Besides the position of the head, the appearance of PAN after intake of *repeated* alcohol doses will depend on (*a*) the course of the blood alcohol level, whether rising, inducing a PAN I, or falling, inducing a PAN II, and(*b*) the nature and intensity of the positional nystagmus, induced by a previous dose. This interplay, depending upon the interaction of the intensities and directions of the existing and the induced nystagmus, will lead to an increase in nystagmus, to a decrease, to a complete block (i.e., a disappearance), or to a reversal (i.e., a change in direction). PAN will change its appearance, for example, after intake of different alcoholic beverages or after CNS-active drugs. The subjective symptoms, corresponding to higher amplitudes of PAN I and II, consist of diplopia, dizziness, vertigo, and sometimes nausea and vomiting.

ROM
These movements show a completely different picture (see Figure 7-3). They are of a sinusoidal character, exist mainly behind closed eyelids with the head in lateral as well as supine directions, and are most probably elicited from the reticular system, being accompanied by subjective sensations of tiredness and sleepiness. Their appearance stands in no simple relation to blood alcohol, but corresponds well to PAN. After alcohol intake an inverse relationship exists between PAN and ROM, an increase in ROM being accompanied by a decrease in PAN (see Figure 7-11). This relationship is changed qualitatively as well as quantitatively by the effect of various CNS-active drugs, and it varies with the type of beverage taken.

Different alcoholic beverages
With the techniques described the effects of intake of different alcoholic beverages were

studied and related to blood alcohol levels. For example, when comparing the effects of whisky and of light wine, given in equal amounts with regard to ethanol, it was noted that besides the differences in blood alcohol curves – whisky inducing higher levels than wine – a clear difference in intensity of subjective mood estimates existed. The changes in subjective degree of intoxication, or in working capacity, for example, followed the time course of the blood alcohol, but wine had less effect. These subjective differences between the effects of the two beverages were, however, *greater* than the differences in blood alcohol levels (see Figures 7-5, 7-6, and 7-7).

The changes seen in ocular phenomena (PAN and ROM) were both quantitative and qualitative (see Figure 7-8). Wine induced less PAN and a higher degree of ROM than whisky, the changes being greater than the differences in blood alcohol levels; the reduction of the hangover phase was obvious. This points to the possibility that the changes are brought about by the differences in concentration of ethanol as well as differences in other constituents. This has been extensively studied with regard to beers (9, 10).

Interaction between alcohol and drugs
One of many ways to get an insight into the mechanisms of action in the CNS is to study the interplay between alcohol and drugs on behaviour, physiological effects, and alcohol metabolism.

The interaction of drugs and ethanol has been extensively studied in our laboratory, effects being observed both on subjective mood estimates and ocular phenomena (PAN and ROM) and on a number of psychological, psychotechnical, and performance tests.

The essential effects of a series of CNS-depressant drugs, ranging from buclozine, chlorpromazine, cyclozine, and hydroxyzine to meclozine, meprobamate, phenoglycodole, promethazine, and tripelenamine, were a decrease in PAN and a corresponding increase in ROM; a reduction of subjective stimulating effects and an increase in tiredness and sleepiness, an increase in area of sway while standing, and a slowing of alpha-frequency in the EEG together

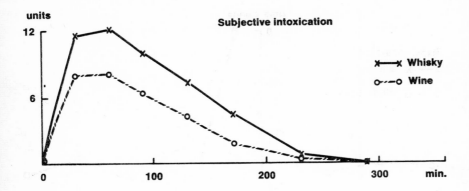

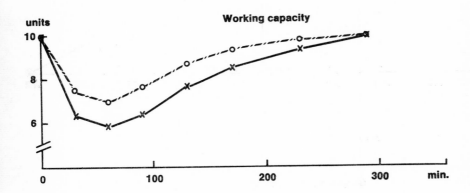

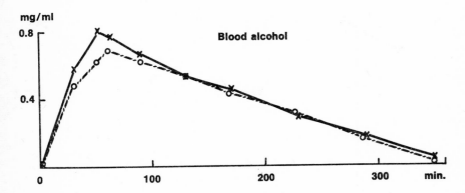

Figure 7-5
Blood alcohol (lower), subjective (upper) and objective tests (middle) after alcohol
0.7 gm/kg as whisky and (44 vol. per cent) white California wine (11.5 vol. per
cent). Average of 16 subjects. Note that differences in effects are larger than
differences in blood levels.

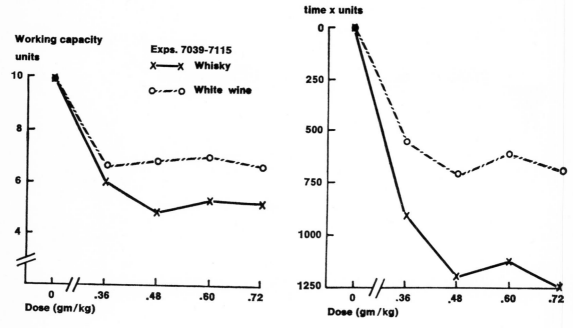

Figure 7-6
Working capacity after four different doses of whisky or white wine, means of four subjects at each dose.

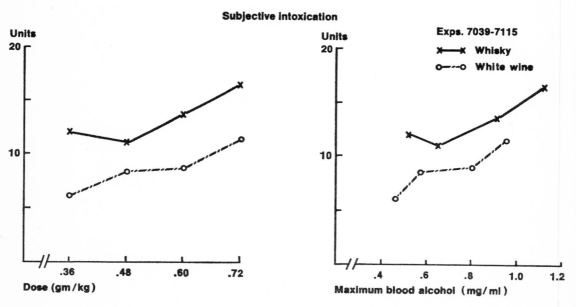

Figure 7-7
Relation between subjective symptoms, dose and blood alcohol levels after whisky and white wine.

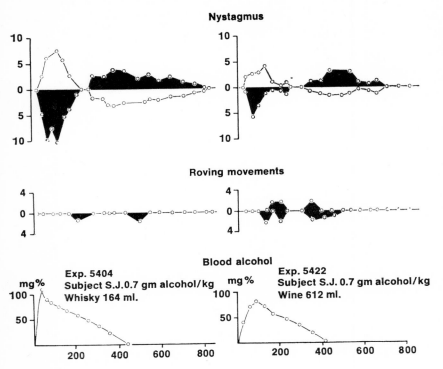

Figure 7-8
Ocular phenomena – positional alcohol nystagmus (PAN) and roving ocular movements (ROM) – after 0.7 gm alcohol as whisky (left) or wine (right).

with an increase in alpha-percentage and amplitude (10, 11).

One example of differential effects on subjective mood estimates and on objective tests is the interaction between alcohol and meprobamate or chlordiazepoxide (7, 12, 14). Chlordiazepoxide (20 mg), during the acute alcohol stage (four to five hours after intake), acts antagonistically to alcohol and diminishes the ethanol effects, both subjectively and objectively, for example, on standing steadiness, reaction time, and a number of performance tests such as hand accuracy. On the other hand, meprobamate (800 mg) in this phase acts synergistically with alcohol, and increases its effects (see Figures 7-2, 7-9, and 7-10). During the *post-alcohol* phase, i.e., six to ten hours after moderate alcohol doses, parallel to PAN II in the hangover phase, both drugs act antagonistically on ethanol, decreasing the impairment normally

seen at this stage after alcohol intake (see Figure 7-11).

The same differential action of meprobamate and chlordiazepoxide is also seen on the PAN and ROM phenomena. Whereas meprobamate, like all other CNS-depressant agents studied, from antihistamines to buclozine and chlorpromazine (11), increases ROM and decreases PAN, chlordiazepoxide is so far the only drug known that reduces both PAN and ROM, the mathematical relation – a rectilinear log-log relation – not being changed (see Figure 7-11).

Thus the interaction between ethanol and drugs depends not only on the type of drug administered, but also on the timing with regard to the phase of alcohol metabolism. However, no changes were found in the alcohol metabolism that could explain the differential effects of the drugs tested. The mechanism of action thus seems to be of a cellular nature, engaging

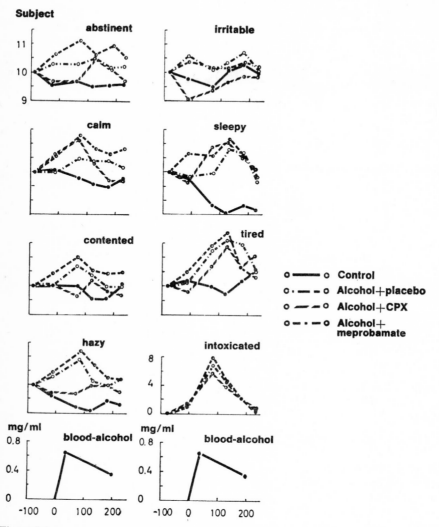

Figure 7-9

Subjective mood estimates. Time course in a dry run and after alcohol plus placebo, alcohol plus chlordiazepoxide, and alcohol plus meprobamate.

receptor sites and possibly mediated by changes in local enzymatic processes and/or in transmittor mechanisms.

Postalcohol effects ("hangover")

Postalcohol or "hangover" effects are in this context defined as the behavioural and subjective changes prevailing for a longer or shorter time after alcohol has left the blood, that is, after the blood alcohol level is zero.

A number of subjective and objective symptoms can be noted in the postalcohol period, from a "specific" pattern, PAN II, of the positional nystagmus (PAN) induced by previous alcohol intake and often accompanied by an increase in ROM (see Figures 7-4 and 7-12), to

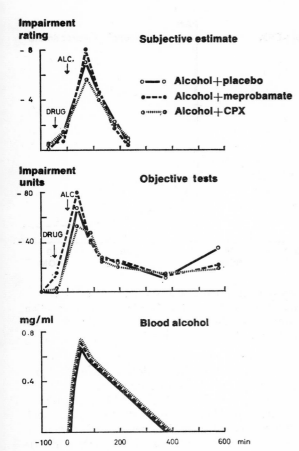

Figure 7-10
Subjective estimates (subj. estim.), objective performance (obj. tests), and blood-alcohol after alcohol 0.7 gm/kg plus placebo (alc. + plac.), alcohol plus 20 mg chlordiazepoxide (alc. + CPX), and alcohol plus 800 mg meprobamate (alc. + MEP). Means of eight subjects and of ten different performance tests. Mean curve of objective tests is the difference between the results of the actual alcohol experiments and of the dry run experiment.

an unspecific impairment in performance tests. This change is often only disclosed after comparison with a placebo or dry-run session (see Figure 7-10).

Intake of a new dose of alcohol during the hangover phase will, by inducing a PAN I for a time, reduce or completely block an existing

PAN II, and at the same time reduce or block some of the subjective symptoms accompanying PAN II, viz vertigo, dizziness, and nausea, parallel to an increase in other symptoms (see Figure 7-12).

The administration of various drugs may, however, profoundly influence signs and symptoms in the hangover phase. A number of drugs decrease PAN II. This decrease is accompanied by a corresponding increase in ROM, corresponding to an increase in tiredness, sleepiness, and fatigue (4, 10, 11). Chlordiazepoxide has so far been the only drug found that decreases both PAN and ROM (12).

Relation between effects and blood alcohol
The subjective mood ratings and objective performance tests of single individuals included most psychotechnical measures, standing steadiness, flicker frequency, corneal sensitivity, and alcohol gaze nystagmus. Most of the effects show a time-course that follows closely the time-course of blood alcohol, peak effects coinciding in time with maximum of blood alcohol. However, all tests studied will have returned to normal before the blood alcohol level is back to zero, indicating a disappearance threshold, its height varying with (*a*) the test employed, (*b*) the constitution of the individual, and (*c*) the individual's alcohol habits (8, 9).

The intensity of most effects studied increased in proportion to the dose (see Figure 7-7). In analysing the durations, whether of subjective or objective effects, it was observed, however, that the effects disappeared earlier than expected, that is, at a higher blood alcohol level (see Figure 7-10). The disappearance thresholds gradually increased with dose. Lacking an explanation of the mechanisms involved, this phenomenon must so far be interpreted as one facet of an adaptation process. The implication of this phenomenon with regard to repeated compulsive intake of alcohol by alcoholics is under consideration.

Some subjective moods – for example, tiredness and subjective working capacity – may for some hours show a course opposite to that of blood alcohol. The same is also true of ROM in most individuals, showing no relation to blood alcohol, but being closely related to subjective

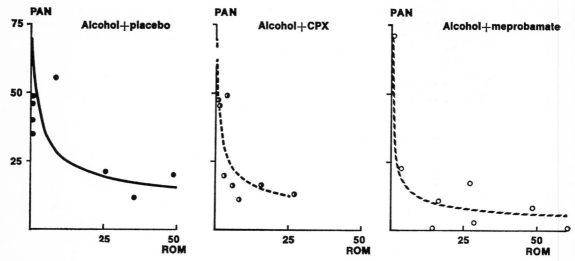

Figure 7-11

Relation between positional alcohol nystagmus (PAN) and roving ocular movements (ROM). Individual cases after alcohol plus placebo and after alcohol plus CNS-active drugs. Individual intensities of PAN (area = duration × intensity), plotted against corresponding intensities of ROM (area = duration × intensity). *Left*: After alcohol plus placebo. *Middle*: After alcohol plus chlordiazepoxide (CPX). *Right*: After alcohol plus meprobamate.

feelings of tiredness. Neither does PAN show any simple relationship to the blood alcohol level (see Figures 7-4 and 7-12). Latency times of PAN I and II and duration of PAN I after single doses are constant and independent of dose. After repeated doses the appearance and duration of PAN depend on the interaction with the blood alcohol gradient, whether rising or falling, and with the intensity and phase of a pre-existing nystagmus.

During the hangover there is also an increase in intensity of some subjective moods such as fatigue, dizziness, and vertigo; this follows a definite time-course even though the blood alcohol is already at zero. The same is true of PAN II in this phase, its intensity being closely correlated with that of subjective moods, vigilance, and ROM.

When studying groups of individuals, three facts emerge: (a) effects of ethanol are essen-tially proportional to the dose of alcohol taken, according to a log probit function (= a log-normal Gauss integral); (b) a higher correlation is found between peak effects and maximal blood alcohol levels than between effects and dosage, because variations in absorption, distri-bution, and disappearance of alcohol do not affect the former comparison; the highest cor-relation was found between peak effects and the difference between blood alcohol maxima and the appearance or disappearance thresholds for the effects studied; and (c) the variations among individuals depend not only on differ-ences in rate of alcohol uptake, distribution, and elimination, but on (i) differences in in-dividual constitutions – what may be termed "inherent resistance" – and (ii) acquired dif-ferences proportional to changes in intensity of alcohol use – what may be termed "acquired tolerance."

Figure 7-12

Hangover phenomena. Positional alcohol nystagmus (upper graph, PAN I and II) and blood alcohol concentra-tions (lower graph). Second dose of alcohol, given 8 1/2 hours after the first dose, when PAN II was at its maximum, counteracts PAN II. Three hours later PAN II returns.

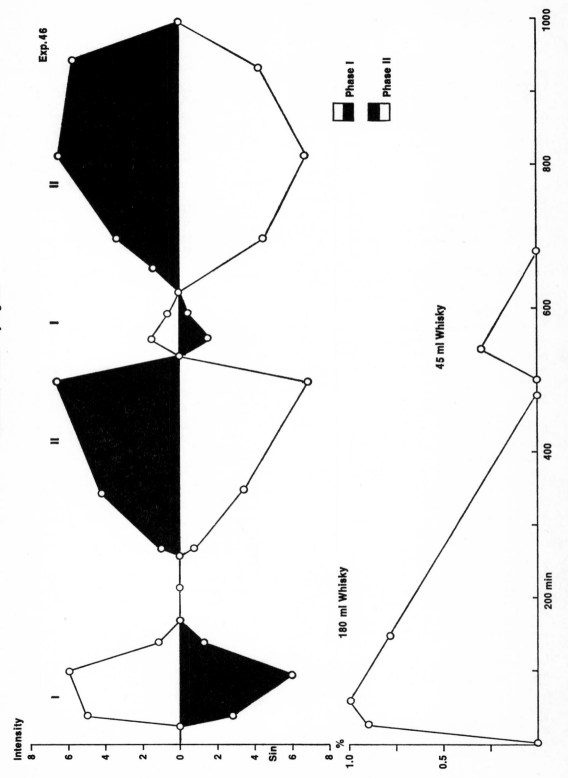

Vestibular Alcohol Nystagmus

Intensity

Exp.46

Tolerance in this respect can be defined as the degree of reaction to a stimulus or even the absence of a reaction, already in the initial testing situation. Tolerance varies greatly within an individual depending on the type of test applied, and between different individuals. An increase in intensity or severity of alcohol habits may bring about a parallel increase in "acquired tolerance" (8, 9, 12).

An adaptation process may in this context be looked upon as part of a normal phenomenon and can be defined operationally as a diminished response or no response to a constant, continuous, or repeated stimulus. The adaptation varies with the type of test applied in one and the same individual, as well as among different individuals. Examples of an adaptation are seen during an experiment when a performance test improves with time, or in repeated experiments when the responses to stimuli, as in performance tests, decrease from day to day. One example of an adaptation to alcohol intake is the diminished response on consecutive days, another is the diminished response with an increase in dosage (8, 9, 12).

To summarize, tolerance indicates the type and intensity of a reaction – whether severe or light – to the administration of a drug. Adaptation indicates the diminished response to a repeated stimulus, whether this be a stressful situation or a drug or any other agent. A series of studies is in progress to elucidate the nature of tolerance and adaptation phenomena.

REFERENCES

1
ASCHAN, G.
Caloric test: nystagmographical study
Acta Soc. med. uppsal., 60: 99, 1955
2
ASCHAN, G., BERGSTEDT, M., GOLDBERG, L., & LAURELL, L.
Positional nystagmus in man during and after alcohol intoxication
Quart. J. Stud. Alc., 17: 381, 1956
3
ASCHAN, G., BERGSTEDT, M., & STAHLE, J.
Nystagmography; recording of nystagmus in clinical neuro-otological examinations
Acta Otolaryng. (Stockholm) Suppl. 129, 1956
4
ASCHAN, G., BERGSTEDT, M., & GOLDBERG, L.
The effect of some antihistamine drugs in positional alcohol nystagmus
Acta Otolaryng. (Stockholm) Suppl., 140: 79, 1958
5
EKMAN, G., FRANKENHAEUSER, M., GOLDBERG, L., JÄRPE, G., & MYRSTEN, A.-L.
Effects of alcohol intake on subjective and objective variables over a five-hour period
Psychopharmacologia (Berlin), 4: 28, 1963
6
EKMAN, G., FRANKENHAEUSER, M., GOLDBERG, L., HAGDAHL, R., & MYRSTEN, A.-L.
Subjective and objective effects of alcohol as functions of dosage and time
Psychopharmacologia (Berlin), 6: 399, 1964
7
FRÖBERG, J.
Unpublished thesis, department of psychology, University of Stockholm, 1963
8
GOLDBERG, L.
Quantitative studies on alcohol tolerance in man. The influence of ethyl alcohol on sensory, motor and psychological functions referred to blood alcohol in normal and habituated individuals
Acta Physiol. Scandinav., 5: suppl. 16, 1943
9
GOLDBERG, L.
Tolerance to alcohol in moderate and heavy drinkers and its significance to alcohol and traffic
Proc. First Internat. Conf. Alc. Road Traffic, 1950, p. 85
10
GOLDBERG, L.
Alcohol, tranquilizers and hangover
Quart. J. Stud. Alc. Suppl., 1: 37, 1961
11
GOLDBERG, L.
Effects and after-effects of alcohol, tranquillizers and fatigue on ocular phenomena
Proc. Third Internat. Conf. Alc. Road Traffic, 1962, p. 123
12
GOLDBERG, L.
Behavioral and physiological effects of alcohol on man
Psychosom. Med., 28: 570, 1966
13
GOLDBERG, L. & RYDBERG, U.
Automated enzymatic micro-determination of ethanol in blood and urine
In Automation in analytical chemistry
Technicon Symposia 1965
New York: Mediad, 1966, p. 595
14
MYRSTEN, A.-L.
Unpublished thesis, department of psychology, University of Stockholm, 1964
15
WIDMARK, E.M.P.
Die theoretischen Grundlagen und die praktische Verwendbarkeit der gerichtlich-medizinischen Alkoholbestimmung
Berlin: Urban & Schwarzenberg, 1932

H. B. MURPHREE

L. M. PRICE

Department of Psychiatry
Rutgers Medical School
New Brunswick, New Jersey, USA

8

Electroencephalographic Effects of Some Alcoholic Beverages

In trying to define ever more rigorously the actions of some drugs upon the central nervous system, we have in recent years turned to various quantitative electroencephalographic techniques. If one accepts the postulate that there is some relationship between behavioural state and electroencephalographic activity, these methods can give numerical values to drug actions upon the brain and thence indirectly to actions upon behaviour. These numbers can then be treated statistically, with all the advantages that entails.

We have also become interested lately in what might be called the psychopharmacology of everyday life: the study of the effects of the numerous drugs with which huge numbers of people dose themselves, often chronically for many years, often without, or even against, medical advice, often for no discernible medical reason. It seems not unlikely that much of this intake is for some variety of mental effect. We include here aspirin and related compounds, antihistamines, various minor tranquillizers or anti-anxiety drugs, stimulants such as caffeine and amphetamine, and of course ethyl alcohol.

Thus far, we have been able to define three classes of drug effects by these methods. Drugs having stimulant subjective and behavioural effects tend to cause a reduction in the electrical energy (wattage, if you like) of the electro-encephalogram and a concurrent reduction in the variability of the energy. This can be related to a sustained flattening or absence of alpha from the EEG. When the alpha is no longer entering and leaving the record in its typical way, this varying source of energy is removed, and only a fine, low-amplitude, rather invariant background remains.

Drugs having depressant or hypnotic behavioural effects, in contrast to stimulants, tend to cause increases in the electrical energy of the EEG and in the variability of the energy. This occurs with the advent of large, slow-wave activity which entails relatively large amounts of

This work was supported in part by grants MH 06713 and MH 04229, US Public Health Service, and by a grant from the American Medical Association Education and Research Foundation.

energy and which, even more than alpha, is highly variable.

The third class of drug effect upon the electroencephalogram relates to drugs having minor tranquillizer or anti-anxiety behavioural effects. Here the picture is more complex. If one looks only at the total energy of the electroencephalogram, the effect is a slight reduction or no change in the mean energy, with an increase in the variance. In this case, it is more informative to employ bandpass filters, so that alpha and slow-wave activity can be studied separately. Typically, anti-anxiety drugs cause some replacement of alpha by slow waves, in the range of one to six per second. Thus there is not so much a change in the overall amount of electrical energy as in its distributions within the spectrum of the electroencephalogram. This switching of distributions accounts for the increases of variance.

We have previously reported (4) that ethanol-containing beverages, in usual clinical dosages, cause quantitative electroencephalographic changes similar to those of several drugs used in the treatment of anxiety. The principal difference is the short duration of action, the half life of the largest doses being only about 90 to 150 minutes. We also have reported (2) that we were unable to find any difference between vodka and bourbon in their quantitative electroencephalographic effects or in their production of nystagmus. These two beverages were chosen because they are at opposite poles in their content of so-called "congeners," that is, the small organic molecules other than ethanol which are present in varying amounts in alcoholic beverages. Vodka is almost pure ethanol in distilled water. Bourbon, which is consumed mainly in the United States, is distilled from a fermented product of maize.

Of several distilled beverages which we assayed by gas (vapour phase) chromatography, bourbon had the richest content of congeners. Some of these compounds are known to have significant pharmacological activity. It seemed to us that persons who chronically consume large amounts of alcoholic beverages would most probably have some effect from whatever congeners are coincidentally imbibed. The present report relates further studies of this possibility.

METHODS

The subjects were normal volunteers, four men and five women, aged 22 to 36, occasional to moderate drinkers by American standards. None had significant medical or psychiatric history. Each trial was begun at about 9:00 AM. Subjects were allowed a light breakfast, such as decaffeinated coffee or orange juice with dry toast. Recordings were made on a Grass Model III G electroencephalograph with monopolar electrodes referenced to both ears and a ground in the midforehead. All recordings were made with the subject supine, eyes closed, in a quiet, partially darkened room. The voltage from the left occipital was recorded simultaneously on an FM magnetic tape recorder for later analysis by means of a high-speed digital computer. The details of the apparatus and technique have been described earlier (1). Recordings were made for 10 minutes before dosage, for 30 minutes after, then for 10 minutes of each half hour up to three hours after dosage. Blood ethanol concentrations were determined with a Breathalyser, and eye movements were monitored by electrographic recording and visual inspection for possible nystagmus.

Two of the beverages were 80 proof vodka and an 86 proof bourbon. Their concentrations of the most commonly encountered congeners are shown in Table 8-1. The concentrations of the same substances in a synthetic ethanol made from petroleum and adjusted to 80 proof with distilled water are shown for comparison. These determinations were made by means of gas chromatography. The third alcoholic beverage used was made by fortifying the same kind of vodka with pure congeners prepared gas chromatographically from the same kind of bourbon. This was to study the effects of increased amounts of congeners with smaller amounts of ethanol. Doses were given according to amounts of absolute ethanol per kilogram of body weight. For the vodka and bourbon, the dose was 1.00 ml/kg. For the superbourbon, the dose was 0.25 ml/kg.

TABLE 8–1

"CONGENER" CONTENTS OF VODKA, BOURBON, AND
SUPERBOURBON (in mg/100 ml)

	Synthetic EtOH	Vodka	Bourbon	Superbourbon
acetaldehyde	0.3	0.3	1.7	54.4
ethyl formate	0.8	0.4	2.7	86.4
ethyl acetate	0.0	0.0	82.5	2640.0
methanol	0.5	0.4	2.6	83.2
n-propanol	0.0	0.0	11.0	352.0
i-butanol	0.0	0.0	25.0	800.0
i-amyl alcohol	0.0	0.0	120.0	3840.0

TABLE 8–2

BLOOD ALCOHOL CONCENTRATIONS AFTER VODKA,
BOURBON, AND SUPERBOURBON (in mg/100 ml)

Time (min)		15	30	60	90	120	150	180
vodka	mean	86	83	78	71	54	44	36
	s.d.	20	18	15	21	25	23	23
bourbon	mean	93	86	83	73	69	61	51
	s.d.	26	18	14	16	16	33	26
superbourbon	mean	25	20	12	5.6	1.1	1.1	1.1
	s.d.	6.1	5.0	6.2	6.8	—	—	—

s.d. = standard deviation.

RESULTS

Table 8-2 shows the blood alcohol concentrations obtained. Note that the values for the vodka and bourbon do not differ significantly, while the values for the superbourbon are smaller, reflecting the smaller dosage of ethanol. Note also that, even after three hours, the concentrations from bourbon and vodka were greater than the 15-minute concentrations from superbourbon.

Figure 8-1 shows sample strips of electroencephalogram of one subject before and 2½ hours after a dose of superbourbon. In the baseline record, there is a moderate amount of alpha activity. In the 2½-hour record, this is no longer clearcut, and there is appreciable slow activity.

Figure 8-2 shows the spectrum of the entire ten-minute baseline recording as plotted by the computer. Means plus or minus standard deviations are shown. Note the smooth alpha peak and relatively narrow limits of the standard deviations above and below the means.

Figure 8-3 shows the spectrum 2½ hours after dosage with superbourbon. Note that the smooth alpha peak is disrupted, with greatly increased standard deviations. Somewhat similar qualitative effects were obtained with the larger doses of bourbon and vodka, but were not so marked or long lasting as with the doses of superbourbon.

Figure 8-4 shows graphs of the total energy, the alpha energy at 10 Hz and the energy at 4 Hz during the baseline recording and during the recording 2½ hours after the superbourbon. During the baseline recording, the alpha and slow-wave activity constitute fairly even proportions of the total, and the time-series statistics, δ^2/s^2, show that there is no significant trend in any of the three functions. During the 2½-hour recording there was an increase in variance of the total energy from 16 to 53. There is a highly significant downward trend

Electroencephalogram 1323
Monopolar left occipital

Baseline

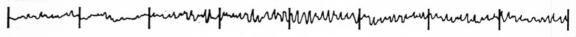

2½ hr. after Superbourbon

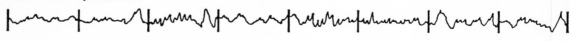

 50 μ V

Figure 8-1
Electroencephalogram of one subject before and 2½ hours after a dose of superbourbon.

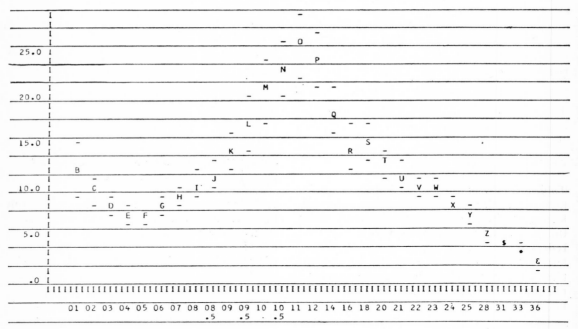

Figure 8-2
Spectrum of ten-minute baseline recording.

in the alpha, showing a tendency of this function to disappear from the record. The δ^2/s^2 is 0.81. Concurrently there is a significant upward trend in the 4 per second activity; δ^2/s^2 is 0.85. In both cases p is less than 0.001.

Table 8-3 shows the incidences of nystagmus among the nine subjects after the three dosages.

The incidence parallels somewhat the blood alcohol concentrations for the bourbon and vodka. However, although the subjects still had appreciable blood alcohol concentrations three hours after bourbon or vodka, nystagmus remained present in only one of the nine. In contrast, the incidence of nystagmus after the super-

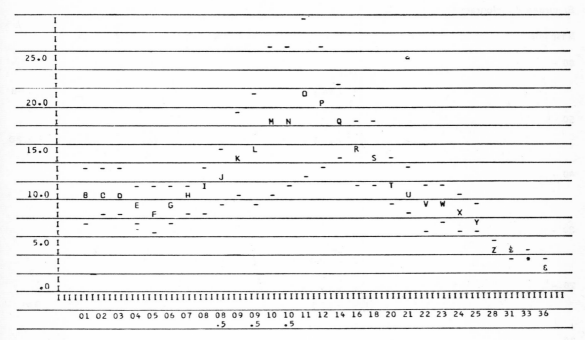

Figure 8-3
Spectrum 2½ hours after dosage with superbourbon.

TABLE 8–3

INCIDENCE OF NYSTAGMUS AFTER VODKA, BOURBON, AND
SUPERBOURBON

Time (min)	15	30	60	90	120	150	180
vodka	5/9	5/9	5/9	4/9	3/9	2/9	1/9
bourbon	5/9	5/9	5/9	3/9	3/9	2/9	1/9
superbourbon	9/9	9/9	9/9	8/9	8/9	8/9	8/9

bourbon remained eight out of nine, although the blood alcohol concentrations had long since become negligible. These findings are reported in greater detail elsewhere (3).

DISCUSSION AND CONCLUSION

The effects reported here might be explained in one of two ways. Either the congeners themselves have direct, long-lasting effects upon the central nervous system, as reflected in the electroencephalogram, or they may somehow retard the metabolism of ethanol so that it has a stronger and more enduring depressant effect. The latter would seem less probable, because the effects were observed well after the blood alcohol concentrations had become unmeasurably small. One would therefore have to postulate that somehow tissue concentrations were maintained even though blood concentrations were not. Accordingly, it appears more likely that one or more of the congeners have direct depressant effects and that these can be separated from those of ethanol, because the former are much longer lasting.

Electroencephalogram 1323

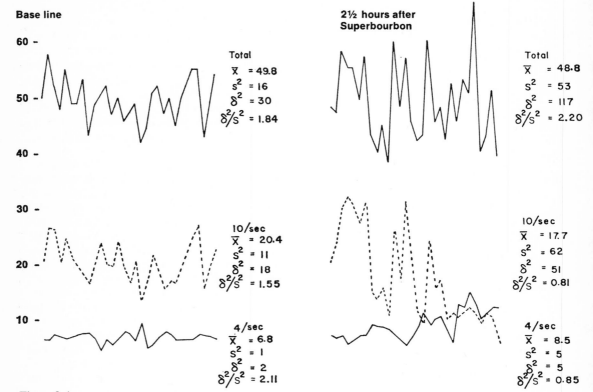

Figure 8-4

Total energy, alpha energy at 10 Hz, and energy at 4 Hz during the baseline recording and during the recording 2½ hours after the superbourbon.

This study is, of course, only preliminary, because just one dose of superbourbon was given, and because the trials were terminated three hours after dosage. Further exploration is needed to determine whether congeners can produce the effects without the presence of ethanol, whether any one congener or set of congeners are responsible for the effects, and whether any dose-effect or dose-duration relationships can be established.

Whatever the exact mechanism, it does appear that beverages with large amounts of congeners, when drunk in excess, may have greater and longer-lasting depressant effects than other beverages, and that these effects may contribute to hangover and to some of the adverse results upon the central nervous system of chronic alcoholics.

REFERENCES

1
MURPHREE, H.B., GOLDSTEIN, L., PFEIFFER, C.C., SCHRAMM, L.P., & JENNEY, E.H.
Computer analysis of drug effects on the electroencephalograms of normal and psychotic subjects
Internat. J. Neuropharmacol., **3**: 98, 1964

2
MURPHREE, H.B. & PRICE, L.M.
EEG effects of bourbon and vodka
Fed. Proc., **24**: 517, 1965

3
MURPHREE, H.B., PRICE, L.M., & GREENBERG, L.A.
Effect of congeners in alcoholic beverages on the incidence of nystagmus
Quart. J. Stud. Alc., **27**: 210, 1966

4
PFEIFFER, C.C., GOLDSTEIN, L., MURPHREE, H.B., & JENNEY, E.H.
Electroencephalographic assay of antianxiety drugs
Arch. Gen. Psychiat., **10**: 446, 1964

RAINER FRIED

Department of Biochemistry
Creighton University Medical School
Omaha, Nebraska, USA

9

Biochemical Studies of a New Anti-Alcoholic Drug, Metronidazole

Metronidazole (Flagyl) was introduced as a trichomonocidal drug by Durel and collaborators (2) in 1959, and has since been used successfully on several thousand patients. The early publications dealing with its pharmacological behaviour have mainly been published in journals of gynecology and of venereal disease. During a study of its side effects, Taylor (14) observed that the drug caused special effects similar to those produced by disulfiram (Antabuse) when taken by patients who were also consuming alcohol.

Metronidazole was reported to cause a reduced tolerance to alcohol, aversion to alcohol, and less severe symptoms during alcohol withdrawal in chronic alcoholics. The side effects of the drug are much less drastic and less dangerous than those of Antabuse, and it is therefore more readily accepted by the patient and preferred by clinicians in the management of alcoholism. At the time of this presentation, only one preliminary publication dealing with the anti-alcoholic effects of metronidazole has been published (14); it reports dramatic success in one fully documented case, which is presented as an example of results obtained with a series of 53 alcoholic patients. More detailed publications are being prepared by Dr. Taylor, and her findings have been confirmed by other investigators.

Metronidazole shows relatively little toxicity. In about 5 per cent of the patients, gastric disturbances can be observed as well as bitter taste, coated tongue, and some mild neurological symptoms. No deaths attributable to the drug have been reported. The most serious possible side effect is a transitory leucopenia. According to Taylor (14), the drugs should not be administered to patients with hypothyroidism, impaired adrenergic function, or severe liver

This investigation was supported in part by a grant from the Scientific Advisory Board of the Licensed Beverage Industries, New York, the American Cancer Society (Nebraska Chapter, grant P-389), and Ayerst Laboratories, New York. Flagyl was kindly provided by Dr. V. A. Drill (G. D. Searle & Co., Chicago) and Antabuse by Dr. T. Robitscher (Ayerst Laboratories, New York). The author is pleased to acknowledge the competent help of Mrs. Lygia W. Fried and Mr. Edward Bottum.

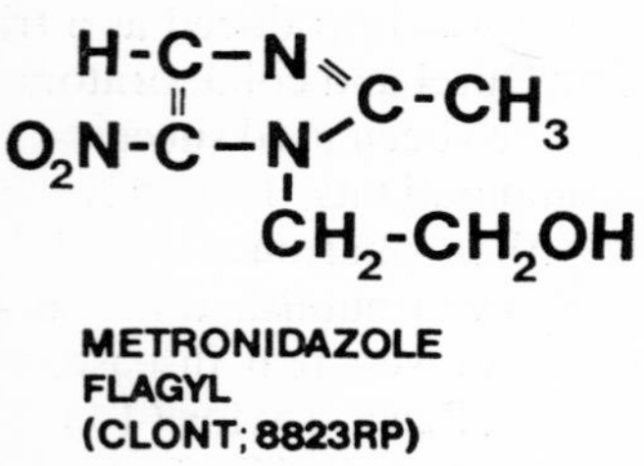

$$H-C-N\begin{matrix}\\ \diagdown\end{matrix}C-CH_3$$
$$O_2N-C-N\diagup$$
$$CH_2-CH_2OH$$

METRONIDAZOLE
FLAGYL
(CLONT; 8823RP)

Figure 9-1
Structure of metronidazole.

damage. This would seem to curtail its application in chronic alcoholics with severe cirrhosis or fibrosis of the liver. Leucocyte counts are probably advisable. Although the drug has been administered to pregnant women without any damage to the fetus or child, it should not be given during the first three months of pregnancy, since it can pass through the placental barrier. Decreases of glucocorticoids and of thyroid-stimulating hormone have also been reported (1, 15).

STRUCTURE OF METRONIDAZOLE

The structure of metronidazole is shown in Figure 9-1. Its chemical name is 1 (2'-hydroxyethyl)-2-methyl-5-nitroimidazole. Note the presence of a -hydroxyethyl side-chain and a nitro-group which may be important for its biochemical mechanism of action and its detoxication. Metronidazole can undergo a series of degradation reactions which include reduction to amino-derivatives, followed by conjugation, intermolecular condensation, and cyclization (10, 11). Several derivatives, including brown pigments, can be demonstrated in the

urine of patients receiving metronidazole, and a red-brown coating of the tongue is also observed occasionally; these pigments are probably azoderivatives of the drug.

The present author has no personal experience with the clinical application of metronidazole. This report deals with biochemical studies of its effects on selected enzymes related to alcohol metabolism. It is hoped that these will contribute to an understanding of the biochemical mechanism of action of metronidazole as an anti-alcoholic drug, about which no data have been available to date.

Ethanol is metabolized according to the following reaction sequence (see Figure 9-2): Ethanol (I) is oxidized in two steps to acetic acid (III) (or acetyl-CoA), which can be utilized in the usual metabolic pathways or be fully burned to carbon dioxide. The product of the first oxidation step, acetaldehyde (II), can be oxidized by several enzymes: NAD-linked or flavo-protein aldehyde dehydrogenases, and also xanthine oxidase. In addition to these oxidation reactions, acetaldehyde and ethanol can also participate in other biological reactions. The present paper deals with the *in vitro* effects of metronidazole on some of the enzymes included in this scheme, namely, alcohol dehydrogenase and xanthine oxidase, as well as another enzyme related to xanthine oxidase, uricase. Parts of the present paper have been previously reported (4, 5).

ABSORPTION SPECTRUM OF METRONIDAZOLE

The absorption spectrum of metronidazole is shown in Figure 9-3. Metronidazole presents

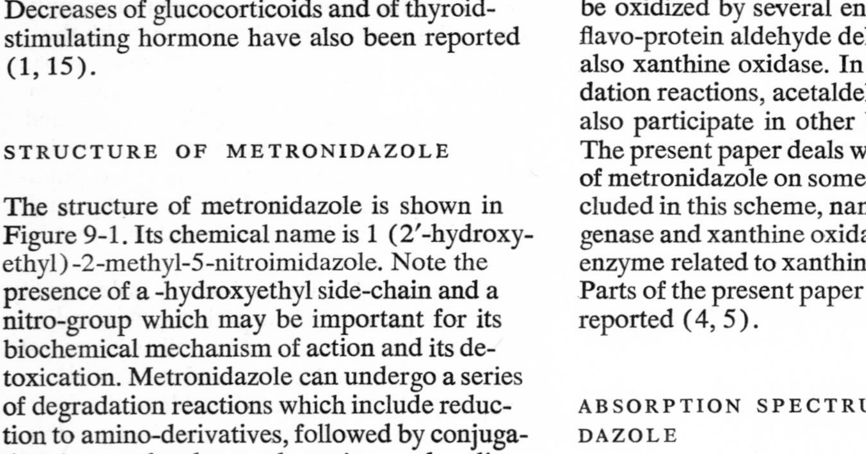

1) $C_2H_5OH + NAD \xrightarrow{\text{alcohol dehydrogenase}} CH_3 . C\overset{\diagup O}{\diagdown H} + NADH + H^+$

    I   II

2) $CH_3 . CHO \xrightarrow[\text{or xanthine oxidase}]{\text{aldehyde dehydrogenase}} CH_3 . COOH$

                                                    III

Figure 9-2
Main pathways of ethanol degradation.

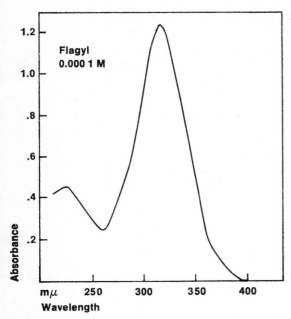

Figure 9-3
Absorption spectrum of metronidazole: 0.0001 M in
0.1 M phosphate; pH 7.8.

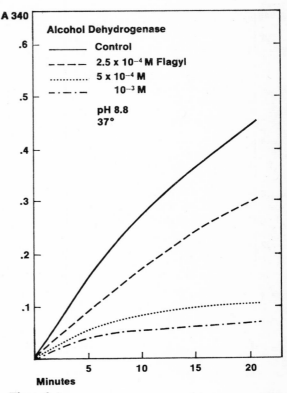

Figure 9-4
Inhibition of alcohol dehydrogenase by metronidazole:
0.10 mg of enzyme; 2 mg NAD; completed to 8.0 ml
with sodium pyrophosphate, 0.032 M, pH 8.8. The
reaction was started by addition of 2.0 ml ethanol,
2.0 M. From Fried & Fried (5), by permission.

absorption maxima at 230 and at 325 mμ. The
latter can be used for spectrophotometric assay,
linear curves being obtained over a wide range
of concentrations. On the other hand, this high
absorption frequently interferes in the spectrophotometric assay of enzymes, and may necessi-
tate special methods or instrumentation for such
procedures.

INHIBITION OF ALCOHOL DEHYDROGE-
NASE BY METRONIDAZOLE*

The first enzyme involved in alcohol metabolism
is NAD-linked alcohol dehydrogenase (ADH).
When metronidazole was tested *in vitro* as inhibitor of ADH (purified horse liver alcohol dehydrogenase, obtained from Worthington) using the spectrophotometric assay (18), the
drug caused about 50 per cent inhibition at a
final concentration of 3×10^{-4}M (see Figure
9–4).

*See addendum.

EFFECT OF Zn ON INHIBITION OF ADH
BY METRONIDAZOLE

Alcohol dehydrogenase is a metallo-enzyme
which contains zinc at its active site. It was
thought that metronidazole might bind zinc and
thus cause inactivation of the enzyme. When
ZnSO$_4$ was added to the incubation mixture, no
effect was observed in either the presence or the
absence of metronidazole (see Figure 9-5).

EFFECT OF METRONIDAZOLE ON ADH
IN THE PRESENCE OF TETRAZOLIUM

It will be remembered that metronidazole itself
contains an "ethanol" group (β-hydroxyethyl)

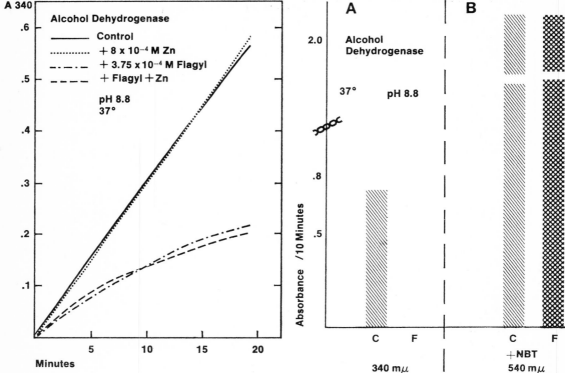

Figure 9-5
Effect of zinc on the inhibition of ADH by metronidazole
assay conditions, as for Figure 9-4.

Figure 9-6
Effect of metronidazole on ADH activity in presence
of tetrazolium. A: Assay as above, read at 340 mμ.
B: Tetrazolium reduction, read at 540 mμ. (c) = control; (F) = metronidazole, final concentration, 0.001 M,
0.5 ml of 0.1 per cent gelatin; 1.0 ml of nitro-BT,
4 mg/ml and phenazine methosulfate 0.5 ml of
0.2 mg/ml.

as a side chain. Thus it is possible that metronidazole could act as a substrate for alcohol dehydrogenase. When the drug was incubated in
the complete system, in the absence of ethanol,
at 37° for up to two hours, no formation of
NADH was observed. This finding indicates that
under the conditions employed, metronidazole
does not act as substrate for ADH.

It was found that ADH could be readily determined by tetrazolium reduction. An assay procedure for ADH was developed by appropriate
adaptation of other tetrazolium reduction
methods (3, 12), using Nitro-BT tetrazolium as
an electron acceptor in the presence of phenazine methosulfate and gelatin. This method is
about eight times as sensitive as the usual spectrophotometric assay. Metronidazole caused
no inhibition of ADH when the tetrazolium
method was used. The addition of phenazine

methosulfate alone had no effect on the inhibition of ADH in the usual spectrophotometric
assay (see Figure 9-6).

EFFECT OF METRONIDAZOLE ON XAN-
THINE OXIDASE

The first oxidation product of ethanol is acetaldehyde, which can be further oxidized by several
enzymes, of which xanthine oxidase is one. The
effect of metronidazole was studied with xanthine oxidase obtained from cream and from
liver; other investigators have shown that these

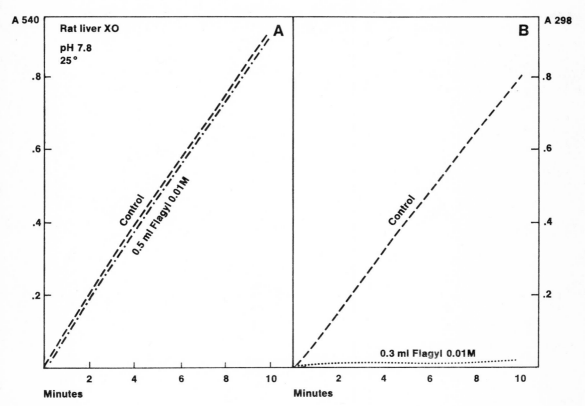

Figure 9-7

Effect of Flagyl on liver xanthine oxidase: A: dehydrogenase activity; 540 mμ: enzyme, 0.08 mg; 0.5 ml of xanthine, 0.001 M; 0.5 ml of gelatin, 0.1 per cent; 0.5 ml of nitro-BT tetrazolium salt, 4 mg/ml; 0.2 ml of phenazine methosulfate 0.2 mg/ml. B: oxidase activity; 298 mμ: 0.08 mg of enzyme; 0.5 ml of xanthine 0.001 M; phosphate, pH 7.8, 0.1 M, to complete 3.0 ml. The rection was started by addition of xanthine. From Fried & Fried (5), by permission.

two enzymes have different biochemical properties. Cream xanthine oxidase was obtained from Worthington and used without further purification. Liver xanthine oxidase was prepared from rat liver homogenate by means of precipitation of inactive proteins at pH 5, followed by ammonium sulfate fractionation of the neutralized supernatant solution. The fraction precipitating between 20 and 50 per cent saturation was used as enzyme source.

Both enzymes were assayed for oxidase and for dehydrogenase activity with graded levels of metronidazole. Oxidase activity was carried out by the spectrophotometric method (7); dehydrogenase was determined by tetrazolium

reduction in the presence of gelatin and phenazine methosulfate (3).

Liver xanthine oxidase activity was found to be completely inhibited *in vitro* when assayed in presence of 0.001 M metronidazole, but liver xanthine dehydrogenase activity was not at all affected by higher concentrations of the drug (see Figure 9-7).

Identical results were observed when cream xanthine oxidase was tested. Again the oxidase activity was completely inhibited by metronidazole 0.001 M. The drug had no effect on the dehydrogenase activity as measured by tetrazolium reduction (see Figure 9-8).

It is interesting to note that with both the liver

68 / *R. Fried*

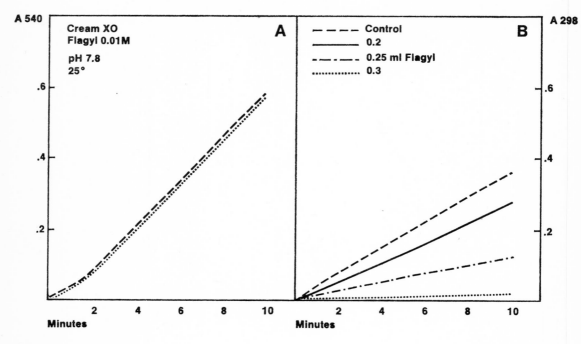

Figure 9-8
Inhibition of cream xanthine oxidase by metronidazole. Assay conditions as for Figure 9-7.

and the cream enzymes the inhibition range is very narrow, since 3×10^{-4}M of metronidazole causes only 5 per cent inhibition.

The inhibition of xanthine oxidase by metronidazole is reversible. Inhibition is no longer observed when the enzyme and metronidazole are preincubated, and the mixture is subsequently dialysed exhaustively before being assayed in the usual manner (see Table 9-1).

Xanthine oxidase has been shown to be inhibited by a compound chemically related to metronidazole, a nitrofuran derivative (Furacin); it also participates in the biochemical degradation of this compound (17). Similar experiments were also carried out with xanthine oxidase and metronidazole. They were preincubated for prolonged periods at 37°; afterwards, an aliquot was removed and xanthine oxidase activity and its inhibition were assayed (see Table 9-2).

Initial concentrations were chosen to give approximately 50 per cent inhibition in relation to the control mixture incubated without the

drug. Prolonged incubation caused a decrease in inhibition due to metronidazole. During this incubation period the enzyme activity of xanthine oxidase alone also decreases. At present two possibilities must be considered: (a) during incubation with the enzyme, metronidazole is

TABLE 9–1

EFFECT OF DIALYSIS ON INHIBITION OF XANTHINE OXIDASE

Preincubation (minutes at 37°)	Flagyl	Dialysis	Activity (percent)
15	−	+	100
15	+	+	100
none	+	−	0
30	+	−	0

Cream xanthine oxidase, 2.0 ml, diluted 1:100 from stock with 0.1 M phosphate, pH 7.8, was incubated in a Dubnoff shaker with 8.0 ml, metronidazole 0.01 M. The mixture was dialysed for two hours against four changes of 50 volumes of buffer, at +2°. For assay, 1.0 ml of the mixture were incubated with 0.5 μM of xanthine in 3.0 ml buffer, pH 7.8 at 25°. Activity was determined as change in absorbance at 298 mμ, during ten minutes.

TABLE 9–2

EFFECTS OF PREINCUBATION
ON INHIBITION OF
XANTHINE OXIDASE BY
METRONIDAZOLE

Preincubation	Control	Flagyl
none	0.82	0.49
90 min.	0.49	0.33
180 min.	0.41	0.30

One millilitre of cream xanthine
oxidase 1:100 was preincubated at 37°
and pH 7.8 with 1.0 ml of 0.01 M
Flagyl. Aliquots of 0.4 ml were
removed for assay. Activity is expressed
as increase in absorbance at 298 mμ,
at 25° for ten minutes.

metabolized to derivatives which cause lower
inhibition; or (*b*) the loss of activity of xanthine
oxidase affects that site of the enzyme which is
related to the inhibition by metronidazole. An
active site to which metronidazole is bound may
be affected in such a manner that binding, and
therefore inhibition, is less efficient. At present
the available experiments do not permit a decision between these two possible mechanisms
which must be clarified by further work. Inhibition did not disappear completely even when
the enzyme and metronidazole were preincubated for 24 hours.

EFFECTS OF METRONIDAZOLE AND DISULFIRAM ON ALCOHOL DEHYDROGENASE

In relation to its effect on xanthine oxidase, metronidazole acts in a manner similar to disulfiram. Disulfiram has been shown to be a potent
inhibitor of xanthine oxidase in the manometric
assay, but the inhibition could be lowered and
even eliminated by the addition of methylene
blue as auxiliary electron carrier (13). Clinical
trials of metronidazole as an anti-alcoholic drug
have revealed that this compound is much less
toxic and causes much less severe physiological
and psychological reactions than observed with
disulfiram. When the two drugs were compared
in vitro as inhibitors of alcohol dehydrogenase,
intense inhibition was caused by metronidazole,
but none by disulfiram (see Figure 9-9).

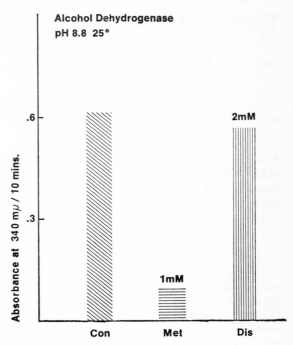

Figure 9-9
Effects of metronidazole and disulfiram on alcohol
dehydrogenase. Con = control; Met = metronidazole;
Dis = disulfiram. Disulfiram was dissolved in ethanol,
with appropriate adjustments for final ethanol concentration.

Lack of inhibition of ADH by disulfiram
(Antabuse) was reported previously, but no experimental data were given (8). This report is
confirmed by the present findings which suggest
a possible explanation for the difference in toxicity between Antabuse and Flagyl. The severe
reaction caused by Antabuse is generally attributed to the accumulation of acetaldehyde,
which alone or in conjunction with Antabuse
is considered the cause of the drastic "Antabuse
reaction."

Thus, the difference in results stemming from
the administration of Antabuse or Flagyl would
stem from a different biochemical mechanism
of action. The two inhibitors act at different
points in the metabolic sequence of alcohol
(see Figure 9-2): Antabuse inhibits acetaldehyde oxidation, and thus lets the toxic acetaldehyde accumulate. On the other hand, Flagyl,

by inhibiting alcohol dehydrogenase, inhibits the first reaction of alcohol, thus preventing the formation of acetaldehyde. The lack of a severe response to Flagyl treatment may be ascribed to the prevention of the accumulation of acetaldehyde.

These findings may not be the sole explanation for the mild reaction caused by Flagyl and the severe reaction caused by Antabuse; possibly other contributing factors will be found. However, these data must be taken into account in attempts to explain the different effects produced by the two drugs. These results also strengthen the hypothesis that the mechanism of action of Antabuse is based on the accumulation of acetaldehyde.

The findings discussed up to this point indicate a possible mechanism of action of metronidazole as an anti-alcoholic drug. Metronidazole has been shown to inhibit two sequential reactions involved in the biological oxidation of ethanol, alcohol dehydrogenase, and xanthine oxidase. It should not be taken to mean that this is the exclusive mechanism of action. Other enzyme systems must also be tested. It is possible that other enzymes which are not directly related to the oxidative degradation of ethanol will be found to be inhibited by metronidazole. Further research will be required to clarify fully how this drug acts in the prevention of alcoholism.

EFFECTS OF METRONIDAZOLE ON URIC ACID FORMATION

The present findings also explain one of the clinical effects of Flagyl therapy: high levels of serum uric acid are observed during intoxication with alcohol (9). When Flagyl is administered to alcoholic patients, the uric acid levels return to normal (16). This can readily be explained by the inhibition of xanthine oxidase, which would cause less uric acid to be formed.

In order to obtain a better understanding of the mechanism of action of metronidazole, xanthine metabolism was studied further. As has been shown above, xanthine metabolism is also impaired, since metronidazole acts as an inhibitor of xanthine oxidase. This enzyme catalyses

the oxidation of xanthine and hypoxanthine according to the following scheme:

$$(1) \quad \text{hypoxanthine} \xrightarrow{\text{xanthine oxidase}} \text{xanthine}$$

$$(2) \quad \text{xanthine} \xrightarrow{\text{xanthine oxidase}} \text{uric acid}$$

$$(3) \quad \text{uric acid} \xrightarrow{\text{uricase}} \text{allantoin}$$

In most mammals, but not in man, uric acid is metabolized further; the first enzyme in this sequence is uricase.

When metronidazole was tested as an inhibitor of uric acid, it was found to inhibit the relevant enzyme at approximately the same concentrations which caused inhibition of ADH and xanthine oxidase (see Table 9-3). Thus at lease one enzyme not directly related to alcohol metabolism is also inhibited in vitro by metronidazole.

During the work with xanthine oxidase a pink colour was observed when metronidazole was incubated at 37° and pH 7.8 and afterwards let stand at room temperature at pH 11.5. Colour formation did not occur at lower pH values. The rate of colour formation was enhanced by the presence of xanthine oxidase during the preincubation phase at 37°, and was further increased by the presence of xanthine (see Figure 9-10). The colour has an absorption maximum at 540. It fades after about 60 minutes at 25°, but reappears when the mixture is aerated; it can be bleached rapidly by ascorbic

TABLE 9–3

EFFECT OF METRONIDAZOLE ON URICASE

Metronidazole (µM)	Activity
0	0.52
1	0.47
2	0.35
3	0.11
5	0.02

Three milligrams of uricase (beef kidney, Worthington); uric acid, 0.1 µM; vol. 3.0 ml.; 0.1 M phosphate, pH 9.0; 25°. Activity $A_{293}/10$ min.

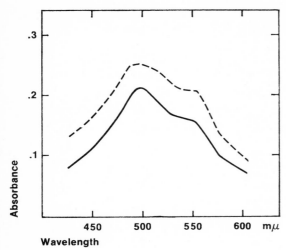

Figure 9-10
Coloured derivative of metronidazole formed in
alkaline solution: 2.0 ml of metronidazole, 0.1 M;
cream xanthine oxidase (1:100), 0.5 ml; 0.1 phosphate,
pH 7.8, to complete 3.0 ml. The mixture was incubated
in Dubnoff shaker for 40 minutes at 37°. One millilitre
of 5 N NaOH was added; final pH 11.5. Colour was
read after standing for 15 minutes at 25°, at 500 mμ.
Phosphate was blank. ——— Metronidazole alone;
————metronidazole incubated with xanthine oxidase.

acid or bisulfite. When HCl is added to a solution of the "pink metronidazole," several colour changes are observed, passing through a rapidly disappearing purple, followed by yellow and white. When alkali is added back, only the yellow colour reappears. It is not known whether the formation of this coloured derivative of metronidazole has any physiological significance. It may be related to the brown pigment found in urine and the reddish coating of the tongue of some patients treated with Flagyl.

SUMMARY COMMENT

The new anti-alcoholic drug metronidazole (Flagyl) has been studied *in vitro* with several mammalian enzymes related to alcohol metabolism. The drug inhibited alcohol dehydrogenase and cream and liver xanthine oxidase, as well as uricase. The first two enzymes are

inhibited only when tetrazolium salts are not included in the reaction mixture. The mechanism of this reaction is not known. In this connection it should be pointed out that tetrazolium reduction methods are widely used for histochemical localization of enzymes, as well as identification of enzyme bands separated by gel electrophoresis. If the absence of inhibition in the presence of tetrazolium salts is not kept in mind, false conclusions might be drawn when metronidazole is tested as an inhibitor. Metronidazole causes a much less severe reaction than disulfiram, probably because metronidazole prevents the formation of acetaldehyde, which accumulates when disulfiram is used as an anti-alcoholic agent.

A new drug which shows promise as an effective anti-alcoholic agent has proved to be a valuable tool for the study of alcohol metabolism and for enzyme research. It is expected that further interesting results will stem from its application.

ADDENDUM

Subsequent experiments revealed that the interpretation of part of the preceding report must be revised. When the inhibition of the alcohol dehydrogenase system was studied in greater detail, it was found that metronidazole interacts with reduced NAD (NAD-H) in the absence of enzyme and ethanol. This mixture results in a decrease in the typical absorbance at 340 nm, which would be interpreted as a decrease or inhibition of alcohol dehydrogenase activity in the usual assay (6).

The nature of the product resulting from the combination of metronidazole with NAD-H is being investigated; it probably involves the formation of a charge-transfer complex. It is possible that during the spectrophotometric assay of alcohol dehydrogenase activity in the presence of metronidazole a steady state of NAD-H is reached, which would be interpreted as inhibition of the enzyme. Whether metronidazole is a true inhibitor of alcohol dehydrogenase must be determined by methods which do not depend on the usual spectrophotometric assay at 340 nm. No interaction was found between disulfiram and NAD or NAD-H.

REFERENCES

1
BAKKE, J.L., LAWRENCE, N., & CAMPBELL, G.
The effect of metronidazole on the synthesis of thyroid stimulating hormone in the hypothyroid rat
Metabolism, 14: 647, 1965

2
DUREL, P., ROIRON, V., SIBOULET, A., & BOREL, L.J.
Essai d'un antitrichromonas derivé de l'imidazome: 8823
RPCR Soc. franc. gynec., 29: 36, 1959

3
FRIED, R.W.
Colorimetric determination of xanthine dehydrogenase by tetrazolium reduction
Anal. Biochem., 16: 427, 1966

4
FRIED, R.W. & FRIED, L.W.
Biochemical studies of metronidazole (Flagyl)
Third International Pharmacological Congress, July 24–30, 1966
Abstracts of short communications, lectures, and symposia, São Paulo, Brazil, p. 32

5
FRIED, R.W. & FRIED, L.W.
The effect of flagyl on xanthine oxidase and alcohol dehydrogenase
Biochem. Pharmacol., 15: 1890, 1966

6
FRIED, R.W. & FRIED, L.W.
Inhibition of oxidizing enzymes by metronidazole
Experientia, 24: 56, 1968

7
KALCKAR, H.M.
Differential spectrophotometry of purine compounds by means of specific enzymes: I. Determination of hydroxypurine compounds
J. Biol. Chem., 167: 429, 1947

8
KJELDGAARD, N.O.
Inhibition of aldehyde oxidase from liver by tetraethylthiuramdisulfide (Antabuse)
Acta Pharmacol. Toxicol., 5: 397, 1949

9
LIEBER, C.S., JONES, D.P., LOSOWSKY, M.S., & DAVIDSON, C.S.
Interrelation of uric acid and ethanol metabolism in man
J. Clin. Invest., 41: 1863, 1962

10
MANTHEI, R.W., HORN, R.S., & FEO, L.G.
Studies on the metabolism of metronidazole (Flagyl)
Pharmacologist, 4: 170, 1962
Abstract

11
MANTHEI, R.W., TO, W., & FEO, L.B.
Characterization of metabolites of metronidazole (Flagyl)
Pharmacologist, 5: 235, 1963
Abstract

12
NACHLAS, M.M., MARGULIES, S.I., GOLDBERG, J.D., & SELIGMAN, A.M.
The determination of lactic dehydrogenase with a tetrazolium salt
Anal. Biochem., 1: 317, 1960

13
RICHERT, D.A., VANDERLINDE, R., & WESTERFELD, W.W.
The composition of rat liver xanthin oxidase and its inhibition by antabuse
J. Biol. Chem., 186: 261, 1950

14
TAYLOR, J.A.
Metronidazole – a new agent for combined somatic and psychic therapy of alcoholism
A case study and preliminary report
Bull. Los Angeles Neurol. Soc., 29: 158, 1964

15
TAYLOR, J.A.
Modification of adrenocortical hyperfunction by an imidazole derivative
J.A.M.A., 181: 776, 1962

16
TAYLOR, J.A.
Personal communication

17
TAYLOR, J.D., PAUL, H.E., & PAUL, M.F.
Metabolism of the nitrofurans: III. Xanthine oxidase in vitro
J. Biol. Chem., 191: 223, 1951

18
VALLEE, B.L. & HOCH, F.L.
Zinc, a component of yeast alcohol dehydrogenase
Proc. Nat. Acad. Sc., 41: 327, 1955

KLAUS SOEHRING

RAINER SCHÜPPEL

Institute of Pharmacology
Hamburg University
Hamburg, West Germany

10

Interactions between Alcohol and Drugs

Drug combinations are relatively frequent in German medicine. The physician expects to find in a combination the known effects of the isolated components, so that if he prescribes an analgesic and a sedative in combination, he might be certain to get both effects for a given identical time. It is difficult to support this expectation, as we can see from the following example: the use of an analgesic rapidly metabolized, in combination with Barbital, which is not metabolized but is slowly eliminated, gives a longer sedative than analgesic effect. Zipf and Hamacher (34) have studied the theory of these combinations, based on Loewe's ideas known since 1953 (15). These papers can be considered as the basis of the mathematical theory of alteraction.

The rapid growth of the pharmaceutical industry has encouraged the use of traditional drug combinations and has also favoured accidental combinations. A great number of patients take drugs other than those prescribed, without any therapeutic reason. Certain social groups accept this habit as normal behaviour.

Loomis (16) stated that in the United States two out of five patients given a prescription take one or more psychoactive drugs as well. Considering the great number of analgesics sold without prescription in the Federal Republic of Germany, for example, it is clear that accidental combinations are frequent and beyond control. It is likely that in these cases experimentally known interactions are not taken into account in medical practice. Nieschulz (20), some years ago, called ethanol the oldest psychoactive drug and suggested the use of this well studied substance as a standard in the evaluation of new compounds of this type.

Considering the consumption of alcoholic beverages in West Germany (about 18 billion DM per year), and of drugs (about 3 billion DM per year), it appears that interactions between alcohol and drugs must be frequent in this population. Therefore, it might be assumed that intensive studies had been performed to establish the pharmacological interaction both on the central nervous system and on the biochemical level; for example, the distribution and metabolism of such drug combinations. However, in the literature up to the middle of this century we find very few reports concerning these matters. A strong stimulus to relevant investigation came from the increase in driving after World War II. We must be prepared to face a continual increase in the number of accidents, if, together with alcohol, other drugs with different effects on the central nervous system are indiscriminately used.

Wagner and Wagner (30) examined about five thousand drivers and found that from 10 to 13 per cent had taken drugs during the past 24 hours before being involved in an accident or being stopped by the police for incorrect driving. Wangel (31), in similar studies, investigated the use of alcohol and drugs in combination. The results for Denmark were as follows: out of 4841 individuals with blood alcohol levels, 18 per cent were influenced by other drugs. In a control group (1226 persons who had not taken alcohol) only 10 per cent drove under the influence of other drugs. The drugs most commonly used were analgesics, hypnotics, and psychoactive drugs. In the "alcohol group" both the frequency and amount of drug taken were significantly greater than in the "control group."

Simultaneous intake of alcohol and drugs is dangerous in road traffic and, at least in Germany, plays an increasingly important role in criminal law. The problem of responsibility under the influence of alcohol and drugs is becoming more and more important, and the lack of information makes investigation in this area correspondingly urgent.

We shall now review attempts to find a solution to these problems in recent years. As pharmacologists, we shall emphasize experimental data rather than the results of psychological or sociological studies. But, in agreement with Goldberg (10), we believe that biochemical and pharmacological data can be useful for the planning of work on higher levels, as in psychology and psychiatry.

As far as we can see, the following research methods have been generally used: accumulation and evaluation of medico-legal and medical observations; psychopharmacological experimentation in animals; psychologic studies in

human volunteers; and biochemical and pharmacological studies *in vitro* and *in vivo*.

ACCUMULATION AND EVALUATION OF OBSERVATIONS

Few references are made to the interaction of alcohol and drugs in published work. In the general index for the last 25 years of the *Archiv für Toxikologie*, a leading journal in Germany, we found only two relevant reports. Most of the information at hand comes from unpublished reports, such as those from special committees, penal verdicts, and the pharmaceutical industry. A bibliography of published and unpublished work is in preparation.

From these sources, we can conclude that the following combinations may be of special interest: hypnotics/antiepileptic drugs; psychoactive drugs (including stimulants); INH and other MAO-blockers; antihistaminic drugs; oral antidiabetic drugs; opiates and synthetic drugs of morphine-like action; and the pyrazolones.

Interaction of alcohol with other drugs may be expected too, but instances are numerically of less importance. This suggests that planning of future work should be concerned first with the combinations mentioned above.

PSYCHOPHARMACOLOGICAL EXPERIMENTS IN ANIMALS

During and after World War II, especially in industrial research, new psychopharmacological methods for the study of drug effects in animals were developed. It is not our task to discuss methodological progress in detail. But it should be mentioned that psychopharmacology today permits the manipulation of psychomotor reactions, the production of different behavioural patterns, the defence against stress, the suppression of instincts, the adaptation to new environments, etc. The methods designed have been used by only a few authors to study the interactions between alcohol and drugs, and this in just the last few years. As an example may be mentioned the work of Hughes and his associates, who showed in 1963 a suppression of the strong sedative effect of meta-amino-diazepoxide by alcohol in rats (13).

PSYCHOLOGICAL STUDIES IN HUMANS

The history of systematic studies in the field of interactions between alcohol and drugs in humans also began in the last few years. Loomis (16), for example, reviewing the literature before starting his own work, found only two studies concerned with the interactions between alcohol and tranquillizers in volunteers, and in which modern psychological methods were employed. Carpenter and Varley (2) note the difficulty of planning experiments in the field of traffic medicine. The differences between the test situation in the laboratory and the actual situation in accidents have not been eliminated so far. Appropriate methods are still lacking. Today's experimental psychology may detect and determine quantitative differences in behaviour, work yield, and even emotion: in this way, interactions between alcohol and drugs can be studied in the laboratory; but it is difficult to estimate the relevance of the results of such work to everyday practice in traffic medicine. From this standpoint, all published psychological work up to now is open to criticism.

Doenicke (3) found that after apparent recovery from intravenous anesthesia or the oral administration of certain barbiturates, work yield, neuromuscular co-ordination, and judgment were impaired again when 7 or 24 hours later 500 ml of beer were given to the subjects. After this combination, and despite the long interval between drug and alcohol, most individuals were subjectively unable to drive a car. In 1964 the author and his coworkers reported similar results with an alcohol-fluphenazine combination.

Wilson *et al.* (32) evaluated the interaction of alcohol and amphetamine with a large battery of tests and came to the unexpected conclusion that the stimulant is unable to suppress all the depressant effects of alcohol. Forney and Hughes (5) likewise could not prove a complete antagonism between caffein and alcohol. Law-

ton and Cahn (14) did not find a decrease in test yields after the administration of alcohol and diazepam. Our own group has studied the combination of alcohol and meprobamate in 80 young healthy individuals of both sexes (17). Antagonism or synergism were observed depending on psychological stability or lability. There was a marked and statistically significant difference between sexes. Zirkle *et al.* (35) obtained similar results but they did not note the difference in behaviour between the sexes.

An interesting experiment designed to improve research methods in man is the so-called multifactorial analysis developed by Bochnik and his colleagues (1). Psychological and somatic data are evaluated together with the results of psychiatric exploration, using modern electronic equipment for calculation and evaluation.

When one considers the high costs and great efforts necessary to assess just one drug, it is not surprising that so few results of studies of the combination of alcohol and drugs have been published as yet. If we consider the great number of psychoactive drugs appearing on the market every year, we easily realize the urgent need for the development of simple and effective methods to detect and grade loss of control in mental and neuromuscular functions.

BIOCHEMICAL AND PHARMACOLOGICAL STUDIES

It is impossible to review the entire subject here, so we shall limit ourselves to the work of our own laboratory during the last six years. By the term "interaction" we understand principally two different patterns: (*a*) alteration of alcohol effects by drugs, and (*b*) alteration of drug effects by alcohol.

For practical reasons, the influence of drugs on alcohol elimination seems to be one of the most important aspects. Tipton *et al.* (28) reported a considerable decrease in rate of alcohol elimination in rabbits after pretreatment with chlorpromazine, and Schleyer and Janitzki (21) confirmed this finding in studies of the same animal. These results could be vitally important for traffic medicine, and therefore Seidel *et al.* (25) decided to repeat the experiments in dogs, as the alcohol elimination rate in these animals is closer to that of man. Alcoholemia was studied for seven hours in dogs pretreated with chlorpromazine before the administration of 0.79 gm/kg alcohol by stomach tube. The authors did not find any change in the curves as compared with dogs not treated with chlorpromazine. Seidel and Soehring (24) extended this work to 41 drugs in frequent use in West Germany, but failed to find any positive or negative influence on alcohol elimination. Wagner (29) studied 15 drugs in a similar manner in human subjects and also was unable to find an effect on the elimination rate. Increase of the alcohol elimination rate by "miracle drugs" seems to exist up to now only in sensational reports in the newspapers. When Fischer and Oelssner (4) saw accelerated alcohol elimination in mice by treatment with hexobarbital, they considered this to be of relatively little importance for all practical purpose in man.

To consider the alteration of drug effects by alcohol, we must differentiate between acute (or sub-chronic) and chronic experiments. It has been generally acknowledged for some time that simultaneous administration of barbiturates and alcohol reinforces the sedative effect of both drugs, as measured by prolongation of sleeping time. On the other hand, every surgeon and anesthetist knows that the administration of barbiturates to chronic drinkers has little effect or even an adverse one; therefore it is difficult to produce barbiturate or thiobarbiturate anesthesia in such cases. In view of its practical implications, we decided to examine the problem further. Frahm *et al.* (8) demonstrated a massive reduction in barbiturate and thiobarbiturate effects in guinea pigs forced to drink 10 per cent alcohol for seven weeks. Sleeping time in these animals was drastically reduced, and in some cases there was no hypnotic effect at all. When alcohol was replaced by water, these effects proved reversible.

Muñoz and Soehring in 1964 performed a similar experiment with "drinking" and "non-drinking" rats from the breeding stock of the Pharmacological Institute of the University of Chile and observed a similar trend. However, they were unable to establish a significant difference. In our laboratory Wissmer (33) showed a decrease of local anesthetic effects in guinea pigs pretreated for several weeks by drinking 10 per cent alcohol. Neithard (18) and Steinhoff (27) observed interactions of alcohol with other drugs, using the enforcement method for several weeks. The prolongation of sleeping time produced by a reserpine-pentobarbital combination decreased in "alcoholic" guinea pigs. With combinations of stimulants and pentobarbital, short-term pretreatment antagonized the awaking effects of the stimulants, while after some weeks on alcohol there was an adverse effect.

All of these experiments contribute to the "phenomenology" of interaction, but do not provide a basis for its comprehension. Accordingly we tried the following hypothesis: previous treatment with alcohol might produce changes in drug distribution or alterations of drug metabolism.

To test the first possibility, Seidel *et al.* (26) determined pentobarbital concentrations in the brains of guinea pigs pretreated for a week with 5 per cent alcohol, and compared the results with those for a non-alcohol control group. The concentration of pentobarbital in "drinking animals" one hour after administration was 30 per cent lower than in the control group ($p < 0.01$). Correspondingly, the blood plasma levels in "drinking animals" were higher than the values found in the control group. Frahm *et al.* (7) found lower levels of pentobarbital in several tissues of alcohol pretreated rats as compared with controls.

These results suggested changes in permeability for pentobarbital after pretreatment with alcohol. Greiser and Soehring (12) therefore studied the distribution of pentobarbital between erythrocytes and a protein-free medium, adding small amounts of alcohol to the system. In control experiments, there was an energy-consuming uptake in addition to the expected diffusion. The uptake of pentobarbital was decreased when small pentobarbital concentrations were used, with 4 per cent alcohol in the suspending medium. Increasing the pentobarbital concentration produced an adverse effect. This suggested the existence of an equilibrium between input and output, both processes being inhibited by alcohol. The results indicate once again that a membrane change results from treatment with alcohol, as discussed many years ago by Hober.

The second possibility – changes in drug metabolism after pretreatment with alcohol – has also been studied intensively in recent years. In liver homogenates of rats treated for months with 10 per cent alcohol, Greiser (11) observed inhibition of hexobarbital metabolism, while Fischer and Oelssner (4) reported enhancement in mice. Difficulties with the separation of metabolites prevented us from continuing this line of work. As Frahm and Streller (9) have recently succeeded in improving the separation methods, we shall soon start again to experiment in this field.

For the reasons mentioned, Schüppel and Soehring (22, 23) turned their attention to another drug. Using the experience of Netter (19) with demethylation methods, we decided to study the demethylation of aminopyrine in rats. Both the major metabolite – 4-amino-antipyrine – and the methyl group that is split off can be determined in the urine, the latter as formic acid. With an alcoholemia between 1 and 5 per cent in acute experiments, the output of both the metabolites decreased in the first six hours after the administration of 150 mg/kg aminopyrine, as compared with control rats on water. In general, the excretion pattern in alcohol treated animals was directly opposite to that in the controls.

These results are open to criticism, but they show an inhibition of aminopyrine demethylation during alcohol oxidation in rats. There may be a real inhibition of the enzymes by alcohol or its first metabolite, acetaldehyde, or, following Forsander (6), a kind of local hypoxia at the sites of demethylation. This might be produced as the oxygen present is used in the first line for alcohol oxidation.

If these results with aminopyrine reflect a general pattern, the importance cannot be overestimated: demethylation is one of the major pathways in the inactivation of many drugs.

Methyl-substituted amines are found for instance in the following groups: analgesics, phenothiazines, psychoactive drugs, morphine, hexobarbital, and anti-epileptics.

It seems desirable to go on with studies of distribution and metabolism. All data collected in this field can be used as a basis for further studies on higher levels such as those of psychology or psychiatry. The pharmacologist can only provide the "bricks," clinical medicine and psychiatry must build with them. To reduce the risks in modern road traffic an effective cooperation between basic and clinical medicine, psychology and psychiatry, seems essential.

REFERENCES

1
BOCHNIK, H.J., *et al.*
Ein Analysemodell für klinische Verbundforschung: Multifaktorielle Untersuchung der Pyrithioxinwirkung nach Schlafentzug bei gesunden Studenten
Fortschr. Neurol. Psychiat., 32: 400, 1964

2
CARPENTER, J.A. & VARLEY, M.
The joint action of tranquillizers and alcohol on driving
Proc. Third Internat. Conf. Alc. Road Traffic, 1962, p. 156

3
DOENICKE, A.
[Infringement of traffic safety by barbiturate moderation and the barbiturate/alcohol combination]
Arzneimittel-Forsch., 12: 1050, 1962

4
FISCHER, H.-D. & OELSSNER, W.
[The effect of barbiturates on alcohol elimination in mice]
Klin. Wschr., 39: 1265, 1961

5
FORNEY, R.B. & HUGHES, F.W.
Effect of caffein and alcohol on performance under stress of audiofeedback
Quart. J. Stud. Alc., 26: 206, 1965

6
FORSANDER, O.A.
Influence of the metabolism of ethanol on the lactate/pyruvate ratio of rat-liver slices
Biochem. J., 98: 244, 1966

7
FRAHM, M., HÖLTJE, W., & SOEHRING, K.
In preparation

8
FRAHM, M., LÖBKENS, K., & SOEHRING, K.

[The influence of subchronic alcohol doses on barbiturate narcosis in the guinea pig]
Arzneimittel-Forsch., **12**: 1055, 1962
9
FRAHM, M. & STRELLER, I.
In preparation
10
GOLDBERG, L.
Personal communication
11
GREISER, E.
In preparation
12
GREISER, E. & SOEHRING, K.
Die Aufnahme von Pentobarbital durch menschliche Erythrocyten *in vitro* und ihre Beeinflussung durch Aethanol
Siebente Frühjahrstagung der Deutschen Pharmakologischen Gesellschaft in Mainz, 24–27 April 1966
In Naunyn-Schmiedebergs Arch. exper. Path. u. Pharmakol., **255**: 17, 1966
13
HUGHES, F.W., ROUNTREE, C.B., & FORNEY, R.B.
Suppression of learned avoidance and discrimination responses in the rat by chlordiazepoxide (Librium) and ethanol-chlordiazepoxide combination
J. Genet. Psychol., **103**: 139, 1963
Abstract in Quart. J. Stud. Alc., **26**: 136, 1965
14
LAWTON, M.P. & CAHN, B.
The effects of diazepam (Valium) and alcohol on psychomotor performance
J. Nerv. & Ment. Dis., **136**: 550, 1963
15
LOEWE, S.
Problem of synergism and antagonism of combined drugs
Arzneimittel-Forsch., **3**: 285, 1953
16
LOOMIS, T.A.
Effects of alcohol on persons using tranquillizers
Proc. Third Internat. Conf. Alc. Road Traffic, 1962, p. 119
17
MUNKELT, P., LIENERT, G.A., FRAHM, M., & SOEHRING, K.
[Sex specific action differences of a combination of alcohol and meprobamate on psychically stable and labile experimental individuals]
Arzneimittel-Forsch., **12**: 1059, 1962
18
NEITHARD, HANSJÖRG
Wirkungsänderungen zweier Analytica durch subchronische Alkoholgaben
Diss. Hamburg, Pharmakol. Inst. Univ., 1964
19
NETTER, K.-J.
Suflhydrlgruppen in Lebermikrosomen
Naunyn-Schmiedebergs Arch. exper. Path. u. Pharmakol., **253**: 76, 1966

20
NIESCHULZ, O.
Dtsche Ges. Verkehrsmedizin, Bad Oeynhausen, 1964
21
SCHLEYER, F. & JANITZKI, U.
[Studies on the effect of megaphon on the blood alcohol level]
Arch. Internat. Pharmacodyn., **141**: 254, 1963
22
SCHÜPPEL, R. & SOEHRING, K.
Vermehrte Ameisensäure-Ausscheidung – ein Mass für gesteigerte Demethylierungsvorgänge *in vivo*?
Naunyn-Schmiedebergs Arch. exper. Path. u. Pharmakol., **251**: 109, 1965
23
SCHÜPPEL, R.
Die Stickstoff-Demethylierung am Phenazon (Anti-pyrin)
Naunyn-Schmiedebergs Arch. exper. Path. u. Pharmakol., **255**: 71, 1966
24
SEIDEL, G. & SOEHRING, K.
Zur Frage der Aenderung der Blutalkoholwerte durch Medikamente
Arzneimittel-Forsch., **15**: 472, 1965
25
SEIDEL, G., STRELLER, I., & SOEHRING, K.
Zur Frage der Beeinflussung des Alkohol-Gehaltes im Blut durch Chlorpromazin
Arzneimittel-Forsch., **14**: 412, 1964
26
SEIDEL, G., STRELLER, I., & SOEHRING, K.
Der Einfluss subchronischer Alkoholgaben auf die Pentobarbitalaufnahme des Meerschweinchenhirns
Naunyn-Schmiedeberg's Arch. exper. Path. u. Pharmakol., **247**: 312, 1964
27
STEINHOFF, CH.
Diss. Hamburg, Pharmakol. Inst. Univ., 1965
28
TIPTON, D.L., JR., SUTHERLAND, V.C., BURBRIDGE, T.N., & SIMON, A.
Effect of chlorpromazine on blood level of alcohol in rabbits
Am. J. Physiol., **200**: 1007, 1961
29
WAGNER, H.J.
Dtsche. Ges. Verkehrsmedizin, Sektion Arzneimittel u. Verkehr, 7. Tagg. Bad Oeynhausen, 1966
30
WAGNER, K. & WAGNER, H.J.
In Sucht und Missbrauch, edited by F. Laubenthal, Stuttgart, 1964, p. 409
31
WANGEL, J.
Alcohol, road traffic, and drugs in Denmark, 1960
Proc. Third Internat. Conf. Alc. Road Traffic, 1962, p. 162
32
WILSON, L., TAYLOR, J.D., & NASH, C.W.
Combined effects of ethanol and amphetamine sulfate

on performance of human subjects
C.M.A.J., **94**: 478, 1966
33
WISSMER, P.-H.
Zur Frage des Einflusses der Alkoholgewöhnung auf
die Wirkung von Lokalanalgetica
Diss. Hamburg Pharmakol. Inst. Univ., 1962
34
ZIPF, H.F. & HAMACHER, J.
Kombinationseffekte: 1. Mitteilung: allgemeine
Fragen der Kombinationsforschung
Arzneimittel-Forsch., **15**: 1267, 1965
35
ZIRKLE, G.A., MCATEE, O.B., KING, P.D., & VAN DYKE, R.
Meprobamate and small amounts of alcohol effects on
human ability, coordination, and judgment
J.A.M.A., **173**: 1823, 1960

H. REMMER
RAINER SCHÜPPEL

Institute of Toxicology
Tübingen University
Tübingen, West Germany

Numerous lipid soluble drugs and other compounds foreign to the organism act on the endoplasmic reticulum of liver cells which contain almost all of the drug-metabolizing enzymes. Substances such as barbiturates, nikethamide, and tolbutamide, which are neither chemically nor pharmacologically related, induce an accelerated synthesis of drug-hydroxylating enzymes (1, 2).

As an example, the time course of the activity of this enzyme system after administration of 100 mg/kg phenobarbital intraperitoneally to rats may be cited (see Figure 11-1). We killed the rats at different times after phenobarbital administration and prepared the liver suprenatant which was incubated with TPN and hexobarbital as substrate. The oxidation rate of hexobarbital decreased during the first four to six hours when the concentration of pheno-

11

The Influence of Ethanol on Drug Metabolism

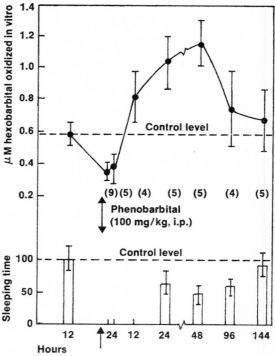

Figure 11-1

Hexobarbital sleeping time and *in vitro* oxidation of hexobarbital in rats after administration of phenobarbital. Figures in brackets are numbers of animals. Vertical bars represent ± SD.

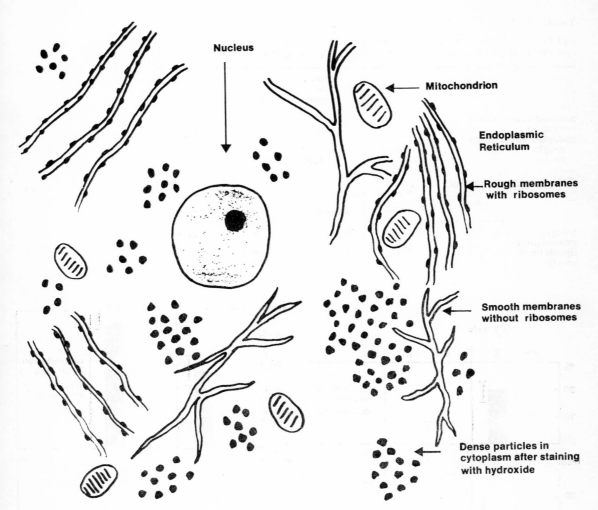

Figure 11-2
Ultramicroscopic structure of the liver cell (schematic).

barbital in the rat was high. Afterwards it began to rise until the second day. After the maximum was achieved the rate fell during the following two to four days.

What was observed *in vitro* could be confirmed with *in vivo* experiments. If these rats were pretreated with just one injection of phenobarbital and given hexobarbital at the times indicated in Figure 11-1, the anesthesia would be considerably shortened. Hexobarbital loses its effects by oxidation, not by excretion. With the rise and fall of the oxidation rate the

duration of the hexobarbital action decreases and increases respectively.

The reduced effect of hexobarbital could be viewed as a particular type of tolerance evoked by an enhanced drug metabolism. (We do not think it is correct to use the term "tolerance" for the phenomenon of enzymic adaptation, as is commonly done in the literature. But to discuss this question would lead us too far from the subject of the present paper.)

If the drugs mentioned are administered to rats, rabbits, and dogs repeatedly for more than

TABLE 11–1

EFFECTS OF PHENOBARBITAL (LUMINAL) PRETREATMENT
ON DIFFERENT CONSTITUENTS OF RAT LIVER CELLS

	Nitrogen (mg)	
	control	luminal
nucleus : mitochondria	11.6	12.0
cytoplasm	10.6	11.2
endoplasmic reticulum		
rough	1.47	1.54
smooth	1.51	3.26

endoplasmic reticulum from 1.0 gm liver

	"Rough" membrane		"Smooth" membrane	
	control	luminal	control	luminal
μM cytochrome b$_5$	4.3	6.6	8.2	24.6
protein (mg)	7.0	7.8	8.9	16.5
lipoids (mg)	2.3	3.4	2.7	6.1
RNA (mg)	1.3	1.1	0.4	0.6

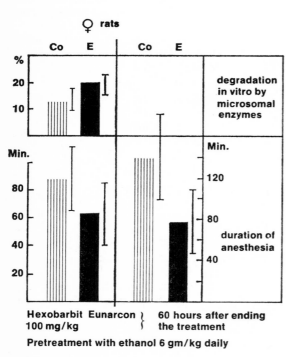

Figure 11-3
Effects of ethanol pretreatment on drug degradation
activity of rat liver preparation and on sleeping time
induced by two barbiturates.

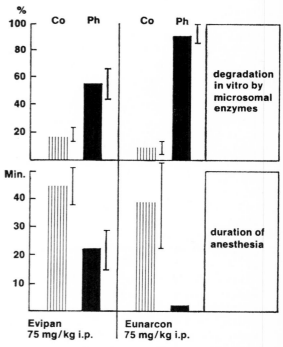

Figure 11-4
Effects of phenobarbital pretreatment (1 × 100 mg/kg
intraperitoneally) on drug degradation activity of rat
liver preparation and on sleeping time induced by two
barbiturates.

TABLE 11–2

COMPOUNDS HAVING SIMILAR EFFECTS ON DRUG
HYDROXYLATION AND THE FORMATION OF SMOOTH
MEMBRANES

	Drug hydroxylation		
	inhibition	activation	new formation of smooth membranes
phenobarbital	+ +	+ + + +	+ + + +
nikethamide	+ +	+ + + +	+ + +
tolbutamide	+ +	+ + + +	+ + +
phenothiazines	?	+ +	?
antihistaminics	?	+ +	?
insecticides: DDT; aldrine	?	+ + +	+
carcinogens: benzopyrene, methylcholanthrene	?	+ +	(+)
ethyl alcohol	+ + +	+	?

three days, a new formation of so-called smooth
membranes of the endoplasmic reticulum is
induced, as shown schematically in Figure 11-2.
What can be seen with the electron microscope
is confirmed by biochemical methods (1, 3), as
indicated in Table 11-1.

We should distinguish between foreign compounds inducing drug-hydroxylating enzymes
as well as new smooth membranes, and those
substances which activate drug-hydroxylating
enzymes only. Table 11-2 shows a selection of
those compounds having similar effects. It is
important to know whether ethyl alcohol has a
similar effect. This question should be answered,
since it is common for sedatives or hypnotics
to be taken before or after alcoholic beverages.
Accordingly, we turn now first to the question
whether alcohol accelerates drug oxidation and
diminishes the effect of some drugs. Then we
shall describe some experiments which show
that alcohol is able to inhibit drug oxidation.

The duration of anesthesia is considerably
shortened if rats are pretreated with ethanol for
8 to 14 days (see Figure 11-3). This might be
explained by a development of tolerance in the
central nervous system produced by ethyl alcohol. But the following three considerations
speak against such an explanation:

First, there is a marked difference in sleeping
time after the intraperitoneal administration of
hexobarbital or Eunarcon to rats pretreated
with ethanol (see Figure 11-3). The same difference was found after one injection of pheno-

barbital (see Figure 11-4). The metabolism
of Eunarcon proceeds much more rapidly than
the oxidation of hexobarbital. Similarly, ethyl
alcohol seems to have a much greater effect on
the metabolism of Eunarcon than on the oxidation of hexobarbital.

Secondly, to test the sleeping time the barbiturates were given 60 hours after the treatment
with alcohol ended. It is not very likely that a

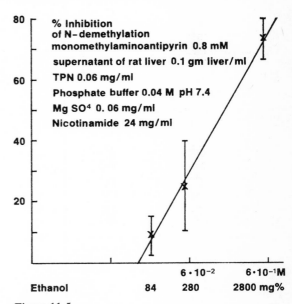

Figure 11-5
Inhibition of N-demethylation in a rat liver preparation
by ethanol *in vitro*.

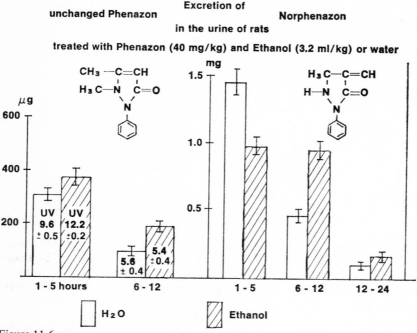

Figure 11-6

Effects of ethanol on the elimination of phenazon and its N-demethylated metabolite (norphenazon) in rats after simultaneous dosing with ethanol and phenazon.

diminished sensitivity of brain tissue would prevail for so long.

Thirdly, the best evidence for "tolerance" by an increased metabolism of barbiturates after pretreatment with ethanol is the fact that liver supernatant metabolizes hexobarbital *in vitro* a little faster if it is prepared from the liver of rats treated with ethyl alcohol.

With the evidence we have now it is impossible to know whether prolonged treatment with ethanol produces an activation of the drug-hydroxylating enzyme system only, or whether it induces a hypertrophy of the smooth membranes of the endoplasmic reticulum. In any case, an alcohol intake for several weeks may produce an accelerated metabolism of drugs.

However, the opposite may be the case if a higher alcohol level prevails in the organism. Ethanol added *in vitro* to liver supernatant causes an inhibition of the oxidative demethylation of monomethylamino-antipyrine. A concentration of ethanol which can be easily achieved

in man after intake of alcohol leads to an inhibition of the oxidation rate (see Figure 11-5).

Non-specific inhibition of enzymic reactions by alcohol *in vitro* can be observed frequently. But in this case it is possible to prove that the metabolism is also inhibited *in vivo*. Thus, such inhibition can be shown after the administration of 40 mg/kg phenazon orally to male rats which received 3.2 ml/kg ethanol at the same time. The excretion of the metabolite norphenazon decreased significantly during the first five to six hours (see Figure 11-6). There is no indication that this decrease was due to diminished overall excretion. One can only assume that the amount of the metabolite in the urine decreases because of an inhibited metabolism in the liver (4).

Activation and inhibition of drug metabolism by ethanol should be taken into consideration when alcoholism is discussed. Moreover, although we are able to present only a very few experiments, we think that research along these lines could produce more and better evidence respecting the influence of alcohol on drug metabolism.

REFERENCES

1
REMMER, H.
Drug tolerance
In Enzymes and drug action, a CIBA Foundation symposium, edited by G.E.W. Wolstenholme
London: J. & A. Churchill, 1962, p. 245

2
REMMER, H.
Drug-induced formation of smooth endoplasmic reticulum and of drug metabolizing enzymes
Proc. Europ. Soc. Study Drug Toxic., **4:** 57, 1964

3
REMMER, H. & MERKER, H.-J.
Enzyminduktion und Vermehrung des endoplasmatischen Retikulums in der Leberzelle während der Behandlung mit Phenobarbital (Luminal)
Klin. Wchnschr., **41:** 276, 1963

4
SCHÜPPEL, R.
Einfluss akuter Aethanoleinwirkung auf die N-Demethylierung zweier Arzneimittel bei der Ratte
Naunyn-Schmiedebergs Arch. exper. Path. u. Pharmakol., **257;** 60, 1967

N. SEGOVIA-RIQUELME

A. HEDERRA

M. ANEX

O. BARNIER

I. FIGUEROLA-CAMPS

I. CAMPOS-HOPPE

N. JARA

J. MARDONES

Institute of Studies on Alcoholism
and Institute of Physical and
Technical Education
University of Chile
Santiago, Chile

12

Nutritional and Genetic Factors in the Appetite for Alcohol

Since 1942 we have been studying in this Institute the appetite for ethanol in rats and the factors modifying it. Initially this research was stimulated by the findings of Richter and Campbell (21) in 1940. They reported that rats can recognize ethanol in concentrations as low as 1.8 per cent, and that under free choice conditions these animals prefer alcohol to water if the solution is less than 5 per cent; the opposite occurs when the concentrations are higher. In the present paper the role of nutritional and genetic factors in the appetite of the rat for alcohol are reviewed.

NUTRITIONAL FACTORS

Mardones and Onfray (13) reported in 1942 that rats fed with the thiamin-deprived diet proposed by Birch and Harris (4) exhibited a gradual increase in alcohol intake, and that this high intake was not reduced by administration of thiamin either alone or together with all the pure B vitamins known at that time. In contradistinction, dry liver or yeast supplements reestablished the alcohol intake to the basic levels.

Two examples of this effect are shown in Figures 12-1 and 12-2. These results suggested that liver and yeast contained a thermolabile factor different from thiamin and other B vitamins which we named factor N (the letter free at that time).

Later on, our group reported (15) that this factor was really a mixture of thiamin and a partial thermolabile factor, named factor N_1. Figure 12-3 summarizes data on the effect of different vitamin factors on the ethanol intake of rats.

In 1955 Beerstecher et al., from the laboratory of R. J. Williams in Austin, Texas (2), reported that some single vitamin deprivations induced an increase in the voluntary alcohol intake of rats, while others did not change it. We have reported that cyanocobalamine does not restore the alcohol intake (16). Table 12-1 summarizes the effects of different vitamin deficiencies.

Investigations of the effect of thiocitic acid on the alcohol appetite (14) showed that this substance induced a partial decrease in the alcohol intake of rats fed on an N_1-deprived

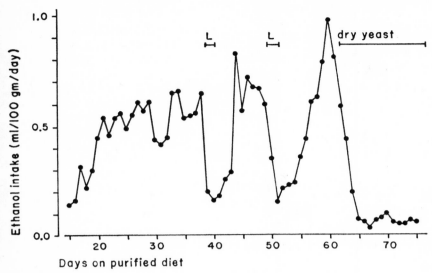

Figure 12-1

Alcohol intake under free choice of six rats fed on a Birch and Harris thiamin-deprived diet. At *L*, dry liver supplement (2 gm/day/rat); at *dry yeast*, replacement of treated yeast by untreated.

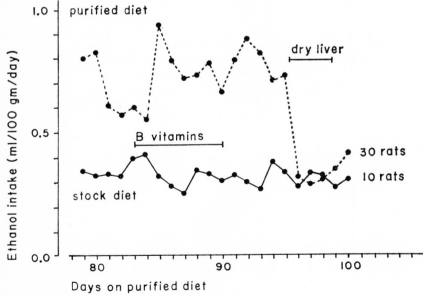

Figure 12-2

Alcohol intake under free choice of rats fed on a Birch and Harris thiamin-deprived diet. At *B vitamins*, a supplement of the following vitamins was given (figures represent µg/day/rat): thiamin HCl, 120; riboflavin, 100; pyridoxine, 120; niacin, 600; calcium pantothenate, 600; inositol, 600; p-aminobenzoic acid, 500; choline chloride, 500; and biotin concentrate, 500. At *dry liver*, a liver supplement of 1 gm/day/rat was given. Each point represents the arithmetic mean.

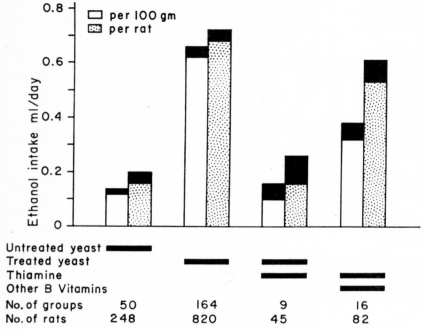

Figure 12-3

Influence of vitamin supplements on the voluntary alcohol intake of rats. *Untreated yeast*, dry commercial brewer's yeast; *treated yeast*, the same heated at 125° C for 90 minutes (10 gm/100 gm diet); *thiamin*, 4 μg/100 gm BW/day; *other vitamins*, daily supplements, in micrograms, as follows: riboflavin, 25; calcium pantothenate, 10; pyridoxine, 10; niacin, 500, and choline chloride, 1,000. The black zone represents the arithmetic mean ± standard error.

TABLE 12–1

SINGLE DEFICIENCY OF VITAMINS INFLUENCING ETHANOL CONSUMPTION OF RATS AS REPORTED BY BEERSTECHER *et al.* (2) AND, FOR VITAMIN B_{12}, BY MARDONES *et al.* (16)

Increase	Mild or no effect
thiamine	biotin
riboflavine	choline
pyridoxine	vitamin A
pantothenate	vitamin B_{12}

TABLE 12–2

DIFFERENCES IN THE ORGANIC COMPOSITION OF DIET WHICH DID NOT INFLUENCE THE ETHANOL INTAKE OF RATS (19)

	Per cent
high carbohydrate	29
low carbohydrate	18
high protein	29
low protein	9
high fat	28
low fat	6

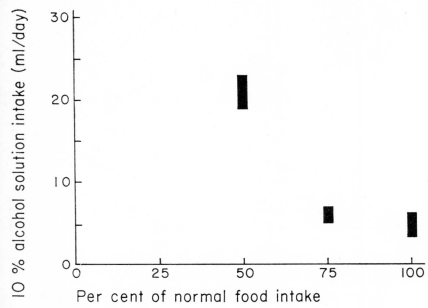

Figure 12-4

Influence of the restriction of food intake on free intake of ethanol by rats (arithmetic mean ± standard error). Based on data from Westerfeld & Lawrow (31).

diet, while a supplement of liver or yeast given subsequently induced a further decrease to the basic level. This effect was not observed when sulfasuxidine was added to the diet (18), suggesting that thiocitic acid could enhance the production by the intestinal flora of an analogue to N_1.

Roger *et al.* (22, 23) observed that glutamine added to a purified diet induced a partial decrease in the alcohol intake. We have confirmed these results, and observed that a subsequent supplement of liver induced a further decrease to the basic level (20).

Changes in the organic composition of the diet did not alter the alcohol intake (19), as shown in Table 12-2.

Westerfeld and Lawrow in 1953 (31) reported that the restriction of food intake to 50 per cent of the basic level induced a significant increase in the voluntary alcohol intake of rats, and that this increase could replace only 40 per cent of the missing calories. These results are summarized in Figure 12-4.

The alcohol appetite observed in all these ex-

periments is not, indeed, a craving, since Lester and Greenberg (9) showed that a third choice of a sugar solution or fat emulsion induced a significant decrease in alcohol intake. We have confirmed this finding (19). Table 12-3 shows the results obtained in third choice experiments.

To summarize: rats exhibit a normal appetite for ethanol, which can be increased by food restriction or by nutritional factors. The most prominent among these are deprivation of thiamin, riboflavin, pyridoxine, panthothenate, or factor N_1. Thiocitic acid or glutamine can partially compensate for the effect of a factor N_1 deficiency.

GENETIC FACTORS

In 1948 we reported (12) clear individual fluctuations in the alcohol intake of rats fed on a diet deprived of factor N_1. We did not observe these individual fluctuations in our earlier experiments because in order to minimize possible errors in the measurement of alcohol intake, we

TABLE 12–3

INFLUENCE OF A THIRD CHOICE OF SUGAR AND FAT ON
THE ALCOHOL CONSUMPTION OF RATS

Third choice	Number of rats	Alcohol intake	Reference
sucrose 11.4 per cent	10	decrease	(9)
sucrose 10.0 per cent	10	decrease	(19)
sucrose 30.0 per cent	9	decrease	(19)
sucrose 70.0 per cent	10	decrease	(19)
sucrose solid	38	no change	(19)
dextrose 10 per cent	10	decrease	(19)
dextrose 30 per cent	9	decrease	(19)
fat 5.8 per cent emulsion	10	decrease	(9)

used a group of rats in each cage. The genetic origin of these fluctuations was demonstrated by a highly significant heredity coefficient ($r = +0.416; p < 0.001$) for the first 7 generations of inbreeding (17). Williams *et al.* in 1949 (32) independently reported individual fluctuations in the alcohol intake of rats and mice fed on either complete or deprived diets. Later, McClearn (11) found similar differences among highly inbred strains of mice. Since 1948 we have selected by inbreeding two strains of rats, one "non-drinker" (A) and one "drinker" (B) strain, starting with parents from the same family.

The general method employed in these experiments was as follows. Rats were offered a free choice between distilled water and a 10 per cent by volume ethanol solution as fluid sources, and a purified solid diet *ad libitum*. The alcohol and water intake were recorded daily. After 60 days on the deprived diet the rats were grouped according to their voluntary alcohol intake in classes with intervals of 0.20 ml of pure ethanol per 100 grams body weight per day. The structure of the original colony, and of the offspring from crossing rats of class 1 (daily alcohol intake < 0.20 ml/100 gm BW) and class 3 or higher (daily alcohol intake > 0.40 ml/100 gm BW), is shown in Figure 12-5.

As can be seen, both structures of the frequency distribution have in common mainly class 2, which appears to be divided in two: 2A (intake 0.20–0.29) and 2B (intake 0.30–0.39). The pedigree of our two strains appears in Fig-

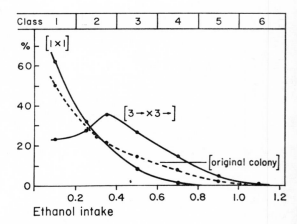

Figure 12-5

Distribution of voluntary alcohol intake in a population of rats: [1 × 1] = 1,614 offspring of "non-drinker" rats; [3→ × 3→] = 1,014 offspring of "drinker" rats.

ures 12-6 and 12-7, and the pedigree relation of the rats starting both strains is shown in Figure 12-8.

It is clear that even after 25 or 30 generations of inbreeding nothing similar to a pure line has been obtained in any of the strains. Thus it is not possible to predict the alcohol intake of each rat simply from knowledge of its pedigree. This also indicates that the appetite for ethanol is not determined by only one pair of alleles. Among the theoretical possibilities with two pairs, one fits the results obtained. This genetic hypothesis (see Table 12-4) assumes that the

Figure 12-6

Pedigree of the "non-drinker" strain A. Figures represent the number of siblings studied in each generation.

Strain A

Siblings

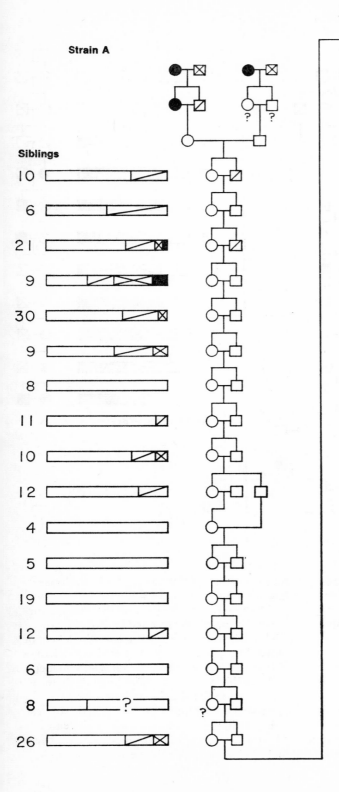

ml alcohol/100gm/day		Class
☐	< 0.2	1
◹	0.2 – 0.4	2
⊠	0.4 – 0.6	3
■	> 0.6	4 →

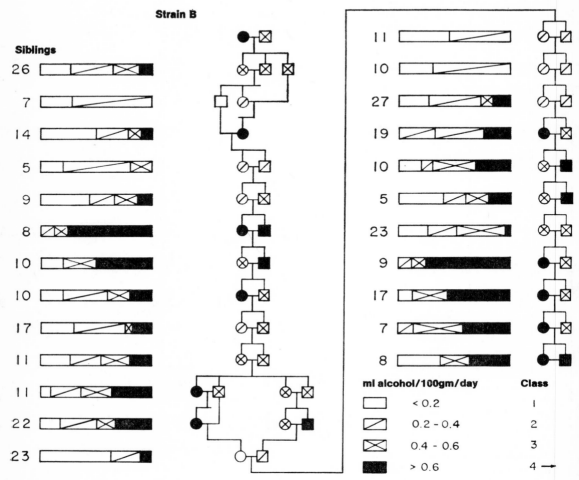

Figure 12-7
Pedigree of the "drinker" strain B. Figures represent the number of siblings studied in each generation.

rats with a dominant gene at both loci are "non-drinker," that those with a dominant gene at one locus are "drinker," and that recessive genes at both loci are lethal. Since the genotype of each phenotype cannot be recognized, it can be assumed that matings are at random. Since class 2 is shared equally by the offsprings of crossing (1 × 1) and (3 plus × 3 plus) we have divided it into two subclasses, as mentioned previously. Class 2A has been classified as "non-drinker" and class 2B as "drinker." The distribution observed in the offspring from the two principal matings and the expected

frequencies according to the Hardy-Weinberg law are shown in Table 12-5.

All these results suggest that the appetite for ethanol is mainly determined by two pairs of alleles. The homozygote-concentrating effect of inbreeding should be counteracted by the lethality of the recessive homozygotes at both loci, and possibly by a higher viability of the heterozygotes over the dominant homozygotes, a phenomenon not uncommon in genetic studies.

Following the idea of Tatum and Beadle (1, 30), "one gene one enzyme," we have been looking for enzymatic differences between the

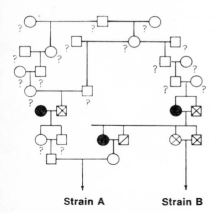

Strain A **Strain B**

Figure 12-8

Pedigree of the ancestors of strains
A and B. Same key as in Figures 12-6
and 12-7.

TABLE 12–4

GENETIC HYPOTHESIS OF DOMINANCE
AT ONE (DRINKER) OR BOTH
(NON-DRINKER) LOCI

Genotype	Frequency			
nondrinkers				
AABB	1			
AaBB	2	$p = 0.66$		$q = 0.33$
AaBb	4			
AABb	2	$u = 0.66$		$v = 0.33$
drinkers				
AAbb	1			
Aabb	2	$p = 0.33$		$q = 0.66$
aaBB	1			
aaBb	2	$u = 0.33$		$v = 0.66$

TABLE 12–5

TEST OF GENETIC HYPOTHESIS

ethanol intake (ml/100 gm/day)	< 0.30	> 0.30	
parents 1 × 1			
observed	1275	329	$\chi^2 \times 0.24$
expected	1283	321	$p > 0.6$
parents 3 → × 3 →			
observed	369	645	$\chi^2 = 1.84$
expected	390	624	$p > 0.15$

"non-drinker" and the "drinker" strains, which
could explain the different appetite for ethanol.
To test this hypothesis, in 1954 we started (with
the Department of Nutrition of the Harvard
School of Public Health) a systematic study of
strain differences in the metabolic rate of various substrates. The rate of recuperation of
the activity of C^{14}-labelled substrates in expired
CO_2 was mainly employed for the purpose.

We have not found any difference in the
metabolic rate of ethanol (25, 27, 28), acetate
(25), pyruvate (25), butyrate (25), citrate
(7), glycerol (5), ribose, galactose, or sorbitol
(unpublished data) in the carbons shown in
Table 12-6, in which the tested doses are also
listed.

The absence of a different rate of ethanol
metabolism excludes the possibility of a difference in the enzymatic systems of ethanol oxidation. The similarity of the metabolic rate
of each of the three carbons of pyruvate in both
strains refutes our former working hypothesis,
namely, that the strain difference could be ascribed to the metabolic transformation of three-
carbon to two-carbon compounds.

Concerning glucose (26), we did not observe
any strain difference in experiments with tracer
doses of this substrate labelled in carbon 1 or 6,
while under glucose overload (10 M/kg BW) a
significant strain difference in metabolic rate

of glucose-1-C^{14} but not of glucose-6-C^{14} was
observed. In fact, the rate of recuperation of the
activity of the carbon 1 of glucose in the expired
CO_2 was higher among "drinker" than among
"non-drinker" rats. In agreement with these
results, the rate of recovery of the activity of
gluconate-1-C^{14} in expired CO_2, when given in
tracer doses, was significantly higher in rats of
the "drinker" strain (24). Thus, the only strain
difference we have observed up to the present
is associated with the oxidative pathway of glucose, commonly known as the pentose pathway.

In general, experiments in which the substrates were given simultaneously with ethanol –
to study eventual strain differences in the influence of ethanol metabolism on that of other
substrates – have given negative results (see
Table 12-7). We have observed that ethanol
induces changes in the metabolic rate of the
following labelled substrates: glucose-1-C^{14}
(26), glucose-6-C^{14} (26), citrate-1-C^{14} (7),

TABLE 12–6

SUBSTRATE EXHIBITING SIMILAR RATE OF OXIDATION TO CO_2 IN "DRINKER" AND "NON-DRINKER" RATS

Substrate	Labelled carbon	Doses (mM/kg)			
ethanol	1			10	44
ethanol	2	0.001			44
acetate	1		1	10	
acetate	2	0.001	1	10	
pyruvate	1	0.5	1	10	
pyruvate	2	0.5	1	10	
pyruvate	3	0.5		10	
butyrate	1	0.5		10	
cytrate	1–5	0.001			
ribose	1	0.001			
glycerol	1			10	
sorbitol	1–6			10	
glucose	1	0.001			
glucose	6	0.001		10	
galactose	1			10	

gluconate-1-C^{14} (6), galactose-1-C^{14}, and sorbitol-1-C^{14} (unpublished data); but the effects have been similar in the rats of both strains.

As a matter of fact, the simultaneous administration of ethanol markedly enhanced gluconate metabolism in both strains in such a way that a difference between strains was not observed. In other words, it would seem as though ethanol enhanced gluconate metabolism in both strains to an equivalent maximum. This is in agreement with the idea that a strain difference in gluconate metabolism might depend on a diverse availability of NAD in relation to NADP. Thus, when ethanol is administered, the decrease of NAD by reduction to $NADH_2$ in both cases would make the difference disappear. Recently we have found a different distribution of the influence of ethanol on glycerol metabolism in each strain.

In general, the significance of the differences observed in all these experiments has been influenced by sex differences in the metabolism of some substrates.

A strain difference observed in another type of study (29) is related to the amounts of lipids found in the liver of rats fed on a stock diet and without access to ethanol. The amount was significantly higher in male rats of the "drinker" than in those of the "non-drinker" strain (see Table 12-8).

TABLE 12–7

SUBSTRATE EXHIBITING SIMILAR RATE OF OXIDATION TO CO_2 GIVEN TOGETHER WITH ETHANOL, IN "DRINKER" AND "NON-DRINKER" RATS

Substrate	Labelled carbon	Doses (mM/kg)	
glucose	1	0.001	10
glucose	6	0.001	10
gluconate	1	0.001	10
citrate	1–5		10
glycerol	1		10
galactose	1		10
sorbitol	1–6		10

In complete agreement with our findings in rats are the results obtained by McClearn and his coworkers using highly inbred mice. They reported that mice of strain C57/BLCrgl spontaneously drank more ethanol than those of strain BALB/cCrgl, coinciding with a higher alcohol dehydrogenase activity in the liver of the former (3), and with a lower duration of sleeping time after a determined dose of ethanol in the latter (10). No difference was observed either in the blood alcohol levels at awakening or in the alcohol content of the brain at 40, 100, and 140 minutes after the test dose (8).

To summarize: it is possible that the appetite

TABLE 12–8

TOTAL LIPIDS IN LIVER OF RATS FED
WITH STOCK DIET WITHOUT ETHANOL,
BY SEX AND STRAIN (PER CENT
OF FRESH TISSUE)

Sex	Strain	N	Liver lipids (gm/100 gm)	p
M	A	28	3.04 ± 0.088	< 0.001
M	B	23	3.73 ± 0.166	
F	A	18	3.22 ± 0.117	> 0.50
F	B	21	3.32 ± 0.091	

for ethanol in rats is determined by two main pairs of alleles, one of them probably influencing the activity of an enzymatic system in the oxidative pathway of glucose. The results which have been reviewed are not yet conclusive evidence of this, but they are highly suggestive, leaving a very interesting question open to further research.

REFERENCES

1
BEADLE, G.W. & TATUM, E.L.
Genetic control of biochemical reactions in neurospora
Proc. Nat. Acad. Sc., 27: 499, 1941
See also reference no. 30
2
BEERSTECHER, E.J., REED, J.G., BROWN, W.D., & BERRY, L.J.
The effects of single vitamin deficiencies on the consumption of alcohol by white rats
In Individual metabolic patterns and human disease: an exploratory study utilizing predominantly paper chromatographic methods
University of Texas, Biochemical Institute Studies IV, 1951
Chap. XIII, p. 115 (University of Texas Publication no. 5109)
3
BENNET, E.L. & HERBERT, M.
University California, Radiat. Lab. Quart., Rep. no. 9208, 1966
4
BIRCH, T.W. & HARRIS, L.J.
Bradycardia in vitamin B₁-deficient rat and its use in vitamin B₁ determination
Biochem. J., 28: 602, 1934
5
FIGUEROLA-CAMPS, I., JARA, N., SEGOVIA-RIQUELME, N., & MARDONES, J.
9a. Reunion Anual Soc. de Biología de Chile, Valparaíso, 1966
6
FIGUEROLA-CAMPS, I., SEGOVIA-RIQUELME, N., CAMPOS, I., & MARDONES, J.
VI Congress ALACF, Viña del Mar (Chile), 1964
Resúmenes de comunicaciones libres
7
JARA, N., FIGUEROLA-CAMPS, I., SEGOVIA-RIQUELME, N., & MARDONES, J.
III International Pharmacological Congress, São Paulo, Brasil, 1966
Abstract of communication, p. 33, 1966
8
KAKIHANA, R., BROWN, D.R., MCCLEARN, G.E., & TALESHAW, I.R.
Brain sensitivity to alcohol in inbred mouse strains
Science, 154: 1574, 1966
9
LESTER, D. & GREENBERG, L.
Nutrition and the etiology of alcoholism. The effect of sucrose, saccharin and fat on the self-selection of ethyl alcohol by rats
Quart. J. Stud. Alc., 13: 553, 1952
10
MCCLEARN, G.E. Genetic differences in the effect of alcohol upon behavior of mice
Proc. Third Internat. Conf. Alc. Road Traffic, 1962, p. 153
11
MCCLEARN, G.E. & RODGERS, D.A.
Differences in alcohol preference among inbred strains of mice
Quart. J. Stud. Alc., 20: 691, 1959
12
MARDONES, J., HEDERRA, A., & SEGOVIA-RIQUELME, N.
Bol. Soc. Biol. Santiago, 7: 1, 1949
13
MARDONES, R.J. & ONFRAY, B.E.
Influencia de una substancia de la levadura (¿elemento del complejo vitaminico B?) sobre el consumo de alcohol en ratas en experimentos de autoselección)
Rev. Chilena Hig. Med. Prev., 4: 293, 1942
14
MARDONES, J., SEGOVIA-RIQUELME, N., ALCAÍNO, F., & HEDERRA, A.
Effect of synthetic thiocitic or alpha lipoic acid on voluntary alcohol intake
Science, 119: 735, 1954
15
MARDONES, J., SEGOVIA-RIQUELME, N., & HEDERRA, A.
Bol. Soc. Biol. Santiago, 5: 27, 1948
16
MARDONES, R.J., SEGOVIA-RIQUELME, N., & HEDERRA, D.A.
Failure of vitamin B₁₂ to reduce alcohol intake in N-deprived rats
Acta physiol. latino-am., 2: 43, 1952
17
MARDONES, J., SEGOVIA-RIQUELME, N., & HEDERRA, A.
Heredity of experimental alcohol preference in rats: II Coefficient of heredity
Quart. J. Stud. Alc., 14: 1, 1953

18
MARDONES, J., SEGOVIA-RIQUELME, N., HEDERRA, A., & ALCAÍNO, F.
Influence of sulfasuxidine on the effect of alpha lipoic or thiocitic acid on the voluntary alcohol intake of rats depleted of factor N
Acta physiol. latino-am., **3**: 140, 1953
19
MARDONES, J., SEGOVIA-RIQUELME, N., HEDERRA, A., & ALCAÍNO, F.
Effect of some self-selection conditions on the voluntary alcohol intake of rats
Quart. J. Stud. Alc., **16**: 425, 1955
20
MARDONES, J., SEGOVIA-RIQUELME, N., HEDERRA, A., & ALCAÍNO, F.
Cited by J. Mardones in
Internat. Rev. Neurobiol., **2**: 41, 1960
21
RICHTER, C.P. & CAMPBELL, K.H.
Alcohol taste thresholds and concentrations of solution preferred by rats
Science, **91**: 507, 1940
22
ROGERS, L.L., PELTON, R.B., & WILLIAMS, R.J.
Voluntary alcohol consumption by rats following administration of glutamine
J. Biol. Chem., **214**: 503, 1955
23
ROGERS, L.L., PELTON, R.B., & WILLIAMS, R.J.
Amino acid supplementation and voluntary alcohol consumption by rats
J. Biol. Chem., **220**: 321, 1956
24
SEGOVIA-RIQUELME, N., CAMPOS, I., SOLODKOWSKA, W., FIGUEROLA-CAMPS, I., & MARDONES, J.
Glucose and gluconate metabolism in "drinker" and "non-drinker" rats
Med. Exper., **11**: 185, 1964
25
SEGOVIA-RIQUELME, N., CAMPOS, I., SOLODKOWSKA, W., GONZÁLEZ, G., ALVARADO, R., & MARDONES, J.
Metabolism of labeled ethanol, acetate, pyruvate, and butyrate in "drinker" and "non-drinker" rats
J. Biol. Chem., **237**: 2038, 1962
26
SEGOVIA-RIQUELME, N., FIGUEROLA-CAMPS, I., CAMPOS-HOPPE, I., JARA, N., NEGRETE, E., & MARDONES, J.
Influence of sex, strain and injection of ethanol on the metabolism of carbons 1 and 6 of glucose in the rat
Arch. Biol. Med. Exper., **2**: 74, 1965
27
SEGOVIA-RIQUELME, N., FIGUEROLA-CAMPS, I., CAMPOS-HOPPE, I., & MARDONES, J.
Ethanol and acetate metabolism in "drinker" and "non-drinker" rat, without substrate overload
Arch. Biol. Med. Exper., **3**: 43, 1966
28
SEGOVIA-RIQUELME, N., VITALE, J.J., HEGSTED, D.M., & MARDONES, J.
Alcohol metabolism in drinking and non-drinking rats
J. Biol. Chem., **223**: 399, 1956
29
SOLODKOWSKA, W., ALVARADO-ANDRADE, R., MUÑOZ, E., & MARDONES, J.
Unpublished data
30
TATUM, E.L. & BEADLE, G.W.
Genetic control of biochemical reactions in neurospora: an "aminobenzoicles" mutant
Proc. Nat. Acad. Sc., **28**: 234, 1942
See also reference no. 1
31
WESTERFELD, W.W. & LAWROW, J.
The effects of caloric restriction and thiamin deficiency on the voluntary consumption of alcohol by rats
Quart. J. Stud. Alc., **14**: 378, 1953
32
WILLIAMS, R.J., BERRY, L.J., & BEERSTECHER, E., JR.
Individual metabolic patterns, alcoholism, genetrophic diseases
Proc. Nat. Acad. Sc., **35**: 265, 1949

ROBERT D. MYERS

Laboratory of Neuropsychology
Purdue University
Lafayette, Indiana, USA

13

Influence of Stress on Alcohol Preference in Rats

From our knowledge of the psychological correlates of alcoholism, it would seem that conflict, tension, or perhaps what is more properly called stress plays an important role in the etiology of this disease. However, relatively few studies are consistent with one another in isolating or identifying the specific attributes of stress which may cause an increase in ethanol intake. For instance, Dember and Kristofferson (5) correlated rats' ethanol intake with their susceptibility to audiogenic seizures and concluded that this relationship was due to the animals' level of emotionality. On the other hand, Rodgers and Thiesson (13) found that increasing the size of a group of mice caused an increase in individual stress levels as reflected by adrenal response, but no elevation in ethanol consumption. In a similar sort of discrepancy, Korman and Stephens (6) showed that neither administration of random shock nor "training" in the consumption of alcohol altered the high water, low ethanol intake ratios in rats. Casey (1), however, reported that random shock elevated ethanol preference in rats but not until 16 days after the shock period had been terminated. It is easy to see why generalizations based on these and other similar studies are difficult to make.

In our laboratory, factors which may mediate the initial consumption of ethanol, such as psychological stress, have been investigated along with the problem of the changes in the central nervous system which sustain ethanol preference once it is established. Each of our experiments has been confronted with the theoretical difficulty of separating psychological from physiological factors in stress.* For in-

This research was supported in part by (US) National Science Foundation grants GB 3874 and GB 7906, by ONR contract N-00014-67-A-0003, and by a grant from the Wallace Laboratories.

*We have been able to differentiate between psychological and physical stressors with respect to volitional alcohol consumption (3). In a self-selection situation, rats increased their alcohol intake when random shock was delivered to a grid floor. This increase occurred only when the unavoidable "punishment" was signalled by a cue, i.e. a warning light. Non-cued unavoidable shock, a physical stressor, did not produce an increase in alcohol intake.

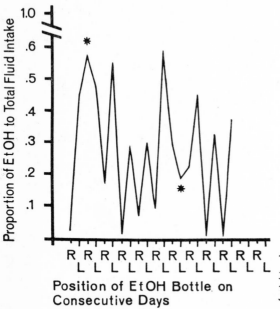

Figure 13-1
Ethanol intake patterns as a function of position habit in the two-choice test for water and 10 per cent ethanol. (Asterisks denote fluctuations in position habit.)

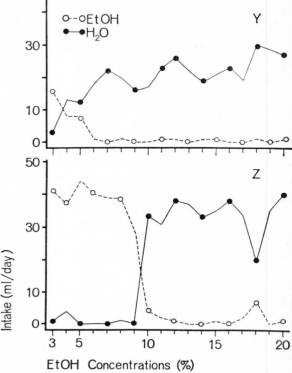

Figure 13-2
Stable ethanol and water intake patterns in two typical rats tested on the modified three-bottle test in which one bottle is empty, but rotated in sequence with the ethanol and water bottles. TOP: Intake of a rat that displayed avoidance of ethanol at all concentrations above 3 per cent; BOTTOM: Intake of a rat that preferred ethanol up to the 10 per cent concentration, then shifted to water immediately in preference to stronger concentrations of up to 20 per cent.

stance, when electric shock is administered in a conditioned avoidance situation, heightened adrenal activity accompanies whatever psychological "disturbances" take place. Similarly, when ethanol is infused directly into the cerebral ventricles of a rat over a prolonged period (7) the ethanol itself may act as a non-specific cellular stressor or may even cause pain much in the same way as shock. In essence, the role of any variable affecting ethanol consumption in animals is difficult to categorize on the basis of one specific system or pathway, be it psychological, physiological, or biochemical.

A second problem is a pragmatic one: the occurrence of a position habit during drinking in a two-choice test. A modified three-bottle method has solved this problem (11). Figure 13-1 shows the daily fluctuations in intake of 10 per cent ethanol which occur simply because the rat prefers the left-hand drinking spout over the right in the two-choice situation. To overcome this, an empty third tube, which serves

simply as a "dummy," is placed beside the two bottles containing water and an ethanol solution. The three tubes are switched randomly every day according to a three position sequence, although only water and ethanol are available. Figure 13-2 presents typical data taken from a group of animals tested in the three-tube situation. Experiments on ethanol preference using two-choice procedures should be viewed cautiously if the data are not plotted on a daily basis. Ethanol and water intake values may simply reflect a position habit.

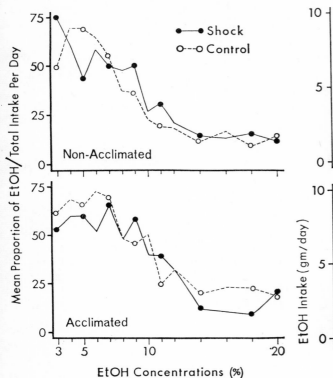

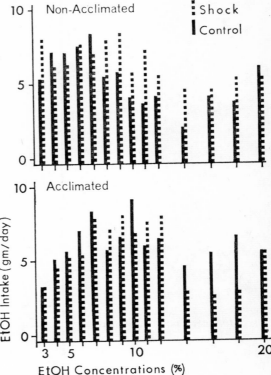

Figure 13-3
Mean ethanol-to-water ratios obtained for rats given shock once per hour (TOP) and for a group of rats acclimated to 12 per cent ethanol for 20 days and given six shocks per hour (BOTTOM). Reprinted by permission from Myers & Holman (10).

Figure 13-4
Total grams of ethanol consumed per group (seven rats) by non-acclimated animals receiving shock once per hour (TOP) and by rats acclimated to 12 per cent ethanol for 20 days receiving six shocks per hour (BOTTOM).

STRESSORS AND VOLUNTARY ETHANOL CONSUMPTION IN ANIMALS

From the vast literature on humans, some relationship would be expected between anxiety or stress levels and alcohol imbibition. In our laboratory three different conditions usually considered to be stressful have been utilized to examine the problem of increasing ethanol preference in rats.

In one experiment unavoidable electric shock delivered intermittently to the cage floors was used as a stressor (10). One group of rats was acclimated to 12 per cent ethanol for 20 days and a second group was not acclimated to

ethanol. The acclimated animals received six shocks every hour, delivered on a variable interval schedule for 14 consecutive days. The non-acclimated groups received one shock every hour on a fixed interval for 14 days. Acclimated and non-acclimated control groups received no shock. Figure 13-3 shows the results of the ethanol versus water preference testing during the administration of shock in which ethanol concentrations were increased daily from 3 to 12 per cent in 1 per cent steps and from 12 to 20 per cent in 2 per cent steps (9). No differences occurred in ethanol preference between groups receiving shock and the controls, whether the group was acclimated or not. The

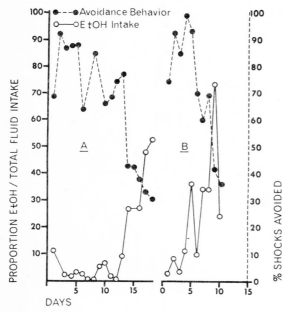

Figure 13-5

Ethanol-to-water ratios plotted together with percentage of shocks avoided in a shock avoidance situation for two rats. From Cicero (2), Myers & Black (3).

amounts of ethanol consumed by shocked and non-shocked groups are presented in Figure 13-4. Total ethanol intake per day in grams is given for both non-acclimated and acclimated shock and control groups. Again, it is clear that unavoidable shock, whether delivered on a fixed or random schedule, produced no significant deviation in the pattern of ethanol consumption.

In a second experiment similar to that of Clark and Polish (4), rats were trained to avoid shock in a simple conditioned avoidance situation (2). If the rat depressed the lever following the onset of a ten-second warning light, shock to the floor of the cage was prevented. The shock avoidance regimen lasted for six hours, followed by a six hour rest period, and was repeated for as many as 18 consecutive days. Water and 10 per cent ethanol were available throughout the experiment. Figure 13-5 shows the increase in the proportion of ethanol consumed as the avoidance task continued in duration. In both animals A and B ethanol con-

sumption increased as the days on this schedule passed and the percentage of shocks avoided during each test session declined with a rise in ethanol intake. These results indicate that the necessity of making an instrumental response to prevent shock constitutes a different kind of psychological stress than the "hopeless" condition in which shock is delivered no matter what is done by the animal. In other words, experimental "responsibility" is stressful.

In a third kind of stress experiment, rats have been maintained in different numbers to determine whether ethanol intake increases under crowded conditions (14). Groups of two, four, and six rats were placed in cages measuring $11 \times 8 \times 8$ inches and designed to house only one rat. Preliminary data suggest that crowding elevates the consumption of ethanol offered in a number of concentrations from 3 to 32 per cent. This does not agree with the report of Rodgers and Thiesson (13), but in their experiment, floor space increased proportionately with the size of the group.

CENTRAL NERVOUS SYSTEM AND ETHANOL PREFERENCE

To simulate the action of alcohol on parts of the brain stem involved in drinking and stress, ethanol in minute amounts has been injected chronically into the cerebral ventricles of rats. A dose-dependent increase in ethanol preference occurs (7). Since the addictive nature of ethanol, following long-term exposure, may rest in the action of one of the intermediaries of ethanol metabolism, we have injected minute amounts of acetaldehyde into the ventricles of rats and monkeys. Recent data indicate that this compound is at least as effective in elevating preference for ethanol as ethanol itself.* One rat infused chronically with 1/2000 concentration acetaldehyde every 10 minutes for 16 days preferred ethanol solutions up to 28 per cent

*Acetaldehyde, methanol, and paraldehyde, micro-infused chemically into the cerebral ventricles of unrestrained rats, causes an unusual elevation of alcohol preference. The increase in alcohol intake is directly dependent on the dose and duration of infusion of these organic substances (12).

over water and even consumed over a gram of ethanol per day when 40 per cent was offered.

Thus far, saline injected in a similar way does not produce these effects.

CONCLUSION

In the consideration of stress as an etiological factor in alcoholism, experimental work is hindered by the fact that physiological adaptation to a given stressor may easily occur, and what is assumed to be a stressful situation may not be one at all. An effort must be made, therefore, to establish conditions which mimic human psychological stress, with all of its physiological concomitants. Within the present limitations of our knowledge about animal psychology, this will be a difficult but not impossible task.

REFERENCES

1
CASEY, A.
The effect of stress on the consumption of alcohol and reserpine
Quart. J. Stud. Alc., **21**: 208, 1960
2
CICERO, T.
The effect of chronic intermittent stress on alcohol ingestion in the albino rat
Unpublished thesis, Purdue University, 1966.
3
CICERO, T.J., MYERS, R.D., & BLACK, W.C.
Increase in volitional ethanol consumption following interference with a learned avoidance response
Physiol. Behav., **3**: 657, 1968
4
CLARK, R., & POLISH, E.
Avoidance conditioning and alcohol consumption in rhesus monkeys
Science, **132**: 223, 1960
5
DEMBER, W. & KRISTOFFERSON, A.
The relation between free-choice alcohol consumption and susceptibility to audiogenic seizures
Quart. J. Stud. Alc., **16**: 86, 1955
6
KORMAN, M. & STEPHENS, H.
Effects of training on the alcohol consummatory response in rats
Psychol. Repts., **6**: 327, 1960

7
MYERS, R.D.
Alcohol consumption in rats: effects of intracranial injections of ethanol
Science, **142**: 240, 1963
8
MYERS, R.D.
Voluntary alcohol consumption in animals: peripheral and intracerebral factors
Psychosom. Med., **28**: 484, 1966
9
MYERS, R.D. & CAREY, R.
Preference factors in experimental alcoholism
Science, **134**: 469, 1961
10
MYERS, R.D. & HOLMAN, R.B.
Failure of stress of electric shock to increase ethanol intake in rats
Quart. J. Stud. Alc., **28**: 132, 1967
11
MYERS, R.D. & HOLMAN, R.B.
A procedure for eliminating position habit in preference aversion tests for alcohol and other fluids
Psychonom. Sc., **6**: 235, 1966
12
MYERS, R.D. & VEALE, W.L.
Alterations in volitional alcohol intake accompanying chronic intracerebral infusions of methanol, acetaldehyde, or paraldehyde
Arch. Internat. Pharmacodyn. & Therap., in press
13
RODGERS, D.A. & THIESSEN, D.
Effects of population density on adrenal size, behavioural arousal, and alcohol preference of inbred mice
Quart. J. Stud. Alc., **25**: 240, 1964
14
VEALE, W.L. & MYERS, R.D.
Increased alcohol preference in rats following repeated exposures to alcohol
Psychopharm., in press

Etiological and Clinical Aspects

During the last 150 years, three major clinical concepts of alcoholism have succeeded one another in Western medicine (6, 7). The first, which prevailed from 1800 to 1850, used a symptomatic criterion to describe the behavioural pattern or overt expression of numerous clinical forms of abnormal drinking. The foremost exponent of this concept, von Brühl-Cramer (10) claimed that drinking to excess was always preceded by a state of depression, a claim that was subsequently limited to one form of alcoholism: classic dipsomania.

The second concept, which took pride of place during the second half of the nineteenth century, used the pathological criterion of Magnus Huss (1). It focussed on the organic damage done by drinking to excess. What this author described as chronic alcoholism is today placed under the rubric of complications caused by abnormal drinking.

About 1900, the addictive-pathogenic concept of alcoholism was first formulated. It found expression in the work of E. M. Jellinek, and more particularly in the book he published in 1960 (5).

Concerned with the definition of physical dependence on alcohol, Jellinek established two clinical forms of alcoholism: (a) gamma, or intermittent, which predominates among drinkers of spirits and is characterized by "loss of control in ingestion" a few minutes after consumption of a small quantity of liquor; and (b) delta, or inveterate, which is mainly found among wine drinkers and is characterized by an "inability to abstain" appearing a few hours after either moderate or excessive intake of alcohol. Dipsomania, which is a form of physical dependence that is known to appear even though the drinker may not have taken any alcohol either minutes or hours beforehand, was not summed up by Jellinek as a precise pathogenic concept, but simply ranked as "epsilon" alcoholism.

The definition of pathological ingestion as a result of physical dependence led necessarily to the definition of other forms of ingestion. On the one hand, there was moderate or normal drinking, and, on the other, simple drinking to excess and complicated drinking to excess, which Jellinek classified as "alpha" and "beta" types of alcoholism, and whose principal motivation is psychological and cultural, respectively.

Jellinek's main contribution to the clinical and pathogenic study of alcoholism as a disease was already embodied in papers published in 1946 (3) and 1952 (4) on the process of evolution from moderate to excessive drinking and from there to pathological ingestion or alcoholism.

It is clear from his work on this subject that a proportion of the total number of excessive drinkers in a community – in which the original motivation for drinking was wholly sociocultural and/or psychopathological – develop at a certain moment an ineradicable biological variation. The adaptation of the tissues to alcohol and the biochemical and neurophysiopathological changes that take place become in themselves the basic pathogenic factors productive of further drinking. This physical dependence is superimposed upon the sociocultural and/or psychopathological motivation, but is often discounted by those who continue to regard any abnormal ingestion of alcohol as nothing more than a symptom of social or psychological maladjustment.

The appearance of "loss of control" or "inability to stop" in gamma or intermittent alcoholism, and of the "inability to abstain" in delta or inveterate alcoholism, marks the crucial difference between alcoholism as a disease – an evolving process with a serious prognosis if not treated in time – and simple drinking to excess.

The result of these considerations has been a new orientation of scientific research (which used to be confined mainly to the study of terminal complications). It seeks now to discover the factors that determine moderate or excessive intake of alcohol; the psychological, and above all, the sociocultural stresses and biological factors that lead to excessive drinking; and the predisposing causes underlying physical dependence on alcohol.

The discussion is now centred on a few key questions inter alia. The first is the relative importance of alcohol as a causative agent in the disease of alcoholism. Physical dependence on alcohol has been produced experimentally in human beings (2) and an attempt is being made to do so in animals (9). But it should be borne in mind that physical dependence does not develop in a large proportion of excessive drinkers and, what is more important, that a primary physical dependence without prior intake of alcohol is found in dipsomania or remittent alcoholism (8). Genetic and epidemiological studies as well as neurophysiological and biochemical studies of alcoholics in a state of abstinence and under the influence of alcohol will help to deter-

mine how much is due to predisposition, how much to environment.

Under what conditions does excessive drinking engender withdrawal symptoms and in what circumstances do these turn into serious disorders or deadly complications of abnormal drinking? The variables involved, e.g. the amount of alcohol taken, how long the previous ingestion lasted, the level of tolerance developed by the subject, need more accurate study, in clinical as well as in epidemiological and experimental terms.

In the past 15 years the number of unknowns has been multiplying steadily in spite of the use of new scientific methods to explore the vast field of normal and abnormal drinking, ranging from cultural anthropology and sociology at one extreme to neurophysiology and biochemistry at the other.

Are there grounds for assuming that a central neuropathogenic mechanism regulates both varieties of physical dependence on alcohol – the primary one, without previous ingestion, as seen in dipsomania or remittent alcoholism, and the secondary one, after ingestion (intermittent or inveterate)? The possibility of using the technique of implanted electrodes in the human brain, and the progress made in studying the central neuronal systems that regulate physiological needs and the pleasure-displeasure balance makes it possible to explore this hypothesis today.

As in other fields of research, a consensus of opinion has been reached on certain basic operational definitions of alcoholism, auguring better medical control of the problem in the next decade, and a vital advance in the difficult task of prevention, in which all members of the community should play a part.

JUAN MARCONI
Department of Psychiatry, University of Chile and Mental Health Unit of the Public Health Service Santiago, Chile

REFERENCES

1
HUSS, MAGNUS
Alcoholismus chronicus eller chronisk
alkolssjukdom, 1849
Chronische Alkohlskrankheit, oder Alcoholismus
Chronicus, translated from the Swedish with revisions
by the author, by Gerhard van dem Busch,
Stockholm: C.E. Fritze, 1852

2
ISBELL, H., FRASER, H.F., WIKLER, A., BELLEVILLE, R.E.,
& EISENMAN, A.J.
An experimental study of the etiology of "rum fits"
and delirium tremens
Quart. J. Stud. Alc., **16**: 1, 1955

3
JELLINEK, E.M.
Phases in the drinking history of alcoholics
Quart. J. Stud. Alc., **7**: 1, 1946

4
JELLINEK, E.M.
Phases in alcohol addiction
WHO Tech. Rep. Series, no. 48, 1952

5
JELLINEK, E.M.
The disease concept of alcoholism
New Haven: Hillhouse Press, 1960

6
MARCONI, J.
The concept of alcoholism
Quart. J. Stud. Alc., **20**: 216, 1959

7
MARCONI, J.
El concepto de enfermedad en alcoholismo
Acta psiquiatr. psicol. Am. lat., **11**: 330, 1965

8
MARCONI, J., POBLETE, M., PALESTINI, M., *et al.*
Un nuevo enfoque del tratamiento del alcohólico
grave recidivante
Acta psiquiatr. psicol. Am. lat., **11**: 340, 1965

9
MARDONES, J.
On the relationship between deficiency of B vitamins
and alcohol intake in rats
Quart. J. Stud. Alc., **12**: 563, 1951

10
VON BRÜHL-CRAMER, C.
Ueber die Trunksucht und eine rationelle
Heilmethode derselben
Berlin, 1919

HARRIS ISBELL

Department of Medicine
University of Kentucky
Lexington, Kentucky, USA

14

Experimental Physical Dependence on Alcohol in Humans

For a considerable period of time a marked difference of opinion existed as to whether abrupt discontinuation of alcohol after prolonged bouts of heavy drinking was responsible for convulsions ("rum fits") and the tremulous, hallucinated alcoholic states. One school believed that these conditions were due not to abstinence from alcohol but rather to the direct toxic effects of alcohol, to nutritional deficiency, or to both. Persons of this persuasion (1, 8) argued that convulsions and deliria were rare in alcoholics admitted to general hospitals; and that alcoholics developed delirium while still drinking as much as a pint of whisky (equivalent to 250 ml of absolute alcohol) daily in a hospital setting. The other school (6, 9) related convulsions and delirious states to abstinence (relative or absolute) from alcohol and pointed to the strong resemblance between the alcoholic states and abstinence from barbiturates.

It was very important that the question be answered definitively, since the mortality rate in delirium tremens averaged 8 per cent, and if delirium tremens was due to abstinence from alcohol it should be prevented or treated by gradual withdrawal of alcohol or some equivalent drug, rather than by abrupt withdrawal. It was not easy to answer the question, however. At that time, all attempts to induce physical dependence on alcohol in animals had failed because of difficulties in maintaining the desired degree of intoxication, in ability to keep the animals alive, etc. It was in this context of pressing need for a definitive answer and of inability to obtain the answer in animals that an experiment in man (4) was undertaken in 1953 at the Addiction Research Center in Lexington.

THE LEXINGTON EXPERIMENT

The subjects who volunteered for the experiment were ten former male morphine addicts. All were abstinent from drugs. Only one had been a heavy drinker. All were physically healthy and all had normal electroencephalograms. They were all classified as having character disorders, but none presented any evidence of psychotic disorder.

After appropriate preliminary observations had been collected, these patients began to drink 95 per cent ethanol diluted with two or three volumes of water every two hours from 6:00 AM to midnight, with a supplementary drink at 2:00 or 3:00 AM. The initial daily dosages of 140 ml of 95 per cent was elevated progressively until the patients were drinking 266 to 489 ml of 95 per cent ethanol daily. Four patients withdrew from the experiment after only 7 to 34 days of drinking. The remaining six drank from 48 to 87 days and consumed from 388 to 489 ml of alcohol daily. Withdrawal of alcohol was abrupt and complete. Two patients who developed severe abstinence syndromes were reintoxicated with barbiturates and slowly withdrawn. All patients recovered completely.

Throughout the experiment patients were provided with a 4,000 calorie diet of high quality and were given daily supplements of all known vitamins that supplied several times the accepted optimal amounts. Massive amounts of additional vitamins were given parenterally just prior to and during abstinence from alcohol.

The amounts of alcohol that the men consumed were higher than had been believed possible prior to the experiment. They ranged, in the case of the six patients who completed the experiment, from 388 to 489 ml daily, the equivalent to 776 to 978 ml of whisky daily. With the particular drinking schedule used, blood alcohol concentrations remained less than 100 mg per 100 ml until 300 ml of alcohol was being taken daily. At steady intakes of about 400 ml daily, blood alcohol levels declined gradually, indicating possibly that the rates of oxidation or elimination of alcohol had increased slightly. Increased intakes of only 2 or 3 ml of alcohol per hour above the dose associated with low blood levels were sufficient to restore blood alcohol to the 200–300 mg/100 ml range.

Patients also became less drunk at given blood alcohol concentrations as the experiment proceeded, indicating some degree of adaptation (tolerance) of the neurons of the central nervous system.

During intoxication patients gained weight and had tachycardia and mild hypertension. Results of liver function tests remained normal. Patients were sometimes tremulous in the morning before the first drink. One patient, who cut his intake of alcohol because of nausea and vomiting, developed hallucinosis as his blood alcohol declined, but the hallucinations disappeared as he resumed drinking. No convulsions or overt deliria occurred as long as the alcohol intake was maintained.

When alcohol was discontinued, the six patients who had drunk for more than 34 days rapidly became tremulous and hyperreflexic, sweated profusely, lost weight, and could not sleep (see Table 14-1). Two of the six had convulsions, five developed hallucinations, and three became disoriented. Two patients (numbers 5 and 10) developed such severe deliria that the experiment had to be terminated and the patients reintoxicated with large amounts of pentobarbital followed by a gradual reduction of this drug. The four patients who drank for only 34 days or less and who drank less than 346 ml of alcohol daily had only mild tremulousness, weakness, and nausea for one to three days, indicating that the length of the bout of intoxication is important as well as the degree of intoxication.

During intoxication with alcohol, EEGs tended to become diffusely slowed (11). Tolerance to this effect developed to such a point that the EEG became more nearly normal even with high blood alcohol concentrations. Following the withdrawal of alcohol, electroencephalographic dysrythmias occurred after 15 to 19 hours of abstinence, even in patients who did not have seizures.

On the basis of these results, it was concluded that both metabolic and tissue tolerance developed to alcohol and that abstinence from alcohol following prolonged drinking can result in tremors, hyperreflexia, fever, convulsions, hallucinosis, and delirium. These symptoms are not due to nutritional deficiency.

THE BOSTON EXPERIMENT

The Lexington experiment has been replicated by Mendelson *et al.* (7). In their study, ten volunteer alcoholics, who had been abstinent from alcohol while confined, drank a mixture of whisky and alcohol (concentration of 43 per

TABLE 14–1

SUMMARY OF THE LEXINGTON EXPERIMENT

Patient	Average alcohol intake (ml/day)	Days of intoxication	Abstinence symptoms				
			tremors	insomnia	disorientation	hallucinations	convulsions
1	286	7	1	0	0	0	0
2	266	16	1	0	0	0	0
3	293	16	1	0	0	0	0
4	346	34	2	0	0	0	0
5	388	78	4	?	4	4	7
6	383	78	4	4	1	4	0
7	448	87	3	2	0	2	0
8	472	48	3	2	0	2	1
9	489	55	4	2	0	0	0
10	458	48	4	4	4	4	0

The numbers indicate the grade of severity of the symptom on a rating scale of 0–4.

TABLE 14–2

SUMMARY OF THE BOSTON EXPERIMENT

Patient	Average alcohol intake (ml/day)	Days of intoxication	Abstinence symptoms			
			tremor	disorientation	memory defect	hallucinations
1	509	24	+	0	+	+
2	509	24	+	0	+	+
3	509	24	+	0	+	+
4	509	24	+	+	+	+
5	509	24	+	0	0	0
6	509	24	+	+	+	+
7	381	24	+	0	+	0
8	509	24	0	0	0	0
9	381	21	+	0	0	0
10	509	24	+	0	+	0

+ indicates that the symptom was present on at least one day.

cent alcohol) every three hours for 24 days in doses increasing from 6 ounces (equivalent to 76.4 ml absolute ethanol) to 40 ounces (equivalent to 509 ml absolute ethanol) daily. As long as the dose of whisky was 30 ounces (equivalent to 381 ml ethanol) daily or less, blood alcohol concentrations remained less than 200 mg/100 ml. When 40 ounces (equivalent to 509 ml of alcohol) were consumed, blood alcohol concentrations increased to more than 200 mg/100 ml and patients became overtly drunk.

When alcohol was discontinued abruptly most of the subjects had tremors, orientation and memory defects, and hallucinations (see Table 14-2). The authors concluded that both metabolic and tissue tolerance to alcohol de-

veloped and that chronic ingestion of alcohol caused definite physiological addiction.

The Boston study also added much important and interesting information on psychomotor performance and metabolic effects of chronic drinking that are beyond the scope of this paper.

SUBSTITUTION OF ALCOHOL FOR BARBITURATES IN BARBITURATE ADDICTS

Impressed by the resemblance of the clinical pictures of alcohol and barbiturate withdrawal, Fraser et al. (3) substituted large amounts of alcohol for barbiturates in ten patients who were ingesting 1.1 to 2.3 grams of pentobarbital or secobarbital daily. Despite difficulties in

TABLE 14–3

INCIDENCE OF MAJOR SYMPTOMS OF ABSTINENCE FROM
BARBITURATES DURING SUBSTITUTION OF ALCOHOL

Symptom	During substitution of alcohol	Controls—no alcohol
convulsions	3 of 9 (33 per cent)	15 of 19 (79 per cent)
delirium	3 of 9 (33 per cent)	12 of 19 (63 per cent)

Figures are the number and percentage of patients who had the indicated
symptom, out of the number in the group; differences are statistically significant
by χ^2: $p < 0.05$.

maintaining satisfactorily high concentrations
of blood alcohol, the incidence of major symptoms of abstinence from barbiturates (convulsions and delirium) was markedly reduced (see
Table 14–3).

The technique of cross substitution has been
a standard method for studying intoxication
equivalence with drugs of the morphine type,
and is based on the hypothesis that if one drug
will entirely or partially suppress symptoms of
abstinence from a second drug known to cause
physical dependence of a certain type, the first
drug will induce the same kind of dependence
as the second when administered chronically.
Thus, the experiment indicated that there was
some common physiological derangement in dependence on barbiturates and on alcohol. It is
now widely accepted that when used to produce chronic intoxication, alcohol, barbiturates,
meprobamate, glutethemide, chlordiazepoxide,
paraldehyde, chloral, and some other central
depressant drugs all induce physical dependence
of a similar kind, which has been termed
"dependence of the alcohol-barbiturate type"
(2).

THE NEED FOR AN ANIMAL MODEL

It would be extremely useful to have a satisfactory and practical method of inducing
physical dependence in lower animals. Only by
this means can the pathophysiological mechanisms responsible for physical dependence on
alcohol be elucidated. Currently we have absolutely no knowledge of these mechanisms.
Hopefully, current work on physical dependence
on alcohol in monkeys will provide such a technique.

THEORETICAL IMPORTANCE OF
PHYSICAL DEPENDENCE ON ALCOHOL

The reality of physical dependence on alcohol
can no longer be doubted. What is the importance of this fact? There is no question of the
importance of psychiatric factors and of psychological dependence on alcohol in the genesis of
alcoholism. The development of physical dependence means, just as it does in the case of
dependence on morphine, that the physically
dependent alcoholic must then drink partly to
ameliorate or to prevent the symptoms of abstinence. The poison that caused the condition becomes the medicine for it. Drinking thus
tends to become continuous, with even greater
damage to the health of the patient. This kind
of alcoholism has been referred to as "delta"
alcoholism by Jellinek (5). Physical dependence on alcohol may also reinforce the psychic
dependence that is already present and could
conceivably lead to the kind of conditioning of
abstinence postulated by Wikler (10) for physical dependence on opiates. Thus physical dependence on alcohol may have even greater
psychological than physiological importance.

TREATMENT OF DEPENDENCE ON
ALCOHOL

Since abstinence from alcohol can cause serious
symptoms, physical dependence on alcohol is
best treated by gradual reduction. In other
types of chronic intoxications, one can use the
drug responsible for the intoxication to reduce
the dose. However, in the case of alcoholism,
alcohol is not a good drug for the purpose because of the narrow margin between the dose

that causes mild intoxication and that which will result in a precipitous drop in blood alcohol, and because of the continuing toxic metabolic effects of the alcohol. For these reasons, alcohol is best replaced by one of the depressant drugs known to cause dependence of the alcohol-barbiturate type. The particular drug used matters little. One can employ barbiturates, paraldehyde, chloral, chlordiazepoxide, or meprobamate. The important thing is to give the depressant drug initially in doses just sufficient to create and maintain a mild degree of intoxication. The proper dose has to be determined individually. Once it has been established, the dose is cut progressively over a period of days. This system is almost 100 per cent effective in preventing convulsions and deliria. The phenothiazine tranquillizers should not be used unless supplemented with the ordinary depressant drugs, since it has been shown that they will not suppress abstinence symptoms of the barbiturate type and since they are weak convulsant drugs.

SUMMARY

Two experiments using human subjects have proved that abstinence from alcohol after protracted, heavy drinking can result in tremors, convulsions, and hallucinated, delirious states. Alcohol will partially suppress abstinence from barbiturates, implying some biological relationship between chronic alcohol and barbiturate intoxication. The mechanisms of physical dependence on alcohol are unknown and an animal model is badly needed. Physical dependence on alcohol is best treated by preventing the appearance of abstinence symptoms. To do this a depressant drug is substituted for the alcohol in doses sufficient to maintain mild drunkenness, and then the dosage is gradually reduced.

REFERENCES

1
BOWMAN, K.M., WORTIS, H., & KEISER, S.
The treatment of delirium tremens
J.A.M.A., **112**: 1217, 1939

2
EDDY, N.B., HALBACH, H., ISBELL, H., & SEEVERS, M.H.
Drug dependence: its significance and characteristics
Bull. World Health Organ., **32**: 721, 1965

3
FRASER, H.F., WIKLER, A., ISBELL, H., & JOHNSON, N.K.
Partial equivalence of chronic alcohol and barbiturate intoxications
Quart. J. Stud. Alc., **18**: 541, 1957

4
ISBELL, H., FRASER, H.F., WIKLER, A., BELLEVILLE, R.E., & EISENMAN, A.J.
An experimental study of the etiology of "rum fits" in delirium tremens
Quart. J. Stud. Alc., **16**: 1, 1955

5
JELLINEK, E.M.
The disease concept of alcoholism
New Haven: Hillhouse Press, 1960

6
KALINOWSKY, L.B.
Convulsions in non-epileptic patients on withdrawal of barbiturates, alcohol and other drugs
A.M.A. Arch. Neurol. Psychiat., **48**: 946, 1942

7
MENDELSON, J.H., ed.
Experimentally induced chronic intoxication and withdrawal in alcoholics
Quart. J. Stud. Alc., suppl. no. 2, 1964

8
PIKER, P.
On the relationship of the sudden withdrawal of alcohol to delirium tremens
Am. J. Psychiat., **93**: 1387, 1937

9
VICTOR, M. & ADAMS, R.
The effect of alcohol on the nervous system
In Metabolic and toxic diseases of the nervous system
Res. Publ. A. Res. Nerv. & Ment. Dis., **32**: 526, 1963

10
WIKLER, A.
On the nature of addiction and habituation
Brit. J. Addict., **55**: 73, 1961

11
WIKLER, A., PESCOR, F.T., FRASER, H.F., & ISBELL, H.
Electroencephalographic changes associated with chronic alcoholic intoxication and the barbiturate abstinence syndrome
Am. J. Psychiat., **113**: 106, 1956

M O R R I S   E . C H A F E T Z

Department of Psychiatry and Alcohol Clinic
Massachusetts General Hospital and
Department of Psychiatry
Harvard Medical School
Boston, Massachusetts, USA

15

Clinical Syndromes
of Liquor Drinkers

Alcohol by itself is a simple substance. But when introduced into a human and his environment, it can effect a wide range of variable responses not only between individual and individual or between culture and culture, but even within the same person from time to time.

In any examination of the clinical syndromes of liquor drinkers, we must resist the temptation to treat them as those other problems of medicine which more easily lend themselves to categorization; we must take a macroscopic perspective that sees alcohol in relation to society and culture before we can single out for microscopic analysis its action on individuals. Let us begin by looking at the drinking behaviour of my countrymen in the United States who are, I am certain, larger consumers of liquor than of wine. (I must add here that for purposes of the program arrangements I have made a distinction between liquor and wine. In my other writings I make no such differentiation because it is the ethyl alcohol content of a beverage that is the main reason for the use of these beverages.)

Many, perhaps a majority of Americans, drink liquor as they live life: rapidly and under tense circumstances. Whether at a cocktail party, a commuter bar, or a private party, the general tendency is to achieve rapid, heightened effects from alcoholic beverages. Coupled with this approach to drinking is the desired end point of being "high." To get "high" (or the many other words used to describe this state), as I understand it, is to get to that delicate point of alcohol effect where one is intoxicated but not sick. By intoxicated but not sick, I mean a state where inhibitions are lost and the individual is without most of his controls, but where gastric upsets and hangover do not appear. In addition to drinking rapidly, my countrymen often drink liquor with little or no food in their stomachs, and in tense, uncomfortable circumstances that often create sufficient anxiety to lead individuals to drink more than intended.

Now the hairline or delicate end point of drink effect just described, is – especially in the

The preparation of this paper was supported in part by National Institute of Mental Health grant MH 01449, and by the Division of Alcoholism, Commonwealth of Massachusetts.

way and in the places where we drink – a difficult target to hit. For the variety of influences that can mediate the imbibing of a definite amount of alcohol are innumerable. The psychological, physical, and social factors that complicate our response to a given quantity of alcohol are not constant. Since responses to alcohol are unpredictable, you can readily see that drinkers who use alcohol to reach a delicate balance between feeling good and feeling sick often cross the border and suffer the complications.

But you must understand: American culture does not disdain intoxication. As a matter of fact, in American culture, to get high or intoxicated (without the unpleasant side effects noted above), is condoned if not acceptable behaviour. We conveniently forget that a state of intoxication, even without the unpleasant symptoms, is a state of illness. By a state of illness I mean a state in which cerebral and motor controls are severely impaired. We drink, therefore, in the United States, with the goal, for the most part, of becoming sick. This is so strongly engraved in American drinking behaviour that one cannot talk about drinking in my country without most people equating it with being drunk.

Recently in a lecture before the New York Academy of Science (2), I proposed exploration of a preventive approach to alcoholism based on didactic and experiential information on alcohol use in the schools in order to develop responsible drinking patterns in our culture. No one in response – serious or jocular – could discuss my proposal without intimating that the students would be intoxicated. Our stage, our television, our writing, nearly always portray drinking liquor as meaning being drunk. By such a cultural attitude we give sanction to and continually reinforce the proposal that an intoxicated state is acceptable. And yet we close our eyes to many peoples of the world who use alcohol, do not sanction the kind of drinking behaviour or acceptance of intoxication described, and suffer minimal alcohol problems; whereas other nations whose drinking behaviour and attitudes approach our own suffer many such problems.

The attitude that drinking means drinking to

an intoxicated state has produced one further complication that results in alcohol problems. To counterbalance the desire for drunkenness, there are powerful forces in favour of abolishing all drinking. In other words, extremes of the continuum exist; it's all right to drink to get drunk; it's destructive to touch any alcohol at all. The latter attitude is as conducive to alcohol problems as the former when both coexist in the same culture. Thus one can see the powerful forces operating to produce alcoholism among liquor drinkers in the United States. I should like, before leaving the macroscopic, to reiterate that the causes of alcohol problems are complex and multifaceted, and I have sorted out only those major forces operating in cultures with a high incidence of alcoholism.

Bearing in mind the points I have noted above, let us now look at some of the syndromes that exist among liquor drinkers. To any student of alcohol problems, a common experience is to find, on examination, that the patient uses liquor as a form of self-medication for depression. The etiology of the depression may be related to external causes and be reactive in nature or it may have deeper roots and be endogenous. Whatever the cause of the depression, the patient begins to use liquor to dull the inner pain and beautify the ugliness within him. The drinking pattern is irregular with these patients: anniversaries or episodes associated with a loss may lead to a drinking bout; rejection or humiliation, however slight, may similarly nudge the patient to the bottle.

What is striking in these patients, however, is the invariable response of the individual to liquor. Some patients who take alcohol to alleviate depression find that alcohol actually deepens depression. They respond by imbibing more and more of the liquor, hoping to achieve the relief they seek. Others find the liquor provides what they seek – relief from depression – and become fearful of giving up the bottle for fear that the pain and ugliness will return. Fortunately for the latter, the physical discomfort and illness an excess of alcohol can sometimes provide yields them a measure of self-punishment which in itself can temporarily afford relief from depression.

In this age of psychiatric sophistication it

would be unfortunate to focus on the obvious problem of self-medication by liquor and not to notice the subtle causative force of the depression. Careful evaluation of the patient's psychopathology and resources for recovery can provide relief by psychotherapeutic and/or psychopharmacological methods, and the need for the unhealthy use of liquor can be avoided.

A second kind of liquor user is the person who employs alcohol to blur his perceptions. Such an individual becomes aware that some socially forbidden impulses are operating within him and he develops uncomfortable sensations. An example of this is the individual who has strong homosexual drives which he represses when he is sober. When he becomes homosexually aroused and anxious because these feelings are so close to the surface, he may use alcohol heavily. The alcohol use under these circumstances serves a dual function: the liquor may obliterate the uncomfortable feelings of homosexual arousal on one level or it may dissolve inhibitions on another to permit the drinker to express his homosexual instincts. If homosexual activity – forbidden during sobriety, but practised during intoxication – occurs, the individual does not consider himself responsible for his actions. He is aware of what has gone on, but his responsibilities and desires are masked to him.

A brief clinical history may illustrate this point: a married patient engaged in frequent and intensive extramarital sexual activity. Whenever sexual situations arose which could question his masculinity and potency, he would drink heavily. At such times he could perform with a woman partner only if she would describe her sexual experiences with some other man, or if he could set up situations where he and some other man presumably shared a woman. Under the influence of alcohol, instead of sharing he would engage in homosexual activities. He would deny to himself when he reflected on these experiences their obvious homosexuality but would attribute the events to the liquor he had consumed.

This patient and others with similar configurations use alcohol to alter their perceptions of their inner selves and their outer worlds. Here, too, the removal of alcohol without

attempting to deal with the contributing factors toward heavy use will result in the development of severe states of anxiety and the onset of various somatic symptoms. My experience with this group of patients has indicated that when they can begin to recognize and deal in different ways with the impulses they pretend do not exist, their need for liquor is significantly lessened.

Another common type of liquor drinker is the individual who uses alcohol to sustain a psychological system of defenses. With this group the oft-noted "blackout" phenomenon is usual. In other words their repressed unconscious desires become a reality, but they have no recollection when sober of what has transpired. People with a sober characterological attitude of complete kindness and abject passivity, showing no hostility, will with liquor become brutal, hostile, and aggressive. A startled employer may find at a company party an intoxicated employee who insults him freely as he would never dare to do when sober. The employee will not remember this once the effects of the liquor have gone and will be incredulous at descriptions of his behaviour while intoxicated.

Similarly, the fastidious, prudish woman can, when intoxicated, become filthy in habit, unclean in dress, and promiscuous in behaviour. Many a puritan woman has awakened with a shock from an alcoholic slumber to find a man peacefully sharing her pillow, and has wondered how he got there. The secret, repressed desires under the façade of social attitudes, respectability, and behaviour are obvious.

Less obvious is that subgroup of individuals who, although heavily under the influence of liquor, do not seem so to the casual observer. These individuals can carry on highly complicated business and social activities and not seem to be any the worse for their drinking. Only when a fall in the blood alcohol level occurs do they suddenly return to their original state of awareness. These people, when they regain their non-drinking selves, do not have an inkling as to the people, places, or events with which they have been in contact, sometimes for hours, days, or weeks. Where at one moment while intoxicated a person may have been the sworn-friend-for-life of another, the "pop" into a sober state brings a response of unfamiliarity startling to all concerned. Not only is the liquor drinker stunned by sudden situations, but innocent sharers of that "other" personality are now confronted with a new individual in an old body.

Treatment in this total group of liquor drinkers is not a simple task. The intensity of denial, the strength of repression, and the alien aspects of behaviour make the therapist's task formidable. The dissociative implications which are to a varying degree present in this syndrome suggest serious psychopathology only a part of which may be amenable to psychiatric treatment.

Since we have just examined a serious syndrome of liquor drinkers, perhaps we ought now to look at one with a less ominous prognosis: the use of liquor to break down psychological barriers. From time to time we are called upon to perform an activity we wish to do but cannot. Our conscious desire to perform is overwhelmed and incapacitated by unconscious restrictions. Try as we will, try as we must, we cannot perform. Liquor for many of these blocked responses is an easy ally; the hounding inhibitions melt quickly before its chemical presence and one can go on. Under such influence the lawyer argues his case before the tribunal, the actor may bring himself to the otherwise terrifying centre stage, the lecturer speak, the author write, the frigid woman respond, and so forth. For this group to drink is to perform, and the horrible anxiety and tension pass from the scene.

This group of liquor drinkers is growing because it seems that the demands of increasingly complex social situations require alcohol to ease the way, and the commuter bars are crowded with men who must fortify themselves before they can even face their families. Unfortunately, alcohol as the means to provide the desired relief is a fickle ally, and its use in increasing amounts to produce the desired effect may lead to states of intoxication and responses not appropriate to the circumstances.

Treatment here may or may not be simple. For some a relationship with a sympathetic, understanding, and supporting human being can supply the source of strength formerly furnished by a bottle. For others, delving into the source of the fear and developing new, less destructive methods of handling the anxiety are desirable. The danger of alcohol fulfilling a tranquillizing role must be guarded against; on the other hand, it may be preferable to reliance on a host of other drugs.

Liquor for a certain segment of the population is not unlike the narcosis achieved by the morphine addict. For these liquor imbibers, one goal is worth drinking for: oblivion. The inhabitants of this unhappy drinking state swallow their drinks quickly to obtain a state of bliss. To them reality is a terror; a dream state of narcosis, the only way to continue. Here we see the patient who ends a drinking bout not because he is ill but because he is unconscious. Here we see the person for whom cirrhosis of the liver, esophageal varices, polyneuropathy, loss of family, loss of job, loss of self-respect, and loss of life are no threat, no deterrent to drinking. Death is more desirable than life without liquor. To be a habitue of skid row with its external social oblivion and internal emotionless life is the all-consuming desire. Although these people are fortunately only a small segment of the problem liquor drinkers, they form the stereotype for most people when they think of alcoholic persons; they also form a major social problem.

Patients who are so bent on self-destruction did not come to this sorry state solely as a result of alcohol. Careful study of their life histories reveals severe disturbances of their pre-alcoholic personalities. Retrospective evidence exists that a disturbance of interpersonal relations exists early in life. Family adjustment and school performance operate at the extremes of a continuum: overcontrolled or undercontrolled behaviour. Goals, seldom achieved, are accomplished only with unwarranted difficulty. Instability of occupation is common; marriage rates are equivalent to those of a non-alcoholic population but with a significantly higher incidence of marital disintegration. In this group the point at which drinking becomes uncontrolled is diffuse and indefinite, and there is some suggestion that social drinking never really exists. Onsets of drinking bouts are unrelated usually to specific external stresses, and the bouts continue until sickness and stupor ensue.

The entire life history pattern as well as the drinking history reveal strong self-destructive and self-defeating patterns of behaviour.

Treatment for this group requires a wide gamut of modalities, not because treatment is futile but because careful tailoring of the therapy to the patient and his resources is essential. Here, too, treatment goals must be based on realistic expectations and perhaps limited objectives. Too often treatment efforts are self-defeating because unrealistic demands are imposed upon patient and therapists. Before leaving this group I must relate an incident told me by a patient. He had been a liquor drinker who essentially fell into the group I have just described. But he was in a controlled, sober state when he took his wife to skid row. His wife was understandably shocked by the sight of intoxicated, oblivious forms lying in doorways and on the street. Noting her response, her husband said, "What is even more shocking is that I envy them their oblivion."

Another clinical syndrome of liquor drinkers we have observed is that in which an intoxicated individual is more tolerable to his social unit than a sober one. This syndrome is most clearly seen in configurations whereby non-alcoholic, extremely dominating mates or parents exist. On the one hand, the non-alcoholic mate or parent appears on the surface to suffer much as a consequence of the alcoholic state of another. If treatment or extraneous events result in sobriety, however, opposition to this state arises in the so-called healthy members. They become proportionately more disturbed as the alcoholic member becomes less alcoholic. What becomes clear is that the pathological drinking behaviour of the alcoholic person, socially unacceptable and readily obvious to society, was a cover-up for disturbances in another area. Improvement in one person exposes the problems in another, and the unhealthy drinking in such cases satisfies, in part, the emotional needs of the second person. Furthermore, we see some mates who cannot tolerate the dependency and demands put upon them when the alcoholic person is sober but can readily provide emotional sustenance instead of rejection when he is drunk.

Treatment of this group when directed toward the alcoholic individual alone is self-defeating.

The subtle and covert influences which an intimate emotional and social situation can bring to bear in an anti-therapeutic way are endless. Unless the symbiotic relationship is understood, treatment will be unsuccessful. Rehabilitation efforts must be directed either toward social manipulation and separation of the patient from his environment, or toward combined treatment of the patient and the significant individuals in his life.

The clinical syndrome of liquor drinkers I shall consider last is the one I feel contributes much to unhealthy alcohol use and may give us some clues to preventive measures: the cocktail party. At least in America, and I suspect that it is spreading to other nations as well, the cocktail party epitomizes unhealthy drinking practices, unfavourable responses to liquor, and unrelating social behaviour (3).

The cocktail party is supreme in emphasizing man's emotional isolation from man; his isolation from what he does, thinks, and feels. People are brought together – many of them unknown to one another – to drink, to talk, to be gay. The drinking is done while standing, gulped rapidly and with the barest minimum of food, and heightened responses toward intoxication are frequent. All factors conducive to heavy alcohol use exist in the cocktail party situation. Drinking under these circumstances provides little of the pleasurable responses of relaxation and socialization alcohol can provide. The talk of the cocktail party emphasizes this. People do not listen; they do not care. All of us are familiar with the habitue of the cocktail party who, while pouring liquor into himself, pours his soul into our ear: intimate details of his life he would never utter to a close friend. The reason for this is fairly obvious: we do not matter; we probably do not care. It is simpler to share intimate details of one's life with an individual with whom we are not emotionally involved than with one with whom we wish to continue our involvement. Words spoken at cocktail parties are often spoken to oneself rather than to another because excess drinking creates a pharmacological barrier to emotional and social communication while healthy alcohol use facilitates communication. Drinking which points in the direction of isolation – epitomized by the cocktail party and the commuter bar – perpe-tuates and intensifies alcohol problems.

If one reflects on the syndromes I have des-cribed, one can see that alcohol use is but one manifestation of a total group of problems of varying intensity; that is, it is symptomatic behaviour. True, the destructive nature of al-cohol problems can be such that one will only focus on the alcoholic disturbance and not upon the underlying physical, psychological, and social causes. If we are to attempt to reduce al-cohol problems on a wide scale, one approach is to understand the factors involved in the choice of alcoholic drinking as a symptom, and then systematically to change those factors.

Centuries of evidence have shown us that some societies drink and yet suffer minimal al-cohol problems, while others drink with major alcoholic disturbances as a consequence (1, 4). Obviously, since all existing societies and cul-tures have problems, the method of coping with the pains of life has been chosen in some out of the alcoholic context – presumably in a non-alcoholic manner and thereby presumably by less destructive social mechanisms. My preven-tive approach aims at removing alcohol as a cop-ing tool of society but does not reach the variable and complex causes of alcohol problems. This proposal is based upon my understanding of the physiological and pharmacological principles of alcohol use, a study of drinking behaviour in non-alcoholic societies, and an understanding of psychological responses to disequilibrium.

This preventive approach aims to inculcate societies with responsible drinking behaviour and to interlard alcohol use with all ordinary social behaviour by teaching young people how to drink with responsibility, without ill effects, and for benefit only. This learning experience for those who will choose to drink and those who will not provides factual information about alcohol use during hygiene instruction at school and college levels. This instruction emphasizes the differing effects of drinking rapidly versus sipping slowly; consuming liquor with food in the stomach versus drinking on an empty stomach; drinking under tense circumstances alone or drinking while relaxed, with people, and in communication; it emphasizes that intoxi-cation is sickness and is unhealthy behaviour.

By providing on a voluntary basis group experi-ences with alcohol under supervision, young people may familiarize themselves with their own responses to alcohol under variable condi-tions and learn how to avoid disastrous, un-healthy episodes. Finally, I would make alcohol available to all so that the attraction provided by that which is forbidden will be removed.

The day is at hand when we can hope to make positive inroads into many of the social and human problems we have long avoided. How-ever, we must guard against the lingering pre-judices of ignorance which continually threaten to defeat our purpose. This is the case with alcohol problems. We have a responsibility to open paths of communication so that people and societies will no longer need to suffer as much from the problems of alcohol.

REFERENCES

1
CHAFETZ, MORRIS E.
Liquor: the servant of man
Boston: Little, Brown, 1965
2
CHAFETZ, MORRIS E.
Alcohol excess
Ann. N.Y. Acad. Sc., 133: 808, 1966
3
CHAFETZ, MORRIS E.
Preventive techniques in alcoholism
Medical Tribune and Medical News, March 13, 1966
4
CHAFETZ, MORRIS E. & DEMONE, HAROLD W., JR.
Alcoholism and society.
New York: Oxford University Press, 1962

P. BAILLY-SALIN

Psychiatric Hospitals of the Seine
Paris, France

16

Clinical Forms of Alcoholism Prevalent among Wine Drinkers

Starting with a trivial consumption of wine, which individuals become dependent on alcohol? How do they reach this state? It is possible to find in this field a clue to the problem of the etiopathogenesis of alcoholism. This is especially tempting for one who is a native of a country where wine is the object of special and extensive consideration and also of special and extensive consumption. The study of the transition from a moderate intake to a pathological state of alcohol intoxication seems to be easier in a country where the consumption of wine is so widespread.

We must first examine the attributes which have been assigned to wine, by a rapid survey of the classic clinical pictures of alcoholism, the relevant literature, and statistical data. It is perhaps not surprising that it is in the mild forms of inebriation that certain differences between the state induced by wine and that induced by consumption of spirituous liquor can be seen. In contrast to liquor the phases previous to inebriety through wine are longer and more gradual, the changing of mood occurs more slowly and insidiously, and the effect is more moderate and without a profound separation of normal personality. The release of impulsive tendencies as well as the removal of anxiety are also less marked after wine. Nevertheless these subtle differences are rapidly lost, and no clinical difference can be recognized in the advanced stage of inebriety whether induced by wine or by liquor.

Concerning abnormal forms of inebriety, the role played by absinth in convulsive alcoholic states is well known. Some authors claim that pathological intoxication is more frequent among liquor drinkers than among wine drinkers; but this is not unanimously accepted. The most important factor seems to be the individual predisposition, so that one might paraphrase the dictum: "alcohol plays the role of the finger triggering the gun."

It is not surprising that we are unable to find any clinical difference between alcoholism induced by wine and that induced by liquors. Some authors have claimed a higher frequency of subacute delirium among wine drinkers, while delirium tremens appears to be more frequent among liquor drinkers. But the clinical picture of these two states does not reveal any factor specifically related to the responsible beverage. As a matter of fact, in a survey of the literature, we did not find any indication as to the influence of the form of alcoholization. Furthermore, no difference attributable to the kind of alcoholic beverage can be observed in simple alcoholic dementia or in pseudo-general paralysis.

In contradistinction, the Korsakoff syndrome seems to be more frequent among liquor drinkers. This statement is supported by the fact that in France this syndrome is more frequent among women, who are very low consumers of wine. On the other hand, the survey on the Gayet-Wernicke encephalopathy by Girard in 1953 did not provide any indication of differences related to the form in which alcohol was ingested.

The present clinical survey cannot omit consideration of the Marchiava-Bignami disease. This illness was first described in 1903. It is characterized by myelin degeneration in the central part of the *corpus callosum* and in the optical bundles. Clinically, the picture resembles alcoholic pseudo-general paralysis in the rapid intellectual and physical decay, dysaphia, psychomotor excitation fits, and deep terminal dementia. It is traditionally accepted that this disease is exclusively associated with chronic intoxication on Italian wines. However, the French scholars Girard, Garde, and Devick have found similar lesions in patients not consuming Italian wines, and they claim that this syndrome should be included in the category of acute hemorrhagic encephalopathies.

Concerning hepato-digestive disorders, and more particularly liver cirrhosis, most authors agree that the main factors are the duration and intensity of the intoxication, and not the source of the ingested alcohol.

The low frequency of mental troubles among patients with alcoholic liver cirrhosis is only partly explained by the fact that the statistics concerning this point originate in gastroenterology services. Many authors have reported that in patients with liver cirrhosis related to wine drinking, practically no personality troubles were present, and consequently they were able to abandon wine without difficulty.

In fact, a clinical study directed more specifi-

cally to the psychological aspects has shown that this is not quite true. In such patients a real dependence on wine, confirmed by the high rate of relapse, is present. Also some personality troubles are evident, but the frequency is much lower than in other alcoholic patients.

It is not possible to discuss here the complex picture of the mental disturbances of alcoholics, which represent, according to personal experience in France, the majority of cases. Everybody knows the patients with varicose face, subjaundiced eyes, tendency to sweating, marked tremor of fingers and tongue, leg muscle cramps, irregular sleeping with nightmares, deficiency of attention, and a parcellated and blurred apprehension of concepts, and in whom affectivity and behavioural troubles appear immediately. These patients are generally good fellows who are helping and kind outside, but at home they are suspicious, irritable, envious, pusillanimous, boastful, deceitful, and hypocritical. The deep malaise they are feeling is revealed only after intensive contact with them. In this advanced stage, is it possible to recognize differences in the symptoms exhibited by the patients consuming only wine and by those consuming other kinds of alcoholic beverages? In practice we find it practically impossible to analyse the clinical picture in terms of the form of ethanol that produced it. One has to study alcoholic behaviour in its earlier phases to discover differences.

As noted previously, it is pertinent to discuss the significance of wine in a country where this beverage is a natural product, where people are widely acquainted with the very original study of Bachard who, at the end of his work on the reveries of the will, gives a substantial psychoanalysis of wine, showing that it is a juice both of the sun and of the earth. As a common and natural product, in contrast to the artificial and concentrated liquors, wine is considered by most people the best beverage and a healthy food for man. Is not the analogy of red wine with blood the origin of certain religious practices and beliefs? But neither its natural origin, its beverage qualities, or its bouquet are sufficient to explain the magnitude of its consumption and the homage paid to it.

As a matter of fact, the mysterious alchemy which transforms the grape juice into a beverage of such different taste, is related to another alchemy able to change situations and psychologies, having a quasi-philosophical power of mutation to make a mighty person from a weak one, a gay from a sad. From a phenomenological and mythological point of view this beneficial alchemical power appears to be followed by a malevolent one; the effect of this healthy, noble, fertile, and rich product is changed into a deleterious one: the weak who became mighty will return to be weak, the sad who became gay will fall in the shadow of anxiety; thus is the spiritual freedom and happiness followed by a deep dullness.

It is not necessary to evoke here Klein's proposition: good breast, bad breast – good milk, bad milk, to understand that all these facts lead us to a deep consideration of the extreme ambivalence in our alcoholic patients, which moves them to break the magic mirror of the good image of wine. Looking for freedom, strength, and happiness, they act neurotically to find servitude, weakness, and anxiety. This opposition is also present in the *social* drinking of alcohol. The good image of wine exhibits it not only as a philtre, but also as something of lasting life, as a prolonged act of a social nature, as a lively and euphoric party. Good wine is tasted slowly in the company of friends, it is the object of a gay cult, which has its own ritual, that cannot be trespassed without risk, the purpose of which is to obtain the best effect, the highest exaltation and Dionysic power. From this point of view, the good image is totally opposed to the brutal, clandestine, and shameful absorption of large amounts of concentrated liquors. In the good image inebriety is an accidental, unpleasant consequence, though in the bad one it is its own purpose. Some factor unique to alcoholics prevents them from assimilating the phenomenological reality of the good image of wine that is held by most of their countrymen.

Let us abandon the phenomenological and mythological aspects of wine and turn to the so-called normal wine drinkers. They are individuals to whom wine is a nice beverage, and who strongly contribute through their moderate and happy consumption to the permanence of the wine totem in a producer country. These individuals do not increase their intake in the course of years; they know how to abstain temporarily when any organic trouble appears; i.e. they do not suffer from dependence. Their consumption is easily admitted and acceptable, and does not cause them to dissemble.

Beside them, but very different, it is possible to describe the excessive drinkers. The somatic examination may show a certain liver overload the pathogenesis of which is difficult to interpret, since drinking is mixed with food excess (particularly of animal fat). The psychological examination does not show the problems, stresses, and difficulties found in alcoholics. Their libido satisfaction is widely extended and polymorphic. Apparently these excessive drinkers cannot be considered sick persons, nor, in many cases at least, as future patients who will develop the classical clinical forms of alcoholism.

Fouquet has described under the term *alcoolité* a form of alcoholism we consider to be applied only to heavy drinkers of wine. They are individuals who drink wine almost exclusively, in large amounts. Generally they drink in company. Their consumption of wine is daily and continuous, in some cases with morning and evening paroxysms. This consumption is determined by an extreme appetite, even love, for the taste of the alcoholic beverage. Inebriety is exceptional. The wine consumption is not affected by any feeling of culpability, and these individuals are initially quite able to evolve rationalizations which satisfy them for a long time. Concerning heredity, it is common to find alcoholism in the father. The family is characterized by a wife generally older than the husband, many children, normal sexual patterns, and a rapid tendency to jealousy.

This picture is decidedly opposed to that described by Fouquet as *alcoolose*, a state characterized by preference for liquor and the aperitif, frequently alone and in secrecy. The alcohol consumption is discontinuous, with many month-long periods of abstinence, which tend to become fewer and shorter. These drinkers have no interest in the taste of alcoholic beverages; sometimes they even have a distaste. They exhibit frequent and atypical inebriety. The feeling of culpability is very clear, and they

report numerous attempts to fight against alcohol.
With respect to the hereditary aspect, it is common to find neuroses or psychoses in one of the
parents. Family life is characterized by early
conjugal differences and important sexual problems.

The marked difference between the "vinic"
forms of alcoholisms and those related to the
consumption of other beverages is clear. The
evolution of vinic *alcoolité* may follow different
patterns. It can remain stable with some decrease in intake and troubles. It can progress
slowly in amount of intake, with aggravation of
all symptoms, until ultimately the mental disturbances of chronic alcoholism, with affectivity
and behavioural troubles, appear. It can progress slowly to the hepato-digestive forms. Episodes of subacute alcoholic delirium or delirium
tremens may appear, giving rise to the mental
troubles of chronic alcoholism. Finally, this
form may evolve into an *alcoolose*, with deep
changes in behaviour.

The inclusion under the term *alcoolité* of a
form of alcoholism which seems more specifically "vinic" is tentative and subject to criticism.
How could one fail to be aware of that in a symposium in memory of such a master as Professor
Jellinek?

ARMANDO ROA

Psychiatric Clinic
University of Chile
Santiago, Chile

17

Alcoholism and Endogenous Psychosis

The relationship between alcoholism and endogenous psychosis is open to several interpretations. One considers the role of alcohol in precipitating endogenous psychosis; another considers alcoholism as one of the relevant symptomatic complexes in such psychosis; a third observes alcoholism remaining as a residue after the core of the psychosis has improved; a fourth is concerned with the consumption of alcohol to cover painful endogenous problems. These conflicting interpretations have so far not been satisfactorily resolved.

The type of crisis preceding massive drinking in some chronic alcoholics (not merely heavy drinkers) is by itself remarkable. Such drinking is preceded by hours or days of intense discomfort and a premonition (*tincada**) of danger to come. And this is the time when the alcoholic will not be able to stop even if he drinks only one or two glasses. However, in the periods between crises he may drink during meals without loss of control; he may get drunk accidentally on the occasion of a birthday or a marriage without any symptom of withdrawal or need to go on drinking.

Some intermittent alcoholics compare the uneasiness felt during the days prior to massive drinking to the tense feeling of a man who desperately wants a woman. One such alcoholic said, "When I don't have the 'feeling,' I drink during meals and I'm not interested in alcohol. I don't go out with my friends after work is over. I go straight home. Suddenly, one morning I awake with this 'feeling,' as if I were a little bit depressed or expecting something unknown; I'm sure that the same day or the next I'm going to give in. I do not refuse my companions anymore, and though I may not accept immediately, I finally go with them saying to myself that one or two glasses will be enough. The way I feel then is quite different from the way I feel when I can drink during meals. Afterwards I keep on drinking for several days two or three times a day, until I'm caught and taken to the hospital."

Another alcoholic reported, "When I'm not

*The Chilean idiom *tincada* means a certain feeling that makes people sure beforehand, and without a reasonable explanation, that something good or evil is going to happen.

drinking day after day, I can see wine and I don't feel any need to drink. Sometimes, if the food is good, I drink even two glasses, but that is only for pleasure. When I'm grabbed by this 'feeling' it's quite different. It's just like when one desires a woman and is desperate to have her. That's the way it starts."

The history of a 44-year-old patient of the clinic is relevant in this respect. He had been drinking for about 30 years and sought treatment. After reflex therapy given to him in 1954, and a subsequent six-year period of abstinence, he began to drink again in 1960: "I started drinking one day, out of my ignorance, and since then I haven't been able to stop. Now I have a drink and I can't stop till I'm drunk." His episodes last eight days with two daily bouts of drinking; he drinks in the morning because he "awakes thirsty and with a hangover." He confesses he might drink water, but he prefers wine because it makes him feel "wealthy, brave, and courageous." In his opinion, he is not a victim of a disease but of a bad habit: "If it was a disease I would always drink. Why is it that I can live two or three months without drinking, after I have been drinking for eight or ten days? When I'm not with this 'feeling' I can go out with friends and have a couple of drinks and I stop; on Saturdays and Sundays I go to the market with my wife and we buy half a litre of wine to drink at home and everything is all right. The desire to go on drinking comes only when I'm with this 'feeling' and I meet friends."

Many chronic drinkers do not recognize the cause of their relapses after having been able to control themselves for months or even years. Statements such as: "I did it to test myself" or "I didn't think it could happen again" do not make clear why they had to test themselves or why they did not choose vacation time for the purpose so as not to fail in their jobs. It is possible that the crisis drinking of many alcoholics represents periodic compulsive phases, similar to the obsessive-compulsive phases of some endogenous depressions or epileptic disthymias. In such cases a long period of consumption would induce the appearance of a periodic endogenous mechanism, which during the weeks of abstinence remains quiescent. The subject would not drink or would be able to drink as anyone else, without losing the capacity to stop.

Only a few of our alcoholics – not psychopaths – showed inability to stop almost from the first. Their crisis drinking had begun at the age of 16, without previous periods of moderate or heavy ingestion. Some drink moderately during the intercrisis periods. It is easy to imagine that in these cases there are endogenous mechanisms which are set into motion by the first flash.

Perhaps the bodily uneasiness of some asthenic and anxious personalities is resolved through the image of liquor. Then the only way to deal with the situation is by drinking, just as the hungry body creates images of delicious foods, or the sexual desire creates images of beautiful women. As a matter of fact, crisis drinking, as in the case of hunger and erotic anxiety, can be suddenly stopped by bad news, an unpleasant situation, or a threat of danger. This is because the source of motivation and action used by the body, which is fantasy, disappears. The fact that crisis drinking is associated with the time of payment of wages or other precise dates does not contradict the notion of endogenicity, or the possible "corporization" of the desire to drink, in which it resembles sexual appetite, since we know that similar situations induce disthymias or depressive states. Christmas, New Year, and anniversary disthymias and endogenous depressions are classical.

In inveterate alcoholics without clinical organic damage we have repeatedly observed symptoms similar to those of endogenous depressions, lasting for months and very difficult to treat successfully. Such symptoms run from a light morning anxiety, sudden and too early awakening, hesitation and tiredness in everyday tasks – characteristics of a subdepression – to open depression with inhibition of thought and action, suicidal compulsions, hand tremors of the depressive type, etc. These symptoms improve a little in the evening. The usual drugs (Tofranil, Surmontil, Dinsidon, Aventyl, Marplan) are of little value even in high doses. But one or two glasses of any alcoholic drink can give some relaxation, as if allowing such men to "untie themselves inside." In spite of this, many patients do not relapse into the drinking habit, and finally overcome their depression.

More frequent is the confession of inveterate alcoholics that they drink to be able to cope with particular situations, for example, when they have to face the boss, a difficult task, or a social party, because otherwise they would be mentally inhibited, they would have a blank mind and would lack courage. It is not clear if these are mere anodyne toxicomania symptoms being relieved by alcohol or if they reflect an endogenous subdepression (which, as is well known, lasts for years and is centred on partial inhibitions). Clinical investigations capable of clarifying the problem are lacking. In some cases we have been able to trace through family history some previous subdepressions.

The classical depressive phases of manic-depressive psychosis do not generally lead to alcoholic drinking. On the contrary, in the manic phases the subject, if he has the opportunity, drinks heavily with friends and very seldom gets drunk. The maniacal person is not after alcohol, nor does he consider it a medicine, but only a source of joy. Hypomanics and hyperthymics also drink with friends solely to be happy. Hypomania and its spontaneous facilitation of all psychic processes is not the cause of inveterate alcoholism. The so-called inability to avoid drinking is the need to find a drug able to "loosen from the inside" and "open life's spontaneity." On the other hand, happiness does not seem to lead to the formation of a habit.

In our country the inability to stop drinking, characteristic of inveterate alcoholics, is largely found among "pettifoggers" and "false witnesses" and people of this sort who hang about trials and law; people who need self-control to perform their jobs. It is possible that fear of being trapped by the law may cause frequent reactive inhibitions, and that such inhibitions may be overcome by alcohol. Alcohol, in moderate doses, is an excellent anti-inhibitor, and inhibition is a basic symptom of the reactive depression, either organic or endogenous. Other symptoms, such as guilt feelings or feelings of a useless past and future, are not found in most of these depressions.

Alcohol may also expedite action in monotonous tasks such as those performed by unskilled workers, and this may be the reason why inveterate alcoholics are so commonly found among them.

Chronic alcoholism enhances the paranoic traits of personality, even in cases when they were not relevant in the past. Thus we can find the litigant alcoholic a champion of justice, the jealous and fanatic ex-alcoholic who has become an enemy of his former habit and a leader in the anti-alcoholic struggle. Many form the centre of anonymous alcoholic associations, but of course this does not mean that all or most of their leaders must be paranoiacs. However, studies performed in our clinic of the personalities of such leaders indicated that some at least were paranoic psychopaths whose overestimated idea was precisely anti-alcoholism. Similar to the case of malaria and general paresis, one disease yields to the other, in this case to paranoia. Some alcoholics suddenly give up drinking through religious conversion – that is to say, when they obtain the overestimated idea they have been longing for. This is a problem of public health and still requires much investigation.

We have observed that those who have stopped drinking after adequate treatment or psychic commotion, without acquiring a symptomatic paranoiac personality, devote themselves to their homes and duties, and rather passively participate or do not participate at all in societies of ex-alcoholics. Besides, it is remarkable that the leaders of such groups are almost always ex-alcoholics who show some signs of organic impairment. There are also found some anti-alcoholic leaders *per se*; these are persons with primitive fanatical personalities whose fanaticism comes from other motivations and not from organic damage. Fanaticism as a consequence of organic damage is not peculiar to alcoholism; it is also produced by severe encephalocranial traumatisms or other organic diseases, which turn into incipient querulent paranoias.

According to Bleuler, dipsomania may be symptomatic in some schizophrenics. They drink to banish stress or anxiety states, and after days of heavy ingestion finish exhausted. Due to their tendency to play the clown – one of the axial symptoms – hebephrenics associate in groups or gangs and drink heavily for long periods; very often they exhibit hallucinosis or delirium tremens, and that is how they happen to be taken to hospital. In other schizophrenics the uncontrolled impulse evolves into alcoholic excesses; it seems they indulge in drinking due to echopraxia (imitation of the master) or automatism of the command. For the same reason they stop drinking when they join non-drinking groups.

It is not known how many schizophrenics drink excessively or are chronic alcoholics, because only those with overt schizophrenia are admitted to hospital, leaving out the larval forms which are the most numerous. They constitute a high percentage of psychiatric pathology, and this is a serious problem because it affects people between 15 and 25 years of age and disables them for the rest of their lives.

In our country there are about 65,000 schizophrenics, and their recognition in the community requires a great deal of clinical skill because of the vague symptomatology of the condition. Classical schizophrenics consulting our hospitals are about 5,000 or 6,000 in number. Epidemiological investigations of this disease are just beginning, though it is as important as alcoholism, since it disables the sufferer for life.

We have rather frequently observed in the last five years paranoiac-catatonic schizophrenics who are hospitalized because of their overt aggressiveness, especially against their wives, after long periods of drinking with daily or weekly drunkenness. They suffer primary jealousy delusions. That is, they establish their suspicions on accidental conversations of the wife with friends, but they neither look for real evidence of infidelity, nor do they submit the wife to exhaustive enquiries, as would be typical in other jealous paranoiacs. During their stay in hospital these ideas come to the fore in the psychiatric exploration or when the wife comes to visit them. The rest of the time they seem to be engrossed in themselves or indifferent, in a kind of autistic state. The drinking bouts are caused by a passive surrender to catatonic impulses. They do not seem worried about them, and neither disguise them nor show them off. At the same time, they are affected by their symptoms, thus giving particular importance

to delirious perceptions, pseudo-perceptions, pseudo-delirious ideas, etc.

Acute alcoholic hallucinosis consists in a state of disturbance of consciousness which is characterized by a dark feeling of being surrounded by dangers, clear auditory hallucinations and vague visual hallucinations, bodily cognition or perception of somebody hiding behind. Sometimes there is guessing, or robbery of their thoughts, guilt feelings, a depressive outlook, insomnia or frightening dreams, whispers from the ceiling which make the patient believe he has overheard a conversation against him. Faced with this threatening environment, the patient usually makes a sudden attempt to escape or shows a tendency to commit suicide. All these symptoms show some schizophrenic signs, more evident still if alcoholism is attached to a larval schizophrenia that would be considered by the inexpert to be simply laziness or bad manners.

If, when lucidity is recovered, the affective state of being frightened by noises or conversations, or suffering from insomnia, tremors, sweating, and muscular twitching, diminishes, but the voices and persecutory ideas still continue amid an objectless life in which work is only a routine, it means that the patient is suffering from schizophrenic hallucinosis as a result of alcohol drinking and in spite of a long period of abstinence. This hallucinosis is of independent evolution. The clinical similarity of alcoholic hallucinosis and hallucinosis originated by causes classed as schizophrenic permits us to place both under the same diagnostic category.

A large number of observations in our clinic have been made of subjects in whom excessive consumption of alcohol began at the age of 16 or 18, and who at that time or one or two years later did not make any effort to get a steady job. They were not interested in taking professional aid courses, and if they did take them, they did not care about failing. They were not concerned with the social standards or prestige values of their milieu, but they also did not exhibit any other neurotic or psychotic symptoms. Such a pathology, consisting in a lack of motivation in life, reluctance to undertake daily tasks, and apparently distant affectivity with respect to the cracking of their personalities, is the very basis of schizophrenia. However, it is occasionally mistaken for psychopathy, neurosis, or simply lack of responsibility. In these cases the excessive consumption of alcohol is symptomatic. In many, after periods of excessive drinking, there appear amnesia, deep depression, anxiety, guilt feelings, ignominious offenses caused by the wife "who has sexual intercourse with anyone who wants to possess her," robbery, guessing and publication of thoughts, stuporous catatonic attitudes, echolalia, echomimia, attempts at suicide, and very often real suicide. These people improve after one or two months, and sometimes it is necessary to use insulin or electroshock therapy. Once amnesia is overcome, the patient remains with his previous larval schizophrenia, which to everybody means normality.

The relationship between schizophrenia and alcoholism could be clarified were it not for the prevalent idea that schizophrenia is a disease centred in thinking and affective disturbances. It is quite possible that most schizophrenics are still in the community, not having consulted a doctor and not showing any disturbance of thoughts, hallucinations, or delirious perceptions. On the other hand, the basic symptoms are the lack of a life purpose, hyperesthesia of affection, unwillingness, weakness before any obstacle in daily tasks, and the lack of genuine boredom in spite of their abandoned state. We consider lack of vital purpose to mean the lack of effective, planned, and persistent efforts towards graded goals that will lead to certain objectives, according to real abilities and possibilities. The schizophrenic patient often retains strong ideals but none of them ever becomes an effective and planned purpose. In comparison to the psychopath, who, faced with similar failures, tries to find clever justifications, the larval schizophrenic offers vague explanations and then only if he is requested to do so; he is not affectively involved, but this does not mean that, deep inside, a very rich and hyperesthesic world is not playing a role.

I do not know whether the problem of alcoholism in children under five (which our group was among the first to emphasize many years ago) could clarify the question of endogenicity of these mechanisms. Some time ago the possibility was suggested that there are three periods related to drinking: the first until five or six years of age, in which there could be a tendency to excessive drinking if alcohol is readily available; the second period from six to fifteen years of age during which there is seldom excessive drinking; and the third period from fifteen onwards. In our records, there are only three cases of chronic alcoholics who began to drink at the age of ten. Recent investigations by Chilean pediatricians in the slums of Viña del Mar have yielded impressive data on drinking in children. Their findings agree well with the clinical observations in our book *Psiquiatria*, published in 1959.

It remains to mention alcoholic melancholy, a disease involving a deep depression of some weeks' duration, and very often ending in suicide. There is no true indecision or thinking inhibition. The patient feels globally overwhelmed, indifferent to future and past. It is not that he does not see his way towards the future, as in the case of the endogenous depressive, but he wants to get rid of the overwhelming present. These patients let the doctor lead them through treatment without the indecision shown by subdepressives or endogenous depressives. This kind of melancholy is produced by alcohol excesses and it is not found in periods of long abstinence. Bleuler was one of the first to describe it as a definite entity.

Summing up, the problem of alcoholism and endogenous psychosis is still to be clarified. Sometimes it is a symptom of automatism to the commands, of echopraxia, of catatonic impulses, or of clownism. In the manic state it is a source of gaiety and very seldom leads to drunkenness. In epileptic disthymias, endogenous subdepressions, and asthenic personalities, it is used as a drug to mitigate tension, as a "spirit releaser," and in certain cases it leads to inveterate alcoholism. It is also observed as inveterate alcoholism in schizophrenics whose key symptom is anxiety. In larval schizophrenia it appears in an intermittent, inveterate, or alternating form. It is rarely observed in overt endogenous depression, perhaps because of psychic and physical inhibition, or because of feelings of distrust in medicines or guilt feelings associated with massive drinking.

JACK H. MENDELSON

NANCY K. MELLO

Stanley Cobb Laboratories for Psychiatric Research
Massachusetts General Hospital
and Harvard Medical School
Boston, Massachusetts, USA
Present address: National Center for Prevention and
Control of Alcoholism
National Institute of Mental Health
Chevy Chase, Maryland, USA

18

Mechanisms of Physical Dependence in Alcoholism

During the past five years our laboratory has carried out a number of studies designed to elucidate some mechanisms of physical dependence in alcoholics. In 1964 we reported our initial studies of long-term inebriation followed by abrupt cessation of drinking by alcoholic subjects studied in a controlled metabolic ward environment (3). The major findings of this study were:

1

Alcohol withdrawal symptoms were observed in eight of the ten subjects. This observation confirms the findings of Isbell *et al.* (1) that alcohol withdrawal symptoms occur as a result of cessation of drinking and not as a consequence of nutritional deficiency.

2

Phenomena of tolerance and behavioural adaptation exhibited by the subjects during the course of the experiment could be correlated with a number of psychophysiological parameters. Correlations obtained between degree of intoxication, amount of alcohol ingested, and serum alcohol levels suggest that the alcoholic individual has developed adaptive physiological processes which affect both the specific sensitivity of receptor sites to alcohol and the general metabolic degradation of ethanol.

3

The psychomotor disturbances that are often designated as physiological criteria of alcohol withdrawal (i.e. tremor, nystagmus, and alterations of deep tendon reflexes) also may be present during periods of active alcohol consumption. Our data indicate that the significance of these criteria as specific manifestations of alcohol withdrawal needs to be re-evaluated.

4

Alteration of cardiac function (significant tachycardia) was associated with both alcohol ingestion and alcohol withdrawal. Specific determinants of this phenomena have not yet been established.

5

Altered hepatic and renal function (other than

These studies were supported in part by research grants MH 10247 and MH 05619 from the National Institutes of Mental Health, United States Public Health Service.

diuresis) was associated with alcohol ingestion. It is postulated that ethanol, in high dosage and without concomitant nutritional deficit, has direct hepatic and renal toxicity. However, the toxic derangement is reversible.

6

The observed relationship between alcohol ingestion and withdrawal and the onset of alcohol gastritis suggest a new hypothesis concerning the association of alcoholism with gastric disease. Specifically, gastrointestinal tolerance may be an extremely important determinant of the amount and periodicity of ethanol ingestion by the alcoholic individual.

7

Derangement of memory function during heavy alcohol ingestion and subsequent withdrawal was frequently limited to a selective lacunar amnesia for recent events, with relatively little impairment of remote memory processes.

8

Anxiety and depression increased rather than decreased as subjects ingested alcohol over a long period of time. This finding is in direct opposition to the prevailing notions about the effect of alcohol on alcoholics.

Data obtained in this study suggested a number of hypotheses which were examined in subsequent experiments. Studies of ethanol metabolism were extended in experiments designed to measure the rate of metabolism of C^{14} ethanol before and after a three- to fourteen-day experimentally induced period of ethanol intoxication in a group of six chronic alcoholic subjects (7). These subjects were in good health with no evidence of hepatic disorder, and the experiment was carried out under metabolic ward conditions. Five subjects showed an increase in rate of C^{14} ethanol metabolism following drinking as contrasted to pre-drinking values. The rate of C^{14} ethanol metabolism decreased in one subject following drinking. These data indicate that rate of ethanol metabolism may change as a function of amount and duration of ethanol ingestion by alcoholics. It was postulated that the increased rate following drinking related in part to the phenomena of increased behavioural tolerance for alcohol shown by these subjects.

In order to further ascertain the role of magnesium deficiency in alcohol withdrawal symptoms, we have carried out studies of exchangeable magnesium in alcoholic patients (5). Magnesium 28 was administered to 13 alcoholic patients who were admitted to the hospital with symptoms of tremulousness following alcohol withdrawal. These patients were also given an intravenous magnesium tolerance test. Data were compared with values obtained from a group of six healthy chronic alcoholic subjects studied during sobriety. Exchangeable magnesium levels and urine loss of injected magnesium following intravenous magnesium loading were significantly lower in the tremulous group. These findings indicate that alcoholic individuals with withdrawal symptoms have a magnesium deficit which may be associated with poor dietary intake plus a variety of intercurrent illnesses. However, these data do not provide unequivocal support for a direct causal relationship between low serum magnesium levels and the onset of alcohol withdrawal symptoms.

Ethanol ingestion is often associated with abnormalities in the transport and metabolism of lipids. In collaboration with other investigators, we have attempted to examine some aspects of lipid metabolism in experimentally induced intoxication and withdrawal (8). Serum triglyceride and free fatty acid levels were determined in ten subjects with chronic alcoholism who ingested a large amount of alcohol under experimentally controlled conditions during a 24-day period. It was found that at moderate blood ethanol levels, striking increases in serum triglycerides occurred. In three subjects a lactescent serum was produced. With higher blood levels, the previously elevated serum triglycerides fell to or below the initial values. At the time when high blood ethanol levels had been achieved, but not before, increased quantities of free fatty acids were present in the serum. Gas chromatographic studies of fatty acids in the serum suggested that an increased mobilization of fatty acids from adipose tissue probably occurred at a time when serum free fatty acid levels were elevated.

It has been postulated that chronic ethanol intake may affect adrenal cortical activity. We have carried out a preliminary study of serum cortisol levels in alcoholic subjects during experimentally induced ethanol intoxication (6). These data were compared with the assessment of serum cortisol levels of non-alcoholics who were also given large quantities of alcohol over a four-day period. Non-alcoholic subjects showed significant elevations in serum cortisol levels when they developed gastrointestinal illness associated with drinking. Alcoholic subjects had elevations of serum cortisol levels which were associated with drinking, but were not caused by gastrointestinal disorders. Hence there was a different cortisol response produced by alcohol ingestion in the alcoholic and non-alcoholic subjects. In addition, the alcoholic subjects showed very high elevations in serum cortisol levels upon cessation of drinking, when they developed alcohol withdrawal symptoms.

Besides the physiological and biochemical assessments discussed above, we have also carried out studies of operant analysis of drinking behaviour of chronic alcoholics (2, 4). We have used two different operant procedures which permit alcoholic subjects to obtain ethanol on a free choice basis. The general findings of these experiments have been:

1

An alcoholic subject, allowed to control the rate and quantity of his alcohol intake, rapidly ingests enough alcohol to raise his blood level to between 150 and 300 mg/100 ml. All subjects achieved high blood levels within the first 24 hours of the experiment.

2

Despite high concentrations of alcohol in the blood, these subjects exhibited only a mild degree of intoxication, which was characterized by a tendency to become more talkative and boisterous without concomitant slurring of speech, ataxia, or gross disturbances of behaviour. Some subjects showed an occasional degree of moderate intoxication which was manifested by a slurring of speech and irregularity of gait. No subject became markedly intoxicated with severe ataxia, dysarthria, or stupor. The absence of severe intoxication in alcoholic subjects with high blood alcohol levels is in agreement with findings obtained in our laboratory during previous studies of experimentally induced intoxication in alcoholic subjects (3).

3

Once relatively high blood alcohol levels were achieved, subjects tended to maintain stable blood levels, although their daily pattern of working at the operant task fluctuated widely. This finding was surprising, since it would be expected that blood levels would correlate with the amount of alcohol ingested, and that an increase in alcohol intake would occur as metabolic tolerance developed during the course of the drinking period. The wide fluctuation in alcohol intake with associated stable blood alcohol levels observed in this experiment suggests that marked fluctuations in the absorption and/or metabolism of ethanol occur in the alcoholic while he drinks. To determine if significant changes in absorption or metabolism of ethanol occur under conditions similar to those observed in this experiment, appropriate assessment of absorption and metabolism of ethanol should be made at relatively short intervals during the drinking period. Whatever factors may be related to fluctuations in blood alcohol levels, it is remarkable that alcoholic subjects can titrate their alcohol intake to produce stable blood values for long periods of time.

REFERENCES

1
ISBELL, H., FRASER, H.F., WIKLER, A., BELLEVILLE, R.E., & EISENMAN, A.J.
An experimental study of the etiology of "rum fits" and delirium tremens
Quart. J. Stud. Alc., **16**: 1, 1955
2
MELLO, N.K. & MENDELSON, J.H.
Operant analysis of drinking patterns of chronic alcoholics
Nature, **206**: 43, 1965
3
MENDELSON, J.H., ed.
Experimentally induced chronic intoxication and withdrawal in alcoholics
Quart. J. Stud. Alc. suppl. no. 2, 1964
4
MENDELSON, J.H. & MELLO, N.K.
Experimental analysis of drinking behavior of chronic alcoholics
Ann. N.Y. Acad. Sc., **133** (art. 3): 828, 1966

5
MENDELSON, J.H., BARNES, B., MAYMAN, C., &
VICTOR, M.
The determination of exchangeable magnesium
in alcoholic patients
Metabolism, **14**: 88, 1965
6
MENDELSON, J.H., STEIN, S., & MC GUIRE, M.T.
Comparative psychophysiological studies of alcoholic
and non-alcoholic subjects undergoing experimentally
induced ethanol intoxication
Psychosom. Med., **28**: 1, 1966
7
MENDELSON, J.H., STEIN, S., & MELLO, N.K.
Effects of experimentally induced intoxication on
metabolism of ethanol–1-C^{14} in alcoholic subjects
Metabolism, **14**: 1255, 1965
8
SCHAPIRO, R.H., SCHEIG, R.L., DRUMMEY, G.D.,
MENDELSON, J.H., & ISSELBACHER, K.J.
Effect of prolonged ethanol ingestion on the transport
and metabolism of lipids in man
New England J. Med., **272**: 610, 1965

JUAN MARCONI

MARIO POBLETE

MARIO PALESTINI

LAURA MOYA

ANDRES BAHAMONDES

Centre for Experimental Psychiatry
University of Chile and
Psychiatric Hospital and Mental Health Unit of the
National Health Service
Santiago, Chile

19

Role of the Dorsomedial Thalamic Nucleus in "Loss of Control" and "Inability to Abstain" during Ethanol Ingestion

The current concept of alcoholism as a simple pharmacological process of addiction is open to doubt because "loss of control" or "inability to stop" (2, 3, 5) can be produced by the intake of a small quantity of ethanol even after prolonged abstinence. Our neurophysiopathological hypothesis, which has been set forth in two recent papers (6, 8), explains this phenomenon in the following way. If a gamma or intermittent alcoholic takes a moderate amount of liquor after a period of abstinence, the ethanol will, in a few minutes, act as a direct stumulant on two closely intermingled central neuronal circuits: one that regulates the desire for ethanol (12) and another that regulates the appearance of anxiety and displeasure (1, 7, 10). The result is an "inability to stop," a need for more ethanol and a concomitant feeling of displeasure or anxiety which makes this need overpowering. In the case of the delta or inveterate alcoholic, the "inability to abstain" springs from the indirect hyperexcitability of the same central neuronal circuits that have been freed from the effects of ethanol through complete abstinence, or because the drinker takes alcoholic beverages at increasingly long intervals, and consequently, through the diminution of a long-standing alcoholemia.

It can be postulated that the circuits that govern the appearance of a thirst for alcohol are located in the hypothalamus, near the circuits that regulate the desire for water (9). As regards the circuits that regulate the appearance of anxiety in man, there are innumerable clinical and experimental data (4, 11) that point to the dorsomedial nuclei of the thalamus as one of the important links in the chain.

If these nuclei are a major link in the neurophysiological regulation of anxiety, it may be assumed that their coagulation would eliminate the reaction of displeasure produced by ethanol, and the compulsive nature of the pathological desire for ethanol as manifested in "loss of control" or "inability to abstain."

The operation is indicated only in the case of patients with a long record of failure in treatment, without active psychotic complications, who have an obvious "loss of control," suffer from bouts of drinking, and are seriously disabled, physically and/or socially, as a result of their alcoholism. Both the patient and the fa-

TABLE 19–1

PREOPERATIVE CLINICAL CHARACTERISTICS OF ALCOHOLIC
PATIENTS TREATED BY THALAMOTOMY

Patient no.	*1*	*2*	*3*
age and sex	42/male	44/male	41/male
occupation	none	secondary school teacher	textile worker
current diagnosis	intermittent alcoholism; psychopathic personality	intermittent alcoholism; addiction to bromoform; depressive anxiety neurosis	intermittent alcoholism
years of alcoholism	21	20	21
maximum length of drinking bout (days)	4	10	15
maximum interval between bouts (months)	4	7	2
number of previous treatments	25	18	15
social disability	severe	severe	severe
signs of organic impairment in mental tests	negative	slight	slight

mily should be fully informed in advance of the purpose, method, and risks of the operation.

PATIENTS OPERATED ON

The clinical data on the patients who have undergone this operation are given in Table 19-1.

PREOPERATIVE EXAMINATION

After an exhaustive medical and psychological examination, an attempt was made to induce "loss of control" by giving each patient (after an adequate and controlled period of abstinence), on six occasions, a single dose of 0.5 gm/kg BW of ethanol in a 20 per cent solution (7). The results of these tests are shown in Figure 19-1.

In three of the tests, patient no. 1 displayed "loss of control" a few minutes after taking ethanol. In five out of the six tests, he also showed an "inability to abstain" accompanied by an urgent need for more ethanol and acute anxiety four or five hours after ingestion.

Patients no. 2 and 3 showed "loss of control" in all tests. Neither, however, had a desire for more ethanol a few hours after the tests. In patient no. 3 the induced "loss of control" was not accompanied by clinical anxiety.

STUDY WITH ELECTRODES IMPLANTED IN THE DORSOMEDIAL THALAMIC NUCLEI

A comparison was made of the behavioural effects of the simple stimulation of each nucleus and the stimuli produced by ethanol during the induced "loss of control" and "inability to abstain." Two experimental sessions were held first to stimulate each nucleus and thereby discover the parameters that produce a behavioural response. Once these had been identified, a third session was held to study the behavioural response to stimulation before and after the ingestion of ethanol (0.5 gm/kg BW) during "loss of control" (15 to 30 minutes after intake) and "inability to abstain" (six to seven hours after intake). The results are given in Figures 19-2, 19-3, and 19-4.

132 / *Marconi et al.*

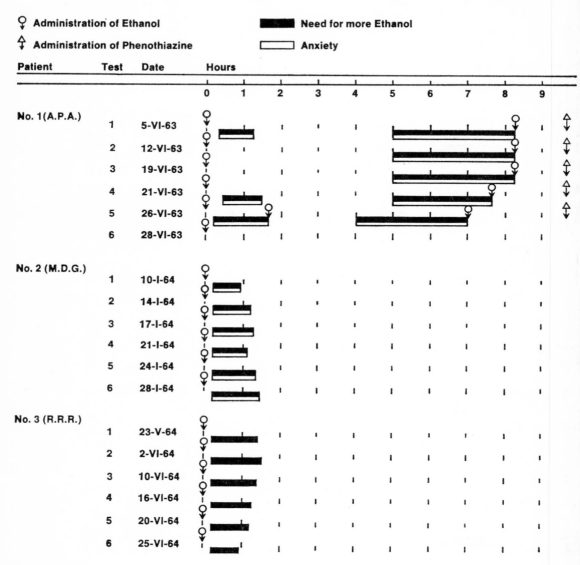

Figure 19-1
Preoperative tests with oral administrations of ethanol (0.5 gm/kg in 20 per cent solution).

To sum up, simple stimulation produced a display of anxiety in all three patients, and in two of them (nos. 1 and 3) it was found that the threshold of the anxiety response to stimulation during "loss of control" and "inability to abstain" tended to be lower than it had been hours or minutes before ingestion. No such comparative study could be made in the case of patient no. 2 because of a state of stress caused by factors unrelated to the experiment (enterocolitis).

POSTOPERATIVE PERIOD

The preliminary work with implanted electrodes made it possible to pinpoint the area to be coagulated. In the case of each patient, the nuclei

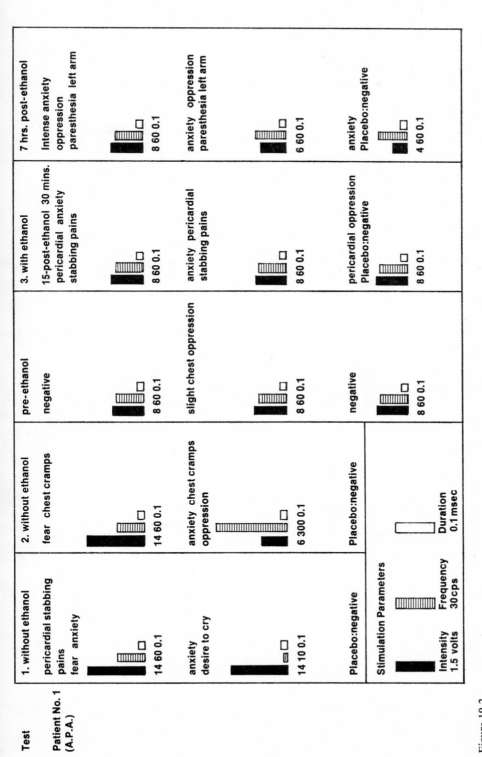

Figure 19-2

Behavioural response and stimulation parameters of the dorsomedial thalamic nucleus before and during an ethanol test (0.5 gm/kg) : patient no. 1.

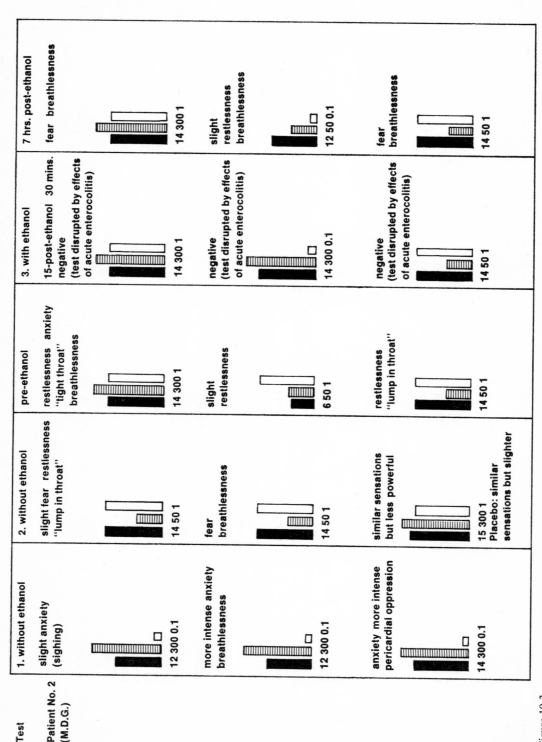

Figure 19-3

Behavioural response and stimulation parameters of the dorsomedial thalamic nucleus before and during an ethanol test (0.5 gm/kg): patient no. 2.

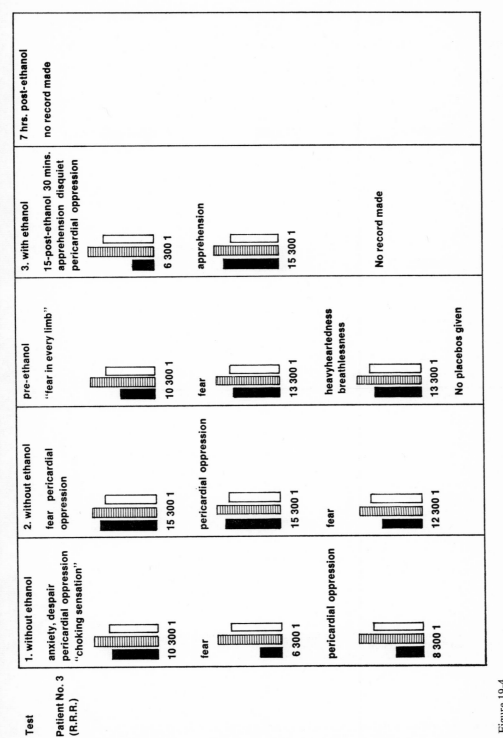

Figure 19-4

Behavioural response and stimulation parameters of the dorsomedial thalamic nucleus before and during an ethanol test (0.5 gm/kg): patient no. 3.

TABLE 19–2

POSTOPERATIVE CLINICAL CHARACTERISTICS OF
ALCOHOLIC PATIENTS TREATED BY THALAMOTOMY AS
REGARDS TYPE OF ORGANIC BRAIN REACTION, ANXIETY
SYNDROME, AND PATTERN OF DRINKING

	First six months after operation
patient 1	
brain syndrome	definite psychic and neurological signs in the first 25 days; slight signs in following months
anxiety syndrome	complaints of more intense anxiety than before the operation; heavy tranquillizer intake
alcohol intake	intake of alcohol on three separate occasions without "inability to stop" but on two of them with "inability to abstain"
patient 2	
brain syndrome	lack of organic signs, even in the immediate postoperative period
anxiety syndrome	no change
alcohol intake	three months of abstinence; during the next three months drank alcohol during drinking bouts with bromoform; no signs of induced "inability to stop" with ethanol
patient 3	
brain syndrome	clear psychic and organic signs, without neurological damage; these lessened considerably after the fourth month
anxiety syndrome	more intense anxiety felt than before the operation
alcohol intake	sporadic heavy drinking marked by an "inability to stop" but without bouts of drinking and without the "inability to abstain"
	Six to thirty-six months after operation
patient 1	
brain syndrome	no signs of organic brain syndrome, save reduction in word fluency capacity in tests
anxiety syndrome	definite lessening of anxiety, irritability, and impulsivity; low tranquillizer intake
alcohol intake	six months of sporadic drinking without "inability to stop"; total abstinence during last 24 months; improved social adjustment
patient 2	
brain syndrome	no signs
anxiety syndrome	no change
alcohol intake	between the sixth and eleventh months the patient had three serious drinking bouts with bromoform and alcohol; during the third he fell into a coma and died
patient 3	
brain syndrome	very slight signs of organic brain syndrome (concretism in tests and perseveration in work performance)
anxiety syndrome	no anxiety apparent
alcohol intake	frequent intake of small quantities of alcohol without displaying an "inability to stop" or "inability to abstain"; very occasionally heavy drinking and inebriety; no bouts have occurred except for one seven-day relapse in July 1966; social adjustment is better

Figure 19-5

Postoperative tests with oral administration of ethanol (0.5 gm/kg in 20 per cent solution).

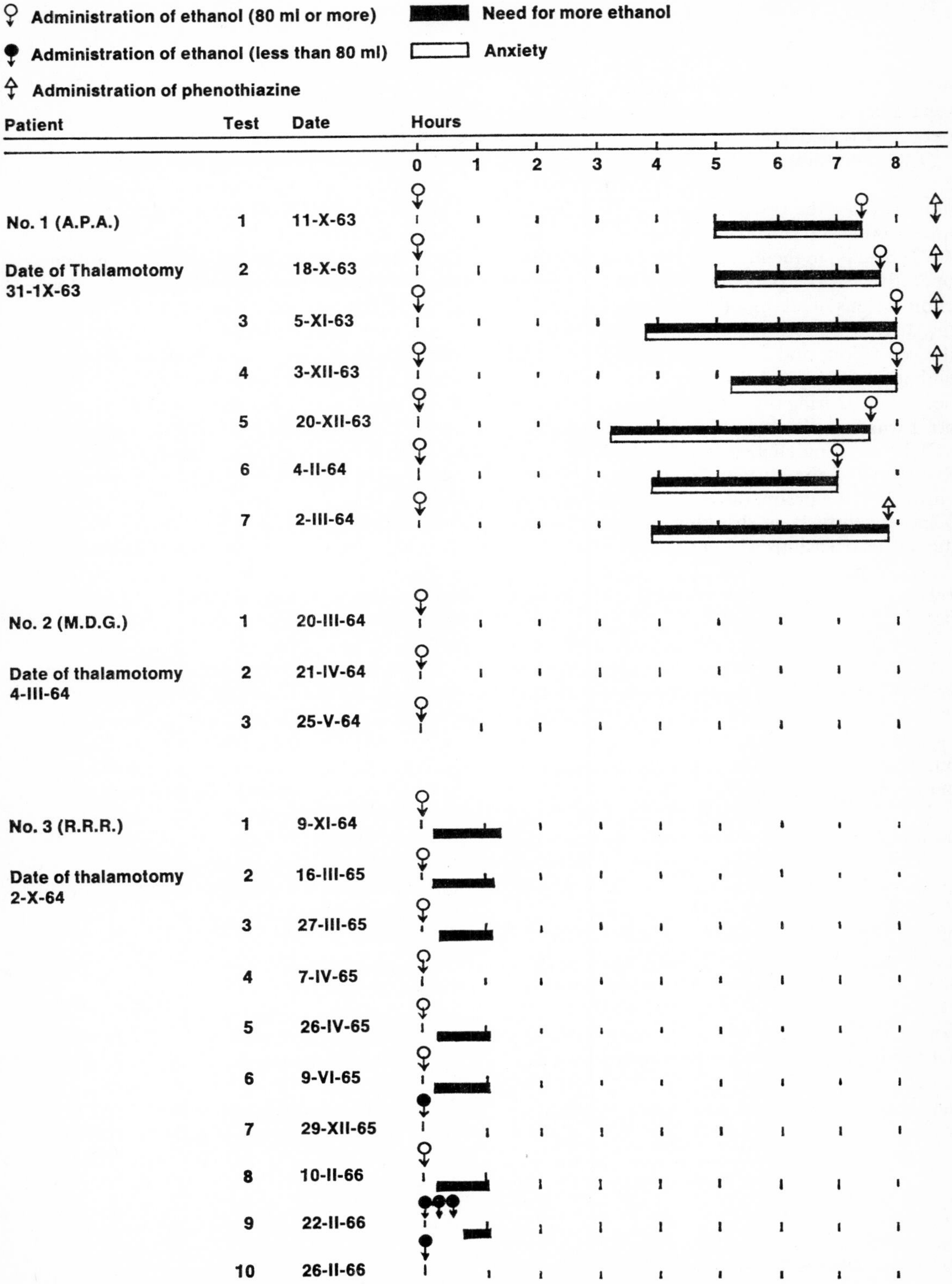

♀ Administration of ethanol (80 ml or more)

● Administration of ethanol (less than 80 ml)

⇕ Administration of phenothiazine

Need for more ethanol

☐ Anxiety

Patient	Test	Date	Hours

0   1   2   3   4   5   6   7   8

No. 1 (A.P.A.) 1 11-X-63

Date of Thalamotomy
31-1X-63 2 18-X-63

3 5-XI-63

4 3-XII-63

5 20-XII-63

6 4-II-64

7 2-III-64

No. 2 (M.D.G.) 1 20-III-64

Date of thalamotomy
4-III-64 2 21-IV-64

3 25-V-64

No. 3 (R.R.R.) 1 9-XI-64

Date of thalamotomy
2-X-64 2 16-III-65

3 27-III-65

4 7-IV-65

5 26-IV-65

6 9-VI-65

7 29-XII-65

8 10-II-66

9 22-II-66

10 26-II-66

on the left and right sides were coagulated separately with an interval of about eight days between the two interventions.

The symptoms of organic brain reaction, anxiety, and drinking habits in the first six months after the operation and in the subsequent follow-up period are indicated in Table 19-2. Briefly, in the first six months of the postoperative period, patients nos. 1 and 3 showed clinical signs of an organic brain reaction, suffered from more intense anxiety than before the operation, and drank sporadically, without embarking on a real drinking bout, on three occasions. During the follow-up period, patient no. 1 was completely abstinent for 24 months, and became much better adjusted socially. Symptoms of anxiety were negligible, as compared with the preoperative period. Patient no. 3 has recently been drinking moderately on numerous occasions without the appearance of "loss of control" or withdrawal symptoms. In July 1966, however, he engaged in a drinking bout lasting for seven days.

Concurrently with the clinical check-ups, the ethanol ingestion tests were repeated during the first six months of the postoperative period in the case of each patient (see Figure 19-5), demonstrating the absence of "loss of control" but the persistence of an "inability to abstain" in patient no. 1.

In patient no. 3, it was later found that an induced "loss of control" continued to exist. A year after the operation on this patient, a second series of four tests were carried out. These showed that the threshold for the appearance of "loss of control" had risen considerably. It was necessary for him to take at least 80 to 100 cc of the 20 per cent solution before physical dependence manifested itself. Before the operation, a very small quantity of alcohol had sufficed to bring this on. After the operation, this patient had no more drinking bouts, except for one in July 1966, and was better adjusted socially.

DISCUSSION

The positive results obtained in the treatment of patient no. 1 were: (*a*) A lowering of the threshold for the appearance of anxiety as a behavioural response to the stimulation of the dorsomedial thalamic nuclei during induced physical dependence on ethanol ("loss of control" and "inability to abstain"). If this finding is confirmed in a larger number of cases and does not manifest itself during the reaction to ethanol in the absence of physical dependence, it will bear out the hypothesis that the nuclei take part in the regulation of physical dependence in the alcoholic patient. (*b*) The nonappearance of an induced "loss of control" in seven postoperative tests with ethanol. (*c*) The clinical disappearance of "loss of control" and of the drinking bouts. (*d*) Total abstinence during the 24 months following the operation owing to the patient's lack of desire for alcohol, and the consequent improvement in his social adjustment.

Running counter to the hypothesis that the neuronal circuits governing "loss of control" and "inability to abstain" are identical is the fact that the latter manifested itself in six of the seven postoperative tests with ethanol and in two periods of clinical ingestion of alcohol.

In the case of patient no. 2, the treatment must be considered a failure, because the patient continued to have serious drinking bouts after the operation (with ingestion of bromoform and alcohol), and died as a consequence of one of them. There are, however, clinical indications that through a technical mistake a mute cerebral area may have been coagulated instead of the dorsomedial thalamic nuclei. Thus, an organic brain syndrome did not appear even immediately after the operation, and the level of anxiety failed to rise during the early months of the postoperative period, as in the other two patients.

The positive results obtained with patient no. 3 were: (*a*) The lowering of the threshold of anxiety as a behavioural response to the stimulation of the dorsomedial thalamic nuclei during the induced "loss of control." (*b*) The almost complete absence of drinking bouts in the postoperative period with a corresponding decrease in social maladjustment. After being in a state of drunkenness, the patient did not suffer from withdrawal symptoms the following day. This was confirmed on numerous occasions at the hospital and by his relatives, and differed sharply from his preoperative pattern of drinking, which was characterized by regular bouts lasting sometimes for as long as 15 days. (*c*) The gradual rise in the threshold for the appearance of the induced "loss of control" during the postoperative period.

Contradicting our hypothesis is the fact that after 22 months of postoperative drinking without bouts, the patient recently had a relapse lasting for seven days.

SUMMARY

A report has been made on the treatment of three alcoholics who were severely maladjusted socially and had a history of 15 to 25 periods of treatment ending in failure. The treatment in the present instance consisted in the coagulation of the dorsomedial thalamic nuclei.

The anxiety that appeared as a behavioural response to the stimulation of the nuclei manifested itself at a lower voltage (descent of threshold) during an induced "loss of control" and "inability to abstain" after ethanol ingestion.

One patient has been followed up for 36 months since the operation. One died 11 months after the operation during a heavy drinking bout with bromoform and alcohol. A third patient is now in the twenty-third month of postoperative study.

In the case of patient no. 1, the clinical drinking bouts and induced "loss of control" ceased after treatment, although induced "inability to abstain" persisted. The patient is better adjusted socially and has been completely abstinent for the last 24 months.

Patient no. 2 failed to respond to treatment, and continued to have heavy drinking bouts with bromoform and alcohol. It is possible that, owing to a technical mistake, the nuclei were not coagulated.

In the case of patient no. 3, clinical withdrawal symptoms have disappeared during the postoperative period, and there have been no drinking bouts, save for one relapse of seven days in July 1966, twenty-two months after the operation. His social adjustment has improved, and the threshold at which "loss of control" appears has risen.

REFERENCES

1
BOVARD, E.
The balance between negative and positive brain system activity
Persp. Biol. Med., **6**: 116, 1962

2
JELLINEK, E.M.
Phases in the drinking history of alcoholics
Quart. J. Stud. Alc., **7**: 1, 1946

3
JELLINEK, E.M.
The disease concept of alcoholism
New Haven: Hillhouse Press, 1960

4
KALINOWSKY, L. & HOCH, P.
Somatic treatments in psychiatry
New York: Grune & Stratton, 1961

5
MARCONI, J.
The concept of alcoholism
Quart. J. Stud. Alc., **20**: 216, 1959

6
MARCONI, J.
El concepto de enfermedad en el alcoholismo
Acta psiquiat. psicol. Am. lat., **11**: 330, 1965

7
MARCONI, J., FINK, K., & MOYA, L.
Experimental study on alcoholics with an "inability to stop"
Brit. J. Psychiat., **113**: 543, 1967
Abstract

8
MARCONI, J., POBLETE, M., PALESTINI, M., *et al.*
Un nuevo enfoque del tratamiento del alcohólico grave recidivante
Acta psiquiat. psicol. Am. lat., **11**: 340, 1965

9
O'KELLY, L.L.
The psychophysiology of motivation
Ann. Rev. Psychol., **14**: 57, 1963

10
OLDS, J.
Hypothalamic substrates of reward
Physiol. Rev., **42**: 553, 1962

11
PALESTINI, M., GALLARDO, R., MARCONI, J., & POBLETE, M.
Registro y estimulación del nucleo dorsomediano del tálamo en pacientes con electrodos dejados a permanencia
Leído en la 6a
Reunión Anual de la Asoc. Argentina de Neurocir. Tucumán, 1964
(To be published)

12
WILLIAMS, R.J.
Biochemical individuality and cellular nutrition: prime factors in alcoholism
Quart. J. Stud. Alc., **20**: 452, 1959

VLADIMIR HUDOLIN

Institute for the Study and Prevention of Alcoholism
Dr. M. Stojanovič Hospital
Zagreb, Yugoslavia

20

Acute Complications of Alcoholism

It is very difficult to present in a relatively short time all the problems associated with acute complications of alcoholism especially since there are various conceptions of the nature of this disorder and many other terminological difficulties. The great lack of a standard terminology considerably hampers every discussion on the topic, and the difficulties encountered in reporting on acute complications of alcoholism are even greater. The very term "chronic alcoholism" does not always refer to the same syndrome, but differs from author to author.

The syndrome being so vaguely defined, what then should we understand by acute complications of the condition? It is obvious that one must first limit the area to be dealt with in this paper. From the many definitions of alcoholism, let us for illustration's sake take the one given by a group of experts of the World Health Organization. This definition has added to the diagnosis of alcoholism some social and economic symptoms and problems of interpersonal relations experienced by persons indulging regularly in excessive drinking. This definition alone indicates that "acute complications" can include a very wide range of symptoms. But other definitions also incorporate in varying degrees the notion of adverse social and economic effects and behavioural changes occurring in alcoholics.

The question evidently is whether by "acute complications" we should understand only complications of acute inebriation, or only those of chronic alcoholism, or both. Furthermore, should these complications include only acute psychiatric complications, acute neurological complications, or only complications affecting individual organs other than the brain (e.g. the liver)? Should they also comprise acute social problems, acute forensic problems, or acute economic complications, and should we also include here the acute problems of interpersonal relations? Should acute complications also embrace injuries at work caused by alcohol, and traffic accidents attributable to alcoholic intoxication?

It is arbitrary to restrict attention to one of these aspects alone. On the other hand, to try to present all aspects in a paper on acute complications resulting from indulgence in alcoholic drinks would mean to describe virtually the entire problem of alcoholism. Difficulties tend to become greater still if one tries to make a distinction between acute and chronic alcoholism and treat them separately. Should an acute state of inebriation be considered alcoholism? Do acute complications, in other words, acute intoxication itself, fall within the framework of this theme, or should acute alcoholism be taken to mean only the so-called pathological states of inebriation, that is, states that differ from some normal state of intoxication? Difficulties arise at the onset, in attempting to distinguish a normal state of inebriation from a so-called pathological state. Every state of inebriation may be viewed as pathological.

Since many problems discussed in this Symposium fall within the category of acute complications of alcoholism, as I see them, I shall confine myself simply to the description of those acute complications not fully covered elsewhere.

Acute complications of alcoholism might be classified as follows:

1) Acute complications of acute alcoholism (i.e., the state of alcoholic intoxication)
a) acute alcoholic intoxication
b) pathological states of inebriation
2) Acute somatic complications of chronic alcoholism
a) neurological complications, including alcoholic encephalopathies and traumas of the central nervous system
b) hepatic complications
c) pancreatic complications
d) cardiac complications
e) complications of heart and blood circulation
f) acute hypoglycemic conditions
g) complications in other organs
3) Acute psychiatric complications of chronic alcoholism
a) alcoholic psychoses
b) acute neurotic reactions
c) suicide
d) acute abstinence symptoms
4) Epilepsy
5) Acute complications in the course of treatment

6) Acute social complications
a) family complications
b) complications at work
c) complications in interpersonal relations in general
7) Traffic accidents and injuries at work
8) Dependence on drugs
9) Susceptibility to disease

I shall now attempt to describe briefly some of these groups of acute complications (see Figures 20-1 to 20-8 inclusive).

ACUTE COMPLICATIONS OF ACUTE ALCOHOLISM

By acute alcoholic intoxication we should understand an acute state of inebriation when it occurs for the first time in one's life, when it occurs more frequently, and finally when it occurs as an acute manifestation of dependence on alcohol in chronic alcoholics. The severity of acute alcoholic intoxication can be measured objectively by the concentration of alcohol in the blood, and by the clinical symptoms manifested by the patient. However, the blood alcohol level and clinical symptoms need not necessarily always coincide. In a chronic alcoholic the metabolism has been severely upset and individual organs damaged, so that acute intoxication does not affect him in the same way it affects a healthy person. It can be particularly severe in a chronic alcoholic with prior organic lesions. In addition, his alcohol tolerance is changed and he lacks certain blood factors which are indispensable for normal metabolism. Treatment of acute alcoholic intoxication, particularly in the case of high blood alcohol levels, is one of the most difficult problems of modern medicine because of lack of reliable means to accelerate the metabolism of alcohol. Death during acute intoxication occurs in a relatively large number of alcoholics.

Particularly severe complications of acute alcoholic intoxication occur in children, since, because of their small body weight, it takes only a minor amount of alcohol to produce a severe clinical picture. And it can quite easily

Figure 20-1
Map of Yugoslavia, showing the six federal republics.

happen that a child will take such a small amount. Acute intoxication in children in Yugoslavia, which is a wine-growing country, is notably common during the period of fruit brandy distillation. It leaves a relatively prolonged clinical picture of the psycho-organic syndrome, which can even reflect permanent, irreversible cerebral lesions. A similar clinical picture also can be seen in children who have taken some alcohol by mistake, for example through an enema, or as a lark in the absence of their parents. Acute alcoholic intoxication in children is often lethal.

The fact should be stressed in particular that in severe alcoholic intoxication it is very difficult to make the right diagnosis, so that each case should be carefully observed until the patient is completely sober to avoid serious diagnostic mistakes, which are unfortunately still rather frequent.

Many authors have been concerned with the problem of therapy for acute alcoholic intoxication, and have advocated various preparations which allegedly speed the disappearance of al-

cohol from the body and thereby hasten the sobering of the patient. Unfortunately, there is as yet no definite evidence that any of these are really effective in this regard. No significant changes have been recently reported in the treatment of severe alcoholic intoxication. Among all the preparations recommended to date we have found centrophenoxine (Lucidril) to produce relatively good results. Good results in individual cases have also been recorded with hemineurine.

Pathological states of inebriation include those disorders occurring during drinking which in their characteristic features differ from so-called normal conditions of intoxication, and which by their psychopathological nature are an indication of more profound disturbances of the patient's personality. I intentionally use the word "state" in the plural since I consider that pathological inebriety is not a single, strictly limited psychopathological entity.

Pathological states of inebriation can manifest themselves in the form of the classical clinical syndrome described in the literature, or they

Figure 20-2
Location of mental hospitals, university neuropsychiatric clinics, and psychiatric wards in general hospitals in Croatia.

may show a different clinical picture in which an acute state of confusion or some other acute psychiatric symptoms prevail. The pathological state of inebriation is in fact an unclear entity. Many authors make a distinction between the classical picture and so-called atypical pathological reactions in the course of acute inebriation. But since all these clinical pictures are fairly well known, I do not propose to dwell on them. I think that the tendency to differentiate individual syndromes has established itself partly under the pressure of forensic practice where the degree of responsibility for the perpetration of an offence is differentiated according to individual syndromes.

Jellinek attempted to classify the various forms of alcoholism, denoting each by a letter of the Greek alphabet. He reported as a separate form alcoholism in Finnish forest workers, who occasionally consume large quantities of alcohol and display markedly aggressive behaviour as a result. Some authors consider that this form of alcoholism is conditioned by the peculiar mode of life of the Finnish forest worker. But similar behaviour has also been described in various groups of alcoholics in other countries. Some of these forms are very similar to the so-called classical pathological state of inebriation, or to pathological reactions manifesting themselves during alcoholic

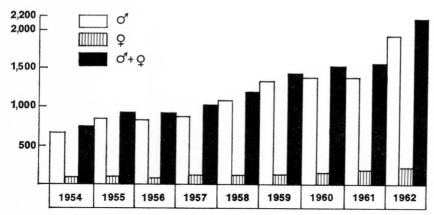

Figure 20-3
Increase in the number of alcoholics treated in psychiatric hospitals in Croatia, 1954–62.

intoxication. This form of alcoholism is probably conditioned by specific ecological factors since it usually occurs in certain limited areas only. In Croatia, one of the federated units of Yugoslavia, this form is relatively frequent and appears in clearly delimited territories. In these areas almost all offenses against life and body are associated with alcoholism. A significant element of this form of alcoholism is loss of control, without, however, an inability to abstain.

I think it appears on the basis of the foregoing that the pathological state of inebriation, the individual forms of pathological reactions in an acute state of inebriation, and the aforementioned aggressive form of alcoholism represent different degrees of a special form of alcoholism. Following Jellinek's system of classification, I propose to call it "zeta alcoholism." The treatment of such cases of alcoholism is relatively complicated. In our case material these were mostly patients with a pyknic constitution, although it is not clear to what extent this constitution can possibly elicit this form of alcoholism.

ACUTE SOMATIC COMPLICATIONS OF CHRONIC ALCOHOLISM

In the course of the last few years a large number of alcoholics have been treated in our institute. All the patients have been subjected to systematic clinical and laboratory examinations. Thus, *inter alia*, pneumoencephalography has been carried out in over 600 chronic alcoholics. In 90 per cent of the cases a more or less developed cerebral atrophy was found, usually in a combined cortical and subcortical form. It is likely that the volume of cerebral lesions caused by alcohol also plays a role in the formation of a certain specific picture of chronic alcoholism.

It seems to us that alcoholic encephalopathies, which sometimes occur in a very acute form, should also be included with neurological complications. On the basis of our own case material and the pneumoencephalograms of a large number of alcoholics, we do not believe that most encephalopathies (Wernicke's disease, Marchiafava-Bignami's disease, etc.) represent clearly distinguished entities. Rather we think that one and the same pathological cerebral process underlies most alcoholic encephalopathies, and that the clinical picture of individual encephalopathies depends on the extent of the process and the location of the most pronounced changes. This group also includes craniocerebral traumas in alcoholics.

Acute complications of alcoholism can also occur as a result of secondary lesions in individual organs (the liver, pancreas, heart ,etc.). Since these lesions are dealt with in other pa-

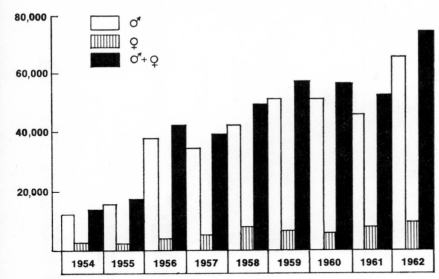

Figure 20-4

Increase in the number of days spent by alcoholics in psychiatric institutions in Croatia, 1954–62.

pers, there is no reason to describe them in detail here. The role of chronic alcoholism in acute complications cannot always be clearly singled out (e.g., in acute pancreatitis or acute decomposition of the liver).

We should, however, mention acute hypoglycemic conditions, since if they are not taken into account considerable diagnostic difficulties may result. The pathophysiology of hypoglycemic states has not yet been entirely settled. Cases have been reported that had normal storage of glycogen. Determination of sugar levels in the blood is today part of the routine examination of patients with a picture of acute alcoholic complications.

ACUTE PSYCHIATRIC COMPLICATIONS OF ALCOHOLISM

The acute psycho-organic syndrome, which appears either in the form of the classical delirium tremens or in the form of pre-delirious clinical pictures, or a prolonged pre-delirious state, has recently been on the increase in most countries. The number of cases of delirium

tremens in Croatia trebled from 1954 to 1962. In recent years instances of a prolonged predelirious picture have become much more frequent than before, while, on the other hand, patients with frank delirium tremens are no longer in the severe state frequently seen in the early post–World War II years. As regards both delirium tremens and pre-delirious states, little new has been discovered in recent years, except that the latest psychopharmacological preparations have helped considerably to improve the prognosis. In addition to these drugs, treatment should also be carried out with other up-to-date therapeutic methods: rehydration, care, vitamin preparations, and cardiovascular therapy.

Particularly interesting are the clinical pictures of pre-delirious states in children, which we have had an opportunity to observe in a large number of cases. These are children from wine-growing regions who begin to drink in their earliest childhood, become dependent on alcohol, and develop pre-delirious or delirious states. The clinical picture does not differ essentially from that in adults. The prognosis of the psychosis is good, but irreversible effects often take place. The prognosis of alcoholism itself in such cases is exceptionally complicated,

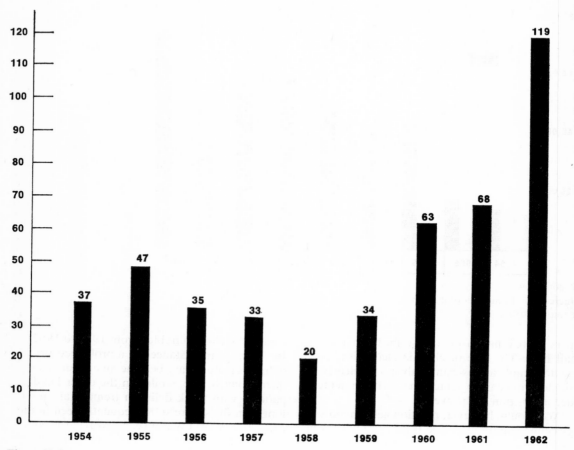

Figure 20-5
Alcoholic psychoses treated in psychiatric hospitals in Croatia, 1954–62.

since severe disturbance in the personality occurs even before its basic characteristics have had time to develop.

Acute psychotic complications in alcoholics include, as is well known, the psychosis of jealousy, alcoholic hallucinosis, various paranoid manifestations, and other atypical forms of psychosis. I think that we should not dwell too much on alcoholic hallucinosis since it has been the subject of many papers recently, and opinions are still divided. In some instances it is probably a schizophrenic state tinted by alcoholism, and in others mainly chronic psychoorganic syndromes.

Much more attention should be devoted in future to the link between a depressive psychosis, or a depressive reaction, and alcoholism. Special attention must be paid to acute paranoid reactions in alcoholics, reactions which we have recently had an increasing opportunity to note in our case material. We have the impression that it is the pre-morbid constitution of the alcoholic after all that plays the principal role in the development of such reactions, although this is not always the case with the schizophrenic variety.

No definite judgment has been reached yet as to the link between depression and alcoholism, but it is clear that chronic and excessive indulgence in drinking may trigger a latent picture of pre-morbid depression, while, on the one hand,

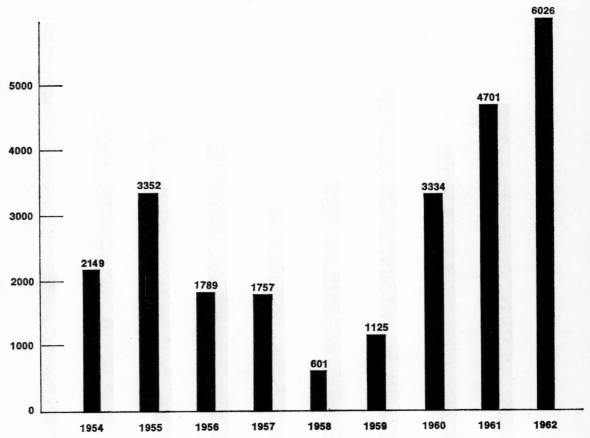

Figure 20-6
Number of days spent by patients with alcoholic psychoses in psychiatric hospitals in Croatia, 1954–62.

the depressive picture may be a direct consequence of alcoholism.

Acute neurotic reactions in the course of alcoholism are more frequent than is usually thought or reported. A large number of such cases are ascribed to the pre-morbid personality of the alcoholic. Here alcoholism is often considered secondary to the neurosis. But it is difficult to accept the view that in wine-growing countries every person is *a priori* mentally upset. It seems to me that such views stem from the fact that in almost all cases alcoholism tends to produce psychic changes, and it is difficult to appraise objectively the pre-morbid personality of an alcoholic after an average of ten years'

addiction to alcohol. It should be noted that individual psychotherapeutic methods in the case of neurotic reactions in alcoholics do not yield particularly good results.

EPILEPSY IN ALCOHOLISM

The occurrence of one or more epileptic seizures is a relatively frequent phenomenon in alcoholics: in acute inebriation, in the course of pathological reactions in acute inebriation, at the beginning of the clinical picture of delirium tremens, and so forth. These isolated seizures are a serious complication and can be a direct

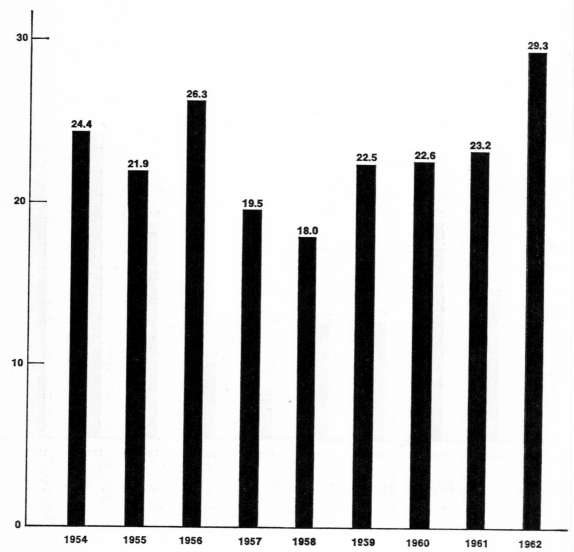

Figure 20-7

Median duration of sick leave per year of an alcoholic in Croatia, 1954–62.

cause of death.

In addition to isolated epileptic attacks, real alcohol epilepsy may occur. The data in the literature differ as to the number of such cases, depending to a large extent on the case material of individual authors. Thus, while some authors observe groups of epileptics and look for alcoholics among them, others describe epileptics in groups of alcoholics.

We have observed a relatively large number of epileptic cases which are most probably related to alcoholism. While we rarely found genuine epileptic EEG manifestations, EEG findings indicating cortical lesions were relatively frequent. The main features in such cases were in the alpha rhythm. Alcoholic epilepsy occurs when definite, irreversible cerebral lesions have occurred. If the patient stops drinking his state usually improves and the number of attacks decreases. The EEG picture also shows some im-

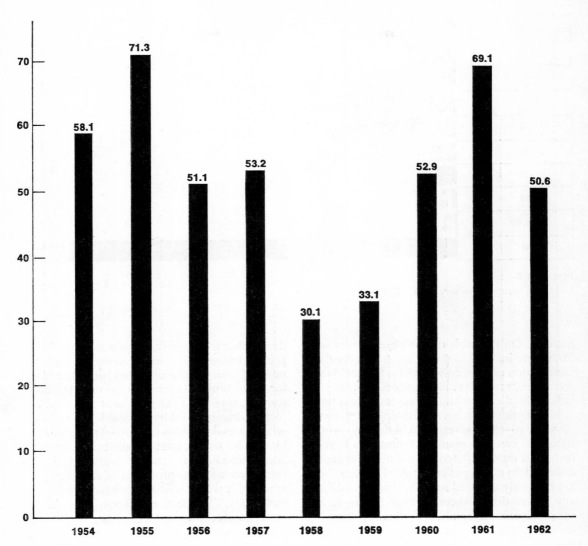

Figure 20-8
Median duration of sick leave per year for alcoholic psychosis in Croatia, 1954–62.

provement, although complete normalization rarely occurs.

COMPLICATIONS DURING TREATMENT

Acute complications occurring in the course of the treatment of alcoholism have not been sufficiently dealt with and have not had sufficient coverage in contemporary medical literature.

Here we have several clinical pictures. One of them, which can constitute a great danger, has the appearance of very complicated abstinence symptoms accompanied by a state of confusion. This complication can be relatively easily prevented with modern psychopharmacological drugs.

Another complication in the course of treatment can be an acute paranoid reaction. Such reactions have been relatively frequent in our

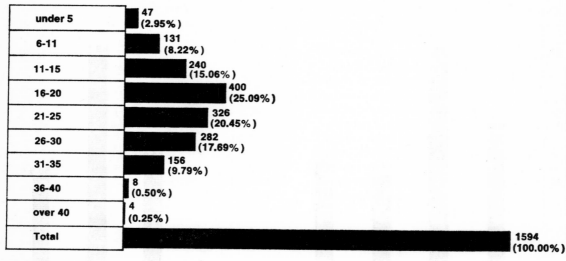

under 5		47 (2.95%)
6-11		131 (8.22%)
11-15		240 (15.06%)
16-20		400 (25.09%)
21-25		326 (20.45%)
26-30		282 (17.69%)
31-35		156 (9.79%)
36-40		8 (0.50%)
over 40		4 (0.25%)
Total		1594 (100.00%)

Figure 20-9
Length of occupational service of 1,594 alcoholics.

patients. On the basis of our observations so far, we are inclined to think that the pre-morbid constitution of the alcoholic plays the decisive role. These reactions may also occur in alcoholics who did not manifest previously any paranoid ideas or symptoms of pathological jealousy.

Acute psychiatric reactions in the course of treatment can also manifest themselves in the form of a marked deterioration of the general mental state of the patient. Indeed, patients who are relatively adjusted and who do not manifest any severe disturbances in their family and social life can, after sudden abstinence, show severe syndromes of maladjustment which call for very cautious evaluation and careful treatment. There seems to be a group of alcoholics, albeit only a small one, in whom the general mental state deteriorates after discontinuation of drinking. In most cases observed by us certain results have been achieved with the use of psychopharmacological preparations. However, the situation must be carefully assessed and efforts made to prevent severe complications, particularly severe states of confusion, depressive reactions, and even suicide.

This brings us to an important complication that occurs both during alcoholism itself and during therapy, namely, suicide in alcoholics. It is a relatively frequent occurrence, for which no satisfactory explanation has been offered so far. An abrupt discontinuation of drinking sometimes results in an early acute depressive picture accompanied by suicidal ideas, or in a mild depression which the patient sometimes hides in his wish to continue to abstain. In the later course of treatment, the depression develops into an acute problem and can even lead to a suicide which at first glance seems to be motiveless. The question that poses itself in such cases is complex. Most authors apparently regard these patients as pre-morbid persons who indulge in drinking only as a means of solving their tensions and depressions. The moment they are deprived of this means they tend to become depressed and contemplate suicide.

In our case material we have had many cases of depression in the course of treatment, and it seems to us that in intellectually well-preserved alcoholics, even those who have otherwise not been burdened with pre-morbid depressions, abstinence itself and their ability to comprehend the situation in which they find themselves can lead to depressive reactions. Recently we carried out a systematic testing of alcoholics during the first few days of abstinence for possible depressive ideas, and wherever a rather pronounced depressive element was noted, preventive antidepressive treatment was initiated. Relatively good results were achieved. There are, however, a few cases where depression becomes an almost permanent state and treatment must be continued for a prolonged period of time. There seems to be a group of patients where it would be better if an improvement could be achieved with treatment which would enable them to recover their ability to control their drinking. However, I do not believe in the possibility of such improvement with present-day therapeutic methods.

Complications that may occur in the course of treatment with disulfiram and apomorphine are well known. We find that disulfiram therapy without the reaction test is equally successful and has fewer complications. Of course, complications in the course of disulfiram therapy demand intensive psychotherapy and work with the family.

Finally, a few words should be said about the delicate problem of acute complications due to psychotherapy. Severe and even lethal complications of psychotherapeutic treatment are neither often nor easily talked about. But it is known that an inappropriate psychotherapeutic procedure can lead to various adverse mental reactions and even suicide. Psychotherapeutic treatment must be entrusted to experienced therapists who are free of *any* (even concealed) aggressive attitudes towards alcoholics. Unfortunately, it is common to find that the therapist only outwardly accepts alcoholism as a disease, while emotionally refusing to accept this view. (See Figures 20-9 to 20-13, inclusive.)

ACUTE SOCIAL COMPLICATIONS OF ALCOHOLISM

So far we have spoken mainly about medical complications of alcoholism, but alcoholism according to most definitions also has an important social aspect. Indeed, according to some definitions, social symptoms of alcoholism are even more critical in the diagnostic sense than somatic-psychiatric ones. Consequently, acute social decompensations in chronic alcoholics represent acute complications of alcoholism which call for swift therapeutic intervention. It is clear that in this therapeutic intervention the principal role will be played by sociotherapy, and the physician will rely heavily on the social worker for help. These acute social decompensations can appear as a result of the gradual deterioration of the personality of the alcoholic. Sometimes, however, they may be elicited by occurrences which the alcoholic indirectly provokes in his surroundings.

It is understandable that such social decompensations will often be combined with psychiatric problems. Most commonly, acute social problems will be accompanied by a depressive reaction with the danger of suicide. The scope of this paper does not permit extensive discussion of the social complications of alcoholism, but we should bear them in mind within the framework of acute complications of alcoholism.

ACUTE COMPLICATIONS OF ALCOHOLISM WHICH MANIFEST THEMSELVES IN INJURIES AT WORK OR TRAFFIC ACCIDENTS

Both injuries at work and traffic accidents represent a special problem of chronic alcoholism. Since this topic will be dealt with in other papers, I shall do no more than mention it within the framework I have set out. (See Figures 20-14 to 20-22, inclusive.)

DEPENDENCE ON OTHER DRUGS

There is another acute complication which perhaps need not be separately dealt with, but which I wish to single out because of the importance and the specific character of the problems involved. What I have in mind here is the combination of alcoholism and addiction to other drugs. Such a combination can constitute an acute complication during the treatment of alcoholism when after a successful abstinence the alcoholic begins to take a habit-forming drug. The relatively frequent combination of

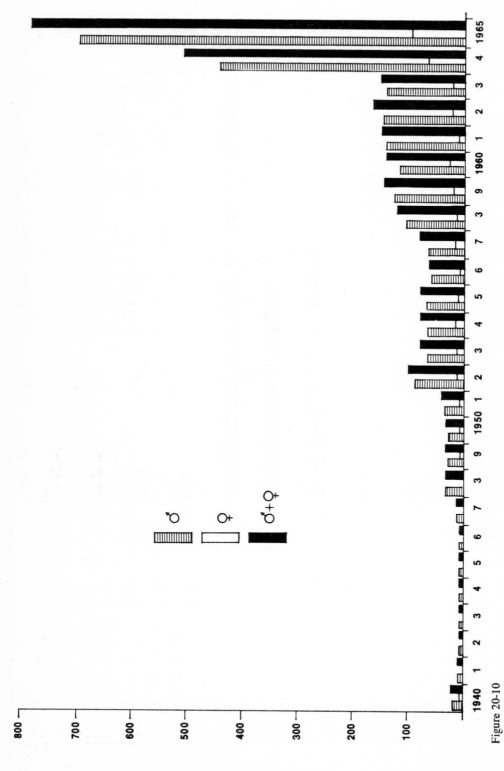

Figure 20-10

Increase in admissions of alcoholics to the psychiatric ward of the general hospital in Zagreb, 1940–1965.

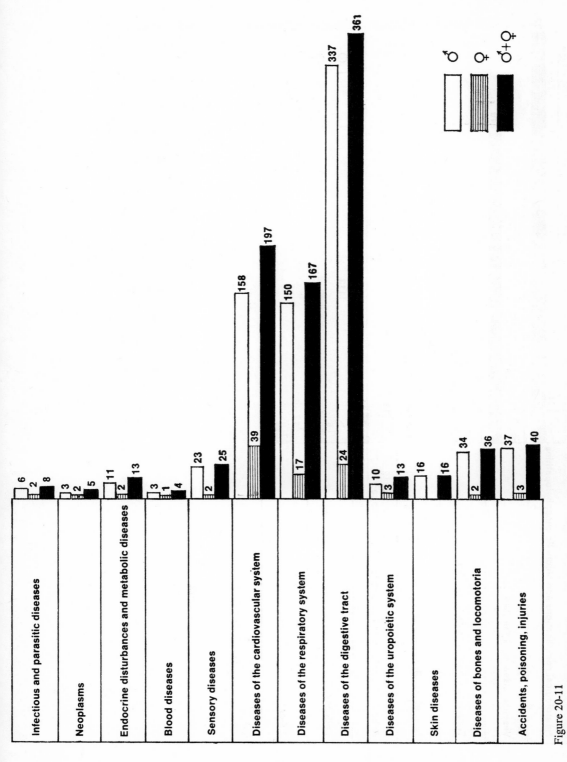

Figure 20-11
Acute somatic complications of alcoholic patients at the time of admission.

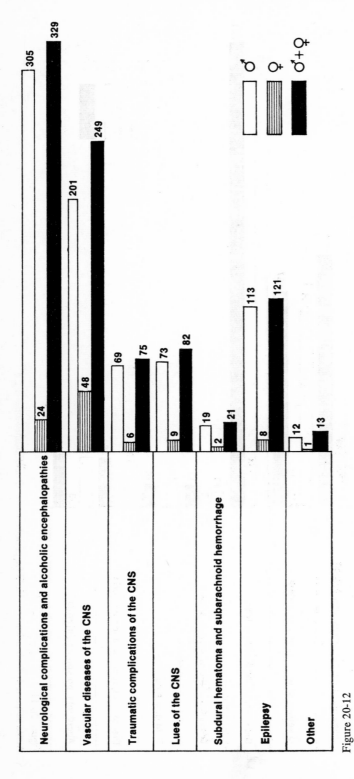

Figure 20-12
Acute neurological complications of alcoholic patients at the time of admission.

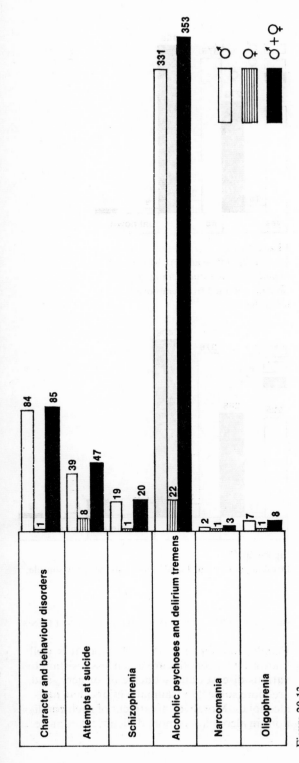

Figure 20-13
Psychiatric complications of alcoholic patients at the time of admission.

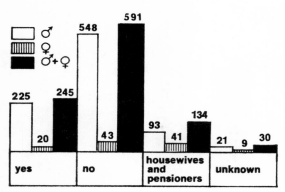

Figure 20-14
Problems at work of the alcoholics in a study sample
of 1,000 families in which one of the marriage partners
was alcoholic.

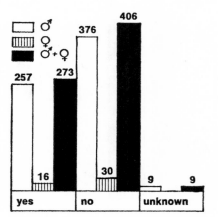

Figure 20-16
Lack of discipline at work of the
alcoholics in the study sample (based
on data obtained from employers
and others).

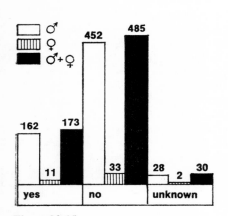

Figure 20-15
Frequency of job changes of the
alcoholics in the study sample.

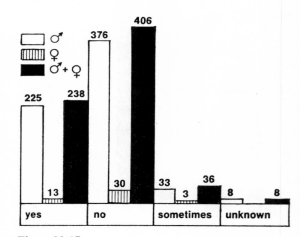

Figure 20-17
Drinking at work of the alcoholics in the study sample.

alcoholism and drug addiction, on the one
hand, and the relatively frequent practice of
switching to some drug after a successful period
of abstinence, on the other, make it necessary
for us to begin to discuss the problems of nar-
comania and alcoholism together, and to extend
our care of alcoholics to the problem of drug
addiction.

SUSCEPTIBILITY TO OTHER CONDITIONS

Finally, to complete this discussion, it is well
known that alcoholics are much less resistant to
various diseases and sequelae of surgery, and
are more subject to traumatic injury than non-
alcoholics. Moreover, treatment of such conditions in alcoholics is more difficult, takes more

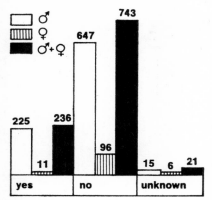

Figure 20-18
Accidents at work of the alcoholics
in the study sample.

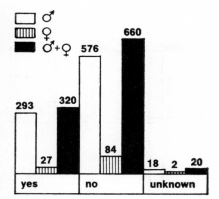

Figure 20-19
Criminal records of the alcoholics in
the study sample.

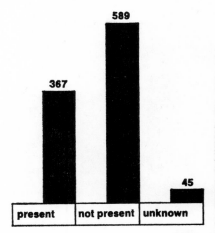

Figure 20-20
Official criminal involvement of the
alcoholics in the study sample.

forth. This makes it necessary for us to engage
more actively in the solution of these problems.
Acute complications of alcoholism have not yet
been clarified, and they manifest themselves in
the form of various syndromes, in the course of
both acute and chronic alcoholism.

In some countries the acute state of inebriation is considered a separate problem and is
taken in charge by a specialized agency. For example, in Czechoslovakia, Poland, and some
other countries special sobering-up centres have
been created. These are mainly concerned with
the accommodation, treatment, and rehabilitation of drunken persons, and are either more or
less medical in orientation or have a repressive
punitive character. In addition to such centres,
which are not concerned with the care of all
acute problems of drinking, and whose principal
aim is not to study the possibilities of their
treatment, there are certain other centres which
are concerned with their treatment and study.

In Zagreb acute complications of alcoholism,
especially those elicited by acute alcoholic intoxication, are taken care of by the emergency
hospital, which also has a rehabilitation department and a department of toxicology. In
studying and treating such cases, this hospital
closely co-operates with the Institute for the

time, and is often attended by many complications.

SUMMARY

All the aforementioned complications indicate
that chronic alcoholism in itself does not present
a single clinical picture but is most probably a
combination of various syndromes producing
primary and secondary somatic and psychiatric
lesions, various social complications, and so

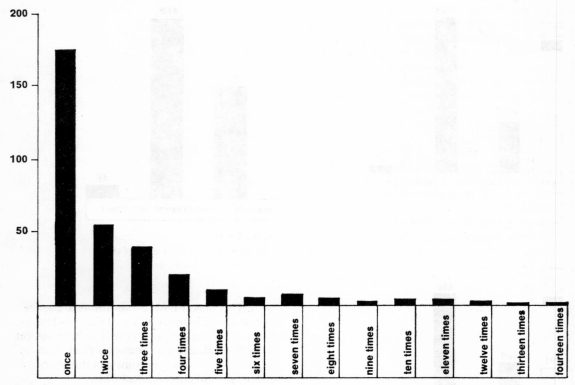

Figure 20-21
Frequency of official condemnations of the alcoholics in the study sample.

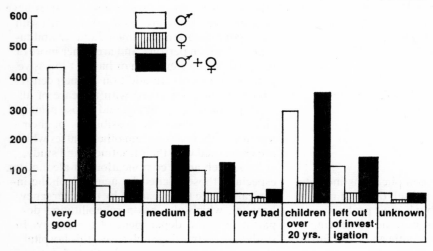

Figure 20-22
Progress in school of the children of the alcoholics in the study sample.

Study and Prevention of Alcoholism. The study of acute alcoholic syndromes is most likely one of the routes to a clearer picture of the pathogenesis of mental disturbances in general, and also one way to help us acquaint ourselves in more detail with the problem of the effect of alcohol and the pathogenesis of chronic alcoholism. Because of this the study and treatment of these syndromes have a great practical and theoretical importance.

Acute complications of alcoholism can be interpreted in various ways. They may be viewed narrowly as connected with alcoholism alone. On the other hand, if chronic alcoholism is taken to be a combination of definite clinical pictures and syndromes and is understood as a single area, then the complications of alcoholism pervade nearly all branches of medicine and some other sciences.

A. VARELA

Psychiatric Clinic and
Institute of Studies on Alcoholism
University of Chile
Santiago, Chile

21

The Role of Personality in Alcohol Abuse

Clinical experience shows that most alcoholic patients exhibit personality abnormalities that differ in nature and degree. In some cases a very definite mental disturbance, such as dysthymias of epileptic origin or an endogenous depressive state of torpid evolution, is present. But in most cases there are only deformations of a neurotic or psychopathic nature.

The cause-effect relation between these aberrations and alcoholism has been discussed for many years. A careful clinical study of each case frequently allows us to determine whether or not a disturbance of the personality constitutes an etiological factor in the development of the abnormal drinking, up to what point it influences the maintenance of alcoholism, and whether or not it is a causal factor in the relapses of abstinent patients.

Generally, the method of the numerous studies performed to discover the personality traits of alcoholic patients is to estimate their prevalence in groups of alcoholics. In these studies, alcoholism tends to be regarded as a single and homogeneous entity, recognized by the analysis of the drinking behaviour. Such studies have revealed that several personality traits are more prevalent in groups of alcoholics than in controls. However, this approach does not give information about the relations between the personality abnormalities and the alcoholism.

I believe that it would be possible to obtain better information regarding this relationship if the notion that alcoholism is a single entity were put aside, and if the different motivations for abnormal drinking were considered independently. If a classification of alcoholic patients according to the relative importance of different motivations were possible, a study to establish the correlations between personality attributes and alcoholism could then be designed. Thus, the different traits of personality, on one hand, and the variable motivations for the abnormal drinking habit, on the other, could be correlated. In the present paper the basis for a study of this type will be discussed.

It is not my intention to describe the different classifications of personality which have been proposed by various authors. I only wish to call attention to those factors motivating alcohol ingestion that could be considered elements for a classification of alcoholic patients. That is, I propose to analyse one of the variables to be correlated, leaving the other – traits of personality – to be classified according to any one of the different schemes proposed in the literature.

In the study of drinking habits, whether in alcoholics or non-alcoholics, it is possible to focus on two different aspects: firstly, behavioural facts related to the intake of alcoholic beverages, and secondly, the tendencies inducing the individual to drink alcohol.

Strictly speaking, the behavioural facts are secondary, since they are the overt manifestations of all the representations, affections, and desires found in the origin of the different types of appetite for alcohol. It is because of its primary and determinant character that the appetite for alcohol is, in my view, the factor of principal importance in this kind of study.

A clinical study of alcoholic patients, as well as of non-alcoholic persons, in which we have explored systematically their attitudes and feelings concerning drinking, has allowed us to distinguish three different types of appetite for alcohol. Firstly, there is the *physiological appetite*. This is similar to the appetite for food, such as sugar, bread, meat, or milk. Secondly, there is the *pharmacological appetite*, which is a desire for the feeling of the characteristic effects of alcohol on the central nervous system. This may vary from the search for a light euphoria to a striving for the alienation characteristic of drunkenness. Lastly, there is the *pathological appetite*, which is a new condition arising in some persons under certain circumstances as a consequence of habitual and prolonged use of alcohol, and which involves an "inability to abstain" or an "inability to stop."

THE PHYSIOLOGICAL APPETITE

Many individuals who habitually drink alcoholic beverages either with or between meals are moved by a natural propensity inducing them to prefer alcohol over other drinks, and not because of the pharmacological effects of alcohol on the central nervous system. Generally, this form of appetite is considered normal and is expressed in a preference for certain wines or beers together with certain foods, or in the use of these beverages and liquors on different social occasions.

Apparently this appetite is related to the peculiar taste of alcoholic beverages, which depends to some extent on the raw material employed in their preparation. On the other hand, since ethanol is an energetic nutriment, under certain circumstances (determined nutritionally and genetically) it could be a preferred substratum for metabolism. All evidence to date leads us to conclude that the preferential drinking of a dilute alcohol solution, when offered alongside water to experimental animals, is the expression of a physiological appetite.

THE PHARMACOLOGICAL APPETITE

When an individual habitually drinks alcoholic beverages with the aim of changing his psychological state – whatever the depth or intensity of this change may be – it can be said that he has a pharmacological appetite for alcohol. A careful exploration of what such persons look for in alcohol shows that some only wish to attain a certain degree of euphoria, while others look for a state of alienation. The latter is an expression of a desire to change one's own psychological state, basically with the intention of "not being oneself" and of "feeling like someone else." In this situation, the most important feature is the desire to lose consciousness of the present self, either in oneself or in relation to the surrounding world. Thus, what is sought is a transitory alienation.

When the desired change is not so radical, but consists only in the desire to obtain a feeling of well-being without losing consciousness of one's identity, we say that it is an appetite for euphoria. What is sought is principally the disappearance of displeasure, which has its origin in affective disturbances or in abnormal traits of character.

Both degrees of pharmacological appetite – euphoria and drunkenness – are often closely related to disturbances of the personality. It is common to observe patients during dysthymic episodes of different types engage in repeated ingestion of alcoholic beverages, inducing a lasting state of drunkenness. Similarly, some persons drink relatively small quantities of alcohol many times during the day, to alleviate light depressive symptoms. In patients suffering from anxiety, small doses of alcohol act as a sedative and relaxant.

The pharmacological action of alcohol on the central nervous system induces psychological changes which not only alleviate physical symptoms but allow the individual to overcome the limitations imposed by abnormal traits. Thus, diverse disturbances of the personality may be part of the genesis of the pharmacological appetite for alcohol. The patient who obtains an advantage, through either the euphoric or the drunken state, from frequently and persistently using the drug is exhibiting the behaviour of psychic dependence. This behaviour is generally characterized by its variable evolution according to affective changes and the difficulties in adaptation caused by psychological disturbances.

The individuals in whom the appetite for euphoria predominates usually drink relatively small amounts of alcohol. They commonly drink daily in the evenings after work, either in public places or at home. In them, only the most careful exploration permits us to recognize whether the habit is in fact determined by a desire for euphoria, by a physiological appetite, or by mere conformity to cultural norms.

In the cases exhibiting a drive towards drunkenness, the pattern of alcohol use is completely different, and consists in drinking at every opportunity until the desired state of intoxication is reached. Clinical study often clearly shows emotional alterations preceding the beginning of each period of drunkenness, this alteration forming an integral part of the clinical picture of the patient.

THE PATHOLOGICAL APPETITE

The habitual and prolonged use of alcoholic beverages may bring about a new condition in the organism, in which a new form of appetite for alcohol arises, the expressions of which are the phenomena called "inability to stop" and "inability to abstain."

The "inability to stop" is the appearance of an urgent need to continue drinking when some amount of alcoholic beverage has been taken – apparently in quantities sufficient to produce a certain blood alcohol level or pharmacological effect, which induces the individual to strive for an intoxicated state that may continue for several days. The "inability to abstain" is also an urgent need to drink alcohol, but in a different way. Here the individual keeps control over the amount he drinks on each occasion, and is able to prevent himself from reaching the state of drunkenness. Nevertheless, he can only abstain for a few hours, and does not have the capacity to give up alcohol, even if he knows it is greatly damaging either his health or social position.

In both conditions the patient has lost control over his desire to drink alcohol. He is the victim of a strong appetite appearing as an ineluctable need for alcohol. This need always arises in relation to previous intake. Thus, when the patient is forced to abstain for a long period, this need is awakened in an abrupt manner immediately after a drink, when the "inability to stop" exists, or it appears insidiously in the case of "inability to abstain."

The fact that the pathological appetite appears after a relatively long period of alcohol abuse leads us to believe that a state of "physical dependence," characterized by the presence of withdrawal symptoms, intervenes in its evolution.

In the case of so-called inveterate alcoholism (Jellinek's "delta") the characteristic symptom of which is the "inability to abstain," it is common to observe a few hours after the last drink clear elements of the withdrawal syndrome, such as tremor, psychomotor restlessness, and anxiety; these are alleviated by the intake of a new dose. In these patients, symptoms are more intense when they awaken in the morning. Their tremor does not allow them to get dressed and they often have nausea; both signs disappear soon after drinking the morning dose.

In the case of the intermittent alcoholic (Jellinek's "gamma"), who suffers from an "inability to stop," the period between doses is so short that the elements of the withdrawal syndrome cannot be noticed. Nevertheless, when these patients have indulged in an episode of continuous heavy drinking and then diminish their intake abruptly, clear signs of withdrawal do appear, the severity of which depends greatly on the duration of the episode. These signs may vary from tremor, nauseau, and neurovegetative disturbances to serious psychotic disturbances such as delirium and convulsive seizures of the grand mal type.

Everything leads us to believe that in these patients some persistent organic alteration has been developed, in such a way that either "inability to abstain" or "inability to stop" are quickly re-established even when there has been a long period of abstinence. It is important, nevertheless, to point out that there are wide variations in the development of this state. As a matter of fact, there are long-time excessive drinkers who do not exhibit any of the "inabilities." On the other hand, young people are not infrequently observed who already have an "inability to stop" a short time after they have taken up drinking. Between these extremes there is a wide range of variation, in length and/or intensity, of the habit necessary for this state to develop.

It is well to bear in mind that the pathological appetite may appear in persons who acquire the habit through either a physiological or a pharmacological appetite, or even in individuals in whom the habit of drinking was caused by cultural factors rather than by a true appetite for alcohol. Since there are wide individual variations in the circumstances inducing the pathological appetite, we are led to think that genetic or environmental factors could influence it.

ACCEPTANCE OF CULTURAL NORMS

The intake of alcoholic beverages is not always determined by an appetite for ethanol. It can also be a consequence of the acceptance of cultural rules. In certain social groups drunkenness is not only accepted, but constitutes a part of the ritual of celebration, or is considered an expression of a virtue such as virility. In other groups, the state of euphoria is a must at parties or other social gatherings, because lack of in-

hibition allows a greater degree of spontaneity in interpersonal relations. It is clear that in all these circumstances alcohol is taken because of its pharmacological effects. Nevertheless, the motivation of many of those who drink alcoholic beverages in these circumstances is not a true pharmacological appetite, but rather their acceptance of the norms peculiar to a group.

CORRELATION OF MOTIVATIONS AND PERSONALITY TRAITS

The analysis of the different causes leading a person into the habit of drinking, and consequently into the state of alcohol dependence, shows that the role played by personality traits in the etiology of abnormal drinking may greatly vary according to the determining cause. In fact, while the psychological characteristics of the personality can be important factors in the origin of the pharmacological appetite for alcohol, they seem to be scarcely important in the origin of the physiological appetite.

The development of the physical dependence peculiar to alcoholism seems to be influenced by the amount and frequency of drinking, as well as by organic structures which may be of genetic origin. Nevertheless, personality traits may influence its establishment through the variable ways of drinking determined by the pharmacological appetite in different personalities. On the other hand, there are characteristics of personality which predispose the individual to cultural pressures to drink. Finally, traits and type of personality as well as its neurotic, psychopathic, or psychotic deformations may give rise to motivations underlying habitual abnormal ingestion of alcohol.

In addition to the disturbances of personality which may produce motivations for abnormal ingestion of alcohol, there is the reverse situation, namely the alterations of personality caused by the alcohol dependence. This seems to be particularly important in the case of physical dependence, not only because of the psychological effect of the loss of liberty with respect to drinking, but also because of the social, economic, and familial consequences.

Studies directed to the establishment of a

correlation between characteristics of personality and motivation require a retrospective analysis in each case, in order to establish the status of both variables during the period leading to dependence, but before the latter had influenced the personality. This form of analysis does not preclude the need to study characteristics of the personality which may intervene in the reinitiation of drinking episodes, commonly observed among alcoholic patients who have been abstinent for a period. The periods of abstinence are a part of the drinking pattern of intermittent alcoholics; but in the case of inveterate alcoholism, abstinence is generally obtained only through treatment. Relapses do not seem to be determined by the pathological appetite – which only appears after the individual begins to drink again – but for other causes, such as social pressure, physiological appetite, or, more often, a search for drunkenness or euphoria. The study of the current relationship between the personality characteristics of each patient and the causes of his relapses supplies particularly important information for his treatment. An effective psychotherapy requires a knowledge of the pathogenic relations between the disturbances of personality and the desire to drink.

GUIDO SOLARI C.

Psychiatric Clinic
University of Chile
Santiago, Chile

22

Psychotherapeutic Methods in Alcoholism

As Scott (14) points out, literature on psychotherapeutic techniques for the alcoholic is scanty in comparison with the bibliography on other aspects of the problem of alcoholism. With few exceptions psychotherapy in alcoholism is spoken of with vagueness and lack of precision (16). We can conceive psychotherapy as the intention to cure or mitigate through words and attitudes, in a specific interpersonal relationship. I should like here to concentrate on some aspects of psychotherapy for the alcoholic.

Within "abnormal drinking" it is necessary to separate the so-called symptomatic alcoholism or symptomatic excessive drinking from the larger grouping of alcoholism. It is undoubtedly impossible to make a strict conceptual and clinical separation, but generally we can leave out that consumption which is a consequence of mental illness, whether an endogenous depression due to brain damage, an altered state of conscience, a psychotic burst, or some other condition which determines by itself the necessary physical and psychic therapy.

The psychotherapeutic approach to the alcoholic involves three considerations: its limits, its objectives, and the methods of obtaining them. I think that the nature of alcoholism or our assumptions about it will determine the limits of a psychotherapeutic approach. In my opinion, at the present state of knowledge there is enough evidence to yield to the belief that the basic symptoms that characterize alcoholism – loss of control and inability to abstain – lie in a physiopathologic alteration which is produced by excessive drinking through time in a predisposed individual. The personality structure, the individual biography, and the socio-cultural circumstances are conducive to excessive drinking, which sometimes leads to alcoholism. But, although excessive drinking is due to psychological and cultural causes, the condition of being an alcoholic lies in a somatic alteration. Moreover, not knowing for the moment its physiopathologic mechanisms, we cannot modify this condition of being an alcoholic, and for all we know it may be modified spontaneously with protracted abstinence.

The "loss of control" and "inability to abstain" put definite limits on the possibilities of modification through psychotherapy. That is why I disagree with those who expect to change these conditions through psychotherapy. These symptoms of alcoholism belong to a different order of phenomena, and therefore cannot be modified psychologically.

Although there is thus a definite limit to the psychotherapeutic scope, it is there where the indication of psychotherapy and its first objective precisely lies (9, 10). Today, strictly speaking, we cannot *cure* the alcoholic, we cannot offer to remove his loss of control and make him a normal drinker. We can only help to prevent his abnormality from being actualized. Abstinence as an improvement criterion can be discussed, but undoubtedly it appears as a condition for the readjustment of the alcoholic patient, although according to Mansell Pattison, its importance may be overestimated (13).

The alcoholic denies his dependence on alcohol. As has been pointed out, one of the most frequent psychic mechanisms in the addict is denial; just as he denies his dependence on the drug, he also denies other vital problems and his own emotional reactions. He defends himself behind a network of rationalizations (4, 11). Even the patient who "surrenders," in Tiebout's sense, defends himself from accepting his dependence (19, 22).

He does not accept it for two reasons: the outrage that it means to his ego – the "humiliation" that dependence implies – and the need he has to resort to alcohol to prevent physical disturbances and to escape vital situations that he has learned to avoid through excessive drinking.

Abstinence as a condition for treatment is then, for the patient, difficult to accept. Only if we succeed in creating consciousness of illness, in other words, the patient's deep acceptance of his dependence on alcohol, and the acceptance of the fact that he has lost his freedom in regard to it; only then can we present to him abstinence as a condition which he will make his own.

Thus, from this first objective, to attain abstinence, emerges the obligation of creating consciousness of illness. In my opinion no aversive or prohibitive treatment will prove successful through time if we have failed to create consciousness of illness. I mean trying to attain in the patient the deep acceptance of his inability to manage alcohol and not merely the notion of illness.

To create consciousness of illness involves destroying rationalization, confronting denial, and supporting the patient who suddenly finds himself face to face with his pathological condition. This task can only be achieved in an adequate doctor-patient relationship. The therapist's art lies in knowing how to obtain it, and in his understanding of the psychodynamics of alcoholics in general and of his patient in particular. This crucial moment, perhaps the most important in psychotherapy for the alcoholic, and in which the greatest technical difficulties reside, highlights a difference as compared with psychotherapy for the neurotic. The emotional contact between therapist and patient, or transference in general terms, should be induced, and the affective dependence of the patient properly used. I agree with Silber when he says (16), "The main therapeutic modification is to induce rapid positive transference. ..."

The attitude and actions of the psychotherapist should be directed to this goal: his capacity for interpersonal relationships, his acceptance, interest, and ability to establish adequate goals are basic factors at this moment. The work of Becker and Israel (1) argues for the usefulness of associating psychotherapy with drug administration, for the symbolic and transferential character of the latter. Kerner (8) also insists on the importance of this initial stage and on the need for therapeutic modifications which consider the peculiar characteristics of the alcoholic. In regard to this, I consider very useful the combination of individual interviews and group meetings. The group situation facilitates extraordinarily the formation of consciousness of illness, no matter which type of group therapy is adopted.

The attainment of a rapid positive transference requires from the therapist an active and participating attitude in therapeutic relations; he must be permanently attentive to manifestations of frustration and the subsequent hostility which so frequently takes the form of treatment abandonment and relapses (5, 15).

The alcoholic comes to treatment suffering the consequences of his abnormal consumption;

anxiety, guilt feelings, depression, low self-estimation, social rejection, maladjustment, etc. are the most frequent expressions that we find in the addict at this stage. The establishment of a therapeutic relationship in which he does not suffer the hostilities that his behaviour has provoked, together with the therapist's attitude and possibly his medical intervention, help at this stage of personality breakdown.

Our objective is not only to treat this secondary neurosis, but also to help the alcoholic to reorganize his life with the acknowledgment that he has lost his ability to manage alcohol. If we concede that the symptoms of stopping and abstaining lie in an alteration of his physiology, for the moment unmodifiable, there is nothing to do but face the patient psychotherapeutically with this reality and guide him in his adjustment to a life of abstinence. Knowledge of his abilities and aptitudes, of his personality structure and his environment, will allow us to state realistically the steps and meaning of his existence. Following Goldstein, this therapeutic action could be called "defect psychotherapy."

Clinical experience shows that the task is not easy. For this there are many and complex reasons: not only does the alcoholic resist acceptance of his irreversible inability to manage alcohol, but he also presents a desire for drinking and seeks it for its pleasant effects; besides, there always is some social pressure, more or less intensive, to start him drinking again. Last and most important, personality anomalies in the alcoholic, when they exist, lead him to seek mitigation or escape in consumption. Knowledge of his symptomatic and characterologic anomalies, whether psychopathic or neurotic, will determine the psychotherapeutic modalities and their probable goals. Personal and circumstantial characteristics will favour the election of one or the other therapeutic modality. Here arises the difficult compromise between what is possible to attain and what the patient expects. The therapist's evaluation of the patient and his circumstances will determine the goals and methods for that patient. In many alcoholics we can observe characteristic behaviour and special psychodynamisms, but in each case there are different structures and different vital situations, so that no two alcoholics are ever the same. The

situation is the same as in psychotherapy for neurotics.

Nevertheless, one aspect should be considered with special thoroughness. As was pointed out by Moore and Krystal (9, 10), the question, What is the patient searching for when he consumes alcohol? not only opens a pass to the understanding of his personality structure and psychodynamics but also shows the difference between psychotherapy for the alcoholic and that for the neurotic. The previous paper has referred to the characteristics of desire and search in alcoholic consumption, its modalities and its meaning in the personality context. A patient who consumes alcohol to remove a social inhibition presents a different problem from the one who drinks to attack a relative. This permits us to concentrate on those anomalies which have a special relationship to abnormal consumption, and these are the symptoms and characteristics that we must necessarily try to modify. Otherwise we would be faced with the need to alter the complete personality, which is only indicated in some cases. I do not mean that psychotherapy should be restricted to the modification of the symptoms and characteristics which lead to consumption. On the contrary, the therapeutic statement must include in its goals the modification of modifiable anomalies that interfere with the personal and social adjustment of the patient, even when not strictly related to consumption. Thus, while the characteristic of being an abnormal drinker imposes certain therapeutic modalities, the goals and methods of obtaining them can only be discovered through an understanding of the personality.

Experience shows the difficulty the alcoholic has in adjusting himself to social life without resorting to drinking. Through the years he has acquired the habit of solving his social problems by means of consumption. We must add the social pressure – which at least in Chile is intensive – to make him drink again with the group. Not only must he learn new social behaviour but frequently he will have to actively resist group pressure. Frequently there will emerge feelings of loneliness, rejection, tediousness, inability to use time, thoughts of inadequateness, need of support, etc. The patient the other way the therapist's ... is our task to help him acquire new ... ocialization and interpersonal contact; we have deprived the patient of his crutch and we must attend him in his efforts to walk on his own feet, guiding him to activities and entertainments, and submitting his difficulties to psychotherapy.

Group psychotherapy, in conjunction with individual interviews, and affiliation with abstinent clubs have proved to be of great utility (6). Not only do they permit the patient to face his present difficulties, but also provide the company, stimulation, and acceptance by others which the alcoholic needs at this stage. In the group situation new ties are established, new interests emerge, and daily work starts to make sense, even if the alcoholic is "converted" to anti-alcoholic proselytism (17, 18).

The methods of group therapy vary according to the conductor's preference, but all of them provide company, new contacts, and new interests. They help resocialization and aid the alcoholic patient in facing the social pressure to which he is subjected (3). Besides, they present another advantage, the management of the patient's affective dependence (7, 23).

Because of his personality characteristics and because of his situation when treatment starts, the alcoholic easily develops dependence on the therapist. In one stage of treatment this dependence is useful, and as I said before, it is advisable to awaken it in the psychotherapeutic situation. However, it should not be maintained. The therapist cannot gratify all the patient's demands. If dependence is not treated it may lead to therapeutic failure. The handling of this abnormal dependence is one of the most difficult tasks for the therapist to solve (2, 12).

Some foresights are helpful in dealing with ambivalent dependence, besides psychotherapeutic elaboration in the interviews. Chafetz has pointed out that his patients are more effectively treated if the therapy is performed in a team that includes the psychiatrist, the social worker, and the psychologist; thus "the task of the therapist becomes somewhat more manageable and the possibilities for arousal of his counterhostility are minimized" (4).

Experience shows the utility of this method. The same can be said for group therapy. Besides the advantages already pointed out, it permits an easier confrontation of dependence with reality.

I have briefly examined different aspects of psychotherapy for the alcoholic which presents, in my opinion, some special characteristics in its limits, objectives, and methods. Although there has been great progress in the field, there is still a long way to go. Our most important weapon for the treatment of the alcoholic requires deep study, refinement of its methods, and evaluation of its results, no matter how difficult it is to systematize the psychotherapeutic experience.

REFERENCES

1
BECKER, G. & ISRAEL, P.
Integrated drug- and psychotherapy in the treatment of alcoholism
Quart. J. Stud. Alc., **22**: 610, 1961
2
BLANC, H.T. & MYERS, W.R.
Behavioral dependence and length of stay in psychotherapy among alcoholics
Quart. J. Stud. Alc., **24**: 503, 1963
3
BRUNER-ORNE, M., IDDINGS, F.T., & RODRIGUES, J.
A court clinic for alcoholics: a description and evaluation of the Stoughton Clinic
Quart. J. Stud. Alc., **12**: 592, 1951
4
CHAFETZ, M.E.
Practical and theoretical considerations in the psychotherapy of alcoholism
Quart. J. Stud. Alc., **20**: 281, 1959
5
DIETHELM, O. & BARR, R.M.
Psychotherapeutics interviews and alcohol intoxication
Quart. J. Stud. Alc., **23**: 243, 1962
6
ESSER, P.H.
Group psychotherapy with alcoholics: its value for significs
Quart. J. Stud. Alc., **22**: 646, 1961
7
GALLANT, D.M.
Group staffing on an alcoholism treatment service
Internat. J. Group Psychotherap., **14**: 218, 1964
8
KERNER, O.J.B.
Initiating psychotherapy with alcoholic patients
Quart. J. Stud. Alc., **17**: 479, 1956

9
KRYSTAL, H.
The problem of abstinence by the patient as a
requisite for the psychotherapy of alcoholism: II
The evaluation of the meaning of drinking in
determining the requirement of abstinence by
alcoholics during treatment
Quart. J. Stud. Alc., **23**: 112, 1962
10
MOORE, R.A.
The problem of abstinence by the patient as a
requisite for the psychotherapy of alcoholism: I
The need for abstinence by the alcoholic patient
during treatment
Quart. J. Stud. Alc., **23**: 105, 1962
11
MOORE, R.A. & MURPHY, T.
Denial of alcoholism as an obstacle to recovery
Quart. J. Stud. Alc., **22**: 597, 1961
12
MYERSON, D.J.
An active therapeutic method of interrupting the
dependency relationship of certain male alcoholics
Quart. J. Stud. Alc., **14**: 419, 1953
13
PATTISON, E.M.
A critique of alcoholism treatment concepts, with
special reference to abstinence
Quart. J. Stud. Alc., **27**: 49, 1966
14
SCOTT, E.M.
The technique of psychotherapy with alcoholics
Quart. J. Stud. Alc., **22**: 69, 1961
15
SELZER, M.L.
Hostility as a barrier to therapy in alcoholism
Psychiat. Quart., **31**: 301, 1957
16
SILBER, A.
Psychotherapy with alcoholics
J. Nerv. Ment. Dis., **129**: 477, 1959
17
STEWART, D.A.
Empathy in the group therapy of alcoholics
Quart. J. Stud. Alc., **15**: 74, 1954
18
STEWART, D.A.
Ethical aspects of group therapy of alcoholics
Quart. J. Stud. Alc., **15**: 288, 1954
19
TIEBOUT, H.M.
The problem of gaining cooperation from the
alcoholic patient
Quart. J. Stud. Alc., **8**: 47, 1947
20
TIEBOUT, H.M.
The act of surrender in the therapeutic process with
special reference to alcoholism
Quart. J. Stud. Alc., **10**: 48, 1949

21
TIEBOUT, H.M.
Surrender versus compliance in therapy with
special reference to alcoholism
Quart. J. Stud. Alc., **14**: 58, 1953
22
TIEBOUT, H.M.
The ego factors in surrender in alcoholism
Quart. J. Stud. Alc., **15**: 610, 1954
23
TIEBOUT, H.M.
Alcoholics Anonymous: an experiment of nature
Quart. J. Stud. Alc., **22**: 52, 1961

GUNNAR A. R. LUNDQUIST

Alcohol Research Clinic
Stockholm, Sweden

23

The Use of Drugs in the Treatment of Alcoholism

In the medical treatment of alcoholism it is first necessary to distinguish the acute from the more chronic stages, and detoxication treatment from dehabituation. In all phases psychotherapeutic and sociotherapeutic measures are of the greatest importance, but it also can be helpful to use different drugs.

The most usual syndromes in the acute stages of alcoholism are the following:

1

Severe alcohol intoxication with excitement, speech difficulties, flushed face, and often anxiety. The blood alcohol level is usually from 250 to 350 mg per cent.

2

Withdrawal symptoms with restlessness, tachycardia, tremor, perspiration, dysphoric state, anxiety, and sleep disturbances.

3

Delirious states or delirium, often part of the withdrawal picture, with tremulousness, hallucinations, and different degrees of confusion.

4

Severe intoxication with coma, pallor, and hyperflexia and blood alcohol levels from 350 to 500 mg per cent.

5

The postalcoholic phase after the cessation of drinking with milder withdrawal symptoms, tiredness, tension, depression, autonomic instability, and loss of appetite. This phase often lasts for two or three weeks.

With respect to the treatment of severe intoxication, there would seem to be no sure and practical way to increase the rate either of the oxidation of alcohol or of its excretion. Many treatments have been tried and different authors have reported sobering effects, for example, of insulin, glucose, fructose, pyridoxine, and analeptics. It has also been stated that oxygen alone or in combination with carbon dioxide increases the rate of metabolism of alcohol. However, the different reports are contradictory and inconclusive.

The sedation of patients with acute severe intoxication with excitement, and of patients with withdrawal symptoms, has been and is still today sought by many physicians through the use of chloral hydrate, paraldehyde, or barbiturates. Personally, for several years I have used the newer psychotropic drugs with tranquillizing effects, such as promethazine (Phenergan, Lergigan), chlordiazepoxide (Librium), diazepam (Valium), trimeprazine (Theralen), and chlormethiazole (Heminevrin). Usually we begin the treatment with rather high doses to get a rapid sedative effect, but the doses depend of course on the patient's state, his body weight, and the degree of excitement or anxiety. We often begin to treat a patient in a severe state of excitement involving motor overactivity and anxiety with three or four tablets or capsules (0.5 gm) of chlormethiazole and repeat the dose after some hours. If necessary we begin with an intravenous injection of 40 to 60 ml of 0.8 per cent solution of chlormethiazole. Often the patient will sleep after a few minutes. When he is awake again he usually can be given tablets or capsules.

Good and rapid results in the sedation of patients in an acute stage have also been attained with injections of 200–300 mg chlordiazepoxide or with 100–200 mg of diazepam. If the patient is known to be a misuser of tablets and perhaps earlier has used large doses of chlordiazepoxide, chlormethiazole, or barbiturates, we prefer to give him promethazine or chlorprotixen (Truxal) or trimeprazine. In general we begin with high doses (200–300 mg) and then try to reduce the doses successively during the following days. If we have begun the treatment with the more rapidly acting drugs such as chlormethiazol or chlordiazepoxide we often can change the drugs after five or six days and turn to the slower acting but longer lasting drugs such as promethazine or chlorprotixen. If necessary we give these drugs for several weeks. If the patient still suffers from anxiety or excitement we add to these drugs small doses of chlordiazepoxide or diazepam.

In delirious states we often must sedate the patient with higher doses and through injection or infusion at the start. The most widely used drug in my clinic for the treatment of delirium is chlormethiazole, which has proved to be an excellent sedative, anticonvulsive, and hypnotic drug. In the very rare cases of severe alcohol intoxication with coma we usually have no need to give sedatives. In such cases we give the patient adrenocortical hormones and oxygen, and eventually even analeptics. We administer antibiotics to prevent pneumonia.

In all acute stages of alcoholism we give vitamins by injection and large amounts of fluids with sugar, and in severe cases infusions of 1 per cent sodium chloride solution.

In postalcoholic phases the patients often manifest depressive symptoms and sleep disturbances. During these periods, it may be necessary to give anti-depressive drugs such as amitriptyline and anti-anxiety drugs such as chlordiazepoxide or diazepam, and hypnotics such as Mogadon or Doriden. If there is an autonomic instability Bellergal is sometimes given, and not infrequently insulin for some weeks is of value. In the postalcoholic phase we have often seen anemia, especially due to iron deficiency. Then we have to give the patient injections of iron.

The acute stages of alcoholism often must be treated in a hospital, but rarely is there any need to hospitalize the alcoholic patient for more than two or three weeks. After this time he has mostly recovered from the acute symptoms and the next phase in the treatment can be carried out on an out-patient basis while the patient is working. Out-patient treatment must continue for a very long time, often for two or three years, and during this time psychotherapy is the most important treatment. The use of drugs is, however, often necessary even at this stage.

The medical treatment during the acute stages constitutes the *treatment of a syndrome*, but the medical and psychological treatment after the acute stage is the *treatment of a person* who must be helped to change his attitude toward drinking, to change his habits, and to learn to abstain from alcohol. This process of dehabituation often creates tensions and insomnia. Therefore, the patient must be supported and sufficiently motivated to live without alcohol. At this point tension-reducing drugs, anti-depressives, and hypnotics can be very helpful. But it is important not to change an abuser of alcohol into an abuser of drugs. Accordingly, the choice of drugs is of great importance. There are two different groups of drugs which now are of value. The first group com-

prises those that give release or mitigate worries
without producing addiction. The second group
comprises drugs which sensitize the organism
to alcohol.

Many different drugs can be used during the
dehabituation or rehabilitation phase. Before
discussing which drugs we use in this connection, I should like to stress again that the goal
of treatment is to make the patient independent
of alcohol *as well as of drugs*. When psychotherapy and sociotherapy are established and
effective there is no need of drugs.

Among the drugs most often used during the
rehabilitation phase are chlorprotixen, levome-
promazine, tioridazine, fluphenazine, and promethazine. These are effective drugs which can
be used for months without risk of addiction.
It is important to give suitable doses. In some
cases very small doses are best, in others it is
necessary for some weeks at least to give large
doses. The distribution of the drug during the
day is also of importance. In certain cases a
patient is best helped by taking the whole dose
in the morning, in other cases it is better to give
the drug four or five times during the day.

In rare cases it can be very helpful to give the
patient amphetamines, dexamphetamines, or
methylphenidate for a short time and under
careful supervision. Particularly at the start of
the rehabilitation phase it can be of value to
give the patient 5–10 mg dexamphetamine or
10–20 mg methylphenidate during the first half
of the day for two or three weeks. The use of
these drugs can lead to dependence, and therefore it is important to select the patients carefully, and to give the drugs only for a short
time.*

The second group of drugs that can be used
in the rehabilitation phase comprises the
sensitizing drugs which make it difficult to
drink. I think that Antabuse treatment has been
the most widely used "drug treatment" of alcoholics during the last 15 years. There is no
doubt that Antabuse or Dipsan can be of value
in many cases, but the selection of patients for
such treatment must be made very carefully. I

have not found it necessary to use either drug
very often, and in any case only for a short
period: a month to six weeks.

An interesting drug which has been introduced recently is metronidazol (Flagyl). It has
been reported that this drug decreases the
craving for alcohol, but as yet I have not been
able to confirm this statement.

*Since July 1, 1968, the medical authorities in Sweden,
owing to frequent abuse by young people, have made
it very difficult for physicians to prescribe amphetamines or similar drugs.

GRIFFITH EDWARDS

Institute of Psychiatry
Maudsley Hospital
London, England

24

Alcoholism: The Analysis of Treatment

Rather similar regimes are today employed in most parts of the world for the treatment of alcoholism. A common element in all the different approaches is that the alcoholic is required to register himself as a patient – a formality that implies that he is to reorientate himself in the sick-role rather than the bad-role. He is then offered a relationship with a therapist and he will be told categorically that he is not to touch a drop of alcohol again. He will probably be given sensible advice about his work and his leisure. To this general approach may be added more or less aversion treatment, more or less hypnosis, and more or less psychotherapy, but probably today most of us treat our patients with a bit of everything. And for many of us this eclecticism perhaps reflects a lack of any very great faith in the supposedly specific treatment methods. The truth is that although we have been using Antabuse (to pick one example) for about twenty years, the contention that patients who take Antabuse do well because well-motivated patients *agree* to take Antabuse and well-motivated patients are those who in any case are going to get better, has hardly been investigated, let alone refuted. Concrete evidence is similarly lacking when we turn to other treatments. Indeed, even the basic evidence that treatment of any sort at all is capable of altering the natural history of alcoholism is, with the exception of Kendell's recent important paper (6), difficult to come by, and Kendell was not really studying two truly comparable groups.

The need in alcoholism is not so much for new treatments but for a proper and scientific assessment of the treatments which we are now using. Wallerstein's monograph (8) was one of the few attempts in this field to bring to bear the methods of controlled trial. Research on alcoholism treatment has for some years seemed

The work reported here was carried out in collaboration with Mrs. Sally Guthrie and will form the basis of a later joint report. We would like to thank Dr. D. L. Davies and Dr. Michael Shepherd for constant advice and encouragement, and Miss Barbara Kingsley for expert statistical assistance. Finally, we would like to thank our secretaries Mrs. Julia Polglaze and Miss Ethane Cross for all their help.

slightly becalmed. Interesting case-series have been reported from many different countries, but it is necessary to proceed beyond the sort of research which is limited to the report of an outcome to investigations which analyze the whys and wherefores of the outcome. How is this to be done?

The answer lies perhaps in taking simple and circumscribed problems and trying to approach them with rigorously designed clinical experiments. Following in the footsteps of Dr. D. L. Davies and his colleagues, whose report (1) was one of the first detailed analyses of prognostic factors, we have recently been trying at the Maudsley Hospital to mount such simple experiments, and this paper presents a brief account of an investigation which compared the value of out-patient (OP) and in-patient (IP) treatment. Both types of treatment obviously have within them many elements, and the present experiment does not try to analyse the components of either treatment, but only the effect of admitting patients to hospital as opposed to giving as nearly as possible the same (multi-factor) treatment without taking them into hospital. We do not pretend that this experiment was a model of its kind; we think indeed that it had several serious shortcomings. Under the successive headings will be considered various aspects of the experimental design and then the results of our investigation, and at each point our procedures will be discussed as illustrating the general problems of an experiment which aims to *measure* the value of any treatment of alcoholism.

THE SAMPLE

Criteria for admission to the trial were that patients should be male, and should have a dependence on alcohol of a pharmacological type usually now referred to as "gamma alcoholism" (5). They had no other significant physical or mental illness and had to state their willingness to co-operate in any form of treatment offered. Vagrant alcoholics were excluded.

Every clinic is apt to treat a different sort of alcoholic and unless the characteristics of the sample are clearly defined, no one can know how generally applicable the results of the experiment are to be regarded. To describe a group of patients in terms which communicate a true idea of the type of patient to a person who works in another clinic, let alone to someone working in another country where differences in psychiatric nomenclature may be considerable, presents real difficulties. Communication may perhaps be helped by giving objective information on the following points:

1
Type of alcoholism – here Jellinek's classification seems at present the most useful one.
2
Demographic features.
3
Personality.
4
Social stability.

In Table 24–1, which also gives data bearing on the comparability of the IP and OP groups, information on the characteristics of patients entering the present trial is set out. Social class is given in terms of the Registrar General's socio-economic classification, in which class I indicates professional occupation, and class V the unskilled labourer. Personality was measured on the E (extraversion) and N (neuroticism) 48-point scales of the Maudsley Personality Inventory (3), and social stability (SS) on a 4-point scale (2, 7). This scale gives one point for each of the following criteria:
1
Subjects had held a steady job for the three immediately preceding years or more.
2
Subjects had had residential immobility for the two preceding years or more.
3
Subjects were living in their own home or in that of relatives or friends.
4
Subjects were married and living with their spouse.

RANDOMIZATION

Our method was to see all alcoholic referrals initially for a clinic interview, to select at this

TABLE 24-1

DEMOGRAPHIC FEATURES, PERSONALITY FACTORS, AND SOCIAL STABILITY OF
20 IN-PATIENT AND 20 OUT-PATIENT MALE ADDICTS, AND OF COMBINED SAMPLE

| | *Mean age (years)* | *Marital status* | | | *Social class* | | | | | *Personality* | | *Social stability* |
		single	*married*	*sep/div*	*I*	*II*	*III*	*IV*	*V*	*E*	*N*	
in-patients	42.3	2	12	6	0	5	10	1	4	24	34	2.4
out-patients	44.3	2	16	2	1	5	8	3	3	24	36	3.0
combined	43.3	4	28	8	1	10	18	4	7	24	35	2.7

See text for explanation of ratings.

interview those who fulfilled the criteria for admission, including the patient's agreeing to any treatment offered, and then to open a sealed envelope, the contents of which determined whether that particular patient should be placed in the in-patient or out-patient group.

The ethical question must obviously always be considered. We felt here that it was legitimate to place patients in the OP group, for there was the safeguard that they could report to the hospital at any time of the day or night in case of emergency.

COMPARABILITY OF GROUPS

That the two groups were satisfactorily comparable is shown by the data set out in Table 24-1. There was no significant between-group difference in any of the items considered.

What are the variables on which comparability should be reported? I would suggest that essentially the same factors have to be considered as when defining the sample, and it is certainly necessary that neither social stability nor personality loading should differ between groups and that a measure of "severity of alcoholism" should, if possible, be introduced.

SIZE OF SAMPLE

Twenty patients were admitted to either group. The size chosen for a sample must of course be related to the degree of difference in outcome which one may be interested in detecting between the two groups. However, relatively small

groups, carefully observed, frequently can provide more valuable information than cursory study of a big series.

THE TREATMENTS

All patients received supportive or more intensive psychotherapy and were introduced to Alcoholics Anonymous; family casework was freely available; help was given with employment and other social problems; and all patients were prescribed citrated calcium carbimide (Temposil) in a dose of 100 mg/day and a test reaction carried out. For those patients who came into hospital the length of stay, and for out-patients the duration of "intensive treatment," was determined by the individual needs of the patient, as judged by the consultant concerned. During the initial intensive treatment period out-patients were seen at least once weekly, and thereafter out-patients and discharged in-patients were seen at least once a month.

Before accepting the findings of any clinical trial one must be persuaded that the treatments under assessment were competently carried out – a negative finding may otherwise imply no more than lack of therapeutic competence. Treatment regimes must therefore be reported in some detail.

RATING THE RESULTS

Each patient was rated each month. In any month he could earn a maximum of two points so that over twelve months his score could range from 0 to 24. The basis of rating was as follows:

Two points: completely sober for the month under consideration or occasional drinking (less than seven days in the month) without interference with social function.

One point: drinking more than occasionally (more than seven days in a month) or drinking occasionally causing mild social incapacity (e.g. patients missing a few days' work).

No points: heavy drinking causing considerable social incapacity (e.g. prolonged unemployment, hospitalization, or imprisonment).

This is really a sociomedical rating and we believe it to be clinically meaningful. From the research point of view, however, a method which mixes two variables – social behaviour and drinking behaviour – is far from satisfactory. It would be better if we were able to rate the patient on several different variables separately, such as sobriety, working capacity, and the wife's report of family harmony.

In all but 11 of 480 monthly assessments there was agreement between two raters, and where there was disagreement the mean was taken. Here, however, our study is certainly open to criticism, for the ratings were not "blind" – the raters knew whether the patients had been receiving in-patient or out-patient care. With a little ingenuity it should be possible to produce the full case records without any clue in them as to which type of treatment any patient had received, and place these records before independent raters.

COLLECTING THE EVIDENCE TO BE RATED

A research social worker carried out the necessary family casework and was responsible for gathering information from home or employer – from some independent source – every month. To this was added all the medical information gained at the clinic visits. It is of course not uncommon to find the patient's own evidence inaccurate, and it would seem rash to place much reliance on any treatment series where the report was not based on independent evidence. If follow-up is not well organized and vigorously pursued there is also the risk that the whole investigation will be marred by sight being lost of 10 to 20 per cent of the patients before the end of the study. A competent and energetic social worker who is capable of keeping a close eye on families and patients without giving any impression of prying, and who can regularly collect accurate and complete information, is therefore the absolute cornerstone of any study of alcoholism treatment.

LENGTH OF FOLLOW-UP

All the patients in the series which we are now reporting have been followed up for twelve months. Alcoholism is, however, a lifetime disease, and before reporting results we should ask how long a follow-up is really required. There is now much evidence (1, 2, 4) that the outcome at six months is a good pointer to later results. If results are collected on the monthly basis described here, then it should be possible to describe the "curve of relapse" and make some predictions as to the likely value of a statement on outcome at the end of any particular period.

THE RESULTS

The treatment given
The average duration of admission for in-patients was 8.9 weeks, and the out-patients on average spent 7.7 weeks in intensive care.

Overall outcome
The results are set out in Table 24-2, which gives the monthly group outcome (maximum possible 20 × 2 points) for each group. Inspection of these figures suggests that the two groups follow courses which are initially rather parallel but after a few months the out-patients fare better. Table 24-3 presents an analysis of variance which confirms that the between-group difference is significant ($p < 0.01$).

Influence of E, N, SS on outcome
Calculation of coefficients of multiple correlation showed no significant correlation between the individual's overall outcome score (os)

TABLE 24–2

MONTHLY GROUP OUTCOME SCORE FOR IN-PATIENT AND OUT-PATIENT GROUPS
FOR EACH OF 12 FOLLOW-UP MONTHS

	Months											
	1	2	3	4	5	6	7	8	9	10	11	12
in-patient group	32	28	29	27	24	21	21	21	23	22.5	21.5	23
out-patient group	32	28	29.5	28	29	24	28	30.5	29.5	28.5	30	25.5

TABLE 24–3

PROGRESS: ANALYSIS OF VARIANCE

	Degrees of freedom	Sums of squares	Mean sum of squares	Variance ratio	Significance
between treatments	1	5.1047	5.1047	6.89	$p < 0.01$
between months	2	6.8307	.62097	.84	not significant
months × treatment interaction	2	1.7641	.16037	.22	not significant
residual	456	337.675	.74052		
total	479	351.3745			

and his E or his N score, but there was a positive correlation between OS and SS score significant at $p < 0.01$ for the IP group and at $p < 0.001$ for the OP group.

CONCLUSIONS

The central argument of this paper is that knowledge of how best to treat the alcoholic can only be advanced by experiments which are designed and executed with due respect for the proper canons of the controlled trial, and it is again worth stressing that our experiment is reported here as much for discussion and criticism of its methods as for any intrinsic interest contained in the results. The investigation appears to demonstrate that for alcohol addiction out-patient is more effective than in-patient treatment, but is this result persuasive?

Results are wholly persuasive only if the experimental design is unimpeachable; the design here had as its most serious shortcoming the lack of "blind" rating of the outcome. We believe therefore that the results are suggestive but that they cannot yet be claimed as conclu-

sive. A further point is that although the mean SS score did not differ significantly between the two groups, the OP group was to some extent more favourably weighted with respect to this factor, and the possible bearing this may have had on outcome requires further analysis. However, it seems that it is safe to make two cautious interpretations: firstly, that out-patient treatment has been undervalued, and secondly, that social stability is even more important in out-patient than in in-patient care in influencing outcome.

SUMMARY

The need in alcoholism is not so much for new treatments but for proper assessment of the treatments now in use. Simple and circumscribed problems should be taken and examined by means of rigorously designed clinical experiments. The general principles involved in planning and executing such investigations are discussed here, and a trial which compared the results of in-patient and out-patient treatment of alcoholism is taken as an example.

In general, attention must be given to the following points: description of patients, with due note of type of alcoholism, demographic features, personality, and social stability; randomization of patients between groups; matching of groups; sample size; description of treatment; rating of results on a defined and objective basis, preferably on several distinct criteria of response, and preferably carried out by two independent observers who are not aware of which treatment any patient has received; collection of complete and valid evidence; adequate length of follow-up; and application of suitable statistical methods to the analysis of results.

Results of the study which forms the basis of discussion suggest that out-patient treatment gives better results than in-patient treatment, but limitations in design mean that this interpretation can only be accepted with caution. In both groups the social stability score correlates positively and significantly with outcome, and the correlation is stronger ($p < 0.001$ as against $p < 0.01$) in the out-patient than in the in-patient group.

REFERENCES

1
DAVIES, D.L., SHEPHERD, M., & MYERS, E.
The two-years' prognosis of 50 alcohol addicts after treatment in hospital
Quart. J. Stud. Alc., 17: 485, 1956
2
EDWARDS, G.
Hypnosis in the treatment of alcohol addiction: controlled trial, with an analysis of factors affecting treatment outcome
Quart. J. Stud. Alc., 27: 221, 1966
3
EYSENCK, H.J.
Manual of the Maudsley Personality Inventory
London: London University Press, 1959
4
GLATT, M.M.
Treatment results in an English mental hospital alcoholic unit
Acta Psychiat. Scandinav., 37: 143, 1961
5
JELLINEK, E.M.
The disease concept of alcoholism
New Haven: Hillhouse Press, 1960
6
KENDELL, R.E.
The fate of untreated alcoholics
Quart. J. Stud. Alc., 27: 30, 1966
7
STRAUS, R. & BACON, S.D.
Alcoholism and social stability. A study of occupational integration in 2,023 male clinic patients
Quart. J. Stud. Alc., 12: 231, 1951
8
WALLERSTEIN, R.S., ed.
Hospital treatment of alcoholism
Meninger Clinic Monograph, no. 11
London: Mayo, 1957

JOSÉ HORWITZ

PEDRO NAVEILLÁN

CARMEN MARAMBIO

MELITTA CORDUA

HILDA GONZÁLEZ

Psychiatric Hospital
National Health Service of Chile
Santiago, Chile

25

Evaluation of the Results of Alcoholism Treatment

Traditions, prejudices and negative attitudes towards the alcoholic and the possibility of his recovery have created a pessimistic atmosphere regarding the results of treatment. This is expressed by physicians and the public in general as a feeling of despair which tends to produce an abandonment of any therapeutic effort. Because of this, health administrators are not inclined to provide the necessary resources to control alcoholism since this illness appears scarcely amenable to successful treatment.

The treatment of alcoholism is difficult and frustrating, but this does not justify the pessimistic attitude which was and still is held by many of us and which does not correspond to reality. Progress in scientific knowledge has led us to an operational definition of alcoholism as psychological and, especially, physical dependence on alcohol. The latter is the pathogenic nucleus of a number of symptomatic manifestations of pathological drinking. We have thus been able to study it more clearly, carefully assessing its clinical syndromes, describing its natural history, and carrying out epidemiological studies which have enabled us to propose preventive programs and patterns of treatment.

We need to have a clear understanding of the objectives and results that can be achieved, and the amount of money required in order to plan a careful program designed to control alcoholism. During the last 25 years a number of evaluation studies of alcoholism treatment have been conducted, but we cannot compare these reports because of: (a) differences in diagnostic criteria; (b) differences in the definition of a "case"; (c) differences in the therapeutic measures applied; and (d) differences in recovery criteria. In any event, most are retrospective analyses made on groups of patients treated years ago, and therefore we are not able to give much credit to the accumulated data. In addition, we are commonly unable to locate a substantial number of the cases in the samples, so the investigation partially loses its validity. These factors explain the apparent variation in the success of treatment as reported in studies before 1953 and as reported since then.

The reports of Voegtlin (17), Lemere et al. (10), Voegtlin et al. (18), O'Hollaren and Lemere (12), Larimer (9), and Hoff and

McKeown (7), for example, provide a more favourable picture than reports published later. The diagnoses are not precise, some are inaccurate, and some patients are included that now would only be classified as excessive drinkers. There is also a marked lack of background information.

The investigations that have been carried out during the last 10 or 15 years have reported less success in treatment, but the proportion is still important. The investigations between 1956 and 1964 of Davies, Shepherd, and Myers (2), Selzer and Holloway (16), Gibbins and Armstrong (4), Pfeffer and Berger (13), Rossi *et al.* (14, 15), Glatt (5, 6), and Dintrans and Arce (3) involved more precise diagnoses based on physical dependence on alcohol in many cases, and therefore are more uniform. Nevertheless, all are retrospective studies except those of Davies *et al.*, Glatt, and Dintrans *et al.*

Davies, Shepherd, and Myers (2) studied the evolution of 50 patients admitted to the Maudsley Hospital in London, England. The treatment consisted in the establishment of a strong physician-patient relationship to create awareness of the disease, plus disulfiram treatment and encouragement to take part in religious activities and in groups or clubs formed by Alcoholics Anonymous. Only one patient was lost during the two-year period of observation. Of the other 49, ten suppressed all ingestion of alcoholic beverages during the whole period; eight had brief relapses. The prognosis was found to be influenced favourably by the following factors: a well-balanced personality, good work history, being married, and consultation for the first time. Other positive factors were: good social standing, prolonged ingestion of disulfiram, and permanent contact with AA. If a patient was able to avoid ingestion during the first six months after the initiation of treatment, the probability of subsequent sobriety was high.

Glatt (6), studied 94 alcoholics during their stay at the Warlingham Park Hospital in London between 1952 and 1954. He followed their progress for periods that fluctuated between 24 and 40 months after discharge from the hospital. Sixteen per cent of the cases were not followed and were classified as not recovered. One-third

of the patients were classified as psychopathic personalities. The results can be summarized as follows: one-third practised abstinence during the whole period of observation; one-third abstained but had one or more relapses; and in one-third the treatment failed. Similar proportions were observed in the total group of 192 alcoholics who were followed up for periods between 6 to 40 months. The first relapse was studied in 100 patients: 76 relapsed during the first to third month; 16 from the fourth to sixth; five between the seventh and twelfth; two between the thirteenth and twenty-fourth; and one between the twenty-fifth and thirty-sixth month. The results were significantly better in men than in women, and were also better in normal subjects than in psychopaths. The treatment was also more successful in patients who had a higher social status.

Dintrans and Arce (3) studied a group of 228 alcoholics who had been admitted to the Division of Internal Medicine of the Hospital in Rancagua, Chile, between December 1957 and December 1962. They were treated with group and individual psychotherapy, and disulfiram, observed by a social worker, and encouraged to participate in the activities of the Club for Recovered Alcoholics. In some cases a special treatment was provided to provoke aversion to alcohol.

The results were: complete recovery (that is, total abstinence) in 17.51 per cent; successful recovery (patients who relapsed an average of less than 20 days per year and voluntarily asked for further treatment) in 22.4 per cent; "doubtful cases" (patients who still came for out-patient consultation but consumed alcohol for periods averaging over 20 days per year) in 30.3 per cent; and failures in 29.81 per cent. Thus, 40 per cent in all were considered recovered.

We made a prospective study designed to obtain complete knowledge of the results obtained by an alcoholic control centre, keeping in mind the social and cultural conditions of the population served and the resources available, in order to prepare a rational plan for treatment that might be applied throughout the country. We observed the progress of 200 patients who consulted at the Alcoholic Centre

TABLE 25–1

AGE AND SEX COMPOSITION OF THE FOLLOW-UP SAMPLE
OF 200 ALCOHOLIC PATIENTS OF THE PSYCHIATRIC
HOSPITAL, SANTIAGO DE CHILE, APRIL 1, 1963 TO
NOVEMBER 30, 1965

Age group	Total sample		Males		Females	
	number	per cent	number	per cent	number	per cent
21–30	29	14.5	27	15.0	2	10.0
31–40	95	47.5	84	46.7	11	55.0
41–50	49	24.5	44	24.4	5	25.0
51–60	20	10.0	18	10.0	2	10.0
61 and older	7	3.5	7	3.9	0	0.0
total	200	100.0	180	100.0	20	100.0
average			34.6 yrs.		38.6 yrs.	

of the Psychiatric Hospital in Santiago, starting in April 1963. We studied all cases without preselection as to medical or neuropsychiatric complications, duration of the disease, premorbid personality, or any other of the many factors that experience shows to be negative influences on prognosis. We completed the series of 200 patients on November 30, 1963, and the study was concluded when the last patient completed a period of two years. Thus, the follow-up period varied between 24 and 31 months.

DEFINITION

Alcoholism was stated as a diagnosis in every patient who presented an irreversible physical dependence on alcohol and who therefore suffered from an "inability to stop" once consumption was initiated (intermittent alcoholism), or an "inability to abstain" (inveterate alcoholism), and who suffered from withdrawal symptoms. Psychological and sociocultural dependence is included by this definition because such dependencies appear prior to or together with physical dependence.

The study included every patient that met one of the following conditions: (*a*) sought treatment for the first time; (*b*) initiated adequate treatment for the first time, even though he had sought treatment; *or* (*c*) had been treated before and had relapsed, but had not

sought treatment for alcoholism for a period of at least one year prior to admission at the time of this study.

A patient was considered recovered if he was able to abstain from alcoholic beverages during the whole period of observation or if his relapses did not exceed a total of 60 days.

CHARACTERISTICS OF THE SAMPLE

As previously noted, we did not select patients except to include only those who lived in Santiago so as to be able to observe their progress in detail. The chosen alcoholics therefore represent the typical alcoholic clients of the Public Health Service in Santiago.

Their distribution by sex (180 males and 20 females) corresponds approximately to the alcoholism prevalence rates observed in the country. Sixty-two per cent of the patients were under 40 years of age. Other studies have a lower percentage for this group; Glatt for example, has only 26.5 per cent of 268 patients in this age group (5).

The great majority of our patients were married (73.5 per cent), whereas only 39 per cent of Glatt's patients were married. Rossi and Bradley (14) report 50 per cent of their sample as married.

Seventy-eight and five-tenths per cent of the patients had received only a primary education or were illiterate. Six per cent had secondary

TABLE 25–2

MARITAL STATUS OF THE FOLLOW-UP SAMPLE OF 200
ALCOHOLIC PATIENTS

	Total sample		Males		Females	
Marital status	number	per cent	number	per cent	number	per cent
single	39	19.5	37	20.5	2	10
married	147	73.5	131	72.9	16	80
widowed	7	3.5	6	3.3	1	5
separated	7	3.5	6	3.3	1	5
total	200	100.0	180	100.0	20	100.0

TABLE 25–3

OCCUPATIONAL AND EDUCATIONAL STATUS OF THE FOLLOW-UP SAMPLE OF
200 ALCOHOLIC PATIENTS

Occupation	Illiterate or first cycle primary	Second cycle primary education	First cycle secondary education	Second cycle secondary or technical or university	No data	Total
professional, managerial, and white collar	4	7	4	7	—	22
skilled workers	18	52	10	1	3	84
unskilled workers	25	28	5	2	—	60
unemployed	6	11	3	2	1	23
military	—	3	3	—	1	7
housewives	—	3	1	—	—	4
total	53	104	26	12	5	200

TABLE 25–4

TYPE AND DURATION OF ALCOHOLISM AND DURATION OF
DRINKING IN THE FOLLOW-UP SAMPLE OF
200 ALCOHOLIC PATIENTS

Type of alcoholism	No. of cases	Average years of drinking	Average years of alcoholism
intermittent	99	11.6	9.2
inveterate	101	13.9	10.2

TABLE 25–5

DURATION OF ALCOHOLISM AND OF DRINKING BY SEX IN
THE FOLLOW-UP SAMPLE OF 200 ALCOHOLIC PATIENTS

Sex	No. of cases	Average years of drinking	Average years of alcoholism
male	180	12.7	10.2
female	20	14.9	5.8

education and very few had a university degree. Eighty-nine per cent were or had been working-men and only 11 per cent were in some business reflecting a higher degree of professional responsibility. This is the reason for the appearance of four persons of low educational level but who worked as independent businessmen.

The group was subdivided into 99 intermittent alcoholics and 101 inveterate alcoholics, which corresponds exactly to the distribution found by Horwitz *et al.* in other studies (8).

The average duration of the habit considered from the first consumption until the appearance of physical dependence was similar in intermittent and inveterate alcoholics (11.6 years and 13.9 years respectively). It was also similar in men and women (12.3 and 14.9 years respectively). The average length of the sickness at the time of consultation was 9.2 years in intermittent alcoholics and 10.2 years in inveterate alcoholics. If we consider the distribution by sex and diagnosis, inveterate alcoholism was more frequent in women: 14 inveterate alcoholics and 6 intermittent; only 87 of the men were inveterate and 93 intermittent. It seems that the social attitude towards excessive ingestion of alcohol beverages in women forces them to hide their habit and therefore to distribute their consumption over the whole day. They maintain this drinking pattern throughout the evolution of their disease.

The study of the family and personal background of the patients revealed only one factor worth mentioning: Forty-one and five-tenths per cent [83] of the patients had one or more relatives who also suffered from alcoholism. Thirty and five-tenths per cent [61] had suffered psychopathological complications such as delirium tremens, or hallucinosis. Twenty-two and five-tenths per cent [45] had suffered encephalocranial traumata of serious nature. Nine and five-tenths per cent [19] had marked signs of psychopathic personality, four and five-tenths per cent [9] were neurotics, two per cent [4] were epileptics, and two suffered from oligophrenia. Some of the patients had more than one of these morbid signs. In all, 104 patients (52 per cent) showed one or more such signs in their personal background.

Unfortunately, the proportion of alcoholic relatives was very high, which provides an indication as to the social and cultural environment in which our patients lived and the negative influence it had on their recovery. Our clinical experience indicates that encephalocranial traumatisms lead to a rapid onset of physical dependence or its aggravation if it already exists. Of our patients, twenty-two and five-tenths per cent had had one or more encephalocranial traumatisms of a serious nature. The frequency of psychopathological complications is another negative factor, since these reflect an advanced stage of the disease.

TREATMENT

The patients were treated on an out-patient basis. A high proportion needed to be hospitalized for a short period (no more than 15 days) to interrupt a crisis of alcoholic ingestion, to start administration of disulfiram, or to initiate special treatment to provoke an aversion to alcohol. We also hospitalized the ones who had psychopathological complications due to alcoholism. Otherwise, the therapeutive measures taken were individual and group psychotherapy, aversive treatment and/or disulfiram, plus the help of the Social Service to assist the patient with problems of social interaction.

The patients were asked to come for medical control every 15 days for the first two months, every 30 days for the next ten months, and every 60 days during the second year. If the patient was not able to come to the hospital, the social worker visited him at his home to determine his condition, his attitude towards ingestion of alcoholic beverages, and his social adaptation. The social workers also educated and informed the patient's relatives about alcohol and its problems.

Some of the patients who frequently relapsed refused to continue the treatment, and therefore their cases were "closed" temporarily, but were kept under observation at less frequent intervals. Many of them returned voluntarily to ask for help.

Every patient who received one or more of the therapeutic measures noted was considered "under treatment," and because of this the

TABLE 25–6

RESULTS OF ALCOHOLISM TREATMENT: MONTHLY AND TOTAL PROBABILITY
OF RELAPSE

x	lx	Wx	rx	Ax	Lx	qx	px	$100\,hpx$	$100\,hqx$
0	200	1	—	1 (D)	199	0.0	100	100.0	0.0
1	198	—	—	—	198	0.0	100	100.0	0.0
2	198	1	13	—	197.5	6.6	93.4	93.4	6.6
3	184	—	16	—	184	8.7	91.3	85.3	14.7
4	168	—	15	—	168	8.9	91.1	77.7	22.3
5	153	—	12	—	153	7.8	92.2	71.2	28.4
6	141	—	14	—	141	9.9	90.1	64.5	35.5
7	127	—	11	—	127	8.7	91.3	58.9	41.1
8	116	—	7	—	116	6	94.0	55.4	44.6
9	109	—	9	1 (D)	108.5	8.3	91.7	50.8	49.2
10	99	—	6	—	99	6.1	93.9	47.7	52.3
11	93	1	5	—	92.5	5.4	94.6	45.1	54.9
12	87	—	2	—	87	2.3	97.7	44.1	55.9
13	85	—	2	—	85	2.3	97.7	43.1	56.9
14	83	—	2	—	83	2.4	97.6	42.1	57.9
15	81	—	5	—	81	6.2	93.8	39.5	60.5
16	76	—	2	—	76	2.6	97.4	38.5	61.5
17	74	1	—	—	73.5	0.0	100.0	38.5	61.5
18	73	—	1	—	73	1.4	98.6	38.0	62.0
19	72	1	—	—	71.5	0.0	100.0	38.0	62.0
20	71	—	4	—	71	5.6	94.4	35.9	64.1
21	67	1	—	—	66.5	0.0	100.0	35.9	64.1
22	66	1	—	—	65.5	0.0	100.0	35.9	64.1
23	65	—	2	21	54.5	3.7	96.3	34.6	65.4
24	42	—	2	14	34	5.9	94.1	32.6	67.4
25	26	—	—	6	23	0.0	100.0	32.6	67.4
26	20	—	—	3	18.5	0.0	100.0	32.6	67.4
27	17	—	—	9	12.5	0.0	100.0	32.6	67.4
28	8	—	—	1	7.5	0.0	100.0	32.6	67.4
29	7	—	—	1	6.5	0.0	100.0	32.6	67.4
30	6	—	—	6	3	0.0	100.0	32.6	67.4

Columns are as follows: month of follow-up (x); cases considered lost to follow-up through death or for other reasons (Wx, Ax); number of relapses (rx); number exposed to risk of relapse (Lx); probability of relapse from one month to the next (qx), and of no relapse (px); probability for original sample of not relapsing by the end of each follow-up period (hpx), and the complementary probability of relapse (hqx).

group includes patients who started treatment but did not come to the clinic subsequently for further consultation.

The patients varied in their adherence to the prescribed treatment regimen. Very few did exactly as told. For example, regular consumption of disulfiram was exceptional. However, this is often found in the case of oral administration of any medication that has to be taken for a long time.

RESULTS

To analyse the results we used the Life Table Method which permitted us to state the probability of "relapse" and "no relapse" during monthly periods, from the beginning of the experience.* This provided a dynamic view of the group during the whole period of observation. Only seven cases were lost (3.5 per cent), and therefore our data are undoubtedly statistically reliable.

Of all patients, 32.6 per cent completed the observation period and were considered "recovered." That is to say, either these patients remained totally abstinent or their relapses did not exceed 60 days. Half of the group can be considered partial failures during the first ten

*We must thank Dr. Enrique Pereda for his valuable help with the statistical analysis of the material and the follow-up techniques. The technical procedures employed will be described in detail in a future communication.

TABLE 25–7

RESULTS OF ALCOHOLISM TREATMENT WITH TOTAL ABSTINENCE DURING THE
WHOLE FOLLOW-UP PERIOD AS RECOVERY CRITERION: MONTHLY AND TOTAL
PROBABILITY OF RELAPSE

x	lx	Wx	rx	Ax	Lx	qx	px	$100\,hpx$	$100\,hqx$
0	200	1	15	1 (D)	199.0	7.5	92.5	92.5	7.5
1	183	—	23	—	183.0	12.6	87.8	81.2	18.8
2	160	1	24	—	159.5	15.0	85.0	69.0	31.0
3	135	—	16	—	135.0	11.8	88.2	60.9	39.1
4	119	—	21	—	119.0	17.6	82.4	50.2	49.8
5	98	—	8	—	98.0	8.2	91.8	46.1	53.9
6	90	—	7	—	90.0	7.8	92.2	42.5	57.5
7	83	—	11	—	83.0	13.2	86.8	36.6	63.4
8	72	—	5	—	72.0	6.9	93.1	34.1	65.9
9	67	—	4	—	67.0	6.0	94.0	32.0	68.0
10	63	—	2	—	63.0	3.2	96.8	31.0	69.0
11	61	1	3	—	60.5	5.0	95.0	29.4	70.6
12	57	—	4	—	57.0	7.0	93.0	27.3	72.7
13	53	—	3	—	53.0	5.7	94.3	25.7	74.3
14	50	—	2	—	50.0	4.0	96.0	24.7	75.3
15	48	—	—	—	48.0	0.0	100.0	24.7	75.3
16	48	—	2	—	48.0	4.2	95.8	23.7	76.3
17	46	—	—	—	46.0	0.0	100.0	23.7	76.3
18	46	—	1	—	46.0	2.2	97.8	23.2	76.8
19	45	1	3	—	44.5	6.7	93.3	21.6	78.4
20	41	—	1	—	41.0	2.4	97.6	21.1	78.9
21	40	—	—	—	40.0	0.0	100.0	21.1	78.9
22	40	—	2	—	40.0	5.0	95.0	20.0	80.0
23	38	—	—	13	31.5	0.0	100.0	20.0	80.0
24	25	—	—	9	20.5	0.0	100.0	20.0	80.0
25	16	—	—	5	13.5	0.0	100.0	20.0	80.0
26	11	—	—	2	10.0	0.0	100.0	20.0	80.0
27	9	—	—	5	6.5	0.0	100.0	20.0	80.0
28	4	—	—	—	4.0	0.0	100.0	20.0	80.0
29	4	—	—	1	3.5	0.0	100.0	20.0	80.0
30	3	—	—	3	1.5	0.0	100.0	20.0	80.0

See note to Table 25–6.

months. But from then on, their probability of relapse increases very slowly. The need for more intensive medical and social therapy during the early months of treatment is clearly indicated by the greater probability of relapse at this time. Nearly all authors agree on this point.

If we take only total abstinence from alcoholic beverages during the whole period of observation as the criterion of recovery, we obtain the results shown in Table 25-7. The overall probability of no relapse is 20 per cent and declines most rapidly during the first six months of treatment.

Considering the matter in its clinical aspect, and employing the broader criterion that relapses should not exceed 60 days, the overall probability of recovery is 36.4 per cent for intermittent alcoholics and 27.9 per cent for in-

veterate alcoholics. This difference is not statistically significant.

If we consider sex differences, 30.7 per cent of the men and 44.4 per cent of the women did not suffer relapses in excess of 60 days. This is a marked difference, but it is also without statistical significance.

With respect to occupational status, there were 11 categories falling into four status groups. Group I included professionals, technicians, directors, businessmen, and public and private employees. Group II included artisans, skilled workers, and transport personnel. Group III included day labourers, unskilled workers, and household servants; and group IV included unemployed persons, soldiers, and housewives. Tables 25–12 to 25–15 show the probabilities of relapse of the four groups. The probability of no excessive relapse in the first group was

TABLE 25–8

RESULTS OF ALCOHOLISM TREATMENT FOR INTERMITTENT ALCOHOLICS:
BIMONTHLY AND TOTAL PROBABILITY OF RELAPSE

x	lx	Wx	rx	Ax	Lx	qx	px	$100\,hpx$	$100\,hqx$
0–1	99	1	—	1 (D)	98.0	0.0	100.0	100.0	0.0
2–3	97	—	13	—	97.0	13.4	86.6	86.6	13.4
4–5	84	—	10	—	84.0	11.9	88.1	76.3	23.7
6–7	74	—	14	—	74.0	18.9	81.1	61.9	38.1
8–9	60	—	5	1 (D)	59.5	8.4	91.6	56.7	43.3
10–11	54	1	5	—	53.5	9.3	90.7	51.4	48.6
12–13	48	—	—	—	48.0	0.0	100.0	51.4	48.6
14–15	48	—	3	—	48.0	6.2	93.8	48.2	51.8
16–17	45	—	1	—	45.0	2.2	97.8	47.1	52.9
18–19	44	1	—	—	43.5	0.0	100.0	47.1	52.9
20–21	43	1	4	—	43.5	9.2	90.8	42.8	57.2
22–23	38	1	1	13	31.0	3.2	96.8	41.4	58.6
24–25	23	—	2	13	16.5	12.1	87.9	36.4	63.6
26–27	8	—	—	5	5.5	0.0	100.0	36.4	63.6
28–29	3	—	—	1	2.5	0.0	100.0	36.4	63.6
30–31	2	—	—	2	1.0	0.0	100.0	36.4	63.6

See note to Table 25–6.

TABLE 25–9

RESULTS OF ALCOHOLISM TREATMENT FOR INVETERATE ALCOHOLICS:
BIMONTHLY AND TOTAL PROBABILITY OF RELAPSE

x	lx	Wx	rx	Ax	Lx	qx	px	$100\,hpx$	$100\,hqx$
0–1	101	—	—	—	101.0	0.0	100.0	100.0	0.0
2–3	101	1	16	—	100.5	15.9	84.1	84.1	15.9
4–5	84	—	17	—	84.0	20.2	79.8	67.1	32.9
6–7	67	—	11	—	67.0	16.4	83.6	56.1	43.9
8–9	56	—	11	—	56.0	19.6	80.4	45.1	54.9
10–11	45	—	6	—	45.0	13.3	86.7	39.1	60.9
12–13	39	—	4	—	39.0	10.3	89.7	35.1	64.9
14–15	35	—	4	—	35.0	11.4	88.6	31.1	68.9
16–17	31	1	1	—	30.5	3.3	96.7	30.1	69.9
18–19	29	—	1	—	29.0	3.4	96.6	29.1	70.9
20–21	28	—	—	—	28.0	0.0	100.0	29.1	70.9
22–23	28	—	1	8	24.0	4.2	95.8	27.9	72.1
24–25	19	—	—	7	15.5	0.0	100.0	27.9	72.1
26–27	12	—	—	7	8.5	0.0	100.0	27.9	72.1
28–29	5	—	—	1	4.5	0.0	100.0	27.9	72.1
30–31	4	—	—	4	2.0	0.0	100.0	27.9	72.1

See note to Table 25–6.

59.1 per cent during the observation period of 31 months; 31.2 per cent in the second group; 29.8 per cent in the third; and 22.9 per cent in the fourth. The difference is statistically significant ($p < 0.01$) between the first group and the three others. The differences among the other groups are not significant.

The same method was used to study the results of the treatment with reference to educational status. The probability of no excessive relapse is higher among patients with a higher educational status, but this difference could be accidental. The great majority of our patients had a low educational status; only 12 had reached the second cycle of secondary education or had some technical or university education.

As previously noted, only 32.6 per cent of the patients could be considered "recovered" on the criterion of not more than 60 days of relapse during the whole follow-up period. But this does not take into account the two-thirds

TABLE 25–10

RESULTS OF ALCOHOLISM TREATMENT FOR MALES:
BIMONTHLY AND TOTAL PROBABILITY OF RELAPSE

x	lx	Wx	rx	Ax	Lx	qx	px	100 hpx	100 hqx
0–1	180	1	—	1 (D)	179.0	0.0	100.0	100.0	0.0
2–3	178	1	27	—	177.5	15.2	84.8	84.8	15.2
4–5	150	—	24	—	150.0	16.0	84.0	71.2	28.8
6–7	126	—	22	—	126.0	17.5	82.5	58.7	41.3
8–9	104	—	15	1 (D)	103.5	14.5	85.5	50.2	49.8
10–11	88	1	9	—	87.5	10.3	89.7	45.0	55.0
12–13	78	—	4	—	78.0	5.1	94.9	42.7	57.3
14–15	74	—	7	—	74.0	9.6	90.4	38.6	61.4
16–17	67	—	2	—	67.0	3.0	97.0	37.4	62.6
18–19	65	1	1	—	64.5	1.5	98.5	36.8	63.2
20–21	63	—	4	—	63.0	6.3	93.7	34.5	65.5
22–23	59	1	2	18	49.5	4.0	96.0	33.1	66.9
24–25	38	—	2	19	27.5	7.3	92.7	30.7	69.3
26–27	17	—	—	10	12.0	0.0	100.0	30.7	69.3
28–29	7	—	—	2	6.0	0.0	100.0	30.7	69.3
30–31	5	—	—	5	2.5	0.0	100.0	30.7	69.3

See note to Table 25–6.

TABLE 25–11

RESULTS OF ALCOHOLISM TREATMENT FOR FEMALES:
BIMONTHLY AND TOTAL PROBABILITY OF RELAPSE

x	lx	Wx	rx	Ax	Lx	qx	px	100 hpx	100 hqx
0–1	20	—	—	—	20.0	0.0	100.0	100.0	0.0
2–3	20	—	2	—	20.0	10.0	90.0	90.0	10.0
4–5	18	—	3	—	18.0	16.7	83.3	75.0	25.0
6–7	15	—	3	—	15.0	20.0	80.0	60.0	40.0
8–9	12	—	1	—	12.0	8.3	91.7	55.0	45.0
10–11	11	—	2	—	11.0	18.2	81.8	44.4	55.6
12–13	9	—	—	—	9.0	0.0	100.0	44.4	55.6
14–15	9	—	—	—	9.0	0.0	100.0	44.4	55.5
16–17	9	1	—	—	8.5	0.0	100.0	44.4	55.6
18–19	8	—	—	—	8.0	0.0	100.0	44.4	55.6
20–21	8	1	—	—	7.5	0.0	100.0	44.4	55.6
22–23	7	—	—	3	5.5	0.0	100.0	44.4	55.6
24–25	4	—	—	1	3.5	0.0	100.0	44.4	55.6
26–27	3	—	—	2	2.5	0.0	100.0	44.4	55.6
28–29	1	—	—	—	1.0	0.0	100.0	44.4	55.6
30–31	1	—	—	1	0.5	0.0	100.0	44.4	55.6

See note to Table 25–6.

who appear as failures, many of whom benefited from treatment, but did not reach the level of recovery established at the outset.

A method that has been little used is the comparison of the number of days of alcohol consumption before treatment with total days of consumption after treatment (4). In this way, a balance of "profit" and "loss" is established using the patient himself as control. It would be better to use other alcoholics not under treatment as controls, but this procedure is fraught with difficulties which need not be enumerated here.

Using the Gibbins and Armstrong recovery criterion we can obtain some information about the patients labelled as failures in the analysis presented above. There was a marked decrease in the number of days of ingestion of alcohol each year, together with other elements of social recovery that are more difficult to tabulate.

In each patient, we compared the number of drinking days in the year preceding the initia-

RESULTS OF ALCOHOLISM TREATMENT FOR DIFFERENT OCCUPATIONAL
STATUS GROUPS: BIMONTHLY AND TOTAL PROBABILITY OF RELAPSE

TABLE 25–12

GROUP I

x	lx	Wx	rx	Ax	Lx	qx	px	$100\ hpx$	$100\ hqx$
0–1	22	—	—	—	22.0	0.0	100.0	100.0	0.0
2–3	22	—	2	—	22.0	9.1	90.9	90.9	9.1
4–5	20	—	3	—	20.0	5.0	95.0	86.3	13.7
6–7	17	—	2	—	17.0	11.8	88.2	76.1	23.9
8–9	15	—	1	—	15.0	6.7	93.3	71.0	29.0
10–11	14	—	—	—	14.0	0.0	100.0	71.0	29.0
12–13	14	—	—	—	14.0	0.0	100.0	71.0	29.0
14–15	14	—	1	—	14.0	7.1	92.9	66.0	34.0
16–17	13	—	—	—	13.0	0.0	100.0	66.0	34.0
18–19	13	1	—	—	12.5	0.0	100.0	66.0	34.0
20–21	12	1	—	—	11.5	0.0	100.0	66.0	34.0
22–23	11	—	1	3	9.5	10.5	89.5	59.1	40.9
24–25	7	—	—	3	5.5	0.0	100.0	59.1	40.9
26–27	4	—	1	1	3.5	0.0	100.0	59.1	40.9
28–29	3	—	—	—	3.0	0.0	100.0	59.1	40.9
30–31	3	—	—	3	3.0	0.0	100.0	59.1	40.9

See note to Table 25–6.

TABLE 25–13

GROUP II

x	lx	Wx	rx	Ax	Lx	qx	px	$100\ hpx$	$100\ hqx$
0–1	84	1	—	—	83.5	0.0	100.0	100.0	0.0
2–3	83	—	8	—	83.0	9.6	90.4	90.4	9.6
4–5	75	—	11	—	75.0	14.7	85.3	77.1	22.7
6–7	64	—	11	—	64.0	17.2	82.8	63.8	36.2
8–9	53	—	9	—	53.0	17.0	83.0	52.9	47.1
10–11	44	—	9	—	44.0	20.4	79.6	42.1	47.9
12–13	35	—	3	—	35.0	8.6	91.4	38.5	61.5
14–15	32	—	1	—	32.0	3.1	96.9	37.3	62.7
16–17	31	—	1	—	31.0	3.2	96.8	36.1	63.9
18–19	30	—	—	—	30.0	0.0	100.0	36.1	63.9
20–21	30	—	1	—	30.0	3.3	96.7	34.9	65.1
22–23	29	—	1	9	24.5	4.1	95.9	33.5	66.5
24–25	19	—	1	9	14.5	6.9	93.1	31.2	68.8
26–27	9	—	—	5	6.5	0.0	100.0	31.2	68.8
28–29	4	—	—	2	3.0	0.0	100.0	31.2	68.8
30–31	2	—	—	2	1.0	0.0	100.0	31.2	68.8

See note to Table 25–6.

tion of treatment with the number in the first
and second years of treatment. We established
the profit or loss in each case, profit in the case
of relative abstinence and loss if the patients
drank more than the year preceding the initiation of treatment. We expressed the difference
in percentages of profit and loss. This analysis
includes 183 of the 200 cases. Seventeen were
lost for want of sufficient data on their behaviour.

During the first year of observation, with five
exceptions, all patients drank for the same
number of days, or less, than during the previous
year. During the second year, nine drank more
than in the year before admission to treatment,
and the rest drank less or in the same proportion. Table 25-16 indicates the profit for each
year.

During the first year, 68.8 per cent of the
patients drank between 50 and 100 per cent

RESULTS OF ALCOHOLISM TREATMENT FOR DIFFERENT OCCUPATIONAL
STATUS GROUPS: BIMONTHLY AND TOTAL PROBABILITY OF RELAPSE

TABLE 25–14

GROUP III

x	lx	Wx	rx	Ax	Lx	qx	px	$100\,hpx$	$100\,hqx$
0–1	60	—	—	—	60.0	0.0	100.0	100.0	0.0
2–3	60	1	11	—	59.5	18.5	81.5	81.5	18.5
4–5	48	—	10	—	48.0	20.8	79.2	64.5	35.5
6–7	38	—	8	—	38.0	21.0	79.0	50.9	49.1
8–9	30	—	2	1 (D)	29.5	6.8	93.2	47.4	52.6
10–11	27	—	—	—	27.0	0.0	100.0	47.4	52.6
12–13	27	—	1	—	27.0	3.7	96.3	45.6	54.4
14–15	26	—	3	—	26.0	11.5	88.5	40.4	59.6
16–17	23	—	1	—	23.0	4.3	95.7	38.7	61.3
18–19	22	—	1	—	22.0	4.5	95.5	37.0	63.0
20–21	21	—	2	—	21.0	9.5	90.5	33.5	66.5
22–23	19	—	—	6	16.0	0.0	100.0	33.5	66.5
24–25	13	—	1	8	9.0	11.1	88.9	29.8	70.2
26–27	4	—	—	3	2.5	0.0	100.0	29.8	70.2
28–29	1	—	—	—	1.0	0.0	100.0	29.8	70.2
30–31	1	—	—	1	0.5	0.0	100.0	29.8	70.2

See note to Table 25–6.

TABLE 25–15

GROUP IV

x	lx	wx	rx	Ax	Lx	qx	px	$100\,hpx$	$100\,hqx$
0–1	34	—	—	1 (D)	33.5	0.0	100.0	100.0	0.0
2–3	33	—	8	—	33.0	24.2	75.8	75.8	24.2
4–5	25	—	3	—	25.0	12.0	88.0	66.7	33.3
6–7	22	—	4	—	22.0	18.2	81.8	54.6	45.4
8–9	18	—	4	—	18.0	22.2	77.8	42.5	57.5
10–11	14	1	2	—	13.5	14.8	85.2	32.0	68.0
12–13	11	—	—	—	11.0	0.0	100.0	32.0	68.0
14–15	11	—	2	—	11.0	18.2	81.8	26.2	73.8
16–17	9	1	—	—	8.5	0.0	100.0	26.2	73.8
18–19	8	—	—	—	8.0	0.0	100.0	26.2	73.8
20–21	8	—	1	—	8.0	12.5	87.5	22.9	71.1
22–23	7	1	—	3	5.0	0.0	100.0	22.9	77.1
24–25	3	—	—	—	3.0	0.0	100.0	22.9	77.1
26–27	3	—	—	3	1.5	0.0	100.0	22.9	77.1
28–29	—	—	—	—	—	—	—	—	—

See note to Table 25–6.

less (in terms of days) than the previous year. Only 10.4 per cent drank the same or more. Thirty and six-tenths per cent drank 100 per cent less. That is, they abstained completely from alcoholic beverages. During the second year, the percentage of patients who drank between 51 and 100 per cent less decreased to 51.4 per cent, and 31.7 per cent abstained completely. During the second year we put together data on all the patients who had lost

contact with the clinic and received no further treatment.

Thus 44.8 per cent of the patients could be considered recovered during the first year and 42.1 per cent during the second. Twenty-four per cent and 9.3 per cent, respectively, ingested alcohol between 51 and 80 per cent less (in terms of days) than the year before, and they can be considered definitely improved. As a conclusion we can say that about 50 per cent

TABLE 25–16

RESULTS OF ALCOHOLISM TREATMENT: PER CENT INCREASE IN DAYS OF
ABSTINENCE IN THE FIRST AND SECOND YEAR FOLLOWING TREATMENT AS
COMPARED WITH THE YEAR PRECEDING TREATMENT

	First year post-treatment		Second year post-treatment	
Days of abstinence	*no. of cases*	*per cent*	*no. of cases*	*per cent*
0 per cent or fewer	19	10.38	67	36.61
1–50 per cent more	38	20.77	22	12.02
51–80 per cent more	44	24.04	17	9.29
81–100 per cent more	82	44.81	77	42.08
total	183	100.00	183	100.00
100 per cent (total abstinence)	56	30.60	58	31.69

of the patients received some degree of benefit from the therapeutic measures.

Finally, 19 out of the 200 patients were psychopaths and ten were neurotics. Three of the 19 psychopaths abstained from alcohol during the whole observation period (15.8 per cent) and seven of the ten neurotics abstained (70 per cent). We included in these figures only those patients who suffered from abnormal characteristics that were manifested prior to the period in which alcohol dependence started. The presence of inadequate character features is frequent during alcoholism and therefore must be considered symptomatic of the disease.

DISCUSSION

As in any abnormality of behaviour, we must consider the number of patients who recover spontaneously in order to evaluate properly the results of treatment. Unfortunately this has been poorly studied. Lemere (11) concluded that 7 per cent of 500 alcoholics studied during the last six years of their lives recovered spontaneously. Amark (1) came to a similar conclusion. The definition of alcoholism is more precise in the second publication.

In our analysis, the rate of recovery based on the excessive relapse criterion was 32.6 per cent in an unselected group. If we analyse the number of days of alcohol ingestion before and after treatment we get more than 50 per cent of pa-

tients recovered. Gibbins and Armstrong (4) obtained inferior results with this method. Only 40.6 per cent of their patients ingested alcohol between 51 and 100 per cent less (in terms of months) than before treatment.

This is a useful way to evaluate the patients only if they can be observed regularly and frequently. Any significant reduction in the number of days of alcohol ingestion represents an improvement for the patient. The relatives of all our patients were interviewed to corroborate or rectify the information they had given about their alcohol habits. We were thus able to get reliable and comprehensive information about the pathological habit, and the exact number of days in which the patient indulged in alcoholic beverages before the beginning of treatment. Likewise, the patients' relatives proved better informants as to the post-treatment evolution of their disease and the details of their relapses than the patients themselves. When Gibbins and Armstrong (4) used the technique of profit or loss respecting alcohol consumption before and after the treatment, they recorded the months of consumption of each patient during the period of observation and they compared this with months of consumption during an equal period before treatment. That is, in the case of a patient whose follow-up lasted four years, the pretreatment period was also taken as four years. We thought it better to study only one year before the beginning of treatment. The patients remember the facts more clearly and if we consider alcoholism to be a disease which aggravates itself instead of improving as time goes on, it is better to consider only the last year before treatment.

The control of the patients is important, however simple it may be. During the first year of our follow-up, 68.8 per cent of the patients drank half the number of days, or less, than they did in the previous year. When our control stopped, because a number of patients refused to continue the treatment, the recovery rate was only 51.4 per cent, and a high percentage drank as much as or more than before the treatment (36.6 per cent). With this method of evaluation one can easily measure the effectiveness of a treatment centre for alcoholics, and we deemed it to be as useful as the usual criteria based on the number of relapses.

Only 15.8 per cent of the patients with psychopathic personalities completed the observation period in total abstinence, a percentage that is inferior to that for the general group (20.0 per cent). But our results are better than those obtained by Glatt (6), whose psychopaths showed a recovery rate of only 2.6 per cent. The other group with an unfavorable prognosis is the neurotic, and our results are therefore surprising: seven of the ten neurotic patients finished the observation period in total abstinence. Therefore we cannot say with complete assurance that such characteristics of personality indicate a poor prognosis.

We must remember that the habit of excessive consumption which is the material cause of the disease is firmly settled in our national culture and especially in the social group that provides the majority of the National Health Service's patients. Education and information about alcohol and alcoholism must be developed, together with the therapeutic action of treatment centres, in order to prevent new cases. At the same time, efforts must be made to modify the environment in which the patients live so as to prevent relapses.

If one considers all the factors involved, and remembers that we made no selection of our cases, our results are promising. They allow us to recommend the development of programs in which treatment and prevention are integrated, so as to control a disease that presents an obstacle to health programs and is of great magnitude.

SUMMARY

We have presented the results of an investigation designed to evaluate the efficiency of an alcoholism treatment centre and thereby to provide the basis of a rational plan for the treatment of alcoholism which could be applied throughout the country.

During a period of 24 to 31 months we studied the progress of 200 patients, all of whom consulted at the Alcoholic Centre of the Psychiatric Hospital in Santiago between April 1 and November 30, 1963. The only selection was as to place of residence; i.e., subjects had to be living in Santiago.

A diagnosis of alcoholism was made when there was irreversible physical dependence on alcohol. The results were analysed by means of the Life Table Method, which gives the probability of relapse in a period of one month, and by the Gibbins and Armstrong Method, comparing for each patient the number of days of consumption during the year prior to treatment with the days of consumption during the first and second years following treatment.

Treatment could be considered successful in 32.6 per cent of the patients on the basis of the excessive relapse criterion of recovery. The proportion was higher in the group of higher occupational status (59.1 per cent). There were no statistically significant differences by age, sex, educational status, or clinical type.

On the basis of the second recovery criterion, improvement in the number of days of abstinence occurred in 44.8 per cent during the first year and 42.1 per cent during the second year of the follow-up. Another 10 to 20 per cent also evidently benefitted from treatment to a lesser degree.

We conclude that education on alcohol and alcoholism must be developed together with therapeutic action in treatment centres, in order to avoid new cases and at the same time to modify the environment in which the patients live and work to prevent future relapses.

REFERENCES

1
AMARK, C.
A study on alcoholism
Acta psychiat. et neurol. scandinav., suppl. no. 70, 1951
2
DAVIES, D.L., SHEPHERD, M., & MYERS, E.
The two years' prognosis of 50 alcohol addicts after treatment in hospital
Quart. J. Stud. Alc., 18: 429, 1957
3
DINTRANS, E. & ARCE, A.
Consideraciones sobre el tratamiento antialcohólico durante cinco años de experiencia en el Hospital de Rancagua
Rev. Soc. Méd. O'Higgins y Colchagua, 3: 18, 1964
4
GIBBINS, R.J. & ARMSTRONG, J.D.
Effects of clinical treatment on behavior of alcoholic patients
Quart. J. Stud. Alc., 18: 429, 1957
5
GLATT, M.M.
Drinking habits of English middle class alcoholics
Acta psychiat. et neurol. scandinav., 37: 88, 1961
6
GLATT, M.M.
Treatment results in an English mental hospital alcoholic unit
Acta psychiat. et neurol. scandinav., 37: 143, 1961
7
HOFF, E.E. & MCKEOWN, C.
An evaluation of the use of tetraethyldisulfide in the treatment of 560 cases of alcohol addiction
Am. J. Psychiat., 109: 670, 1953
8
HOROWITZ, J., MUÑOZ, L.C., et al.
Investigaciones epidemiológicas acerca de morbilidad mental en Chile
Rev. serv. nac. de Sal., 3: 277, 1958
9
LARIMER, R.C.
Treatment of alcoholism with Antabuse
J.A.M.A., 150: 79, 1952
10
LEMERE, F., VOEGTLIN, W.L., BROZ, W.R.,
O'HOLLAREN, P., & TUPPER, W.E.
The conditioned reflex treatment of chronic alcoholism
J.A.M.A., 120: 269, 1942
11
LEMERE, F.
What happens to alcoholics?
Am. J. Psychiat., 109: 674, 1953
12
O'HOLLAREN, P. & LEMERE, F.
Conditioned reflex treatment of chronic alcoholism: results obtained in 2,323 cases from 3,125 admissions over a period of ten and a half years
New England J. Med., 239: 331, 1948
13
PFEFFER, A.Z. & BERGER, S.
A follow-up study of treated alcoholics
Quart. J. Stud. Alc., 18: 624, 1957
14
ROSSI, J.J. & BRADLEY, N.J.
Dynamic hospital treatment of alcoholism
Quart. J. Stud. Alc., 21: 432, 1960
15
ROSSI, J.J., STACH, A., & BRADLEY, N.J.
Effects of treatment of male alcoholics in a mental hospital
Quart. J. Stud. Alc., 24: 91, 1963
16
SELZER, M.L. & HOLLOWAY, W.H.
A follow-up of alcoholics committed to a state hospital
Quart. J. Stud. Alc., 18: 98, 1957
17
VOEGTLIN, W.L.
The treatment of alcoholics by establishing a conditioned reflex
Am. J. Med. Sc., 199: 802, 1940
18
VOEGTLIN, W.L., LEMERE, F., BROZ, W., & O'HOLLAREN, P.
Conditioned reflex treatment of alcoholic addiction: VI Follow-up report of 1042 cases
Am. J. Med. Sc., 203: 525, 1942

Organic Complications of Alcoholism

For a long time we faced in Chile an inexplicable medical attitude towards alcoholism. Clinical and general hospitals deemed alcoholism a problem beyond their sphere of action and its treatment was left exclusively in the hands of a number of devoted psychiatrists, who were the first to understand the extent of the problem and its enormous socioeconomic gravity. But psychiatrists soon realized that they were unable to face alone a problem which is so common among our people and hence turned to the internists for help. The Division of Internal Medicine, under the direction of Professor Rodolfo Armas Cruz, was the first to respond to the call, and took charge of a centre for alcoholic treatment which started functioning in the area covered by the San Juan de Dios Hospital. Later, similar institutions in Santiago and in the different provinces throughout Chile followed this example.

Psychiatrists were right in being seriously concerned, for alcoholism not only causes neurological and mental disorders but is also responsible for a number of pathological conditions which fall within the field covered by internal medicine, as we shall see in the course of these remarks. Although it is true that alcoholic patients frequently end up as psychiatric cases, at the beginning they are not; they start the habit as a result of social pressure and certain cultural and other tendencies which I shall not attempt to analyse here.

Alcohol damages various systems and organs in the human body. I shall enumerate a few to show that alcoholism is an important etiological factor in medical illnesses, and that we must work hand in hand with psychiatrists and other experts in the fight against alcoholism if we really intend to develop an effective social medicine.

CARDIOVASCULAR SYSTEM

Chabonel and other French scholars have demonstrated that cerebro-vascular accidents — especially hemorrhages in young people — occur frequently without hypertension or congenital aneurysms or arteriosclerosis. Such etiologies were discarded by careful microscopic and X-ray studies. The only positive element in these cases was a marked chronic alcoholism. These investigators deem that alcohol alone is capable of producing alterations in the mechanisms of blood coagulation and a striking decrease in prothrombin time, which on some occasions can fall below 50 per cent. English investigators also think that certain primitive myocardiopathies have an alcoholic origin, together with a degenerative process of the myocardial fiber, hypertrophy, and cardiac insufficiency. The expansion of the left ventricle would sometimes cause a non-lesional mitral insufficiency, difficult to differentiate from a true rheumatic valvulopathy or from one of a different origin. In any event, alcoholism interferes with the treatment of cardiac insufficiency, whatever the etiology of the latter, and makes compensation of such patients difficult.

It is also known that alcoholics drink more in the afternoon and evening, hours during which they should avoid excessive ingestion of liquids because of the increased risk of circulatory accidents at night caused by hypervolemia (pulmonary edema, paroxysmal dyspnea, etc.). The ingestion of a great quantity of liquids at these times is by itself capable of aggravating the condiiton of the cardiac patient, by placing excessive stress on the heart. If we add to this the toxic effect of alcohol on the myocardial fibre, we get an annulment of all our therapeutic efforts, and cardiac tonics and other compensatory measures become ineffective. It is probable that an adequate treatment of alcoholism in any cardiopathy would avoid future decompensations which weigh excessively on our already too heavy medical work. The same considerations apply to the treatment of arterial hypertension.

RESPIRATORY SYSTEM

The respiratory system is also affected by alcohol. The alcoholic is more vulnerable than other persons to common colds and acute bronchitis due to cold. The etiology of acute pulmonary affections is closely related to alcoholism through three different mechanisms:

1

Typical pneumopathy caused by prolonged exposure to cold. In these cases, the normal mechanisms of defence of the respiratory system fail, and the nasopharyngeal secretion falls directly to the lungs by the bronchial tubes, especially the right bronchus which is in a more vertical position. It is a common way of acquiring pneumonia in the cold season,

particularly among alcoholics who are apt to expose themselves to cold during the sleep which follows intoxication.

2

Alcoholics are also exposed to atypical pneumopathies, some of which are localized on the apical portions of the lungs. Sometimes these are caused by germs other than the pneumococcus and therefore are more serious and resistant to the usual treatments, especially to penicillin. For example, pneumopathies caused by Klebsiella and staphylococcus are more frequent in alcoholics and often complicated by pulmonary abscesses.

3

In daily practice, we have encountered a third mechanism which has received little attention up to the present, and which causes pneumonia in alcoholics: the aspiration of vomitus resulting from acute gastritis of alcoholic origin. The contents of the stomach can enter the respiratory system and rapidly produce pneumonia. Recently we saw a typical case of this nature.

Aside from the mechanisms mentioned, we must remember that alcoholism aggravates any pneumopathy. For example, some febrile alcoholics easily develop delirium tremens which is a very serious complication often ending in death. It should also be pointed out that alcoholism both seriously interferes with the treatment of pulmonary tuberculosis and aggravates this illness considerably, not only by decreasing the natural defences of the body but by its tendency to make the individual either forget to come to the hospital for periodic checkups or else abandon treatment altogether.

DIGESTIVE SYSTEM

Alcohol plays an important role in the illnesses of the digestive system. To begin with, alcohol is responsible for gastric damage, causing acute and chronic gastritis. Medical treatment of duodenal ulcer fails frequently in alcoholic patients. Although alcohol has nothing to do with the etiology of ulcers, it seriously endangers therapy since, unless alcohol ingestion can be suppressed, ulcerous crises occur more frequently and take longer to overcome.

Processes of duodenitis and enteritis with mal-

absorption syndromes have also been attributed to alcohol, but for the time being there is no definitive opinion as to the truth of this attribution.

After a survey of our clinical records, we concluded that a considerable number of digestive hemorrhages occurred after abundant and continued alcohol ingestion. On certain occasions the patients required emergency hospitalization and massive blood transfusions. These hemorrhages were caused by erosive gastritis and acute ulcerations, which, although superficial, can bleed abundantly. The patients had no record of ulcers, and hence X-ray studies had proved negative. At the moment it is difficult to state the percentage of digestive hemorrhages due to alcoholism, but there is no doubt that they exist. The Mallory-Weiss syndrome, commonly known to cause abundant bleeding due to the laceration of a zone in the stomach, frequently occurs after heavy alcohol ingestion.

Acute pancreatitis often follows excessive alcohol consumption and some authors have described pancreatic damage in autopsies of chronic alcoholics. Ramón Guerra and other Uruguayan authors have described hypoglycemic syndromes produced by alcohol, some of a serious nature. Hypoglycemia reached figures of 0.60 and even 0.30 gm/100 ml, especially in children given alcohol for experimental purposes.

The liver is without doubt the organ which suffers most from the harmful effects of alcohol. We have two hepatic pathologies with an alcoholic etiology: one (acute) is fatty infiltration of the liver and the other (chronic) is Laënnec's cirrhosis.

In 1958 Zieve described a pathology of alcoholic origin, characterized by hyperlipemia, jaundice, and hemolytic anemia, together with fatty infiltration of the liver. Hyperlipemia is sometimes so high that the blood serum assumes a milky appearance. Total lipids in blood normally fluctuate between 500 and 800 mg/100 ml, but in this syndrome they can rise to 1,500 mg/100 ml or more. Blood cholesterol levels also rise and it may be that the increase in lipids can produce a degree of hemolysis of the red blood corpuscles. Jaundice would be due to intrahepatic ectasia with a variable degree of cellular damage. Sometimes this pathology is accompanied by a painful crisis from the right hypocondrium which can simulate an hepatic colic. Kessel believes that together with hepatic

damage there is a pancreatic lesion, with insufficient production of the hormone which regulates the level of blood lipids. This condition, known as the Zieve Syndrome, recovers if alcohol consumption is stopped. Otherwise, it can end in cirrhosis or cause death by hepatic insufficiency, as was the case with the two patients we had in the Medical Division of the San Juan de Dios Hospital.

Myerson and his associates have described cases of acute anemia after alcoholic excesses, associated with fatty infiltration of the liver and a rise of lipids in the blood serum. These workers impute the anemia to medullar depression and hemolysing factors.

Portal or Laënnec's cirrhosis is recognized as caused largely by alcohol associated with malnutrition. This condition is very common in Chile and makes a substantial contribution to mortality rates (8 to 9 per cent of the general adult mortality rate) especially of citizens of middle age, that is, just the age when the individual is most useful to his family and community, and his work yields maximum returns.

Alcohol not only influences the etiology of hepatic cirrhosis, but also frustrates the treatment of a great number of cases since, despite the risk of death, patients continue to drink after discharge from hospital. Sermons and advice are not enough, nor even telling the patient, as some do with rude frankness, that his life is in danger. Cirrhotic patients, dependent on alcohol, commonly continue to drink even after difficult and costly compensation in hospital. In these cases, the patient requires a long educational process and a strong antialcoholic treatment which must rest in the hands of the physician treating the cirrhosis. Probably we would get better results if this treatment were started in the hospital after compensation of the cirrhosis. Without alcohol consumption, this illness becomes more accessible to treatment and we would not have to face as many failures as we now do, or so high a rate of mortality. If we changed our attitude we could avoid frequent rehospitalizations and make our work lighter.

Digestive hemorrhages which so often kill the cirrhotic patient, are also closely related to alcoholism. It is frequent to observe rupture of esophageal varices after alcoholic excesses, due not only to portal hypertension by hypervolemia, but *also to the vomiting which usually follows these transgressions. The vomiting, a violent effort in itself, causes a flow of acid to the esophagus and hence digestion of the frail venous walls.*

SUMMARY COMMENT

In this paper I have referred to some systems and organs of the human body which are damaged by alcoholism, and probably many more exist. But the main object of these preliminary remarks is to show that alcoholism is not solely a psychiatric problem. It is necessary for all physicians to change their attitude towards this illness. Confronted with any pathology, specialists in all fields should investigate the possibility of an alcoholic record in their patients and if their findings are positive, consider this as a second illness which also requires treatment. It is also necessary that all physicians be trained in the problem, especially in prevention and therapy. And, finally, I would recommend that students of medicine be informed about alcoholism so that they may become accustomed from the beginning to investigate the problem carefully and note it in the clinical history of their patients during the hospital training period.

RAÚL YAZIGI J.
Department of Medicine, University of Chile and San Juan de Dios Hospital
Santiago, Chile

CHARLES S. LIEBER

Liver Disease and Nutrition Section
Bronx VA Hospital and
Mt. Sinai School of Medicine
New York, New York, USA

26

Pathogenesis of Fatty Liver and Cirrhosis: Biochemical Approach

The disorders associated with alcoholism, especially those affecting the liver, have been traditionally attributed to nutritional deficiencies accompanying alcoholism rather than to ethanol itself. This concept was based primarily on the publications of Best, Hartroft, and their associates (1). More recent studies, however, indicate that in addition to dietary deficiencies, alcohol *per se* exerts a number of direct effects on hepatic and intermediary metabolism (18, 22, 24, 25). It is the purpose of this presentation to summarize those of our studies which describe and, in part, explain some of the direct effects of alcohol upon the liver, especially with reference to the pathogenesis of alcoholic fatty liver.

ALCOHOL AS A DIRECT CAUSE OF FATTY LIVER

Previous attempts by Volwiler *et al.* (59) and Summerskill *et al.* (57) failed to detect deleterious effects of alcohol administered to patients recovering from alcoholic fatty liver. In their studies, however, the amount of alcohol given was less than the usual intake of alcoholics. In contrast, Menghini (43) found, presumably with larger amounts of alcohol, that the clearing of the fat from alcoholic fatty liver was prevented by alcohol ingestion. These studies were concerned with the effect of alcohol in subjects recovering from established fatty liver, leaving unanswered the question whether in individuals with a morphologically normal liver ingestion of alcohol in amounts comparable to those consumed by chronic alcoholics is capable of injuring the liver, even in the absence of dietary deficiencies.

To resolve this question, ten volunteers with a history of alcoholism, but whose hepatic morphology had returned to normal, were given adequate diets under metabolic ward conditions, with either addition of alcohol to the diet (30,

Original studies reported in this paper were supported by research grants MH 14263, MH 15558, AM 09536, AM 10893, and AM 12511 from the United States Public Health Service.

TABLE 26–1

FATTY ACID COMPOSITION* OF ADIPOSE TISSUE LIPIDS AND LIVER TRIGLYCERIDES IN A SUBJECT GIVEN THE DIETS ILLUSTRATED IN FIGURE 26–2

| | *Control corn oil diet* | | *Ethanol coconut oil diet* | | *Control low fat diet* | | *Ethanol low fat diet* | |
| | *biopsies A* | | *biopsies B* | | *biopsies C* | | *biopsies D* | |
Fatty Acids†	*liver*	*adipose*	*liver*	*adipose*	*liver*	*adipose*	*liver*	*adipose*
12:0 + 14:0		1.6	16.4	2.9		3.0		2.9
16:0		23.0	36.8	23.5		19.6	27.3	19.6
16:1		8.7	8.1	9.6		9.5	4.5	10.4
18:0			4.0			1.8	6.1	1.6
18:1		47.6	28.0	45.1		44.4	56.1	44.7
18:2		19.0	5.5	17.8		19.4	6.1	20.1
total lipids (mg/gm)			155.5		43.5		63.4	
triglycerides (mg/gm)			108.2				32.1	

*Expressed as per cent of total fatty acids.
†Acids designated as chain length:double bond.

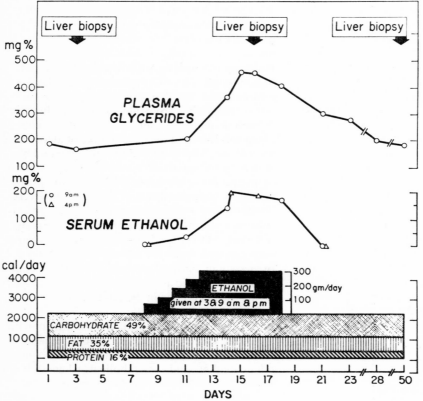

Figure 26-1
Scheme of the composition of the diet and its relationship to the hyperglyceridemia associated with the intake of alcohol and to the liver biopsies (hematoxylin-eosin stains) done before intake (A), after eight days of ethanol (B), and one month after ethanol withdrawal (C). From Lieber, Jones, and DeCarli (30).

32) or as isocaloric substitution for carbohydrates (30, 32, 37). In all ten individuals, alcohol administration resulted in hepatic steatosis, evident both on morphologic examination, as illustrated by the representative cases shown in Figures 26-1 and 26-2 or by the direct measurement of the lipid content of the liver biopsies, as indicated in Table 26-1.*

Since all the individuals studied admitted a history of alcoholism the possibility remains that they were more susceptible to an alcoholic insult than non-alcoholic individuals. Our studies in rats, however, indicate that in experimental animals, normal livers respond to an alcoholic insult in a manner similar to that of our alcoholic volunteers.† We succeeded in overcoming the natural aversion of rats for alcohol by incorporating the ethanol in a totally liquid, adequate diet, to the extent of 36 per cent of total calories given as carbohydrate to the controls (see Figure 26-3). The nutritional adequacy of this diet was evidenced by continued growth as well as normal hepatic morphology and fat content in the pair-fed sucrose controls. With isocaloric substitution of sucrose to the extent of 36 per cent of total calories by ethanol, hepatic steatosis was consistently produced (see Figure 26-4), with an average eight-fold rise of hepatic triglycerides after 24 days. Isocaloric replacement of carbohydrate by fat instead of ethanol did not produce steatosis, demonstrating that the capacity of ethanol for generating a fatty liver is greater than that of fat itself. No fatty liver developed when sucrose (to the extent of 18 or 36 per cent of total calories) was omitted from the control diet, indicating that the steatosis observed with isocaloric substitution of sucrose by ethanol was not simply due to a lack of carbohydrate calories. Steatosis was also produced in rats given ethanol in liquid diets containing dextrin-

maltose instead of sucrose, casein instead of the expensive amino acid mixture, and only 35 per cent of total calories as fat (instead of 43 per cent), an amount less than that of the average American diet (4).

ORIGIN OF THE FATTY ACID ACCUMULATION IN ALCOHOLIC FATTY LIVER

As illustrated in Figure 26-4, lipids which accumulate in the liver can originate from three main sources: dietary lipids, which reach the blood stream from the gut as chylomicrons (mechanism 1); adipose tissue lipids, which are transported to the liver as free fatty acids (FFA) (mechanism 3); and lipids synthesized in the liver itself (mechanism 5).

In rats, one very large dose of ethanol produced moderate hepatic accumulation of fatty acids resembling those of adipose tissue (2, 39, 54); in contrast, after prolonged ethanol intake, the fatty liver was more pronounced and had a fatty acid composition different from depot fats. To differentiate the origin of the fatty acids which accumulate in the liver, rats were given ethanol after a preliminary period of "pre-labelling" of their adipose tissue through feeding of diets containing oils with a characteristic fatty acid pattern: either coconut oil (containing a large fraction of laurate and myristate) or linseed oil (rich in linolenate). Growing rats received these diets for three weeks *ad libitum*; at the end of this period they had doubled their body weight and their adipose tissue fatty acid had been "labelled" with the characteristic fatty acids to the extent of more than 30 per cent. As illustrated in Figure 26-5, when ethanol was introduced in the diet, simultaneously, the characteristic dietary oil was changed, to allow differentiation of dietary from depot fatty acids. After 11 days of alcohol, there was, compared to the controls, an average 3.5-fold increase of hepatic triglycerides which contained fatty acids derived to a large extent from the diet, rather than from depot fat. Similarly, in rats which developed a fatty liver after ethanol and low-fat diets hepatic triglycerides had a fatty acid composition very

---

*We have now extended these observations to alcoholic volunteers given a diet in which 25 per cent of total calories, or twice the recommended amount, was protein. In all subjects, isocaloric replacement of carbohydrate by ethanol resulted in the development of fatty liver (35).

†We have now shown that non-alcoholic volunteers also develop fatty liver when given ethanol with non-deficient diets, even when with a dietary supplement of 10 gm of choline per day (50).

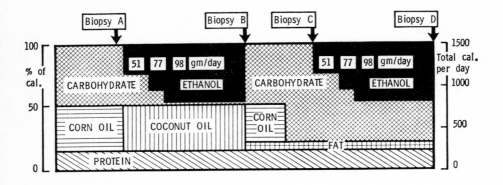

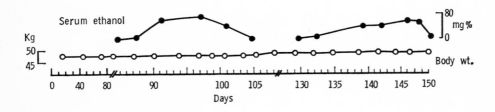

Figure 26-2
Composition of the diet, body weights, and serum ethanol concentrations in their relationship
to the liver and adipose biopsies. Hepatic morphology (hematoxylin-eosin stains) before and
after each ethanol period are indicated in A-D. From Lieber and Spritz (37).

different from that of adipose tissue, with a
linolenate concentration five times lower, but
more endogenously synthesized fatty acids such
as palmitate (see Figure 26-6).

Results obtained in alcoholic volunteers were
similar to those observed in rats. As illustrated
above in Figure 26-2 and Table 26-1, after the
ingestion of alcohol and a fat-containing diet
the fatty acids of the triglycerides accumulated
in the fatty liver had a large component of dietary
fatty acids, while after ingestion of ethanol and
low-fat diets, endogenously synthesized fatty
acids such as palmitate and oleate were predominant. In both types of alcoholic fatty livers,

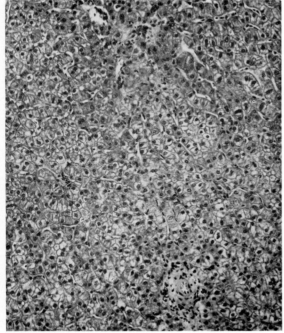

Figure 26-1 A

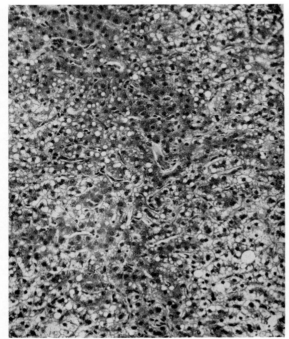

Figure 26-1 B

Figure 26-1 C

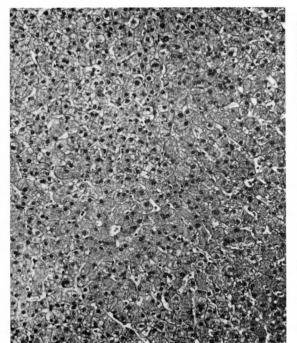

Figure 26-2 A

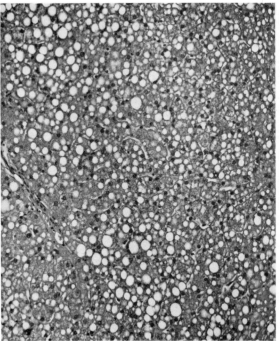

Figure 26-2 B

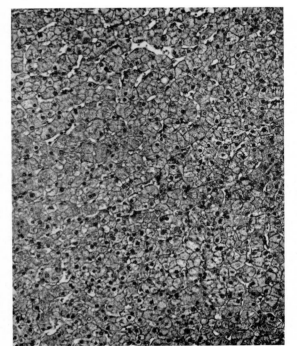

Figure 26-2 C

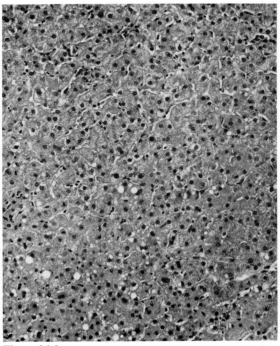

Figure 26-2 D

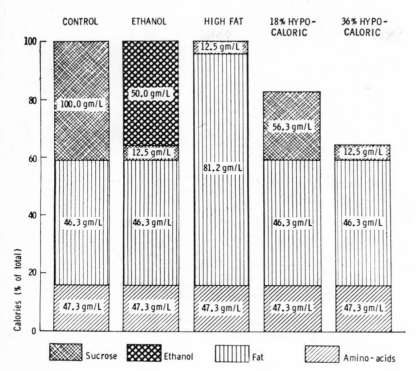

Choline Cl. - 0.25 gm/L, Vitamins - 0.05 gm/L, Salts - 10.00 gm/L, Sod. Carrageenate - 4.00 gm/L

Figure 26-3

Composition of five types of liquid diet fed to rats for 24 days.

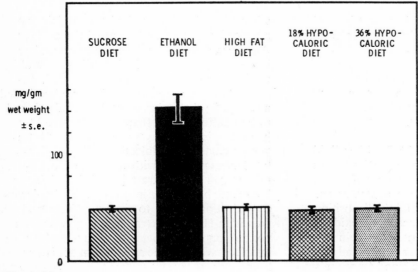

Figure 26-4

Total hepatic lipids in rats given the diets represented in Figure 26-3.

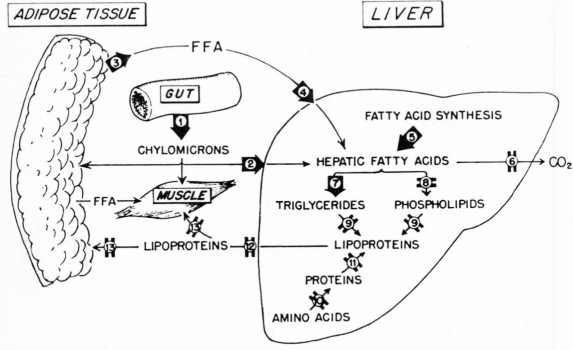

Figure 26-5
Schematic representation of lipid transport and metabolism, with some possible mechanisms for fatty liver production, either through increase (———→) or decrease (—‖→) of existing metabolic pathways. From Lieber (23), by permission of the Williams & Wilkins Co., Baltimore, Md., USA.

fatty acid composition of hepatic triglycerides was found to be different from that of the corresponding adipose tissue.

MECHANISMS RESPONSIBLE FOR THE HEPATIC LIPID ACCUMULATION PRODUCED BY ALCOHOL

As illustrated in Figure 26-5, either lipid accumulation in the liver can result from an excessive supply from one or more of the three lipid sources discussed above, or steatosis could result from a disturbance of lipid disposition from the liver through reduced lipid oxidation (mechanism 6), insufficient lipoprotein formation (mechanisms 9–11), or diminished transport of lipoprotein into the blood (mechanism 12).

As illustrated in Figure 26-6 and Table 26-1,

when ethanol is given with diets containing an amount of fat similar to that of the average American diet, dietary fatty acids accumulate in the liver. To explain this finding, several possible mechanisms were investigated. Increased lipid absorption could not be implicated and hepatic chylomicron uptake was also found to be unaffected by ethanol, as measured by hepatic lipid labelling ten minutes after intravenous chylomicron injection (39) or in isolated livers perfused with ethanol and chylomicron (34). In contrast, hepatic lipid labelling both three hours after intravenous chylomicron-C^{14} injection or two to six hours after oral palmitate-H^3 administration was greater than normal, suggesting that ethanol in some way interferes with hepatic metabolism of dietary lipids.

Whether, under normal circumstances, the liver metabolizes circulating chylomicron *per se*

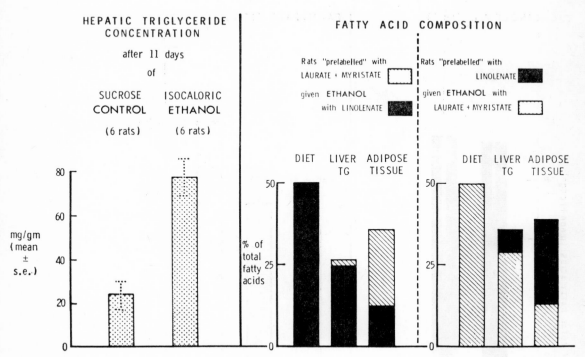

Figure 26-6

Role of dietary fatty acids in hepatic triglyceride accumulation after 11 days of ethanol. The concentrations of the characteristic dietary fatty acids (linolenate and laurate + myristate) have been measured in liver triglycerides and adipose tissue lipids. From Lieber, Spritz, and DeCarli (39).

or whether these are first hydrolyzed in peripheral tissue remains the subject of some debate (9, 44, 46). The rate of oxidation of chylomicrons in isolated perfused livers, although very low with control substrates, was even lower in the presence of ethanol (34) indicating that further metabolism of chylomicrons trapped by the liver is impaired in the presence of ethanol. Since hepatic oxidation of chylomicrons-C^{14} and fatty acids-C^{14} to $C^{14}O_2$ was affected to a similar degree by ethanol (34), the block of chylomicron metabolism appears to be at the stage of the oxidation of the long-chain fatty acids rather than of the conversion of chylomicron to fatty acids.

Our previous observation (36) that the reduction of $C^{14}O_2$ production from palmitate-C^{14} in the presence of ethanol was paralleled by a similar decrease in $C^{14}O_2$ evolved from acetate-C^{14} (see Figure 26-8) suggests that the

decrease in fatty acid oxidation may result from decreased citric acid cycle activity, possibly as a consequence of the enhanced formation of reduced nicotinamide adenine dinucleotide ($NADA_2$)* produced by the metabolism of ethanol in the liver, as illustrated in Figure 26-9. A diminution in citric acid cycle activity has been recently confirmed by the observation of a reduction in the absolute amount of CO_2 produced in livers perfused with ethanol, without change in oxygen consumption (10, 34); reduced citric acid cycle activity would offer a satisfactory explanation for the hepatic accumulation of fatty acids originating from the diet.

Decreased fatty acid oxidation could also play a role in the hepatic accumulation of endogenously synthesized fatty acids, when ethanol is given with low-fat diets (see Figures

*Previously called DPNH.

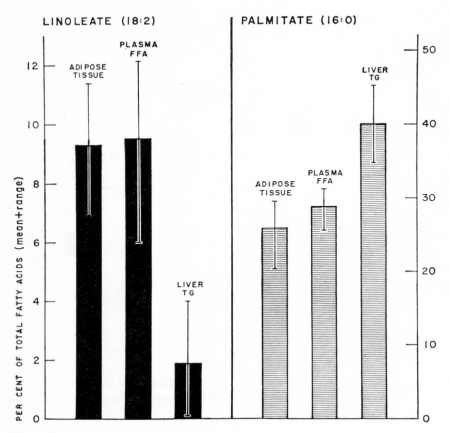

Figure 26-7
Fatty acid composition in adipose tissue, plasma FFA, and liver triglycerides (TG)
of four rats that developed fatty liver after 24 days of ethanol and low-fat (2 per
cent of calories) diet. From Lieber, Spritz, and DeCarli (39).

26-2 and 26-7, and Table 26-1). Hepatic
accumulation of endogenously synthesized
lipids however could result more directly from
a stimulation by ethanol of hepatic fatty acid
synthesis (26, 31) (Figure 26-5, mechanism
5) and triglyceride production (11, 48)
(Figure 26-5, mechanism 7). Theoretically,
increased fatty acid synthesis could be considered as another means for disposing of the
excess hydrogen produced on ethanol oxidation
in the liver (25). Indeed, an NADH₂-generating
system such as sorbitol was found, in liver
slices, to increase the incorporation of acetate-
C¹⁴ into fatty acids, relative to the C¹⁴O₂ produced, in a manner similar to ethanol (28, 36).

Ethanol could exert these effects directly
through enhanced production of NADH₂, which,
as well as NADPH₂,* stimulates fatty acid synthesis (11, 60).

Ethanol may also act via NADPH₂ through
transhydrogenation from NADH₂; it must be
pointed out, however, that recent studies have
indicated that NADH₂ is as great or sometimes
an even greater source of hydrogen for fatty acid
synthesis than NADPH₂ (19, 52); ethanol could
also act via an increase of alpha-glycerophosphate which was found to accumulate after
alcohol ingestion (45) and to stimulate fatty

*Reduced nicotinamide adenine dinucleotide phos-
phate, previously called TPNH.

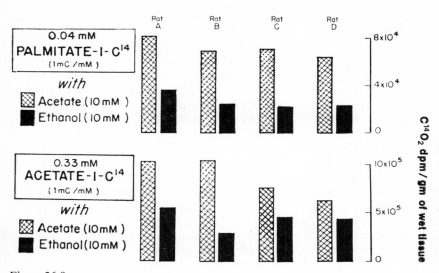

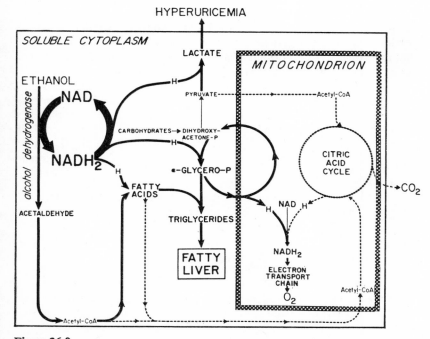

Figure 26-8

Effect of unlabelled ethanol or acetate on $C^{14}O_2$ production by randomized liver slices, incubated with either acetate-1-C^{14} or palmitate-1-C^{14}. From Lieber and Schmid (36).

Figure 26-9

Hepatic oxidation of ethyl alcohol and some of its effects, through increases (———→) or decreases (—‖→) of metabolic pathways. From Lieber (24), by permission of the Williams & Wilkins Co., Baltimore, Md., USA.

acid synthesis (13). In any event, increased alpha-glycerophosphate accumulation could contribute to hepatic triglyceride formation through enhanced production of the glycerol moiety of triglycerides. Thus, the changes in the hepatic $NADH_2/NAD$ ratio resulting from the oxidation of ethanol seems to play a key role in the alterations of hepatic lipid metabolism produced by ethanol.

In addition to lipogenesis other metabolic pathways can serve as hydrogen acceptors. For instance, the oxidation of ethanol is known to be coupled in part with the reduction of pyruvate to lactate (Figure 26-9). Increased blood lactate concentration produces a diminution in urinary uric acid output, which explains, at least in part, the hyperuricemia which we observed in subjects intoxicated with alcoholic beverages (31). A further effect, possibly related to the hyperlactidemia, includes increased splanchnic blood flow, observed after large doses of ethanol (42, 56).

The studies discussed above indicate that, both in man and in rats given ethanol over prolonged periods of time, adipose tissue fatty acids represent only a small portion of the fatty acids accumulating in the liver; therefore, excessive FFA mobilization from depots (Figure 26-5, mechanism 3) does not represent a major mechanism for development of hepatic steatosis under these experimental conditions. In contrast, after the administration of a very large single dose of alcohol by gastric tube to fasting rats, adipose tissue fatty acids were found to accumulate in the liver (2, 39, 54). This was considered to be due to increased peripheral fat mobilization since, under these experimental conditions, circulating FFA were found to be increased (2, 41). However, under apparently similar experimental conditions, other investigators found no rise in FFA (7) and no evidence of enhanced mobilization of fatty acids from labelled fat pads (47). In man, large amounts of alcohol (400 gm per day) were found to raise circulating FFA, but with more moderate quantities of ethanol, up to 300 gm per day for as long as 18 days, circulating FFA remained unchanged (32); fatty liver was nevertheless observed with these moderate amounts of ethanol. Given to volunteers over short periods

of time, ethanol decreased circulating FFA (15, 33), with a reduction in FFA turnover (16), V–A difference in FFA across the extremities (33), and plasma glycerol (8). Moreover, in subjects studied by hepatic vein catheterization, net splanchnic FFA uptake seemed to be reduced rather than increased (29).* Thus, except for experimental conditions with administration of a very large amount of alcohol, peripheral fat mobilization has not been found to represent a major factor in the pathogenesis of the alcoholic fatty liver.

Decreased hepatic lipoprotein formation (Figure 26-5, mechanisms 9–11) or release (Figure 26-5, mechanism 12) has been proposed as an explanation for the fatty liver produced by a variety of toxic agents. On the basis of hepatic perfusion studies, a similar mechanism has been proposed for the alcoholic fatty liver (53). In contrast with the *in vitro* perfusions of livers with large amounts of ethanol, *in vivo* administration of alcohol was not accompanied by a fall, but rather by an increase in blood lipids, especially triglycerides (15, 30, 32). These findings suggest that decreased transport of lipids from the liver is not the primary factor in the production of the alcoholic fatty liver, if one assumes no major change in peripheral fat utilization. The pathogenesis of alcoholic hyperlipemia, however, has not been fully clarified. Decreased lipolysis may play a role in the rare individual suffering from marked hyperlipemia, the so-called "Zieve Syndrome" (40, 61). This is suggested by the observations, in some of these subjects, of low lipoprotein lipase activity (40) and a circulating inhibitor of lipoprotein lipase (17). Delayed clearing of post-prandial hyperlipemia due to ethanol has also been reported in man (58) and in the rat (6). Furthermore, in addition to the production of lipoproteins, the liver is also responsible (together with other tissues) for the removal of an important fraction of the circulating lipoproteins (Figure 26-5, mechanism 13). Theoretically, alteration of this function by alcohol, possibly in association with steatosis, could also lead to hyperlipemia.

*The reduction of plasma FFA produced by ethanol in man has now been shown to be due to acetate, a metabolite of ethanol (3).

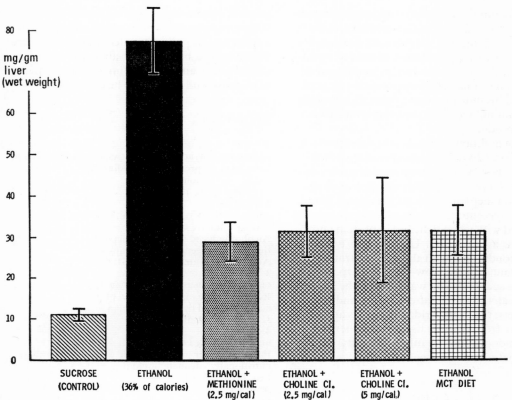

Figure 26-10

Hepatic triglycerides (mean ± SE) in rats fed liquid diets containing either sucrose (controls) or isocaloric amounts of ethanol (36 per cent of calories) with or without various additives. In the ethanol-MTC diet the long-chain triglycerides of the regular diet (mixture of olive and corn oils: 41 per cent of calories) were isocalorically replaced with medium chain triglycerides (MCT). From Lieber and DeCarli (26), by permission of the Williams & Wilkins Co., Baltimore, Md., USA.

PREVENTION AND AGGRAVATION OF ALCOHOLIC FATTY LIVER BY DIETARY AND CHEMICAL FACTORS

The fatty liver produced by prolonged alcohol ingestion was reduced by decreasing the fat content of the diet, both in man (37), and in rats (39), underlining the important role of dietary lipids in the pathogenesis of the alcoholic fatty liver. A similar effect was obtained by replacing dietary fats with medium-chain triglycerides as shown in Figure 26-10. In contrast, a series of agents, such as asparagine or antioxidants, some of which had been found to reduce fat accumulation in the liver follow-

ing administration of one large dose of alcohol (5, 21), were found ineffective with prolonged ethanol intake (26). Ethyl alpha-p-chloro-phenoxyisobutyrate, a drug used to reduce hyperlipemia, was found to be partially protective under these conditions (55).

In experimental animals, the fatty liver produced by small amounts of alcohol in conjunction with diets deficient in lipotropic agents can be prevented by simple correction of the dietary deficiency (1). With larger amounts of alcohol, fatty livers were produced in rats on prolonged alcohol intake despite diets containing adequate amounts of lipotropic agents (0.25 mg choline chloride and 1.5 mg DL-methionine per calorie

(30, 32). Supplementation with larger amounts of methionine (2.5 mg per calorie) or choline chloride (2.5 mg per calorie) resulted in a decrease of fat accumulation produced by alcohol, but the protection was incomplete and could not be enhanced by doubling the dose of choline. This indicates that, although lipotropic factors undoubtedly play an important role, alcohol produces steatosis through effects other than or in addition to those related to lipotrope metabolism (26). The importance of dietary adequacy however has been underlined recently by the observation that the direct effects of alcohol on hepatic lipid accumulation are strikingly potentiated when alcohol intake is combined with a diet deficient in protein and lipotropic agents (38). Under these experimental conditions, with the administration of ethanol and deficient, low-fat diets, hepatic triglyceride accumulation was found to be several times greater than that after ethanol and adequate diets; the triglyceride fatty acids again did not derive from adipose tissue but rather comprised endogenously synthesized fatty acids, such as palmitate and oleate (38).

ALCOHOLIC LIVER CIRRHOSIS

In contrast to the problem of the fatty liver, not much progress has been made in unravelling the pathogenesis of alcoholic cirrhosis. It is not clear which hepatic lesions have to be considered as "precursors" of the cirrhosis, for instance, whether alcoholic fatty liver *per se* leads to cirrhosis, or whether independent of the fatty liver or in conjunction with it, other lesions are necessary. In addition to fat accumulation, alcoholic individuals may have a variety of hepatic lesions which have been grouped under the term "alcoholic hepatitis." It has not yet been established to what extent these lesions are due to alcohol *per se* or to associated factors such as dietary deficiencies. It has been shown however that even in the absence of dietary deficiencies, both in man and in rats, administration of alcohol under controlled conditions results not only in steatosis, but also in the early development of marked alterations of the endoplasmic reticulum (14, 20) and various altera-

tions in the mitochondria (14, 20, 49). In which way these morphologic changes, which appear very rapidly after alcohol ingestion, are linked to the biochemical abnormalities described above and to the ultimate development of cirrhosis still remains to be established.*

REFERENCES

1
BEST, C.H., HARTROFT, W.S., LUCAS, C.C., & RIDOUT, J.H.
Liver damage produced by feeding alcohol or sugar and its prevention by choline
Brit. Med. J., ii: 1001, 1949
2
BRODIE, B.B., BUTLER, W.M., JR., HORNING, M.G., MAICKEL, R.P., & MALING, H.M.
Alcohol-induced triglyceride deposition on liver through derangement of fat transport
Am. J. Clin. Nutr., 9: 432, 1961
3
CROUSE, J.R., GERSON, C.D., DECARLI, L.M., & LIEBER, C.S.
Role of acetate in the reduction of plasma free fatty acids produced by ethanol in man
J. Lipid Res., 9: 509, 1968
4
DECARLI, L.M. & LIEBER, C.S.
Fatty liver after prolonged intake of ethanol with a nutritionally adequate liquid diet
Fed. Proc., 25: 304, 1966
Abstract
5
DI LUZIO, N.R.
Prevention of the acute ethanol-induced fatty liver by the simultaneous administration of antioxidants
Life Sc., 3: 113, 1964
6
DI LUZIO, N.R. & POGGI, M.
Abnormal lipid tolerance and hyperlipemia in acute ethanol-treated rats
Life Sc., 10: 751, 1963
7
ELKO, E.E., WOOLES, W.R., & DI LUZIO, N.R.
Alterations and mobilization of lipids in acute ethanol-treated rats
Am. J. Physiol., 201: 923, 1961
8
FEINMAN, L. & LIEBER, C.S.

*The microsomal fraction of the liver (which comprises the endoplasmic reticulum) has now been shown to have ethanol-oxidizing activity which is inducible by ethanol feeding and has cofactor requirements and other characteristics comparable to those of hepatic microsomal drug detoxifying enzymes (26). Ethanol feeding was also found to increase the activity of a variety of other hepatic microsomal drug detoxifying enzymes, both in the rat (45) and in man (46).

Effect of ethanol on plasma free fatty acids
(FFA) in man
Am. J. Clin. Nutr., **20**: 400, 1967
9
FELTS, J.M. & MAYES, P.A.
Lack of uptake and oxidation of chylomicron
triglyceride to carbon dioxide and ketone bodies
by the perfused rat liver
Nature, **208**: 195, 1965
10
FORSANDER, O.A., RÄIHÄ, N., SALASPURO, M., &
MÄENPÄÄ, P.
Influence of ethanol on the liver metabolism of
fed and starved rats
Biochem. J., **94**: 259, 1965
11
HARLAN, W.R., JR., & WAKIL, S.J.
The pathways of synthesis of fatty acids by
mitochondria
Biochem. Biophys. Res. Commun., **8**: 131, 1962
12
HORNING, M.G., WAKABAYASHI, M., & MALING, H.M.
Biochemical processes involved in the synthesis of
accumulation and release of triglycerides in the liver
In: Internat. Pharmacol. Meeting, First
Effects of drugs on synthesis and mobilization of
lipids, proc. **2**, ed. by Horning, E.C.
Oxford: Pergamon, 1963. p. 13
13
HOWARD, C.F. & LOWENSTEIN, J.M.
The effect of alph-glycerophosphate on the microsomal
stimulation of fatty acid synthesis
Biochim. Biophys. Acta, **84**: 226, 1964
14
ISERI, O.A., LIEBER, C.S., & GOTTLIEB, L.S.
The ultrastructure of fatty liver induced by
prolonged ethanol ingestion
Am. J. Path., **48**: 535, 1966
15
JONES, D.P., LOSOWSKY, M.S., DAVIDSON, C.S., &
LIEBER, C.S.
Effects of ethanol on plasma lipids in man
J. Lab. Clin. Med., **62**: 675, 1963
16
JONES, D.P., PERMAN, E., & LIEBER, C.S.
Free fatty acid turnover and triglyceride metabolism
after ethanol ingestion in man
J. Lab. Clin. Med., **66**: 804, 1965
17
KESSLER, J.I., KNIFFEN, J.C., & JANOWITZ, H.D.
Lipoprotein lipase inhibition in the hyperlipemia of
acute alcoholic pancreatitis
New England J. Med., **269**: 943, 1963
18
KLATSKIN, G.
Alcohol and its relation to liver damage
Gastroenterology, **41**: 443, 1961
19
LAMDIN, E., SHREEVE, W.W., OJI, N., & SCHWARTZ, I.L.
Transfer of tritium from succinate and other
carbohydrates into liver fatty acids of mice *in vivo*

Fed. Proc., **24**: 343, 1965
Abstract
20
LANE, B.P. & LIEBER, C.S.
Ultrastructural alterations in human hepatocytes
following ingestion of ethanol with adequate diets
Am. J. Pathol., **49**: 593, 1966
21
LANSFORD, E.M., JR., HILL, I.D., & SHIVE, W.
Effects of asparagine and other related nutritional
supplements upon alcohol-induced rat liver
triglyceride elevation
J. Nutr., **78**: 219, 1962
22
LIEBER, C.S.
Metabolic effects produced by alcohol in the liver
and other tissues
Adv. Intern. Med., **14**: 151, 1968
23
LIEBER, C.S.
Pathogenesis of hepatic steatosis
Gastroenterology, **45**: 760, 1963
24
LIEBER, C.S.
Hepatic and metabolic effects of alcohol
Gastroenterology, **50**: 119, 1966
25
LIEBER, C.S. & DAVIDSON, C.S.
Some metabolic effects of ethyl alcohol
Am. J. Med., **33**: 319, 1962
26
LIEBER, C.S. & DE CARLI, L.M.
Study of agents for the prevention of the fatty liver
produced by prolonged alcohol intake
Gastroenterology, **50**: 316, 1966
27
LIEBER, C.S. & DE CARLI, L.M.
Ethanol oxidation by hepatic microsomes: adaptive
increase after ethanol feeding
Science, **162**: 917, 1968
28
LIEBER, C.S., DE CARLI, L.M., & SCHMID, R.
Effect of ethanol on fatty acid metabolism in liver slices
Biochem. Biophys. Res. Commun., **1**: 302, 1959
29
LIEBER, C.S., GEORGE, W.S., & STEIN, W.
Effect of ethanol on plasma free fatty acids
(FFA) in man
Clin. Res., **8**: 242, 1960
Abstract
30
LIBER, C.S., JONES, D.P., & DE CARLI, L.M.
Effects of prolonged ethanol intake: production of
fatty liver despite adequate diets
J. Clin. Invest., **44**: 1009, 1965
31
LIEBER, C.S., JONES, D.P., LOSOWSKY, M.S., &
DAVIDSON, C.S.
Interrelation of uric acid and ethanol
metabolism in man
J. Clin. Invest., **41**: 1863, 1962

32
LIEBER, C.S., JONES, D.P., MENDELSON, J., &
DE CARLI, L.M.
Fatty liver, hyperlipemia and hyperuricemia produced
by prolonged alcohol consumption, despite adequate
dietary intake
Trans. Assoc. Am. Physicians, **76**: 289, 1963

33
LIEBER, C.S., LEEVY, C.M., STEIN, S.W., GEORGE, W.S.,
CHERRICK, G.R., ABELMANN, W.H., & DAVIDSON, C.S.
Effect of ethanol on plasma free fatty acids in man
J. Lab. Clin. Med., **59**: 826, 1962

34
LIEBER, C.S., LEFÈVRE, A., FEINMAN, L.,
SPRITZ, N., & DE CARLI, L.M.
Differences in hepatic metabolism of long- and
medium-chain fatty acids: the role of fatty acid
chain length in the production of the alcoholic
fatty liver
J. Clin. Invest., **46**: 1451, 1967

35
LIEBER, C.S. & RUBIN, E.
Alcoholic fatty liver in man on a high protein and
low fat diet
Am. J. Med., **44**: 200, 1968

36
LIEBER, C.S. & SCHMID, R.
The effect of ethanol on fatty acid metabolism;
stimulation of hepatic fatty acid synthesis *in vitro*
J. Clin. Invest., **40**: 394, 1961

37
LIEBER, C.S. & SPRITZ, N.
Effects of prolonged ethanol intake in man: role of
dietary adipose and indogenously synthesized fatty
acids in the pathogenesis of the alcoholic fatty liver
J. Clin. Invest., **45**: 1400, 1966

38
LIEBER, C.S., SPRITZ, N., & DE CARLI, L.M.
Hepatic effects of ethanol given with deficient diets
Am. J. Clin. Nutr., **18**: 309, 1966
Abstract

39
LIEBER, C.S., SPRITZ, N., & DE CARLI, L.M.
Role of dietary adipose and endogenously synthesized
fatty acids in the pathogenesis of the alcoholic
fatty liver
J. Clin. Invest., **45**: 51, 1966

40
LOSOWSKY, M.S., JONES, D.P., DAVIDSON, C.S., &
LIEBER, C.S.
Studies of alcoholic hyperlipemia and its mechanism
Am. J. Med., **35**: 794, 1963

41
MALLOV, S.
Effect of ethanol intoxication on plasma free
fatty acids in the rat
Quart. J. Stud. Alc., **22**: 250, 1961

42
MENDELOFF, A.I.
Effect of intravenous infusions of ethanol upon
estimated hepatic blood flow in man
J. Clin. Invest., **33**: 1298, 1954

43
MENGHINI, G.
[The morphobioptic aspect of the liver of the alcoholic
(non-cirrhotic) and its evolution]
Bull. Schweiz. Akad. Med. Wiss., **16**: 36, 1960

44
MORRIS, B.
The metabolism of free fatty acids and chylomicron
triglycerides by the isolated perfused liver of the rat
J. Physiol., **168**: 564, 1963

45
NIKKILA, E.A. & OJALA, K.
Role of hepatic L-alpha-glycerophosphate and
triglyceride synthesis in production of fatty liver by
ethanol
Proc. Soc. Exper. Biol. Med., **113**: 814, 1963

46
OLIVECRONA, T., GEORGE, E.P., & BORGSTRÖM, B.
Chylomicron metabolism
Fed. Proc., **20**: 928, 1961

47
POGGI, M. & DI LUZIO, N.R.
The role of liver and adipose tissue in the pathogenesis
of the ethanol-induced fatty liver
J. Lipid Res., **5**: 437, 1964

48
RUBIN, E., HUTTERER, F., & LIEBER, C.S.
Ethanol increases hepatic smooth endoplasmic
reticulum and drug-metabolizing enzymes
Science, **159**: 1469, 1968

49
RUBIN, E.R. & LIEBER, C.S.
Early fine structural changes in the human liver
induced by alcohol
Gastroenterology, **52**: 1, 1967

50
RUBIN, E. & LIEBER, C.S.
Alcohol-induced hepatic injury in non-alcoholic
volunteers
New England J. Med., **278**: 869, 1968

51
RUBIN, E. & LIEBER, C.S.
Hepatic microsomal enzymes in man and rat:
induction and inhibition by ethanol
Science, **162**: 691, 1968

52
ROGNSTADT, R. & KATZ, J.
Metabolism of tritium labeled glucose by
adipose tissue
Fed. Proc., **24**: 291, 1965
Abstract

53
SCHAPIRO, R.H., DRUMMEY, G.D., SHIMIZU, Y., &
ISSELBACHER, K.J.
Studies on the pathogenesis of the ethanol-induced fatty
liver. II, Effect of ethanol on palmitate-1-C-14
metabolism by the isolated perfused rat liver
J. Clin. Invest., **43**: 1338, 1964

54
SCHEIG, R. & ISSELBACHER, K.J.
Pathogenesis of ethanol-induced fatty liver
3. In vivo and vitro effects of ethanol on hepatic
fatty acid metabolism in rats
J. Lipid Res., **6**: 269, 1965

55
SPRITZ, N. & LIEBER, C.S.
Disease of ethanol-induced fatty liver by ethyl
alpha-p-chlorophenoxyisobutyrate
Proc. Soc. Exper. Biol. Med., **121**: 147, 1966

56
STEIN, S.W., LIEBER, C.S., LEEVY, C.M., CHERRICK, G.R.,
& ABELMANN, W.H.
The effect of ethanol upon systemic and hepatic blood
flow in man
Am. J. Clin. Nutr., **13**: 68, 1963

57
SUMMERSKILL, W.H., WOLFE, S.J., & DAVIDSON, C.S.
Response to alcohol in chronic alcoholics with liver
disease; clinical, pathological, and metabolic changes
Lancet, **i**: 335, 1957

58
TALBOTT, G.D., & KEATING, B.M.
Effects of preprandial whiskey on postalimentary
lipemia
Geriatrics, **17**: 802, 1962

59
VOLWILER, W., JONES, C.M., & MALLORY, F.B.
Criteria for measurement of results of treatment in
fatty cirrhosis
Gastroenterology, **11**: 164, 1948

60
WAKIL, S.J.
Mechanism of fatty acid synthesis
J. Lipid Res., **2**: 1, 1961

61
ZIEVE, L.
Jaundice, hyperlipemia and hemolytic anemia: a
heretofore unrecognized syndrome associated with
alcoholic fatty liver and cirrhosis
Ann. Intern. Med., **48**: 471, 1958

W. STANLEY HARTROFT

E. A. PORTA

Research Institute
Hospital for Sick Children
Toronto, Ontario, Canada

27

Pathogenesis of Fatty Liver and Cirrhosis: Histopathological Approach

The production of various types and degrees of severity of fatty livers in animals consuming alcohol has now been reported under both acute (5, 11, 17) and chronic (2, 13, 14, 16, 18) conditions. In only a few models have these lesions included a fibrotic element (2, 7), and in none has cirrhosis developed in the sense of a distortion of architecture associated not only with fibrosis but also with the formation of monolobular or multilobular regenerative nodules.

This presentation will review briefly the types of fatty liver (with and without fibrosis) achieved, in other laboratories as well as our own, in animals consuming alcohol, and will evaluate the present concensus regarding the relation of the fatty liver to fibrosis and cirrhosis. Attempts to produce models of true cirrhosis in which alcohol acts as the precipitating factor in experimental animals have not to date been successful. Possible reasons for failure will be discussed.

FATTY LIVER AND ALCOHOL

The abnormal accumulation of fat in the liver of man accompanies nearly every stage of hepatic injury associated with the excessive consumption of alcohol (4). Only in the end-stage of the atrophic type of multilobular cirrhosis is fat an inconspicuous feature, but in all other phases, from the early acutely enlarged liver to the initial stages of fibrosis and monolobular cirrhosis, fat is a prominent feature. At one time, the lobular distribution of fat was considered important in relation to etiology, and the fatty liver of the alcoholic was variously described as centrolobular or periportal. With our animals models (see below), we have now been able to demonstrate in recent experiments that the distribution of fat throughout hepatic lobules of rats consuming appreciable amounts of alcohol varies not only with the composition of the basal diet but also with time. If these same factors are operative in

The original experiments which were carried out during the past five years and referred to in this paper have been supported by the Addiction Research Foundation, Toronto, Ontario, and the Medical Research Council (block grant MA-1904) of Canada.

alcoholic man, it would appear that the lobular distribution of fat can no longer be regarded as a primary feature or a consistently useful clue to the etiology of fatty liver in an individual patient.

Although cirrhosis has not been produced as the result of allowing rats or other animals to consume large amounts of alcohol even over long periods of time, fatty livers can be produced at will even after administration of just single large doses (6 gm absolute alcohol per kg body weight suitably diluted) (6). This acute model has proven a useful source of considerable information concerning biochemical mechanisms, but differs significantly in certain essential features from the fatty liver accompanying chronic consumption of alcohol (one to four months). This type of acute fatty liver, which is transient and therefore without a direct relation to cirrhogenesis, will not be discussed further at this time.

FATTY LIVERS IN ANIMALS CONSUMING
ALCOHOL OVER SEVERAL MONTHS

For many years, investigators failed to produce fatty livers in animals given alcohol over long periods of time. These experiments, carried out during the 1930s by the late F. B. Mallory and others, failed for at least two reasons which are now evident. These early trials used the rabbit, which we now know is an unsuitable choice because, unlike the rat, it does not readily consume unnatural food stuffs. Furthermore, it is very susceptible to hepatic parasitisms; and the importance of the background diet was not recognized at that time so that the alcohol was administered with highly nutritious mixtures of natural foods.

Shortly after World War II, a group in Texas (1) returned to the problem. They used the rat this time but again failed to produce an alcoholic fatty liver when they gave 15 per cent alcohol in the drinking water along with a normal, natural laboratory diet. Professor Best and his group (2), of which one of us (W.S.H.) was at that time a member, repeated this experiment and showed that when alcohol was added to a diet, which contained only enough lipotropic factors (choline or methionine-containing protein) to prevent a fatty liver when the diet alone was consumed (see Figure 27-1), a fatty liver and even

fibrosis resulted (see Figure 27-2). The same result could be achieved by an isocaloric supplement of sucrose, thereby demonstrating that the alcohol *per se* had not been responsible for the abnormal accumulation of fat but was the result of the additional calories provided by either alcohol or sucrose. Furthermore, a generous supplement of choline given to either group completely protected the liver in both cases, conclusively demonstrating that the fatty liver in this model was not the result of a hepatotoxic effect of alcohol (or sucrose) but had been produced by a relative deficiency of choline induced by the empty calories of either the alcohol or sucrose. This relative choline deficiency could be corrected by adding more choline to that in the basal diet, even though the latter was balanced in its lipotropic content as long as neither alcohol nor sucrose was consumed in addition. This experiment was soon confirmed and extended by Klatskin *et al.* of Yale (14) and more recently by Lieber and De Carli (15).

It is now evident that the principle employed here – the induction of a relative deficiency of an essential food factor (choline in this case) by the abundant, nutritionally empty calories of alcohol (or sucrose) with consequent harmful effects to the liver – is an important one. Probably other factors are involved in addition to choline which are essential for maintaining the liver, including protein *per se*, essential fatty acids, other members of the vitamin B-complex and tocopherol. Using the model devised by Lieber *et al.* (16), in which alcohol and a completely liquid basal diet (employing amino acids instead of protein can be simultaneously administered, we have been able to demonstrate that this concept, first developed with choline, does indeed apply to other essential food factors: particularly the total availability of protein in terms of calories consumed, including, most important, those provided by alcohol (or by isocaloric sucrose controls). Our results are in agreement with those of others working in the field including Jones (13) and Jabbari *et al.* (12).

The composition of the first diet which we employed is illustrated diagrammatically in Figure 27-3. In these experiments alcohol is the source of 36 per cent of the total calories provided by the liquid mixture. Using the pro-

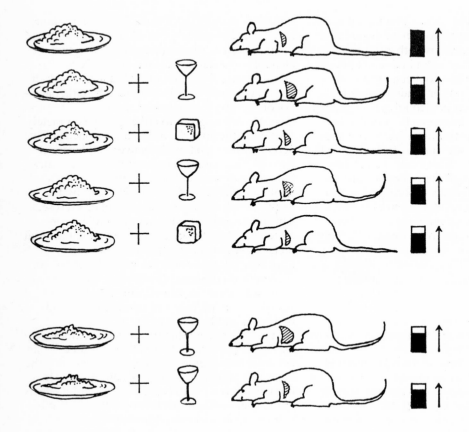

Alcohol, choline and the liver

Figure 27-1

Diagrammatic representation of the design of the first experiment to produce fatty and fibrotic livers in rats by conditioning with alcohol. The symbols (glasses or cubes) represent supplementation with alcohol (15 per cent in the drinking water) or sugar (in amounts isocaloric with the alcohol) of the basal diet. The latter contained just enough lipotropic factors to take care of the calories in the basal diet except in the third, fifth and seventh groups from the top. In these cases additional supplements of choline were given to take care of the alcohol or sucrose supplements. As indicated in the schematic drawings of the animals' livers, those receiving supplements of either sucrose or alcohol without additional choline developed enlarged livers which were fatty and fibrotic (see Figure 27-2). Livers of those rats receiving the additional choline supplements remained normal even when they also received additional calories from either sucrose or alcohol.

portions of fat, carbohydrate, and protein (supplying respectively 43, 5, and 16 per cent of total calories) originally employed by Lieber we were able to confirm his findings that a fattier liver developed in alcohol-consuming rats than in those given the sucrose-control diet. The fat was centrolobular in distribution (see Figure 27-4) and in neither case did fibrosis (let alone cirrhosis) develop even after three months. In a further experiment, the amount of protein was

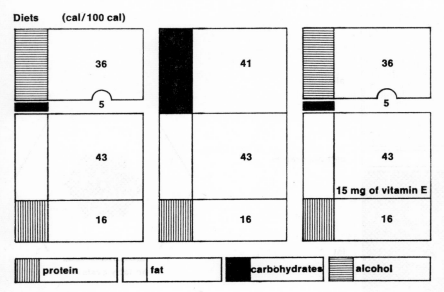

Figure 27-3

Figures 27-3 to 27-7
Graphic depictions of the proportions of calories derived from alcohol, protein, fat, and carbohydrate in the various experiments employing modifications of Lieber's liquid diets (containing amino acids instead of protein). The photomicrographs illustrate the distribution of fat within the lobules which is also shown diagrammatically in each case. Note that the position of the fat varies with the various diets: centrolobular in Lieber's original formula (Figures 27-3 and 27-4), midzonal when the basal diet is high in fat (Figure 27-5), and periportal with fatty cyst formation when the basal diet is high in carbohydrate (Figure 27-6). But when the amino acids supplied 25 per cent of the calories, the livers of the rats in this group were completely protected from any fatty change associated with the high intake of alcohol (Figure 27-7).

reduced and the fat increased. Again a mild degree of fatty liver resulted, particularly in the alcohol-consuming rats, despite the presence of an adequate choline supplement. The fat was now midzonal in distribution, presenting a remarkably different architectural pattern (see Figure 27-5). But when the amount of dietary fat was reduced and the carbohydrate elevated along with either the alcohol (or its sucrose substitution) still supplying 36 per cent of total calories, fat was present in periportal regions and even fatty cysts had formed (see Figure 27-6). This latter point we consider important from the cirrhogenic standpoint as will be outlined later.

Despite the fact that all the above food-mixtures contained adequate choline, fatty livers developed in all groups, particularly those consuming alcohol (rather than sucrose). We suspected and soon confirmed that protein (although it had been present in the form of amino acids equal to 16 per cent protein) had been the limiting factor. When the amount of amino acids was increased sufficiently to provide 25 per cent of the total calories, a fatty liver was prevented even when the animals still received 50 per cent of their calories in the form of alcohol (see Figure 27-7). It appeared that under these conditions, alcohol had increased the protein requirement of these animals and a fatty liver induced by a relative deficiency of protein would result unless the level of the latter was raised beyond that normally considered adequate for the (non-alcohol-consuming) rat. It is significant however that neither in any of these experiments nor in those conducted by Lieber and others was a fibrotic or cirrhotic change produced. Not even in our own experiments, which we continued for

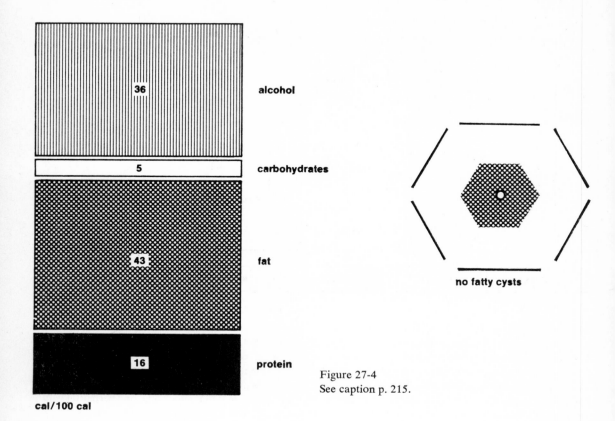

cal/100 cal

Figure 27-4
See caption p. 215.

much longer periods (four months) than did Lieber, did fibrosis and cirrhosis develop.

Electron microscopy studies of these livers showed that the accumulation of fat was accompanied (particularly in rats consuming alcohol without the high-protein supplement) by two cardinal changes. The first involved mitochondria. We consider this lesion the most significant and fundamental one at the ultrastructural level. The mitochondria in both the acute model, briefly mentioned at the outset, and the chronic experiments, described above, undergo bizarre changes in size and shape. They become enlarged, greatly elongated, and frequently form unusual target shapes (see Figure 27-8). In extreme form, they become so big that individual mitochondria are larger than nucleoli and even approach nuclear dimensions (see Figure 27-9). These megamitochondria, as we have named them, are clearly several micra in diameter. They

should therefore be evident even under the lower magnifications of the light microscope. They have in fact been observed for nearly half a century by light microscopy and were first described by Mallory. These megamitochondria are indeed the main constituent of Mallory bodies or the so-called intracellular hyaline seen so frequently in the livers of alcoholic patients. We have even demonstrated this identity of Mallory bodies with megamitochondria by combined light and electron microscopy of the same body. An inclusion identified by light microscopy as a classical Mallory body proved, in serial sections of the same structure examined by the electron microscope, to be a clearly recognizable but grossly enlarged and deformed mitochondrion (see Figure 27-10). Previously we had been able to show, somewhat less clearly, a similar relationship between megamitochondria and Mallory bodies in choline-deficient rats.

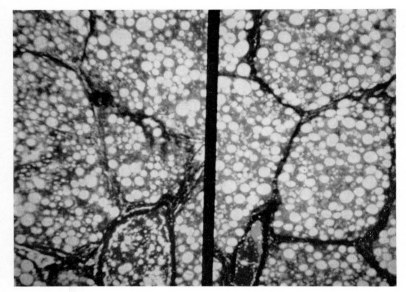

Figure 27-2

Fatty and fibrotic change in sections of liver from rats on the basal diet without supplementary choline. That on the left is from an animal receiving alcohol as well as the basal diet; that on the right from an animal receiving sucrose in an amount isocaloric with the alcohol. Both livers contain much fat in the form of fatty cysts and are penetrated by abnormal fibrous trabeculae. These lesions were completely prevented in comparable control animals given additional choline.

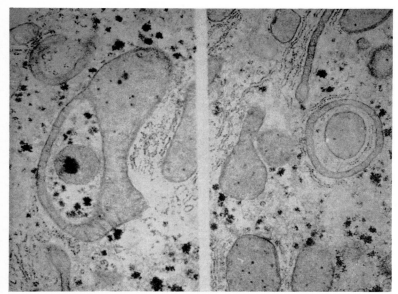

Figure 27-8
Two fields from electronmicrographs of livers of rats consuming a low-protein, high-alcohol liquid diet. Note the extremely bizarre shape of the mitochondria with "target formations" ($\times$ — 10,000).

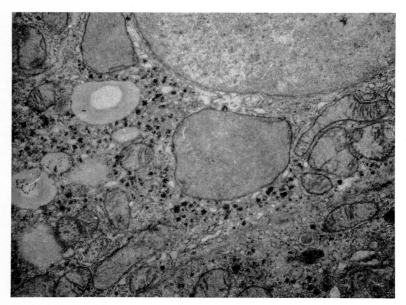

Figure 27-9
Electronmicrograph of the liver of an animal given a low-protein, high-alcohol diet. In the centre a greatly enlarged mitochondrion is shown – a megamitochondrion. It is larger than the nucleolus ($\times$ — 10,000).

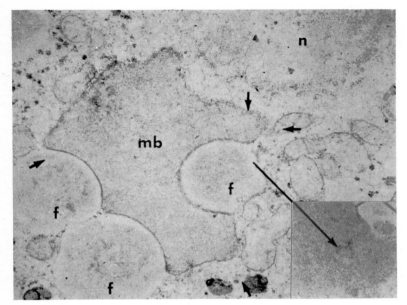

Figure 27-10
Electronmicrograph from a rat fed alcohol showing an inclusion labelled
"mb." This was identifiable as a distorted mitochondrion and in the light
microscopic section (inset) a serial section of the same inclusion was
identifiable as a Mallory body.

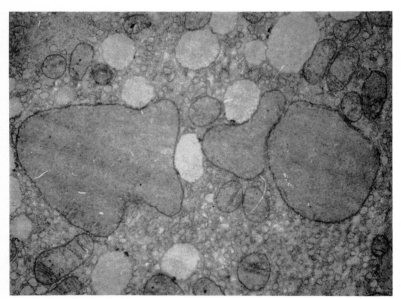

Figure 27-11
Electronmicrograph of the liver of an alcohol-fed rat showing increased
vesiculated ergastoplasm and smooth ER between the bizarre megamitochondria. ($\times$ — 10,000).

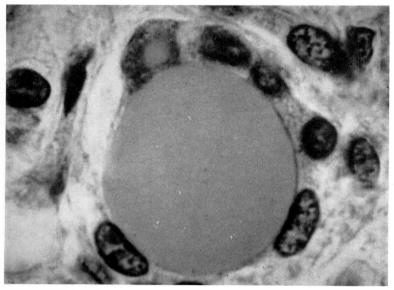

Figure 27-12
Frozen section stained for fat and prepared from the cirrhotic liver of a young
female alcoholic (age 34) showing a large fatty cyst. One of the mural nuclei
(at 11 o'clock on the wall of the cyst) is filled with fat, a not uncommon
finding in severely fatty livers produced by any method ($\times$ — 600).

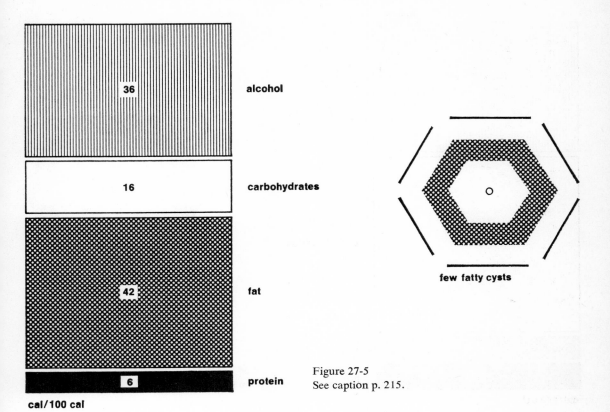

alcohol — 36

carbohydrates — 16

fat — 42

protein — 6

cal/100 cal

few fatty cysts

Figure 27-5
See caption p. 215.

The second ultrastructural change, which we consider less important, affects the ergastoplasm which becomes vesiculated with a transformation of rough ER to smooth ER at an early stage of the experiment (see Figure 27-11). This aspect of the electron microscopic changes has been emphasized by others (3) but we do not agree that altered ergastoplasm is a major or uniform constituent of the Mallory body.

THE RELATION OF THE FATTY LIVER TO FIBROSIS AND CIRRHOSIS

Although this portion of the paper may be the only one directly related to the title, "Pathogenesis of Fatty Liver and Cirrhosis," we have left its consideration to the end. We have done this because the foregoing descriptions of experiments in which the oral consumption of alcohol and the induction of liver damage have been studied serve to emphasize that the fatty liver is the chief form of hepatic damage induced by alcohol under suitable dietary conditions. As pointed out at the beginning, fatty liver precedes and accompanies every stage but the final atrophic one in the cirrhosis associated with chronic and excessive consumption of alcohol by man. Even in the final atrophic form, the persistence of intratrabecular fatty cysts (9) betrays the previous fatty nature of this final multilobular ("post-hepatitic," "post-necrotic") stage of advanced alcoholic cirrhosis.

But, given sufficient time, will a fatty liver necessarily or even frequently progress into true fibrosis and cirrhosis? This question has been debated for decades. On the one extreme are those who believe that the fat, the fibrosis, and the architectural distortion are simply coexistent lesions not pathogenically related. At the other

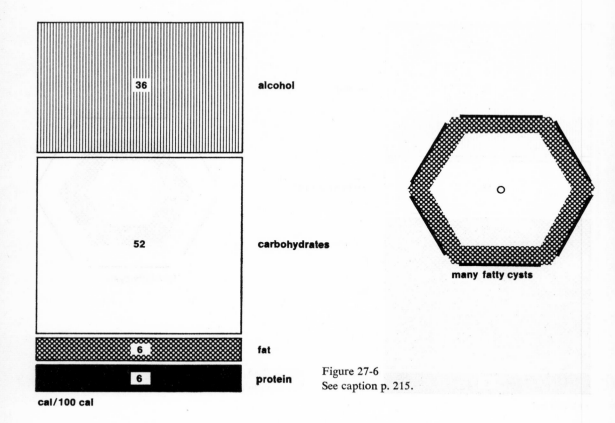

36 alcohol

52 carbohydrates

6 fat

6 protein

cal/100 cal

O

many fatty cysts

Figure 27-6
See caption p. 215.

extreme, are those, including the writer, who believe that under appropriate conditions some types of fatty liver will inevitably progress to extreme degrees of cirrhosis. That is, some fatty livers, but not all, are cirrhogenic.

The conditions of fatty liver and cirrhosis are traditionally associated in the minds of pathologists since they constantly perform autopsies on patients and frequently encounter both lesions in the same liver. However, this association is much less common in the experience of the experimental hepatopathologist. In fact the only dietary model in which fatty livers of experimental animals are consistently accompanied by fibrosis and cirrhosis is that of choline deficiency. There are a host of dietary methods now available to the investigator for the production of fatty livers in animals, including simple protein deficiency, very high-fat diets, starvation, obesity, and deficiencies of essential fatty acids, riboflavin, or

pyridoxine. Some of these livers are characterized by periportal accumulations of parenchymal fat and others by centrolobular distributions. But there are no reports of any of these dietary imbalances (other than choline deficiency) being followed by fibrosis and cirrhosis.

Even the addition of large amounts of cholesterol to the diet will not *per se* produce cirrhosis in rats unless accompanied either by some other dietary change (high fat, inclusion of bile salts or thiouracil) or hepatotoxic factors (amounts of carbon tetrachloride or chloroform which are below those levels necessary to produce liver damage without the addition of dietary cholesterol).

These considerations suggest that perhaps something more than a single dietary deficiency at a time is necessary for the production of cirrhosis and that somehow the conditions under which choline deficiency is usually studied set the

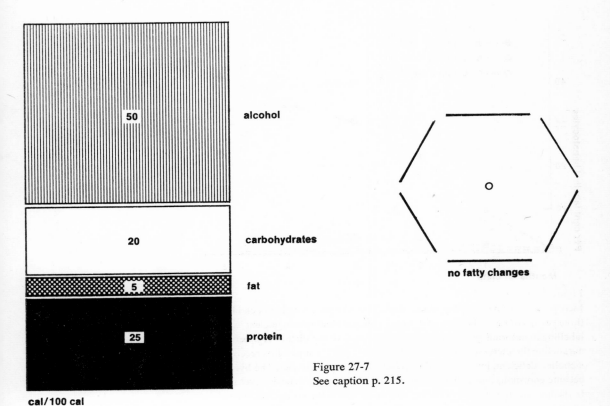

50	alcohol
20	carbohydrates
5	fat
25	protein

cal/100 cal

no fatty changes

Figure 27-7
See caption p. 215.

stage for the development of cirrhosis more aptly than do other hepatolipogenic deficiencies.

This answer has proved in fact to be the most likely one. Because the rat (and other animals) is able to synthesize choline from methionine-containing protein, the experimental diets usually employed are not only free of appreciable amounts of either free or bound choline, but also low in protein. This restriction of protein is necessary in order that only enough methionine will be available to support total body growth of the rat but no appreciable amount will be left over for choline synthesis from labile methyl groups donated by any methionine not used for growth. An examination of the literature indicates that the diets used successfully by every investigator to date to produce cirrhosis in rats are low not only in choline but also in total protein. There are no exceptions to this statement. Handler and Dubin (8) were among the first to

emphasize this point nearly two decades ago. They concluded that the fat and the fibrosis were separate but coexistent lesions, the former caused by choline deficiency and the latter by protein deficiency. We cannot agree with this interpretation if for no other reason than that protein deficiency without a coexisting deficiency of choline does not result in cirrhosis with or without fat.

Over the years, a series of extensive studies of the pathogenesis of dietary cirrhosis in the rat by our group have provided a possible explanation for the above phenomenon in terms of pathogenic events. Our notion is based on the concept that the critical circumstance necessary for the development of a cirrhotic from a fatty liver is an excessive accumulation of fat *per parenchymal cell* which is not necessarily reflected by a simple measurement of the total amount of liver fat such as the percentage of the

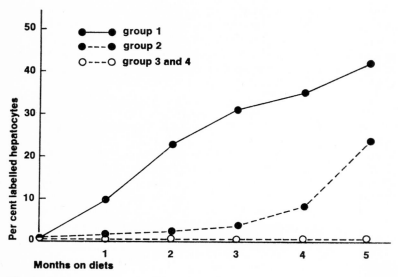

Figure 27-13

Incorporation of tritiated thymidine into the DNA of proliferating nuclei in
three groups of rats. The top curve shows a prompt increase in nuclear
labelling in autoradiographs beginning at the start of the dietary regimen and
paralleling the increase in liver fat (not shown). This group of rats received
a choline-deficient, low-methionine, relatively high-protein diet. The livers
became enormous and very fatty but neither fibrosis nor cirrhosis developed.
In the lower curve, nuclear labelling was much less in the group of animals
which received the same choline-deficient, low-methionine but low-protein
diet. Formation of new liver cells proceeded only slowly until the last month
when a spurt represented the development of compensatory regenerative
nodules. These livers, even though containing less *total* fat than the first
group, were both fibrotic and cirrhotic. The lowest line represents nuclear
labelling in a group of animals receiving the low-methionine, relatively
high-protein diet supplemented with choline. These livers were not abnormally
fatty and nuclear labelling was also normal: fibrosis and cirrhosis were of
course absent.

total wet weight of the liver or per 100 grams of
body weight as is usually done.

Some years ago at Washington University in
St. Louis, one of us (W.S.H.) and a former colleague, Dr. J. W. Grisham, were able to show
that even when the methionine was kept both
low and constant in choline-deficient diets, cirrhosis would only develop in those rats fed a
low-protein, low-choline diet. Enormous fatty
livers without cirrhosis developed in other rats
pair-fed an equally choline-deficient, low-
methionine diet but one containing a higher

amount of total protein. In the large fatty, non-
cirrhotic livers, the DNA-content increased parallel with the increase in fat right from the start.
As we determined microscopically, the amount
of fat per cell in these livers was never sufficiently
great to rupture them and instigate formation of
fatty cysts (lipodiastemata) which we first described quite some years ago (see Figure 27-
12). Only in the livers of the rats fed the low-
protein, low-choline diet did fatty cysts form
from overloading of individual parenchymal cells
by abnormal amounts of lipid. The amount of

fat *per cell* was excessive and harmful, not necessarily because of the *total* amount of liver fat was any greater than in the non-cirrhotic, high-protein group but because there had not been a comparable increase in DNA (see Figure 27-13). Only *after* the cirrhosis was initiated did the DNA-content of these livers suddenly spurt upwards. This late increase corresponded to the formation of regenerative nodules (i.e. cirrhosis). We have described elsewhere the manner in which fatty cysts in their turn rupture, lose their fat with condensation of supporting reticulin to form fibrous trabeculae which accompany the development of architectural distortion incident to the compensatory hyperplasia leading to nodule formation.

An adequate level of protein is necessary to provide not only methionine but also the other amino acids essential for the synthesis of protein attendant to formation of new liver cells, and as reflected by an increase in DNA in the livers of rats fed the choline-deficient, high-protein diet. Without these essential building blocks, even though the stimulus for the formation of new liver cells was present (the fat induced by choline deficiency) sufficient new liver cells could not be formed in the absence of adequate dietary protein in the low-choline, low-protein fed rats, to share the burden of the excessive fat storage. DNA content did not increase along with the increase in fat, individual liver cells were overloaded with fat to the bursting point, fatty cysts formed and ruptured with resulting fibrotic scars replacing them. The final compensatory burst of formation of new liver cells in regenerative nodules came too little and too late to prevent damage as it did in the low-choline, adequate-protein group where DNA increased from the beginning of the dietary regimen.

From the foregoing it is evident that the fatty cyst is the cytometaplastic link in the pathogenesis of fatty cirrhosis. The regenerative power of the liver is so remarkable that the amount of fat per cell will never be sufficiently great to stimulate cyst-formation unless dietary protein, as well as choline, is sufficiently low to prevent new parenchymal formation. Alcohol fed to rats will apparently, under suitable dietary conditions, stimulate deposition of excess fat. But to date, even when the dietary protein has been restricted, the critical ratio of abnormal fat to DNA content has apparently not been reached so as to result in cirrhosis. Our current attempts to produce an alcohol-conditioned cirrhosis in the rat by dietary means are formulated in accordance with this last hypothesis.

IS ALCOHOL A HEPATOTOXIN?

We cannot close without emphasizing that all the foregoing data taken together strongly suggest that in both man and experimental animals the chronic consumption of large amounts of alcohol is not hepatotoxic. Any liver damage associated with chronic alcoholism can be explained by the induction of relative deficiencies of vitamins or essential food factors including distortion of optimal carbohydrate, fat, and protein dietary balances. Recently Dr. A. Takada and Dr. E. A. Porta have successfully brought about dramatic regression of previously well-established multilobular dietary cirrhosis in rats by feeding them large amounts of alcohol (36 per cent of total calories) and a "super" diet containing several times the usual amounts of proteins and vitamins. How can this nectar of the gods be a hepatotoxin if, when suitably administered, it even permits recovery of a previously damaged liver?

REFERENCES

1
ASHWORTH, C.T.
Production of fatty infiltration of liver in rats by alcohol in spite of adequate diet
Proc. Soc. Exper. Biol. Med., **66**: 382, 1947
2
BEST, C.H., HARTROFT, W.S., LUCAS, C.C., & RIDOUT, J.H.
Liver damage produced by feeding alcohol or sugar and its prevention by choline
Brit. Med. J., **ii**: 1001, 1949
3
BIAVA, C.
Mallory alcoholic hyalin: a heretofore unique lesion of hepatocellular ergastoplasm
Lab. Invest., **13**: 301, 1964
4
CONNOR, C.L.
The etiology and pathogenesis of alcoholic cirrhosis of the liver
J.A.M.A., **112**: 387, 1939

5
DILUZIO, N.R,
Effect of acute ethanol intoxication on liver and
plasma fractions of the rat
Amer. J. Physiol., **194**: 453, 1958

6
DILUZIO, N.R,
Prevention of the acute ethanol-induced fatty liver by
simultaneous administration of antioxidants
Life Sc. **3**: 113, 1964

7
GÓMEZ-DUMM, C.L.A. & PORTA, E.A.
Protein and hepatic injury associated with experimental
chronic alcoholism
Fed. Proc., **25**: 304, 1966
Abstract

8
HANDLER, P. & DUBIN, I.N.
The significance of fatty infiltration in the development
of hepatic cirrhosis due to choline deficiency
J. Nutr., **31**: 141, 1946

9
HARTROFT, W.S.
Diagnostic significance of fatty cysts in cirrhosis
Arch. Path., **55**: 63, 1953

10
HARTROFT, W.S.
Experimental reproduction of human hepatic diseases
In Progress in liver diseases, ed. by M. Popper &
F. Schaffner
New York: Grune & Stratton, 1961

11
HARTROFT, W.S., PORTA, E.A., & SUZUKI, M.
Effects of choline chloride on hepatic lipids after
acute ethanol intoxication
Quart. J. Stud. Alc., **25**: 427, 1964

12
JABBARI, M., BAKER, H., & LEEVY, C.M.
Factors influencing accumulation and removal of
liver fat
Am. J. Clin. Nutr., **16**: 382, 1965
Abstract

13
JONES, D.P.
The importance of a high fat diet in the pathogenesis
of alcoholic fatty liver
Am. J. Clin. Nutr., **16**: 381, 1965
Abstract

14
KLATSKIN, G., KREHL, W.A. & CONN, H.O.
The effect of alcohol on the choline requirement:
I, Changes in the rat's liver following prolonged
ingestion of alcohol
J. Exper. Med., **100**: 605, 1954

15
LIEBER, C.S. & DE CARLI, L.M.
Study of agents for the prevention of fatty liver
produced by prolonged alcohol intake
Gastroenterology, **50**: 316, 1966

16
LIEBER, C.S., JONES, D.P., MENDELSON, J., &
DE CARLI, L.M.
Fatty liver, hyperlipemia and hyperuricemia produced
by prolonged alcohol consumption, despite adequate
dietary intake
Trans. Assoc. Am. Physicians, 76: 289, 1963

17
MALLOV, S. & BLOCH, J.L.
Role of hypophysis and adrenals in fatty intoxication
of liver resulting from acute ethanol intoxication
Am. J. Physiol., **184**: 29, 1956

18
PORTA, E.A., HARTROFT, W.S., & DE LA IGLESIA, F.A.
Hepatic changes associated with chronic alcoholism
in rats
Lab. Invest., **14**: 1437, 1965

W. SOLODKOWSKA

R. ALVARADO-ANDRADE

N. SEGOVIA-RIQUELME

E. MUÑOZ

J. MARDONES

Institute of Studies on Alcoholism
University of Chile
Santiago, Chile

28

Ethanol Metabolism in Experimental Liver Cirrhosis

It is well known that chronic intoxication with carbon tetrachloride induces fatty infiltration of the liver followed by cirrhosis (2, 8). Sirnes in 1953 (9) observed that rats intoxicated with this substance increased their voluntary alcohol intake, a finding which we have confirmed (1). It was pertinent to study the effect of CCl_4 on ethanol metabolism to determine whether the resulting lesions influenced the activity of alcohol dehydrogenase and to find an explanation for the increased appetite for alcohol.

Experiments performed in our Institute (1) with CCl_4-intoxicated rats involved the administration of 1.55 g per kg body weight of ethanol-1-C^{14} by intraperitoneal injection and the determination of the activity of the expired CO_2. It was found that during the first four hours the rate of ethanol oxidation to CO_2 did not differ from the controls, while between the fourth and sixth hour the activity of the expired CO_2 was significantly lower than in the preceding four hours and than in the controls. These results are shown in Figure 28-1 and the statistical analysis in Table 28-1.

To determine the origin of this difference, we studied in the same rats the changes in blood alcohol level through time after an intraperitoneal injection of ethanol. The results, summarized in Figure 28-2, show that the rate of ethanol elimination from the blood was significantly higher in the intoxicated rats than in the controls. This accounts for the difference in CO_2 activity between the fourth and sixth hours, since the blood ethanol reached levels below the saturation point of alcohol dehydrogenase in the intoxicated rats earlier than in the controls.

It seemed desirable to seek the origin of this higher rate of alcohol elimination from the blood of rats exposed to CCl_4. Since the maximal rate of ethanol oxidation was similar in both groups, we had to look for a difference in the metabolic pathways of ethanol which did not lead rapidly to CO_2. One of these pathways is lipid synthesis, in which the carbons of ethanol are incorporated into fatty acids and glycerol. We performed experiments in which liver slices from rats intoxicated with CCl_4 and from controls were incubated with labelled ethanol at a concentration of 0.2 mg/ml. In these experiments the CO_2 was recovered in a central

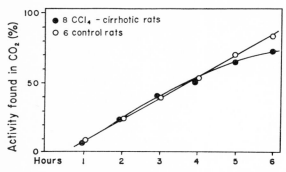

Figure 28-1

Cumulative activity as a percentage of injected activity in expired CO_2 of cirrhotic and control rats after intraperitoneal injection of 1.55 gm ethanol-1-C^{14} per kg body weight. Each point represents the arithmetic mean. From Campos *et al.* (1).

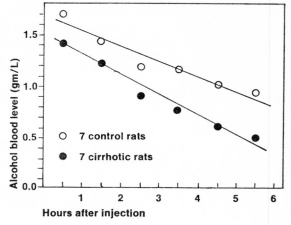

Figure 28-2

Evolution of ethanol blood levels in cirrhotic and control rats after intraperitoneal injection of ethanol 1.55 gm/kg BW. Each point represents the arithmetic mean. The value of β expressed in mg of ethanol per ml of blood per hour were: $-.236 \pm .016$ and $-.157 \pm .012$, respectively ($p < .005$). Based on data in Campos *et al.* (1).

tube containing 30 per cent KOH solution; the activity of the CO_2 and of the lipids of liver slices were determined at the end of the experiment.

The data provided in Table 28-2 show that there was no significant difference between the liver slices from CCl_4-intoxicated rats and those from controls, either in the activity of the recovered CO_2 or in lipids. Thus, the ability of liver cells to oxidize ethanol appears not to be altered by CCl_4 intoxication, and the incorporation of ethanol into lipids by liver slices seems not to be different in normal and CCl_4-intoxicated rats.

It is well known that in the rat adipose tissue is a relevant site of formation of triglycerides (11) and that this tissue is able to incorporate acetate into fatty acids (4, 6). Accordingly, we next sought to determine whether the incorporation of ethanol into lipids by adipose tissue slices was modified by chronic intoxication with CCl_4. *In vitro* experiments were performed using slices of mesenteric adipose tissue from CCl_4-intoxicated rats and from controls. The data given in Table 28-3 show that ethanol oxidation to CO_2 was similar in both groups, while the incorporation of the carbon one of ethanol into lipids was significantly higher in the slices from CCl_4-intoxicated rats.

The experiments of Winegard and Renold (12) and of Trew and Begg (10) have shown

that acetate incorporation into lipids of adipose tissue *in vitro* is considerably increased by the presence of glucose. For this reason we performed experiments in which adipose tissue slices of intoxicated rats and controls were incubated with labelled ethanol (2 mg/ml) in the presence of glucose and of fructose (3.6 mg/ml), and in the absence of any substrate. No significant difference in the oxidation of ethanol to CO_2 by adipose tissue slices in the presence or absence of these substrates was observed in slices from either intoxicated or control rats (see Table 28-4).

The data on the incorporation of the labelled ethanol into lipids are provided in Table 28-5. These data show that even in the presence of hexoses the incorporation of ethanol into lipids of slices from CCl_4-intoxicated rats was significantly higher than in the controls.

Glucose appears to enhance significantly more than fructose the incorporation of ethanol into lipids. This is consistent with the ability of adipose tissue to phosphorilate both hexoses and is much higher for glucose than for fructose (3, 5).

TABLE 28–1

STATISTICAL ANALYSIS OF THE DIFFERENCE IN THE
ACTIVITY OF $CH_3{}^{14}CH_2OH$ RECOVERED IN CO_2 FROM CCl_4
INTOXICATED RATS AND CONTROLS

Hours	Controls		Treated		2p
	N	b	N	b	
0 to 4	6	15.2±1.3	8	16.6±1.8	>0.5
4 to 6		15.0±1.2		9.6±1.2	<0.01
2p		>0.8		<0.01	

Values of *b* are from the formula $y = a + bx$, where y = cumulative per cent recovery,
and x = hours after injection.

TABLE 28–2

INFLUENCE OF CHRONIC INTOXICATION OF RATS WITH
CCl_4 ON THE OXIDATION OF $CH_3{}^{14}CH_2OH$ TO CO_2 AND ITS
INCORPORATION INTO LIPIDS BY RAT LIVER SLICES

	N	Oxidation to CO_2 (μM/gm/2 hours)	Incorporation into lipids (μM/gm/2 hours)
treated	16	2.91±0.28	0.37±0.03
controls	16	2.56±0.18	0.31±0.03
2p		>0.30	>0.10

Experimental conditions: Ringer-Krebs phosphate solution, pH 7.2 plus $CH_3{}^{14}CH_2OH$
(0.2 mg/ml). About 500 mg of liver slices were incubated at 37 °C for two hours. The
CO_2 was recovered in a central tube with 30 per cent KOH. The activity was measured
as $^{14}CO_3Ba$ in infinitely thick layer.

TABLE 28–3

INFLUENCE OF CHRONIC INTOXICATION OF RATS WITH
CCl_4 ON THE OXIDATION OF $CH_3{}^{14}CH_2OH$ TO CO_2 AND ITS
INCORPORATION INTO LIPIDS BY ADIPOSE TISSUE SLICES

	N	Oxidation to CO_2 (μM/gm/2 hours)	Incorporation into lipids (μM/gm/2 hours)
treated	16	0.63±0.04	0.76±0.05
controls	16	0.68±0.03	0.35±0.02
2p		>0.30	<0.001

Experimental conditions as in Table 28–2 except that adipose tissue was used instead of
liver slices.

Finally, it was important to clarify the question as to whether the higher incorporation of ethanol into lipids of adipose tissue from intoxicated rats takes place in the fatty acids or in the non-saponifiable fraction or in both. Therefore, we performed experiments in which the fatty acids were separated by saponification and acid extraction with petroleum ether. The corresponding activity of glycerol was calculated from the difference between the activity in total lipids and in fatty acids, since it is known that rat adipose tissue contains triglycerides almost exclusively (7). To obtain additional information these experiments were performed with ethanol labelled either in carbon one or carbon two.

TABLE 28–4

INFLUENCE OF CHRONIC INTOXICATION OF RATS WITH CCl_4 AND OF THE PRESENCE OF HEXOSES ON THE OXIDATION OF $CH_3{}^{14}CH_2OH$ TO CO_2 BY ADIPOSE TISSUE SLICES

| *Hexoses* | *Treated* | | *Controls* | | *2p* |
	N	μM/*gm*/*2 hours**	N	μM/*gm*/*2 hours**	
—	52	3.42 ± 0.15	62	2.82 ± 0.15	< 0.01
glucose†	35	3.23 ± 0.27	35	2.86 ± 0.21	> 0.2
2p		> 0.5		> 0.8	
fructose†	17	3.72 ± 0.39	27	3.11 ± 0.22	> 0.1
2p		> 0.4		> 0.2	

*Arithmetic mean ± standard error.
†3.6 mg/ml.
Experimental conditions as in Table 28–2 except that concentration of ethanol was 2 mg/ml.

TABLE 28–5

INFLUENCE OF CHRONIC INTOXICATION OF RATS WITH CCl_4 AND OF THE PRESENCE OF HEXOSES ON THE INCORPORATION OF $CH_3{}^{14}CH_2OH$ INTO LIPIDS BY ADIPOSE TISSUE SLICES

| *Hexoses* | *Treated* | | *Controls* | | *2p* |
	N	μM/*gm*/*2 hours*	N	μM/*gm*/*2 hours*	
—	37	0.72 ± 0.10	51	0.25 ± 0.02	< 0.001
glucose	20	3.61 ± 0.37	18	0.77 ± 0.11	< 0.001
2p		< 0.001		< 0.001	
fructose	17	1.20 ± 0.07	17	0.35 ± 0.02	< 0.001
2p		< 0.001		< 0.001	

Experimental conditions as in Table 28–2 except that the activity in the lipids was measured directly.

Table 28-6 shows the values of ethanol oxidized to CO_2 by slices from CCl_4-intoxicated animals and from controls. In general, the activity of carbon one of ethanol was recovered in CO_2 in higher proportion than that of carbon two. The explanation is that carbon one is oxidized to CO_2 in higher proportion than carbon two within the first turns of the TCA cycle. Furthermore, the CO_2 released by decarboxylation of oxalacetate arises in higher proportion from carbon one of ethanol.

The fact that in experiments with adipose slices from CCl_4-intoxicated rats, the proportion of CO_2 coming from carbon two was significantly higher than in the controls, leads to the hypothesis that the turning rate of the TCA acid cycle is higher in the intoxicated animals. The results concerning the incorporation of carbon one and two into fatty acids and glycerol are summarized in Table 28-7.

If the incorporation into fatty acids took place exclusively as: acetylCoA → acetoacetate, the incorporation of both carbons should be similar. However, the proportion is clearly higher for carbon two, whether in slices from intoxicated rats or controls. This leads one to suspect that some formation of fatty acids occurs through the following sequence: oxalacetate → pyruvate → acetylCoA – a pathway involving exclusively carbon two of ethanol.

The incorporation of ethanol into fatty acids by adipose tissue of treated rats was clearly higher than in the controls, the incorporation of carbon two being higher than carbon one.

TABLE 28–6

INFLUENCE OF CHRONIC INTOXICATION OF RATS WITH
CCl_4 ON THE OXIDATION OF $CH_3{}^{14}CH_2OH$ OR ${}^{14}CH_3CH_2OH$
TO CO_2 BY ADIPOSE TISSUE SLICES

	N	*Activity recovered in CO_2 ($\mu M/gm/2$ hours)**		
		$CH_3{}^{14}CH_2OH$	*${}^{14}CH_3CH_2OH$*	*2p*
treated	17	3.70 ± 0.46	2.56 ± 0.18	0.05
controls	27	3.81 ± 0.23	1.87 ± 0.14	<0.001
2p		>0.8	>0.005	

Experimental conditions as in Table 28–4.
*Arithmetic mean ± standard error.

TABLE 28–7

INFLUENCE OF CHRONIC INTOXICATION OF RATS WITH CCl_4 ON THE
INCORPORATION OF $CH_3{}^{14}CH_2OH$ OR ${}^{14}CH_2CH_2OH$ IN FATTY ACIDS AND
GLYCEROL BY ADIPOSE TISSUE SLICES

	Ethanol	*Treated*		*Controls*		*2p*
		N	*$\mu M/gm/2$ hours*	N	*$\mu M/gm/2$ hours*	
fatty acids	$1\text{-}{}^{14}C$	16	0.13 ± 0.02	16	0.10 ± 0.01	<0.05
fatty acids	$2\text{-}{}^{14}C$	16	0.24 ± 0.03	16	0.15 ± 0.01	<0.01
2p			<0.005		<0.001	
glycerol	$1\text{-}{}^{14}C$	16	0.19 ± 0.04	16	0.06 ± 0.02	<0.01
glycerol	$2\text{-}{}^{14}C$	16	0.15 ± 0.03	16	0.11 ± 0.02	>0.2
2p			>0.6		>0.05	

Experimental conditions as in Table 28–4.

Concerning the incorporation of ethanol into glycerol, the proportion of the activity of carbon one and two recovered in the tissue of treated rats was higher than in the controls. The difference was clearly significant in the case of carbon one but not as clear in the case of carbon two. This is in agreement with the hypothesis that the higher formation of fats in CCl_4-intoxicated rats is linked with a greater availability of glycerophosphate formed by reversible glycolysis.

It would be desirable to study what happens with labelled acetate in order to discover the role played by the NADH$_2$ produced during ethanol metabolism. The possibility of glycerol formation from alcohol by a metabolic pathway different from reversible glycolysis also deserves study, since the proportion of carbon one of ethanol found in glycerol was significantly higher in animals chronically intoxicated with CCl_4.

REFERENCES

1
CAMPOS, I., SOLODKOWSKA, W., MUÑOZ, E.,
SEGOVIA-RIQUELME, N., CEMBRANO, J., & MARDONES, J.
Ethanol metabolism in rats with experimental liver cirrhosis
I. Rate of combustion of labeled ethanol and rate of decrease of blood ethanol level
Quart. J. Stud. Alc., **25**: 417, 1964
2
DIANZANI, M.U.
The content of adenosine polyphosphates in fatty livers
Biochem. J., **65**: 116, 1957
3
FAIN, J.N.
Effects of dexamethasone and 2-deoxy-D-glucose on fructose and glucose metabolism by incubated adipose tissue
J. Biol. Chem., **239**: 958, 1964
4
FELLER, D.D.
Metabolism of adipose tissue; incorporation of acetate carbon into lipids by slices of adipose tissue
J. Biol. Chem., **206**: 171, 1954

5
FROESCH, E.R. & GINSBERG, J.L.
Fructose metabolism of adipose tissue
I. Comparison of fructose and glucose metabolism
in epididymal adipose tissue of normal rats
J. Biol. Chem., **237**: 3317, 1962
6
GELLHORN, A., BENJAMIN, W., & WAGNER, M.
The in vitro incorporation of acetate -1-C^{14} into
individual fatty acids of adipose tissue from young and
old rats
J. Lipid. Res., **3**: 314, 1962
7
HIRSCH, J., FARQUHART, J.W., AHRENS, E.H., JR.,
PETERSON, M.L., & STOFFEL, W.
Studies of adipose tissue in man
A microtechnic for sampling and analysis
Am. J. Clin. Nutr., **8**: 499, 1960
8
RECKNAGEL, R.O. & ANTHONY, D.D.
Biochemical changes in carbon tetrachloride fatty liver:
separation of fatty changes from mitochondrial
degeneration
J. Biol. Chem., **234**: 1052, 1959
9
SIRNES, T.B.
Voluntary consumption of alcohol in rats with
cirrhosis of liver; preliminary report
Quart. J. Stud. Alc., **14**: 3, 1953
10
TREW, J.A. & BEGG, R.W.
In vitro incorporation of acetate-1-C^{14} into adipose
tissue from normal and tumor-bearing rats
Cancer Res., **19**: 1014, 1959
11
VAUGHAN, M.
The production and release of glycerol by adipose
tissue incubated in vitro
J. Biol. Chem., **237**: 3354, 1962
12
WINEGARD, A.I. & RENOLD, A.E.
Studies on rat adipose tissue in vitro
I. Effects of insulin on the metabolism of glucose,
pyruvate, and acetate
J. Biol. Chem., **233**: 267, 1958

G. UGARTE

I. INSUNZA

H. ALTSCHILLER

H. ITURRIAGA

Department of Medicine
University of Chile
Alcoholism Program of the Central Area of Santiago
National Health Service of Chile
Santiago, Chile

29

Clinical and Metabolic Disorders in Alcoholic Hepatic Damage

The association of alcoholism and hepatic damage has long been acknowledged. Vesalius is said to have recognized this relationship and Addison observed that patients who died of liver failure after overindulgence in drinking showed a fatty liver at autopsy (1). In the nineteenth and early twentieth centuries, French clinicians wrote that cirrhosis was induced, among other causes, by excessive drinking, and since then ethanol has been connected in one way or another with the pathogenesis of this disease (11, 12).

In the medical services of our University, as in other medical services in Santiago, Laënnec or septal cirrhosis of the liver is the first cause of admissions and mortality. In Chile the prevalence of problem drinking as revealed by field surveys is very great: 5 per cent of the adult population are addicts and 14 per cent excessive drinkers (19). In our cases, after a careful medical and social history was taken, it was found that problem drinking (in both excessive drinkers and addicts) existed in 90 per cent of male patients (and 86 per cent of both male and female) with liver cirrhosis. These percentages are higher than others given in literature, and we believe that the differences are probably due to the double check that we have made through interviews with relatives of the patients, regarding their history of alcoholic consumption. It has been the experience of the social workers and psychologist in our group that it is more difficult to obtain data from female patients than from males (29). Cirrhosis in Chile is the third most frequent cause of mortality in the adult population. In the United States, there has been a steady increase in the number of deaths from cirrhosis since the repeal of Prohibition, and the only diseases that outrank cirrhosis as causes of death at ages 45 to 64, are heart disease, cancer, and cerebral hemorrhage (22, 35).

The evidence suggests a strong relationship between alcoholism and Laënnec cirrhosis. However, this type of cirrhosis has been found in some areas of the world related to chronic malnutrition instead of alcoholism (10). In England it is said that alcoholism plays a minor influence in the development of cirrhosis. However, Rowntree in 1927 reported that death rates from cirrhosis in England and Wales fluctuated with deaths due to alcoholism (33). Cirrhosis in England today is thought to be mainly cryptogenic or posthepatitic, but in a recent visit we could not find statistics on alcohol consumption based on field surveys. This brings out the point that viral hepatitis, prevalent in some countries such as Chile, may lead to a cirrhosis of the liver indistinguishable from alcoholic-nutritional cirrhosis in the terminal stage. Howard and Watson found a higher prevalence of antecedent hepatitis in patients with Laënnec cirrhosis than in a control group (20). Armas-Cruz *et al.* in Chile, on the other hand, found no significant difference respecting antecedent hepatitis in patients with cirrhosis and controls (2).

Another problem which should be considered in the relationship of problem alcohol intake and liver damage is that not all alcoholics actually develop liver abnormalities. In our experience, based on liver biopsies, 21.6 per cent of alcoholic patients had liver cirrhosis and 55 per cent, fatty liver in varying degrees (21, 39). Possibly the answer to this problem should be sought in genetic and dietary differences among alcoholics. We have observed some families with several members suffering from alcoholic cirrhosis even though not living together. Cruz-Coke has reported a higher prevalence of colour blindness among alcoholics with liver cirrhosis than among the normal Chilean population and patients with other types of liver failure (7). We should not forget that liver cells have different sensitivities to toxins, both in different species and among individuals of the same species. This also holds true for dietary deficiencies: not all Sprague Dawley rats develop cirrhosis although they are much more sensitive to cirrhogenic diets than other varieties. Thus, it is quite possible that the incidence of liver damage in alcohol addiction varies according to genetic differences.

A low protein intake has been found by us in alcoholic patients with and without cirrhosis. However, due to the difficulties in obtaining accurate dietary data, it is impossible to say if there is a quantitative difference in protein consumption. Of the several explanations offered for the apparent relationship between chronic problem drinking and cirrhosis, the one most widely accepted is that alcohol acts indirectly so that food intake and especially protein consumption is relatively limited. This view is supported usually by the following evidence:

1
Cirrhosis has been produced in animals only with diets deficient in protein and choline. Alcohol *per se*, when the diet is adequate, does not produce liver cirrhosis in experimental animals, although fatty liver has been reported (10, 11, 24, 26, 30, 37).

2
There is a high incidence of malnutrition in human alcoholic cirrhosis, and high-protein diets have been known since Dielafoy and the work of Patek *et al.*, to be effective in the treatment of this form of cirrhosis (11, 30).

3
Patients with Laënnec cirrhosis have been reported to improve on such diets even when alcohol was not completely removed (37).

4
A similar form of cirrhosis had been reported as a sequel to kwashiorkor in non-alcoholic areas of the world (10).

This evidence indicates there can be little doubt that nutritional deficiencies play a very important role in the pathogenesis of Laënnec cirrhosis. However, this does not mean that alcohol cannot have a direct deleterious effect on liver cells. Lieber *et al.* have recently reported, in patients recovered from fatty liver related to alcohol intake, fatty infiltration of the liver when placed on a controlled adequate diet with the addition of ethanol (24). Klatskin *et al.* have proved that in animals alcohol enhances the requirement for choline and also that patients with cirrhosis may recover after alcohol withdrawal without dietary supplementation (23). Our experience is in agreement with the latter observation, although what is usually seen is an improvement in appetite and food intake after alcohol withdrawal.

Further evidence pointing towards a direct hepatotoxic effect of alcohol is the report of a decreased transaminase content of liver cells in rats fed an alcohol solution (18). Bang *et al.* in Denmark, have reported increased serum

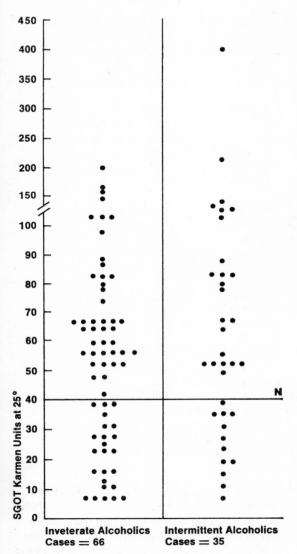

Figure 29-1

SGOT values in alcoholic patients upon admission to hospital. Each dot represents one patient.

glutamic-oxaloacetic transaminase (SGOT) in chronic alcoholics shortly after an episode of acute intoxication, and they were able to reproduce this effect by oral administration of alcohol to alcoholics, but no increase was found in healthy controls (4).

In our laboratory, we found an increase in SGOT in 66 alcoholic patients admitted to the ward shortly after intoxication, but only seven cases were over 100 Karmen units at 25° (39). The distribution is shown in Figure 29-1. On the other hand, we have been unable to demonstrate in the same group of alcoholic patients, a consistent increase in SGOT following intravenous infusion of 1.5 ml 95 per cent alcohol per kg in normal saline. The fluctuations observed may reflect in some cases variations in the method (see Figure 29-2).

These results agree with observations reported by Galambos *et al.* who gave smaller doses of alcohol intravenously (16). Perhaps different routes of administration exert a different effect on the release of this enzyme by the liver. In any event, observations such as these suggest that alcohol has a direct noxious effect in addition to its indirect effect on the liver through a caloric protein imbalance. But the facts presently known do not permit us to ascribe to ethanol a direct cirrhogenic effect.

ALCOHOL METABOLISM IN ALCOHOLICS AND LIVER DAMAGE

It has been reported that the activity of alcohol dehydrogenase is altered after alcohol administration and in liver disease. The results published are somewhat controversial. Dajani *et al.* reported an increase of ADH in the liver of Sprague Dawley rats previously treated orally with ethanol (8). McClearn *et al.* have recently reported a similar increase in mice and have shown that such increase is a function of the substrate ingestion (27). However, the increase in ADH is much less than that observed for other enzymes induced by their substrates.

Figueroa and Klotz did not find a change in liver ADH of Sprague Dawley rats intoxicated through intraperitoneal administration of ethanol, but have reported an increase of ADH activity after three weeks of forced alcohol ingestion followed by a decrease in activity six weeks later (13, 14). A decrease in alcohol dehydrogenase in the liver of choline-deficient cirrhotic rats has been found by Mikata, Dimakulongan and Hartroft (28). Figueroa and Klotz and also Asada and Galambos have found a decrease in ADH activity in human cir-

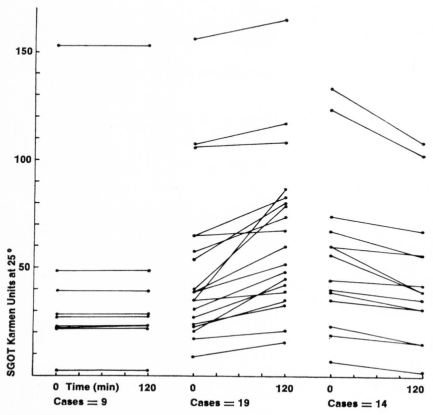

Figure 29-2

Changes in SGOT values 120 minutes after intravenous administration of ethanol.
Each line represents one case, each dot one determination.

rhotic liver as compared with normal controls (3, 15). But while Asada and Galambos did not find a difference in the rate of alcohol metabolism in patients with cirrhosis of the liver, Liebermann demonstrated a diminished metabolic rate only in cirrhotic patients with hepatic failure (25). Earlier, Danopoulos *et al.* (9) and von Bauer (42) reported a low rate of alcohol metabolism in cirrhosis. However, their data are insufficient to determine if the differences are statistically significant.

We recently studied hepatic ADH in liver biopsies of six normal controls (moderate drinkers), 18 alcohol addicts with normal liver histology, 12 alcohol addicts with fatty liver, and six alcoholics with liver cirrhosis. All cases except the controls were admitted to our alco-

holic ward intoxicated and were studied from two to five days after admission (41). Alcoholic liver samples showed a significant decrease in ADH as compared with samples from moderate drinkers. No difference was encountered in the hepatic ADH of alcoholic patients with cirrhosis or fatty infiltration as compared with alcoholics with normal livers (see Figure 29-3 and Table 29-1).

Our results respecting a significant decrease in ADH in alcoholics without liver damage, agree with those of Schwarzmann *et al.* in France (34). Our normal values are lower than those reported by von Wartburg in this Symposium. The discrepancy may be due to the different enzymatic (Bonichsen) and protein method used by us, or by loss of the enzyme in the

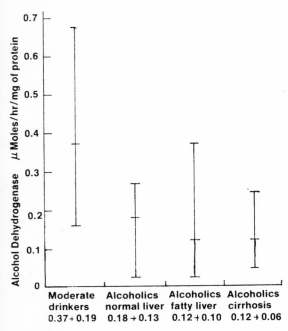

Figure 29-3
Hepatic alcohol dehydrogenase. Vertical lines represent the range and horizontal lines the mean. From Ugarte *et al.* (41), by permission.

TABLE 29-1

HEPATIC ALCOHOL DEHYDROGENASE IN MODERATE DRINKERS AND ALCOHOLICS WITH AND WITHOUT LIVER DAMAGE (41)

	ADH *(μM/hr/mg of protein)*		
	N	mean	s.d.
moderate drinkers	6	0.37	0.12
alcoholics without liver damage	18	0.18	0.13
alcoholics with steatosis	13	0.12	0.09
alcoholics with cirrhosis	6	0.12	0.08

biopsy procedure with the Menghini needle (41). We believe that the low hepatic ADH in alcoholics observed shortly after intoxication, irrespective of alterations in liver histology, may be related to reported abnormalities in zinc metabolism, or to a defect in protein synthesis.

We have also studied in our laboratory the

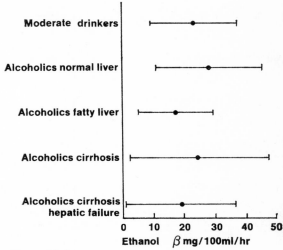

Figure 29-4
β of Widmark (mg per cent per hr). The dots represent the average and the lines the two standard deviations.

rate of removal from the blood of alcohol given intravenously (1.5 ml per kg in normal saline), and the increase in lactic acid content of blood in eight moderate drinkers, and 53 alcohol addicts (20 with fatty infiltration, and 15 with liver cirrhosis). Eight of the cirrhosis cases registered liver failure with jaundice. The alcoholic history of these patients ranged from three to 20 years, with an average of 15 years. All were inveterate alcoholics except eight intermittent drinkers. All, except the controls (moderate drinkers) were studied shortly after admission while intoxicated to the alcoholic ward. In this sample, we failed to find significant differences either in the rate of alcohol metabolism or in the increase in blood lactic acid content (40) (see Figures 29-4 to 29-6 and Table 29-2).

The values of β and of the rate of ethanol metabolism are higher than reported for man. This may result from the dose of alcohol used and the intravenous route. Thus, Newman and Lehman have shown an increase in β and r values when alcohol is given intravenously (41). Our β values agree with those recently reported by Asada and Galambos after giving 1.0 ml of alcohol intravenously (3).

234 / *Ugarte et al.*

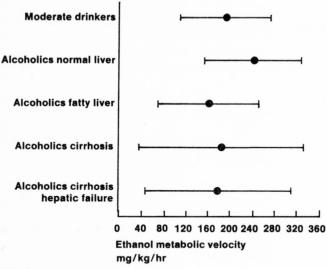

Figure 29-5
Ethanol disappearance rate (mg/kg/hr). The dots represent the average and the lines two standard deviations.

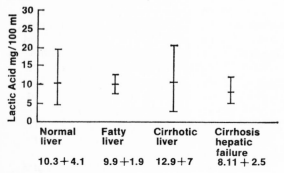

Figure 29-6
Blood lactic acid increase after intravenous ethanol administration. The horizontal lines represent the mean and the vertical lines two standard deviations.

CLINICAL AND HISTOLOGICAL FINDINGS IN ALCOHOL-INDUCED NUTRITIONAL LIVER DAMAGE

Time does not permit a detailed discussion of the different manifestations of alcoholic liver disease, so we shall restrict ourselves to comments on the broad aspects of this disorder as observed in the liver clinic and medical wards, and in the alcoholic ward.

Since 1964, we have been operating a research, prevention, and treatment program for alcoholism in the San Francisco de Borja Hospital which covers the central area of Santiago. The program, staffed by internists, psychiatrists, psychologists, biochemists, social workers, and nurses, falls within the Gastrointestinal Division and Clinical Research Laboratories of Chair A of Medicine in the University of Chile. This organization has permitted us to study, with the same methodology, patients admitted to the medical wards or to the alcoholic ward.

In the last ten years, we have seen 453 cases of liver disease related to alcohol intake and malnutrition. The history of alcohol intake revealed that 54 per cent were inveterate alcohol addicts and 22 per cent were intermittent; 10 per cent had a history of continuous excessive drinking, with frequent alcoholic sprees over weekends, and 14 per cent were moderate drinkers (over 106 cases). It is interesting to note that three of the moderate drinkers were diabetics.

The average period of problem drinking was twelve years. Although some of the patients seen in the medical wards had fatty liver, early cirrhosis, or well-developed inactive cirrhosis

TABLE 29–2

RATE OF DISAPPEARANCE OF ETHANOL FROM THE BLOOD

	N	β *(mg/100 ml/hr)*	*Ethanol metabolic rate (mg/kg/hr)*
normal drinkers	7	17 ± 6	162 ± 45
alcoholics			
normal liver	20	19 ± 8	178 ± 48
fatty liver	18	24 ± 11	184 ± 75
cirrhosis	15	23 ± 7	193 ± 41

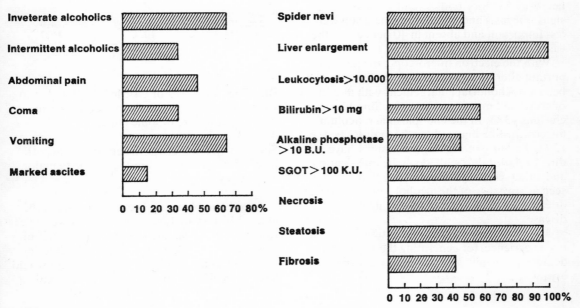

Figure 29-7

Clinical, biochemical and histologic derangements in 30 alcoholics with acute liver failure.

without liver failure, the great majority presented some form of serious hepatic failure. From a clinical point of view, these patients present two rather different types of liver disease. The first and most frequent clinical form is characterized chiefly by marked ascites, muscle wasting, hematemesis due to bleeding varices, moderate or low-grade jaundice, and sometimes encephalopathy. Second, at autopsy, or in liver biopsy specimens, a well-developed cirrhosis with small nodules, marked fibrosis, variable inflammatory changes, and moderate or little steatosis and necrosis is observed.

In addition to the above cases, there are others who exhibit deep jaundice, fever, stupor and little or no ascites. These patients are sometimes misdiagnosed as having obstructive jaundice because of the frequency of abdominal pain, fever, leucocytosis, and laboratory signs of obstruction. This syndrome has been variously called "acute hepatic insufficiency of the chronic alcoholic," "acute alcoholic hepatitis," and "acute fatty metamorphosis of the liver" (5, 17, 31). Figure 29-7 summarizes the most important clinical and laboratory findings in our experience with such cases.

The most relevant findings were deep jaundice, spider nevi, hepatic coma, little or moderate ascites, vomiting, diarrhea, and important liver enlargement. In the laboratory study, the presence of the very high leucocytosis, alkaline phosphatase values over 10 Bodansky units and SGOT higher than 100 Karmen units were striking features as compared with the advanced cases of septal cirrhosis. Our clinical and laboratory findings agree with reports in literature. At autopsy or liver biopsy, the most important signs were diffuse and severe steatosis, necrosis, Mallory bodies, and inflammatory signs. Fibrosis and nodular regeneration were less important and absent in 40 per cent of the cases.

With the electron microscope, the most important alteration described in the literature has been mitochondrial enlargement with alterations of crests and matrices with crystalline-like inclusions (38). In the endoplasmic reticulum fingerprint-like figures have been described (32). In our experience, these signs have a direct relationship with alcoholic intoxication and other complicating factors, and can be seen at any stage of the alcohol-nutritional liver disease, or as we prefer to call it, Laënnec's disease.

The most important complicating factors in our experience, for generating the syndrome of acute hepatic failure in alcoholics, are the following:

1
Alcoholic spree: Several of our patients significantly increased their alcohol consumption for days or weeks prior to the development of jaundice, and/or encephalopathy, bleeding, and ascites. We have observed patients who had been drinking 2 to 3 litres of wine daily increase that amount to 6 or 8 litres or add distilled liquors. Usually during these crises all food intake ceased.
2
Intercurrent infections: Pneumonia, diarrhea, urinary infections, etc., aggravated the condition of many patients. Paradoxically, two cases of superimposed viral hepatitis did not alter the course of arrested septal cirrhosis. The diagnosis was based on epidemiological data and very high SGOT levels (values over 400 Karmen units).

TABLE 29-3

CLINICAL AND BIOCHEMICAL DISORDERS IN 114 ALCOHOLIC PATIENTS

	Inveterate alcoholics (per cent)	Intermittent alcoholics (per cent)
10 or more years of alcoholism	64	61
liver enlargement	38	42
ascites	0	0
total bilirrubin > 2 mg/100 ml.	4.5	4.9
floculations +	10.4	16.2
SGOT > 80 K.U.	21.0	39

3
Bleeding: Episodes of gastric bleeding due to varices, peptic ulcer, or alcoholic gastritis induced liver failure in some patients.
4
Surgery: In a few cases, the episode of hepatic insufficiency followed anesthesia due to major emergency surgery.

In order to obtain an accurate picture of the natural history of Laënnec's disease, we have studied the clinical and laboratory evidence of liver disease in alcoholics admitted while intoxicated to the alcoholic ward and who would have been difficult to manage on an out-patient basis. Table 29-3 provides the clinical and laboratory data for 114 patients seen in the ward in 1965.

The most frequent finding was a high SGOT, probably indicating acute damage. It is interesting to note that in spite of long histories of problem drinking and recent alcohol intoxication in these cases, not one showed overt signs of liver failure. However, this fact is partly due to selection, because patients with severe hepatocellular failure such as ascites, jaundice, gastrointestinal bleeding, or hepatic coma, usually stop drinking spontaneously and are admitted to the medical wards.

The histological findings are summarized in Table 29-4. Cirrhosis was found in 21.6 per cent, and exclusive steatosis in 55 per cent, but the latter was moderate or marked in about half of these (see Figures 29-9 and 29-10). Minor non-specific abnormalities such as small areas

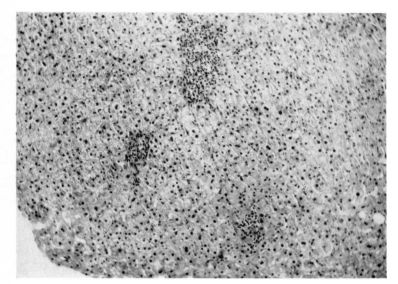

Figure 29-8
Non-specific abnormalities. Small foci of inflammatory
reaction. (Hematoxylin-Eosin × 128).

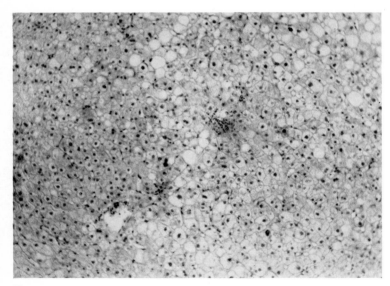

Figure 29-9
Moderate steatosis. (Hematoxylin-Eosin × 128).

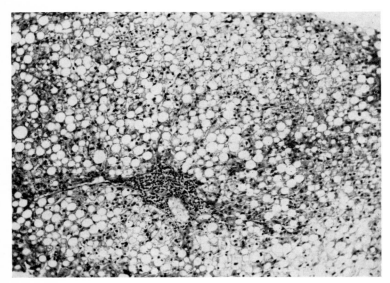

Figure 29-10
Marked steatosis. (Hematoxylin-Eosin × 128).

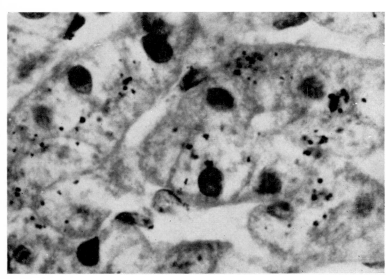

Figure 29-11
Iron deposit in liver cells. Perles reaction.
(Hematoxylin-Eosin × 765).

TABLE 29–4

HISTOLOGICAL DIAGNOSIS IN 75 LIVER
BIOPSIES FROM ALCOHOLICS

	Inveterate alcoholism (per cent)	Intermittent alcoholism (per cent)	Total (per cent)
normal liver	8.7	0	5.5
nonspecific derangement	17.4	20.8	19.2
steatosis			
minimum	34.7	25.0	32.8
moderate	8.7	25.0	13.7
marked	6.5	12.5	8.5
cirrhosis	24	16.7	21.6

of degeneration, necrosis, and inflammation, were observed in 19 per cent of the cases (see Figure 29-8). Although the number of alcoholic cases biopsied to date is small (75 cases), it is interesting to note that cirrhosis was more frequent in the inveterate drinkers, and steatosis in the intermittent alcoholics. Steatosis complicating cirrhosis was found in 50 per cent of the cirrhotic livers.

Mallory bodies were observed without using special methods in only three cases and we were impressed by the considerable iron deposition in eight patients (see Figure 29-11). These findings could be related to the high iron content of impure wines usually sold in a clandestine manner. This problem is now under investigation by our group.

The absence of liver failure in patients with hepatic damage and a long history of alcoholism is interesting and suggests that we should always search for aggravating factors in alcoholic nutritional liver disease with hepatic insufficiency.

Our material shows a greater incidence of cirrhosis among Chilean alcoholics than the 10 per cent reported at this Symposium for France by Boivin, or than the figure reported by Klatskin (22).* This supports Hartroft's

*Further studies in our department indicate that the incidence of cirrhosis among alcoholics depends on the duration of the alcoholism. The figure given in this paper pertains to alcoholics who had been drinking excessively for more than 16 years. If cases with five to 35 years of alcoholism are considered, the overall incidence of cirrhosis in 200 biopsied cases is 12.6 per cent.

suggestion that it would be desirable to undertake a geographical investigation of the incidence of cirrhosis and alcoholism taking into account dietary and genetic differences in alcoholic populations in different parts of the world.

REFERENCES

1
ADDISON, T.
Fatty degeneration of the liver
Guy Hosp. Rept., 1: 476, 1836
2
ARMAS-CRUZ, R., YAZIGI, R., LÓPEZ, O., MONTERO, E., CABELLO, J., & LOBO, G.
Portal cirrhosis; analysis of 208 cases, with correlation of clinical, laboratory and autopsy findings
Gastroenterology, 17: 327, 1951
3
ASADA, M. & GALAMBOS, J.T.
The relationship between liver disease, hepatic alcohol dehydrogenase and alcohol metabolism in the human
Gastroenterology, 45: 67, 1963
4
BANG, N.U., IVERSEN, K., JAGT, T., & MADSEN, S.
Serum glutamic oxalacetic transaminase in acute acute activity and chronic alcoholism
J.A.M.A., 168: 156, 1958
5
BECKETT, A.G., LIVINGSTONE, A.V., & HILL, K.R.
Acute alcoholic hepatitis
Brit. Med. J., ii: 1113, 1961
6
CASIER, H. & DELAUNOIS, A.L.
L'intoxication par l'alcool ethylique
Paris: Masson, 1947. p. 116
7
CRUZ-COKE, R.
Asociación de defecto de clores y cirrosis hepática
Rev. Méd. Chile, 93: 519, 1965
8
DAJANI, R.M., DANIELSKI, J., & ORTEN, J.M.
The utilization of ethanol. II. The alcohol acetaldehyde dehydrogenase system in the liver of alcohol treated rats
J. Nutr., 80: 196, 1963
9
DANOPOULOS, E., MARATOS, K., & LONGOTHETOPOULOS, J.
Studies on alcohol metabolism in patients with atrophic cirrhosis
Acta med. scandinav., 148: 485, 1954
10
DAVIES, J.N.P.
The essential pathology of kwashiorkor
Lancet, i: 317, 1948
11
DIELAFOY, G.
Manuel de pathologie interne
Paris: Masson, 1908, pp. 725 & 760

12
FIESSINGER, N.
Foie et pancreas
Paris: E. Maloine, 1920, p. 147
13
FIGUEROA, R. & KLOTZ, A.P.
Alterations of alcohol dehydrogenase and other
hepatic enzymes in experimental liver disease
Metabolism, **11**: 1169, 1962
14
FIGUEROA, R. & KLOTZ, A.P.
Alterations of alcohol hepatic dehydrogenase and
other hepatic enzymes following oral alcohol
intoxication
Am. J. Clin. Nutr., **11**: 235, 1962
15
FIGUEROA, R.B. & KLOTZ, A.P.
Alterations of liver alcohol dehydrogenase and other
hepatic enzymes in alcoholic cirrhosis
Gastroenterology, **32**: 10, 1962
16
GALAMBOS, J.T., ASADA, M., & SHANKES, J.Z.
The effect of intravenous ethanol on serum enzymes
in patients with normal or diseased liver
Gastroenterology, **44**: 267, 1963
17
GOLDBERG, M. & THOMPSON, C.M.
Acute fatty metamorphosis of the liver
Ann. Intern. Med., **55**: 416, 1961
18
HENLEY, K.S., WIGGINS, H.S., HIRSCHOWITZ, B.I., &
POLLARD, H.M.
The effect of oral ethanol on glutamic pyruvic and
glutamic oxalcetic transaminase activity in the rat liver
Quart. J. Stud. Alc. **19**: 54, 1958
19
HORWITZ, J. & HONORATO, R.
Importancia del alcoholismo y de los problemas
derivados del alcohol
In Simposium alcoholismo y problemas del alcohol
Santiago, Chile: Imprenta del SNS 1959, p. 13
20
HOWARD, R. & WATSON, C.J.
Antecedent jaundice in cirrhosis of the liver
Arch. Internat. Med., **80**: 1, 1947
21
ITURRIAGA, H., INSUNZA, I., UGARTE, G., & ALTSCHILLER, H.
Patologia hepática en pacientes alcohólicos. I. Aspectos
morfológicos básicos
Rev. Méd. Chile, **94**: 399, 1966
22
KLATSKIN, G.
Alcohol and its relation to liver damage
Gastroenterology, **41**: 443, 1961
23
KLATSKIN, G., KREHL, W.A., & CONN, H.O.
The effect of alcohol on the choline requirement:
I. Changes in the rat's liver following prolonged
ingestion of alcohol
J. Exper. Med., **100**: 605, 1954

24
LIEBER, C.S., JONES, D.P., & DECARLI, L.M.
Effects of prolonged ethanol intake
Production of fatty liver, despite adequate diets
J. Clin. Invest., **44**: 1009, 1965
25
LIEBERMAN, F.L.
The effect of liver disease on the rate of ethanol
metabolism in man
Gastroenterology, **44**: 261, 1963
26
LOWRY, J.V., ASHBURN, L.L., DAFT, F.S., & SEBRELL, W.H.
Effect of alcohol in experimental liver cirrhosis
Quart. J. Stud. Alc., **3**: 168, 1942
27
MCCLEARN, G.E., BENNET, E.K., HERBERT, M.,
KAHINA, R., & SCHLESINGER, K.
Alcohol dehydrogenase activity and previous ethanol
consumption in mice
Nature, **203**: 793, 1964
28
MIKATA, A., DIMAKULANGAN, A.A., & HARTROFT, W.S.
Metabolism of ethanol in rats with cirrhosis
Gastroenterology, **44**: 159 1963
29
NUMHAUSER, J. & UGARTE, G.
Enfoque sicosomático del enfermo cirrótico
Rev. Méd. Chile, **91**: 745, 1963
30
PATEK, A.J., POST, J., RATNOFF, O.D.,
MANLAIN, H., & HILLMAN, R.W.
Dietary treatment of cirrhosis of the liver; results in
124 patients during a 10 year period
J.A.M.A., **138**: 543, 1948
31
PHILIPS, G.B. & DAVIDSON, C.S.
Acute hepatic insufficiency of the chronic alcoholic
Arch. Int. Med. (Chicago), **94**: 585, 1954
32
PORTA, E.A., BERGMAN, B.J., & STEIN, A.A.
Acute alcoholic hepatitis
Am. J. Pathol., **56**: 657, 1965
33
ROWNTREE, L.G.
Considerations in cirrhosis of the liver
J.A.M.A., **89**: 1590, 1927
34
SCHWARZMANN, V.L., JULIEN, C., BORENSTEIN, P.,
ETEVÉ, J., & BERTHAUS, N.
L'alcool dehydrogenase hepatique chez les alcoholiques
Rev. franc. étud. clin. biol., **7**: 762, 1962
35
Statistical Bulletin, Metropoliton Life
Insur. Co., **35**: 8, 1957
Quoted in Diseases of the liver, edited by Schiff, Leon
Philadelphia: Lippincott, 1963, p. 575
36
SULLIVAN, J.F. & LANKFORD, H.G.
Urinary excretion of zinc in alcoholism and
post alcoholic cirrhosis

Am. J. Clin. Nutr., **10**: 153, 1962

37
SUMMERSKILL, W.H.J., WOLFE, S.J., & DAVIDSON, C.S.
Response to alcohol in chronic alcoholics with
liver disease
Lancet, **i**: 335, 1954

38
SVOBODA, D.J. & MANNING, R.T.
Chronic alcoholism with fatty metamorphosis
of the liver
Mitochondrial alterations in hepatic cells
Am. J. Path., **54**: 645, 1964

39
UGARTE, G., INSUNZA, I., ITURRIAGA, H., & ALTSCHILLER, H.
Trastornos clínicos y metabolicos en el daño
hepático alcohólico
Rev. Hosp. San Borja, **1**: 14, 1966

40
UGARTE, G., PEREDA, T., PINO, M.E., LORCA, F.,
& SEPULVEDA, B.
Velocidad metabolica del etanol y lacticidemia en
bebedores moderados y adictos alcohólicos con y sin
daño hepático
Rev. Méd. Chile, **95**: 67, 1967

41
UGARTE, G., PINO, M.E., & INSUNZA, I.
Hepatic alcohol dehydrogenase in alcoholic addicts
with and without hepatic damage
Am. J. Dig. Dis., **12**: 589, 1967

42
VON BAUER, H.A.
Der vereinfachte Alkohol Test als
Leberfunktionsprüfung
Gastroenterologia, **74**: 341, 1948

HÉCTOR ORREGO-MATTE

Department of Gastroenterology
José J. Aguirre Hospital and
Department of Medicine
University of Chile
Santiago, Chile

30

Portal Hypertension in Laënnec's Cirrhosis

Portal hypertension in liver cirrhosis induces vascular and hemodynamic alterations which directly or indirectly cause esophageal varices frequently followed by bleeding, portal encephalopathy, (38, 42, 44, 49) and ascites (2, 16, 18, 19, 22, 31), the three main complications of liver cirrhosis. Diet and alcohol withdrawal stop cellular injury and improve the damaged hepatic functions in a great number of patients (36, 50). Nevertheless, in some, portal hypertension remains established at a high level even when hepatic function has almost recovered. The portal pressure depends mainly on three factors: (1) blood flow in splanchnic circulation; (2) resistance opposed by the hepatic vascular system; and (3) capacity of splanchnic blood vessels.

The flow depends on the pressure gradient between the resistance systems at the entrance and exit of the splanchnic circulation. The main entrance resistances are those located in the digestive tract where 90 per cent or more of the resistance is given by the intestinal vessels having a diameter less than 0.5 mm corresponding to precapillary arterioles (47). The blood flow through the intestinal vessels may widely change as a consequence of by-pass from the arterial to the venous system, through which the blood avoids the capillaries (4, 5, 14). Both the flow and oxygen content of the blood increase in the portal system when these arteriovenous by-passes in the gastrointestinal wall are open (21). When hepatic resistance does not decrease simultaneously with this increase in blood flow, the portal vein pressure would be expected to increase. Therefore, two types of therapy for decreasing portal pressure are possible: decreasing portal blood flow, or diminishing the resistance at the liver level.

The most accepted concept today is that portal hypertension found in liver cirrhosis is the consequence of mechanical factors acting upon hepatic resistances (23, 39, 41). Obviously this interpretation has led to the employment of a therapy which acts mechanically by decreasing portal flow. In liver cirrhosis, resistance to hepatic flow occurs mainly in the drainage zone of hepatic circulation, i.e., it is post-sinusoidal (25, 33, 34, 35). It is generally accepted that the constriction of these blood vessels is a consequence of irregular growth of regenerative nodules (3, 23, 26, 45). The small branches of the suprahepatic vein, in contrast to those of the intrahepatic portal vein, are only covered with fibrous tissue in the upper divisions, far from the central veins where tissue compression of any kind is easily possible (11, 20).

When india ink is infused through a cirrhotic liver (13) the intrahepatic portal veins appear distributed irregularly in contrast to their normal distribution. In some cases the only vessels appearing injected are the perilobular ones; while nodules are scarcely injected and sometimes are crossed by the perilobular vessels. Furthermore, anastomosis connecting all the vascular systems are also observed. The consequence of this anatomical picture is stasis in the exit territory of the liver accompanied by an increase in the capacity of the portal territory and a decrease in that of the suprahepatic vein (8, 26). Therefore, the obstruction being post-sinusoidal, both the sinusoidal and the portal systems share the hypertension.

The importance of these mechanical factors may be obvious but the role played by concomitant functional factors in portal hypertension has not been thoroughly studied. The functional factors may enhance the effect of the anatomical ones either in the intestinal territory by increasing blood flow or in the hepatic territory by increasing resistance.

There are certain physiological factors which increase splanchnic blood flow and portal pressure. One of them is diet (7, 12). We have observed that a protein-rich diet causes a rapid increase in hepatic blood flow, as estimated by clearance of albumin labelled with I^{131}. This increase can be more than twice the basic value: average increase was 1.523 ± 0.222 L/min, 1.73 m^2 body surface. A concomitant rise in portal pressure (measured by means of a catheter placed in the suprahepatic vein) and an increase in O_2 saturation in the venous blood were observed. This effect of protein diet on hepatic blood flow can be prevented by the administration of anticolinergic drugs.

Neither carbohydrate, nor fat-rich diets, nor N_2 intravenous administration of amino acids, which induce an increase in liver oxygen consumption (7, 30), alter the splanchnic flow. Ammonium chloride given orally in doses of 10 grams increases hepatic blood flow but does not change either portal pressure or oxygen content of the suprahepatic venous blood.

To summarize, among the physiological factors mentioned, only after administration of a protein-rich diet was there an increase in portal pressure and hepatic blood flow. This double effect is difficult to explain by some mechanism operative at the level of the hepatic blood vessels. The most probable cause is the opening of gastrointestinal, arterio-venous by-passes which would explain the increase in blood flow and also the arterialization of the portal and suprahepatic blood. The rise in portal pressure could be a consequence of an inadequate adaption of hepatic resistance to the increase in splanchnic blood flow.

It is possible that this functional factor could aggravate portal hypertension in liver cirrhosis. Therefore it would be desirable to diminish or even suppress it in these patients.

Concerning hepatic resistance, Bradley (6) has reported that liver blood flow increases in patients with liver cirrhosis when serum albumin is injected intravenously. This increase, without a simultaneous rise in portal pressure, can only be the consequence of a decrease in vascular resistance in the liver. If only a mechanical obstruction were present, it would be expected that the vascular network located behind the place of maximum resistance would show maximum vasodilation as a compensatory reaction. Bradley deduced that, in addition to mechanical obstruction, vasoconstriction has to be present. Epinephrine and norepinephrine injected into the portal vein induce a marked increase in hepatic vascular resistance, a rise in portal pressure and a decrease in hepatic blood flow (1, 24, 29, 40, 46, 48). It has been reported that the catecholamine level in portal venous blood of patients with portal hypertension caused by cirrhosis, is higher than normal (17, 43). However, this has not been subsequently confirmed.

Our group (27, 28) has studied the effect of antiadrenergic drugs such as Regitine, and of sympathicoplexic drugs such as Reserpine (9, 10) on portal hypertension in liver cirrhosis. Regitine (5 mg intramuscularly) rapidly decreases portal pressure measured with a catheter in the suprahepatic vein of patients with liver cirrhosis and portal hypertension. We did not observe the same effect in normal subjects or in cirrhosis patients without portal hypertension. The effect of this drug is transient, so that about 15 minutes after injection, the pressure returns to its basic level. We have also studied the effect of Regitine on the cardioportal circulation time, i.e., the time taken by a radioactive shot to pass from the heart to the liver through the portal vein. Regitine caused a shortening of this time in all cases in which the drug was administered. These changes in portal pressure were not correlated with concomitant changes in systemic arterial pressure.

Administration of Reserpine (in doses of 2.5 mg intramuscularly) caused a reduction of portal pressure in a period of one hour in patients with portal hypertension and liver cirrhosis. This effect was not observed in normal controls. Intrasplenic pressure was measured in two cases, before, and 24 hours after Reserpine administration (2.5 mg intramuscularly). In one of the cases, the pressure dropped from 28 to 21 mm Hg, and in the other no significant change was observed. We have also studied the effect of Reserpine on cardioportal circulation time, and we have observed that in all cases the time was shortened and this effect persisted for as much as 30 hours after the injection.

It is our feeling that these observations warrant the postulation that functional factors are implicated in the maintenance of portal hypertension in patients with liver cirrhosis. Although this does not reduce the importance of mechanical factors, it is nevertheless of therapeutic significance since it gives hope for medical control of portal hypertension. Regitine is not a suitable drug for this purpose because of its transient effect. Reserpine appears more promising but its stimulant effect on gastric secretion when administered parenterally (15, 37) involves a potential risk in patients suffering from esophageal varices. The use of oral Reserpine or some similar substance which does not affect secretion deserves study.

REFERENCES

1
ANDREWS, W.H.H., HECKER, R., MACGRATH, G.V., & RITCHIE, H.O.
The action of adrenaline, noradrenaline, acetycholine and other substances of the perfused canine liver
J. Physiol., **128**: 413, 1955

2
BAGGENSTOSS, A.H. & CAIN, J.C.
Further studies on the lymphatic vessels at the hilius of the liver of man; their relation to ascites
Proc. Staff Meet. Mayo Clin., **32**: 615, 1957

3
BALDUS, W.P. & HOFFBAUER, F.W.
Vascular changes in the cirrhotic liver as studied by the injection technic
Am. J. Dig. Dis., **8**: 689, 1963

4
BARCLAY, A.E. & BENTLEY, F.H.
The vascularization of the human stomach
Brit. J. Radiol., **22**: 62, 1949

5
BARLOW, T.E.
Vascular patterns in the alimentary canal
In Visceral circulation, a CIBA Foundation Symposium, ed. by Wolstenholme, G.E.W.
London: J. & A. Churchill, 1952, p. 21

6
BRADLEY, S.E.
Clinical aspects of hepatic vascular physiology
In Liver injury, ed. by F.W. Hoffbauer
New York: J. Macy, Jr. Found., 1951, p. 71

7
BRANDT, J.L., CASTLEMAN, L., RUSKIN, H.D., GREENALD, J., KELLY, J.J., & JONES, A.
The effect of oral protein and glucose feeding on splanchnic blood flow and oxygen utilization in normal and cirrhotic subjects
J. Clin. Invest., **34**: 1017, 1955

8
BRITTON, R.C., BROWN, C.H., & SHIREY, E.K.
Intrahepatic veno-occlusive disease in cirrhosis with chronic ascites: diagnosis by hepatic phlebography and results of surgical treatment
Ann. Surg., **158**: 370, 1963

9
BURN, J.H.
A new view of adrenergic nerve fibres, explaining the action of reserpine, bretylium, and guanethidine
Brit. Med. J. i: 1623, 1961

10
BURN, J.H. & RAND, M.J.
Noradrenaline in artery walls and its dispersal by reserpine
Brit. Med. J., i: 903, 1958

11
BURTON, A.C.
Relation of structure to function of the tissues of the wall of blood vessels
Physiol. Rev., **34**: 619, 1954

12
CASTLEMAN, L., BRANDT, J.L., & RUSKIN, H.
The effect of oral feedings of meat and glucose on
hepatic vein wedge pressure in normal and cirrhotic
subjects
J. Lab. Clin. Med., **51**: 897, 1958

13
CAYUELA, M.L., ORREGO, H., & BARAHONA, R.
Estudio de la vascularización intrahepática en la
cirrosis hepática
Rev. Méd. Chile, **86**: 309, 1958

14
CHAMBERS, R. & ZWEIFACH, B.W.
Topography and function of the mesenteric circulation
Am. J. Anat., **75**: 173, 1944

15
CLARK, M.L. & SCHNEIDER, E.M.
The effect of intravenous reserpine on gastric acidity
in man
Gastroenterology, **29**: 877, 1955

16
DUMONT, A.E. & MULHOLLAND, J.H.
Alterations in thoracic duct lymph flow in hepatic
cirrhosis: significance in portal hypertension
Ann. Surg., **156**: 668, 1962

17
EVANS, C.S. & KAY, A.W.
Catecholamines in portal venous blood in portal
hypertension
Lancet, **ii**: 387, 1964

18
FREEMAN, S.
Recent advances in the physiology and biochemistry
of the liver
Med. Clin. N. Am., **37**: 109, 1953

19
GRAY, H.K.
Clinical and experimental investigation of the
circulation of the liver
Ann. Roy. Coll. Surg. Eng., **8**: 354, 1951

20
HARKNESS, M.L.R. & HARKNESS, R.D.
The relation of collagen content of the liver to body
weight in the rat
J. Physiol., **125**: 447, 1954

21
HENNING, N. & DEMLING, L.
Blood flow in the liver
In Progress in liver disease,
ed. by Popper, H. & Schaffner, F.
New York: Grune & Stratton, 1961, p. 162

22
HYATT, R.E., LAWRENCE, G.H., & SMITH, J.R.
Observations on the origin of ascites from experimental
hepatic congestion
J. Lab. Clin. Med., **45**: 274, 1955

23
KELTY, R.H., BAGGENSTOSS, A.H., & BUTT, H.R.
The relation of the regenerated liver nodule to the
vascular bed in cirrhosis
Gastroenterology, **15**: 285, 1950

24
KOHN, P.M., CHARMS, B.L., & BROFMAN, B.L.
Effect of epinephrine and posterior pituitary extract
on the wedged-hepatic vein pressure in normal patients
and in those with liver disease
New England J. Med., **261**: 323, 1959

25
KROOK, H.
Circulatory studies in liver cirrhosis
Acta med. scandinav., **156**: 318, 1956

26
MADDEN, J.L., LORÉ, J.M., GERDD, F.P., & RAVID, J.M.
The pathogenesis of ascites and a consideration of its
treatment
Surg. Gynec. Obst., **99**: 385, 1954

27
MENA, I., ORREGO, H., BARAONA, E., & MÁRQUES, S.
Efectos de la Regitina y reserpina sobre la
hipertensión portal
Rev. Méd. Chile, **91**: 96, 1963

28
MENA, I., ORREGO, H., BARAONA, E., & MÁRQUES, S.
Effects of Regitine and reserpine on portal hypertension
Am. J. Dig. Dis., **8**: 895, 1963

29
MORENO, A.H., ROUSSELOT, L.M., BURCHELL, A.R.,
BONE, R.F., & BURKE, J.H.
Studies on the outflow tracts of the liver
II. On the outflow tract of the canine liver with
particular reference to its regulation by the hepatic
vein sphincter mechanisms
Ann. Surg., **115**: 427, 1962

30
MYERS, J.D.
The effect of the intravenous administration of
glucose and amino acids on the hepatic blood flow
and splanchnic oxygen consumption of man
Fed. Proc., 7: 83, 1948

31
NIX, J.T., MANN, F.C., BOLLMAN, J.L., GRINDLAY, J.H.,
& FLOCK, E.V.
Alterations of protein constituents of lymph by specific
injury to the liver
Am. J. Physiol., **164**: 119, 1951

32
ORREGO, H., MENA, I., BARAONA, E., & PALMA, R.
Modifications in hepatic blood flow and portal
pressure produced by different diets
Am. J. Dig. Dis., **10**: 239, 1965

33
PETERSON, L.H.
Properties and behavior of living vascular wall
Proc. Symp. Vasc. Smooth Muscle Physiol. Rev., **42**:
(suppl.) 309, 1962

34
POPPER, H. & ELIAS, H.
Histogenesis of hepatic cirrhosis studied by the
three-dimensional approach
Am. J. Path., **31**: 405, 1955

35
POPPER, H., ELIAS, H., & PATTHY, D.E.

Vascular pattern of the cirrhotic liver
Am. J. Clin. Path., **22**: 717, 1952

36
POST, J. & SICAM, L.
The clinical course of Laënnec's cirrhosis under
modern medical management
Med. Clin. N. Am., **44**: 639, 1960

37
RIDER, J.A., MOELLER, H.C., & GIBBS, J.O.
The effect of reserpine on gastric secretion and its
possible site of action
Gastroenterology, **33**: 737, 1957

38
SCHWARTZ, R., PHILIPS, G.B., SEEGMILLER, E.J.E.,
GABUZDA, C.J., & DAVIDSON, C.S.
Dietary protein in the genesis of hepatic coma
New England J. Med., **251**: 685, 1954

39
SHALDON, S., DOLLE, W., GUEVARA, L., IBER, F.L.,
& SHERLOCK, S.
Effect of Pitressin on the splanchnic circulation in man
Circulation, **24**: 797, 1961

40
SHALDON, S., PEACOCK, J.H., WALKER, R.M.,
PALMER, D.B., & BADRICK, F.E.
The portal venous content of adrenaline and
noradrenaline in portal hypertension
Lancet, **i**: 63, 1962

41
SHERLOCK, S.
The investigation and classification of portal
hypertension
Minerva Cardioangiol., **9**: 303, 1961

42
SHERLOCK, S., SUMMERSKILL, W.H.J.,
WHILE, L.P., & PHEAR, E.A.
Portal-systemic encephalopathy
Neurological complications of liver disease
Lancet, **ii**: 453, 1954

43
SIEGEL, J.H. & HARRISON, T.S.
Portal venous catecholamines in portal hypertension
Lancet, **ii**: 1357, 1963

44
SUMMERSKILL, W.H.J., DAVIDSON, E.A., SHERLOCK, S.,
& STERNER, R.E.
The neuropsychiatric syndrome associated with
hepatic cirrhosis and an extensive portal collateral
circulation
Quart. J. Med., **25**: 245, 1956

45
TAYLOR, W.J. & MYERS, J.D.
Occlusive hepatic venous catheterization in the study
of the normal liver, cirrhosis of the liver and
non-cirrhotic portal hypertension
Circulation, **13**: 368, 1956

46
TERAMOTO, S. & SHUMACKER, H.B., JR.
Influence of L-norepinephrine upon hepatic blood flow
Surg. Gynec. Obst., **116**: 443, 1963

47
TEXTER, E.G.
Small intestinal blood flow
Am. J. Dig. Dis., **8**: 587, 1963

48
WAKIM, K.G.
The effect of certain substances in the intrahepatic
circulation of blood in the intact animal
Am. Heart J., **27**: 289, 1944

49
WALSHE, J.M.
Biochemical studies in hepatic coma
Lectures on the Scientific Basis of Medicine, **8**: 407,
1958–9

50
YAZIGI, R., ARMAS-CRUZ, R., PIWONKA, J., PAREDES, E.,
MAIRA, J., GONZÁLEZ, E., & JEDLICKY, A.
Resultados del tratamiento de la cirrosis portal
descompensada
Rev. Med. Chile, **89**: 833, 1961

SERGIO TEZANOS-PINTO

Department of Internal Medicine
Hospital Deformes
National Health Service
Valparaiso, Chile

During recent years we have made a clinical study of hepatic damage in alcoholic patients referred by the Anti-Alcoholic Centre (1, 23, 24). The object has been to determine the functional and anatomical state of the liver, and to establish the indications and contraindications for the use of potentially hepatotoxic drugs in the treatment of alcoholism (Antabuse) or associated syndromes (chlorpromazine).

The ideal method for the diagnosis of alcoholic hepatopathy (liver disease induced by alcohol) should indicate the anatomical and functional state of the liver safely and rapidly. Since to date none of the methods in use meets these requirements, we are obliged to learn through experience what each may offer us.

Laboratory tests now used in the study of hepatic affections do not indicate the etiology and anatomy of the patient's disease and, consequently, do not help us in differential diagnosis and detection of early stages of damage (8). Symptomatic characteristics of hepatic pathology are not sufficiently specific or defined according to the various anatomical pictures. This is particularly true of alcoholic hepatopathy, since it presents many types of damage which originate from a common source and whose differentiation is of great importance (9, 13, 20). I should like to emphasize here our belief that a good diagnosis should take account of the fact that affections presenting similar clinical symptoms but with different underlying histological injuries involve great differences in prognosis. The prognosis depends on an exact diagnosis.

31

Early Diagnosis of Alcoholic Hepatic Damage

FACTORS CONTRIBUTING TO EARLY DIAGNOSIS OF ALCOHOLIC HEPATOPATHY

We shall analyse the contributions of the clinic, the laboratory, and the liver biopsy. Alcoholic hepatopathy starts asymptomatically in most cases and its diagnosis is slower than in the hepatic affections of other groups of patients. The data obtained through questioning the patient contributes very little to the diagnosis of alcoholic hepatopathy. This is attributable to the degree of psychic dullness of the patients and to the confusion of the general symptoms inherent in their alcoholic habits.

From the case histories of our patients, we seek three types of information: (a) indications of previous hepatic affection,. whether of an alcoholic nature or not; (b) actual symptoms suggestive of hepatic affection; and (c) a history of his alcoholism, feeding habits, concomitant illnesses, etc.

In five of 82 cases investigated we found either evidence of symptoms related to previous hepatic damage (ascites, icterus) or the diagnosis of a hepatic problem upon previous hospitalization or consultation.

Reports of suggestive symptoms from patients are not helpful in formulating an early diagnosis because they are unclear and unspecific; asymptomatic lesions (10) are frequent or lesions with few symptoms peculiar to them. As regards the symptomatology of our patients with acute alcoholic hepatitis (4, 25, 26, 27) only the presence of psychic disturbance was of any value, but its specificity is not absolute. Nor could we find a significant contribution to the early diagnosis of alcoholic hepatitis in the third type of anamnesic information. The duration of heavy alcohol ingestion did not show a proportional relation to hepatic lesions. We found patients who had been drinking heavily for over 46 years with sound livers, and others who after six years exhibited hepatic cirrhosis. On the other hand, ingestion of excessive amounts of alcohol over extended periods proved a useful indication of acute liver damage (24), a fact verifiable in 28 of 33 patients in whom we found particularly acute fatty livers.

Food habits did not contribute to the diagnosis of the lesion presented by the patient, as the great majority (96 per cent) had insufficient diets, and the same dietetic antecedents were found in different types of hepatic pathology. This is in agreement with the findings of others (12). The type of alcohol taken was not studied since Chilean alcoholics are almost exclusively drinkers of wine.

Knowledge of the history and intensity of coincident pathology could provide clues to the alcoholic liver lesion and lead us to an early diagnosis. That is, we think there might be correlations between alcoholic hepatopathy and more easily detected conditions. We proceeded to study the involvement of the nervous system (46 cases out of 82), the digestive tract (34 cases out of 40), and associated disorders (12 cases out of 82). We were especially interested in neuropsychiatric involvement since it was easy to recognize and more precocious. The results were unfortunately negative. Thus, in patients with delirium tremens we found no vestige of hepatic lesion, and in patients who had not shown neuropsychic symptoms, we found constituted, irreversible hepatic cirrhosis.

Physical examinations only provided non-specific data which did not allow early differentiation of the type of alcoholic hepatopathy presented by the patient.

The clinical laboratory in a general hospital appears to have only a limited contribution to make to the early diagnosis of hepatic damage in an alcoholic (2). We had the following results:

1
The hemogram did not reveal the characteristic alterations either in the red or white series: both leucopenia and leucocytosis were found in eight cases of alcoholic hepatitis. Sedimentation did not permit us to incline our suspicions one way or another.
2
High bilirubin proved an element of value in the diagnosis of hepatic damage generally, but not its anatomic type. The test was of value in the diagnosis of acute alcoholic hepatitis when the prompt reacting bilirubin was low, accompanied by high cholesterol and without any signs of hemolysis (26).
3
Flocculations lacked specificity.
4
Cholesterol, brought down at the expense of its sterified portion, indicated parenchymatous involvement, but non-specifically as to form. This is the same as with high retention of bromosulphalein.
5
The pyruvic transaminase test allowed us to differentiate some of our cases of acute alcoholic hepatitis but did not present the elevation appropriate to the initial period of the viral forms (6).

TABLE 31–1

RESULTS OF HEPATIC BIOPSIES
ON 90 ALCOHOLIC PATIENTS

Histological diagnosis	No. of cases
normal liver tissue	22
Laënnec's cirrhosis	12
non-specific alterations	12
hepatic carcinoma	1
acute fatty liver	2
moderate fatty infiltration	12
minimum fatty infiltration	13
intense fatty infiltration	5
alcoholic hepatitis	8
failure of biopsy	3
total	90

The lack of specificity of clinical laboratory tests obliged us to resort to biopsies, which were done with a Menghini needle (14–18, 20). The histological diagnoses based on biopsies performed on 90 alcoholic patients are shown in Table 31-1.

It seemed to us that hepatic biopsy was the only method permitting: (*a*) exact diagnosis of the chronic or acute alcoholic hepatic damage in the excessive drinker (5, 19); (*b*) recognition of the type of lesion presented by an alcoholic patient at any given stage in its evolution (22); (*c*) the tracing of the development of damage; and (*d*) wide scope for experimental and other approaches to the study of the deleterious effects of alcohol on the human liver (3, 11, 21).

Our experience and that of others as reported in the literature leads us to conclude that alcoholic hepatopathy suspected from clinical examination and laboratory tests can be established at an early stage only by means of hepatic biopsy.

REFERENCES

1
ALCAYAGA, T.
Biopsia hepática en alcohólicos
Método de Menghini
Tesis de Grado
Universidad Católica de Valparaiso
2
ASADA, M. & GALAMBOS, J.T.
Liver disease, hepatic alcohol dehydrogenase activity and alcohol metabolism in the human
Gastroenterology, **45**: 67, 1963

3
ASHWORTH, C.T., WRIGHTSMAN, F., & COOPER, B., *et al.*
Cellular aspects of ethanol-induced fatty liver: a correlated ultrastructural and chemical study
J. Lipid Res., **6**: 258, 1965
4
BECKETT, A.G., LIVINGSTONE, A.V., & HILL, K.K.
Acute alcoholic hepatitis
Brit. Med. J., **ii**: 1113, 1961
5
BROHULT, J. & REICHARD, H.
Liver damage after a dose of alcohol
Lancet, **ii**: 78, 1965
6
CHILDS, A.W.
Effects of ethyl alcohol on hepatic circulation, sulfobromophthalein clearance, and hepatic glutamic oxalacetic transaminase production in man
Gastroenterology, **45**: 176, 1963
7
COLMAN, R.W. & SHEIN, H.M.
Leukemoid reaction, hyperuricemia and severe hyperpyraxia complicating fatal case of acute fatty liver of the alcoholic
Ann. Int. Med., **57**: 110, 1962
8
DAHL, S.
Studies on liver function in chronic alcoholics
Wien. Ztschr. inn. Med., **45**: 550, 1964
9
EDMONSON, H.A.
Needle biopsy in differential diagnosis of acute liver disease
J.A.M.A., **191**: 480, 1965
10
GREEN, J.R.
Subclinical acute liver disease of the alcoholic
Aust. Ann. Med., **14**: 111, 1965
11
KIESSLING, K.H., PILSTRÖM, L., & STRANDBERG, J. *et al.*
Ethanol and the human liver
Correlation between mitochondrial size and the degree of ethanol abuse
Acta med. scandinav., **178**: 633, 1965
12
LIEBER, C.S., JONES, D.P., & DECARLI, L.M.
Effects of prolonged ethanol intake
Production of fatty liver despite adequate diets
J. Clin. Invest., **44**: 1009, 1965
13
MANESIS, J.G. & SULLIVAN, J.F.
Primary sclerosing cholengitis
Arch. Int. Med. (Chicago), **115**: 137, 1965
14
MENGHINI, G.
Un effettivo progresso nella tecnica puntura-biopsia del fegato
Rass. Fisiopat. Clin. Ter., **29**: 756, 1957
15
MENGHINI, G.
One-second needle biopsy of the liver
Gastroenterology, **35**: 190, 1958

16
MENGHINI, G.
Two-operator needle biopsy of the liver: a new, easier
and safer version of the one-second technic
Am. J. Dig. Dis., **4**: 682, 1959
17
NORRIS, T.S., SINGH, M.M., & MONTUSCHI, E.
Liver biopsy: experience with a new needle
Lancet, **ii**: 560, 1958
18
PARETS, A.D., SCHAFFNER, F., & BLACK, H.
Liver biopsy with the Menghini needle
Am. J. Dig. Dis., **4**: 693, 1959
19
SANES, S., BAHN, R.C., CHAPPLE, W.H.C., & CHASSIN, N.
Needle biopsy of liver in alcoholic patients
New York State J. Med., **49**: 2677, 1949
20
SCHAFFNER, F.
Hepatocellular cytoplasmatic changes in acute
alcoholic hepatitis
J.A.M.A., **183**: 3434, 1963
21
SHERLOCK, S.
Biochemical investigations in liver disease: some
correlations with hepatic histology
J. Path. Bact., **58**: 523, 1946
22
SEIFE, M., KESSLER, B.J., & LISA, J.R.
Functional and needle biopsy study of liver in
alcoholism
Arch. Int. Med. (Chicago), **86**: 658, 1950
23
TEZANOS-PINTO, S., ALCAYAGA, T., & SILVA, L.
Biopsia hepática en alcohólicos
Método de Menghini
Gaceta Sanit., **20**: nl/2, 1965
24
TEZANOS-PINTO, S., OLAVARRÍA, F., & SILVA, L.
Patologia hepática en el alcohólico
Rev. Méd. Chile, **93**: 522, 1965
25
TEZANOS-PINTO, S., OLAVARRÍA, F., & SILVA, L.
Hepatitis aguda alcohólica
Rev. Méd. Chile, **93**: 528, 1965
26
TEZANOS-PINTO, S., OLAVARRÍA, F., & SILVA, L.
Hepatitis aguda alcohólica ictérica
Rev. Méd. Valparaíso, **19**: 1, 1966
27
WELCH, C.E. & CASTLEMANN, B.
Case records
M.E.J.M., **274**: 271, 1966

RAÚL YAZIGI J.
BERNARDITA LAZO

Service of Internal Medicine
San Juan de Dios Hospital and
Department of Medicine
University of Chile
Santiago, Chile

Pancreatic Damage in Alcoholism

In our medical practice we have become aware that acute pancreatitis and acute crises of chronic pancreatitis often coincide with excessive consumption of alcohol. We agreed to examine the topic on the basis of our observations for this Symposium, but we did not realize how difficult it would be to reach definitive conclusions on the subject. In fact, the role of alcoholism in pancreatic damage proved to have been little studied and not properly recorded in the clinical file of patients.

In different text-books of internal medicine, and in various papers, it is recognized that the etiology of acute and chronic pancreatitis is unclear. Close relationships with gall-bladder pathology, allergy, and viral processes are noted, and most authors consider that alcohol plays a role.

Dávila et al. (1) postulated that the mechanism of alcohol action was the direct stimulation of gastric acid secretion resulting in an increase of secretin which, in turn, stimulated pancreatic juice secretion. On the other hand, alcohol induces edema of the duodenal mucous membrane and spasm of the Oddi sphincter. The association of both factors, results in an intracanalicular hypertension, which may cause the rupture of the pancreatic acini. Depending on the intensity of the process and the number of broken acini, acute pancreatitis or progressive fibrosis, which can finally lead to chronic pancreatitis, would occur.

Fox (2) pointed out that pancreatitis is frequent among chronic alcoholics. Inadequate diet associated with the irritative action of alcohol are factors in recurrent crises of pancreatitis, either mild or severe. Gambill, of the Mayo Clinic (3), also states that pancreatitis is frequently associated with the consumption of large amounts of alcohol.

We have searched the files of the San Juan de Dios Hospital from 1960 to date, and the files of our private practice in which eight cases were found. In the hospital files, we found records of 67 women in whom pancreatitis was given as a tentative or confirmed diagnosis and all of whom had gall-bladder pathology requiring surgery. The surgeon in these cases, without biopsy and on the basis of manual exploration only, reported that the pancreas was hardened or enlarged. A background of alcoholism was noted in five of the records but no information concerning its degree or duration was recorded. In the other cases, drinking habits had not been explored showing a serious deficiency in clinical recording.

It seems clear that among women pancreatitis is almost always associated with gall-bladder pathology. Unfortunately, we are not in a position to assert whether alcoholism also participates, owing to a lack of comprehensive clinical histories. However, it is well known that in Chile alcoholism is less frequent among women and that when it exists, it is usually denied.

We found clinical records of 80 male patients for whom a diagnosis of acute or chronic pancreatitis was recorded from 1960 to 1965. In 60 of these cases the diagnosis was sufficiently confirmed by clinical data, laboratory tests, surgery or autopsy. Their ages ranged from 16 to 70 years and almost all were workers with low incomes. Therefore, we suppose that those who had alcoholic habits, generally drank beer or wine of inferior quality.

Ten of the reports of 60 cases of confirmed pancreatitis contained no information whatsoever regarding alcohol consumption. In another five cases the question of alcoholic behaviour had been investigated but the findings were categorically negative, so that the pancreatitis has to be attributed to some other cause. The remaining 45 cases had a clear previous history of alcoholism but 15 of them also suffered from some other concomitant and etiologically relevant pathology (liver cirrhosis, gall-bladder disease, gastroduodenal ulcer, etc.). Thus, in 30 cases of confirmed acute or relapsing chronic pancreatitis, alcoholism appeared as the main causal factor. All were excessive drinkers and in many of them the episodes of acute pancreatitis had occurred after consumption of large amounts of alcoholic beverages. Unfortunately, we were not able to identify the type of alcoholism of these patients, because their clinical records provided no details but simply emphasized the fact that they were excessive drinkers.

Two of the eight cases from our private practice were women, one of whom suffered from a gall-bladder disease and the other had alcoholic liver cirrhosis, confirmed by biopsy. The six men did not exhibit other associated pathology. All were alcoholics, some intermittent, and their pancreatitic crises coincided with excessive consumption of alcohol. This group usually drank wine or spirituous liquors.

DISCUSSION

The data presented suggest that alcoholism actually causes pancreatic damage, and the three authors cited concur in this. At the same time the data reveal two facts of importance, which by themselves justify the effort we have made about the problem:

1

Physicians do not investigate alcoholic habits adequately in patients suffering from pancreatitis, even though alcoholism clearly has etiological significance.

2

It is curious to note that only five of the patients receiving treatment for chronic pancreatitis received treatment for alcoholism at the same time. Lately, this attitude has changed and the Gastroenterology Department refers such patients to specialized centres for treatment of alcoholism if this is deemed necessary.

CONCLUSIONS

A marked relation between acute and chronic pancreatitis and alcoholism exists among men; but it seems that the main factors in pancreatitis in women are various liver diseases. It is important to investigate alcoholism carefully in patients suffering from acute pancreatitis and to classify it according to type, time of consumption, type of alcoholic beverage, etc. All patients who suffer from pancreatitis and have records of alcoholism should receive treatment for the alcoholism with all available resources. We consider it advisable for the physician treating the patient's pancreatitis to undertake as well the treatment of his alcoholism. This will require a change of attitude on the part of many physicians concerning the serious problem of alcoholism. They must study it, know it better, and be able to provide suitable treatment.

REFERENCES

1
DÁVILA, M., PARROCHIA, E., & RUFÍN, F.
Monografía sobre enfermedades del pancreas
1960
2
FOX, V.
Alcoholism
Disease-A-Month, Jan. 1965, pp. 1–34
3
GAMBILL, E.
Current practices in general medicine: acute and
chronic relapsing pancreatitis
Proc. Mayo Clin., **35**: 17, 1960

PIERRE BOIVIN

PAUL OUDEA

RENÉ FAUBERT

Department of Clinical Medicine
University Hospital
Nantes, France

33

Acute Alcoholic
Liver Damage

In the present paper we consider under the heading "acute alcoholic liver damage" the joint group of reversible forms of liver damage observed among alcoholics. Though such disturbances develop along with liver cirrhosis, patients suffering from this disease were excluded from our study.

We have systematically studied the liver conditions of 60 alcoholic patients, hospitalized for the most diverse causes, and either with or without a previous history of hepatic injury. The first clinical, biological, and histological examinations, including biopsy for electron microscopy, were performed in 20 of them shortly after withdrawal from alcohol. The systematic character of the study distinguishes it from others, which have focussed on liver lesions in samples selected according to a clinical sign, a histological finding or a special kind of developmental sequence. In fact, many papers are concerned only with the study of fatty liver (8–10, 20, 25, 28, 29, 50).

Recently many authors have insisted on hepatocellular degeneration and attempted to isolate different evolutionary stages under special terms: subacute cytolitic hepatitis (1); toxic hepatitis (18); fatty liver with hepatocellular degeneration (40, 41); steatonecrosis (53); overt cirrhosis (42); acute alcoholic hepatitis (4, 5, 23); sclerosing hyaline necrosis (16); active liver disease of alcoholics (14); and acute liver deficiency of chronic alcoholics (38).

Nevertheless, the reported data are not homogeneous; some correspond to real liver cirrhosis, which is beyond our scope. The case series which comes closest to ours is that of Green (22), who reported a systematic study of 29 cases under the heading: "subclinical acute liver disease of alcoholics." Only this type of study, performed systematically without any selection, can provide useful information concerning the prevalance, type and prognosis of reversible liver injuries induced by alcohol.

In this paper the following topics will be dealt with: (*i*) clinical symptoms, physical signs and pathophysiological tests; (*ii*) the prevalence of certain clinical and biological features; (*iii*) histological and ultrastructural lesions; (*iv*)

TABLE 33–1

CLINICAL SYMPTOMS IN A SAMPLE
OF 60 HOSPITALIZED ALCOHOLICS

Symptom	Per cent of cases
asthenia	40
anorexia	42
loss of weight	22
abdominal pain	22
vomiting	28
diarrhea	5
gastric hemorrhage	5
neuropsychiatric problems	47
loss of consciousness	5

correlations between different anomalies; and
(*v*) prognosis.

CLINICAL SYMPTOMS

Most of our patients are chronic alcoholics.
Some of them exhibit a peculiar type of (intermittent) psychogenic intoxication, alternating
with more or less prolonged periods of abstinence. Most had recently been through a period
of intoxication. The accompanying anorexia had
increased the nutritional imbalance, characterized by an excess of alcohol calories in relation
to those of protein.

The most frequent causes of hospitalization
were neuropsychiatric disturbances, which involved 47 per cent of our cases (see Table 33-
1). There is seldom a true delirium tremens;
the most frequent symptoms are tremor and
agitation, but no real delirium.

Anorexia, either for all foods or only for
meat, and physical and psychic asthenia appear
with about the same frequency. Loss of weight,
observed in 22 per cent of our patients, appears
to be directly related to food restriction. Digestive disturbances are also frequently observed,
vomiting was present in 28 per cent of our cases
and abdominal pain in 22 per cent. This pain,
which has been mentioned in other studies (4,
10, 20, 23, 25, 29) reporting a similar incidence, is generally non-systematized, epigastric,
and frequently located in the right hypochon-
drium. On certain occasions it can be attributed
to alcoholic gastritis, but more frequently it is

related to a liver disturbance exhibiting the
topographic pattern of hepatalgia; the pain
could be explained by liver enlargement following massive steatosis. Three of our patients (5
per cent) exhibited hematemesis without any
sign of portal hypertension or gastroduodenal
lesions. Some of the patients suffered from diarrhea.

Three patients were hospitalized in a state
of unconsciousness; hypoglycemia was found in
one, but we have not been able to find any
satisfactory explanation for the condition of the
other two. However, it should be mentioned
that in these particular cases the determination
of blood sugar was done after a delay of several
hours.

Few of these initial presenting symptoms are
related to liver injury; most seem rather to be
related to alcohol intoxication and its concomitant nutritional disturbances.

PHYSICAL SIGNS

The two most common signs were hepatomegaly
and fever (see Table 33–2). Hepatomegaly
was present in 75 per cent of the cases and its
magnitude varied greatly. It could be diffuse,
sometimes enormous, and predominantly located in the left lobe; this characteristic was
mentioned by Trousseau (49) in reference to

TABLE 33–2

PHYSICAL SIGNS IN A SAMPLE OF
60 HOSPITALIZED ALCOHOLICS

Sign	Total cases
hepatomegaly	75
fever	60
splenomegaly	3
ascites	0
collateral venous circulation	2
edema of lower extremities	5
jaundice	5
stellate angioma	12
palmar erythrosis	14
gynecomastia	5
Dupuytren's disease	4
polyneuritis	14
Gayet-Wernicke encephalopathy	5
Korsakoff's syndrome	3
ecchymosis	10

TABLE 33–3

TESTS OF LIVER FUNCTION—GLOBAL

Test	Number of cases (pathological/total)	Per cent pathological results
BSP clearance < 12 per cent	20/28	71
gold clearance < 14 per cent	6/23	26

steatosis. Scintographically, the liver appears in a square form. The hepatomegaly can be explained by fatty overload: the liver surface is smooth, regular, firm but not hard, and its inferior border dull. Manual exploration is often somewhat painful. Though hepatomegaly is very important, in some cases it does not occur, as noted by Green (22).

Several studies, of samples including many cases of established liver cirrhosis, have noted the prevalence of splenomegaly, ascites, and edema of the lower extremities. Nevertheless, we have the impression that these conditions are not common in alcoholics examined systematically, and not selected on the basis of signs of liver damage (see Table 33–2). The same can be said concerning the prevalence of jaundice; we have observed it in only 5 per cent of our cases, although it constitutes a common finding in certain cases of "acute alcoholic hepatitis," in which the clinical picture is similar to that of an acute viral hepatitis.

The other signs we have seen rarely are: stellate angioma (12 per cent); gynecomastia (5 per cent); Dupuytren's disease (4 per cent), and palmar erythrosis (14 per cent). Neurological complications of alcoholism are less frequent: polyneuritis (14 per cent), Gayet-Wernicke encephalopathies (5 per cent), and Korsakoff's syndrome (3 per cent). Green's findings are similar (22). A condition that has not been reported before so far as we are aware and which appeared quite frequently (10 per cent) is ecchymosis, with no apparent traumatic etiology.

Sixty per cent of our patients had fever, almost always moderate (38°–38.5° C), which tended to disappear spontaneously, together with the hepatic lesions, after a few days or weeks. Some authors (23, 28) consider that fever is a sign of hepatocellular necrosis, but so

far this has not been proved. In any case, there was no infectious disease present to account for the fever.

As with the clinical symptoms, some disturbances revealed by the examination were not specific to hepatic damage.

PATHOPHYSIOLOGICAL TESTS

Because of the reversible character of the hepatic lesions of interest and their biological consequences, functional tests must be conducted immediately after the admission of the patient, otherwise transient disturbances may be missed. The tests performed are discussed below in accord with the pathophysiological classification used in our laboratory.

Global
Clearance of bromsulphalein (BSP) was disturbed in three-quarters of our cases, a frequency similar to that reported by other authors (9, 20, 22, 23, 40, 50). It can be as low as 3 per cent. Clearance of colloidal gold from Kupfer cells was disturbed in one case in four.

Cholestatic syndrome
Jaundice seldom appeared and when it did it was always moderate. Total bilirubin was only as high as 8 mg/L in a quarter of the cases. Hyperbilirubinemia is made up mainly of nonconjugated bilirubin which had a similar frequency. Total cholesterol was higher than 2 gm/L in 57 per cent of the cases. Total lipids were 8 gm/L in one fourth of the cases. Alkaline phosphatase was increased in only 24 per cent of the cases, and clearly dissociated from the changes in leucine-aminopeptides which were increased in 82 per cent of the cases.

Our studies reveal a prevalence of jaundice

TABLE 33-4

TESTS OF LIVER FUNCTION—CHOLESTATIC SYNDROME

Test	Number of cases (pathological/total)	Per cent pathological results
total bilirubin > 8 mg/L	11/40	27
non-conjugated bilirubin > 8 mg/L	11/40	27
total cholesterol ⩾ 2 gm/L	23/40	57
total cholesterol < 2 gm/L	17/40	43
total lipids > 8 gm/L	4/17	23
alkaline phosphatase > 2.5 B.U.	17/70	24
leucine aminopeptides > 400 C.U.	27/33	82

TABLE 33-5

TESTS OF LIVER FUNCTION—CELLULAR INSUFFICIENCY SYNDROME

Test	Number of cases (pathological/total)	Per cent pathological results
quick standard ⩽ 80 per cent	11/40	32
true prothrombin ⩽ 80 per cent	14/39	36
complex VII ⩽ 80 per cent	11/39	28
proaccelerin ⩽ 80 per cent	13/39	33
esterified cholesterol < 1 gm/L	11/40	27
serum albumen ⩽ 30 gm/L	7/40	17

lower than that reported in other papers (2, 4, 23, 39, 51). But a selection of the patients, biassed in favour of those with cholestatic forms of alcoholic steatosis, gives a false impression of the general incidence of jaundice in acute alcoholic liver conditions.

On the other hand, it is possible that among hepatic lesions, steatosis *per se* may be exclusively responsible for the cholestatic syndromes.

Hepatocellular insufficiency syndrome
Disturbances in the prothrombin complex were relatively frequent, appearing approximately in one out of three patients. These are moderate and reversible and the levels were not lower than 60 per cent of the normal. A fall of esterified cholesterol to 1 gm/L was found in 27 per cent of the cases. Hypoalbuminemia lower than 30 gm/L was observed in 17 per cent of the cases but always in a mild form. To summarize, the biological signs of hepatocellular insufficiency were inconstant and not severe.

Inflammatory "immunologic" syndrome
Gamma globulin higher than 17 gm/L was observed in one out of four patients. The rise was parallel to a positive MacLagan thymol reaction, but so far we have not found a Hanger reaction higher than + +. On the other hand, the Gros reaction, which is more significant because it is influenced by either albumin or globulin levels, was positive in 50 per cent of the cases. Thus, the inflammatory syndrome also appeared to be inconstant, and in agreement with most other studies, it was mild.

Liver lesion syndrome
This syndrome is of considerable pathophysiological importance. The absence of its elements in some reports, especially those concerned with alcoholic steatosis, seems to be due to a delay in performing the test. This disturbance is transitory and disappears in the first few days following alcohol withdrawal. Nevertheless, most published reports confirm our results (3–5, 19, 20, 22, 23, 44, 51, 52); Green (22) has postulated that the rise in SGOT is the best diagnostic evidence of liver lesions in alcoholics.

Concerning our cases, SGOT was increased in 86 per cent, SGPT in 77 per cent, ornitin-carbamil-transpherase (OCT) in 78 per cent, F-1-6P aldolase in 67 per cent, sorbitol-dehydrogenase

TABLE 33-6

TESTS OF LIVER FUNCTION—INFLAMMATORY
"IMMUNOLOGIC" SYNDROME

Test	Number of cases (pathological/total)	Per cent pathological results
gamma globulin > 17 gm/L	10/40	25
Gros reaction < 1.8 ml	18/35	51
hanger reaction > + +	0/40	—
thymol reaction > 12 v.u.	9/40	22
thymol reaction: floculation	6/40	15

TABLE 33-7

TESTS OF LIVER FUNCTION—HEPATIC LESIONAL SYNDROME

Test	Number of dosages (pathological/total)	Per cent pathological results
s.g.o.t. > 60 c.u.	63/73	86
s.g.p.t. > 40 c.u.	57/74	77
o.c.t. > 1 γ	22/28	78
f 1-6-p aldolase > 8 c.u.	22/33	67
s.d.h. > 1 u.	16/33	48
i.c.d. > 250 u.	15/32	47
g.d.h. > 0.9 u.	8/9	
serous iron > 180 µg/100 ml	11/37	30

(SDH) in 48 per cent, isonitric-dehydrogenase (ICD) in 47 per cent. The increases were rather mild and in only two cases did the amount of SGPT exceed 500 u. The change in glutamic dehydrogenase (GDH) is particularly interesting, because of the mitochondrial localization of the enzyme. We have not yet had much experience with this measure, but we found a marked increase (20 times higher than normal) in eight out of nine cases.

The iron level in plasma has been included in the picture of the syndrome on analogical grounds, in view of its increase in cytolytic acute hepatitis. It was, in fact, increased in only 30 per cent of the cases, but we must take into account that both fever and the "inflammatory syndrome" discussed below tend to decrease the plasma iron level. In summary, we can say that in our patients the liver lesion syndrome was severe and almost constant.

Biological inflammatory syndrome
We have frequently observed a special type of biological inflammatory syndrome. It includes a rise in the erythrosedimentation rate (see Table 33-8), which is nearly always moderate, but which can rise as high as 60 mm during the first hour. It is accompanied by an increase of fibrin to 3.5 gm/L and by an increase in alpha-2-globulin to 5 gm/L. We have no clear explanation for this syndrome. Some authors (7, 17) have reported finding it in the course of delirium tremens, but we have observed it in cases without any neuropsychiatric troubles. Green (22) ascribed both fever and the increase in sedimentation rate to lesions of hepatocellular necrosis; but no direct evidence is available to confirm this hypothesis.

Hematological changes
Anemia of less than 4,000,000 RC/mm³ was observed in two-thirds of the cases (see Table 33-9). It was macrocytic rather hyperchromic, and similar to that observed by other authors (20, 36). It was accompanied by signs of mild hyperhemolysis with medullar erythroblastic reaction and an increased peripheral reticulocytosis of 3 to 4 per cent. The half life of

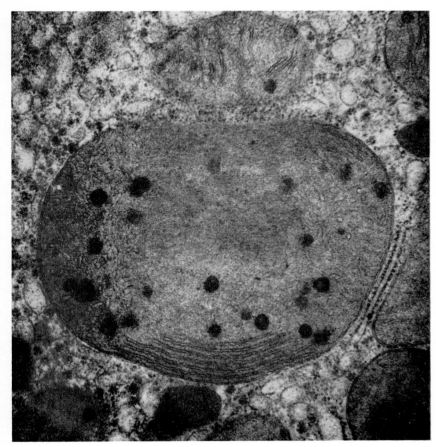

Figure 33-1
Giant mitochondria with persisting abnormally arranged cristae, and a heterogeneous
matrix containing numerous opaque, probably calcified, granules (× 28,000).

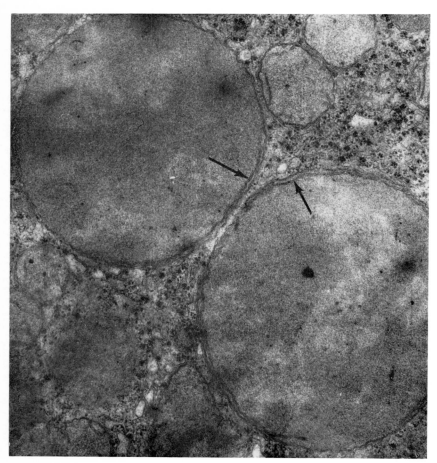

Figure 33-2
Giant mitochondria undergoing transformation into an amorphous globule.
Double membrane still visible. A second double membrane undulates close to the
circumference of the organelle (arrows) and seems to be a remnant of the cristae.
The matrix contains fine fibrillar aggregations ($\times$ 25,000).

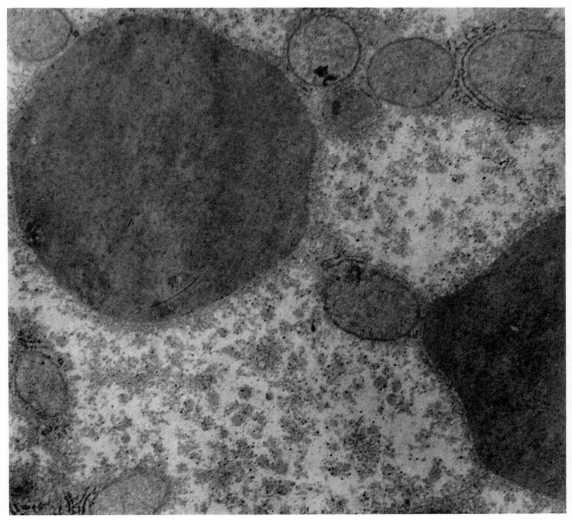

Figure 33-3

Amorphous globule with gluteraldehyde prefixation. The opacity of this globule distinguishes it from the very light fat droplets in this patient. The difference is confirmed by staining with toluidine blue: these globules are then bright blue while the fat is yellow and the pigments are black or greenish brown. In this patient most of the cells contain one or two globules of this type. The globules appeared much less opaque when gluteraldehyde prefixation was not used. ($\times$ 28,000).

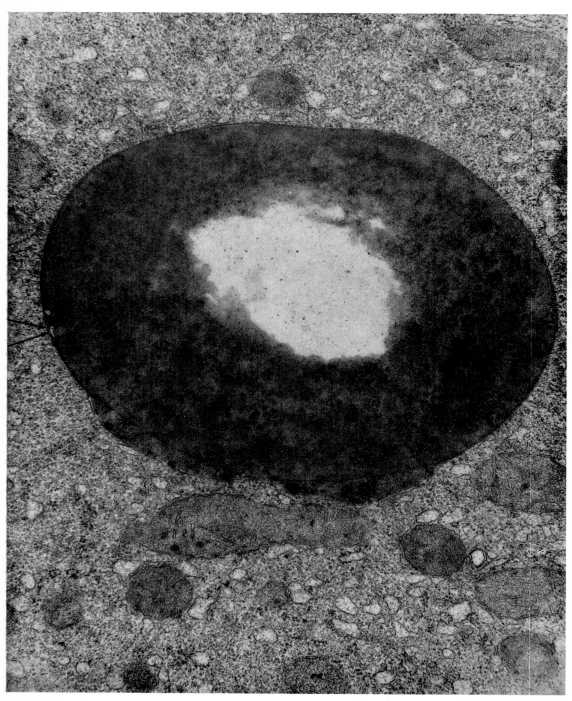

Figure 33-4
Globule apparently limited by double membrane (arrows) while its content seems to be of a ceroid nature. Its origin cannot be stated definitely ($\times$ 22,000).

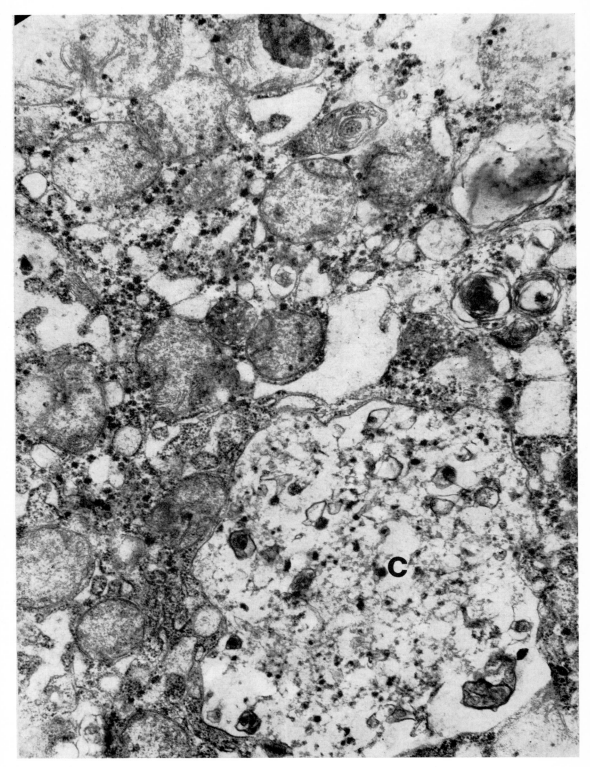

Figure 33-5
Large cytolysomes (c) or foci of cytoplasmic degeneration ($\times$ 27,000).

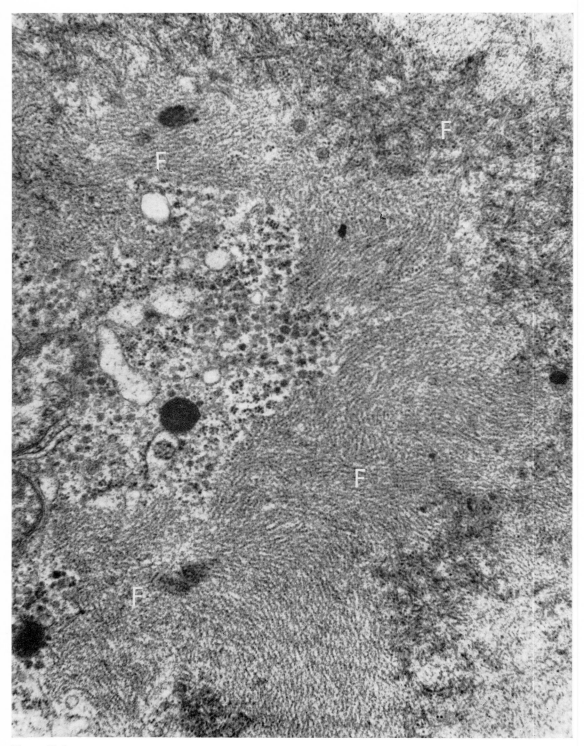

Figure 33-6
Fibrillar degeneration of cytoplasm (F); serpiginous aggregations of variously oriented fibrils invade the whole cell ($\times$ 35,000).

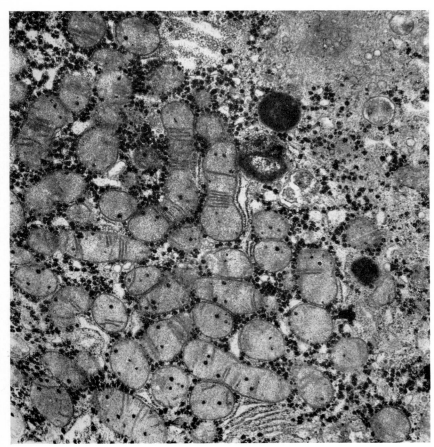

Figure 33-7
Massed mitochondria with parallel cristae (oncocytoid cells of Biava). This
appearance has been very rarely encountered ($\times$ 16,700).

TABLE 33–8

OTHER PATHOPHYSIOLOGICAL TESTS—BIOLOGICAL INFLAMMATORY SYNDROME

Test	Number of cases (pathological/total)	Per cent pathological results
erythrosedimentation rate > 20 mm first hour	26/34	76
fibrin > 3.5 gm/L	31/38	81
alpha-2-globulin > 5 gm/L	20/40	50

TABLE 33–9

OTHER PATHOPHYSIOLOGICAL TESTS—HEMATOLOGICAL

Test	Number of cases (pathological/total)	Per cent pathological results
red cells < 4 × 10^6/mm^3	23/35	66
white cells > 10,000/mm^3	5/35	14
platelets ≥ 350,000/mm^3	7/38	18
platelets ≤ 100,000/mm^3	2/38	5

erythrocytes was measured with 51 CR in six cases and found to be either at the low normal limit or a little less. The anemia tended to be cured after a few weeks. Three hypotheses have been postulated to explain it:

1
Changes in blood lipids inducing hyperhemolysis, as postulated by Zieve (52). But we have not found any increase in lysolecithin after chromatographic separation of plasma lipids.

2
Direct action of alcohol on the production of erythroblasts, as shown by MacCurdy et al. (35), inducing vacuolization of erythroblasts identical to that observed with chloramphenicol.

3
Alcohol interaction in folate metabolism, i.e. blocking hepatic folate reductase.

So far none of these hypotheses has been confirmed.

In some cases a hyperleucocytosis over 10,000 per mm^3, with neutrophilic polynucleosis, was found (see Table 33-9). No case exceeding 20,000 per mm^3 appeared in our sample. Similar findings have been reported (4, 10, 20, 22, 38), and considered without evidence, to be a consequence of hepatocellular

necrosis. In some cases, hyperleucocytosis can represent a veritable leukemoid reaction (13, 14).

In our series, thrombopenia was rare (see Table 33-9), and hyperplaquetosis rather more frequent (7 out of 38, with platelets over 350,000). The latter was usually mild and below 500,000, but in one case it was 980,000/mm^3. These disturbances were also transient.

Blood lactate level
An increase in blood lactate level during acute alcoholic intoxication has been pointed out by some authors. It may be a consequence of alcohol-dehydrogenase activity increasing hepatic DPNH. This is suggested by the decrease in the ratio DPN/DPNH. The need to use the excess of DPNH leads to an increase of pyruvate reduction into lactate under the influence of alcohol-dehydrogenase. The excess of lactate causes a decrease in renal uric acid clearance, which would explain the hyperuricemia observed in the course of acute alcoholism and demonstrated experimentally (30, 33).

We have measured blood lactate by an enzymatic method in ten patients, and have not observed any significant changes. However, this may be because the tests were delayed in relation to alcohol ingestion. We have also systematically studied the urate blood level in almost all our patients. In general, this level was markedly increased.

Glucose regulation

We did not find a regular pattern of disturbances in glucose regulation (30). The most interesting such disturbances are those leading to hyperglycemia, which have been widely studied, for example by Neame and Joubert (37).

The true incidence of hypoglycemia has not been established. In order to determine it, systematic measurements should be made on acutely intoxicated patients immediately after admission to hospital. Most of our measurements were made 12 to 24 hours after admission so that some transitory cause of hypoglycemia may have escaped observation.

PREVALENCE OF CERTAIN CLINICAL
AND BIOLOGICAL FEATURES

Cholestatic forms of alcoholic liver disease correspond to lesions of massive steatosis and are characterized by the intensity of the cholestatic type of jaundice with predominance of bounded bilirubin, bilirubinuria, hypercholesterolemia and hyperlipemia, as well as increased alkaline phosphatase, negative flocculation tests and mildly increased transaminases (2, 39, 51). To date, we have seen only one case of this type.

The exploration of the portal system has not been performed systematically. We have found varicose dilation of esophageal veins in only two cases out of 19. Intrasplenic pressure was measured in some patients but was found to be high in only one case. Splenoportography performed in eight patients failed to reveal any abnormal by-passes. Nevertheless, Chiandussi *et al.* (12) have demonstrated portal hypertension associated with massive steatosis, which could be the consequence of a blockade of pre-sinusoidal type.

In 1958, Zieve (52) described a syndrome comprising general weakness, nausea or vomiting, anorexia, fever, upper quadrant abdominal pain, and jaundice (non-specific). It involved massive steatosis, plasmatic hyperlipemia, and hemolytic anemia. The evolution is favourable, the disturbances disappearing after four to six weeks. According to Zieve, the hyperlipemia and jaundice are related to liver injury and the hemolytic anemia is the result of an increase in the blood level of lysolecithin, a lipid with known hemolytic action. The 20 cases studied by Zieve are heterogenous from the anatomical point of view, and some patients were actually cirrhotic. Other authors have critically discussed his conclusions (26). It seems that he may only have associated disturbances frequently found among alcoholics, but which can also occur independently from one another. We have observed jaundice, anemia, and hyperlipemia in nearly 20 per cent of our patients. It is possible that the "Zieve Syndrome" is only an eventual coexistence of these features. Actually we have seen three cases which correspond to the Zieve Syndrome.

Finally, there is *Beckett's acute hepatitis* which is the most severe of the various acute alcoholic liver problems. We have found only two cases; these can be classified as such because of the rise of transaminases to over 500 U. On the whole, the frequency of this disease seems to be rather low.

HISTOLOGICAL AND ULTRASTRUCTURAL
LESIONS

Routine histological examinations of the liver have revealed steatosis in almost all our alcoholic patients. Only two were free of the lesion; this proportion is lower than the 15 out of 65 cases reported by Seife *et al.* (47), or the 19 out of 66 of Leevy *et al.* (31). The importance of the steatosis in our sample is rather unequal. When the results were classified in three groups according to the percentage of hepatocytes containing fat droplets (< 30 per cent, 30–70 per cent, > 70 per cent) the three groups were quite similar. Steatosis does not exhibit a uniform distribution in the liver lobulin. The fat droplets were decidedly variable in size. It is often difficult to establish the presence of fatty pseudocysts.

Mallory bodies were observed in 15 early biopsies out of 57, and cellular clarification in 17. Bile pigments were observed in two cases and siderosis in four. The glycogen content was normal in four-fifths of the cases.

Hyperplasia of Kupffer cells was frequent. Mild inflammatory infiltration either portal or periportal was observed in two-thirds of the cases. Periportal fibrosis, generally mild, was indicated in 27 biopsies, and became more apparent after the regression of steatosis. Pencil-shaped stroma infiltrated the lobulin.

The study of about 2,000 electron micrographs, based on 20 biopsies, is not yet completed. However, three types of cytoplasmic lesion of liver cells have been distinguished: mitochondrial lesions, unspecific signs of cellular injury, and fibrillar degeneration of cytoplasm.

Mitochondrial lesions have been described by Schaffner (45, 46), Porta (43), Kiessling (27) and Svoboda (48). They can be recognized in any degree of steatosis. Some of the mitochondria are about the same size as the nucleus (see Figure 33-1). This giantism is accompanied by full disorder of the peaks. The matrix may loose its fine granulations, increase in density, and adopt the homogeneous appearance of lipids (see Figure 33-2). At the end of this evolution the mitochondrion becomes an amorphous globule, similar to the cytosomes of renal tubules (see Figures 33-3 and 33-4). These giant mitochondria as well as the amorphous globules, which seem to derive from them, appeared in almost all the cells in the biopsies from six patients. Their prevalence was very low in another seven biopsies, and we have not observed them in other patients. It is pertinent to remember that, according to Porta (43), these structures are the Mallory bodies. This picture differs greatly from the myelin degeneration of mitochondria, which was also observed in some of our patients. Other commonly observed features are: fat inclusions in the mitochondria, central peaks, and big granules similar to the calcic granules found after intoxication by carbon tetrachloride.

We understand by signs of unspecific cytoplasmic injury, focal cellular degeneration, cytolysomes, intravacuolar lamellar bodies, intracytoplasmic myelin forms, and also lipofuchsin masses. All these features, which we have found in almost every biopsy, represent a partial cytolysis controlled by the cell. The most diffuse cytoplasmic lesions, such as swelling of the reticulum, were much less common.

Fibrillar cytoplasmic degeneration, described by Biava (6) as hyaline Mallory substance, seems to us to be specific to alcoholism. It appears that its evolution ends in the rupture of the cells (see Figures 33-5 to 33-7). We found this lesion in four patients with an overt liver cirrhosis, who had been admitted to the hospital initially for an acute alcoholic liver problem, which is the reason for their inclusion in our sample. Numerous giant mitochondria and a large number of cytolysomes were also found in their biopsies.

Less frequently we have observed masses of perioxysomes, fingerprint formations, rare canallicular anomalies, and biliar vacuoles. The tissue spaces frequently contained large numbers of precollagen fibriles as well as collagen fibres. A basal membrane was only exceptionally observed. The endothelial cells frequently appeared without an overt fibroblastic character.

Many of the Kuffer cells contained fat globules, which also could be observed in a free state in the sinusoids or stroma, where they appear as a residue of cellular destruction. We have not yet studied a sufficient number of biopsies to establish the regression rate of these lesions.

CORRELATIONS BETWEEN DIFFERENT ANOMALIES

As in the case of all previous authors, we were unable to find any satisfactory relationship between clinical signs and biological lesions. Even massive steatosis may exist without hepatomegaly, and fever is neither more frequent nor more severe when hepatocellular degenerative lesions are present.

There was a significant correlation between BSP clearance and the intensity of steatosis, and between the prevalence of giant mitochondria and SGOT level. But these correlations do not necessarily indicate a cause-effect relationship. No other significant correlations could be established, although hyperplaquetosis was observed only in cases of mild steatosis.

PROGNOSIS

As soon as intoxication subsides and nutritional conditions return to normal – although we do not know the role played by each element in the process – acute alcoholic liver problems disappear in most cases after a short period.

From a prognostic standpoint, two problems call for special consideration. First is the question of repetitive episodes of steatosis. Second, and often a subject of passionate debate, is the evolution of cirrhosis and its relationship to steatosis. Our experience in regard to these questions has been as follows. In a short period, it is common to observe a rapid clinical, biological, and anatomical recovery. The outlook is even more optimistic when it is based on initial hepatic biopsies, which permits elimination of severe cases of liver damage at the outset. Our research design was affected by this bias.

Clinically, the liver size diminishes; in the rare cases in which splenomegaly is present, it returns to normal and temperature reaches a normal level. In the absence of edema, increase in weight is the best sign of recovery. Inflammatory conditions appear rather more marked in some of our patients after a few weeks and disappear only gradually. BSP clearance is an excellent and constant sign of functional recovery of the liver.

The study of successive liver biopsies allows us to state that the recovery is also anatomical. The disappearance of fat deposits is more rapid for intracellular (three weeks) than for extracellular fat (four to six weeks). Routine histological examination does not reveal degenerative lesions after a short time. We have been able to confirm that the recovery of steatosis occurs without any specific therapy, either lipotrophic or protective, both of which have been proven ineffective.

A fatal evolution is the consequence of hypoglycemia or fatty embolism (11, 15, 21, 34). Sudden death has been ascribed to one of these causes, in patients showing massive steatosis as the only necropsic finding. Fatty embolism is confirmed by the rupture of lipid cysts into the hepatic circulation, directly revealed by examination of tissue fixed with osmic acid. Even more exceptional is a type of severe jaundice, only one case of which has been reported (10).

Protracted observation has shown that a variety of outcomes are possible; four of these may be noted as follows:

1

Clinical as well as biological and anatomical recovery are possible, provided intoxication is stopped.

2

When alcohol intoxication is maintained, steatosis may remain established with astonishing tolerance.

3

In some cases, withdrawal of alcohol brings about clinical, biological, and anatomical recovery, but after new episodes of intoxication a relapse occurs with the same clinical, biological, and histological characteristics. Many of our observations provide examples of this evolutionary pattern.

4

In the sequence, acute alcoholic liver to cirrhosis, four cases in our series are examples. It is significant that the fibrillar degeneration, described by Biava (6), was observed in these four cases, and only in them.

SUMMARY AND CONCLUSIONS

From the clinical, biological, histological, and sometimes ultrastructural study of 60 non-cirrhotic alcoholics, the following statements may be made:

1

Routine microscopic examination of the liver revealed in almost all patients a steatosis, the importance of which was variable.

2

Electron microscopy, complemented by optical microscopic studies on slices prepared from the same blocks, is the only way to get a correct appreciation of certain lesions, which include in order of increasing severity: cytoplasmic focal degeneration, giant mitochondria leading to amorphous globules, and fibrillar degeneration (Biava's hyaline bodies). The importance of these ultrastructural lesions is independent of that of steatosis.

3
Pathophysiological changes are almost always observed, mainly those revealing cytolitic lesions, and among them, a rise in SGOT and SGPT levels, ornityl-carbymil-transpherase and glutamic-dehydrogenase, all mitochondrial enzymes.

4
No correlation between steatosis and pathophysiological changes was observed, with the possible exception of BSP clearance.

5
It seems that no relationship between BSP clearance and the severity of utrastructural lesions exists. But these lesions are most severe in patients with higher SGOT levels.

6
Both lesions and their biological consequences appear to be rapidly reversible once alcohol has been withdrawn and a normal diet established. This conclusion should be taken as tentative only because of the incompleteness of ultrastructural studies on the point. Many alterations subsumed under the heading of "acute alcoholic liver damage" can only be detected when examination is made immediately after withdrawal from alcohol.

REFERENCES

1
ALBOT, G., SCHLUMBERGER, C.S., FAYE, C.M., RUFFINO, J., & RAIMBAULT, S.
Le gros foie des alcooliques
Sa formule biologique et ses deux aspects histologiques
Arch. Mal. Appar. Dig., **45**: 585, 1956
2
BALLARD, H., BERNSTEIN, M., & FARRAR, J.T.
Fatty liver presenting as obstructive jaundice
Am. J. Med., **30**: 196, 1961
3
BANG, N.U., IVERSEN, K., JAGT, T., & MADSEN, S.
Serum glutamic oxalacetic transaminase activity in acute and chronic alcoholism
J.A.M.A., **168**: 156, 1958
4
BECKETT, A.G., LIVINGSTONE, A.V., & HILL, K.R.
Acute alcoholic hepatitis
Brit. Med. J., **ii**: 1113, 1961
5
BECKETT, A.G., LIVINGSTONE, A.V., & HILL, K.R.
Acute alcoholic hepatitis without jaundice
Brit. Med. J., **ii**: 580, 1962
6
BIAVA, C.
Mallory alcoholic hyalin: a heretofore unique lesion of hepato-cellular ergostoplasm
Lab. Invest., **13**: 301, 1964
7
BOUDIN, G., LAURAS, A., LANIECE, M., & KREBS, H.
Syndrome biologique du delirium tremens
Press. Med., **40**: 1469 & **41**: 1503, 1960
8
BRADUS, S., KORN, R.J., CHOMET, B., WEST, M., & ZIMMERMAN, H.J.
Hepatic function and serum enzyme levels in association with fatty metamorphosis of the liver
Am. J. Med. Sc., **246**: 36, 1963
9
BUCK, R.E.
Observations on alcoholic fatty liver: the use of intervalle needle biopsy and liver function tests
J. Lab. Clin. Med., **33**: 555, 1958
10
CACHERA, R., LAMOTTE, M., LAMOTTE-BARILLON, S.
Etude clinique, biologique et histologique des stéatoses du foie chez les alcooliques (à propos de 71 observations)
Bull. Mém. Soc. Méd. Hôp. Paris, **66**: 276, 1950
11
CHALMERS, T.C. & JONES, W.A.
Hepatic failure in alcoholic patient
(Case rept. Massachusetts Gen. Hosp.)
New England J. Med., **267**: 200, 1962
12
CHIANDUSSI, L., GRECO, F., INDOVINA, D., CESSANO, L., VACCARINO, A., & MURATORI, F.
Hepatic steatosis and portal hypertension with presinusoidal obstruction
Report of a case
Gastroenterology, **44**: 532, 1963
13
COLMAN, R.W. & SHEIN, H.M.
Leukemoid reaction, hyperuricemia and severe hyperpyrexia complicating a fatal case of acute fatty liver of the alcoholic
Ann. Int. Med., **57**: 110, 1962
14
DAVIDSON, C.S. & MACDONALD, R.A.
Recovery from active hepatic disease of the alcoholic
Arch. Int. Med., **110**: 592, 1962
15
DURLACHER, S.H., MEIER, J.R., FISHER, R.S., & LOVITT, W.V.
Sudden death due to pulmonary fat embolism in

persons with alcoholic fatty liver
Am. J. Pathol., 30: 633, 1954
16

EDMONDSON, H.A., PETERS, R.L., REYNOLDS, T.B., & KUZMA, O.T.
Sclerosing hyaline necrosis of the liver in the chronic alcoholic: a recognizable clinical syndrome
Ann. Int. Med., 59: 646, 1963
17

FONTAN, M., FLAMENT, G., & CARIDROIT, M.
Anomalies des alpha 2-globulines d'éthyliques chroniques
Lille Méd., 8: 443, 1963
18

GALL, E.A.
The diagnosis of hepatites by needle biopsy
In Hepatitis frontiers, ed. by F.W. Hartman, G.A. Lo Grippo, J.G. Mateer, & J. Barron
Boston: Little & Brown, 1957, p. 475
19

GEFFROY, T., FABLET, J., LELIEVRE, L., & DESHAYES, P.
Intéret du dosage de l'ornithine carbamyl transférase sérique en pathologie hépatobiliaire
Rev. Internat. Hépat., 12: 685, 1962
20

GOLDBERG, M. & THOMPSON, C.M.
Acute fatty metamorphosis of the liver
Ann. Int. Med., 55: 146, 1961
21

GRAHAM, R.L.
Sudden death in young adults in association with fatty liver
Bull. Johns Hopkins Hosp., 74: 16, 1944
22

GREEN, J.R.
Subclinical acute liver disease of the alcoholic
Aust. Ann. Med., 14: 111, 1965
23

GREEN, J.R., MISTILIS, S., & SCHIFF, L.
Acute alcoholic hepatitis
A clinical study of fifty cases
Arch. Int. Med., 112: 67, 1963
24

HED, R.
Clinical studies on chronic alcoholism
IV. Studies on serum transaminase activity in chronic alcoholism
Acta med. scandinav., 165: 161, 1959
25

KEEFER, C.S. & FRIES, E.D.
The fatty liver
Its diagnosis and clinical cause
Tr. A. Am. Physicians, 57: 283, 1942
26

KESSEL, L.
Acute transient hyperlipemia due to hepatopancreatic damage in chronic alcoholics (Zieve's syndrome)
Am. J. Med., 32: 747, 1962
27

KIESSLING, K.H., LINDGREN, L., STRANDBERG, B., & TOBE, U.
Electron microscopic study of liver mitochondria

from human alcoholics
Acta med. scandinav., 176: 595, 1964
28

LAMELIN, J.P., ORCEL, L., BOIVIN, P., & FAUBERT, R.
Etude clinique et biologique de 25 cas de stéatose hépatique éthylique
Arch. Mal. Appar. Dig., 54: 737, 1965
29

LEEVY, C.M.
Fatty liver: a study of 270 patients with biopsy proven fatty liver and a review of the literature
Medicine, 41: 249, 1962
30

LEEVY, C.M., FINEBERG, J.C., WHITE, T.J., & GNASSI, A.M.
Hyperglycaemia and glycosuria in chronic alcoholic with hepatic insufficiency
Clinical observations in 10 patients
Am. J. Med. Sc., 223: 88, 1952
31

LEEVY, C.M., PATRYLO, I., & DOODY, W.
Hepatic abnormalities in alcoholics with delirium tremens
Quart. J. Stud. Alc., 14: 568, 1953
32

LIEBER, C.S.
Hyperuricemia induced by alcohol
Arthritis Rheum., 8: 786, 1965
33

LIEBER, C.S., JONES, D.P., LOSOWSKY, M.S., & DAVIDSON, C.S.
Interrelation of uric acid and ethanol metabolism in man
J. Clin. Invest., 41: 1863, 1962
34

LYNCH, M.J., RAPHAEL, S.S., & DIXON, T.P.
Fat embolism in chronic alcoholism: control study on incidence of fat embolism
Arch. Path. (Chicago), 67: 68, 1959
35

MACCURDY, P.R., PIERCE, L.E., & RATH, C.E.
Abnormal bone marrow morphology in acute alcoholism
New England J. Med., 266: 505, 1962
36

MYERSON, R.M. & GILBERT, D.
Observations on acute anemia of alcoholism
Am. J. Med. Sc., 244: 696, 1962
37

NEAME, P.B. & JOUBERT, S.M.
Postalcoholic hypoglycaemia toxic hepatitis
Lancet, ii: 893, 1961
38

PHILIPS, G.B. & DAVIDSON, C.S.
Acute hepatic insufficiency of the chronic alcoholic
Clinical and pathological study
Arch. Int. Med., 94: 585, 1954
39

PHILIPS, G.B. & DAVIDSON, C.S.
Liver disease of the chronic alcoholic simulating extrahepatic biliary obstruction
Gastroenterology, 33: 236, 1957

40
POPPER, H. & SCHAFFNER, F.
Nutritional hepatic injury
Arch. Int. Med., **94**: 795, 1954

41
POPPER, H. & SZANTO, P.B.
Fatty liver with hepatic failure in alcoholics
J. Mount Sinai Hosp. NY, **24**: 1121, 1957

42
POPPER, H., SZANTO, P.B., & PARTHASARATHY, M.
Florid cirrhosis: a review of 35 cases
Am. J. Clin. Path., **25**: 889β, 1965

43
PORTA, E.A., BERGMAN, B.J., & STEIN, A.A.
Acute alcoholic hepatitis
Am. J. Path., **46**: 657, 1965

44
SATALINE, L.R. & MATRE, W.J.
Significance of hyperphosphatasemia in alcoholics
with liver disease
An analysis of fifty-eight cases with histologic diagnosis
Am. J. Med., **35**: 323, 1963

45
SCHAFFNER, F., LOEBEL, A., & WEINER, H.A.
Hepatocellular changes in acute alcoholic hepatitis
J.A.M.A., **180**: 768, 1962

46
SCHAFFNER, F., LOEBEL, A., WEINER, H., & BARKA, T.
Hepatocellular cytoplasmic changes in acute
alcoholic hepatitis
J.A.M.A., **183**: 343, 1963

47
SEIFE, M., KESSLER, B.J., & LISA, J.R.
Clinical, functional and needle biopsy study of the
liver in alcoholism
Arch. Int. Med., **86**: 658, 1950

48
SVOBODA, D.J. & MANNING, R.T.
Chronic alcoholism with fatty metamorphosis
of the liver
Mitochondrial alterations in hepatic cells
Am. J. Path., **44**: 645, 1964

49
TROUSSEAU, A.
De l'alcohlisme
Clinique médicale de l'Hôtel Dieu, Baillière
Edit., **2**: 383, 1913

50
ULEVITCH, M., GALL, E.A., ABERNATY, E.L., & SCHIFF, L.
Needle biopsy of the liver
Observations in fatty vacuolation of the liver
Gastroenterology, **18**: 1, 1951

51
VARAY, A., ORCEL, L., BERTHELOT, J., FABRE, J.C.,
VITERBO, G., & MENACHE, D.
Sur un syndrome de stéatose – ictère cholostatique –
Les stéatoses ictérigènes
Arch. mal. appar. dig., **51**: 5, 1962

52
ZIEVE, L.
Jaundice hyperlipemia and hemolytic anemia:
a heretofore unrecognized syndrome associated with
alcoholic fatty liver and cirrhosis
Ann. Int. Med., **48**: 471, 1958

53
ZIMMERMAN, H.J.
The evolution of alcoholic cirrhosis: clinical,
biochemical and histological correlations
Med. Clin. N. Am., **39**: 241, 1955

SERGIO FERRER

IBCIA SANTIBÁÑEZ

MARIO CASTRO

DINA KRAUSKOPF

HELIETTE SAINT-JEAN

Neurological Service and
Institute of Neurosurgery
Salvador Hospital
Centre of Studies on Mental Health
and Psychiatric Clinic
University of Chile
Santiago, Chile

34

Permanent Neurological Complications of Alcoholism

In the present paper we intend to examine those neurological complications of alcoholism in which signs of permanent damage to the central nervous system can be shown. We will not consider the conditions which are commonly treated in psychiatric or emergency services. These apparently do not leave organic lesions, and include acute intoxication and syndromes attributable to alcohol withdrawal such as delirium tremens, alcoholic hallucinosis, oneiroid episodes, and epileptic seizures (7, 26, 27, 38).

The permanent neurological complications of alcoholism considered here are classified in the literature as a group of anatomico-clinical syndromes according to the area of the nervous system affected (1, 3, 12, 16–18, 31, 41). The following are included: upper hemorrhagic polioencephalitis of Wernicke; Morell's laminar cortical sclerosis; Korsakoff's polyneuritic psychosis; Marchiafava-Bignami's axial degeneration of the corpus callosum; epilepsy in alcoholics; Marie-Foix, Alajouanine, and Adam's late cerebral cortical degeneration; Adam and Lapresle's central pons myelinosis; spinal syndromes; alcoholic polyneuritis; and alcoholic myopathy and myocardiopathy.

We have not found in the extensive literature on the topic either a critical revision of this classification or a proposal of new criteria to include evolutionary aspects and maintain the clinical point of view (5). Although in Chile there is a high prevalence of alcoholism, clinical papers on permanent neurologic complications are scarce (29). Systematic pathological studies are lacking, and no publications on syndromes diagnosed on the basis of pathological findings are available.

The main purpose of the present communication is to report the results of a study of a group of chronic alcoholics with permanent neurological damage, to describe the different syndromes and degree of psychic impairment, to correlate these syndromes with the psychological and pneumonencephalographic findings, and to consider the relevance of such etiopathogenic factors as drinking habits, nourishment, liver function, and gastric secretion.

MATERIALS AND METHODS

The study sample was selected from the 72

chronic alcoholic patients admitted to the Neurology Service of El Salvador Hospital between May 1, 1964 and July 30, 1966. All were referred by general physicians attached to different services in Santiago. The selection criteria were as follows:

1
Only patients younger than 60 years with central neurological lesions and clinical signs of psychic impairment were included.
2
Patients with antecedent encephalocranial traumatism, cerebrovascular accident, or epilepsy not caused by alcoholism were excluded.
3
Patients with neurological symptoms ascribed to alcohol withdrawal were excluded when no permanent neurological disturbances were evident after the acute phase.

On the basis of these criteria the study group was reduced to 23 patients (3 women and 20 men). All sample patients were submitted to neurological examination, most of them on several occasions so as to observe the evolution of their symptoms. The history of their alcoholism and their nutritional, educational, and socio-economic background were also explored. The data obtained from the patient on these topics were checked against those obtained from his family. Sixteen of the 23 patients were submitted to a series of psychological tests to explore the verbal and manual areas. Seven patients were excluded because they did not appear when required.

The verbal area was evaluated by means of the Binet Word Evocation Test, Binet Word Vocabulary Test, Wais Comprehension Test and the Wechsler Similarity Test. The manual area was studied by means of the Grassi Block Substitution Test and the Minnesota Perception-Diagnosis Test (MPD). The Vocabulary Test was applied to assess the loss of previously acquired concepts. The Word Evocation Test provides information as to initiative and the ability to associate systematic thoughts. The Comprehension Test evaluates judgment, considered as the ability to adapt emotionally and intellectually to an ordinary situation. The Similarity Test is used to determine the verbal

conceptualization level. The Grassi Test is designed to determine any slight psychic impairment in the spheres of abstract and concrete behaviour, and the MPD Test, based on gestalt theory, estimates organic damage through the distortion of the spatial orientation of figures presented.

Liver function was studied in all the patients through flocculation tests and blood bilirubin, transaminases, and prothrombin levels. Gastric secretion was studied in 11 patients. In each case the time elapsed between the performance of these tests and the withdrawal of alcohol was reported.

A cerebrospinal fluid test (CSF) was performed in 17 cases, EEG in 18, and a fractioned pneumoencephalogram (NEG) in 17 of the 23 patients. The results were assessed according to the criteria of Lindgram. NEG was refused by four patients and there were medical contraindications in three cases.

The patients were grouped according to the predominant syndrome, and classified as acute or chronic according to the stage of development.

The acute forms were characterized by sudden onset of neurological symptoms after a period of excessive alcohol ingestion together with deficient diet, inducing disturbances of consciousness. The end of the acute episode was indicated by the attenuation or disappearance of the main neurological signs of the predominant syndrome and recovery from confusion. Such acute episodes evolve into chronic residual forms. The chronic forms were defined by a partial or total irreversibility of neurological damage with acute or insidious onset, affecting predominantly a specific level of the nervous system and usually accompanied by psychic impairment.

NEUROLOGICAL FINDINGS

Seven patients were admitted with an acute episode, and the rest with a more or less stabilized neurological damage which apparently had begun insidiously.

In both groups it was difficult to determine the moment at which the neurological damage appeared because of its insidious evolution and because usually the only available information was untrustworthy anamnestic data from the patient and his family. The neurological damage could be prior to the acute manifestations or to the onset of a chronic disease.

During the observation period, chronic forms showed only quantitative variations, while the acute forms generally evolved towards residual syndromes with a different qualitative configuration. For instance, an acute Parkinson syndrome changed towards spastic paraparesis and then towards a non-specific syndrome with generalized tonus alteration and psychic impairment.

Four types of acute episode were recognized in our material:

Pseudo-encephalitic episode (1 case)
It did not adopt the typical Gayet-Wernicke form, since neither ocular paralysis nor nystagmus were present. The patient had deep conscious disturbances, showed primary responses such as suction and prehension reflexes, alteration of tonus and catatonia, oppositional hypertonia, cogwheel, involuntary movements such as postural clonus and high amplitude tremor, asinergic involuntary movements and bilateral pyramidal signs. In short, the patient exhibited diffuse encephalic damage revealed also by severe EEG alterations in both hemispheres.

Parkinson Syndrome (2 cases)
These patients had hypomimia, hypokinesia, plastic increase of tonus and tremor, in common with Parkinson's Disease. Their condition differed from the latter because the signs were associated with a slight conscious disturbance without psychotic productivity, they did not show postural alterations of the body axis, the difficulties in gait were derived from leg weakness and lack of equilibrium, the tremor was predominantly postural and not proportional to the cogwheel as in a Parkinson tremor of certain intensity, and most important, these symptoms disappeared within a few days and were replaced by derivative syndromes.

In summary, the two patients showed a generalized involvement of the nervous system evoking encephalitic symptomatology, and their condition was classified as an extrapyramidal syndrome because of the importance of the tremor.

Cerebellar syndrome (2 cases)
Here the picture was more clearly defined and involved certain peculiarities: (*a*) symptoms appeared abruptly after a drinking episode and persisted, though partially attenuated, during the whole period of observation; (*b*) the cerebellar signs predominated in the lower extremities; (*c*) there was no nystagmus; (*d*) the alterations in gait suggested tabes rather than cerebellar ataxia; (*e*) instead of the classical hypotonia, there was spastic hypertonia of the lower extremities; and (*f*) the scanned voice was only transitorily present.

Acute non-specific forms (2 cases)
Two patients who later showed clear signs of psychological impairment and neurological damage, were admitted with oneiroid syndrome; one of them clearly configurated a delirium tremens. The latter patient had liver cirrhosis and the delirium appeared after alcohol withdrawal in response to digestive bleeding. As the delirious episode was severe and the confusional condition persisted, the possibility of an encephalopathy induced by high blood ammonia level was postulated, but not confirmed by blood and CSF analysis. The other patient, suffering from a residual alcohol epilepsy, was admitted with an oneiroid episode involving paranoid ideas. The latter induced aggressive behaviour which evolved towards an alcoholic hallucinosis of relatively short duration.

The residual or chronic neurological syndromes of the 23 patients were grouped in five categories regardless of whether or not these syndromes followed acute episodes or exhibited a chronic evolution. It must be emphasized that in each case the neurologic signs remained irreversible and changed only in intensity during observation.

Psychic deterioration syndrome with global alterations in tonus (12 cases)
This was a non-specific neurological condition similar to that of brain damage from other causes. It appeared generally as a background

to every other neurological disturbance observed among the alcoholics. From the psychological point of view, it was characterized by impairment indicated mainly through alterations in memory, affective indifference, and a progressive loss of work efficiency and social adaptation. From the neurological point of view, it is characterized by generalized dystonia, expressed by hypomimia, hipokinesia, perseveration in imposed attitudes, coenervation, inability to relax the tonus during passive movements (without reaching the oppositional hypertonia as in pseudo-encephalitic acute pictures), motor iteration, and generalized spasticity or rigidity.

These tonus disturbances, inducing slow performance, contrast with the precipitous actions and excessive movements usual in such patients, and give the impression of an automatic and careless activity.

In this group of patients, some forms of psychic impairment symptomatic of cerebral damage were seen, such as simple mental deterioration, general pseudoparalysis (because of euphoria and disartria), and epilepsy.

Cerebellopathies (4 cases)

The clinical picture of acute cerebellopathies only diminishes in intensity when it becomes chronic, but maintains its characteristics. These patients exhibited signs equivalent to the acute forms already described: occasionally nystagmus, asinergy, and dysmetria predominating in the lower extremities, and ataxic gait with spastic components.

Spastic paraparesis (3 cases)

This form was characterized by the presence of spasticity of the lower limbs, with conservation of muscular power and generalized exaltation of the myotactic reflexes, including that of the chin. Diminution and even abolition of the ankle reflexes was commonly observed. The Babinsky sign was rarely present, but the Chaddock was frequently found. Deep and superficial sensitivity was generally undamaged, but occasionally vibration perception was abolished in the toes.

Polyneuropathies (3 cases)

These did not exhibit any differences from neuropathies due to other causes. The skin of the feet was red, humid, and hot with a velvety aspect. Subjectively the patients complained of heat in this region and of hyperalgesia to cutaneous stimuli. They all presented clear signs of psychic impairment.

Alcoholic myopathy and myocardiopathy (1 case)

The patient was admitted for a cardiac illness but also exhibited asthenia, muscular pains, and generalized muscular atrophy, which predominated in the proximal segments of the upper extremities. A biopsy of the right biceps revealed signs of intense degeneration of the muscular fibres, without inflammatory elements.

Considering the 23 patients as a whole, some common clinical elements can be recognized. All showed psychic impairment and generalized disturbance of muscular tonus. In some cases spasticity predominated and in others plastic hypertonia was the main sign. In fact, all patients could be included in the first group of chronic syndromes. But the other groups include those patients who also exhibited signs of lesions at other levels.

It is also important to emphasize that effective indifference and impulse inertia was a prominent feature of patients' behaviour. Their lack of interest was revealed also in the small importance they attributed to their physical defects and their frequent ignorance of their intellectual deficiencies. This psychic picture is reminiscent of the frontal syndrome. On the other hand, the tonus alterations in these patients suggest the tonic perturbations resulting from damage to the extrapyramidal frontal areas. For these reasons, it can be assumed that the cerebral damage is primarily located in the cortex or frontal connections.

DRINKING PATTERNS

The average age of the group was about 45 years, and the distribution in the third, fourth, and fifth decade was almost equal (8-8-7, respectively). The average age when the patients started excessive drinking was 19.4 years. In eleven cases the patient was younger than 20 years.

Most of the patients were wine drinkers and six also drank spirits (Aguardiente). The average daily wine intake was about 3.5 L. Seventeen patients exhibited patterns of inveterate alcoholism and six of intermittent.

Analysis of the time sequence of the onset of withdrawal symptoms and neurological disturbances shows that the patients did not recognize neurological symptoms until the appearance of a withdrawal syndrome. It is important to note that two of the women exhibited symptoms of physical dependence almost from the beginning of excessive drinking.

NUTRITIONAL DATA

An inquiry about habitual diet was made in 21 patients. Food intake during the alcohol drinking episodes was insufficient in 16 cases. Generally, diet was hypocaloric and high in carbohydrates. Some patients had no other source of food than alcoholic beverages for months and even years.

HEPATIC AND GASTRIC INVOLVEMENT

Seven patients (25 per cent) had alterations in the liver function tests. Three had liver cirrhosis and one, a fatty liver (both verified by biopsy). All of these patients were admitted during a period of excessive drinking.

RESULTS OF EEG, NEG, AND CSF TESTS

The EEG was normal in 14 cases and altered in four: one had rapid activity and the other three exhibited non-specific abnormalities in the theta waves. The CSF was studied in 17 cases; three of which showed a slight increase of albumin and cells. The NEG revealed hemispheric atrophy (cortical, internal, or mixed) in 14 patients. In one case, there was only cerebellar atrophy; in two cases the NEG was normal; and six showed cortical or diffuse cerebellous atrophy.

PSYCHOLOGICAL FINDINGS

The occupational and educational data on the patients indicated that they belonged to the lower middle class of Chile. Most of them were workers, and only three had occupations of higher social prestige. The biographic and educational data for 16 patients showed that the intellectual level prior to the illness was normal in 11, subnormal in one and deficient in four.

Table 34-1 shows the median and range of the test scores and of educational level and age. The scores are tabulated according to degree of intellectual disturbance in Table 34-2. Scores which do not indicate impairment occur in three cases on the similarity test, one case on the MPD, and none on the Grassi test.

As is well known, the scores of comprehension and vocabulary tests, are not greatly altered by intellectual impairment and generally reflect the school level. Only one case showed in both tests scores lower than those expected on the basis of his educational level, and two cases with very little schooling had a comparatively high score on one of the two tests. This would suggest that taken by itself educational level is not a reliable indicator, and indeed the correlations between the test scores and educational level were not statistically significant for the most part. The coefficients are provided in Table 34-3. The score of the word evocation test was the only one exhibiting a significant correlation with educational level.

Table 34-4 summarizes the correlation coefficients between scores of the different tests. The vocabulary, comprehension, and similarity tests appear well correlated, revealing the presence of a common factor – perhaps of general mental ability. The Grassi test was also well correlated with the similarity and vocabulary tests, showing that it too was influenced by the capacity for abstract thinking.

Since the group comprised patients with severe brain damage, it is easy to explain the small dispersion observed in the Grassi and MPD tests (see Table 34-1). Nevertheless, it is important that there was no correlation between the impairment levels explored by each of these tests – hence the desirability of using both tests

TABLE 34–1

MEDIAN AND RANGE OF THE TEST SCORES AND OF EDUCATION
LEVEL AND AGE

Test	Units	Median	Scores (range)
vocabulary	mental age (years)	10	8–16
similarity	point in standard scale	5	1–9
comprehension	point in standard scale	7	4–12
word evocation	words per minute	17	9–37
Grassi (GBST)	points	12	1–19.5
MPD	degree	58	14.5–150
educational background	years of study	grade 3	illiterate–grade 10
age	years	45 years	33–60 years

TABLE 34–2

SCORES ON THE GRASSI, MPD, AND SIMILARITY TESTS BY DEGREE
OF INTELLECTUAL DISTURBANCE

Diagnosis	Grassi range	N	MPD range	N	Similarity range	N
deterioration	0–15.5	10	60–150	8		
mental decay	16–19	5	21–59	7	<9	13
normal	19.5–26	0	0–20	1	9–11	3

TABLE 34–3

CORRELATION COEFFICIENTS
BETWEEN THE SCORES OF THE
TESTS AND EDUCATIONAL LEVEL

	r_s	p
vocabulary	0.21	>0.10
comprehension	0.40	>0.10
similarity	0.36	>0.10
word evocation	0.58	<0.02
MPD	0.14	>0.10
Grassi (GBST)	0.44	>0.10

together to detect the type of alteration (15). Furthermore, the MPD did not correlate significantly with educational or previous intellectual levels, indicating its efficiency as a means of recognizing mental deterioration. It is important to note that the similarity test, which is not correlated with educational level, correlates well with the Grassi test. The common characteristics that they detect may be organicity and abstractive function as reflected in manual and verbal performance.

RELATIONS BETWEEN RESULTS OF NEG
AND MPD AND GRASSI TESTS

It was desirable to determine whether or not the organic alterations revealed by the NEG had a detectable psychological expression. Since our group was very small only the presence or absence of brain atrophy and the areas involved were considered. Three groups were formed according to the diagnosis indicated by the two tests: (I) normality, (II) weakness, and (III) serious deterioration (see Table 34–5).

The severe alteration shown by the test scores agrees with the presence of atrophy involving both cerebral areas in six of the 13 patients. There is a lower degree of deterioration revealed by the tests in two patients with only one area involved. The relation is not clear in three patients who had atrophy in only one area and obtained a bad score on the tests, and in two with normal NEGs for whom the tests revealed severe deterioration. The reason for this apparent contradiction may be that these

270 / *Ferrer et al.*

TABLE 34–4

CORRELATION COEFFICIENTS BETWEEN THE SCORES OF THE DIFFERENT
TESTS (INFERIOR TRIANGLE) AND SIGNIFICANCE LEVEL (SUPERIOR TRIANGLE)

	Vocabulary	Comprehension	Evocation	Similarity	Grassi	MPD
vocabulary		<0.05	>0.10	<0.001	<0.05	>0.10
comprehension	0.48		>0.10	<0.01	>0.10	>0.10
word evocation	0.32	0.09		>0.10	>0.10	>0.10
similarity	0.72	0.64	0.29		<0.01	>0.10
Grassi	0.51	0.35	0.34	0.68		>0.10
MPD	0.16	0.05	0.07	0.26	0.15	

TABLE 34–5

DISTRIBUTION OF NEG RESULTS BY LEVEL OF
DETERIORATION (ACCORDING TO GRASSI AND MPD TESTS)

Deterioration Grassi, MPD	Internal and cortical	Cortical	Internal	Normal
III–III	3			
III–II	3	1		1
II–III		1	1	1
II–II		1		
II–I			1	

TABLE 34–6

DISTRIBUTION OF NEG RESULTS BY AGE

Age (years)	Internal and cortical	Cortical	Internal	Normal
50 or older	4		1	
40–49	2	2	1	
39 or less		1		2

two patients were the only ones under 36 years of age.

To determine whether the frequency distribution indicates a relation between the results of the NEG and the tests, arbitrary ranks, 3, 2, 1, and 0, were assigned to the pneumoencephalographic results, indicating atrophy in both areas, cortical atrophy, internal atrophy, and normal condition, respectively. The correlation coefficient is 0.68 showing that the distribution is not random ($p < 0.01$).

Since the two youngest patients appeared inversely placed in the distribution, it seemed pertinent to consider age as a factor in the psychologic expression of atrophy indicated by the NEG (see Table 34-6). The atrophy involving both areas was found to be more frequent among the older patients. The correlation coefficient for this variable was 0.67 ($p < 0.01$), which indicates that even though our group was rather young, the extension of the atrophy is related to age.

RELATION BETWEEN DEGREE OF
NEUROLOGICAL DISTURBANCE AND
PSYCHOLOGICAL DETERIORATION

In general, all the patients exhibited tonus disturbances recognized by most of the following signs: coenervation, hypomimia, hypokinesis, relaxing difficulty during passive movements, abundant movements, perseveration of imposed attitudes, motor iteration and spasticity or generalized rigidity. They also exhibited organic alterations in psychological performance, showing intellectual deterioration of different degrees. Nevertheless, the intensity of the tonus disturbances and the degree of psychological deterioration were not significantly correlated. This may be because the tonus disturbances are a consequence of different forms of CNS damage than those which induce alterations in psychological tests. Since our group comprised very deteriorated patients, either from a neurological or a psychological point of view, it was not possible to obtain further information concerning the relation between the two kinds of disturbance.

A comparison of patient behaviour during the psychological interviews with that observed by the neurologists, showed some traits in agreement: low self-criticism, little effective resonance, loss of impulse, indifference towards physical disability, and lack of consciousness of psychic illness. During the administration of the psychological tests these traits were recognized through the lack of interest in looking for new solutions, absence of catastrophic reactions, and a characteristic pattern of perseveration, which appeared to be the consequence of general apathy.

CORRELATION BETWEEN NEUROLOGIC SYNDROMES AND OTHER VARIABLES

The study of the age of onset of the different neurological syndromes showed that only the cerebellous type was sufficiently regular, since it started in all patients after 45 years of age. The chi-square test for age and appearance (corrected for continuity) was 5.8 with 1 d.f. ($p < 0.02$).

No significant correlations between the form of severity of the neurological syndromes and drinking habits, daily alcohol intake, or commonly used alcoholic beverages were found. With respect to the influence of diet, approximately one fourth of the patients had a rather balanced diet; the remainder exhibited marked nutritional deficiency.

It is interesting to point out that six of the 23 patients exhibited lesions of tuberculosis (four active, two inactive). These six patients were distributed randomly in the groups of neurological syndromes, and only two of them had a slight anemia, showing that this disturbance was not an important etiological factor in neurological damage.

DISCUSSION

We should like to discuss first the usefulness of the generally accepted classification of the multiple clinical forms of neurological complication of alcoholism. Since most authors have studied these forms without considering simultaneous damage at other CNS levels, they have been led to deduce erroneously that in each syndrome alcohol damages exclusively one CNS structure.

The main criticisms of the classification can be summarized as follows:
1
The limits between syndromes are not precise, and the anatomico-pathological substratum of the whole symptomatology is not sufficiently established.
2
Some of the syndromes are exclusively characterized by anatomico-pathological findings.
3
Clinical forms with known causal factors are grouped together with diseases of controversial pathogenesis. Thus, the Gayet-Wernicke syndrome is generally considered a cerebral beri-beri; while the factors inducing the axial demyelination of the *corpus callosum* in the Marchiafava-Bignami disease is under discussion (24).
4
The evolution of acute forms is not considered.

Concerning the lack of precision as to the limits between syndromes, many authors agree that Wernicke's syndrome and Korsakoff's disease cannot be differentiated by their symptomatology. Furthermore, Marchiafava-Bignami's disease and Morell's cortical atrophy are considered as only one disease by some.

Respecting the evolution of acute forms, in

our group of patients these were followed by syndromes which generally did not fit any of the classical descriptions. We considered that it would be convenient to classify the permanent neurological damage observed in alcoholics into two classes according to the form of onset: (*a*) clinical pictures with acute onset, and (*b*) clinical pictures with insidious onset. This difference should be based only on anamnestic data, since once the damage is established, no differences between the two forms can be recognized.

Possibly the most important result of our study is the finding that once a permanent neurological complication of alcoholism has been established, all levels of the CNS are more or less involved. In fact, during the course of a case of overt polyneuropathy, diffuse damage of the CNS could be demonstrated by clinical, psychological and NEG examinations. This has also been observed in cerebellopathies and spinal syndromes. Furthermore, in three patients without cerebellar signs, the NEG showed atrophy of the cerebellar cortex. Other authors have found similar results by taking a NEG in cases of alcoholic polyneuropathy (21, 23, 30). The natural consequence of this finding is that classification should be based on the predominant signs rather than on the limits of the damage. It is rather surprising that in our group the EEG was normal in 13 of 17 patients examined.

As far as etiopathogenesis is concerned, experiments in animals and humans (volunteers and prisoners in concentration camps) have definitely demonstrated that Wernicke's syndrome, Korsakoff's polyneuritic psychosis, and polyneuritis are consequences of thiamin deficiency, acute in encephalopathies and chronic in polyneuropathies (2, 10, 11, 13, 19, 20, 22, 28, 35, 37). Thiamin deficiency may also induce subclinical polyneuropathy, as is suggested by studies of neural conduction time in chronic alcoholics (25, 40). On the other hand, pathogenic factors in cerebellopathies, Marchiafava-Bignami's disease, pons myelinosis, spinal syndromes, and myopathies, are yet unknown. In general, the authors who have discussed these conditions stress the importance of nutritional deficiencies (especially of vitamins), and of gastric and liver complications.

A high percentage (75 per cent) of our patients, both in the periods of drinking and during abstinence, had a diet deficient in proteins and vitamins. Neurological changes could not be ascribed to niacin deficiency, since none showed signs of pellagra (34). The symptom of burning feet, which was present in the patients with polyneuropathy, has been considered a symptom of deficiency of pantothenic acid (4). The importance of thiamin and pyridoxine deficiency in our group could only be suspected from the nutritional data.

In our group there were only three cases of liver cirrhosis, one of fatty liver, and three of liver damage revealed only by liver function tests. This suggests that excessive ingestion of alcohol damages the liver and CNS independently, and that neurological damages are not a conseqeunce of disturbances in liver function. Cyanocobalamine deficiency seems also to be irrelevant as a cause of CNS damage in alcoholics, since anemia was rarely observed in our group.

As for psychological deterioration, this can be ascribed to cerebral atrophy, since there was a significant correlation between performance on the psychological test and the extension of the atrophy. Age seems also to play a role, the deterioration being more pronounced in older patients.

Unfortunately, there are too few comparable studies on psychic deterioration and brain damage from causes other than alcoholism. Thus, it is not possible to know whether or not a form of mental decay peculiar to alcoholism exists. Generally, the behaviour of our alcoholic patients appeared similar to that observed in non-alcoholic patients with frontal syndrome.

SUMMARY

Twenty-three alcoholic patients exhibiting permanent neurological damage were studied from the neurological and psychological points of view. The results showed that in every patient practically all levels of the CNS were involved, and that all exhibited psychological impairment of different degree. No differences were observed between the cases with acute as opposed to insidious onset of the neurological or psychological damage. It was found that the neurological syndromes could evolve without liver damage, and that the role of nutritional deficiency was not clear, since in some cases neither liver damage nor nutritional deficiencies were observed. The generally accepted classification of alcoholic neurological syndromes was criticized on the basis of the results obtained in the present study.

REFERENCES

1
ADAMS, R.D., VICTOR, M., & ELLIOTT, L.
Central pontine myelinolysis
Arch. Neurol. & Psychiat., **81**: 154, 1959
2
ALAJOUANINE, TH., CASTAIGNE, P., & FOURNIER, E.
Biochimie des manifestations encéphaliques de l'alcoolisme
Rev. Neurol., **94**: 447, 1956
3
BACHER, F., CHANOIT, P., ROUQUETTE, J., & VERDEAUX, G.
Épilepsie et alcoolisme
Études statistiques comparatives de critères EEG
Rev. Neurol., **103**: 228, 1960
4
BEAN, W.B., HODGES, E.E., & DAUM, K.E.
Pantothenic acid deficiency induced in human subjects
J. Clin. Invest., **34**: 1073, 1955
5
BENNETT, A.E., MOWERY, G.L., & FORT, J.T.
Brain damage from chronic alcoholism
The diagnosis of intermediate stage of alcoholic brain disease
Am. J. Psychol., **116**: 705, 1960
6
BERNARD, A., DELATTRE, A., & LAMELIN, P.
Le mécanisme d'action de l'alcool sur la muqueuse gastrique, sa propiété higroscopique et déshydratante
Acta gastroentérol. Belge, **27**: 129, 1964
7
BÜHRER, O.A.
Ueber 204 Fälle von Delirium Tremens
Münch. med. Wchnschr., **106**: 1016, 1964
8
DELAY, I., BOUDIN, G., BRION, S., & BARBIZET, J.
Étude anatomo-clinique de huit encéphalopaties alcooliques
Encéphale, **47**: 99, 1958
9
DELAY, J., BRION, S., ESCOUROLLE, R., & SANCHEZ, A.
Rapports entre la dégénerscence du corps calleux de Marchiafava-Bignami et la sclérose laminaire corticale de Morel
Encéphale, **48**: 281, 1959

10
DE WARDENER, H.E. & LENNOX, B.
Cerebral beriberi (Wernicke's encephalopathy)
Lancet, **i**: 11, 1947
11
DREYFUS, P.M. & VICTOR, M.
Effects of thiamine deficiency on the central nervous system
Am. J. Clin. Nutr., **9**: 414, 1961
12
EKBOM, K., HED, R., KIRSTEIN, L., & ASTROM, K.E.
Muscular affections in chronic alcoholism
Arch. Neurol., **10**: 449, 1964
13
FENNELLY, I., BAKER, H., FRANK, O., & LEEVY, C.M.
Peripheral neuropathy of the alcoholic
I. Aetiological role of aneurin and other B-complex vitamins
Brit. Med. J., **ii**: 1290, 1964
14
GIRARD, P.F., DEVIC, M., & GARDE, A.
L'encéphalopathie de Gayet-Wernicke des alcooliques
Rev. Neurol., **94**: 493, 1956
15
GRUNER, I.E.
Sur la pathologie des encéphalopathies alcooliques
Rev. Neurol., **94**: 682, 1956
16
HÉCAEN, H. & DE AJURIAGUERRA, J.
Les encéphalites alcooliques subaiguës et chroniques
Rev. Neurol., **94**: 528, 1956
17
HED, R., LUNDMARK, C., FAHLGREN, H., & ORELL, S.
Syndrome musculaire aigu chez les alcooliques chroniques
Acta med. scandinav., **171**: 585, 1962
18
HIBBS, R.G., BLACK, W.C., FERRAUS, V.J., WEILBAECHER, D.G., & BURCH, G.E.
Alcoholic cardiomyopathy, an electromicroscopic study
Am. Heart J., **69**: 766, 1965
19
HOCKADAY, T.D.R., HOCKADAY, J.M., & RUSHWORTH, G.
Motor neuropathy associated with abnormal pyruvate metabolism unaffected by thiamin
J. Neurol. Neurosurg. Psychiat., **29**: 119, 1966
20
HORNABROOK, R.W.
Alcoholic neuropathy
Am. J. Clin. Nutr., **9**: 398, 1961
21
LAFON, R., PAGES, P., PASSOUANT, P., LABAUGE, R., MINVIELLE, J., & CADILHAC, J.
Les données de la pneumoencéphalographie et de l'électroencéphalographie au cours de l'alcoolisme chronique
Rev. Neurol., **94**: 611, 1956
22
LEEVY, C.M., BAKER, H., TENHOVE, W., FRANK, O., & CHERRICK, C.R.

B-complex vitamins in liver disease of the alcoholic
Am. J. Clin. Nutr., **16**: 339, 1965

23
LEREBOULLET, J., PLUVINAGE, R., & AMSTUTZ, C.L.
Aspects cliniques et électroencéphalographiques des atrophies cérébrales alcooliques
Rev. Neurol., **94**: 674, 1956

24
MANCALL, E.L.
Some unusual neurological diseases complicating chronic alcoholism
Am. J. Clin. Nutr., **9**: 404, 1961

25
MAWDSLEY, C. & MAYER, R.F.
Nerve conduction in alcoholic polyneuropathy
Brain, **88**: 335, 1965

26
MICHAUX, L. & BUGE, A.
Étude clinique des délires alcooliques aigus
Rev. Neurol., **94**: 480, 1956

27
NIELSEN, J.
Delirium tremens in Copenhagen
Acta psychiat. scandinav. (suppl. 187), **41**, 1965

28
NORTH, I.P.C. & SINCLAIR, H.M.
Nutritional neuropathy (chronic thiamin deficiency in the rat)
Arch. Pathol., **61**: 351, 1956

29
NUÑEZ, R.
Polineuritis y sindrome espástico en el alcoholismo crónico
Santiago de Chile, Universidad de Chile, 1954

30
POSTEL, J. & COSSA, P.
L'atrophie cérébrale des alcooliques chroniques, étude pneumoencéphalographique
Rev. Neurol., **94**: 604, 1956

31
SCHULLER, E.
Les encéphalopathies carentielles de l'ethylisme chronique
Presse Méd., **69**: 1025, 1961

32
SCHULLER, E. & ENDTZ, L.J.
Épreuves fonctionelles biochimiques en neurologie
L'épreuve de pyrucicemie après surcharge glucosée
Presse Méd., **68**: 1933, 1960

33
SCHULLER, E. & ENDTZ, L.J.
Épreuves fonctionelles biochimiques en neurologie
L'épreuve de xanthurenurie après charge en tryptophane
Presse Méd., **68**: 2037, 1960

34
SPIES, T.D. & DE WOLF, H.F.
Observations on the etiological relation of severe alcoholism to pellagra
Am. J. Med. Sc., **186**: 521, 1933

35
SWANK, R.L. & PRADOS, M.
Avian thiamin deficiency
Arch. Neurol. & Psychiat., **47**: 97, 1942

36
THIEBAUT, I., ROHMER, F., & ISCH, F.
Considérations à propos de 3 cas d'encéphalopathie alcoolique
Rev. Neurolog., **94**: 594, 1956

37
TREMOLIÈRES, J., GRIFFATON, G., & LOWY, R.
Aspects biochimiques de l'oxydation de l'alcool
Rev. alcoolisme, **5**: 39, 1959

38
VICTOR, M. & ADAMS, R.D.
On the etiology of the alcoholic neurologic disease
Am. J. Clin. Nutr., **9**: 379, 1961

39
VICTOR, M., ADAMS, R.D., & MANCALL, E.
A restricted form of cerebellar cortical degeneration occurring in alcoholic patients
Arch. Neurol., **1**: 579, 1959

40
WANAMAKER, W.M. & SKILLMAN, T.G.
Motor nerve conduction in alcoholics
Quart. J. Stud. Alc., **27**: 16, 1966

41
WIESER, S.
Alkoholismus II: Psychiatrische und neurologische Komplikationen
Fortschr. Neurol. Psychiat., **33**: 349, 1965

42
WORMS, R., BERTRAND, I., GUILLAIN, G., & GONDA, M.H.
Le cerveau des cirrhotiques
A propos de 30 observations anatomo-cliniques
Bull. Mém. Soc. Méd. Hôp. (Paris), **76**: 1152, 1960

MARIO CASTRO

Department of Radiology
Institute of Neurosurgery
University of Chile
National Health Service of Chile
Santiago, Chile

35

Alcoholic Encephalomyelopathies: Pneumoencephalographic Studies

The increasing use of air examinations for the study of neurological and psychiatric patients during recent years has revealed that brain involvement in alcoholic patients is not an exceptional occurrence (4, 6, 7, 15). Pneumoencephalography permits the study of the brain *in vivo*, and in experienced hands provides full information on the state of the cortex and ventricular system; their enlargement is indicative of a reduction in the size of the brain, i.e. atrophy (1, 3, 14).

MATERIAL AND METHODS

Seventeen patients with a diagnosis of chronic alcoholism and with neurological involvement were submitted to radiological studies. In all of them an air lumbar encephalogram was taken according to the Robertson-Lindgren technique of fractional pneumoencephalography (9, 13). The average amount of air injected was 45 cc per examination. Spinal fluid was not withdrawn unless specially requested for analysis; the mean quantity removed was 6.5 ml.

The patients were divided into four groups according to the main symptoms dominating the clinical picture. All exhibited impairment of intellectual performance in some degree. The groups were as follows:

I
patients with hypertonicity, spasticity, and pyramidal signs (nine patients);

II
patients with cerebellar dysfunction (four patients);

III
patients with paraparesis as the main neurological disturbance (two patients);

IV
patients with a diagnosis of polyneuropathy (two patients).

The evaluation of the pneumoencephalograms was accomplished by measuring the septum-caudate line in the anterior-posterior projection (2, 16). This line represents the shortest distance between the attachment of the septum pellucidum in the corpus callosum to the nearest point of the caudate nucleus. The

TABLE 35-1

PNEUMOENCEPHALOGRAPHIC FINDINGS IN 17 ALCOHOLIC
PATIENTS BY DIAGNOSTIC GROUP (SEE TEST)

	Group I	Group II	Group III	Group IV	Total
normal pneumoencephalogram	1	–	–	–	1
cortical atrophy	1	–	–	–	1
internal atrophy	2	1	–	–	3
diffuse atrophy	5	2	1	2	10
cerebellar atrophy	–	1	1	–	2
total	9	4	2	2	17

appearance of the subarachnoid sulci compared to what is seen in normal cases provided an indication of cortical atrophy. The pneumoencephalogram permits one to distinguish three types of atrophy: (*a*) central or periventricular, which is manifested in dilation of the lateral ventricles and the third ventricle; (*b*) cortical, which involves a widening of the subarachnoid sulci with confluence in some cases to produce images that may be compared to hollow pouches; and (*c*) mixed or diffuse, which is the result of a combination of the first two types.

RESULTS

The findings are summarized in Table 35-1.

DISCUSSION

The high frequency of degenerative cerebral disorder might be in part because use was not made of our routine system of evalution of different degrees of ventricular dilation. We preferred to use measurements since, as Troland *et al.* point out: "measurement would 1) aid in obviating the factor of personal judgment in analyzing encephalograms for evidence of dilation, 2) form a basis of comparison between cases and 3) provide comparison between repeat examinations in the same cases" (16). However, the incidence of radiologically demonstrable atrophy in our patients (94.11 per cent) was higher than that reported by others for larger series of alcoholic patients: for example, Postel and Cossa – 77.27 per cent of 34 patients (12); Lafon *et al.* – 78 per cent

of 100 patients (5); and Lereboullet, Pluvinage, and Amstutz – 50 per cent of 150 encephalograms (8). This higher percentage is probably due largely to the selection of our series from patients with definite clinical signs of organic brain disease.

Diffuse atrophy, i.e. the combination of the internal or periventricular and the cortical varieties, was the most frequent type found in our cases. The cortical involvement affects the frontal lobes mainly, as other authors have pointed out, and in three of our cases we observed dilation of the sulci corresponding to the corpus callosum and cinguli gyri.

In group II, composed of four alcoholics with cerebellar symptomatology, we were able to demonstrate a reduction in size of the cerebellum in two; in its pure form in one and in the other with diffuse involvement of the brain. The other two patients in this group had diffuse atrophy. The lack of cerebellar atrophy in these two cases is perhaps not surprising since in other cases (one of group I and another from group II) evident structural abnormalities of the cerebellum were found although the patients did not present clinical symptoms of cerebellar dysfunction. This is, therefore, the converse of Murphy and Arana's point that "air study of the brain, particularly in lateral views with the occipital region of the head superior, can reveal unexpected cerebellar disease" (10).

We do not feel that the size of the cisterna magna is a suitable indicator of the size of the cerebellum since there are variations in the size of the cisterna and Robertson has described anomalies of this structure without evidence of atrophy of the cerebellum.

Since our sample was very small and selected,

reliable conclusions cannot be drawn. However, it may be pointed out, in agreement with Peron and Gayno (11), that we consider cerebral atrophy in the alcoholic patient to be an unfavourable prognostic sign.

REFERENCES

1
BERG, K.J. & LÖNNUM, A.
Ventricular size in relation to cranial size
Acta Radiol. [Diagn.] (Stockholm), **4**: 65, 1966
2
ENGESET, A., & LÖNNUM, A.
Third ventricles of 12 mm diameter width or more
A preliminary report
Acta Radiol., **50**: 5, 1958
3
HAUG, J.O.
Pneumoencephalographic studies in mental disease
Acta psychiat. scandinav., **38**: Suppl. 165, 1962
4
KIRCHER, J.P. & PIERSON, C.-A.
Toxicomanies et atrophie cérébrale; essais thérapeutiques basés sur la pneumoencéphalographie
Rev. Neurol., **94**: 607, 1956
5
LAFON, R., PAGES, P., PASSOUANT, P., LABAUGE, R., MINVIELLE, J., & CADILHAC, J.
Les données de la pneumoencéphalographie et de l'électroencéphalographie au cours de l'alcoolisme chronique
Rev. Neurol., **94**: 611, 1956
6
LEDESMA JIMENO, A.
Estudios neumoencefalográficos en el alcoholismo
Rev. Clin. Española, **68**: 161, 1958
7
LEREBOULLET, J. & PLUVINAGE, R.
L'atrophie cérébrale des alcooliques
Ses conséquences médico-sociales
Bull. Acad. Nat. Méd., **140**: 398, 1956
8
LEREBOULLET, J., PLUVINAGE, R., & AMSTUTZ, CL.
Aspects cliniques et électroencéphalographiques des atrophies cérébrales alcooliques
Rev. Neurol., **94**: 674, 1956
9
LINDGREN, E.
Encephalography in cerebral atrophy
Acta Radiol., **35**: 277, 1951
10
MURPHY, J.P. & ARANA, R.
The pneumoencephalogram of cerebellar atrophy
Am. J. Roentgen., **57**: 545, 1947
11
PERÓN, N. & GAYNO, M.
Atrophie cérébrale des ethyliques
Rev. Neurol., **94**: 621, 1956
12
POSTEL, J. & COSSA, P.
L'atrophie cérébrale des alcooliques chroniques, étude pneumoencéphalographique
Rev. Neurol., **94**: 604, 1956
13
ROBERTSON, E.G.
Pneumoencephalography
Springfield, Ill.: Charles C. Thomas, 1957
14
RUGGIERO, G.
L'encéphalographie fractionnée
Paris: Masson, 1957
15
SKILLICORN, S.A.
Presenile cerebellar ataxia in chronic alcoholics
Neurology, **5**: 527, 1958
16
TROLAND, CH., BAXTER, D., & SCHATZKI, R.
Observations on encephalographic findings in cerebral trauma
J. Neurosurg., **3**: 390, 1946

STEFAN WIESER

Municipal Clinic for Nervous Diseases
Bremen, West Germany

36

Treatment of the Chronic Neuropsychiatric Complications of Alcoholism

It is well known that the fundamental work on the clinical classification of the neuropsychiatric complications of alcoholism was done by Thomas Sutton, who first described the clinical features of delirium tremens, and by Marcel, who introduced the term "alcoholic hallucinosis." Further landmarks in the field were the descriptions of alcoholic encephalopathies and polyneuropathies by Korsakoff and Wernicke. Finally, Bonnhoeffer completed the basic work with his comprehensive monograph, "The Acute Mental Diseases in Habitual Drinkers," which appeared in 1901. This system of disease entities, consisting of acute intoxication, delirium tremens, alcoholic hallucinosis, Korsakoff psychosis, and alcoholic brain deterioration, has been accepted by clinicians throughout the world. It has proven quite stable for many decades; not one of the various schools of psychiatry of the last hundred years has deviated from it very greatly.

In the 1940s a reappraisal of these traditional concepts began to take place. The first new impulse came from Isbell and his coworkers as a result of their basic study on the alcohol withdrawal process. Their findings have been confirmed by many subsequent clinical and pathophysiological studies of the withdrawal syndrome.

Less well known, but nevertheless of great importance, is the work of Spillane on nutritional disorders of the nervous system. His studies of the neurological syndromes in such disorders gave us new insights into the pathophysiology and clinical classification of the encephalo-, myelo-, and polyneuropathies in alcoholics.

According to a more modern clinical classification (as shown in Table 36–1) it is necessary to distinguish first between intoxications of the excito-inhibitory type (so-called "normal" drunkenness) and other forms of alcohol intoxication as well as the hangover syndrome. With the latter we also have to include some epileptic seizures occurring in alcoholics.

The withdrawal syndrome also represents a group of psychiatric complications with a rather acute course. Since I have to limit myself to the chronic neuropsychiatric complications, I shall not deal with the treatment of hyperesthetic-

TABLE 36–1

CLINICAL CLASSIFICATION OF THE
NEUROPSYCHIATRIC COMPLICATIONS
OF ALCOHOLISM

Acute intoxications

excito-inhibitory type ("normal" drunkenness)
deviant types ("pathological" intoxication and other
atypical reactions to alcohol)
hangover syndrome (e.g. epileptic seizures)

Psychoses in chronic intoxication
acute hallucinosis
paranoid and paranoid-hallucinatory psychoses (about
10 per cent are chronic hallucinoses of verbal and visual
type and paranoid-hallucinatory (schizoform) psychoses
confusional states
other symptomatic psychoses (Bonhoeffer)

Withdrawal syndromes
hyperaesthetic-emotional syndrome
delirium tremens
epileptoid seizures

Psychoses in medical complications of alcoholism
somnolent and comatose states (e.g. liver insufficiency)

Neuropsychiatric syndromes in encephalopolyneuropathies
acute confusional state (Korsakoff's psychosis)
pseudoencephalitis Wernicke
dementia of Korsakoff type
chronic mental deterioration
epileptic seizures of grand mal and psychomotor types
polyneuritis
nicotinic acid deficiency
chronic polyneuritis
systematic cerebellar atrophy
Marchiafava-Bignami disease

emotional syndrome, delirium tremens, and
epileptoid seizures during withdrawal, which
belong to the acute category of disorders.

The next diagnostic category comprises the
symptomatic psychoses in chronic alcohol intoxication. The concept "alcoholic hallucinosis,"
as used in classical psychiatry, has been shown
to be too narrow. Though hallucinatory states
are quite common, other types of acute exogenous reaction occur as well. Among the most
frequent are the transient acute acoustic hallucinoses, acute paranoid conditions which resemble short schizophrenic episodes, visual hallucinoses with complete orientation in reality,
short confusional conditions, and states of psychotic excitement. In chronic alcoholism it

would seem that not only paranoid-hallucinatory
psychoses may occur, but any of the known
exogenous psychotic episodes.

Although most of these episodes are of
rather short duration, about 10 per cent persist
even after the individual has stopped drinking.
These conditions, which begin as clear-cut cases
of transient exogenous psychoses and end as
chronic schizoform and hallucinatory or delusional psychoses, have led to much discussion
about the concepts of exogenous and endogenous psychoses. For present purposes theoretical considerations are of secondary importance, especially since therapy is directed not
towards etiology but towards the predominant
symptoms of the disease. Freyhahn has aptly
called this approach the treatment of target
symptoms.

These cases, as well as chronic delusional
psychoses of the Kraepelin paranoia type and
delusions of jealousy should be treated with
phenothiazines alone or combined with butyrophenones. Among the phenothiazines we prefer
trifluperazine, chlorperphenazine, or dyxirazine.
Among the butyrophenones we have found
haloperidol and triperidol to be most valuable.
Different drugs of these two groups with recommended dosages are listed in Table 36-2.

The so-called "alcoholic epilepsy" is the link
between the psychoses and the neurological
complications of chronic alcoholism. The term
is, however, too broad. Actually there is no such
disease entity as "alcoholic epilepsy," and therefore it is preferable to speak of epileptic seizures
in different phases and organic complications of
alcoholism. The following points are relevant
in this respect:

1
Patients with genuine and residual epilepsy who
later in life become alcoholics are by no means
rare. In such cases therapy will be directed towards the basic illness. In other words, the complete arsenal of anti-epileptic drugs is indicated
according to the particular form of the seizures.
2
A latent liability to seizures can be activated in
the hangover phase of relatively heavy intoxication.
3
Epileptiform fits sometimes also occur in the

TABLE 36–2

RECOMMENDED DOSAGES OF PHENOTHIAZINE AND
BUTYROPHENONE DRUGS

	Generic name	Commercial name	Daily dosage (mg)
phenothiazines	chlorpromazine	Largactil	100–500
	levomepromazine	Nozinan	50–300
	prochlorpemazine	Tementil	40–125
	thioproperazine	Majeptil	10–70
	perphenazine	Trilifan	15–60
	trifluoperazine	Terfluzine	20–120
	fluphenazine	Moditen	10–40
	thioridazine	Melleril	50–500
	dioxyrazine	Esucos	50–100
	propericiazine	Neuleptil	20–60
butyrophenones	haloperidol	Haloperidol	5–15
	haloanison	Sedalande	60–120
	triperidol	Triperidol	1–6
	benperidol	Frenactil	2–6

withdrawal phase after previous adaptation to alcohol.

4
Seizures often occur in the late phases of alcoholism, without relation to particular states of acute or chronic intoxication. As a rule in such cases, the seizures are manifestations of irreversible anatomico-pathological processes. Usually these are brain atrophies, based either on alcoholic encephalopathies or on nutritional disorders of the nervous system caused indirectly by alcohol.

The generally accepted treatment schedule of epileptic seizures in chronic encephalopathies in alcoholics is based on the distinction between grand mal and psychomotor seizures. Most frequently grand mal seizures are seen and are best controlled by a combination of hydantoines and barbiturates. We start with 1/4 tab of a barbiturate and 1/2 tab of a hydantoine twice a day, and increase the dosage gradually to the level of tolerance. Psychomotor seizures are rather rare and sometimes occur in the final states of alcoholic dementia. In such cases a combination of anti-epileptic drugs is indicated, with an increased amount of barbiturate.

If I am to adhere strictly to my topic, the chronic neuropsychiatric complications of alcoholism, my contribution must be limited to what I have said. I have not touched on the treatment of chronic mental deterioration in alcoholics,

but there is not much to be said about such treatment since it is largely a matter of custodial care. The situation is similar in the case of chronic polyneuritis and systematic cerebellar atrophy. Nor am I able to contribute to the problems of Marchiafava-Bignami disease therapy. Since this syndrome apparently occurs only in Italian and Latin-American populations, I have had no personal experience with it and hope to profit from contributions to the topic presented by others at this Symposium.

Epidemiological and Preventive Aspects

Epidemiology, that is, the study of disease as a problem of human masses, taken as populations and smaller groups, is the basic instrument of social medicine. Here man is studied in his environment, which is defined as everything outside himself.

According to Leavell the environment includes the society in which the man lives, as well as the numerous complex interpersonal relationships which may markedly influence his health. In this sense, social medicine is almost synonymous with preventive medicine, broadly defined by Winslow, as the science and art of preventing disease, prolonging life, and promoting the health and the physical and mental efficiency of man. The epidemiological method, in its widest modern meaning, is fundamental to the study of preventive and social medicine.

Any epidemiological study requires an accurate definition of the disease investigated as well as adequate bases for proper diagnosis. The lack of good operational definitions in the field of mental diseases has impaired progress in research.

Around 1940, as Jellinek said, there emerged a "new approach to alcoholism," which established scientifically the criteria necessary to analyze this problem in a more systematic way. We owe to him the diagnostic criteria for distinguishing different types of drinkers and for studying the developmental sequences from the moderate consumption of alcoholic beverages to the ultimate disease of alcoholism. In his monograph, Phases in the Drinking History of Alcoholics, *he established the natural history of the disease through the clinical study of two thousand cases and proved that the final phase of this process is indeed a disease. It is possible to define this disease in terms of clinical symptomatology, to follow its evolution, and to isolate it from other forms of excessive drinking. It is possible also to systematize information respecting other forms of pathological drinking, and to study the organic disturbances regarded today as complications of the pathological process referred to as alcoholism. The goals of treatment, the necessary elements for prophylaxis, and the lines of systematic action to improve mental health with respect to alcohol can now be clearly appreciated.*

It is desirable to emphasize that this new approach to alcoholism sprang basically from the same source as the study of psychopathological problems, namely, clinical work. The clinical studies that followed Jellinek's research have demonstrated that psychological and especially physical dependence on alcohol are the fundaments from which all other serious manifestations of the disease emerge; the studies have indicated also that such dependence is irreversible, at least in the present state of our knowledge. This irreversibility shows that the disease – no matter what initiated the habit of excessive ingestion of alcoholic beverages – involves pathophysiological substrata conditioning physical dependence and probably located in the central nervous system.

Consequently the goal today in the treatment of alcoholism is complete abstinence from alcoholic beverages; preventive action is directed towards discouraging the habit of excessive drinking, the first step towards alcoholism, and improvement in mental health in relation to alcohol use is sought through education to change sociocultural patterns fostering intemperance.

In summary, alcoholism is defined by psychological, and above all, physical dependence on alcohol. It is a pathogenic entity appearing after a long process in which psychological, biological and sociocultural elements all play a role; and these elements have organic, psychological, and sociocultural consequences which affect the patient's life.

Alcoholism is not an exception in mental pathology, since its etiology is multiple and its clinical manifestations are multiform. The tentative conclusion of Böök that any unitary explanation of etiology, even when the condition is considered a special type of mental disease or clinical entity, will not contribute to the development of psychiatric research fits very well in the case of alcoholism. The diffusion of this concept of alcoholism among medical professionals and the general public has produced good results, which can be appreciated in the field of pathophysiological and clinical research. At the same time it has encouraged epidemiological investigations, which are necessary in order to discover the ecology of a disease having so many sociocultural repercussions. A satisfactory operational definition of alcoholism makes possible prevalence studies to measure the extent of the problem, and these in turn provide the basis of all health programs designed to achieve more rational control of the disease.

When alcoholism is defined as psychological and physical dependence on alcohol, the objectives of a preventive program are as follows:
1
Tertiary prevention (of death or severe disablement) is designed to treat and rehabilitate alcoholics who suffer from medical complications (e.g. hepatic cirrhosis), psychiatric complications (e.g. psychosis), neurological complications (e.g. encephalopathy), and / or marked socioeconomic maladaptation (e.g. unemployment, family problems, etc.). Medical and social therapists are responsible for these measures.
2
Secondary prevention (of complications and social damage), also one of the main objectives of medical therapists, seeks to arrive at an early diagnosis and start treatment before irreversible complications have appeared.
3
Primary prevention (of the risks of acquiring alcoholism and of associated social damage) is designed to control and modify sociocultural patterns encouraging excessive ingestion of alcoholic beverages. These activities are beyond the scope of medical institutions and are the responsibility of various state organizations and of the community in general. Systematic education on alcohol and alcoholism as part of health education programs at all educational levels is one of the most important instruments of primary prevention. Similarly, adult education at every opportunity in community life and with the co-operation of the health services is an important element. State organizations related to the production and distribution of alcoholic beverages, and to legislation and enforcement respecting alcohol use and abuse, all have a potentially significant role to play in primary prevention.

It would be desirable if these diverse activities were considered by a committee comprising representatives of departments of health, education, agriculture, economy, treasury, and justice, to co-ordinate harmoniously the various aspects of the program. Hence it is important to encourage and co-ordinate relevant investigations in the alcohol field, to ensure awareness of the conditions leading to excessive drinking in each sociocultural group and thereby the ability to take measures necessary for its control.

A number of reports are included in this section of the Symposium, which have direct relevance to these problems and I am sure will have great significance for the primary prevention of alcoholism.

JOSÉ HORWITZ
Psychiatric Hospital
National Health Service of Chile
Santiago, Chile

R. CRUZ-COKE

A. VARELA

Department of Medical Genetics
José J. Aguirre Hospital and
Institute of Studies on Alcoholism
University of Chile
Santiago, Chile

37

Genetic Factors
in Alcoholism

During an investigation of the genetics of common diseases performed with the Gene-Disease Association method (2) we discovered a highly significant association between colour blindness and cirrhosis of the liver (3, 4). In the group studied, the association between cirrhosis and alcoholism was similar among those exhibiting colour blindness and those with normal colour vision. Subsequent study of a sample of male alcohol addicts also revealed a significant association between alcoholism and colour blindness (7). The triple phenotypic association between colour defectiveness, alcoholism, and cirrhosis of the liver is shown by the data summarized in Table 37–1. These phenotypes are connected through a colour vision defect in the Hubbard-Wald vision cycle. Two of the enzymes involved alcohol dehydrogenase (ADH) and hepatic retinene isomerase (HRI) are known. The genetic control of ADH, demonstrated in Drosophila, is achieved through the action of two alleles, ADH^F and ADH^S (Grell *et al.* 1965). These findings and the fact that colour blindness is a recessive X-linked characteristic, suggested the possibility that a genetic factor in alcoholism was located on the X chromosome.

According to McKusick (13), to apply an X-linked model of inheritance in the case of a common disease, requires among other steps that an X-linkage be suggested by the relative frequency of affected males and females. If the trait is recessive the frequency of affected females should be the square of the frequency of affected males. In a survey of the prevalence of alcoholism among the adult population of a suburb of Santiago, Marconi *et al.* (14) found 8.3 per cent male and 0.6 per cent female alcoholics, according to the following criteria: (*a*) frequent drunkenness, (*b*) habitual ingestion of alcoholic beverages before breakfast, and (*c*) frequent and prolonged bouts of drinking ("sprees"). Table 37-2 shows that the genetic analysis of these proportions is in complete agreement with an X-linked recessive model.

According to the X-linked mechanism of inheritance, we would postulate that females are the heterozygous carriers of a supposed alcohol mutant gene. Classical genetic theory holds that female carriers of sex-linked recessive traits do not show any manifestations of the

TABLE 37–1

PHENOTYPIC ASSOCIATION BETWEEN COLOUR DEFECTIVENESS AND CHRONIC
ALCOHOLISM IN MALES IN FOUR HOSPITAL POPULATIONS

	Hospitals			
	Seattle Medicine* *(1)*	*Aguirre Psychiatry†* *(2)*	*Aguirre Medicine‡* *(3)*	*Arica Medicine§* *(4)*
male population sample	24	100	450	50
Caucasian admixture‖	0.99	0.63	0.63	0.47
colour defective subjects	10	18	44	9
alcoholic subjects	20	100	63	8
gene-disease association methods	Retrospective (Woolf)		Prospective (CCLi)	
relative risk (x)	8.92	4.41	4.53	7.60
chi square	27.91	55.9	36.60	9.40
$p <$	0.001	0.001	0.001	0.01

*Fialkow *et al.* (9).
†Cruz-Coke and Varela (7).
‡Cruz-Coke (4).
§Cruz-Coke (5).
‖Estimated value m for gene I_A.

TABLE 37–2

GENE FREQUENCIES AND PHENOTYPE DISTRIBUTION
BY SEX OF THE ALCOHOLIC TRAIT (q) ON SUPPOSITION
OF X-LINKED INHERITANCE IN A GENERAL
POPULATION SAMPLE OF 1,976 PERSONS OF A SUBURB
OF SANTIAGO (MARCONI *et al.*, 14)

	Observed males	*Expected females*	*Observed females*
gene frequency p	0.9170	0.9170	0.9226
gene frequency q	0.0830	0.0830	0.0774
	1.0000	1.0000	1.0000
phenotypes			
normal	p 0.9170	p^2 0.8409	q^2 0.8511
carriers	—	$2pq$ 0.1522	$2pq$ 0.1429
alcoholics	q 0.0830	q^2 0.0069	q^2 0.0060
	1.0000	1.0000	1.0000

defect carried. Thus, the heterozygous carrier of a colour vision defect should be normal on the various colour vision tests. However, several reports, using more sensitive methods of testing, have shown that so-called normal carriers of colour defectiveness are in fact abnormal (10). This agrees with the hypothesis of Lyon (12) that most carriers would be expected to show some degree of abnormality. Random X-inactivation in the normal human female produces a mosaic of cells, some of which contain active maternal-derived X chromosomes and others,

active paternal-derived X chromosomes. The nature and detectability of an abnormality will depend on the size of the abnormal patches and the overall balance between normal and abnormal areas (10). Consequently, it seemed to us that it would be necessary to use a more sensitive test to detect abnormality in the heterozygous carriers of our samples.

The Farnsworth-Munsell 100-hue test is a simple method for testing differential wave length discrimination. The pattern of colour defectiveness is identified by bipolarity: a

TABLE 37–3

DISTRIBUTION OF THE NUMBER OF CAP ERRORS ON THE FARNSWORTH–MUNSELL 100-HUE TEST IN THE CHILDREN OF ALCOHOLIC AND NON-ALCOHOLIC CONTROL SUBJECTS PROPOSITI

| | | | Over 100 errors | | |
	Subgroup	*Sample number*	N	*per cent*	*Number of errors (mean and standard error)*
non-alcoholic controls propositus (mean age 38.0 ± 11.77)	a	35	6	17.1	58 ± 5.32
sons	b	21	2	9.5	45.9 ± 9.03
daughters	c	21	1	4.7	36.3 ± 6.00
alcoholics propositus (mean age 40.9 ± 8.55)	d	21	13	61.9	152.2 ± 23.6
sons	e	14	4	28.5	83.8 ± 21.8
daughters	f	21	9	42.8	116.8 ± 17.5

Significant differences at $p < 0.01$ level: $(a–d)(c–f)(d–e)(d–b)$.

clustering of errors in two regions of the spectrum. This test detects a significant peculiarity of colour-defectives, namely, the inability to recognize changes in wave length in certain areas of the spectrum. Krill (10) was able to detect low discrimination ability in 13 heterozygous carriers of colour vision defect who had normal colour vision when tested by the classical plates of H-R-R and Ishihara. Table 37–3 shows our preliminary results, using this test in 20 families of alcoholics and 10 families of control non-alcoholic subjects. The mean discrimination ability of the alcoholics is significantly lower than the control subjects (152 errors against 58). Only daughters of alcoholic and control subjects differ significantly in their discrimination ability (116 and 36 errors, respectively). Moreover, the discrimination ability of the non-alcoholic daughters of alcoholics is highly correlated with the ability of their alcoholic fathers, and the mean cap errors do not differ significantly (116 and 152 errors, respectively). This correlation does not appear in the case of fathers and sons. These sex differences agree with the X-linked model, on the supposition that females are the carriers of both the alcoholism factor and the colour vision defectiveness.

If we suppose that alcoholism is "predetermined" by a mutant X-linked gene with a relatively high frequency (0.083) in the general population of Santiago, it could be considered,

like colour blindness, a genetic polymorphism. Now, to maintain a polymorphism it is necessary to have a selection balance favouring heterozygotes. If the mechanism of inheritance were X-linked, only females could be heterozygotes, and the balance would have to be maintained by them. A selection balance is maintained by mortality and fertility differences. For example, the persistence of the sickle-cell gene in Africa is maintained mainly by mortality differences, and differential female fecundity is of minor importance (1). But in Central America, fertility differences are sufficiently strong to maintain the sickle-cell gene, even in the absence of differential mortality due to malaria (1). In our supposed alcohol polymorphism, the data in Table 37-4 show that fertility differences are greater among heterozygous females than among normals and supposedly homozygous alcoholics. This agrees with the finding of Smart (18) in Canada, that the percentage of alcoholics who came from large families was significantly greater than expected. We have not yet studied the problem of mortality differences.

If we suppose that the selectional balance is maintained by fertility differences alone, the equilibrium condition of our postulated polymorphic system will be established when the mutant reaches a value of $q = 0.243$, as shown in Table 37-5. This figure is very close to the equilibrium condition of the sickle-cell trait (15). But our polymorphism has been detected

TABLE 37–4

PROVISIONAL ESTIMATES OF FITNESS BY FERTILITY DIFFERENCES ALONE IN SIBSHIPS ACCORDING TO THE PHENOTYPE OF MOTHERS OF ALCOHOLIC PATIENTS ON SUPPOSITION OF SEX-LINKED INHERITANCE

| | Type of sibship | | | |
| | *Santiago general population** | *alcoholic cirrhotics hospital†* | *children of alcoholic females* | |
			survey‡	*adjusted§*
mean age of mothers	65–84	over 70	47.4	65–84
mean age of sibship	45–49	47	20	45–49
number of mothers	36.716	72	12	
mean sibship size at birth	4.84	5.84	1.75	2.13
Fitness (*w*)				
Aa = 1.0	0.82	1.00	0.30	0.44
AA = 1.00	1.00	1.21	0.35	0.53
phenotype of mother	normal	carrier	alcoholic	
supposed genotype	AA	Aa	aa	

*Census 1960. Includes an estimated 0.6 per cent of alcoholic females.
†Prospective hospital sample (Cruz–Coke (4)).
‡Same sample as in previous column.
§Adjusted to the same age as in first two columns.

TABLE 37–5

SELECTIONAL BALANCE WITH HETEROZYGOTE SUPERIORITY IN FITNESS BY FERTILITY DIFFERENCES ALONE ON SUPPOSITION OF X-LINKED INHERITANCE FOR MUTANT ALCOHOLIC ALLELE ($q = 0.0830$)

Genotype	*Frequency before selection* f	*Fitness* w	*Frequency after selection* fw	*New gene frequency* q'	*Genotypic proportion in next generation* f'
AA	0.8409	0.82	0.6895	$p' = 0.9063$	0.8213
Aa	0.1522	1.00	0.1522	$q' = 0.0936$	0.1697
aa	0.0069	0.44	0.0030		0.0087
	1.0000		0.8447		0.9997

$\Delta q = q' - q = 0.0106.$ $\bar{q} = 0.2430.$

in a period of transition with a mutant allele rapidly increasing at a rate of 1 per cent in each generation. This spreading of the postulated alcohol mutant agrees with the increasing prevalence of alcoholism in Chile, as indicated by the change in the mortality rate of alcoholic cirrhosis from 5 to 25 per 100,000 during the last 50 years (17). Moreover, according to the latest vital statistics for Santiago, in 1965 cirrhosis of the liver was the most frequent cause of death in the male adult population.

The evolutionary pattern of our postulated mutant gene has been investigated recently by us (5). We performed a survey of alcohol behaviour and colour vision in human populations currently living at different stages of cultural evolution and with decreasing possibilities for total natural selection (6). Table 37–6 shows the highly significant correlation existing between increasing prevalence of alcoholism and colour defectiveness, and in association with evolution from nomadic to industrial cultural levels and increasing Caucasian admixture. These results are in accord with the suggestion of Post (16) that natural selection against colour blindness has been completely relaxed during cultural evolution, with a resultant increase in the frequency of the mutant gene. Of course we do not know the cause of the emergence of this supposed alcoholic polymorphism. Nevertheless, this anthropological concordance agrees with the sociological

TABLE 37–6

CORRELATION BETWEEN THE PREVALENCE OF COLOUR DEFECTIVENESS AND ALCOHOLISM IN MALES IN A CONTEMPORARY CULTURAL GRADIENT OF TYPE OF ALCOHOL CONSUMPTION (AYMARA-SPEAKING PEOPLE OF NORTHERN CHILE)

Population surveyed*	Culture	Type of alcohol consumption†	Sample size	m‡	Colour defectives (per cent)	Alcoholics (per cent)
Huallatire	semi-nomadic	I–II	70	0.15	2.8	1.4
Molinos	rural	II	70	0.09	5.7	2.8
Chapiquiña	rural	II–III	65	0.09	1.6	0.0
Belen	rural	II–III	33	0.02	6.0	3.0
Azapa	rural	II–III	37	0.02	0.0	0.0
Arica§	urban	III–IV	50	0.47	18.0	16.0
Santiago§	urban	III–IV	450	0.63	9.8	14.0

*Cruz–Coke (5).
†Fallding's typology (8): I–community-symbolic; II–facilitation; III–assuagement; IV–relational.
‡Coefficient of Caucasian admixture, allele *A*.
§Hospital samples.
Correlation: $r = 0.952$; $p < 0.00001$.

concordance respecting types of alcohol consumption proposed by Fallding (8), who considers that drinking patterns have evolved from an "independent-ornamental symbolic type" characteristic of primitive societies to a "dependent relational type" in urban civilizations.

We consider that all these concordances support the result obtained in our exploration of the first step suggested by McKusick for the detection of an X-linked mechanism of inheritance in a common disease. Unfortunately, it is difficult to take the next step, i.e., to establish agreement between types of mating with the proportions expected on the basis of gene frequencies in males. Before a specific phenotype for alcoholism linked to an enzymatic defect could be discovered, we would have to be able to perform a direct Mendelian analysis of the families of alcoholics. Consequently, any conclusion about the inheritance of alcoholism is as yet only tentative.

REFERENCES

1
ALLISON, A.C.
Polymorphism and natural selection in human population
(Cold Spring Harbor) Symp. Quant. Biol., **29**: 137, 1964

2
CLARKE, A.C.
Genetics for the clinician
Oxford: Blackwell, 1961

3
CRUZ-COKE, R.
Colour-blindness and cirrhosis of the liver
Lancet, **ii**: 1064, 1964

4
CRUZ-COKE, R.
Colour-blindness and cirrhosis of the liver
Lancet, **i**: 1131, 1965

5
CRUZ-COKE, R.
Association between opportunity for natural selection, color blindness and chronic alcoholism in different human populations
Arch. Biol. Med. Exper., **3**: 21, 1966

6
CRUZ-COKE, R. & BIANCANI, F.
Demografia genética de Arica
Rev. Méd. Chile, **94**: 63, 1966

7
CRUZ-COKE, R. & VARELA, A.
Colour-blindness and alcohol addiction
Lancet, **ii**: 1348, 1965

8
FALLDING, H.
The source and burden of civilization illustrated in the use of alcohol
Quart. J. Stud. Alc., **25**: 714, 1964

9
FIALKOW, P.J., THULINE, H.C., & FENSTER, H.L.
Lack of association between cirrhosis and the common types of color blindness
New England J. Med., **275**: 5847, 1966

10
KRILL, A.E. & SCHNEIDERMAN, A.
A hue discrimination defect in so-called normal
carriers of color vision defects
Invest. Ophtal., **3**: 445, 1964

11
LI, C.C.
Human genetics
New York: McGraw-Hill, 1961

12
LYON, M.F.
Gene action in the X-chromosome of the mouse
(Mus musculus L.)
Nature, **190**: 372, 1961

13
MCKUSICK, V.A.
On the X chromosome of man
Washington, DC: Am. Inst. Biol. Sc., 1964

14
MARCONI, J., VARELA, A., ROSENBLATT, E., SOLARI, G.,
MARCHESE, I., ALVARADO, R., & ENRIQUEZ, W.
A survey on the prevalence of alcoholism among
the adult population of a suburb of Santiago
Quart. J. Stud. Alc., **16**: 438, 1955

15
MAYNARD-SMITH, S.
Appendix to notes on sickle-cell polymorphism
Ann. Hum. Genet., **19**: 51, 1954

16
POST, R.H.
Selection against "colorblindness" among
"primitive" populations
Eugen. Quart., **12**: 28, 1965

17
ROMERO, H., MEDINA, E., MASSAD, F., YRARRÁZABAL, M.,
& KAEMPFFER, A.M.
Hepatic cirrhosis as a public health problem
Rev. Méd. Chile, **89**: 829, 1961

18
SMART, R.G.
Alcoholism, birth order, and family size
J. Abnorm. Soc. Psychol., **66**: 17, 1963

VERA EFRON

Center of Alcohol Studies
Rutgers University
State University of New Jersey
New Brunswick, New Jersey, USA

38

Sociological and Cultural Factors in Alcohol Abuse

The existence of abuse of alcohol, or excessive drinking, or alcoholism, as it is variously called, presupposes the existence of normal drinking or norms in drinking; in other words, drinking customs. And it is not possible to discuss abuse of alcohol without discussing its normal use. These norms differ widely from society to society, and even among ethnic subgroups within a society; what is considered abuse in one group may be normal drinking behaviour in another. It is normal for an Italian to drink a tumblerful of wine with his midday meal, but it would seem suspicious behaviour, indeed, in many North American groups. The taking of cocktails before a meal and without food is regularly done by many North Americans but would be highly deviant behaviour, especially for women, among Russians who always have a bite of food with their vodka, even just a crust of stale bread, if nothing better is available (3).

Drinking customs in some groups are accompanied by well-defined ritual, either specific to the drinking or related to some other forms of societal customs. Or drinking may be restricted to certain occasions, such as weddings, or fiestas, as in Latin America. The rituals which accompany drinking may be simple or elaborate. Here is an example of ritual which was observed in a hotel restaurant during a late meal hour (3). Around a large table some 20 men were finishing their meal. A great many bottles were on the table and even more on a side table where the waiter put them as they became empty. For each tall wine bottle there were two squat bottles of mineral water. As the men sipped their diluted wine there was always one of them, glass in hand, who stood and spoke, sometimes at considerable length. At the end of his speech, sipping from his glass, the man would toast one or more of his companions, and the rest would touch glasses and sip from theirs. As soon as one sat down another got up and spoke. The toasts continued, one after the other, pleasantly and peacefully. Then

Preparation of this article was aided by grant MH-05655, to the Rutgers Center of Alcohol Studies, from the National Institute of Mental Health, US Public Health Service. I thank Professors Selden D. Bacon and Mark Keller for advice and criticism.

a rather different behaviour was observed. One speaker drained his glass and invited the others to do the same; they smiled pleasantly at him but sipped as before. Instead of sitting down this man made another speech and again drained his glass, turning it upside down this time, and obviously getting irritated at the others. His voice rose unpleasantly. His neighbour then got up and began to shove him gently around the table and toward the door, allowing him to speak and shout as he wished. In a few minutes they were both outside the door. The neighbour returned soon after, the other man did not. This took place in Tbilisi, the capital of the Georgian Republic of the Soviet Union. Clearly, the man who drained his glass did not behave according to the ordinary drinking customs accepted by his group; his was deviant behaviour. But he was only mildly intoxicated and such behaviour would have been regarded as normal, or at least acceptable, in almost any Western European or North American society. This scene was an example of highly ritualized and highly civilized drinking. Nearly every sip was accompanied by elaborate toasting, and the enjoyment of the group was twofold: good drink and good oratory.

Examples of differing customs which accompany drinking can be multiplied almost indefinitely. And so can examples of individual drinking behaviour which fall within the norm in one group but are deviant in another. And as the norms differ, so the abuses take on different forms.

From the various forms of deviation, differing drinking pathologies develop. These pathologies E. M. Jellinek described as species of alcoholism and labelled alpha, beta, gamma, and delta alcoholisms (5). Not everyone agrees that they are all alcoholisms, and he himself allowed that at least one of them was not a disease. At any rate they certainly represent different types of drinking pathologies, different forms of alcohol abuse. As an example one may cite the drinking pattern of French alcoholics who drink continuously through the day without reaching drunkenness (5), in contrast to the Chilean alcoholics described by Varela and Marconi (10), among whom 80 per cent of the men drink in bouts with episodes of continuous

drunkenness lasting more than a day.

It is not only ways of drinking and deviations that differ from group to group, but also psychotic manifestations consequent on abuse. Thus Auersperg and Derwort (1) have described a special type of psychosis which forms what they call a "bridge" between alcoholic hallucinosis and delirium tremens and which, they believe, is specific to the milieu of a certain class of man in Chile.

It is common knowledge that rates of alcoholism, or drinking pathologies, differ in different groups. Statistics in the United States are particularly suitable for comparisons between groups because of the variety of cultural backgrounds found within a population which is subject to the same laws. Because of this, pathologies among various ethnic groups can be compared more meaningfully than the same groups in their native countries. A striking example is the rejection rates of military recruits in the Boston area during World War II (4). The same rejection standards for alcoholism were applied to all ethnic groups, but the rates were 3 per cent among the Irish, 1.2 per cent among the Italians, and 0.2 per cent among the Jews. The Irish rejection rate for alcoholism, in other words, was more than twice that of the Italians and 15 times greater than that of the Jews.

As long as I have given a glimpse into the drinking rituals of the Georgians it might be of interest to mention a rare statistic which pertains to their rate of alcoholism: of a population of four million in Georgia, about 20 per cent are Russians, but among hospitalized alcoholic patients, 80 per cent are Russians (3).

The issue of differential rates leads to the question of deviation in drinking behaviour from the norm. Why does deviation appear more often in some groups than in others? One answer to this question, suggested by S. D. Bacon (2), emphasizes the matrix of drinking customs, for far from existing in a vacuum, drinking customs are enmeshed in a complicated network of general mores which govern the forms of behaviour of individuals and groups. It is the extent of this nexus of drinking customs with other customs that is the important factor in the likelihood of deviation. If the two are closely integrated, rewards and punishments meted out to the individual for his various forms of behaviour encompass also his drinking behaviour, and deviation in this behaviour will be less likely to occur. When drinking customs are more independent of other practices the transgressing individual will be more likely to "get away with it" and hence deviation and ultimately pathologies will be more frequent. Once more, the scene in the Georgian restaurant may serve as example: the elaborate ritual of speech-making, combined with drinking, defines the rules of behaviour. Deviation is dealt with firmly at its inception and will therefore not likely develop into serious pathology.

In seeking explanations of the causes of alcohol abuse, it is not enough to know that people drink to be sociable, to allay anxieties, or to reduce tensions. The motivations are much more complicated than that. The physiological and psychological effects of alcohol on man are not sufficient to explain the differences in drinking pathologies among different cultures and thus sociocultural factors also need to be taken into etiological consideration.

Such factors also have to be taken into account in attempts to cope with alcohol abuse, and in the planning of treatment programs. What helps patients with a puritan Anglo-American background will not necessarily work with an alcoholic of Latin, Catholic upbringing who has experienced very different sanctions and formed a quite different ideology. A description of such a situation is given by W. Madsen (7) in his study of the anglicized Mexican-Americans living in a Texas community. The Latin Americans (called simply Latins) generally constitute the lower class in this community, the employees; the Anglo-Americans (called the Anglos), are the upper class, the employers. The Latin who seeks to better himself by adopting Anglo ways, the so-called *agringado*, loses his community and becomes unsure of his identity. He tries to emulate the drinking of Anglos and becomes enmeshed in customs and values he has not fully integrated. He sometimes misinterprets drinking with Anglos as acceptance in the Anglo world, only to be rejected by them; if his drinking is to continue Anglo-style, the road to alcoholism is easy. Then, as an alcoholic, the *agrin-*

gado needs help, and what he finds is a clinic designed for the Anglos and staffed with kindly therapists who have no knowledge of the Latin's world view. To their dismay, their attempts to rehabilitate the Latin patient invariably fail.

In Russia, whose alcoholics seem not too different from North America's, treatment is primarily by conditioned reflex. The technique of creating aversion is similar to that of other countries. But what a difference in approach! The authoritarian paternalistic attitude of the therapist is accepted by the Russian patients, for it is in keeping with cultural traditions of the country (3). Such attitudes probably would not make much headway in the United States.

Another example of culturally divergent types of treatment is one described from Japan by R. A. Moore (8). Since drinking among Japanese is nearly universal and is considered an indispensable part of life, some Japanese psychiatrists think it futile to expect the alcoholic to become an abstainer. With a proper adjustment of a cyanamide compound (Temposil) which, like disulfiram, sensitizes the organism to alcohol, it is possible to let the alcoholic patient consume up to 200 cc of saké daily. This is called "temperance therapy." American psychiatrists who heard this style of treatment described at a congress in Tokyo were shocked. One need not go looking for exotic examples of treatments which fit one culture and do not fit another. In the United States, E. M. Pattison and his colleagues (9) report from an alcoholism clinic in Ohio that the lower classes of the community lacked the background and skills to use the therapeutic facilities available there. Psychotherapy, which presupposes extensive verbal communication between patient and therapist, is not operative among groups with low verbal fluency.

Now that I have stressed the differences between peoples and cultures, I want to assert the opposite; I want to ask: Aren't all men alike, all subject to the same laws of nature, physiological and psychological? Despite the different roads which alcohol abusers travel on their way to the disease of alcoholism, they end up with attributes which are the same throughout the world. The physiological and psychological effects of many years of excessive drinking are the same in Protestants and Catholics, Slavs and Japanese, rich and poor. What characterizes an alcoholic, irrespective of the particular drinking customs he grew up with, is that he drinks repetitively in a way that implies there is something wrong about his drinking, and he experiences injury from the drinking in his health, or his social or economic functions. (This definition has been plagiarized freely from M. Keller (6).) What unites all alcoholics the world over is their helplessness in the face of alcohol (loss of control or inability to abstain) and their suffering because of it. This suffering, and its repercussions among those around the alcoholic, are the universal elements in alcoholism.

REFERENCES

1
AUERSPERG, A.P. & DERWORT, A.
Beitrag zur vergleichenden Psychiatrie exogener Psychosen vom sozio-kulturellen Standpunkt
Nervenarzt, **33**: 22, 1962
2
BACON, S.D.
Sociology and the problems of alcohol; foundations for a sociologic study of drinking behaviour
Quart. J. Stud. Alc., **4**: 402, 1943
3
EFRON, V.
Notes from a visit to the Soviet Union: treatments and studies of alcoholism; education about alcohol; drinking in Georgia
Quart. J. Stud. Alc., **26**: 654, 1965
4
HYDE, R.W. & CHISHOLM, R.M.
Studies in medical sociology
III. The relation of mental disorders to race and nationality
New England J. Med., **231**: 612, 1944
5
JELLINEK, E.M.
The disease concept of alcoholism
New Haven: Hillhouse Press, 1960
6
KELLER, M.
Definition of alcoholism
Quart. J. Stud. Alc., **21**: 125, 1960
7
MADSEN, W.
The alcoholic agringado
Am. Anthrop., **66**: 355, 1964
8
MOORE, R.A.
Alcoholism in Japan

Quart. J. Stud. Alc., **25**: 142, 1964
9
PATTISON, E.M., COURLAS, P.G., PATTI, R., MANN, B., & MULLEN, D.
Diagnostic-therapeutic intake groups for wives of alcoholics and nonalcoholics
Quart. J. Stud. Alc., **26**: 605, 1965
10
VARELA, A. & MARCONI, J.
Addicción al alcohol: estudio de la evolución de la enfermedad en pacientes chilenos
Rev. Psiquiat., Santiago, **17**: 19, 1952

ROBERT E. POPHAM

Addiction Research Foundation
Toronto, Ontario, Canada

39

Indirect Methods of Alcoholism Prevalence Estimation: A Critical Evaluation

To the student of epidemiology, alcoholism appears to be almost unique among the so-called mental or behavioural disorders. For example, in the case of psychotic and neurotic conditions, unless a costly and time-consuming field survey is undertaken, one must depend very largely upon hospital admission statistics (with all the reporting and other errors to which these are liable) for data upon which to base estimates of prevalence. On the other hand, whatever else it may involve, alcoholism is always characterized by the repetitive intake of alcohol, usually in rather large quantities, and with various damaging consequences. Accordingly, it may be expected that the behaviour of alcoholics *en masse* will be reflected not only in hospital admissions, but in a number of other statistics regularly reported for most European and American jurisdictions. These include convictions for drunkenness and other alcohol-related offences, beverage alcohol sales data, and statistics of such causes of death as alcohol poisoning or liver cirrhosis which are wholly or partly attributable to the consumption of alcohol.

I do not mean to suggest that these data are not also subject to various errors, although sales and vital statistics are ordinarily much more completely reported and less subject to the selection biases associated with hospital admission statistics. The point is simply that, relatively speaking, the documentary data available for the epidemiological study of alcoholism are unusually good. When this fact is considered together with advantages of economy and flexibility, it is not surprising that considerable effort has been devoted to a search for a satisfactory *indirect* method of prevalence estimation; that is, a method to arrive at prevalence through the use of a documentary statistic known to vary with the rate of alcoholism. This is in contrast to case-finding or survey methods designed to obtain a direct count of the alcoholics in a population sample.

The writer would like to thank Mr. Jan de Lint and Dr. Wolfgang Schmidt for their many helpful suggestions respecting the content of this review. He is also grateful to Mrs. Jean Bronetto who calculated all of the coefficients shown in Table 39–1.

In the present review, I shall endeavour to evaluate the results to date of efforts to develop a fully acceptable indirect method. In so doing, I hope to clarify the nature and shortcomings of existing attempts, particularly the controversial Jellinek Formula, and to indicate in which direction it seems to me most profitable to proceed in future epidemiological research in the alcoholism field.

THE IPSEN-MOORE-ALEXANDER METHOD

One of the first indirect methods of prevalence estimation to be applied, and which for convenience has been given the name of its authors (Ipsen, Moore, Alexander), was reported in 1952 (14). The method was developed in the course of a study of deaths from poisoning in the state of Massachusetts. It utilizes as its primary source of data the death certificates issued by official medical examiners. In this state, the latter are obliged to certify the cause in all violent and sudden deaths. It is argued that alcoholism, when present, is likely to be reported by these examiners, who are not affected by the "regard to discretion which inhibits the reporting of alcoholism by the family physician."

The authors assume that the rate of alcoholism among violent and sudden deaths due to causes *in no way* associated with alcoholism will constitute an estimate of the prevalence of alcoholism in the general population. To approximate this rate for Massachusetts, a large sample of examiners' records were tabulated according to primary death cause. For each such cause the proportion of cases in which the examiners had reported alcoholism as a secondary condition was determined. Where this proportion proved high, relative to the average and after correction for age and sex differences among the cause categories, the deaths involved were assumed to be due to causes positively associated with alcoholism (e.g., deaths from suicidal and accidental poisoning). Accordingly, these were excluded from the sample. Adjustments were made to allow for age and sex differences between the remainder of the sample and the population of the state. The resulting average rate of mention of alcoholism was

taken to be an estimate of general prevalence in Massachusetts.

The prevalence figure obtained by this method was compared with an estimate based on the Jellinek Formula (to be considered in the next section). In the view of the authors, "the two methods of estimating prevalence are as close as can reasonably be expected." In fact, their estimate exceeded that based on the Jellinek method by more than 74 per cent – rather poor agreement as will be evident from the data in Table 39-2. Popham (36) has suggested that the discrepancy may have been due to a faulty assumption on the author's part, namely, that the alcoholics reported by the medical examiners were all "alcoholics with complications." This was assumed on the grounds that the state of alcoholism must be "rather advanced in order for it to be known to a medical examiner called to view a deceased who is unknown to him." However, the definition of "complication" underlying the Jellinek method is a very narrow one (36). Consequently, direct evidence (e.g. from autopsies) of complications in all cases would be necessary before the two estimates could be considered strictly comparable.

As far as the writer is aware, no attempt has yet been made to apply the method in any area other than Massachusetts. This situation may be due in part to the absence of a comparable system of death certification in most other jurisdictions. But in any event logical objections to the calculation procedures involved have been raised by Seeley (46). Furthermore, at least two of the principal assumptions underlying the method may be seriously questioned. First, it is probably true that medical examiners are not similarly influenced by the attitudes which lead family physicians to under-report alcoholism on death certificates. Nevertheless it does not follow that their detection even of alcoholism with complications, is comprehensive. Indeed, the fact that the deceased is unknown to the examiner would render it in many cases unlikely that sufficient personal history data would be available for such a diagnosis. Second, it is difficult to think of almost any category of sudden or violent death among adults in which victims would not be liable to show a higher frequency of alcoholism than the general population.

In conclusion, it cannot be categorically asserted that a further attempt to apply the method would not repay the effort. However, if such an attempt were made it is clear that: (*a*) careful attention would have to be given to the basis upon which diagnoses of alcoholism were made by the physicians certifying causes of death; and (*b*) detailed studies would have to be undertaken to ensure that the death cause categories chosen for analysis were in fact unrelated to alcoholism.

THE JELLINEK METHOD

The Jellinek Estimation Formula is by far the best known and most widely applied method yet devised for estimating alcoholism prevalence. Estimates based upon it have been reported for each state of the United States (15, 20, 23), for the larger US cities (24), for Canada and its provinces (1, 37) and for Australia, Chile, the United Kingdom and a number of European countries (11, 37). Certain of the trend analyses and other studies which eventually led to the development of the method were reported in 1942 (21). The formula itself was first described in 1951 (11), but a comprehensive account of the method and of the evidence in support of it did not appear until 1956 (36).

Official mortality from liver cirrhosis constitutes the primary data employed by the method. To obtain an estimate of prevalence in a given jurisdiction, this vital statistic is entered in the formula:

$$(PD/K)R,$$

where D = the total number of deaths from liver cirrhosis reported officially for a given year in the jurisdiction of interest; P = the proportion of such deaths which may be considered attributable to alcoholism; K = the annual death rate from liver cirrhosis among alcoholics with complications; R = the ratio of all alcoholics to alcoholics with complications.

Many persons have been sceptical or plainly incredulous of the validity of the Jellinek method, but few have published their views,

much less undertaken a systematic examination of the method. The most commonly heard criticisms are that official mortality figures underreport the true incidence of liver cirrhosis as a cause of death, and that it is not a satisfactory index of alcoholism because the trend may be distorted for varying periods of time by transient causes such as epidemic hepatitis (14). In a direct study of Finnish mortality data, it was shown (6) that more deaths were apt to be reported as due to liver cirrhosis when certifications were based on autopsy findings than when based on clinical diagnoses. Since in most jurisdictions only a relatively small percentage of all deceased are autopsied, it is probably true that this cause of death is commonly underreported. Indeed, the actual rate may exceed the reported rate by as much as 50 per cent (6). However, since selection for autopsy (e.g. police cases, homeless men) may often favour those with liver cirrhosis, it is likely that the discrepancy is generally much less than this.

With respect to causes of liver cirrhosis other than alcoholism, the author of the formula stressed that it was "imperative to determine P for each country from a thorough analysis of trends as well as from a knowledge of various conditions of the liver which enter into the certification of death from cirrhosis" (11). Moreover, he felt that it should not be applied at all in oriental and other countries where there are many deaths from parasitic liver diseases included in the reported mortality from liver cirrhosis (18). It would also seem valid to rule out the method where there is evidence of distortion in the mortality trend due to a high prevalence of infectious hepatitis (14, 55). Denmark during the early 1940s is a case in point (13).

Another criticism is based on the observation that liver cirrhosis mortality rates sometimes show considerable, apparently random, fluctuations from one year to the next. Jolliffe and Jellinek (21) noted that such variation is to be expected in the case of a minor cause of death, and that it is especially marked in populations of less than 300,000. However, Seeley and Schmidt (54) found that correlations between liver cirrhosis mortality and alcohol consumption rates through time ceased to be statistically significant in populations of less than a million. It may be concluded in this regard that the formula is inapplicable to areas of less than 300,000 persons. But in the case of other populations of up to a million persons, most of the chance variation can be removed by averaging the mortality data over several years. For populations over a million the use of centred two-year moving averages has been found satisfactory (36).

The strongest objections to the formula have been directed against the methods employed by Jellinek to derive values for the three factors: *P, K,* and *R.* Seeley (47) demonstrated clearly that the calculation procedure used to obtain *P* values from trend data (21, 36) was incorrect. Furthermore, he showed that the value of *P* may be expected to vary not only from one country to another, but also in accord with temporal changes and regional differences in the prevalence of alcoholism in the same country. The latter point had been made earlier by Popham (36), who noted that, as a consequence, the formula may *underestimate* prevalence when the liver cirrhosis death rate exceeds that for the year to which the *P* value applies. On the other hand, *overestimation* may occur when the rate is lower than in the latter year.

Jellinek obtained a value for *K* by averaging frequency data based on autopsy samples of "alcoholics with complications," and reported by different workers in many different countries. He regarded *K* as a constant for all countries (11). However, Popham (36) argued that, even if the frequency of deaths from liver cirrhosis among alcoholics suffering from the disease were constant from country to country, the frequency of other organic complications might be expected to vary: for example, with the nutritional status of the population. As a consequence, the prevalence of liver cirrhosis among "alcoholics with complications," and hence the rate of death from it in this group (*K*), would also be subject to international variation. The constancy of *K* through time may be doubted on the same grounds.

Sjővall (55) questioned the validity of averaging results from a diversity of autopsy samples. He noted that differences in diagnostic criteria among pathologists and in the influence of such conditions as infectious hepatitis might cause wide fluctuations in the frequencies of liver cirrhosis reported for different areas. But the most serious criticism has been that of Seeley (47) who argued that since the value of *K* provided by Jellinek was based on autopsy data, it could not logically be equal to the death rate from liver cirrhosis among *living* alcoholics with complications. Indeed in his view, Jellinek's value (.694 per cent) should exceed the true rate by a factor equal to the average duration of life of an alcoholic after onset of a complication (i.e., probably by a factor of at least four assuming a death rate of 25 per cent for alcoholics with complications). Since *K* is in the denominator of the formula, gross underestimates of prevalence should result unless a compensating error is operative.

Finally, the value assigned by Jellinek to the *R* factor for the US and some other countries (11) has been questioned both on empirical grounds (36), and from a logical standpoint (47). Seeley noted that, where the value was derived from clinical samples, it is apt to be too small. Thus, the presence of one of the organic diseases attributable to alcoholism may be one of the reasons why many alcoholics seek admission to clinics. If so, then the proportion of alcoholics with complications will be greater in the clinical population, and, therefore, the ratio employed in the formula will be smaller than that in the general alcoholic population. This error would also be expected to result in the underestimation of prevalence by the formula.

PROPOSED MODIFICATIONS OF
THE JELLINEK METHOD

Following the publication of Seeley's critique (47), and in part prompted by it, a number of modifications were proposed in an effort to overcome the objections to the Jellinek method. Jellinek himself (19) offered new values for *K* and *R* (without, however, meeting Seeley's criticisms of their method of derivation), and proposed an alternative method.* Keller (22) argued that the Jellinek Formula estimates for the years 1940–5 were probably accurate, and that the rate of alcoholism with complications had not changed substantially since that period. Therefore, in his view, estimates of the size of the alcoholic population in any recent year could be obtained simply by multiplying the 1940–5 rate by the appropriate population figure for the year of interest, and multiplying the result by 5.3 to get the number of alcoholics with and without complications. The 5.3 multiplier is Jellinek's revised US value for R (19). Keller's proposal is unacceptable for three reasons: (*a*) the logical objections to the method apply as well to its use in the 1940s as to its use today; (*b*) the empirical evidence (discussed below) in support of the accuracy of estimates based on the method applies largely to the last 15 years; and (*c*) the proposal fails to allow for the evident increase in the general rate of alcoholism during the period after World War II in the United States and many other countries (6, 33, 37, 42, 44, 54).

Brenner (2, 3) proposed a modification of the numerator in the formula to meet objections respecting the variability of the P factor. However, Seeley (49) showed that the modified formula was logically unsound partly for the same reasons as the original version. Seeley then proposed an alternative formula of his own (50), and endeavoured to clarify the theoretical basis of prevalence analysis (45, 48). His proposal has also been criticized (8). However, its chief shortcoming seems to be that it re-

*Essentially, Jellinek's alternative involves determination of the total number of alcoholics among all deaths in the population of a country in a given year. This number is divided by an estimate of the death rate of alcoholics to obtain the total number alive during all or part of the year in point. The method was applied by Jellinek to data for Switzerland where he considered the reporting of alcoholism on death certificates to be comprehensive. However, as often noted, regard for the possible stigma on the deceased's family commonly inhibits reporting of this condition. In addition, the necessary anamnestic data to make a diagnosis of alcoholism are frequently not available to certifying physicians. These factors are apt to result in such gross under-reporting as to render the method inapplicable in most jurisdictions at the present time.

quires a knowledge of seven quantities, five of which would be very difficult to estimate accurately at present.

Lastly, Popham and Schmidt (38) maintained that the minimum requirements for the application of the Jellinek method in a given country were: (*a*) the determination of the death rate from liver cirrhosis among *all* alcoholics (i.e. K/R) through studies of reported liver cirrhosis mortality in areas where the size of the alcoholic population is known through field surveys; (*b*) the derivation of a P value for reported liver cirrhosis mortality utilizing the direct method developed for the purpose in Finland (6); and (*c*) a knowledge of the principal factors other than alcoholism effecting differences in the rate of liver cirrhosis mortality from year to year, and area to area in the country of concern. If these requirements are accepted, we are left with the practical question whether or not the return on this method would be proportional to its evident cost in time and money. I shall return to this question after a brief review of the empirical evidence in its favour.

EVIDENCE IN SUPPORT OF
THE JELLINEK METHOD

Paradoxically, in view of its serious logical shortcomings, there is a good deal of empirical evidence which favours the Jellinek method. First, with respect to the principal assumption underlying it – that there is a relationship between alcoholism and liver cirrhosis mortality – one can but agree with Keller (22) that this is established beyond dispute, and "in agreement with clinical experience wherever inebriety is observed." The clinical and statistical evidence up to 1942 was summarized by Jolliffe and Jellinek (21), and since then considerably more has been accumulated. Recent statistical evidence is chiefly in the form of demonstrated correlations (for various jurisdictions and periods of time) between rates of liver cirrhosis mortality and hospital admissions for alcoholism (18, 36, 44), convictions for drunkenness (6), and alcohol consumption as reflected in per capita beverage sales (4, 5, 42, 43, 51, 54).

TABLE 39–1

TEMPORAL AND REGIONAL CORRELATIONS BETWEEN
RATE OF LIVER CIRRHOSIS MORTALITY AND PER CAPITA
ALCOHOL CONSUMPTION*

Area	Series	Correlation coefficient	Probability
Australia	1938–59	.65	< .005
Belgium	1929–59 (less 1940–5)	.75	< .001
Canada	1927–60	.88	< .001
Alberta	1929–60	.85	< .001
Manitoba	1935–60	.86	< .001
Nova Scotia	1932–60	.60	< .001
Ontario	1930–60	.89	< .001
Quebec	1929–60	.43	< .05
Saskatchewan	1943–60	.77	< .001
Canada	9 provinces 1955	.81	< .01
Finland	1933–57	.78	< .001
France	1925–58	.62	< .001
France	23 départements 1950	.76	< .001
Holland	1927–58	.57	< .001
Sweden	1926–56	.45	< .05
United Kingdom	1931–58	− .68	< .001
United States	1934–58	.60	< .005
United States	45 states 1939	.61	< .001
United States	48 states 1944	.78	< .001
United States	46 states 1950	.76	< .001
United States	46 states 1957	.86	< .001
International	11 countries 1956†	.78	< .005

*Correlation studies of these two variables have been reported previously for nearly
all of the series shown (4, 5, 21, 26, 42, 43, 51). However, for the purposes of the
present review, the original series were extended wherever possible and new coefficients
calculated. In all instances, liver cirrhosis mortality was expressed as an
unstandardized rate: deaths per 100,000 population aged 20 and older; and the
measure of alcohol consumption comprised sales of alcoholic beverages expressed as
imperial gallons of absolute alcohol per capita of population aged 15 and older.
†Includes Australia, Belgium, Canada, Denmark, France, Finland, the Netherlands,
Sweden, Switzerland, the United Kingdom, and the United States.

To indicate something of the degree of relationship, correlations between liver cirrhosis
mortality and alcohol consumption rates for a
number of temporal and spatial series are shown
in Table 39–1. Several different countries are
represented and, in fact, which areas were included depended simply on whether or not the
appropriate data happened to be readily available. All of the coefficients are statistically
significant and most are very large. Unfortunately for the researcher's peace of mind, one
of them (for the United Kingdom) is a highly
significant *negative* correlation. A purely
statistical explanation for this could be offered,
but it would not account for the failure of the
data to conform to the general pattern. In any
event, it serves to illustrate one of the shortcomings to which an analysis of this type may be
liable: the assumption of normal variation

underlying Pearsonian correlation technique
may not be met by secular trend data so that
spurious indications of correlation may occur.
Another shortcoming is that all of the geographic units in the tabulation are not strictly
independent (e.g. the provinces of Canada).
Consequently, the overall degree of association
between the two variables is somewhat exaggerated.

The most important evidence to consider in
an evaluation of the Jellinek method is the
extent to which estimates based upon it agree
with estimates derived by entirely independent
methods. In Table 39–2 are assembled all instances to date (so far as the writer is aware)
in which a comparison can be made. An account
of the various independent methods involved is
beyond the scope of this review. Suffice it to say
that in all but two instances (Massachusetts

TABLE 39–2

ALCOHOLICS PER 100,000 POPULATION AGED 20 AND OVER IN VARIOUS AREAS
ESTIMATED BY THE JELLINEK FORMULA AND INDEPENDENT METHODS

Area	Year*	Source†	Jellinek method	Independent method	Percentage difference
England & Wales	1948, 1960–63	(11, 57)	1,100	865	−21.4
Finland	1951–57	(6)	1,120	1,330	+18.8
Ontario	1951	(37, 12)	1,600	1,600	0.0
Denmark	1948	(11)	1,950	1,750	−10.3
Switzerland	1953, 1947	(18, 11)	2,100	2,700	+28.6
Kansas	1953, 1954	(23, 7)	2,350	1,580	−32.8
Ontario	1961	(1, 33)	2,460	2,375	− 3.5
Iowa	1957, 1958	(32)	3,260	3,000	− 8.0
New York (Monroe Co.)	1961	(58)	3,580	3,500	− 2.2
Chile	1950, 1953	(18, 31)	3,610	4,150	+15.0
Massachusetts	1938–48	(14)	4,060	7,090	+74.6
New Jersey	1945	(40)	4,080	3,945	− 3.3
Florida	1953, 1954	(28)	4,310	4,150	− 3.7
Michigan	1953, 1955	(23, 29, 30)	4,490	4,300	− 4.2
France	1951	(17, 25)	5,200	7,300	+40.4
Illinois	1953	(23, 39)	5,250	5,250	0.0

*A dash separating two years indicates that the prevalence estimates represent averages for the period. Where two
years are separated by a comma, the first is the year to which the Jellinek estimate applies.
†Where two reference numbers are shown, the first indicates the source of the Jellinek estimate.

and France) direct case-finding methods were
employed. It should also be noted that the
authors of the independent methods usually
cannot be held responsible for the form in which
their results appear in this tabulation. In several
cases it was necessary to alter the figures reported by them (e.g., from a rate of "alcoholism
with complications" to a general rate of alcoholism) so that all estimates might be expressed
on a comparable basis.* No changes were made
which would in any way bias the comparison
for or against the Jellinek Formula.

In eight instances the agreement may be
classed as *excellent*: the difference is either
non-existent or less than 10 per cent. In another
three it might be classed as *good* (difference
less than 20 per cent), and in five cases as *fair*
or *poor*. The linear correlation coefficient for

*In several instances, the prevalence estimate for the
area shown represents a projection from the results of
a survey of a much smaller area within the province
or country in question. In one such case (Michigan)
the authors of the survey report explicitly and justi-
fiably refrained from generalizing their results beyond
the single community studied. However, the Jellinek
Formula could not be safely applied to so small a
population. Accordingly, with apologies to these
authors, for present purposes their prevalence estimate
was assumed to hold for the larger political area.

the 16 pairs of estimates is .88 which indicates
that the Jellinek Formula is very likely to estimate in the same order of magnitude as independent methods.

It is not difficult to explain away such dis-
crepancies as exist by appeal to probable
sources of error in the independent methods
(36). For example, the independent estimate
for Chile was based on a survey of an urban
population (31). Since urban rates of alcoholism generally exceed rural rates (15, 24, 52),
it could be said that a discrepancy in the prevalence estimates, of the size and direction
found, was to be expected. But with equal
facility one might challenge the instances of
very close agreement. For example, the survey
in Ontario 1951 was conducted in an area
distinctly more rural than the province as a
whole (12). Accordingly, instead of perfect
agreement one would have expected an independent estimate smaller than that based on the
Jellinek Formula. However, for present purposes, the point I wish to make is simply that –
taken essentially as reported in the literature –
the overall agreement in the 16 comparisons
surely cannot be attributed solely to chance as
Keller (22) and Seeley (47) maintain. Rather
would the explanation appear to lie in the values

commonly assigned to the three factors in the formula: P, K and R.

The value usually assigned to P in order to estimate prevalence in the United States and elsewhere during the 1950s has been about 49 per cent.* In a direct study of liver cirrhosis mortality in Finland – a country for which the relevant trends closely parallel those for North America – a conservative P value of 38 per cent was obtained for the years 1954–5 (6). And in an attempt to determine the P value empirically for us data, a tentative estimate of 40 per cent was obtained (34). The values usually given K and R have been .694 per cent and 4, respectively (11). When converted to a single quantity (K/R), these values imply a death rate among alcoholics with and without complications of about 0.17 per cent. The data necessary to calculate direct estimates of this death rate are available as a result of the Finnish study just mentioned, and two surveys conducted in Ontario (12, 33). For the city of Helsinki the estimated rate is 0.15 per cent, and for Ontario it is 0.26 per cent.†

These data indicate that – albeit by accident rather than design – the values for P and K/R ordinarily employed in the Jellinek Formula are probably close to their true values for most of the period after World War II. It is suggested that this very likely accounts for the agreement between formula and independently derived estimates of prevalence. Certainly the empirical evidence does not indicate that the rate of death from liver cirrhosis among alcoholics has been greatly overestimated. The value assigned to P by Jellinek is larger than the estimates obtained by direct study. However, it is quite possible that this served to compensate in some degree for the tendency (previously noted) to underreport liver cirrhosis as a cause of death.

*Weighted average of the value 62.8 for males and 21.6 for females provided by Jellinek (16).
†The rate for Helsinki was based on the results of a sample survey which indicated a probable alcoholic population of 10,000, and on the finding in a separate study of 30 reported deaths from liver cirrhosis attributable to alcoholism in two years. The rate for Ontario was based on the occurrence of two deaths from liver cirrhosis among 698 alcoholics identified in the first survey (1951) and three such deaths among 1231 in the second survey (1961).

In summary, the weight of evidence favours the conclusion that most Jellinek Formula estimates published to date are sufficiently accurate for purposes of education and program development. However, this assumes that in these activities interest is primarily in the *total number* of alcoholics at a given time in a particular jurisdiction. If, on the other hand, the concern is with *differences in prevalence* both through time and from one jurisdiction to another, then most of the objections to the method cannot be ignored. To establish that an apparent temporal or spatial difference is not artifactual (e.g., due to demographic differences) is often a quite difficult problem (27, 35), and the use of Jellinek Formula estimates simply introduces an additional and unnecessary complication. A promising beginning towards the study of variations in alcoholism prevalence has already been made by relying entirely on the primary mortality data and various basic alcohol statistics. The work of Ledermann (26), Schmidt (41, 43) and Seeley (51, 54) is particularly noteworthy in this regard. Accordingly, it is the writer's view that the expenditure of time, energy, and money required to achieve a logically sound modification of the Jellinek Formula would be better directed to the furtherance of ecological (i.e. etiologically oriented) research on the problems of variation in the primary indices of alcoholism, especially liver cirrhosis mortality rates.

ESTIMATION OF ALCOHOLISM PREVALENCE FROM ALCOHOL SALES DATA

This review would not be complete without mention of attempts to utilize alcohol sales data as an index of alcoholism prevalence. Indeed it is surprising that so little attention has been given to the epidemiological possibilities of such data, since it seems obvious, as Wallgren (56) has remarked, "that there should be a connection between the level of alcohol consumption and the harmful effects of drinking." Nevertheless, until quite recently, the only systematic attempt to explore the connection appears to have been that of Ledermann (26).

Following a detailed examination of a variety

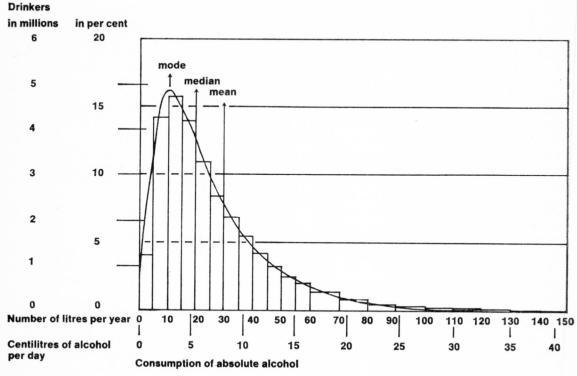

Figure 39-1
Theoretical distribution of alcohol consumption in France. Based on Ledermann (26).

of alcohol statistics and the results of a number of direct studies of drinking habits, Ledermann concluded that the distribution of alcohol consumption in any population could be described theoretically by a logarithmic normal curve. He then constructed such a curve for France on the basis of reported alcohol sales per capita and certain other data. This enabled him to estimate the proportion of the population falling above any given per capita consumption level (see Figure 39-1). An examination of various definitions of alcoholism and the findings of a number of physiological studies led to the view that an intake of 20 centilitres of absolute alcohol or more per day (the equivalent of at least two litres of 10 per cent wine) could be safely considered pathological consumption. Reference to the theoretical distribution indicated that 7 per cent of the adult population could be expected to

drink at this level or higher. The figure of 7 per cent was taken to be an estimate of the prevalence of alcoholism in France.

In the writer's opinion, Ledermann's method is the most theoretically sophisticated yet developed, and deserves much closer attention than it has received outside of France to date.* Its application may pose certain (but by no means insurmountable) difficulties in countries where a substantial proportion of the adult population does not consume alcoholic beverages. For example, in the United States and

*Recently, de Lint and Schmidt (10a) showed that the normal logarithmic model provided an excellent fit to data on the distribution of alcohol buying in Ontario, Canada. They subsequently employed the model to estimate the prevalence of alcoholism in this province (43a), and obtained a figure in very close agreement with that based on the Jellinek Formula.

Canada, between 30 and 40 per cent of adults are reported to be total abstainers, and there are indications of a change in the proportion through time (37). As a consequence, per capita alcohol sales figures underestimate the consumption of users, and changes in such figures may reflect changes in the number of drinkers rather than in average individual intake.

These considerations would lead one to expect that any method which utilizes per capita sales data might tend to underestimate prevalence in areas such as North America or Scandinavia. Recently, de Lint and Bronetto (9), and Seeley (53) have sought to develop a method based on: (*a*) the mean annual alcohol consumption of an alcoholic, estimated on the basis of the reported intake of a clinical sample; and (*b*) the percentage of all consumption contributed by alcoholics, derived from the mean intake per alcoholic, the estimated total number of alcoholics in the province of Ontario, Canada, and the total sales of alcoholic beverages in the province in one year. The values obtained for (*a*) and (*b*) provide two "constants" which can be applied to reported alcohol sales in other areas to obtain an estimate of prevalence. Application of the method to the provinces of Canada and the states of the United States (9) resulted in quite considerable departures from Jellinek Formula estimates in many instances; and as expected, in 46 of the 56 jurisdictions the prevalence estimate based on alcohol sales data was the lesser of the two. On the other hand, a rank order coefficient of .67 indicated a significant tendency for the two methods to place the various jurisdictions in the same order with respect to the relative magnitude of the problem.

It seems appropriate to conclude this review with a reference to promising current research which seeks to estimate prevalence through a study of alcohol buying habits (10). This investigation grew in part out of a dissatisfaction with the conventional per capita sales figure as an index of alcohol consumption. It is being conducted in Ontario, and depends for data on direct observation of buyers and the purchasing slips which have to be filled out to obtain alcoholic beverages. These sources of data are providing the means to determine the number of very frequent, probably alcoholic buyers in the population. But in addition, evidence has been found that a few readily ascertained facts, such as the number of buyers during the first opening hour of the stores and the proportion of all alcohol bought in the form of the cheapest source, constitute indices of one segment of the alcoholic population, namely, impoverished pathological drinkers.

Clearly an indirect method of general applicability cannot be expected from research of this sort. The behaviour under study is partly dependent on local tradition and regulations. However, it serves to indicate another alternative to the direct case-finding survey, and one which eventually should provide more and sounder information respecting the character and magnitude of the problem in a given jurisdiction than any of the indirect methods yet devised.

SUMMARY

There have been a number of attempts to develop methods to estimate alcoholism prevalence from documentary statistics, including records of sudden and violent death, reported liver cirrhosis mortality, and beverage alcohol sales data. All of these methods are either limited in applicability to one or a few areas, are economically impractical, or suffer from more or less serious logical shortcomings. Empirical evidence indicates that most estimates obtained to date by the Jellinek method, which is the most widely used, are probably sufficiently accurate for educational or planning purposes; that is, where interest is chiefly in the total number of alcoholics in a particular area. If, as in etiologically oriented research, interest is in temporal and spatial variation, then the method introduces an unnecessary and undesirable complication. It is suggested that, relative to other behavioural disorders, more satisfactory documentary data are available to the student of alcoholism, and that it would be better to direct attention to the nature and extent of variation in the primary indices of this condition than to engage in costly attempts to revise existing indirect methods of estimation.

REFERENCES

1
Annual report of the Alcoholism and Drug Addiction Research Foundation, 1964
Appendix III
Toronto: Addiction Research Foundation 1965

2
BRENNER, B.
Estimating the prevalence of alcoholism: toward a modification of the Jellinek Formula
Quart. J. Stud. Alc., **20**: 255, 1959

3
BRENNER, B.
Estimating the prevalence of alcoholism from vital rates
Quart. J. Stud. Alc., **21**: 140, 1960

4
BRESARD, M.
Consommation d'alcool et mortalité par cirrhose du foie à Saint-Étienne et à Marseille
Bull. Inst. Nat. Hyg. (Paris), **14**: 367, 1959

5
BRONETTO, J.
Studies of the relation between alcohol price, alcohol consumption and death by liver cirrhosis
Toronto: Addiction Research Foundation, Substudies 1–8–60 to 1.7–8–63, 1960–63

6
BRUUN, K., KOURA, E., POPHAM, R.E., & SEELEY, J.R.
Liver cirrhosis mortality as a means to measure the prevalence of alcoholism
Helsinki: The Finnish Foundation for Alcohol Studies Publication no. 8, part 2, 1960

7
Community Studies, Inc.
Alcoholism survey: State of Kansas
Prepared for the Kansas State Commission on Alcoholism, Topeka 1954

8
DE LINT, J.E.E.
Alcoholism prevalence: an alternative estimation method – three critical comments
Toronto: Addiction Research Foundation, Substudy 4–10–60, 1960

9
DE LINT, J.E.E. & BRONETTO, J.
Alcoholism prevalence estimation and alcohol consumption
Toronto: Addiction Research Foundation Substudy 3–10 & 8–64, 1964

10
DE LINT, J.E.E. & SCHMIDT, W.
Studies of the distribution of wine consumption and certain characteristics of the wine-using population
Toronto: Addiction Research Foundation, Substudies 1–10 & 4–61 to 6–10 & 5–63, 1961–1963

10a
DE LINT, J.E.E. & SCHMIDT, W.
The distribution of alcohol consumption in Ontario
Quart. J. Stud. Alc., **29**: 968, 1968

11
Expert Committee on Mental Health
Report on the first session of the Alcoholism Subcommittee
Geneva: World Health Org., Tech Rept. Series no. 42, 1951

12
GIBBINS, R.J.
Alcoholism in Ontario: a survey of an Ontario county
Quart J. Stud. Alc., **15**: 47, 1954

13
IPSEN, J.
An epidemic of infectious hepatitis, predominantly of adults, and highly fatal for elderly women.
Am. J. Hyg., **51**: 255, 1950

14
IPSEN, J., MOORE, M., & ALEXANDER, L.
Prevalence of alcoholism in the population and among suicides and accidents from poisoning
Massachusetts 1938–1948
Quart. J. Stud. Alc., **13**: 204, 1952

15
JELLINEK, E.M.
Recent trends in alcoholism and in alcohol consumption
Quart. J. Stud. Alc., **8**: 1, 1947

16
JELLINEK, E.M.
The estimate of the number of alcoholics in the U.S.A. for 1949 in the light of the Sixth Revision of the International Lists of Causes of Death
Quart. J. Stud. Alc., **13**: 214, 1952

17
JELLINEK, E.M.
International experience with the problems of alcoholism
Geneva: World Health Org., Document WHO/MENT/58, WHO/APD/ALC/12, 1954

18
JELLINEK, E.M.
Personal communications, August 1954 and July 1956

19
JELLINEK, E.M.
Estimating the prevalence of alcoholism: modified values in the Jellinek Formula and an alternative approach
Quart. J. Stud. Alc., **20**: 261, 1959

20
JELLINEK, E.M. & KELLER, M,
Rates of alcoholism in the United States of America, 1940–1948
Quart. J. Stud. Alc., **13**: 49, 1952

21
JOLLIFFE, N. & JELLINEK, E.M.
Cirrhosis of the liver. In: Effects of alcohol on the individual, vol. 1, ed. by E. M. Jellinek,
New Haven: Yale University, 1942, p. 273

22
KELLER, M.
The definition of alcoholism and the estimation of its

prevalence. In: Society, culture, and drinking patterns,
ed. by D. J. Pittman & C. R. Snyder
New York: Wiley, 1962, p. 310
23
KELLER, M. & EFRON, V.
The prevalence of alcoholism
Quart. J. Stud. Alc., **16**: 619, 1955
24
KELLER, M. & EFRON, V.
Alcoholism in the big cities of the United States
Quart. J. Stud. Alc., **17**: 63, 1956
25
LEDERMANN, S.C.
La mortalité par causes dans ses rapports avec
l'alcoolisation de la population
Inst. Nat. d'Études Démographiques (Paris),
Séance no. 2, 1954
26
LEDERMANN, S.C.
Alcool, alcoolisme, alcoolisation
Inst. Nat. d'Études Démographiques (Paris),
Traveaux et Documents, Cahier no. 29, 1956
27
LIPSCOMB, W.R. & SULKA, E.
Some factors affecting the geographic comparison of
alcoholism prevalence rates
Quart. J. Stud. Alc., **22**: 588, 1961
28
MACLACHLAN, J.M.
Personal communication, March 1955
29
MANIS, J.G.
Personal communication, June 1963
30
MANIS, J.G. & HUNT, C.L.
The community survey as a measure of the
prevalence of alcoholism
Quart. J. Stud. Alc., **18**: 212, 1957
31
MARCONI, J. *et al.*
A survey on the prevalence of alcoholism among
the adult population of a suburb of Santiago
Quart. J. Stud. Alc., **16**: 438, 1955
32
MULFORD, H.A. & MILLER, D.E.
Drinking in Iowa. v. Drinking and alcoholic
drinking
Quart. J. Stud. Alc., **21**: 483, 1960
33
NEWMAN, A.F.
Alcoholism in Frontenac County: a survey of the
characteristics of an alcoholic population in its
native habitat
PH.D. thesis, Queen's University, 1965
34
ORIEL, A.E.
Personal communication, November 1954
35
PEARL, A., BUECHLEY, R. & LIPSCOMB, W.R.
Cirrhosis mortality in three large cities: implications

for alcoholism and intercity comparisons.
In: Society, culture, and drinking patterns, ed. by
D. J. Pittman & C. R. Snyder
New York: Wiley, 1962, p. 345
36
POPHAM, R.E.
The Jellinek Alcoholism Estimation Formula and its
application to Canadian data
Quart. J. Stud. Alc., **17**: 559, 1956
37
POPHAM, R.E. & SCHMIDT, W.
Statistics of alcohol use and alcoholism in Canada
1871–1956
Toronto: University of Toronto Press, 1958
38
POPHAM, R.E. & SCHMIDT, W.
A decade of alcoholism research
Toronto: University of Toronto Press, Brookside
Monograph no. 3, 1962
39
Portal House of the Chicago Committee on Alcoholism
The public alcoholic in Chicago and Cook County
Chicago, 1955
40
RILEY, J.W. & MARDEN, C.F.
The medical profession and the problem of alcoholism
Quart. J. Stud. Alc., **7**: 240, 1946
41
SCHMIDT, W.
The ecology of alcoholism
Selected papers presented at the 27th International
Congress on Alcohol & Alcoholism, Frankfurt-
am-Main 1964, vol. 1, p. 43.
42
SCHMIDT, W. & BRONETTO, J.
Death from liver cirrhosis and specific beverage
consumption – United States – 1934–1958
Toronto: Addiction Research Foundation
Substudy 1.1–4 & 8–61, 1961
43
SCHMIDT, W. & BRONETTO, J.
Death from liver cirrhosis and specific alcoholic
beverage consumption USA – 1950
Am. J. Pub. Health, **52**: 1473, 1962
43a
SCHMIDT, W. & DE LINT, J.E.E.
Estimating the prevalence of alcoholism from alcohol
consumption and mortality data
Quart. J. Stud. Alc., in press
44
SCHMIDT, W. & SMART, R.G.
Admissions of alcoholics without psychosis to mental
institutions, and the estimated prevalence of
alcoholism: Ontario, 1948–55
Canad. J. Pub. Health, **50**: 431, 1959
45
SEELEY, J.R.
Alcoholism prevalence analysis: the basic transactions
Toronto: Addiction Research Foundation,
Mathematical Memo 9–1–58, 1958

46
SEELEY, J.R.
Prevalence of alcoholism: The Ipsen-Moore-Alexander
Method
Toronto: Addiction Research Foundation, Substudy
13–1–58, 1958
47
SEELEY, J.R.
Estimating the prevalence of alcoholism: a critical
analysis of the Jellinek Formula
Quart. J. Stud. Alc., **20**: 245, 1959
48
SEELEY, J.R.
Sampling error in estimations of the Jellinek
Alcoholism Prevalence Formula type
Toronto: Addiction Research Foundation,
Mathematical Memo 12–1–59, 1959
49
SEELEY, J.R.
Estimating the prevalence of alcoholism: a critical
analysis of the Brenner Formula
Toronto: Addiction Research Foundation, Substudy
19.1–1–60, 1960
50
SEELEY, J.R.
Alcoholism prevalence: an alternative estimation
method
Quart. J. Stud. Alc., **21**: 500, 1960
51
SEELEY, J.R.
Death by liver cirrhosis and the price of
beverage alcohol
C.M.A.J., **83**: 1361, 1960
52
SEELEY, J.R.
The ecology of alcoholism: a beginning
In: Society, culture, and drinking patterns,
ed. by D. J. Pittman & C. R. Snyder
New York: Wiley, 1962, p. 330
53
SEELEY, J.R.
An approach to the estimation of alcoholism in a
population based on mean alcohol consumption
Toronto: Addiction Research Foundation,
Substudy 27–1–63, 1963
54
SEELEY, J.R. & SCHMIDT, W.
Studies in the ecology of liver cirrhosis mortality
Toronto: Addiction Research Foundation,
Substudies 1–1 & 4–58 to 1.8–1 & 4–60, 1958–60
55
SJÖVALL, E.
Alkohol und Lebercirrhose
Deutsche Ztschr. ges. gerichtl. Med., **41**: 10, 1952
56
WALLGREN, H.
Alcoholism and alcohol consumption
Alkoholpolitik, **23**: 177, 1960
57
WILLIAMS, G.P.
Chronic alcoholics: a report on the incidence in

Harrow, Peterborough, York, Salford and Gateshead
London, Eng.: Steering Group on Alcoholism
(Joseph Rowntree Social Service Trust) 1965
(See also G. P. Williams & M. M. Glatt
Brit. J. Addict., **61**: 257, 1966.)
58
ZAX, M., GARDNER, E.A., & HART, W.T.
A survey of the prevalence of alcoholism in
Monroe County, N.Y., 1961
Quart. J. Stud. Alc., **24**: 316, 1967

ALFREDO SAAVEDRA

JAVIER MARIÁTEGUI

Department of Psychiatry
Cayetano Heredia Peruvian University
Department of Psychology
San Marcos University
Lima, Peru

40

The Epidemiology of Alcoholism in Latin America

This paper is concerned with the nature and extent of alcoholism in Central and South American countries. It has been made possible through the generous co-operation of many colleagues who provided publications and a variety of information for their respective countries. However, we must emphasize that because of the complexity of the problem, which is differently manifested in each country, and the scarcity of the requisite data in many instances, our effort constitutes only a first, tentative approximation to a general epidemiology of alcoholism in Latin America. Although we have some data for Argentina, Brazil, Colombia, Costa Rica, Chile, Mexico, and our own country, Peru, we have little or no information for the remaining Latin American countries. Furthermore, the sources of information in those countries where the problem has been studied in detail are direct surveys of small population groups, and indirect rates that give only a rough estimate of prevalence. It is difficult to compare the survey results for such countries, because different methodological criteria have been used. Certainly the work which has been accomplished by a small group of investigators is worthy of praise; but the problem of determining the factors influencing alcoholism rates in Latin America requires further organized analysis of each aspect, using similar criteria, exploration methods of unquestionable validity, and a firmly established socioeconomic and cultural frame of reference.

In general, there are two types of factors which influence the epidemiology of alcoholism: internal, i.e. depending on the individual himself, such as biological or psychological vulnerability; and external, i.e. social and cultural. Both factors usually act together in such a way that it is almost impossible to separate them. By way of background information we shall first consider the figures for alcoholic beverage consumption, and then analyse some direct and indirect attempts to estimate alcoholism prevalence, the indirect methods being based on consequences of the drinking habit.

CONSUMPTION OF ALCOHOLIC BEVERAGES

The main beverages used in Latin America are of the fermented type: wine, pulque, chicha, and beer. Among the distilled beverages used are brandy, rum, tequila, whisky, and certain combinations of alcohol and distilled spirits with fruit or plant juices, or infusions of tobacco and alcohol with other components; these have different names in each region. A large proportion of all alcoholic beverages is produced illegally and therefore is not reported in official statistics. In some countries, such as Peru, Bolivia, Colombia, Venezuela, and some parts of Central America, the spirits are distilled but not properly rectified. In Peru only 30 per cent of spirits are rectified (7).

Argentina

In 1965, the general consumption of wine was 19,175,640 hectolitres, that is 85.23 litres per capita, an amount which ranks third in world rates. In 1962–3 and 1963–4, the consumption of distilled spirits amounted to 123,541,968 and 157,523,279 litres, respectively. Beer consumption was 9.98 litres per capita in 1965. (In 1950 it was 21.62.) The consumption was mainly of distilled drinks in provinces near Paraguay and Patagonia, and wine in Buenos Aires and provinces such as Litoral, Cuyo, and Cordoba. In 1964 the annual consumption of wine was almost 90 litres per capita.

Brazil

The only information we have indicates that in 1964, 14,277 distilleries were in operation (1).

Chile

In 1960, the production amounted to 8,507,516 litres of absolute alcohol (in brandy, pisco, and other liquors), and 485,274,000 litres of wine in 1961 (13, 49). This gives an annual consumption rate of 2.33 litres of alcohol and 130 litres of wine per capita older than 15 years.

Colombia

In 1964, the consumption of domestic beer was 654,972,224 litres, and of imported beer, 34,293. There were 1,003,853 litres of imported liquors and wines consumed (27).

Guatemala

The consumption of alcoholic beverages in 1965 was 8,090,810 litres (12).

Mexico

In 1959 1,086,078 litres of fermented drinks were produced (chiefly beer and pulque) and 72,744 litres of distilled spirits of high alcoholic concentration, that is, 33.48 and 2.23 litres respectively, per capita. If we consider that the male adult population between 22 and 44 years of age was about 5,000,000, more realistic estimates may be derived, namely, 217.22 and 14.55 litres per capita, respectively. The states with highest consumption rates were Veracruz, Puebla, Sinaloa, and Jalisco (14, 50).

Peru

The consumption in 1965 was 168,266,176 litres of beer, 18,588,000 of rum, 1,848,556 of brandy, 3,159,138 of various liquors, 9,853,413 of common wine, 783,348 of sweet wine, 514,616 of champagne, and 1,912,828 of vermouth (11).

Venezuela

The consumption in 1962 (49) was 19 litres of strong alcoholic beverages and 102 of beer (18) per adult.

DIRECT EPIDEMIOLOGICAL SURVEYS

The prevalence of alcoholism has been investigated in some countries by both direct and indirect methods. The former seek to estimate the percentage of alcoholics through surveys of population samples. Such surveys have been conducted in Argentina, Brazil, Chile, Mexico, and Peru. Physicians, employers, clergymen, police, staff of social agencies, and other relevant groups have participated in the interviews.

Argentina

The National Institute for Mental Health, through its Department of Statistics and Psychiatric Epidemiology, has started to obtain data on prevalence, incidence, and risks of mental pathology according to a three-year plan (3). Twenty-two regions representative of the different social strata and the geographic distribution of the population have been chosen. The region of Buenos Aires was studied in consultation with Professor Tsung-Yi Lin of the World Health Organization. The first pilot studies were made in urban and suburban areas. In an urban area (the federal capital), out of 2,735 interviews 0.7 per cent alcoholics were found in the population over 15 years of age. Mental pathology was found in 6.43 per cent of the samples, and alcoholism occurred in slightly over 10 per cent of those exhibiting such pathology. In a suburban area (Mendoza) 3.3 per cent adults of the 1,268 persons surveyed proved to be alcoholics. This higher rate was associated with a frequency of 12.24 per cent mental disorders.

We do not yet know the full results of these epidemiological studies, or the selection criteria and other techniques. We also lack the information needed to associate the results with the social structure of Argentina. Nevertheless, it is now evident that the consumption of fermented drinks (preference being given to wine) is very common in this country; 90 per cent of the persons interviewed in Lanus and Buenos Aires drank wine with their meals seven days a week (15, 55).

Brazil

Two hundred and three persons (88 men and 115 women) were interviewed in Villa Santa Teresinha (1), a workers quarter of Riberirao Preto (São Paulo) with 260 inhabitants. The study included only those over ten years of age with the exception of one younger person because his unusual alcoholic beverage ingestion was known to the whole community. There were found to be 6.4 per cent alcoholics and 13.3 per cent excessive drinkers in this sample. Most alcoholics were males (13.6 per cent of all men and 0.9 per cent of all women), while among excessive drinkers the sex difference was not as great (17 per cent of all men and 10.4 per cent of all women). These findings are similar to those found in a study of hospitalized addicts (30). Moreover, the latter study confirmed the responses obtained by the questionnaire in 92.3 per cent of the cases, thus indicating the validity of the epidemiological method used.

Chile

Since 1954, a number of surveys of selected areas have been made to estimate the prevalence of abnormal use of alcohol. The first survey was of a working-class population (21). It found 4.2 per cent alcoholics and 13.2 per cent periodic excessive drinkers among those over 15 years; the sex ratio was 13 men to one woman. A second survey (35) was conducted in October 1955 and July 1956 in Santiago, and was also of a working-class population. It found 5.7 per cent alcoholics, with a sex ratio of 25 to one. In 1958, a study was made of different forms of mental pathology (with special emphasis on alcoholism) in samples chosen from two areas of Santiago – Ñuñoa and San Miguel – which have much in common with the city as a whole (35). In this study, 5.1 per cent alcoholics were found (inveterate, 2.5 per cent; intermittent, 2.6 per cent) and 7.7 per cent excessive drinkers. The latter were not considered alcoholics but persons with a serious risk of becoming so. The alcoholic sex ratio was 14 men to one woman.

In 1958 in Quilpué, a small town near Valparaíso, 1.5 per cent alcoholics and 10 per cent excessive drinkers were found among children 6 to 15 years of age in a small working-class area (52). The very early start of the problem and the high social acceptance of alcohol ingestion is clear. In 1965 a survey of the northern area of Santiago, nearly all middle-class, showed a prevalence of 1.9 per cent alcoholics among those over 15 years (39). Studies of various unorganized communities around Santiago show a high prevalence of alcoholism: as great as 15 per cent of the adult population (34). An investigation made in Chiloé (43), with an 80 per cent rural population, revealed 3.4 per cent alcoholics among those over 15. A survey of the prevalence of alcoholism in the Chilean Indian populations (Araucanians), found chiefly in Malleco, Antofagasta, Santiago, and Cautín, is planned (42).

Mexico

In 1958, a group of public health physicians undertook a direct survey of an area in Mexico City and found an alcoholism rate of 6.8 per 1,000 of general population. This was in close agreement with the rate estimated by the Jellinek

Formula (6.9 per 1,000). When the rate is based on adult population, it becomes 1.8 per cent or one alcoholic in each 55 individuals at the most productive stage of their lives. The ratio of men to women was 15:1. In some areas, as for example among the Indian population of Chamula, there are a number of sociocultural factors favouring alcoholism. Thus, alcohol use is an integral part of all civic and religious activities (14).

A survey of neurological and psychiatric diseases was made in 1960, in which physicians all over the country were requested to complete a questionnaire on patients seen by them during a ten-day period. The data obtained in this manner indicated an alcoholism prevalence rate of 5.48 per 1,000 of general population or about 1 per cent of the population over 18 years of age. This result was later confirmed through studies of other samples (41).

In 1964, another survey was made by professional nurses of a sample of public employees, that is, a sample with an educational and socio-economic level higher than the average for the general population. The alcoholism rate was 12.2 per thousand adults (50).

In the rural community of Morelos with 850 inhabitants, and ranking third in alcohol consumption per capita after Mexico City and Puebla, an alcoholism survey was undertaken by Dr. Felipe Sánchez over a five-year period. He found 14.4 per cent alcoholics, and 13 per cent excessive drinkers among persons older than 15 years (28). Among those over 40, 32 per cent were alcoholics and 16 per cent excessive drinkers. Problems attributable to alcoholism in this community included aggressive behaviour, family disorganization, and economic unproductiveness.

Peru

A first study of the prevalence of mental disorders was made in 1958 (44, 45) in a district of Central Lima called Mendocita, which is relatively isolated from the rest of the urban area. This district was the object of a series of social psychiatric studies conducted through interviews, survey and tests. The inhabitants comprised a low-income group with unstable employment histories, and were mainly emigrants from the provinces; social disorganization was evident and the delinquency rate was high (46, 47).

A sample of 239 individuals from this population was studied with reference to psychiatric pathology. On the basis of the Cornell Medical Index, significant evidence of pathology was found in 42.5 per cent of the sample. The alcoholism prevalence rate was 8.8 per cent with four men to one woman. Alcoholism appeared to be more frequent among people coming from the Andes regions, and among migrants whether from the coast or the mountains. In disintegrated domestic groups the prevalence was also higher showing the important protective function of an adequate family organization.

In Lince, representative of the urban middle-class population of Lima, we undertook in 1962 (37) a prevalence survey of 4 per cent of all families as given in the national census of 1961 (10). The sample included 593 families or a total of 2,901 individuals. The selection of the families was at random from the community of 14,860 persons. The results indicated that 18.7 per cent of the population had some current emotional or mental problems. Concerning alcoholism, we counted only regular excessive drinkers and addicts, and found 51 cases or 1.8 per cent of the population over 14 years of age. Alcoholism was present in 9.4 per cent of the cases with a diagnosis of pathological disturbance, and 12.4 per cent if based on the adult population only.

Peru is a part of what was Tawantinsuyo, which, at the arrival of the Spaniards, included Peru, Bolivia, Ecuador, southern Colombia, northern Chile, and a small portion of north-eastern Argentina. After the conquest, with the disintegration of the controls imposed by Incan society, the Peruvian Indian began to consume much larger amounts of alcohol than had previously been his custom. Before the arrival of the Spaniards, religious feasts were usually accompanied by heavy drinking, but social demands were sufficiently strong to prevent excessive inveterate drinking. The Spanish conquest, which shattered one social organization but did not replace it with another, upset this balance, and from then on the Indian moved increasingly towards the use of alcohol as a drug. He began to seek escape from his continual deprivations both in alcohol and in coca (also used in ancient Peru), and in the high regions of the Andes these two substances became dangerous means of survival for the chronically hungry Indian.

Little is known of the characteristics, extent, and incidence of alcohol problems among Peruvian Indians or among the inhabitants of the area comprising ancient Tawantinsuyo. We also know nothing of the combined effects of alcohol and coca, but we suspect such effects to be at the root of their social stagnation, apathy, and episodic aggressiveness. Many millions of Latin Americans in the Andean regions from northern Argentina to southern Colombia, and in Ecuador and Brazil, but especially in Peru and Bolivia, chew coca and drink wine (26, 48). For example, the consumption of coca leaves in Peru is about 10,000,000 kg per year, and 4,000,000 kg in Bolivia. The estimated coca consumption for all Latin America is over 15,000,000 kg and there are some 4,000,000 users. A study in Vicos, an Indian village in El Callejón de Huaylas (32, 46) indicated the cultural motivations leading to alcohol drinking and its differential characteristics. All inhabitants over ten years of age drink chicha or rum. They drink together, never alone, and apparently there are no conflicts about the role played by alcohol in the community. It is impossible to have some kind of celebration without alcohol: "people can't understand life without feasts, or feasts without alcohol" (32).

In Lunahuaná (51) a study of the population of "mestizos" revealed the integration of habits of alcohol consumption in the cultural background, and found less frequent pathological ingestion or alcoholism.

When natives migrate so that traditional community controls are no longer effective, their drinking behaviour is apt to create difficulties for them. Among migrants to the coastal regions where the social support is no longer present and the prevalent attitudes towards alcohol differ from those of their original community, conflict inevitably occurs; and its consequences are easily seen in the ghettos (*barriadas*), first and unavoidable destination of migrants from the Andes. Alcohol is dissociated from its primitive

functions in the home community, and excessive consumption becomes a means to relieve the tension inherent in any process of adaptation to a different environment. The high proportion of alcoholism in the suburbs of Lima and other cities of the coast is undoubtedly related to this process.

Alcohol consumption in native populations fulfils integrative and social functions. Its eradication or replacement means a complicated change of attitudes which has to start with a radical change in customary modes of living, and in the economic structure of the country, which involves a repressive and exploitative system inherited by the Republic from the early Spanish conquerors. Thus, social factors appear of fundamental importance for the comprehension of alcoholism and its problems in the native population.

Venezuela
A survey performed in 1950 (18) among 1,650 oil workers found 0.37 per cent alcoholics, while rates for the general population fluctuate between 1.34 per cent and 3.95 per cent.

JELLINEK FORMULA ESTIMATES OF PREVALENCE

Estimates of the prevalence of alcoholism based on the Jellinek Formula have been calculated for Chile and Mexico.

Chile
In 1957 (19, 23), 5 per cent alcoholics, 14 per cent excessive drinkers and 62 per cent moderate drinkers were found, and therefore in the population over 15 years of age (about 3,600,-000), 180,000 were estimated to be alcoholics. The sample was taken from Santiago, Ñuñoa and San Miguel, and the estimate coincided with that found by direct survey in 1954 (20).

Mexico
In 1960, the prevalence of alcoholism was estimated to be 15 per cent in the Federal District, a proportion similar to that found after five years' observation of a selected rural population (10 per cent) (28). For Mexico as

a whole, the Jellinek Formula gave 6.8 per thousand or about 255,300 alcoholics, of whom 194,765 lived in the Federal District (4).

DEATHS FROM ALCOHOLISM AND ASSOCIATED CAUSES

Here we shall consider only cases in which death occurred as a direct consequence of alcohol or of complications induced by its continuous use. Various studies have revealed that death from liver cirrhosis, cardiovascular diseases, esophageal and gastric cancer, and chronic tuberculosis occur more frequently among alcoholics. Liver cirrhosis is a consequence of nutritional deficiencies induced by alcohol consumption. The final report (24) of the Latin American Seminar on Alcoholism, held in 1960, noted that the mortality rate from liver cirrhosis was 4.7 per 100,000 for Argentina (1956); 2.9 for Bolivia (1954); 5.1 for Colombia (1958); 4.6 for Costa Rica (1958); 3.7 for Ecuador; 6.8 for El Salvador; 6.8 for Guatemala; 2.0 for Honduras; 5.6 for Nicaragua; 4.8 for Peru; 9.1 for the Dominican Republic; 3.8 for Panama; and 1.7 for Paraguay (all in 1957); 5.9 for Uruguay (1955); 7.3 for Venezuela (1955); 19.6 for Mexico (1956); and 20.0 for Chile (1958).

In Buenos Aires, the mortality rate in 1964 (55) due to causes associated with alcoholism was 0.08 per 100,000 for alcoholic psychosis, 0.10 for alcoholism, and 1.6 for liver cirrhosis.

HOSPITAL ADMISSIONS FOR ALCOHOLISM AND ASSOCIATED CONDITIONS

According to the final report of the Latin American Seminar (24), it can be estimated that 10 per cent of the alcoholics in Latin America in 1958 developed an alcoholic psychosis.

Argentina
In 1956, there were 13.7 per cent alcoholics among admission to psychiatric hospitals. In 1954, alcoholism was diagnosed in 8 per cent of the patients of the Lanus Department of Psychology and Neurology (55). In the Neuro-

psychiatric Hospital for men, 24 per cent of admissions were alcoholics in 1965. In the Neuropsychiatric National Hospital, 78 per cent were inveterate alcoholics and 22 per cent intermittent. In the Melchor Romero Neuropsychiatric Hospital in 1965, 33 per cent of total patients were suffering from sub-acute alcoholism. In the Avellaneda Psychopathological Institute in 1965, 10 per cent of first admissions were alcoholics. In the Model Institute in 1965, 5 per cent of diagnoses comprised liver cirrhhosis, alcoholism, and alcoholic psychosis. In the Grondona Institute in the same year, 2.51 per cent were alcoholics. The proportion of psychiatric admissions to the general hospitals was 13.7 per thousand.

Brazil
In Brazil (1), alcoholism is the second major cause of admission to mental hospitals after schizophrenia. Thus in 1963, 13.6 per cent of the total of 484,448 patients were hospitalized because of alcoholism.

Chile
A study of the morbidity of mental disorders, carried out in 1957 (20, 23), disclosed 5.1 per cent alcoholism. The proportion with alcoholic psychosis among the latter was 15.7 per cent. The percentage of psychiatric admissions to general hospitals was 24.8.

In 1961 the prevalence and incidence of alcoholic psychosis, absolute and relative, was enormous in comparison to the small number of hospitalizations for alcoholism without psychotic complications. The average rate of hospitalization for men was 32.3 per cent, and 32 per cent of these cases were treated for psychotic complications (delirium tremens, alcoholic hallucinosis, etc.). This rate for the country is higher than the frequency of psychotic consequences found in drinkers of the province of Concepción, or in the statistics reported by any other similar psychiatric department.

Of the total number of discharged patients (38) from the Psychiatric Hospital in Chile in 1964, 25.7 per cent were diagnosed as having alcoholism; and over 10 per cent suffered from alcoholic psychosis.

Mexico

In the Federal District of 6,500,000 inhabitants (6), three rehabilitation departments hold 68 new alcoholic consultations daily, and an average of 60 patients receive different therapies each day. The Federal Psychiatric Hospital admits an average of 32 alcoholic patients per month.

Peru

Delirium tremens is the main cause of admission for alcoholic psychosis to the Victor Larco Herrera Hospital, and admissions for alcoholism in general rank third after schizophrenia and epilepsy.

Venezuela

In 1962 (18) the percentage of hospital admissions due to alcoholism was 1.2 per cent, and less than 5 per cent of these were to private institutions.

Other countries

The number of psychiatric admissions involving alcoholism was 50.8 per cent in Guatemala between 1955 and 1957; 51 per cent in Honduras in 1956; 4.6 per cent in Panama in 1958; and 3 per cent in Colombia in 1958. In 1965 in Costa Rica, 3,169 individuals underwent treatment for alcoholism, and 185 patients were admitted for detoxication.

ALCOHOL-RELATED LEGAL OFFENCES

Another indirect approach to the prevalence of alcoholism in Latin America is through illegal behaviour associated with alcohol use. It is important to emphasize that the relationship between the consumption of alcoholic beverages and crime is direct, and that between crime and alcoholism is indirect, except in the case of psychiatric complications. Most alcohol-related offences are committed during acute or subacute intoxication.

Argentina

From an annual average of 25,004 offences, 60 to 158 were homicides, and of these an estimated seven to ten were induced by alcohol

(54). Among over 300 suicides, alcohol appeared to be responsible for 250. In 1961 (5), 67 per cent of those arrested in "villas miserias" were alcoholics.

Chile

A study made in 1966, showed that the alcohol-crime rate for Santiago in 1964 was 50 per 100,000 inhabitants; abnormal alcohol ingestion was responsible for 4.6 per cent of traffic accidents. A study made in a metallurgical industry (49) showed that 12.7 per cent of work accidents were related to alcohol. In Antofagasta, 69 per cent of all crimes were related to alcohol; in Valdivia, 60 per cent; and in Concepción, 69 per cent. In Santiago's penitentiary, 33 per cent of the convicts had committed the crime while drunk; 31.7 per cent of pedestrian victims of traffic accidents and 3.5 per cent of drivers showed high blood alcohol levels.

Guatemala

The Public Welfare Council showed that in 1956 51,334 of a total of 80,967 convicted persons were drunk when arrested (12).

Mexico

In 1953 in the Federal District (50), 66 per cent of all acts of violence were related to alcohol (fights, traffic accidents). Another study (4) showed that alcohol was involved in 60 per cent of all homicides, and 70 per cent of deaths in traffic accidents. If we add deaths caused by fights, homicides, and suicides, the mortality rate from alcoholism become 3 per cent. This study also mentions the work of Quiroz Cuarón in 1959, who, together with Marcoz and Meza, found that in Cruz Verda 27 per cent of admissions were under the influence of alcohol. Many authors report that a high proportion (ranging from 63 to 85 per cent) of antisocial behaviour is induced by alcohol. Of the total number of suicide attempts, 6.7 per cent occurred while the individual was severely intoxicated; of these 5.07 per cent were successful, that is a rate of 17 per 1,000 (6).

Peru

Between 1951 and 1955, 30,000 persons were arrested for problems related to alcoholism. In

1956, 60 per cent of all cases arrested were punished for inebriety. A study made in this year (8) found that 35 per cent of collisions and 9 per cent of pedestrian accidents in Lima, were attributable to alcoholic intoxication. Crimes committed under the influence of alcohol amounted to one-third of the total, and 80 per cent of all offences involving aggression were committed while drunk. During 1955 and 1956, 58,000 individuals were arrested for inebriety, a number higher than that for any other offence. Pedestrian accidents and collisions in Lima, Callao and Balnearios, which occurred under the influence of alcohol amounted to 58 per cent of the total in 1955.

Venezuela

The rate of homicide in 1950 (18) was 17.04 per thousand. Crimes under the influence of alcohol ranged from 30 to 50 per cent. In the state of Miranda in 1957, alcohol was a factor in 46.4 per cent of the total number of crimes; 58.2 per cent in the state of Tovar; 78.7 per cent in Mesa Bolivar; 45.4 per cent in Anzoategui; and 42.8 per cent in Sucre.

DISCUSSION

It does not seem necessary to examine critically all of the investigations mentioned in order to compare the different Latin American countries. However, it is true that since different methods of epidemiological research were employed, the value of the findings for comparative analysis is impaired. The various population samples require further examination, with similar definitions (21, 22), to permit a clear delimitation of concepts and an adequate evaluation of the sociocultural parameters of the groups investigated (36). Taking this as a starting point, the studies will reflect reality and will be ready for application to all regions of a given country to measure regional changes and the sociocultural circumstances that condition them.

The extent of alcoholism revealed by the data presented, must seriously retard the development of Latin American countries. In urban districts we find similar rates for Mexico City (1.8 per cent), Lima (1.8 per cent), and for a sample of the middle-class of Santiago (1.9 per cent). The highest rate is that for Santiago as a whole (5.1 per cent), and the lowest is for Buenos Aires (0.7 per cent).

The relationship between socioeconomic status and the pathological consumption of alcohol is indicated by the rates for such lower-class suburbs as Ribeirao Preto in San Pablo (6.4 per cent), Mendocita in Lima (8.8 per cent), and for working-class areas in Santiago (4.2 and 4.7 per cent). The rate of alcoholism seems especially high in the peripheral population around Santiago (15 per cent); there it is similar to that found in the rural community of Morelos in Mexico (14.4 per cent). Though different methods were used, these similarities are no doubt significant.

All investigators note that drinking is not disfavoured in most of the Latin American countries and is even considered a sign of manhood. Most of the native population drink on all special civic, religious, and social occasions. Business transactions and, among adolescents of higher educational level, sports events are accompanied by drinking; alcohol appears everywhere to be an important means of establishing social contacts. In rural towns, lack of interest and motivation, and of other recreation and work, bring about indifference and boredom which are main factors in excessive drinking (2, 3, 5, 25, 26, 28, 29, 40).

Insecurity is a general characteristic of Latin American populations – insecurity due to fragile socioeconomic structures and deficient instruction. Most people work only to obtain the minimum required for survival; of 180,000,000 Latin Americans 40,000,000 over 15 years of age are illiterate (13). In Argentina a study of the relationship between alcoholism and educational standard (13) revealed that 57 per cent of alcoholics were illiterate, a phenomenon that is common to all Latin American countries. Among alcoholics admitted to the Melchor Romero Hospital, 21 per cent were illiterate, as were 23 per cent of their relatives. Surveys of the *villas miserias* in Buenos Aires found 19 per cent illiterate.

The *favelas* in Brazil, *ranchos* in Caracas, *barriadas* in Lima and *villas miserias* in Argentina (13) are deficient in housing and sanitary facilities, and the educational poverty is outstanding. In all of these areas, alcohol (and in

some, coca as well) is the normal sedative anti-
dote that makes survival possible and tolerable
in such a difficult life situation.

Intensive advertising, through all the principal
media of communication, is conducted systematically by the alcoholic beverage industry. This
contributes to an increase in alcohol consumption. Millions are spent to advertise the quality
of certain types of beverage (14).

This brief review of epidemiological data and
research on alcoholism in Latin America offers
some insight into the extent and seriousness of
the problem. However, it should be emphasized
that most of the studies have been concerned
only with urban populations. We know little or
nothing about the problems of alcohol in rural
areas, and even less of those in the native populations which occupy large sections of the continent.

It is clear that a complete study of the basic
factors that condition alcoholism and the problems derived from it in every Latin American
country would be highly desirable (16, 22).
The group responsible for epidemiological investigation has emphasized (17) the need to
start new research designed to define the problem and determine its extent, so that the assistance required and basic elements of a program of prevention can be assessed. This group
has suggested the following topics for study:
(*a*) the prevalence of different types of normal
and abnormal drinkers, through direct surveys
of populations; (*b*) medical and socioeconomic
consequences of abnormal alcohol ingestion;
(*c*) methods to evaluate the results of present
alcoholism treatment; and (*d*) the attitudes of
the population towards alcoholism as a disease.
The group also cites the technical difficulties and
lack of resources in each country as factors impairing research to date. They recommend accordingly a united effort on the part of interested
countries to seek the help of international organizations in developing the programs outlined.

SUMMARY

Available statistics of alcohol use and alcoholism
in Latin American countries are reviewed as a
first approach to an epidemiological picture of
the nature and magnitude of the problem. Special attention is given to data obtained through
direct surveys of population samples and to estimates of alcoholism prevalence obtained by indirect methods such as the Jellinek Formula.
The findings are discussed in relation to socioeconomic and cultural conditions, and the importance of comparable parallel investigations
in all Latin American countries is emphasized
as a means to an adequate evaluation of the alcoholism problem and a sound basis for prevention and treatment.

REFERENCES

1
AZOUBEL NETO, D. & RIBEIRO DA COSTA, M.C.
Contribuicâo para o estudo epidemiologico do
alcoholismo. II. Estudo da conduta de ingestâo de
bebidas alcoolicas em um bairro de Riberâo Prêto
(not published).
2
BEJARANO, J.
La experiencia colombiana en la campaña contra la
chicha y la coca
In: Informe final de la Conferencia Nacional de
Alcoholismo, Lima, 1957
3
BONHOUR, A.
Discurso del presidente del primer seminario
internacional sobre desarrollo de la comunidad en
salud mental
Buenos Aires, July 1965
4
CABILDO, H.M.
Consideraciones epidemiológicas sobre el alcoholismo
en la República Mexicana
Neurolog. y Neurocir.-Psiquiat., México, **6**: 21, 1965
5
CALDERON NARVAEZ, G.
Consecuencias sociales y económicas de la ingestión
abnormal de alcohol
Presented at the Study Group on the Epidemiological
Investigation of Alcoholism in Latin America,
San José, Costa Rica, June 1966
6
CALDERON, N.G. & CABILDO, H.M.
Aspectos relacionados con el problema del
alcoholismo en México
Presented at the Study Group on the Epidemiological
Investigation of the Problems of Alcoholism,
San José, Costa Rica, June 1966
7
CARAVEDO, B.
Trabajo y salud mental
Rev. psiquiat. per. **2**: 91, 1959
8
CARAVEDO, B. & ALMEIDA VARGAS, M.
El alcoholismo, problema de salud pública
(Investigatión de algunos aspectos en el Perú)

Informe del Ministerio de Salud Pública y Asistencia
Social, Departamento de Higiene Mental, 1956
9
CARAVEDO, B., ROTONDO, H., & MARIÁTEGUI, J., eds.
Estudios de psiquiatria social en el Perú
Lima: Sol 1963
10
Censo Nacional de Población
Resultados de Primera Prioridad, Instituto Nacional
de Plantificación, Lima, 1964
11
Datos proporcionados por el Departamento de
Recaudación del Banco de la Nación del Perú
(Departamento de Alcoholes y Azúcar) sobre el
consumo de beidas alcohólicas en 1965
12
Datos sobre alcoholismo proporcionados por el
Consejo de Bienestar Social de Gautemala y extractados
de la Tesis de T. S. Concha F. de Ordonez, 1965
13
FERRARA, F.
Alcoholismo en América Latina
Buenos Aires: Palestra 1961
14
FERRER, T.F.
El alcoholismo como problema sanitario
Secretaría de Salubridad y Asistencia, Dirección
General de Neurología, Salud Mental y
Rehabilitación, México s/f
15
GOLDENBERG, M., SLUZKI, C.E., KORN, F.,
& TARNOPLSKY, A.
Actitudes frente al alcohol, el alcoholismo y el
alcoholista
Acta psiquiát. psicol. Am. Lat. In press
16
Grupo de Estudio sobre la Investigación Epidemio-
lógica del Alcoholismo en América Latina
Estudios comparativos básicos acerca de los patrones
culturales de ingestión, los problemas del alcohol y
el alcoholismo en diversos paises de América Latina
(Proyecto de Investigación), San José, Costa Rica,
June 1966
17
Grupo de Estudio sobre la Investigación Epidemio-
lógica del Alcoholismo en América Latina
Informe final
San José, Costa Rica, June 1966
18
HERRERA, LUQUE F.
Influencia alcohólica y criminalidad en Venezuela
Temas de neuro-psiquiat. y psicol., 1: 7, 1962
19
HORWITZ, J.
Investigaciones epidemiológicas acerca de la morbilidad
mental en Chile (alcoholismo, epilepsia, psicosis,
neurosis, 1957)
Rev. psiquiat. per., 2: 7, 1959
20
HORWITZ, J.
La obra de Elwin Morton Jellinek y su importancia
para el conocimiento del alcoholismo en Chile

Acta psiquiat. psicol. Am. lat., 11: 81, 1965
21
HORWITZ, J. & MARCONI, J. eds.
Evaluación de definiciones transculturales para
estudios epidemiológicos en Salud Mental
Aspectos Metodológicos
Publicación provisional, Servicio Nacional de Salud,
Universidad de Chile, Santiago de Chile, 1965
22
HORWITZ, J, & MARCONI, J.
Estudios acerca del hábito de beber, los problemas
del alcohol y del alcoholismo en América Latina
Presented at the Study Group on the Epidemiological
Investigation of Alcoholism in Latin America, San
José, Costa Rica, June, 1966
Alcoholism (Zagreb), 3: 3, 1967 (in English)
23
HORWITZ, J., MUÑOZ, L.C., ALVAREZ, M., BECERRA, M.,
GONZÁLEZ, M., MARTINEZ, L., MERCADO, N.,
ORELLANA, N., & PLAZA, J.
Investigación epidemiológica acerca de morbilidad
mental en Chile
Rev. serv. nac. sal (Chile), 3: 277, 1958
24
Informe final de los documentos de trabajo
participantes en el Seminario Latinoamericano
sobre Alcoholismo, Santiago de Chile, 1960
25
JERI, R.
Efectos psicológicos del alcohol
In: Informe final de la Conferencia Nacional de
Alcoholismo, Lima, 1957
26
KUCZYNKI, GODARD, M.H. & PAZ SOLDAN, C.E.
Disección del indigenismo peruano (un examen
sociológico y médico social)
Publ. del Instituto de Medicina Social, Lima, 1948
27
LÓPEZ PARDO, A.
Datos del Director del Departamento Administrativo
de Protección y Asistencia Social
Bogotá, 1966
28
MACCOBY, M.
El alcoholismo en una comunidad campesina
Rev. psicoanál. psiquiat. y psicol., México, 1: 38, 1965
29
MALPICA, S.S.C.
Crónica del hambre en el Perú
Lima: Francisco Moncloa, 1966
30
MANFREDINI, J.
A incidencia do alcoolismo psicopatico no Brasil,
no lustro 1950–54
J. brasil. psiquiat., 5: 141, 1956
31
MANGIN, W.P.
Alcoholismo en las comunidades indígenas.
In: Informe final de la Conferencia Nacional de
Alcoholismo, Lima, 1957
32
MANGIN, W.P.

Drinking among Andean Indians
Quart. J. Stud. Alc., **8**: 55, 1957
33

MARCONI, J.
The concept of alcoholism
Quart. J. Stud. Alc., **20**: 216, 1959
34

MARCONI, J.
Evaluación del programa nacional de prevención y
tratamiento del alcoholismo en Chile, Abril 1966
Presented at the Study Group on the Epidemiological
Investigation of Alcoholism in Latin America,
San José, Costa Rica, June 1966
35

MARCONI, J., VARELA, A., ROSENBLAT, E., SOLARI, G.,
MARCHESE, I., ALVARADO, R., & ENRIQUEZ, W.
A survey on the prevalence of alcoholism among
the adult population of a suburb of Santiago
Quart. J. Stud. Alc., **16**: 438, 1955
36

MARIÁTEGUI, J.
Estudios de morbilidad por alcoholismo
Presented at the Study Group on the Epidemiological
Investigation of Alcoholism in Latin America,
San José, Costa Rica, June 1966
37

MARIÁTEGUI, J. & ALVA, V.
Epidemiológia psiquiátrica en un distrito urbano de
Lima (Lince)
In press
38

MORENO HENRIQUEZ, A.
El alcoholismo y sus secuelas en el ambiente
psiquiátrico de Concepción (Chile)
Rev. neuro-psiquiat., Lima, **24**: 310, 1961
39

MOYA, L.C., HORWITZ, J., MARCONI, J. *et al.*
Prevalencia de seis desórdenes mentales en tres distritos
del área norte de Santiago
In press
40

PACHECO E. SILVA, A.C.
Intoxicación crónica en América Latina
Rev. psiquiat. per., **2**: 159, 1959
41

Primer Censo de Enfermedades Neurológicas y
Psiquiátricas
México, D.F.: La Secretaria de Salubridad 1960
42

RUIZ, E.
Desórdenes mentales en un reducto mapache
aislado de la provincia de Malleco
In press
43

RUIZ, E. *et al.*
Estudio de prevalencia de desórdenes mentales
en Chiloé
In press
44

ROTONDO, H.
Problemas de salud mental en el área urbana de
Mendocita. El proyecto

In: Estudios de psiquiatría social en el Perú, ed. by
B. Caravedo, H. Rotondo, & J. Mariátegui
Lima: Sol, 1963
45

ROTONDO, H., ALIAGA, P., & GARCIA-PACHECO, C.
Estudios de morbilidad psiquiátrica en le populación
urbana de Mendocita; la prevalencia de los desórdenes
mentales
In: Estudios de psiquiatria social en el Perú, ed. by
B. Caravedo, H. Rotondo, & J. Mariátegui
Lima: Sol, 1963
46

ROTONDO, H., MARIÁTEGUI, J., BAMBAREN VIGIL, C.,
GARCIA-PACHECO, C., & ALIAGA, P.
Un estudio comparativo de la conducta antisocial
de menores en áreas urbanas y rurales
In: Estudios de psiquiatría social en el Perú, ed. by
B. Caravedo, H. Rotondo, & J. Mariátegui
Lima: Sol, 1963
47

ROTONDO, H., MARIÁTEGUI, J., BAMBAREN VIGIL C.,
GARCIA-PACHECO, C., & ALIAGA, P.
Un estudio de conducta antisocial en un área urbana
en estado de desorganización (Mendocita)
In: Estudios de psiquiatria social en el Perú, ed. by
B. Caravedo, H. Rotondo, & J. Mariátegui
Lima: Sol, 1963
48

SAAVEDRA, A.
El cocaísmo en América Latina
Acta neuro-psiquiát. Arg., **5**: 143, 1959
49

SAN MARTIN, H. & MERINO, R.
Epidemiología y implicancias sociales del
alcoholismo en Chile
Actas del IX Congreso Médico Social Panamericano
Lima, Peru: Federación Médica Peruana, 1966
50

SILVA MARTINEZ, M.
El alcoholismo en la salud individual y colectiva
Higiene (México), **15**: 70, 1963
51

SIMMONS, O.G.
Ambivalence and the learning of drinking behavior in
a Peruvian community
In: Society, culture and drinking patterns, ed. by
D. J. Pittman & C. R. Snyder
New York: Wiley, 1962
52

STEGEN, G.
Consumo de bebidas alcohólicas en la población
infantil
Rev. Chile pediat., **30**: 53, 1959
53

URIBE COALLA, G.
Problemas sociales de la comunidad en Colombia
Rev. pisquiat. per., **2**: 64, 1959
54

VIDAL, G.
Contenidos básicos de los programas nacionales de
prevención, tratamiento y rehabilitación del
alcoholismo

Presented at the Study Group on the Epidemiological
Investigation of Alcoholism in Latin America,
San José, Costa Rica, June 1966
55
VIDAL, G.
El alcoholismo en la Argentina
Report of answers to the questionnaire of the CPS for
the Study Group on the Epidemiological Investigation
of Alcoholism in Latin America, San José, Costa Rica,
June 1966

BENJAMÍN VIEL

DANILO SALCEDO

SERGIO DONOSO

ANÍBAL VARELA

Department of Hygiene and Preventive Medicine
Department of Pathology
Institute of Studies on Alcoholism
University of Chile
Santiago, Chile

41

Alcoholism, Accidents, Atherosclerosis, and Hepatic Damage

The influence of immoderate use of alcoholic beverages in the etiology of hepatic cirrhosis of the Laënnec type is still being debated. There are several opinions converging to the assertion that excessive and continued ingestion of alcohol has a direct effect through a process not yet well established; among these we can mention Klatskin and Yesner (6). Others, including Patek (9), think that there is not a direct influence and that the predominant etiological factor is malnutrition. This latter position is based ultimately on the observation that alcoholics are generally people who do not have a proper diet.

In Chile, surveys of representative samples of the adult population of Santiago (4, 8) have shown a high prevalence of heavy drinkers and alcoholics, mainly among males. At the same time the mortality rate from cirrhosis among individuals older than 40 shows a tendency to increase, and according to Steiner (12) the present mortality from cirrhosis is the third highest in the world. West Berlin has a rate of 32.6, France 26.7, and Chile 25.1 per 100,000 inhabitants. It is interesting to note that the same author records Egypt as the country with the lowest rate – 0.9 per 100,000 – in spite of the fact that Egypt's population is underfed; however, its religious beliefs reduce the consumption of alcoholic beverages to a minimum.

A desire to determine empirically the relationship between drinking habits and hepatic damage led us to study persons who had died violently in the city of Santiago. Our purpose was to obtain the results of a histopathological examination of the liver, and data on drinking habits through interviews with next of kin.

THE SAMPLE

According to Chilean law every individual who dies violently or under suspicious circumstances

The authors wish to thank the US National Institute of Health for grant 07366 which made this work possible. We also thank Dr. Raúl Alessandri, who helped to diagnose the hepatic lesions, and Dr. Alfredo Vargas, Director of the Institute of Legal Medicine of Santiago, for the data-gathering facilities which he provided.

must be autopsied before his burial. This is done in a medicolegal centre of which there are several scattered through the country; in Santiago, the Institute of Legal Medicine is closely associated with the Chair of Legal Medicine in the University of Chile.

The autopsy is also compulsory for those patients who die in the hospitals of the National Health Service. However, a majority of these patients are of low socioeconomic status; this was the reason for choosing the sample for the present study from those autopsied at the Institute, since a more representative sample of the metropolitan population of Santiago could be obtained there than from the state hospitals. In addition, it was important to minimize the presence of sickness as a cause of death in order to generalize the findings. Violent deaths provided a sample of individuals, many of whom could be assumed to be healthy prior to their death.

The authors are aware that the sample is not entirely representative of Santiago's population, because it contains those persons who are more prone to die in accidents or from causes which are more frequent in groups characterized by a higher degree of social disorganization. This explains why there is an over-representation of males and an age distribution a little different from that of the general population, and why greater percentages of heavy drinkers and alcoholics were found than in surveys of the general population.

The total sample, collected during the period 1960–64, comprised 1,662 subjects over 15 years of age. These were selected within 24 hours of death, and all died from a violent external cause. Moreover, the selection took into account some personal antecedents indicating that the individual had lived a more or less normal active life. It is important to point out that the cause usually provoked death almost immediately, but in no case did the individual survive for more than three days.

METHODS

Each corpse was weighed and measured, and all the anthropological measurements recommended by the International Project on Atherosclerosis

(10) were recorded. Each was classified according to the ratio of real to ideal weight (i.e., the amount an individual should weigh according to height, age, and sex). For this calculation the tables for the Chilean population were used (13). A ratio between 0.90 and 1.09 was considered normal; a ratio less than 0.90, subnormal; and a ratio above 1.09 was taken to indicate obesity.

The cardiac weight was determined and any valvular lesion recorded. A macroscopic evaluation of the liver was made, and samples were taken from heart and liver for histopathological study. The latter examination was made after staining with hematoxylin-eosin and Van Gieson. Each sample was observed independently by two pathologists; their diagnoses were then matched and differences discussed. The findings were classified according to the following code:

0   Complete lack of fatty vacuoles.
1   Presence of a few small vacuoles in each microscopic field.
2   Presence of small vacuoles in moderate numbers in each microscopic field.
3   Presence of vacuoles in many hepatic cells in each microscopic field.
4   Infiltration of abundant fat with development of lipodiastems and interstitial inflammatory reaction (acute or subacute fatty liver).
5   Existence of alterations described in 4, plus a noticeable increase in fibrous tissue (incipient cirrhosis).
6   Existence of abundant fibrous tissue and replacement of a lobular structure by regenerated nodules (advanced cirrhosis).
7   Various lesions of other types such as cholangitis with canalicular fibrosis.

The socioeconomic data and information pertaining to drinking habits were obtained through interviews conducted by trained personnel with the nearest relative of the deceased or a close friend when there were no relatives. The interview was conducted within ten days after the death.

The interview schedule was constructed to obtain data on variables relevant for the determination of socioeconomic status, such as education, income, main occupation, social participation,

TABLE 41–1

DRINKING HABITS OF 1,662 INDIVIDUALS OLDER THAN 15 YEARS, WHO DIED
FROM VIOLENT CAUSES; DISTRIBUTED ACCORDING TO SEX, SANTIAGO 1960–64

Drinking habits	Males N	Males per cent	Females N	Females per cent	Total N	Total per cent
abstemious	174	13.2	172	50.6	346	20.8
normal drinker	509	38.5	129	38.0	638	38.4
heavy drinker	295	22.3	12	3.5	307	18.5
intermittent alcoholic	112	8.5	10	2.9	122	7.3
inveterate alcoholic	232	17.5	17	5.0	249	15.0
total	1,322	100.0	340	100.0	1,662	100.0

housing. Each variable was weighted to permit the construction of a scale from which we could establish three groups: low, medium, and high socioeconomic status.

Drinking habits were determined through a set of questions which differentiated various aspects considered important in drinking behaviour. The data on each individual were analysed carefully and formed the basis of the following classification:

Abstemious
The individual who did not consume alcohol at all.

Normal drinker
The individual who drank moderately with his meals, or during social events, and who did not become intoxicated more than six times a year. That is, no indication of dependence on alcohol was evident.

Heavy drinker
The individual who had all the characteristics of the normal drinker, but in addition, was accustomed to drinking on weekends to the point of inebriation. He also remained inebriated for two or more consecutive days, not more than three times a year, and sometimes drank after work to the point of intoxication.

Intermittent alcoholic
All the characteristics of the heavy drinker applied with two additional patterns. First, the individual had an overall dependence on alcohol, drinking all day long, and was often "tipsy" for periods over two days; drinking took place before breakfast and during or after work. Second, his drinking episodes were separated by shorter or longer periods of abstinence.

Inveterate alcoholic
The individual with the same characteristics as the intermittent alcoholic, but who maintained his drinking throughout the year with no periods of abstinence. In short, he had a total dependence on alcohol.

The findings of the histopathological examination of the liver were not known by the team concerned with the interviews; to avoid bias, the data were kept separate until the final analysis.

RESULTS

The drinking habits of the sample according to sex are shown in Table 41-1. As found in other Chilean surveys, the immoderate use of alcoholic beverages was practically restricted to the male sex. The differences between the sexes in frequency of heavy drinkers and alcoholics of both types are statistically significant ($p < 0.01$).

It proved interesting to examine the association between the amount of alcohol in the blood of the deceased and their drinking habits as learned through the interviews. In Table 41-2 the results are presented for only 1,201 cases (72.2 per cent of the total), since in some instances it was not considered necessary to test for alcohol. The blood alcohol level is significantly related to drinking habits, which indicates that there is a high degree of consistency between the laboratory data and that obtained through the

TABLE 41-2

BLOOD ALCOHOL LEVELS OF 1,201 INDIVIDUALS OLDER THAN 15 YEARS, WHO DIED FROM VIOLENT CAUSES; DISTRIBUTED ACCORDING TO SEX AND DRINKING HABITS, SANTIAGO 1960–64

| | Males | | | | | |
| | *drinking habits determined by interviewing* | | | | | |
Amount of alcohol (gm/kg)	*abstemious*	*normal*	*heavy*	*intermittent*	*inveterate*	*total*
0–0.50	100.0	58.5	32.4	35.2	37.1	52.0
0.51–1.00	0.0	10.7	9.1	6.8	4.7	7.7
1.01–1.50	0.0	10.9	12.3	9.1	13.5	10.2
1.51–2.00	0.0	8.1	17.4	19.3	12.3	10.9
2.01 and over	0.0	11.8	28.8	29.6	32.4	19.2
total	100.0	100.0	100.0	100.0	100.0	100.0
number of cases with amount of alcohol undetermined	54	116	76	24	62	332
per cent over total	31.0	23.0	25.8	21.5	26.8	25.2
	Females					
0–0.50	100.0	75.6	14.3	50.0	25.0	82.0
0.51–1.00	0.0	14.1	0.0	12.5	0.0	5.7
1.01–1.50	0.0	7.7	28.6	0.0	25.0	5.2
1.51–2.00	0.0	0.0	14.3	25.0	8.3	1.9
2.01 and over	0.0	2.6	42.8	12.5	41.7	5.2
total	100.0	100.0	100.0	100.0	100.0	100.0
number of cases with amount of alcohol undetermined	66	51	5	2	5	129
per cent of total	38.4	39.8	41.7	20.0	29.4	38.0

interviews. Appreciable blood alcohol levels (over 0.5 gm/kg) do not occur in any subject classified as abstemious. Values over 1.5 gm/kg occur significantly more often among heavy drinkers and alcoholics than among normal drinkers. This indicates the validity of the interview information even though given by persons other than those to whom it applies.

The influence of socioeconomic status on drinking habits was analysed for 777 males in our preliminary report (14). However, in the present paper persons under 15 years of age have been excluded and females have been included. In Figure 41-1, socioeconomic status is taken as the independent variable, and drinking habits as the dependent variable. The data show very clearly that among males it is more common to find heavy drinkers and inveterate alcoholics when socioeconomic status is low. The association is statistically significant ($p < 0.01$). Females are less frequently found in the excessive drinker categories, and differences in the proportion of women among the socioeconomic groups are not significant ($p > 0.01$).

Excessive alcohol intake is inversely related to socioeconomic status; that is to say, the lower the status the greater the probability of alcoholic behaviour. The proportions of heavy drinkers and inveterate alcoholics differ significantly among the socioeconomic groups ($p < 0.01$). However, there are no such differences with respect to intermittent alcoholism ($p > 0.01$).

The influence of age on drinking habits is analysed for males only. Figure 41-2 shows the distribution of heavy drinkers, and of intermittent and inveterate alcoholics, and also of the sum of these three groups, according to socioeconomic status and age. The figure clearly indicates that those of low socioeconomic status began to abuse alcohol at an earlier age and in a greater proportion than those in the other two socioeconomic groups.

After 55 years of age there is a decrease in the proportion of heavy drinkers and alcoholics. This could be due to the sickness or death of those who previously drank immoderately. This explanation is supported by the fact that a majority of the deaths from hepatic cirrhosis of the

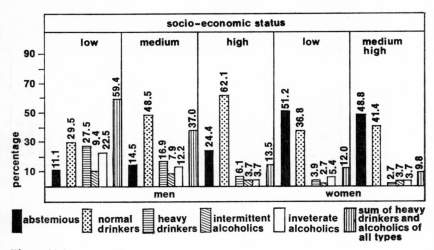

Figure 41-1
Socioeconomic status and drinking habits according to sex in 1,662 individuals autopsied following violent death.

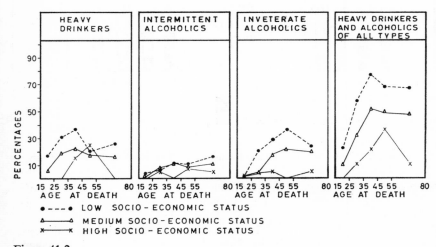

Figure 41-2
Drinking habits and socioeconomic status according to age in 1,332 males autopsied following violent death.

Laënnec type in Chilean hospitals occur between 50 and 60 years of age.

The intermittent alcoholics appear again as a distinct group. Among them are found a greater proportion of younger individuals, regardless of socioeconomic status.

Main occupations were classified according to whether the work was primarily manual or intel-

lectual in character. Although it is sometimes difficult to draw the line, we classified as "manual" all occupations characterized by a greater physical effort, those not well defined socially, and unknown jobs, since there was a greater probability that they would be manual. In Figure 41-3 the distribution of 1,622 cases according to occupation, drinking habits, and sex

324 / *Viel et al.*

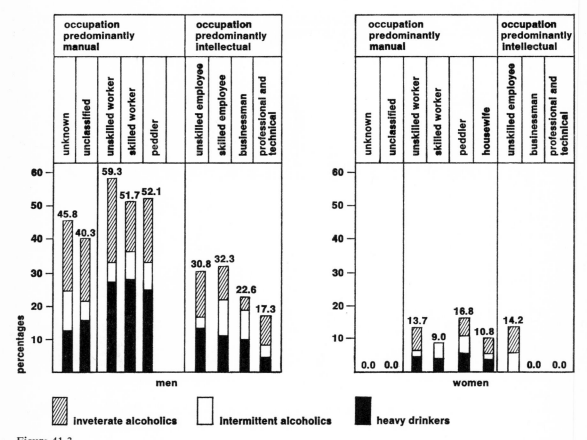

Figure 41-3
Drinking habits and main occupation according to sex in 1,622 individuals autopsied following violent death.

is shown. It is clear that the proportion of heavy drinkers and alcoholics in the manual occupation group is substantially greater than in occupations of the intellectual type: an average of 54.6 per cent and 29.1 per cent respectively. The difference is statistically significant ($p < 0.01$). Furthermore, within the predominantly intellectual occupations, as job responsibility increases, the relative frequency of alcohol abuse appears to diminish. Among the females there do not appear to be any important differences in this regard.

The relation between education and drinking habits is shown in Figure 41-4. Among males there is a direct relationship between education and excessive use of alcohol: the higher the educational level, the lower the proportions of heavy drinkers and alcoholics. However, among females no relationship is evident, which suggests

that the factors influencing the development of alcoholism in women differ from those etiologically relevant in males.

The proportions of heavy drinkers and alcoholics among males are quite remarkable when we compare different levels of education. In Table 41-3 the illiterates are grouped with the individuals having an education equivalent to grade three or less. There are significant differences among heavy drinkers and inveterate alcoholics, but the proportion of intermittent alcoholics does not vary with educational level.

With respect to alcoholism and family situation, in Figure 41-5 we distinguish first the presence or lack of family, and second the different relationships that the individual maintained with his family, namely, being a son or being with or without children. It should be emphasized that

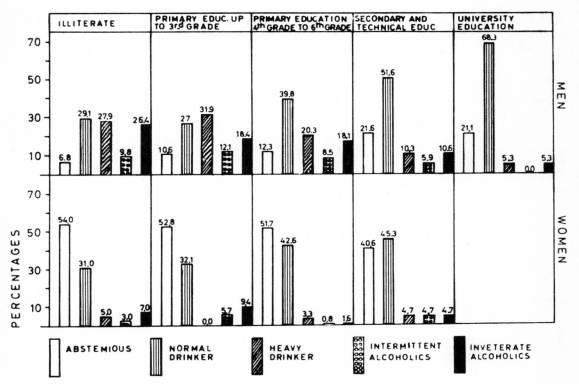

Figure 41-4
Drinking habits and educational level according to sex in 1,643 individuals autopsied following violent death.

here "family condition" refers only to a structural description; behavioural aspects of the relationship between the individual and his family, such as adjustment or conflict, are not investigated.

The figure indicates that the greater proportion of individuals who abuse alcohol are found among those who did not have a family or lived as a protégé. The number of inveterate alcoholics without family ties is significant, but when we compare the proportions of alcoholics among those with children and those without, the differences are not significant. It would seem that the responsibility of having children is not a sufficient incentive to use alcohol moderately. It would be of considerable interest to examine the functional disturbances in families having one or more alcoholic members.

Alcoholism and accidents
The impairing effect of alcohol on the reflexes of

the nervous system, and therefore on the co-ordination of movements, is indicated by the frequency with which alcoholics are involved in accidents. Out of 1,662 subjects studied, 1,151 died as a consequence of various accidents, and the great majority of these were traffic accidents (59.6 per cent of the total sample). The greatest number of traffic accident victims were run over; if it had been possible to determine the degree of intoxication of the drivers involved, the proportion of inebriated persons involved in accidents might have been greater.

Table 41-4 shows the different types of accident distributed according to sex. The figures demonstrate that males have a greater proportion of accidents than females, and this is not due to chance ($p < 0.01$). The explanation of this difference probably lies in the greater risk of accident to which a man is subjected in his daily activities; this is reflected in the greater percentage of work accidents that occur among males. Also,

TABLE 41-3

LEVEL OF EDUCATION AND DRINKING HABITS OF 1,301 MALES AUTOPSIED
FOLLOWING VIOLENT DEATH (PERCENTAGES)

Level of education	Heavy drinker	Intermittent alcoholic	Inveterate alcoholic	Heavy drinker and alcoholic
illiterate and primary education up to grade 3	28.4	10.8	23.0	62.2
primary education from grades 4 to 6	20.3	8.5	18.1	46.9
x/σ	2.9*	1.2	1.9	4.8*
primary education from grades 4 to 6	20.3	8.5	18.1	46.9
secondary and technical education	10.3	5.9	10.6	26.8
x/σ	4.0*	1.4	3.4*	6.0*
secondary and technical education	10.3	5.9	10.6	26.8
university education	5.3	0.0	5.3	10.6
x/σ	0.8	—	1.0	2.2*

*Significant at 1 per cent level.

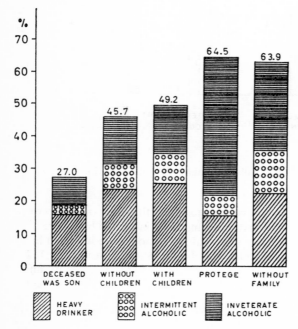

Figure 41-5
Drinking habits and family condition in 1,332 males
autopsied following violent death, 1960–64.

a sexual difference in drinking behaviour is an
important factor.

In Table 41-5, we relate drinking habits to
traffic accidents. The data show quite clearly that
among males there is a greater probability that
those who die in traffic accidents tend to abuse
alcohol, since 41.0 per cent of the males were
heavy drinkers or alcoholics, as compared to only
5.5 per cent of the females.

We felt that it was not sufficient to study only
the pattern of drinking behaviour; it was also important to know if the persons who died in traffic
accidents were intoxicated or not at the time of
the accident. Data are presented in Table 41-6
showing the amount of alcohol found in the
blood of fatal accident victims. Alcoholemia was
determined in 74.4 per cent of the males and
86.7 per cent of the females.

From the data in Table 41-6 we can conclude
that the lower proportion of traffic accidents
among females is due in part at least to the
smaller influence of alcohol, since only 6.4 per
cent of the females had an alcoholemia over 1
gm/kg as compared with 46 per cent of the
males. Although we do not have a control group
with which we can establish a valid comparison,
the latter figure constitutes evidence that there is
an increased risk of death in traffic accidents
when the blood alcohol level exceeds 1 gm/kg.
This conclusion is supported by the increase in
the proportion of such deaths with increasing
blood levels.

Alcoholism and nutritional status
It is also of interest to consider the effect of alcoholism on the nutritional status of the individual.
The index of nutritional status employed was the
ratio of real to ideal weight. Undoubtedly this is
a gross index, but no other quantitative procedure was available to us for the purpose.

The index could be calculated for 1,361 males

TABLE 41–4

TOTAL NUMBER OF VIOLENT DEATHS DISTRIBUTED BY
TYPE OF ACCIDENT AND SEX

	Males		Females	
	N	*per cent*	N	*per cent*
total number of violent deaths	1,332	100.0	340	100.0
deaths by accidents	981	74.2	170	50.0
domestic accidents	37	2.8	19	5.6
traffic accidents	596	45.1	90	26.4
work accidents	65	4.9	3	0.9
other types of accidents	283	21.4	58	17.1

TABLE 41–5

DEATHS BY TRAFFIC ACCIDENTS DISTRIBUTED ACCORDING
TO SEX AND DRINKING HABITS

Drinking habits	Males		Females	
	N	*per cent*	N	*per cent*
heavy drinker	142	23.8	3	3.3
intermittent alcoholic	33	5.5	–	–
inveterate alcoholic	70	11.7	2	2.2
abstemious and normal drinker	351	59.0	85	94.5
total	596	100.0	90	100.0

TABLE 41–6

ALCOHOLEMIA AT THE MOMENT OF
DEATH IN 521 INDIVIDUALS WHO DIED
IN ACCIDENTS; DISTRIBUTED
ACCORDING TO SEX

Alcoholemia (gm/kg)	Males		Females	
	N	*(per cent)*	N	*(per cent)*
0.0 –0.50	210	47.5	68	87.2
0.51–1.00	29	6.5	5	6.4
1.01–1.50	48	10.8	2	2.6
1.51–2.00	58	13.1	–	–
2.01 & over	98	22.1	3	3.8
total	443	100.0	78	100.0

and 248 females, but the small proportion of females who abused alcohol made it advisable to conduct the analysis for males only. Figure 41-6 exhibits the percentages of males with a real/ideal weight ratio below or above normal, distributed according to age and drinking habits. The data show that before 35 years of age, alcohol does not exercise a significant influence on nutritional condition. Whatever the drinking habit may be, the differences between the percentage of individuals below and above normal could occur by chance. After 35 years of age, there is an overall higher proportion of individuals whose real/ideal weight ratio is above normal. However, as the degree of alcohol use increases, the proportion below normal increases, and the proportion above normal diminishes significantly.

Alcoholism and cardiovascular pathology
Average weight of the heart was taken as one index of possible alcohol-induced cardiovascular pathology. Subjects with valvular lesions were omitted. Another index employed was the extent to which fibrous plaques covered the surface of the intima of the left anterior descending coronary artery. Figure 41-7 shows the data for 1,046 males on cardiac weight, real/ideal weight ratio, drinking habits, and age. Females are not shown since we found no relation between cardiac weight and ingestion of alcohol.

The data indicate that among individuals under 35 years of age the average cardiac weight in abstemious and normal drinkers of the same

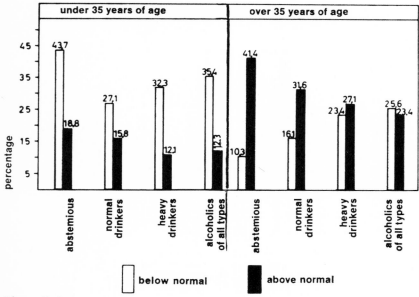

Figure 41-6

Per cent above and below the normal real/ideal weight ratio, according to drinking habits and age, in 1,013 males autopsied following violent death.

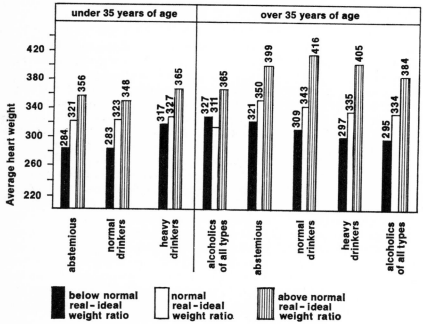

Figure 41-7

Average cardiac weight according to age, real/ideal weight ratio, and drinking habits in 1,046 males autopsied following violent death.

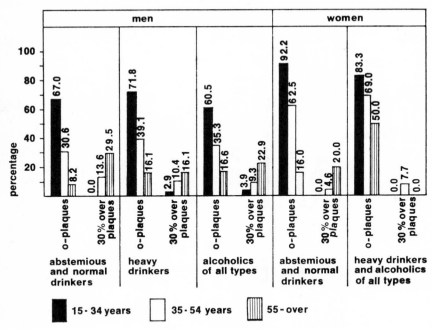

Figure 41-8
Distribution of coronary atherosclerosis according to sex, age, and drinking habits in 1,340 individuals autopsied following violent death.

real/ideal weight ratio are almost identical. The same is true of heavy drinkers and alcoholics of both types. But if we take the group with a real/ideal weight ratio below normal and compare the average cardiac weight of the abstemious and the alcoholics, the difference is statistically significant ($p < 0.01$). Consequently, it would appear that heavy alcohol consumption has some relation to an increase in cardiac weight when the individual has a real/ideal weight ratio below normal. However, it is well to recall that a greater proportion of alcoholics occurred among those whose main occupation involved manual work. This might be a factor contributing to the difference observed. Since there were no significant differences among the groups over 35 years of age, it would appear that alcohol is not an influential factor in cardiac weight with increased age, despite diverse nutritional conditions.

In our previous study (14) we did not find any relationship between abuse of alcohol and the presence of fibrous plaques in the intima of the abdominal aorta of 777 males. In the present

case, we looked for arterial damage in the left anterior descending coronary in both sexes. The results are presented in Figure 41-8. Data for 1,080 men and 260 women are distributed by age and drinking habits in two extreme categories: complete lack of fibrous plaques, and 30 per cent or more of the surface covered. The latter category comprises the most severe cases of coronary sclerosis.

The data are consistent with the well-established principle that the amount of fibrous plaques increases with age, and the process is less pronounced among females than males. The existence of a small number of individuals over 55 years of age with severe atherosclerotic damage and who were abusers of alcohol is not statistically significant when compared with frequencies for the abstemious and normal drinkers of similar characteristics.

Alcoholism and hepatic damage
Histopathological examinations of liver samples were conducted for 1,618 subjects. That is to

percentages

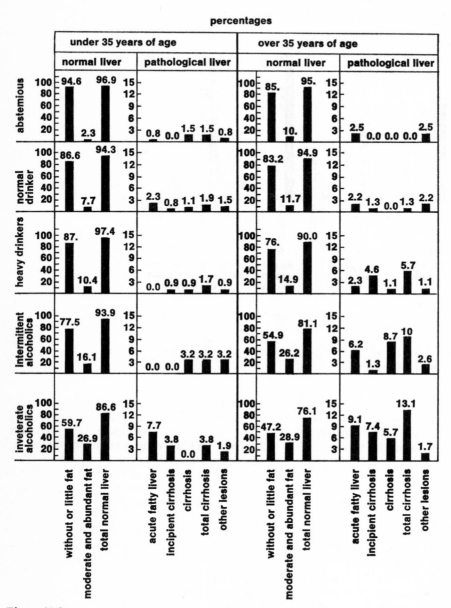

Figure 41-9

Results of histopathological examination of the livers of 1,294 males autopsied following violent death, according to age and drinking habits.

say, samples were obtained from all but 44 of the original 1,662. The results of these examinations are shown in Figures 41-9 and 41-10, distributed according to sex, age, and drinking habits. Under "cirrhosis" both incipient and advanced cases are included, because once fibrosis has occurred the pathological process is irreversible.

Cirrhosis occurred in 56 out of 1,294 males (4.3 per cent), and in 10 out of 324 females (3.1 per cent). Among males, the proportion

percentages

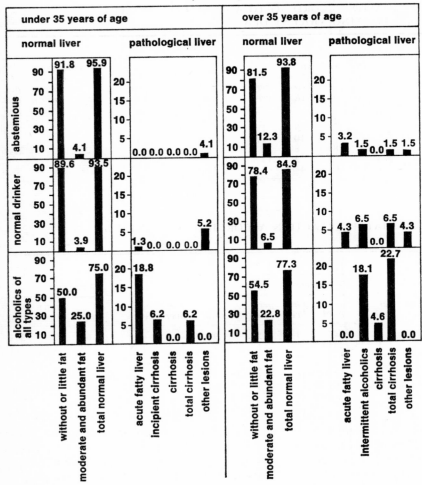

Figure 41-10
Results of histopathological examination of the livers of 324 females autopsied
following violent death, according to age and drinking habits.

suffering from cirrhosis becomes higher as the abuse of alcohol becomes more pronounced; among the abstemious it is only 1.5 per cent, while among alcoholics of both types it reaches 10.5 per cent. Among the women, 1.3 per cent of the abstemious and 10.3 per cent of the alcoholics suffered from cirrhosis. Thus the two sexes present almost the same proportions of cirrhosis when similar patterns of drinking behaviour are compared.

In Table 41-7, the frequency of cirrhosis is shown in relation to drinking habits, age and sex. Among both men and women, the proportion of individuals older than 35 with cirrhosis increases as the abuse of alcohol increases. The differences between abstemious and normal drinkers, on the one hand, and heavy drinkers and alcoholics, on the other, are highly significant. However, among individuals of both sexes younger than 35, the proportion of cirrhosis is almost equally

TABLE 41–7

CIRRHOSIS AND DRINKING HABITS ACCORDING TO AGE AND SEX IN 1,618 INDIVIDUALS AUTOPSIED FOLLOWING VIOLENT DEATH

Drinking habits	Males						Females					
	< 35 years			*> 35 years*			*< 35 years*			*> 35 years*		
	total	*cir-rhosis*	*per cent*	*total*	*cir-rhosis*	*per cent*	*total*	*cir-rhosis*	*per cent*	*total*	*cir-rhosis*	*per cent*
abstemious	130	2	1.5	40	—	—	98	—	—	65	1	1.5
normal drinkers	262	5	1.9	233	3	1.3	77	—	—	49	3	6.1
heavy drinkers	115	2	1.7	175	10	5.7⎫						
intermittent alc.	31	1	3.2	80	8	10.0⎬	13	1	7.7	22	5	22.6
inveterage alc.	52	2	3.8	176	23	13.0⎭						
total	590	12	2.1	704	44	6.2	188	1	0.2	136	9	6.6

TABLE 41–8

FATTY LIVER WITH INFLAMMATORY REACTION ACCORDING TO DRINKING HABITS, AGE, AND SEX

Drinking habits	Males						Females					
	< 35 years			*> 35 years*			*< 35 years*			*> 35 years*		
	total	*fatty liver*	*per cent*	*total*	*fatty liver*	*per cent*	*total*	*fatty liver*	*per cent*	*total*	*fatty liver*	*per cent*
abstemious	130	1	0.8	40	1	2.5	98	—	—	65	2	3.1
normal drinker	262	6	2.3	233	5	2.1	77	1	1.3	49	2	4.1
heavy drinker	115	—	—	175	4	2.3⎫						
intermittent alc.	31	—	—	80	5	6.2⎬	13	3	23.0	22	—	—
inveterate alc.	52	4	7.7	176	16	9.1⎭						
total	590	11	1.9	704	31	4.4	188	4	2.1	136	4	2.9

distributed over the different drinking habits. Therefore, it would seem that while the drinking habit is an important factor among older persons, hepatic cirrhosis has a different etiology among those under 35 years of age.

As indicated in Figures 41-9 and 41-10, not only cirrhosis, but also fatty liver with inflammatory reaction seems to be a more frequent lesion among alcohol abusers. Data relevant to the occurrence of this condition are provided in Table 41-8.

Among males older than 35 years of age the proportion in alcoholics of both types with fatty liver with inflammatory reaction (15.3 per cent) is significantly greater than that observed among heavy drinkers (2.3 per cent). This condition is also more frequent in both male and female alcoholics younger than 35 years.

When the livers classified as normal were examined, fatty vacoules – in moderate or abundant quantities – were found more frequently among the individuals who drank immoderately. Thus, the data in Table 41-9 indicate an increase in the frequency of persons with moderate or abundant liver fat both with age and with greater alcohol consumption. The differences between the group of abstemious and normal drinkers and the group of alcoholics – for both sexes and age groups – were statistically significant at the 1 per cent level of confidence. It seems that individuals who abuse alcohol have an increased tendency to deposit fat in their livers even though the morphological structure of the liver can still be classified within the limits of normality.

From the evidence presented so far, it is possible to infer that the normal processes leading to an increase in deposits of hepatic fat become more rapid and pronounced with the abuse of

TABLE 41–9

MODERATE AND ABUNDANT FAT IN NORMAL LIVERS ACCORDING TO
DRINKING HABITS, AGE, AND SEX

Drinking habits	Males						Females					
	< 35 years			*> 35 years*			*< 35 years*			*> 35 years*		
	total	*fat*	*per cent*	*total*	*fat*	*per cent*	*total*	*fat*	*per cent*	*total*	*fat*	*per cent*
abstemious	130	3	2.3	40	4	10.0	98	4	4.1	65	8	12.3
normal drinkers	262	20	7.6	233	26	11.1	77	3	3.9	49	3	6.1
heavy drinkers	115	12	10.4	175	26	14.8⎤						
intermittent alcoholics	35	5	14.3	80	21	26.2⎬	13	4	30.8	22	8	36.3
inveterate alcoholics	52	14	27.0	176	51	29.0⎦						
total	590	54	9.1	704	128	18.3	188	11	5.8	136	19	13.9

TABLE 41–10

THICKNESS OF THE ADIPOSE PANNICULUS UNDER THE ABDOMINAL SKIN,
ACCORDING TO DRINKING HABITS, AGE, AND SEX (PERCENTAGES)

Drinking habits	0–10 mm	11–20 mm	21 mm or more	0–10 mm	11–20 mm	21 mm or more
	Males under 35			*Females under 35*		
abstemious	59.4	32.4	8.2	13.5	60.8	25.7
normal drinkers	41.7	45.1	13.2	20.3	42.4	27.3
heavy drinkers	50.0	43.1	6.9	50.0	50.0	0.0
intermittent alc.	38.4	53.8	7.8⎤	0.0	42.9	57.1
inveterate alc.	33.3	58.9	7.8⎦			
total	46.8	43.3	9.9	16.6	52.1	31.3
	Males 35 or older			*Females 35 or older*		
abstemious	16.1	45.1	38.8	9.9	39.2	50.9
normal drinkers	18.7	55.1	26.2	13.3	23.3	63.4
heavy drinkers	35.1	44.1	20.8	42.8	28.5	28.5
intermittent alc.	33.8	38.7	27.5⎤	12.5	75.0	12.5
inveterate alc.	32.6	40.0	27.4⎦			
total	28.1	46.1	28.5	14.6	36.4	50.0

alcohol. Moreover, this phenomenon appears as a selective process of the liver, as if the excess fat were blocked in this organ instead of being evenly distributed through the body. This conclusion is supported by the findings respecting the thickness of the adipose panniculus under the abdominal skin. Thickness was measured in the same spot in all the corpses and then classified into three groups: 0 to 10 mm, 11 to 20 mm, and 21 mm and over. The results in relation to drinking habits are shown in Table 41–10. The data conform to the generally accepted pattern of increasing thickness with age, and a thicker adipose layer among females than males. However, there are no indications of increased thickness with heavier drinking, such as would be expected if the extra fat were equitably distributed over the body.

DISCUSSION

The sexual differences in the pattern of drinking behaviour can be explained in terms of the different social norms acting upon men and women, and consequently, of the different social sanctions which prevail. In our country it is not acceptable for a woman to drink heavily or become intoxicated. In contrast, people are complacent toward the exaggerated ingestion of alcohol by men, and there are several cultural inducements for them to drink heavily.

The proportion of heavy drinkers and of alcoholics among men is directly related to socioeconomic status. That is to say, the lower the socioeconomic level, the higher the percentage of those who abuse alcohol. When the problem is analysed in terms of the components of the socioeconomic status, we find that some components are more closely associated with drinking behaviour than others, education and type of occupation being the most relevant. The higher the level of education, the lower the proportions of heavy drinkers and alcoholics. Since education determines, at least in part, occupational possibilities, it is not surprising that we also found different rates of alcoholism as between intellectual and manual types of work.

Education is a determinant for the individual of possibilities of many sorts; hence we may conclude that it is in a sense a mechanism of defence against boredom and alcoholic behaviour. But the smaller proportion of alcoholics among individuals of higher education may be determined also by the stronger social sanction against deviant behaviour imposed upon those from whom society expects the most. Education and social norms are inseparable factors, but the first is perhaps the most influential since it operates on two levels: first, that of the individual, and second, that of the group. Thus, whether alcoholic behaviour is accepted or rejected by the group depends on the general educational level.

Considering the therapeutic and prognostic difficulties, the importance of education as a preventive technique becomes evident. When the rather disparate drinking patterns are compared, it would seem that the intermittent alcoholic suffers from a special mental illness of a different nature from that suffered by the inveterate alcoholic. In support of this contention, there is the relatively smaller influence that educational level and type of work have on this particular group, and also the different age distribution which is evident when members of the group are compared with heavy drinkers and other alcoholics.

When family structure and abuse of alcohol are examined, the group with filial status had smaller percentages of heavy drinkers and alcoholics of both types. However, this is not surprising since the individuals included were among the younger subjects studied. Among the individuals who lived in foster homes or in an ill-defined family situation, the percentage of inveterate alcoholics was high. It may be that these individuals were precocious heavy drinkers and alcoholics, and this impeded them from forming a normal family or taking part in one. When the individuals who were family heads with children are compared with those who were childless family heads, no difference appears in the proportions who abuse alcohol. This leads to a negative conclusion, namely, that children do not constitute a restraint against exaggerated intake of alcohol, and it may well be that the damage produced affects not only the drinker, but also his children's welfare. Among the children of heavy drinkers and alcoholics of both types, it is probable that there is a higher frequency of malnutrition and infant mortality.

With respect to organic damage due to alcohol consumption, we only examined the possible effects on the nervous system, nutritional status, the cardiovascular apparatus, and the histopathological condition of the liver.

The nature of the material made it impossible to study the nervous system with respect to personality or neurological signs. It was only possible to analyse the impairing influence of alcohol on reflexes as reflected in the frequency of accidents. The greater frequency of fatal accidents among the male sex proved to be due not only to greater exposure, but also to more frequent abuse of alcohol. The determination of alcoholemia at the moment of the fatal traffic accident revealed that 46 per cent of the males involved had an amount of alcohol in excess of 1 gm/kg. It is therefore logical to conclude that the probability that a man will die in a traffic accident increases with the blood alcohol level.

The influence of alcohol abuse on nutritional status was studied using the real/ideal weight ratio as a gross indicator. If this indicator is accepted tentatively, it is possible to conclude that alcohol is largely without effect on the nutritional status of individuals under 35 years of age. But among older individuals the greater proportion of those with real/ideal weight ratios below normal probably reflect a deterioration due to heavy alcoholic intake. This may indicate that alcoholics tend to lose weight as they become older, i.e., when the abuse of alcohol is prolonged. In contrast, those who are abstemious or normal drinkers tend to gain weight. In spite of the deficiencies of the real/ideal weight ratio as an index, the data support the hypothesis that immoderate and prolonged ingestion of alcohol induces malnutrition.

The possible damage that alcohol may produce in the cardiovascular system was examined in terms of two indicators: cardiac weight and extent of atherosclerotic lesion on the surface of the intima of the left anterior descending coronary. The findings with respect to cardiac weight did not permit any new conclusions. Some already well-known facts were reaffirmed, namely that the average cardiac weight is greater among males than among females of comparable age, and that it tends to increase with age, regardless of sex. The apparent causal relationship between alcohol abuse and greater cardiac weight in some thin individuals under 35 is not consistent with the findings for normal and obese individuals over 35, who also abuse alcohol. Accordingly, our conclusion is that a greater amount of fibrous plaques on the intima is not associated with a smaller or greater consumption of alcohol; the atherosclerotic condition is distributed uniformly among the diverse patterns of drinking behaviour.

The nervous system and the liver are the two areas in which the most significant pathological findings associated with alcoholism were found. The existence of heavy fat deposits in the liver was clearly related to an increase in the consumption of alcohol in both sexes. This condition would seem to be the first stage in a progression, since fat deposits in livers of normal structure appear more frequently among alcoholics under 35 than among abstemious and normal drinkers of all ages. This phenomenon is independent of nutritional status, since, as already stated, the real/ideal weight ratio among those under 35 is not related to alcohol use. If our interpretation is

correct, then alcohol induces a blocking effect in the liver, and the extent of such blocking could be proportional to the amount of alcohol consumed. This line of reasoning is supported by the experimental work of Isselbacher and Greeberger (5), and also by the finding that the thickness of the adipose panniculus is not affected by abuse of alcohol, as it probably would be if the increase of fat induced by alcohol were uniformly distributed in the body.

The existence of fatty liver with inflammatory reaction appears as a later manifestation of hepatic disease in alcoholics older than 35. Our data induce us to think that continued abuse of alcohol produces structural changes in the liver in the sense that the fat blocked by alcohol gives rise to fatty liver with inflammatory infiltration in a precocious form when the amount of alcohol consumed increases. If it is accepted that this stage of damage, which is transitory and reversible, evolves into cirrhosis, which is permanent, then it is quite understandable that incipient and advanced cirrhosis appeared in our data in individuals older than 35 years of age. Among those under 35, cirrhosis was not clearly related to the abuse of alcohol, but for the older age group it was quite evident that the greater the consumption of alcohol the greater the likelihood of cirrhosis, and this was true for both sexes. Our conclusion is that abuse of alcohol is the cause of a process of liver damage in which the first stage is a blockage of normal fat distribution causing an early increase in fatty deposits in livers of normal structure, followed by inflammatory reaction, and finally fibrosis of the Laënnec type.

With respect to the possible association of alcohol use and malnutrition, it is true that our data do not shed much light on the subject, probably because of the crudity of the index employed. However, the fact that the alcoholics under 35 did not show a deterioration in their real/ideal weight ratio at an age when the hepatic fat-blocking effect begins to be evident, leads us to think that alcohol is a factor in the etiology of cirrhosis, independent of malnutrition. To support this line of reasoning, there is the survey of Caroli and Péquignot (2), who were able to observe nutritional conditions in detail because they studied living individuals. These authors concluded that out of 116 patients suffering from cirrhosis of the Laënnec type, 88 did not diminish their normal food ration until the first symptoms of the disease appeared. For these authors, the malnutrition that is observed in the cirrhotic is not the cause of the sickness – as maintained by some students who have observed a diminished protein intake in such cases (1) – but a consequence of the lack of appetite that the sickness itself induces. A similar conclusion was reached by Sepúlveda *et al.* (11), who pointed out that although malnutrition alone could induce fatty liver, cirrhosis appeared only when there was ingestion of alcohol.

If the increase in fat deposits is accepted as the initial stage of the sickness, then the question arises as to why such deposits also exist – albeit less frequently – in some normal drinkers and even in abstainers, and do not develop into cirrhosis. Undoubtedly the problem is worthy of investigation, since it is improbable that the deposits reflect simply total body fat. Probably alcoholics develop a hepatic fat deposit of different quality from that deposited in those who do not drink excessively or do not drink at all. This view is supported by the work of Lieber *et al.* (7), who have shown that the liver has an endogenic gestation independent of fat deposition in other parts of the organism.

The potential value of a comparative qualitative analysis of the hepatic fat deposits of abstainers and alcoholics is indicated particularly by various relevant findings in experimental pathology. For example, one may cite Holstin's successful induction of cirrhosis in rabbits by gastric instillation of 3-monohydroxy cholastic acid (3). Unquestionably, if it were demonstrated that the hepatic fat deposits in alcoholics were qualitatively different from those in non-alcoholics, this would represent an important step in understanding the pathogenesis of Laënnec's cirrhosis.

SUMMARY

A study has been reported of 1,322 males and 340 females over 15 years of age who were autopsied following violent death in Santiago de Chile, during the period 1960–64. The objects were: (*a*) to determine the relationships between drinking habits and socioeconomic status, education, type of occupation, and family structure; (*b*) to relate alcoholism and frequency of fatal accidents; (*c*) to find the extent to which alcohol influences nutritional status; (*d*) to assess the relationship between ingestion of alcohol and cardiovascular pathology; and (*e*) to relate abuse of alcohol to hepatic damage. The principal sources of data were: (*a*) interviews with the nearest relatives of the deceased persons to obtain information on socioeconomic characteristics and patterns of drinking behaviour; (*b*) calculations of the real/ideal weight ratios of the subjects according to sex, age, and height; (*c*) quantitative determinations of the amount of fibrous plaques covering the surface of the intima of the arteries and (*d*) histopathological examination of liver samples.

The analysis indicated that: (*a*) alcoholism was primarily a masculine pattern of behaviour in Chile: 48.3 per cent of the males and only 11.4 per cent of the females were heavy drinkers or alcoholics; (*b*) alcoholism was relatively more frequent among individuals of low socioeconomic status and appeared at an earlier age among such persons; (*c*) individuals with predominantly manual jobs included a relatively greater proportion of heavy drinkers and alcoholics; (*d*) alcoholism among males was clearly associated with illiteracy and low education; (*e*) there was a greater proportion of alcoholics among individuals who did not have family ties or lived in foster homes; (*f*) 46 per cent of the males and 6.4 per cent of the females who died in traffic accidents were intoxicated at the time of their death; (*g*) abuse of alcohol tended to be related to malnutrition among individuals over 35 years of age; (*h*) the average cardiac weight was probably influenced by alcohol only among individuals with a low real/ideal weight ratio, regardless of sex; (*i*) alcoholism was not significantly related to the presence or absence of fibrous plaques on the intima of the arteries; (*j*) immoderate ingestion of alcohol was clearly associated with an increase of fat deposits in the liver, regardless of sex; (*k*) exaggerated and prolonged ingestion of alcohol may give rise to a blocking effect which induces fatty liver with inflammatory reaction; (*l*) the increase of fat induced by alcohol in the liver did not affect the thickness of the adipose panniculus; (*m*) alcoholism was clearly associated with cirrhosis among individuals of both sexes over 35 years of age; and (*n*) a study of possible qualitative differences in the fat deposits of abstainers, normal drinkers, and alcoholics might prove a rewarding line of research.

REFERENCES

1
ARMAS CRUZ, R., YAZIGI, J.R., LÓPEZ, P.O.,
& MONTERO, O.E.
Consideraciones etiológicas sobre la cirrosis
hepática
Rev. Méd. Chile, **76**: 538, 1948
2
CAROLI, J. & PÉQUIGNOT, G.
Enquête sur les circonstances diététiques de la
cirrhose alcoholique en France
World Congress of Gastroenterology and Fifty-ninth
Annual Meeting of the American Gastroenterological
Association, **1**: 661, 1958
3
HOLSTON, P.
Cirrhosis of the liver induced in rabbits by gastric
instillation of 3-monohydroxycholanic acid
Nature, **186**: 250, 1960
4
HORWITZ, J., MUÑOZ, L.C., *et al.*
Investigación epidemiológica acerca de la
morbilidad mental en Chile
Rev. Serv. Nac. Sal., **3**: 277, 1958
5
ISSELBACHER, K.J. & GREENBERGER, N.J.
Metabolic effects of alcohol on the liver
New England J. Med., **270**: 2351, 1964
6
KLATSKIN, G. & YESNER, R.
Factors in treatment of Laënnec cirrhosis. Clinical and
histological changes observed during control period of
bed rest, alcohol withdrawal and minimal basic diet
J. Clin. Invest., **28**: 723, 1949
7
LIEBER, CH.S., PRITZ, N., & DE CARLI, L.M.
Role of dietary, adipose, and endogenously synthetized
fatty acid in the pathogenesis of the alcoholic fatty
liver
J. Clin. Invest., **45**: 51, 1966
8
MARCONI, J. & VARELA, A.
Encuesta sobre la prevalencia de alcoholismo en la
población de una zona de Santiago
Rev. Psiquiat., **18–20**: 14, 1953–55
9
PATEK, ARTHUR J., JR.
Portal cirrhosis (Laënnec's cirrhosis)
In: Diseases of the liver, 2nd ed. Edited by Leon Schiff
Philadelphia: Lippincott, 1963

10
Proyecto Internacional de Arteriosclerosis, Institute
Central Americano de Nutrición (INCAP) y Louisiana
State University, Protocole standard de Operación,
Guatemala, 1962
11
SEPÚLVEDA, B., HERNÁNDEZ DE LA PORTILLA, R.,
ROJAS, E., & MACÍAS, J. DE
Malnutrition and liver diseases
Gastroenterology, **33**: 249, 1957
12
STEINER, P.E.
World problem in the cirrhotic diseases of the liver:
their incidence, frequency, types, and aetiology
Trop. Geogr. Med., **16**: 172, 1964
13
VALIENTE, S. & TAUCHER, E.
Peso aceptable para adultos
Bol. Hosp., San Juan de Dios, **8**: 1961
14
VIEL, B., DONOSO, S., SALCEDO, D., *et al.*
Alcoholism and socioeconomic status, hepatic damage,
and arteriosclerosis
Study of 777 autopsied men in Santiago, Chile
Arch. Internat. Med. (Chicago), **117**: 84, 1966

HARRISON M. TRICE

School of Industrial and Labor Relations
Cornell University
Ithaca, New York, USA

42

The Alcoholic Employee and His Supervisor: A General Management Problem

"I just don't know what to do with him. He's a first class headache – but I can't send him over to them (the Medical Department). The whole thing could blow up in my face and then I'd really be in a fix. So, I don't do anything – except worry." This is how one work supervisor recently described his reaction to one of his alcoholic employees. In this brief statement the supervisor went to the core of the major cost of ethyl alcohol to our industrial society. Because the alcoholic is normally employed during most of his illness, the largest burden of these costs falls upon the employing organization. Not only do these costs include the "hard" economic loss traceable to sick pay for absenteeism, and the loss of the employee's potential contribution through a shortened career; they also include the anxiety, frustation, and ulcerating indecision which such employees create for the operating manager.

In this article I shall explore some of the dimensions of the problem which alcoholism poses for business and industry. Specifically, attention will be given to: (*a*) the nature of the alcoholism problem and some of the difficulties it raises in business and industry; (*b*) the traditional policy and program approach to this problem; (*c*) several reasons why the traditional approach seems to fall short; (*d*) several methods to bridge the gap between policy and effective implementation.

It is important to note at the outset that much of our discussion concerning alcoholic employees is also relevant to a wide range of other kinds of problem employees including the neurotic, the poorly placed, the aging, and the employee who is technologically obsolete. While the central focus of this article is on the alcoholic, it is worthwhile to bear in mind that there is a close relationship between the methods outlined to deal with this particular type of problem employee and methods to improve management performance across the board. Since in many important ways the problems raised by an alcoholic employee are similar to those posed in a broad spectrum of management situations, the following discussion should sharply illustrate the development and application of sound management practices.

PREVALENCE OF ALCOHOLISM

According to the best estimates, there are between four and five million alcoholics in the United States. Not only does alcoholism appear to be a male problem, with males comprising approximately 80 per cent of the total number, but it is concentrated in the productive years between 35 and 50. The problem seems to cut across social class lines, with alcoholics appearing in sizable numbers in all social strata. Furthermore, contrary to the popular image of the "skid row bum," the vast majority of those afflicted with alcoholism continue to work, remain at home with their families, and more or less function in society. This is particularly true of alcoholics in the white collar, professional, and executive occupations. The alcoholic in the blue collar group, because of his greater visibility, is more likely to become a statistic in some public hospital, jail, or court (7). As a result, most of the popular published material deals mainly with the working class blue collar alcoholic. This myopic view is unfortunate, since the real problem for business may well be the alcoholic manager or engineer rather than the alcoholic punch press operator.

Before examining the impact which alcoholism has on the work world, it is necessary to grapple with the problem of defining alcoholism in a relevant fashion. In US society, where alcohol is viewed at one and the same time as a highly desirable social lubricant and as a "demon" to be avoided, it is extremely difficult to evolve an objective definition. For example, alcoholism cannot be equated with heavy drinking, though heavy drinking may be one indication of alcoholism. Technically speaking, an alcoholic is a person who has lost control of his ability to drink and has become dependent upon alcohol. However, it is a fact that most people drink and, at one time or another, may become drunk without being alcoholic. From the business point of view, a useful pragmatic and behavioural definition is: any individual whose repeated or continued use of alcohol interferes with the efficient performance of his work. This definition, which emphasizes consistent job impairment, is the definition upon which we rely.

IMPACT ON THE WORK WORLD: OCCUPATIONAL AND PSYCHOLOGICAL COSTS

With this definition of alcoholism, it is possible to point out the specific impacts it has on the business world. Evidence clearly indicates that absenteeism is one of the major operational costs. The employee may be absent for a full day or a partial day, or he may be absent while on the job by frequently leaving his work station. The pattern of absenteeism will vary according to the occupational status of the employee. Indications are that executive and professional alcoholics are more likely to be absent for a part of a day, often coming to work even when suffering from severe hangovers. The blue collar employee, on the other hand, tends to group full-day absences (1,3). Several studies have demonstrated that blue collar alcoholic employees are absent three to five times as often as other employees. Their absence records are also chronic, i.e., the absentee pattern continues over a period of time, and absences are often unreported (2,5).

In contrast to absenteeism, neither turnover nor on-the-job accidents seem to pose a cost burden to the employing organization. While popular thought holds that alcoholics are accident prone, recent evidence demonstrates that blue collar alcoholics have few on-the-job accidents, though off-the-job accidents do increase sharply (3). These drinkers seem to avoid on-the-job accidents by remaining away from work or by exercising extra caution while on the job. The latter is the alcoholic's way of proving to himself that there is nothing wrong with him. For much the same reason alcoholics tend not to be job hoppers but try to remain with the same employer. For instance, a recent study indicated that alcoholics in one company had 21 to 30 years of service (3).

A far more serious operational cost which alcoholics pose to a company is inefficient job performance. Supervisors of blue collar alcoholic employees consistently rate them as poor employees due to decreases in both quantity and quality of work and evidence of an uneven work pace. However, since most of the published information deals only with these blue collar

TABLE 42–1

FREQUENCY OF SIGNS OF DEVELOPING ALCOHOLISM AS
REPORTED BY SUPERVISORS OF ALCOHOLICS AND
ALCOHOLICS THEMSELVES*

Type	Supervisors	Alcoholics
I noticed early and frequently thereafter	leaving post temporarily absenteeism: half day or day more unusual excuses for absences lower quality of work mood changes after lunch red or bleary eyes	hangover on job increased nervousness/jitteriness hand tremors
II noticed later but frequently thereafter	less even, more spasmodic work pace lower quantity of work hangover on job	red or bleary eyes more edgy/irritable avoiding boss or associates
III noticed fairly early but infrequently thereafter	loud talking drinking at lunch time longer lunch periods hand tremors	morning drinking before work drinking at lunch time drinking during working hours absenteeism: half day or day more unusual excuses for absences leaving post temporarily leaving work early late to work
IV noticed late and infrequently thereafter	drinking during working hours avoiding boss or associates flushed face increase in real minor illnesses	mood changes after lunch longer lunch periods breath purifiers lower quality of work lower quantity of work

*Reprinted by permission of the American Management Association from Trice (4).

employees, the total cost of inefficiency may be rather deeply buried in the profit and loss statement. The executive, professional, or white collar alcoholic who insists upon coming to work regardless of his condition also poses a serious potential cost to his organization. Since such employees are relatively free of direct supervision and are highly mobile, it is almost impossible to check their work performance accurately. Yet one poor decision by such a "half man" could cost an organization millions.

To the significant operational cost of absenteeism and job impairment must be added the "psychological costs" of necessarily increased supervisory time and attention and the creation of a frustrating situation for the alcoholic's superior. As the quotation at the beginning of this article indicates, the supervisor of an alcoholic is confronted with what he perceives as a "no-win situation." While we will explore this feeling in

depth in a later section, it is already apparent that the supervisor must spend an inordinate amount of time supervising and worrying about the alcoholic. This diverts his energies from more productive channels and adds immeasurably to the costs of alcoholism to industry.

Re-examining the job behaviour of the alcoholic which result in the operational and psychological costs mentioned above, it is possible to isolate those signs which can aid in the early identification of alcoholism. Table 42–1 presents the results of some recent research which shows the signs of developing alcoholism as reported by supervisors of blue collar employees (4). Contrary to popular belief, developing alcoholism is anything but hidden. Both alcoholics themselves and managers who have supervised alcoholic employees report a cluster of persistent on-the-job signs. These syndromes centre around impaired work performance and different forms of absenteeism. Compared with early work, later quantity and quality of work decline, and this decline is often apparent in a spasmodic work pace. Absences from the job increase, including on-the-job absences such as disappearances from the work station. The alcoholic uses unlikely and almost unbelievable excuses to explain these absences as well as his declining work. Hangovers on the job with physical symptoms such as red or bleary eyes are also a part of the early warning signs. Sharp mood changes, particularly after lunch, and unusual personality changes, such as relatively sudden increases in loud talking, are frequently cited in the developing alcoholic. Though the professional and managerial alcoholic, because of his relative freedom from observation, may be more difficult to isolate than the blue collar alcoholic, he too will demonstrate the cluster of early warning signs which indicate the existence of a drinking problem. Thus, early identification of developing alcoholism is a realistic possibility in all types of occupation.

THE COMPANY POLICY AND
PROGRAM APPROACH

In an effort to identify the problem employee and to minimize the losses he can create, many US companies have devised special policies and programs.* In general there are five main ingredients of these programs. These are: (*a*) a policy understood and accepted by management which clearly defines alcoholism as an illness, not a moral defect; (*b*) motivation of the line manager to identify alcoholics and refer them to treatment; (*c*) motivation of the alcoholic employee to accept treatment; (*d*) the establishment or support of treatment and rehabilitation facilities; and (*e*) follow-up to insure consistent application.

It has been frequently argued that a special alcoholism policy, separate and distinct from the general health program of the organization, is necessary. This argument is based on the belief that the alcoholic is different from

*For a good summary of some of these programs see *A basic outline for a company program on alcoholism.* New York: The Christopher D. Smithers Fndn., 1968.

patients with other ailments such as heart disease, tuberculosis, or diabetes, because he hesitates to identify himself and voluntarily ask for treatment. Even if the alcoholic is identified by others, only with extensive urging will he accept the treatment offer. Without wishing to be drawn into the fray, I think that the essential first step in any program is definitive management thinking about the problem, with a clear-cut desire to improve the situation. Once the mental commitment is made, it seems to matter little whether the procedures are formalized into a policy or carried out informally.

The necessity for motivating the alcoholic employee to accept treatment is a unique part of an alcoholism program and deserves a word of comment. Most employees are reluctant to identify themselves as having a drinking problem. "I can stop anytime I want to" is the frequent boast of an alcoholic. To break through the elaborate crust of defences which the alcoholic has cleverly constructed over many years requires a crisis or "hitting bottom" (as defined by Alcoholics Anonymous). Serious threats to the individual can lead to the realization that life with alcohol is far more complicated and difficult than life without it.

Many companies seek to create such a crisis through the application of "constructive coercion." Simply put, this approach identifies alcoholism as an illness and offers the alcoholic a way back to normal life through treatment. This is the constructive phase of the policy. However, if the alcoholic refuses treatment and does not make progress through therapy, his job is clearly in jeopardy. This is the coercion aspect. To render this particular part of the program operative, consistent application of coercion up to and including discharge is essential. Alcoholics are master manipulators who are adept at playing one supervisor against another. The motivation of the alcoholic to accept treatment through the application of constructive coercion is crucial to the success of the program.

THE POLICY-PRACTICE GAP

Despite the neatness, orderliness, and rationality of the program outlined above, there are at least three major defects which create a gap between policy intention and actual practice. In the first place, it has been our experience that supervisors of white collar, clerical, professional, and executive personnel do not use the company program. Their reluctance probably stems from the widely held stigma of alcoholism which creates the desire to keep the mention of a drinking problem out of the company records. Such supervisors, because of their position, probably realize the partial fiction behind the anonymity of company medical and personnel records. They know that in matters of promotion or transfer, "confidential files" can and often are made available. Therefore, drinking problems involving employees in the high status occupations are usually handled informally through groups of fellow executives or in co-operation with private doctors and clinics. This almost total exclusion of a large segment of the organization is a serious handicap for any company program. Ironically, the executive-professional group probably poses the highest potential costs of alcoholism to the organization. However, it is clear that in actual practice most programs deal almost exclusively with the blue collar alcoholic.

The second gap-creating factor is a reluctance on the part of the immediate supervisor to confront the alcoholic and refer him for treatment. As previously pointed out, because of the alcoholic's unpredictability in both attendance and work the supervisor is generally aware of the drinking problem. Even so, though he recognizes the early signs and bears the main brunt of the alcoholic's poor performance, the supervisor continues to vacillate in deciding what to do about the problem.

Discussion with many supervisors indicates that this vacillation is a typical reaction to many employee problems for several reasons. First and foremost, the supervisor believes that it is his responsibility to help the employee overcome his problem. This "do it myself" attitude stems from both cultural norms and from many management publications which cross the supervisor's desk. From his point of view, outside help, such as referral to the medical department, is an admission of his failure as a boss.

Because the administration of company alco-

holism programs is usually done by staff specialists, such as the medical director or the personnel director, and because first level supervisors are inclined to view such staff as tools of management brought in for control of "the lower line," the "do it myself" attitude is reinforced. The line supervisor is likely to view his part in many staff-inspired programs as "taking all the risks, doing all the work, and getting none of the credit."

Strong group feelings among his immediate subordinates that drinking problems should be "kept among the boys" also serves to exercise pressure on the supervisor not to report the deviant employee. We have found this same work group norm to be present not only among blue collar workers but also among executives and professionals. We recently observed the alcoholic presidents of two large organizations. In both cases, their staffs went to great lengths to insulate them from the balance of the organization and to keep the drinking problem known among only a small executive group.

In addition to the lack of support from subordinates, many first level supervisors have considerable doubts concerning their support from management. There emerges from our research a very clear view of the rift between higher management and the first level or two of supervision. Supervisors have told us that frequently they have taken action on a problem employee only to have upper management reverse them. As a result, in many instances the supervisor waits until the situation is so serious that he is absolutely certain of top management support.

The absence of support from either above or below means that the supervisor must be very certain in his mind about the problem before he takes any action. Most programs cast the supervisor in the role of a diagnostician – a role almost impossible to avoid. The very process of identification and referral to the medical department involves diagnosing and a labelling and is apparent to all parties concerned – the supervisor, the employee involved, other employees, and the supervisor's boss. This placing of the supervisor in a role that he is not medically equipped to perform adds to his reluctance to identify and confront the alcoholic until he is absolutely certain that the problem exists.

Therefore, most referrals, even in the best of programs, are apt to occur only in the late stages of the disease. By this time the supervisor or the work group can no longer tolerate the drinking, and referral becomes the lesser of two evils. Unfortunately, by this time chances for treatment and rehabilitation are slim. While concrete evidence is unavailable, it would seem that the rehabilitation rate averages only between 25 and 40 per cent (6). This means that better than three out of five referred alcoholics do not respond to treatment, and under the policy of constructive coercion are probably terminated. The line supervisor, seeing the termination of his referred alcoholic employee, or hearing about it from other fellow supervisors, is likely to say "I told you so – we send one of our boys over to them (the Medical department) and they discharge him. It will be a cold day in July before I send another over there." This sets in motion the vicious cycle of late referral, separation, supervisor resentment, and still later referral. Thus, the "do it myself" feeling, the lack of support from above and below, and the poor results from treatment all feed back to reinforce the supervisor's reluctance to confront and refer an alcoholic employee.

Closely related to the reluctance of supervisors to confront the problem is a third major obstacle to the successful implementation of the program: the absence of treatment facilities. Fortunately this does not pose as serious a problem as the other two. Treatment facilities take one of two forms: individually based treatment or group therapy. Individual treatment facilities include family doctors and psychiatrists who are equipped to handle alcoholics. The National Council on Alcoholism maintains a list of doctors so equipped for most areas, and usually, through some research, these doctors can be found. The principal group treatment for alcoholics is through Alcoholics Anonymous. While only a small percentage of the total number of alcoholics are amenable to treatment by AA, for those who do become involved it is very effective therapy. Also useful for group treatment facilities are out-patient or in-patient clinics in many general hospitals.

Regardless of the current availability of treatment outlets, it has been our experience that when industry becomes interested, the community usually responds with treatment facilities. It must be borne in mind, however, that unless referral takes place earlier than usual, most treatment still has a success rate of only 25 to 50 per cent. Several examples of treatment success ranging up to 70 per cent have been reported, but these are exceptional.

In summary, despite the real cost of an alcoholic employee, both in economic and psychological terms, and the existence of a soundly conceived policy and program, the three major obstacles outlined above create a gap between the existence of a policy and the implementation of the program. It is worth noting again that many of the situations mentioned apply to a wide range of management actions. For instance, the isolation and lack of support felt by the front level supervisor influence his technical as well as his personal decisions. When discussing the alcoholic and analysing management actions and attitudes towards this type of deviant, it is possible to gain insights into a wide range of management activities.

SOME BRIDGES ACROSS THE POLICY-PRACTICE GAP

Against this depressing backdrop of obstacles there are at least three promising approaches to bridging the gap between policy and practice. The first and most obvious is through training. If the line supervisor could simply be given training in identifying and handling the alcoholic employee, he might change his attitude which, in turn, might lead to earlier referral. Recent experience with two large organizations indicates that one possible way to avoid all of the stigmas and defences usually surrounding a training program on alcoholism is to broaden the base and discuss many types of problem employees of which the alcoholic is only one. If training is geared to the problem employee in general, and not just to the alcoholic employee, supervisors will probably show less resistance to the new information and be more willing to act upon it. We are currently involved in an extensive research project with one organization to test this hypothesis. In general, however, present evidence leads us to be less than sanguine about the prospects for dramatic behavioural change through training.

The second major approach is the use of a non-threatening staff person with some specialized knowledge in the area of alcoholism. The industrial nurse seems ideally suited to this role. Because of her position, she frequently observes many of the early medical signs, such as upper respiratory ailments, and also absentee patterns. Her central location in the organization's grapevine also assures that she will hear about "John, who's been drinking a lot lately." Not only is the nurse in a position to identify the alcoholic employee, but, because of her organizational neutrality and medical expertise, she is capable of influencing the first level line supervisor to take some action. Other low level staff people, such as the employment interviewer, the assistant personnel director, or the safety inspector might also be in a position to observe the early identification signs and, through influence with the line manager, encourage some early action. It is, however, easy to overemphasize the utility of this alternative. As we previously pointed out, the first level supervisor tends to develop many defences against the encroachment of staff personnel. Increased surveillance by the industrial nurse or the safety inspector may be met with increased defences rather than with co-operation.

The use of staff personnel to accumulate control statistics, such as absentee information, suggests the third alternative for action. In the final analysis, the obstacles outlined in the previous pages are the results of misguided management. The supervisor who tolerates a partially productive alcoholic is likely also to tolerate other partially productive employees. A supervisor who is reluctant to confront an alcoholic employee is also likely to be reluctant to deal with an employee who has been frequently absent. Therefore, the third approach hits hard on such factors as costs, waste, and absenteeism, and applies additional pressure on general management performance, leaving the first level supervisor with less ability to absorb the poor producer, including the alcoholic. This management strategy can precipitate

a crisis for the front level supervisor, forcing earlier action. Thus, it might be said that one way to deal with the problem of alcoholism in industry is to strengthen and improve general management practices across the board. This is a possible alternative because, in many respects, the problems posed by an alcoholic are similar to those raised in many other personnel situations. If the supervisor's ability to handle general management problems is improved, he will also be more competent to handle the alcoholic. Conversely, it is also possible to improve overall management competence through improving the supervisor's ability to handle the alcoholic.

Perhaps the best means to bridge the policy-practice gap would be a combination of the three approaches outlined. The pressure for improvement in overall management performance might well generate a supervisory crisis which convinces the supervisor that he must do something about the ineffective performer. Training might be expected to stimulate referral and treatment and offer the supervisor a way out of his difficulty. Such action is less costly to him than continuing to absorb the employee's erratic performance. At the same time it is more in the interest of the employee. The use of non-threatening staff neutrals can provide for this alternative a source of support which the supervisor does not have in his current situation. In short, a combination of all three approaches might prove an effective way to translate policy intention into concrete action.

SUMMARY

In this paper the costs of alcoholism to industry have been noted, and a company policy and program have been outlined, designed to minimize these costs. Three major causes of a gap between policy and practice were pointed out. The supervisor's reluctance to confront the alcoholic employee was examined and it was concluded that his vacillation is a general phenomenon arising out of his feelings of lack of support and his desire to help the employee. To overcome these obstacles, three approaches were suggested: (*a*) training, (*b*) the use of non-threatening staff neutrals, and (*c*) pressure for improved general management performance. It was concluded that the line manager could deal most effectively with the alcoholic and the problems of alcoholism in industry through a combination of these three approaches.

REFERENCES

1
MAXWELL, M.A. & WASSON, J.
Social variables and early identification of alcoholism on the job
Unpublished ms, 1963
2
OBSERVER & MAXWELL, M.A.
A study of absenteeism, accidents and sickness payments in problem drinkers in one industry
Quart. J. Stud. Alc., **20**: 302, 1959
3
TRICE, H.M.
The job behavior of problem drinkers
In: Society, culture, and drinking patterns, edited by D. J. Pittman & C. R. Snyder
New York: Wiley, 1962, p. 493
4
TRICE, H.M.
New light on identifying the alcoholic employee
Personnel, Sept.–Oct. 1964
Reprinted as no. 162 in the Reprint Series, NYSSILR Cornell University
5
TRICE, H.M.
Alcoholic employees: a comparison with psychotic, neurotic and "normal" personnel
J. Occup. Med., **7**: 94, 1965
6
TURFBOER, R.
The effects of in-plant rehabilitation of alcoholics
Med. Bull. Standard Oil, N.J., **19**: 108, 1959
7
WELLMAN, M.M., MAXWELL, M.A., & O'HOLLAREN, P.
Private hospital alcoholic patients and the changing concept of the "typical" alcoholic
Quart. J. Stud. Alc., **18**: 388, 1957

CARL L. ANDERSON

Alcoholism and Drug Abuse Section
National Institute of Mental Health
Bethesda, Maryland, USA
(Retired June 1967)

43

Control of Alcoholism

Since other papers in this Symposium consider in some detail the organization of services for the treatment and control of alcoholism in various countries, I shall confine myself here to the question of the framework within which such programs may be developed.

"Control" has many meanings, but for present purposes two appropriate definitions are "to exercise restraint or direction over; dominate; command" and "to hold in check, curb." Sometimes control may be expressed by legislative action. For example, the United States in 1919 adopted a constitutional amendment, which was repealed later, making it illegal to produce alcoholic beverages. After repeal, the individual states adopted their own laws governing the sale and distribution of such beverages. With the enactment of recent legislation in the state of Mississippi, none of the states is legally "dry" any longer. State laws differ in their provisions for the sale of such beverages and the taxes imposed upon them. The details of alcoholic beverage control laws are the subject of much discussion and disagreement. For example, should the sale of alcoholic beverages be a state monopoly through state-owned stores? Should states permit local options enabling individual counties to decide whether or not to permit the distribution and sale of alcoholic beverages? Should taxes received from alcoholic beverage sales become part of the general revenue or should they be used in whole or in part to support programs of alcoholism research, treatment, and prevention? Should 18 or 21 years be the minimum age of persons to whom alcoholic beverages may be sold? It is doubtful if such questions are unique to the United States.

Alcoholism and alcohol-related problems in individuals can be curbed by early case-finding and diagnosis, care, treatment, and rehabilitation. In the United States, the development of treatment services has been handicapped by the lack of facilities and by the limited professional interest in the alcoholism field. At the present time, many clinics, social agencies, general hospitals, medical personnel, and others have been relatively non-functional in caring for and treating the alcoholic. Increased attention to treatment and rehabilitation has been influenced by two recent court decisions which state essentially: (*a*) that a chronic alcoholic may not be stamped a criminal if his drunken public display is the involuntary result of disease, and (*b*) that there may be appropriate detention of the chronic alcoholic for treatment and rehabilitation so long as he is not marked a criminal.

The community seeking to check alcoholism also must take into account the alcoholic's family and immediate social environment. The total framework of community effort and planning should make appropriate and effective use of such resources as the general practitioner, the clergy, clinics, general hospitals, public health and welfare services, courts, rehabilitation facilities, correctional institutions, and probation and parole services; in short, the agencies and institutions having some responsibility for the provision of helping services to people, and upon whom individuals call for help in time of distress.

Control of alcoholism is aided by co-ordinated planning to develop and strengthen services to the alcoholic and his family, and to stimulate better working relations between actual and potential resources. In some instances, specialized agencies providing services to the alcoholic are quite isolated from the rest of the community. As a result, they are unable to draw upon the strengths of other agencies or to influence their policies or practices relative to alcoholism. Staff consultation, case conferences, and other methods can be used by the specialized alcoholism agency to establish collaborative relationships with others.

In-patient services, out-patient services, partial hospitalization services, emergency services, and consultation and education services are basic elements in coping more successfully with a community's alcoholism problem and in checking its progress in individuals and families. For effective use of resources, it is essential to establish criteria for admitting alcoholics to different parts or units of the treatment program, as well as for the progression of the patient from in-patient services to out-patient services to partial hospitalization to community living. For each unit, it will be important to develop and adopt policies and procedures to carry out the functions upon which agreement has been reached. Although various units may be operated, sometimes by different agencies, it is possible to blend them into a viable community mental health framework of services to alcoholics and their families (3).

The concept of "progressive patient care" has aroused much interest in the hospital and medical field and is pertinent to the control of alcoholism (4). The central theme of the concept is the organization of facilities, services, and staff around the medical and nursing needs of the patient. The patients are grouped according to their degree of illness and need for care. The staff serving each of these groups is selected and trained to provide the kind of services needed by its own group.

The present concept of progressive patient care embraces five elements. Four of them are contained in the hospital and the fifth is an extension of services into the community. They are: intensive care, intermediate care, self care, long-term care, and organized home care. In curbing the progressive development of alcoholism, it is probable that the intensive care unit, and possibly the intermediate care unit, would be the only elements requiring an in-patient facility such as a general hospital. Some of the elements might operate under different auspices, public or private, but they should be closely related to maximize continuity of care and accountability for the alcoholic's health status.

The intensive care would provide the medical, nursing, and other care needed by the critically and seriously ill patients regardless of primary diagnosis. Its staff would be trained to work with that type of patient. The intermediate care unit would have the patients who required a moderate amount of nursing care, not of an emergency type, who may be ambulatory for brief periods, and who are capable of participation in the planning of their own care. The self-care unit is for the ambulatory and physically self-sufficient patients requiring therapeutic or further diagnostic study, or who may be convalescing. Long-term care is for those needing skilled prolonged medical and nursing services. Rehabilitation, occupational therapy, and other services may be essential also.

The community mental health framework and the concept of progressive patient care provide models within which broad treatment services can be developed. They deal with the areas of secondary and tertiary prevention in the control of alcoholism. But the community mental health framework is also involved in endeavours related to primary prevention. Halfway houses, sheltered workshops, residential lodges, foster home placement, day-night centres, work release programs, and related approaches could be more fully developed to give better recognition to the general medical, nursing, psychiatric, social, spiritual, and vocational needs of the alcoholic.

In recent years, there has been a shift from almost exclusive concentration upon diagnosis and treatment of illness to diagnosis and treatment of the person in totality and of his family. Within this change, attention is being given to the physical and social environment in which the treatment is occurring (1, 2). The treatment of the alcoholic becomes much more than an organizational chart, a staffing pattern, and established procedures for interagency co-operation. These are important factors, but the social environment necessary for their functioning should not be overlooked. It can be a powerful force in helping to provide direction over the course of alcoholism.

Care, treatment, and rehabilitation services for the alcoholic and his family are needed. There is the necessity also for manpower, professional and non-professional, to provide these services and evaluate their effectiveness. What other things are needed for more effective control of alcoholism?

The long-range attempts to curb alcoholism should be similar to those used toward any other public health problem (5). Public health workers point out that there is no evidence of the control or elimination of any disease solely as a result of activities directed at early diagnosis and treatment in individuals. This does not deny that much good is done for the individuals who are diagnosed and treated, but that does not necessarily decrease the incidence of a disease such as alcoholism.

So far, the bulk of time, money, personnel, and effort has been devoted to the individual approach to alcoholism. It is necessary to devise community approaches, that is, public health procedures. What is the environment which is fostering and producing the alcoholism and alcohol-related problems? How do non-users of alcohol cope with alcoholic beverages in their environment, and how do they use intra-psychic and social resources during a particular stage of life or when faced with environmental challenges? Have alcoholics progressed through a typology of crises? Can these crises be anticipated, can ways be learned to cope with them in which alcohol is not the tension reducer?

In keeping with the public health approach, it is necessary to modify our single causal theory and recognize that many factors contribute to alcoholism. What may be causal under certain conditions may not be the crucial factor under different circumstances. The multi-causal approach helps us to face alcoholism as a community problem, not as an individual one (5). This means that alcoholism, as a community disease, can be diagnosed and treated in each community with every community being different from its neighbour. The diagnosis requires community study to learn the factors which make alcoholism more prevalent in one place than in another. What are the crucial environmental factors that are conducive to alcoholism? The environment has physical, social, economic, religious, political, psychological, ethnic, educational, and other components. The community diagnosis requires the skill, knowledge, and competence which is not possessed by any one individual, agency, profession or group. It requires a team of able professionals from the necessary disciplines to examine, test, diagnose, and prescribe for each community. Self-evaluation has merit and is helpful in obtaining community understanding and co-operation, but the community should have the services of individuals qualified to undertake the community study of alcoholism. At the present time it would be hard to identify, let alone obtain, the services of such personnel. However, a step towards remedying this would be to initiate the identification of possible causal factors in the community through pilot projects, using various community diagnostic approaches.

The control of alcoholism has prevention as

its goal and this will not be achieved easily or in isolation. Alcoholism is a community problem, a team problem, requiring community approaches and research. The people active in this work will be of different backgrounds and approaches. They will have or will develop the competence to identify the causative environmental factors which can be modified or eliminated to curb the prevalence of alcoholism and alcohol-related problems. They will have opportunities for creativity and innovation in the development of procedures for control and in the evaluation of their effectiveness.

REFERENCES

1
BROWN, E.L.
Newer dimensions of patient care: Part I
The use of the physical and social environment of the
general hospital for therapeutic purposes
New York: Russell Sage Foundation, 1961
2
BROWN, E.L.
Newer dimensions of patient care: Part II
Improving staff motivation and competence in the
general hospital
New York: Russell Sage Foundation, 1962
3
The comprehensive community mental health center
Washington, D.C.: Superintendent of Documents,
U.S. Govt. Print. Off., 1964
(Public Health Service Publication no. 1137)
4
Elements of progressive patient care
Washington, D.C.: Superintendent of Documents,
U.S. Govt. Print. Off., 1962
(Public Health Service Publication no. 930-C-1)
5
MC GAVRAN, E.G.
Facing reality in public health
Paper presented at the Conference on Key Issues
in the Prevention of Alcoholism, Pittsburgh, 1962

ERNESTO MEDINA L.

Department of Hygiene and Preventive Medicine
University of Chile
Santiago, Chile

44

The Role of Alcohol in Accidents and Violence

The role played by a previous ingestion of alcohol in an individual case of casualty or violence can not be evaluated, because of individual differences in tolerance to alcohol and because various other factors are commonly involved. On the other hand, when the situation is judged collectively, a great amount of evidence reveals the importance of the role played by alcohol.

Under the influence of the drug the concept of self and environment is changed. The liberation of deep features of the personality frequently awakens aggressive tendencies, and the individual tends to overvalue his mental and physical abilities; his self-confidence is increased and he is induced to act carelessly. Even the ingestion of small amounts of alcohol can lower the perception of sensory stimuli and the ability to judge correctly auditory and visual changes including shades of colour, besides disturbing the memory for recent events.

Alcohol also delays automatic reactions, disturbing first the finest co-ordinations and then the capacity to receive two stimuli at the same time. It impairs those judgments and discriminations which enable the individual to react adequately in an emergency. This combination of pharmacological actions constitutes the background of the role of alcohol in accidents and acts of violence.

These effects differ in each individual case, rendering difficult the assessment of the contribution of alcohol alone. The determination of the amount of ingestion through blood, urine, or breath analysis provides valuable information. The average values of alcoholemia under experimental conditions are shown in Figure 44-1; the amount ingested determines the maximum blood levels as well as the rate of disappearance from the blood. However, the blood alcohol curve changes with dosage, gastric occupation, type of food consumed, the appearance of vomiting, and previous habits of drinking.

In different groups studied (11,13), a significant correlation was found between blood level and clinical signs of alcohol effects, especially drunkenness. In general, drunkenness appears with blood levels under 50 mg/100 ml in one of ten individuals; with blood levels from 51 to 100 mg it appears in one out of three; in two out of three with 101 to 150 mg; and in 99 per cent

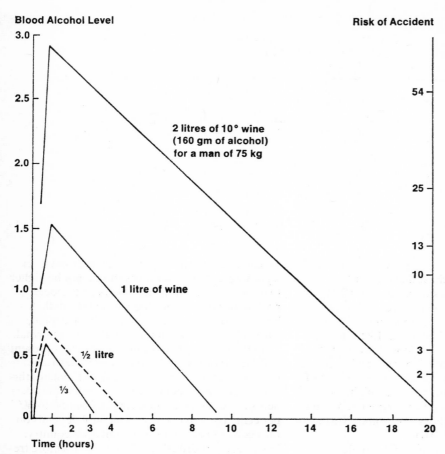

Blood Alcohol Level

Risk of Accident

2 litres of 10° wine
(160 gm of alcohol)
for a man of 75 kg

1 litre of wine

½ litre

⅓

Time (hours)

Figure 44-1
Blood alcohol levels and accident risk according to amount of alcohol consumed
and time following consumption.

when blood levels are higher than 250 mg/100 ml. These data show the great extent of individual variation, depending, among other things, on body weight, form of alcohol ingestion, and above all on the different effect of the same blood level when the curve is rising or falling. We must also add the factor of marked differences among investigators in judging the disturbances induced by alcohol in each case.

The association of alcohol ingestion with violence or accidents appears to differ from one country to another. It varies with the alcohol habits of the community, the extent of determination of blood alcohol levels, and the situation of the cases studied (murder victims, drivers,

hospitalized or deceased accident casualties, etc.). In the case of Chile, the situation can be summarized as follows: (*a*) the annual alcohol intake is 14 litres per capita in persons aged 15 and older; (*b*) three to five per cent of adults in urban areas are alcohol addicts, 8 to 12 per cent are excessive drinkers, 50 per cent are moderate drinkers and 30 per cent are abstainers; (*c*) there is a marked sex difference in alcoholism, namely, 13 male addicts to one woman (1, 4, 5, 10).

It is easy to understand that under these circumstances alcohol frequently appears associated with violence and accidents. Research carried out in the Criminology Institute of the State Prison for Men in Santiago showed that in

TABLE 44-1

PERCENTAGE OF SAMPLES SHOWING A BLOOD ALCOHOL LEVEL
HIGHER THAN 49 mg/100 ml IN VIOLENCE VICTIMS IN
SANTIAGO DE CHILE (BASED ON LEYTON (9))

	Men		Women	
Type of violence	number of samples	over 49 mg/100 ml (per cent)	number of samples	over 49 mg/100 ml (per cent)
homicides	208	62	20	35
suicides	193	36	64	14
accidents in public places	203	53	44	23
traffic accidents	354	44	70	19
home accidents	72	39	19	21
other accidents	88	34	8	38
total	1,118	45	225	21

one of every three cases (35 per cent) the crime was committed under the influence of alcohol: 58 per cent of the crimes were murders; 28 per cent were robberies with violence, and the remainder other robberies, arson, and miscellaneous crimes. The Medico-Legal Institute of Santiago registered blood alcohol levels of 50 mg/100 ml or higher in 62 per cent of men and 35 per cent of women brought in as victims of homicides. These frequencies are higher than those reported for other Latin American countries and similar to those for some North American cities (6, 15, 16).

The association of alcohol and suicide fluctuates in various countries between 2 and 10 per cent (14). In Chile, alcohol is reported in 36 per cent of male suicides and 14 per cent of female (8). Table 44-1 shows the association of alcohol with different types of violence and accidents in the city of Santiago (9). Traffic accidents are more easily prevented than others and therefore are especially interesting. Numerous investigations confirm the disturbing effect of alcohol on ability to drive or to avoid a car. The occurrence of alcohol in such accidents ranges from 10 to 75 per cent in the various reports.

The evaluation of the role of alcohol can be achieved in different ways. Figure 44-2 presents Swedish figures showing the frequency of accidents in abstainers and drinkers, and the increased risk observed by comparison of the blood levels of persons in accidents with those of individuals chosen at random. From this information

we can conclude that the maximum blood level legally accepted as harmless should not be higher than 50 mg/100 ml which shows an accident probability three times higher than normal. A limit of 100 mg/100 ml cannot be accepted, since it gives a risk ten times higher than normal.

In the USA the influence of alcohol was present in 20 to 30 per cent of drivers and pedestrians involved in fatal accidents (12). In England, this figure reaches 18 per cent (7). In non-fatal accidents in the USA the figure ranges from 50 to 60 per cent. The importance of alcohol depends on the accident pattern prevalent in each country. In Chile, overt drunkenness is 2.2 times more frequent in cases of pedestrian injuries and falls from vehicles than in collisions. This is important because out of 100 deaths in traffic accidents, 57 are pedestrian deaths, 13 are the result of falling from a vehicle, and 13 result from collisions. This distribution differs widely from that of other countries.

In Chile, the information given by the police on the prevalence of drunken drivers gives a lower figure than that obtained from emergency services, where the frequency reaches 41 per cent of drivers involved in some kind of accident (2, 3). The blood alcohol levels of victims of traffic accidents, based on data of the Asistencia Pública de Santiago – an emergency service – is shown in Table 44-2.

For an adequate interpretation of this information, it is necessary to point out that of the patients admitted to the service 51 per cent were

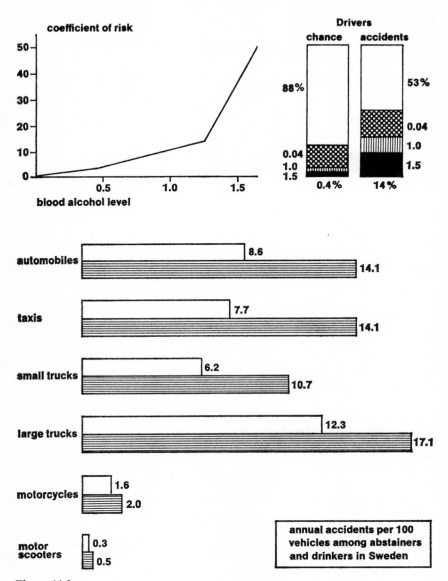

Figure 44-2
Frequency of accidents in abstainers and drinkers and the increase in risk with increased blood alcohol level.

pedestrians, 11 per cent fell from a vehicle, and 38 per cent were victims of collisions or turnovers. Among the deceased, the proportion of pedestrians was 66 per cent; falls from a vehicle constituted 6 per cent and other accidents 28 per cent. A clear sex difference is also indicated by the data in this table. The difference in blood alcohol level by hour of the day is shown in Table 44-3.

To summarize, the role played by alcohol in accidents and violence is always important, but its importance is in relation to a variety of factors.

TABLE 44–2

BLOOD ALCOHOL LEVELS IN PERSONS ADMITTED TO THE ASISTENCIA PÚBLICA DE SANTIAGO OR DEAD AT THE SCENE OF THE ACCIDENT (BASED ON ZAPATA (17))

Alcohol blood level (mg/100 ml)	Admitted to AP		Died in AP		Died in accident	
	men (per cent)	women (per cent)	men (per cent)	women (per cent)	men (per cent)	women (per cent)
> 99	53	13	45	20	69	0
21–99	21	30	23	13	17	28
0–20	26	57	32	67	14	72
number of cases	678	174	124	28	130	26

TABLE 44–3

DISTRIBUTION OF PERSONS ADMITTED TO THE ASISTENCIA PÚBLICA DE SANTIAGO FOLLOWING A TRAFFIC ACCIDENT, BY BLOOD ALCOHOL LEVEL AND TIME (1960) (BASED ON ZAPATA (17))

Time of day	Number of cases	Alcohol blood level (mg/100 ml)		
		> 99 (per cent)	20–99 (per cent)	0–19 (per cent)
0– 6 AM	109	47	17	36
6–12 M	157	10	15	75
12– 6 PM	230	15	17	68
6–12 PM	319	44	15	41

The possibility of control through both legislation and education is related to the establishment of a low limit of tolerance for alcoholemia, with severe punishment for transgressors and continuing offenders.

REFERENCES

1
ACEVEDO, L., MARTY, L., ROBINSON, A., & SAAVEDRA, M.
Rev. Méd. Valparaiso, 12: 121, 1959
2
ADRIASOLA, G., ARMIJO, R., & TERRAZAS, F.
Algunos hallazgos en encuesta sobre accidentes del transito
Soc. Chil. salubridad, 1954
3
ADRIASOLA, G., KAEMPFFER, A.M., LEYTON, A., MAIRA, J., & OPASO, A.
Rev. Chil. hig. med. prev., 14: 219, 1952
4
HONORATO, R., GARCÍA, P., & OXMAN, M.
Rev. Chil. neuropsiquiat., 2: 144, 1958
5
HORWITZ, J., MUÑOZ, L.C., ALVAREZ, M., BECERRA, M., GONZÁLEZ, M., MARTINEZ, L., MERCADO, N., ORELLANA, N., & PLAZA, J.
Investigación epidemiológica acerca de morbilidad mental en Chile
Rev. Serv. nac. sal., 3: 277, 1958
6
Informe final del Seminario Latinoamericano sobre alcoholismo
Talleres educacion para la salud, Servicio nacional de salud, Santiago, 1961
7
JEFFCOATE, G.O.
The importance of alcohol in road accidents
Brit. J. Addict., 55: 37, 1958
8
LEDERMANN, S.
Alcool, alcoolisme, alcoolisation
Travaux et documents de l'institut national d'études demographiques
Cahier 29
Presses universitaires de France, 1956
9
LEYTON, A.

Algunos aspectos epidemiológicos de las muertes
violentas registradas en Santiago
Tesis de médicos cirujanos
Edit. Universitaria, Santiago, 1954
10
MARCONI, J., VARELA, A., ROSENBLATT, E., SOLARI, G.,
MARCHESE, I., ALVARADO, R., & HENRIQUEZ, W.
Rev. psiquiat., **18**: 11, 1954
11
MEDINA, E.
Epidemiológia de los accidentes del transito
Relato al I Congreso de Medicina Sanitaria
Mendoza, Argentina, 1961
12
National Safety Council
Accident Facts
1960
13
ROMERO, H., MEDINA, E., & YRARRÁZAVAL, M.
Rev. Méd. Chile, **90**: 999, 1962
14
SCHNEIDMAN, E.S. & FARBEROW, N.L.
Clues to suicide
Pub. Health Rep., **71**: 100, 1956
15
WOLFGANG, M.E. & STROHM, R.S.
The relationship between alcohol and criminal
homicide
Quart. J. Stud. Alc., **17**: 411, 1956
16
ZAMORANO, M. & MUNIZAGA, C.
Crimen y alcohol
Santiago de Chile: Pacifico, 1963
17
ZAPATA, R., TORRES, F., WELCH, J., & GROSSLING, S.
Repercusión en la salud y la economía de los
accidentados del tránsito en Santiago en 1960
Soc. Chil. de salubridad, 1961

KETTIL BRUUN

The Finnish Foundation for Alcohol Studies
Helsinki, Finland

45

Legislation
and Alcoholism

Considering the prevailing views of the nature of alcoholism, it may seem odd to postulate an interrelation between legislation and this condition. In etiological theories, genetic, metabolic, neurophysiological, psychological, and sociological factors are enumerated, but legislation is generally not included in the list of causes. However, there is some empirical evidence that legislation under certain conditions influences alcoholism. I shall present a number of specific cases and from this base try to arrive at more general conclusions. It is convenient to divide the discussion into two sections: first, instances where legislation either directly or through the changes it creates in alcohol consumption has influenced the prevalence of alcoholism in general or of one type of alcoholic; secondly, the effects of legislative actions aimed at defining alcoholism.

LEGISLATION, ALCOHOL CONSUMPTION, AND ALCOHOLISM

During and after World War I, national prohibition laws were enacted in the United States and in Finland. According to the literature (3, 6), in both countries a considerable decline in rates of death from liver cirrhosis occurred during a short period immediately after the introduction of prohibition – a period which has been labelled "effective prohibition." There is evidence that this decline was due to a decrease in consumption of alcoholic beverages and to a lower rate of alcoholism during this period. However, it must be emphasized that this decline was only temporary; not only did the prevalence of alcoholism later increase, but the prohibition had a number of negative consequences. For instance, in Finland there was a considerable increase in crimes against man (11). Because of such negative effects on society at large, prohibition laws were ultimately abolished. The experiments with prohibition clearly show how legislative measures may influence behaviour and the prevalence of alcoholism. However, the basic assumption underlying prohibition was wrong. Customs embedded in the culture serve social functions which cannot be eliminated by mere legislation.

An interesting example of something that might be called a temporary "unintended prohibition" is worth noting in this connection. In Sweden there was a two-month strike in the alcohol beverage industry in 1963. During this period spirits were hard to obtain and a large number of liquor stores closed. The impact of this strike on the society was very considerable. Most interesting from the point of view of the present topic is that the number of patients in institutions for alcoholics decreased greatly (4).

The foregoing examples concern situations where traditional legal channels of alcoholic beverage distribution have been disrupted. It is pertinent also to consider instances of dramatic changes in the availability of alcoholic beverages. As far as I know, the most radical example is provided by Denmark, where the price of a litre of akvavit (Danish vodka, 40 per cent) increased from 0.90 kronen in 1917 to 11.00 kronen in 1918. The new price was thus 12 times higher than the old one, whereas the price of beer remained practically unchanged. Because of this price change, the consumption of distilled spirits decreased from 5.1 litres of absolute alcohol per inhabitant to 1.1 litres. Although the consumption of distilled spirits later increased somewhat, essentially Denmark has been a beer drinking country since 1918. A recent investigation (8) shows that delirium tremens and deaths from chronic alcoholism decreased remarkably. The number of delirium cases dropped from 27.2 per 100,000 inhabitants (annual mean for 1911–16) to 1.7 in 1918, and this level has prevailed since then despite minor variations. The decrease in deaths due to alcoholism was from 14 per 100,000 inhabitants before the reform to less than 2 afterwards. Evidently, drastic price changes influenced not only the structure of consumption but also the prevalence of alcoholism – or, to be more cautious – at least the prevalence of one type of alcoholism.

The price policy adopted by the Finnish State Alcohol Monopoly has been guided by the results of econometric studies (9), and it is now quite clear that price policy exerts a powerful influence on the structure of consumption. In contrast to the Danish example, price changes have been moderate and there is no evidence of an influence on the prevalence of alcoholism.

Dramatic changes in the availability of alcoholic beverages, however, are not confined to price regulations. In countries like Finland and Norway there is what could be labelled partial prohibition. In Finland this means that the laws prohibit the sale of alcoholic beverages in rural areas.* In Norway, on the other hand, sale in local areas is determined by local referendums. There have been some systematic studies of changes in drinking habits when liquor stores are opened in previously dry areas. An experimental study done in Finland (7) has shown that the introduction of wine and beer stores has some effect, but not a very large one, on the consumption level, whereas no changes were observed in the frequency of intoxication in the communities studied. Similar results have been obtained in Norway (1). And a study of drinking habits among male teenagers in four Scandinavian capitals showed only minor differences in drinking habits, despite the fact that differences among these cities in the laws and their enforcement are indeed large (2).

All of these studies clearly indicate that legal attempts to limit the level of consumption are generally unsuccessful; but it does seem possible to change the structure of consumption. This certainly has some bearing on the problem of alcoholism, which is evident from Jellinek's ample discussion of the relationship between types of alcoholism and attitudes toward alcohol and drinking habits. Thus, it is at least to some extent possible to influence the distribution of types of alcoholics through rational alcohol policies. Sudden changes, such as prohibition or radical price regulations, may have large effects, but so far the number of such attempts have been far too few to permit general conclusions about the permanence of changes and the conditions necessary to achieve explicitly stated goals.

ALCOHOLISM DEFINED BY LEGISLATIVE ACTION

There is another area of legislation which certainly influences the social situation of the alcoholic and probably also the prevalence of alcoholism. In some countries, for instance Finland,

*New legislation in 1968 abolished the distinction between rural and urban areas.

Norway and Sweden, there are special laws concerning alcoholism in which an alcoholic is defined. According to Finnish law he is a person who is addicted to drinking or who otherwise repeatedly misuses alcoholic beverages in that he: (a) is violent, maltreats his wife or children, or is a menace to himself or to the health or personal safety of others; (b) has been convicted during the previous 12-month period of driving a motor or other vehicle while drunk or under the influence of any intoxicant; (c) is guilty of disorderly conduct at home or elsewhere; (d) has been arrested during the previous 12-month period three or more times for drunkenness; (e) neglects to support and care for dependents or repeatedly neglects to do his job; (f) has become a burden to his kith and kin; or (g) is in need of social welfare (10).

What does the introduction of a legal definition of alcoholism mean for the prevalence of alcoholism? The mere existence of a definition does not influence prevalence; but presumably it affects the number of *recognized* alcoholics. In addition, the manner of applying the law may have some bearing on prevalence. As far as Finland is concerned, the most commonly applied criterion of legal alcoholism is arrest for drunkenness more than three times in a given 12-month period. Very few of those punished for drunken driving are labelled as alcoholics, even though under the law this is possible provided there is evidence of repeated misuse (and this could mean anything). The legal definition of an alcoholic is therefore usually a person who for some reason is arrested often because of acute intoxication. Such a person, once defined as an alcoholic by society, may be warned or placed against his will in an institution for alcoholics. It is hard to judge how this process of control influences the prevalence of alcoholism. The concept of "legal alcoholism" may influence the meaning of the concept "alcoholic" in Finnish culture in general, and also beliefs concerning the possibilities of treating alcoholics.

In addition to the law respecting alcoholics, a general health insurance system was recently introduced in Finland, under which alcoholism is accepted as a disease. Since the introduction of this system, alcoholics more often have gone voluntarily to institutions; if an alcoholic voluntarily enters an institution he receives a daily allowance based on the health insurance law; if he is there for compulsory treatment he does not. Thus the new law influences the willingness to accept the label "alcoholic."

Another example of how the situation of at least a subpopulation of alcoholics has been changed remarkably through legislation is provided by a Norwegian investigation (5). At the turn of the century there was much discussion in Norway concerning those who were imprisoned for drunkenness frequently but for short terms. Because the punishment was considered ineffective, a new law was proposed in parliament. According to this proposal a person could be sentenced for three years for repeated public drunkenness. However, the parliament considered this punishment too harsh in comparison with sentences for crimes against man and for theft. But an ingenious solution was found. Punishment was called "treatment," and then the law was passed. Since that time members of a subpopulation of Norwegian alcoholics are kept in a special institution where no treatment is given and which is considered by the inmates harder than a prison. Introducing the term "treatment" in the text of the law thus meant more severe punishment. The situation of the alcoholics changed considerably.

DISCUSSION

Examples have shown that legislation may affect alcoholism in at least the following ways:

1
a) by determining whether or not alcoholic beverages are prohibited;
b) by imposing limitations on the availability of alcoholic beverages (age, type of community, price).
2
a) by defining alcoholism;
b) by defining how an alcoholic should be perceived: as a patient or as a sinner, and accordingly, whether he should be treated or punished;
c) by defining ways of rehabilitation (for instance, stipulating that employers are obligated to hire former alcoholics).

All in all, concerning the first point, legislation may influence the level of consumption of alcoholic beverages – or at least the structure of consumption – and indirectly also the prevalence of types of alcoholics. Concerning the second point, legislation structures the situation of an alcoholic and influences beliefs about and perceptions of the alcoholic.

It should be noted that the content of the concept of alcoholism has not been discussed. It is not relevant in the present context, though it is evident that the influence of legislation – if any – depends on what concept of alcoholism is current. In any event, all concepts have at least one thing in common. An alcoholic is always defined as such by social interaction; he becomes an alcoholic not by his drinking alone but through the perception of his drinking by others, and through his own perception of how other people view his drinking. Thus, even if the etiological background of alcoholism cannot be manipulated by legislation, the social consequences of alcoholism are socially defined, and therefore influenced by legislation.

The purpose of legislation is to solve conflicts between human beings and to influence the behaviour of people. Many times legislation represents the acceptance of changing customs; in some instances it attempts to initiate changes in customs. Actual behaviour, attitudes, the power of the legislator, and the enforcement of laws are all influential in the outcome of legislative actions. And because social structure differs from society to society, it is hard to generalize from the few empirical findings available as to the general effects of legislation on alcoholism. However, if legislative action is to be used to fight alcohol problems, empirical study of the effects of such action should be conducted and, wherever feasible, an experimental approach systematically employed.

REFERENCES

1
AMUNDSEN, A.
Hva skjer når et nytt vinutsalg åpnes?
Statens institutt for alkoholforskning, 1965
[Mimeographed]

2
BRUUN, K., et al.
Drinking habits among northern youth; a cross-national study of male teenage drinking in the northern capitals
Translated from Swedish and Norwegian by F.A. Fewster
Helsinki: Finn. Fdn. Alc. Stud. Publication no. 12, 1963

3
BRUUN, K., KOURA, E., POPHAM, R.E., & SEELEY, J.R.
Liver cirrhosis mortality as a means to measure the prevalence of alcoholism
Helsinki: Finn. Fdn. Alc. Stud., Publication no. 8, Pt. 2, 1960

4
CFN (Centralförbundet för nykterhetsundervisning)
Då alkoholen försvann
Uppsatser om spritstrejken 1963 från Alkohhol-frågen 6–9, 1963

5
CHRISTIE, N.
Tvangsarbeid og alkoholbruk
Oslo, 1960

6
JOLLIFFE, N. & JELLINEK, E.M.
Cirrhosis of the liver
In: Effects of alcohol on the individual, vol. I, edited by E.M. Jellinek
New Haven: Yale University Press, 1942, p. 273

7
KUUSI, P.
Alcohol sales experiment in rural Finland
Translated by A. Westphalen
Helsinki: Finn. Fdn. Alc. Stud., Publication no. 3a, 1957

8
NIELSEN, J.
Delirium tremens in Copenhagen
Acta psychiat. scandinav. (suppl.), **41**: 187, 1965

9
NYBERG, A.
Alkoholijuomien kulutuksen vaihteluista Suomessa vuosina 1949–64 sekä hintapolitiikasta alkoholijuomia myyvässä monopoliyhtiössä
Helsinki. In press

10
TIRKKONEN, J.
Alcoholism in Finland from the standpoint of psychiatry
Alcoholism (Zagreb), **2**: 6, 1966

11
VERKKO, V.
Homicides and suicides in Finland and their dependence on national character
Copenhagen: G.E.C. Gads, Scandinav. Stud. Sociol. no. 3, 1951

LUIS C. MUÑOZ

AÍDA PARADA

Mental Health Section
National Health Service of Chile
and Department of Education
University of Chile
Santiago, Chile

46

Teaching about Alcoholism in the Schools

Anthropoloical sciences have provided objective ways to investigate the problems of alcoholism. The quest of the pure sciences has been matched by that of the practical sciences, mental hygiene and education. Education studies the values operating in a culture so as to fulfil its main purposes: the provision of norms that will allow the individual to achieve a dynamic adjustment.

Obviously, there is a common tendency among these sciences to investigate phenomena that might be categorized under "axiological pathology." There is, in fact, a multiplicity of factors that may alter the norms and values in a cultural community to produce lack of understanding, aggression and the loss of incentives for production and creation. Thus, anomalous standards may arise which threaten the superior values of human proficiency and which grant validity, instead, to the power of prejudice, creating false values or strengthening the blind requirements of uncontrollable instincts.

The positive cultural objectives are theoretically open to all individuals within a group. The dynamic forces, however, that lead the individual either towards good or evil lie within his own nature, in the satisfaction – or lack of satisfaction – of his biological needs, in his impulse to succeed or achieve prestige, as well as in his desire for love and companionship.

Our societies are going through a period of crisis. There is a general clamour for changes in social life, for expedient channels to ensure a better collective life. These changes cannot be left to chance; they must be clearly conceived, planned, and guided by people who are well acquainted with the community's real needs and interests. Indices of underdevelopment in Chile are lack of food, social stratification, inadequate sanitary conditions, low education level, disorganized administrative structures, and high rates of birth and mortality. These conditions are so deeply ingrained that they have a pathological effect on the society. Among the symptoms of malaise, alcoholism and the habit of excessive drinking stand out; their irrational basis promote the strengthening of attitudes, symbolic beliefs, and prejudices of great emotional power and dynamism.

The solution to these problems requires much more than the action of either state or private institutions considered in isolation; it calls for the state as the regulator of relationships of harmony and co-operation among its members to solve problems that involve a large portion of the population and produce phenomena of social pathology. State action, planned and with suitable resources, could co-ordinate the action of different social structures and carry out a national campaign to erase abnormal habits of excessive drinking with all their derivative problems.

In the legislation of every country, provision is usually made for imparting instruction about problems of alcoholism. In Chilean legislation, this is incorporated in the Alcohol Law as revised in 1964. Article 16 states that primary, secondary, and special schools must teach hygiene along with notions of physiology and temperance, using audio-visual aids to illustrate the consequences of abuse of alcoholic drinks. This is to be a required subject at schools, for which credit must be obtained to be promoted to the next grade. The article also states that cinemas must show anti-alcoholic advertisements for five minutes. And article 17 specifies that the state is to provide the schools with adequate materials for anti-alcoholic teaching. So far the effects of this law have been virtually nil, and the beliefs and prejudices favouring the excessive intake of alcoholic drinks have not been broken. There are, however, some promising developments that reveal a change of attitude of some state agencies, stimulated, no doubt, by the pioneers who have searched unremittingly for solutions to these problems. Thus, the following initiatives have been taken:

1

By the General Directory of Health: the setting up of the Committee of Experts on Alcohol and Alcoholism, 1957; the creation of the Mental Health Section, 1960; the creation of the Advistory Committee on matters connected with alcohol and alcoholism, 1961; and the approval of the National Program for the Control of Alcoholism and Problems of Alcohol, by the Technical Council of the National Health Service, 1965.

2

By the National Congress: the creation of a special investigating committee to consider a general campaign to fight alcoholism in Chile.

3

By various ministries: the creation of a mixed committee to co-ordinate the sum total of actions to be undertaken in matters of alcohol and alcoholism, 1966.

We think that such organizations have a very complex task to fulfil and that it is therefore necessary for the state to secure sufficient budget resources for the purpose.

If we consider that the greatest risk associated with excessive drinking is the development of the alcoholic disease, then primary prevention should be oriented towards reducing the likelihood of excessive intake. This would fundamentally mean a modification of the property system assigned to alcohol in relation to values; that is to say, a new system of socialization would have to be devised through technical action from multiple sectors, including all the many shades of education from non-systematic (that absorbed through childhood experiences) to systematic.

All those who carry out functions of leadership, and especially professionals, are looked upon as models and constitute a reference group for the majority within a community, which tries to raise its own status by absorbing and imitating the norms and values of its leaders. Bearing this in mind, a line of research in connection with primary prevention may be tackled, namely, a study of the leaders of a community to determine how far they are capable of participation in a program of preventive action.

Between 1944 and 1960 a number of investigations were carried out to determine if there were differences in psychological features between students from homes with alcoholic or abnormal parents and those coming from homes with normally drinking or abstemious parents. In all studies statistically significant differences were found in school achievement and antisocial features of temperament and character (4).

In 1958 we found with Horwitz negative correlations, not accounted for by chance, between intemperance in drinking and educational level, occupational level, and salary (3). Later, through the Mental Health Section of the National Health Service, we have tended to guide the direction of non-systematic education in this area on the grounds that bio-psycho-social

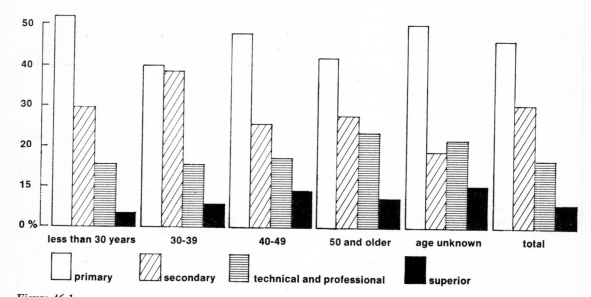

Figure 46-1

Distribution of ages in the sample of teachers according to the level of school taught.

deterioration caused by alcoholism exercises a negative influence on cultural development and produces a circular relation: disease–poverty–lack-of-culture.

It becomes clear that to modify positively the habit of excessive drinking which leads towards alcoholism, it is necessary to develop educational programs for all groups in the social structure. Particularly important is the educational effort in schools, and so it is obviously most essential to instruct teachers in mental hygiene, especially in matters related to alcohol and alcoholism (5). The teacher is the person most in contact with the child and the adolescent, and he can therefore effectively contribute towards the desired socialization, acting as its primary tool.

But to what extent are teachers at present prepared to take on this responsibility? To find out objectively how familiar teachers were with problems of alcohol and alcoholism, and to determine their attitudes, a survey was carried out covering a representative sample of teachers in primary, secondary, and technical-professional schools as well as in higher education in Greater Santiago. A stratified random sample was taken, which included 7 per cent of all teachers. The age distribution of the sample by level of school taught is shown in Figure 46-1.

To describe the teacher's situation, the following questions were included in the research:
1
What is the teacher's attitude towards excessive drinking?
2
How far does he share in factors that predispose towards excessive drinking? In other words, how far does he assign positive qualities to alcohol in relation to values?
3
What information does the teacher have about alcoholism?
4
What experiences has he had with respect to excessive drinking?
5
How does he feel about participation in co-ordinated educational action aimed at prevention?
6
What is his degree of preparation for such participation?

Some revelant findings may be summarized as follows:
1
Information of the teacher about problems of alcohol. Out of a variety of questions to deter-

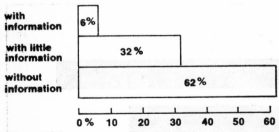

Figure 46-2
Amount of information concerning the problems of alcohol and alcoholism.

mine the teachers' knowledge of alcoholism, a few were selected to construct an index. These questions referred to characteristics of excessive drinking, and of alcoholism and its treatment. The results, as shown in Figure 46-2, indicated that 62 per cent of the teachers did not have any information on the subject, 32 per cent had very little, and only 6 per cent had some knowledge, and that not as satisfactory as might be wished. This lack of information applied to all types of teacher, although those in secondary schools and higher tended to be a little better informed.

2

Teachers' attitudes towards excessive drinking. The form of drinking considered most acceptable by the teachers was moderate; however, some also accepted excessive drinking. This acceptance increased considerably when it involved teachers' friends or happened on a special occasion, such as a party. Heavy drinking at a party was tolerated by 2 per cent and accepted by 39 per cent, as long as it was not accompanied by evident symptoms of drunkenness or did not become embarrassing to others. The attitude of tolerance towards excessive drinking was not related to sex, type of teacher, or degree of information about alcoholism. This may be quite significant as it seems to indicate that mere "information" does not promote a real educational experience or a change of attitude regarding excessive drinking. Although there are no similar studies of representative samples of the population at large, the question arises whether the teachers' attitude is the same as that of the rest of the population. Our impression is that there is little difference.

3

Acceptance of prejudices by teachers. The rela-

tion between degree of knowledge about problems of alcohol and alcoholism and acceptance or rejection of erroneous beliefs indicated that acceptance was more common in persons less well informed, while rejection was more common among those who had a relatively greater knowledge. Overall, 57 per cent of the teachers rejected erroneous beliefs, while 43 per cent accepted them. The percentage of teachers holding various beliefs about alcohol is shown in Figure 46-3.

4

Participation of teachers in a prevention program. Although teachers at large understand the importance of education for the prevention of alcoholism, only 28 per cent indicated that they would be willing to participate personally in a preventive program. Willingness to participate was not linked either to sex or type of teacher, although the largest number of willing collaborators was found among primary school teachers and the smallest among teachers working in technical and professional schools. On the other hand, as shown in Figure 46-4, teachers with more information on the subject of alcoholism were more often willing to participate than those less well informed. Among the former, 37 per cent were ready to participate wholeheartedly, while only 24 per cent of the latter expressed willingness to do so.

Regarding the form in which teachers conceived their participation, the following findings are relevant: (*a*) 34 per cent noted certain conditions, the most important of which was that the program be systematic and responsible; (*b*) among those who noted conditions, a distinction was made as to the place where their participation should be expected: inside or outside the school. The majority favoured action *outside* school, especially primary teachers and those in higher education. Secondary, technical, and professional school teachers seemed to favour action *inside* the school.

To sum up the survey results, teachers do not seem to have sufficient information, and they appear to share fully in the prejudices and traditions existing in their culture. A negative attitude towards excessive drinking is not sufficiently established among them, so that they do not have the motivation to educate their pupils in matters connected with alcohol and alcoholism.

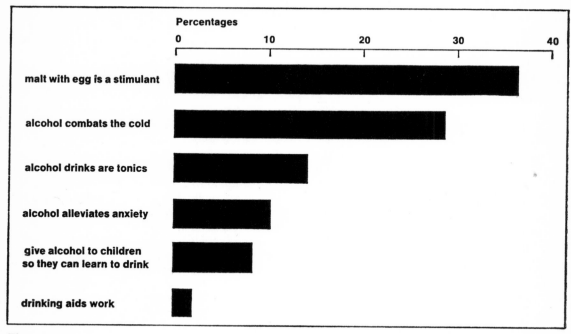

Figure 46-3
Proportion of teachers holding erroneous beliefs about alcohol.

To develop the fundamental educational programs for the prevention of a disease that has the characteristics of an epidemic with serious consequences for our national life, the inclusion of mental hygiene courses in the curriculum of all teacher-training institutions is of the utmost importance. And these courses must comprise substantial sections on alcohol and alcoholism. Trained pedagogical advisers who have specialized in mental hygiene are also urgently needed. They would supervise the activities of teachers in all educational services and initiate prevention programs.

ELEMENTS OF A PLAN OF TEACHING ACTION

Teamwork with the participation of all experts in the field (health, education, and community leaders, in the present case) is nowadays a widely accepted approach. Because of his multiple functions as an instructor, counsellor, cultural agent of the community, and active operator in professional proficiency, we think that the teach-er can most effectively act to modify the cultural patterns that favour the excessive intake of alcoholic drinks, if he does so in accordance with a well directed educational campaign. The health expert must bring together the scientific material to be included in the educational subjects, adding to it all pertinent data and experience that different experts on problems related to alcoholism can offer. We think that both in the curriculum and in school life itself, situations tinged with emotion and reflecting real life may best provide learners with experience and contribute towards the weakening of prejudices and the forging of desirable attitudes.

With respect to the content of the curriculum, the following topics should be introduced, where suitable, in the official programs of biology, social sciences, the mother language, mathematics, and the plastic arts: (*a*) Excessive drinking, the process leading towards alcoholism. (*b*) Psychophysical risks of excessive drinking. (*c*) Socioeconomic factors determining excessive drinking. (*d*) Effects of excessive drinking on family organization. (*e*) Economic damage to

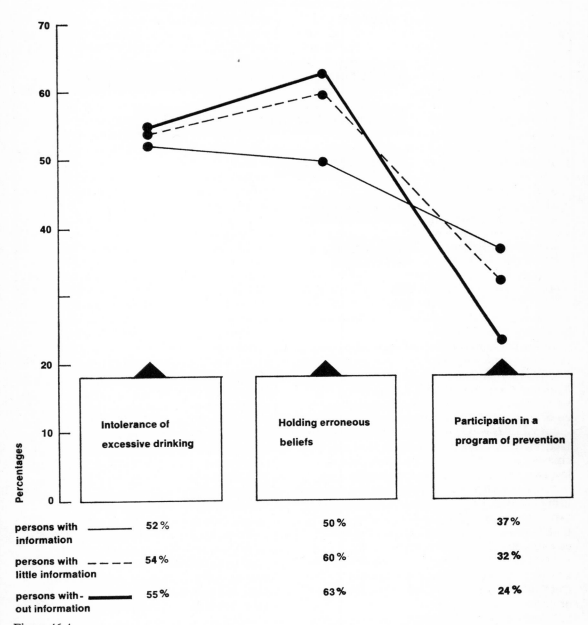

Figure 46-4
Amount of information in relation to intolerance of excessive drinking, holding erroneous beliefs, and willingness to participate in a program of prevention.

the national budget produced by excessive drinking. (*f*) Cultural patterns that favour the habit of abnormal drinking.

At a symposium held in Santiago some years ago, attention was drawn to a number of prevalent beliefs which might be expected either to initiate or to strengthen the urge to consume alcoholic beverages (5). These were as follows.

"To get drunk is a sign of manliness," or *"He who drinks more is more of a man."* It is not uncommon to see a group of youngsters around a table crowded with beer or wine bottles. Nausea as well as actually being sick are carefully concealed to avoid being thought a "sissy." It is easy to show how inconsistent this belief is. It is precisely the "less manly" individual – the weak, the sickly, the fearful, the cowardly, the frustrated – who needs to drink to stimulate his energies and feel strong.

" Alcohol increases the capacity for physical work" is another erroneous belief widely held. It is true that shortly after the first drink there is a brief period of excitement, but it is followed as quickly by one of fatigue.

Intimately connected with this belief is another currently found among football players and athletes: *"A certain amount of alcohol increases agility and co-ordination."* This is palpably wrong. It has been proved that alcohol impairs co-ordination of movements.

"Alcohol is good protection against cold." In fact, increased blood to peripheral areas increases the loss of heat by irradiation, and this loss is greater the colder the surroundings.

"Alcohol is a food." It is true that the metabolism of alcohol produces calories, but no food expert would consider alcohol genuinely nutritious because of its toxic effects and the lack of essential elements for forming new cells.

"Old wine (vino añejo) is a reconstituent," is a belief found even among some health experts. But "old wine" is actually more toxic than "new" or current wine.

"Beer and wine stimulate the secretion of the mammary glands." This belief was the one most frequently accepted by those in our research sample (36 per cent). But it is established that milk – and not wine – is the first liquid chosen to help increase mammary production and strengthen the mother.

"Alcohol aids digestion." It is true that small doses excite the production of gastric juices, but not in a larger proportion nor more effectively than food. A concentration of 5 to 10 per cent alcohol retards digestion, and if it is higher produces irritation of the gastric mucosa.

"Alcohol increases the quantity and quality of intellectual work." The truth, on the contrary, is that alcohol hinders judgment, most particularly on moral issues, which is very dangerous, since the judicial function is the main activity of reason and intellect. Alcohol also weakens attention, increasing perceptive errors and lengthening reaction time. Finally, it also diminishes the power to fix and recall events.

"The intake of alcohol fortifies the will." The "will" may be said to operate whenever the individual is faced with two or more desires, and chooses that having greater social importance. This choice presumably cannot be made by the alcoholic who is unable to deny himself pleasure or to prefer ethical and social forms of behaviour.

"Alcohol is a source of joy." Alcoholic intoxication produces an initial euphoric state and liberates emotions inherent to temperament, but it also has special after effects, usually by no means of a joyful nature.

"Wine increases friendship." But the opposite is most frequently the case. The release of inhibitions and weakening of judgment often leads to violence, resentment, distrust, jealousy, etc. Intoxication frequently weakens and destroys the most noble features of social behaviour.

Such erroneous beliefs as these, if considered as possible subject matter for an educational program, have to be selected, graded, and correlated by the teacher according to a pedagogical criterion, and he will have to know the socio-cultural conditions that prevail in his community. The ideas outlined could be incorporated into a general and well organized educational policy, directed towards all members of a community in an unselfish, integral and democratic manner, and leading towards the full development and adjustment of the individual. Special education, as a complement of general education to provide the individual with a trade or profession, will have to emphasize the risks of excessive drinking in connection with work.

In spite of all the limitations that have made it difficult for schools to fulfil their task as specific agents for socialization throughout the centuries, their historical development shows their increasing effectiveness and gradua*l approchement* towards achieving what philosophically oriented anthropologists call the elaboration of universal values leading to the highest degree of integrated community life (1, 2, 6).

The teacher's attitude has to be one of serene mutuality. It is as undesirable to preach abstinence as it is to stimulate moderate drinking. A passionate or aggressive attitude usually stimulates the tendency to fight in children and adolescents. Above all, vocational interests, fortified by a number of aptitudes, must be taken into account. The instinct for survival if adequately guided, leads a young person to choose and dedicate himself to a profession which satisfies a cultural need as well. To achieve this, the didactic procedure chosen has to start from a psychological point of view according to the learner's interests and needs, and has to finish with a logical point of view, namely the acquisition of knowledge. Between these two poles the teacher has to display all his creative power and ingenuity to carefully promote the development of desirable attitudes towards alcohol.

Where is this educational task best accomplished? The educational system in each country differently subdivides the process of schooling. However, it is worthwhile to remember that the best period in which to achieve desirable attitudes towards alcohol is that of adolescence, when awareness of absolute values emerges and the main features of the moral character are strengthened. Let us not forget, on the other hand, that adult life is regarded nowadays as a period of enrichment and that education tries to cultivate these possibilities universally. In this instance, convincing adults that excessive drinking leads almost inevitably to alcoholism constitutes, to a great extent, a fruitful process of prevention.

SUMMARY AND CONCLUSIONS

Alcoholism, before becoming a disease, is preceded by a period of excessive drinking funda-mentally conditioned by sociocultural motives. There is an apparent correlation between a low standard of living and the existence of an "axiological pathology" favouring excessive intake. The possibility of carrying out effective primary prevention of alcoholism is dependent on the modification of habits that promote excessive drinking, as well as on socialization to develop scientifically desirable forms of conduct in matters related to alcohol. The descriptive survey carried out allows us to conclude that the teachers of Santiago are not prepared – at any level – to participate successfully in a program of preventive education. Their attitude, however, is generously understanding, hence we strongly recommend a better training of teachers in matters connected with mental hygiene and alcoholism. Finally, we recommend that all educational programs devised should carefully consider the analysis of those erroneous beliefs that favour the excessive intake of alcoholic drinks.

REFERENCES

1
BRAMELD, TH.
Bases culturales de la educación
Buenos Aires: Eudeba, 1961
2
HAVIGHURST, ROBERT J.
La sociedad y la educación en América Latina
Buenos Aires: Eudeba, 1958
3
HORWITZ, J., MUÑOZ, L.C., ALVAREZ, M., BECERRA, M., GONZÁLEZ, M., MARTINEZ, L., MERCADO, N., ORELLANA, N., & PLAZA, J.
Investigaciones epidemiológicas acerca de morbilidad mental en Chile
Rev. Serv. nac. sal. (Chile), **3**: 277, 1958
4
MUÑOZ, L.C.
Antecedentes para el estudio del escolar Chileno
(Conjunto de investigaciones – 1944 a 1960 – inéditas)
5
MUÑOZ, L.C.
Bases para un programa de educación en alcohol y alcoholismo
Simposium sobre alcohol y alcoholismo
Santiago de Chile: Serv. nac. de salud, 1958
6
Planes y programas de estudio de la educación (1961)
Chile

IRMA MORALES DE FLORES

Alcoholism Commission
San José, Costa Rica

47

Organization of Local Services for Alcoholism Control

Alcoholism has been considered the world's most serious problem by some, not only in the field of mental health but in that of general welfare as well. During the late 1930s and 40s little attention was given to excessive drinking or alcoholism except from the social angle. The anti-alcohol campaigns of the time were carried out for the purpose of making people abstain altogether from drinking, in their own interest, but by presenting horrifying images. No one bothered to look into the crucial question of motivation: "Why do people drink in the first place?"

In the Central American Isthmus, Costa Rica was the first country (in 1950), followed shortly by Guatemala, to undertake open and continuing campaigns against alcoholism, painting to the public the carnage that was brought about by drinking alcoholic beverages.

Culturally, the Central American Isthmus has much in common with Latin America as a whole, but each country presents its own local characteristics which will be analysed later in connection with the discussion of specific aspects of programming. Guatemala, for example, exhibits special problems which have been described by Ruth Bunzel (1). The author shows the consequences of alcoholic intoxication in two indigenous groups, one in Guatemala, the other in Mexico. The study demonstrates that to understand the present problem of alcoholism in Central America one must take into account the historic context which shows how the consumption of intoxicating drinks was traditionally a part of religious life.

There is or has been a strong contrast between the Spanish and indigenous cultures in Central American countries. However, at present such a contrast hardly exists in Costa Rica, with its preponderance of inhabitants of Caucasian descent, and a relatively small number of aborigines (about 4 per cent) who are almost totally integrated into the general population. Such demographic and cultural variables are of particular importance in planning a treatment program. It is also important to recognize the social maturity of a community or group for which a program is planned, and the potential for action that it may develop.

It is possible to see how programs in Costa Rica were established on what appear to be quite solid grounds. For over twenty years the community felt the urge to do something about the problem of alcoholism. There was a committee working continuously towards the enlightenment of the public. Campaigns aimed at prevention through education reached the youth in schools and colleges. Several members of the old Committee of the Anti-Alcohol Campaign helped constitute the Committee on Mental Health which was established in 1950. Later, in 1952, there came a "parting of the ways," and these members left to form the National Committee on Alcoholism, which continued to work intensively until 1955 when the Costa Rican government passed an act creating the present semi-autonomous Alcoholism Commission and providing funds for its program. This growth, upwards from the community to the state, has given the program certain distinctive characteristics and the dynamic spirit which prevails today.

It is essential that alcoholism programs evolve as a result of action by the community. In all its functions, including hospitalization and treatment of the alcoholic, treatment and guidance of the family, prevention, and education, it must be supported by the very groups to which such services are directed.

In Guatemala the Anti-Alcoholic Association, a private undertaking was founded in 1945. From the beginning, its plans included the possibility of making Guatemala, in due course, the site of a Central American institute of research on alcoholism. Apparently the program, which was well financed at the start, succeeded in building a sanitarium for alcoholics but failed to gain the interest and co-operation of the community.

Eventually the funds assigned to the program were incorporated in the nation's general budget. The Institute was then left in a difficult economic position, since the amounts assigned fluctuated according to the varying criteria of the legislators. The budget assigned became so stringent that at one time only a small amount was available for the prevention campaign, leaving the sanitarium without any income whatsoever. However, since 1959 the grants have remained fixed for both the sanitarium and the prevention campaign. At this point the program was reorganized and took the form it has today.

Chile, unlike either Costa Rica or Guatemala, commenced an intensive research program in 1948. However, comprehensive epidemiological surveys through family sampling were begun as early as 1945. The Institute of Studies on Alcoholism in Santiago has what is recognized as the most thorough research program in Latin America, and has shed much light on many of the problems involved in the organization of such programs. Thus in Chile we have an instance of a program which has succeeded in filtering down from the government to the community, instead of the other way round.

In Colombia we have no record as yet of an institution specializing in the treatment of alcoholism. Dr. Bejarano in Bogota, however, was successful in making peasants aware of the perils of drinking home-made liquors.

It is noteworthy that in Panama, according to a recent report, there is allegedly no serious problem of alcoholism. The notion among Panamanians is that alcoholism constitutes a serious problem in neighbouring Central American republics to the north, but that in Panama it is comparatively unimportant. This view may be quite incorrect. One has seen analogous situations in other countries where lack of concern about matters related to alcohol was based on entirely false impressions. Under such circumstances the need for relevant research becomes particularly important.

In other countries of Central and South America, the number of Alcoholics Anonymous groups would seem to indicate that although there are no governmental programs an attempt to cope with the problem has sprouted from the community itself. The latest AA World Directory (1966) provides a population breakdown as shown in Table 47-1.

There are no government-supported or private organizations responsible for an integrated program on alcoholism. By way of contrast, it is interesting to note that in Boston, Massachusetts, USA, for example, the State Commission under the Department of Public Health maintains sixteen hospital-level clinics for the treatment of alcoholics. This program began in 1955 and its efforts are directed as well towards those persons who have not yet accepted treatment. A 24-hour service is maintained in these clinics, and the staff is well trained in the field of alcoholism, as I can attest as a result of a recent visit.

Another American city, Cleveland, Ohio, has a program on alcoholism that has managed,

TABLE 47–1

ALCOHOLICS ANONYMOUS
MEMBERSHIP IN CERTAIN LATIN
AMERICAN COUNTRIES

El Salvador	population	2,500,000
	active members	5,081
	registered groups	178
Colombia	population	18,750,000
	active members	3,035
	registered groups	128
Panama	population	1,300,000
	active members	8
	registered groups	1
Canal Zone	population	50,000
	active members	55
	registered groups	2

through the Department of Welfare, to transform a house of correction with a capacity for 500 inmates into a regular treatment centre. Inmates may choose to remain voluntarily in the centre for further treatment after they have completed their period of compulsory confinement. There are two programs in operation: one for older alcoholics which is run along the lines of an old people's home, and another for younger patients. Cases are referred to the centre by all manner of agencies. The house of detention is open; no bars or barriers.

To sum up, of the local programs of the five Latin American countries that have been discussed, it may be concluded that only Costa Rica and Chile have integrated programs, and both are in process of development. It may be observed further that in most programs attention is exclusively directed towards detoxification of the patient. From the experience in Costa Rica, where the program has been developing for eleven years, a number of conclusions have been drawn which may be of help in the future organization of local programs.

OBJECTIVES AND TREATMENT

The treatment of alcoholism must proceed in three directions: physical, psychological, and social. Inasmuch as the disease affects these three areas, it follows that treatment must be directed

to each. The program must be well integrated and not concentrated on a single aspect.

In general, a program can be based on the following objectives, bearing in mind the social, economic, and cultural aspects of each country or area:

1

To persuade the community through the use of all possible promotional means to create an organization or establishment to manage the program, which may be either publicly or privately run.

2

To promote the drafting and execution of legislation appropriate to the treatment of alcoholics.

3

To promote research and investigation on all phases of the problem.

4

To carry out an educational program directed towards all segments of the population and designed to convey enough knowledge for their own protection.

5

To establish information centres for both the alcoholic and his family, and to encourage all clinics and hospitals to initiate and maintain services for the alcoholic patient, wherever these are not already available.

6

To co-ordinate all efforts being made by local and international institutions in the same field and to awaken interest in others.

7

To prompt the specialization of the personnel necessary to the development of the various aspects of the program: medical, anthropological, etc.

PERSONNEL

Any program under development necessarily must have access to a source of competent personnel, which should possess not only scientific training but personalities suitable for this work. In addition, research personnel are needed, as well as qualified therapists. In Costa Rica the program has been developed through the efforts of social workers, physicians, and a few psychiatrists. A general practitioner interested in mental health can be of great assistance in this field, while using a trained nurse with a similar interest. The social worker must be proficient in the methods employed by this profession and must also be capable in community organization.

In the complete absence of trained personnel, persons possessed of deep humanitarian feeling and civic spirit, such as teachers, nurses, priests or ministers, and citizens of many walks of life, with full understanding of the problem and appropriate guidance, may serve as agents in the rehabilitation of the diseased individuals. Alcoholics who have taken treatment and enjoyed periods of sobriety can be enormously useful if they will co-operate. In small communities especially, the organization of local civic committees and the maintenance of their interest is an indispensable means of providing continuing support for the program. Parenthetically, all the programs I studied recognized the need to encourage a much larger number of persons to specialize in the field of alcoholism.

METHODS OF OPERATION

To develop a program successfully, it is necessary to select methods which function in an integrated fashion in all respects. Casework is indispensable at the beginning of treatment and for evaluation of the patient's life situation. The period of hospitalization for detoxification provides an excellent opportunity to motivate the patient to carry on subsequently with other aspects of treatment. This is indispensable to divert the dependency of the alcoholic. As an example of failure of one-phase treatment, the program of Guatemala may be cited. There, despite the availability of extensive medical facilities, it did not fulfil expectations due to the lack of follow-up treatment facilities.

The grapevine questionnaire employed by Dr. Jellinek, the "liquor test" of Dr. Seliger, and other similar devices offer the patient the opportunity to make his own decision as to whether he does or does not suffer from alcoholism, and in many instances, this one step is sufficiently strong motivation to break his resistance to treatment. Tape recordings of programs, appropriate music,

and other audio-visual aids also help in alcoholism therapy. A periodic publication, such as the monthly *Boletin* which is published in Costa Rica, keeps patients throughout the country informed of local events, progress, or needs, and also spreads widely the philosophy of the program.

REFERENCE

1
BUNZEL, RUTH
The role of alcoholism in two Central
American Cultures
Bol. Inst. Indig. Nac., 3: 27, 1957

JAROSLAV SKÁLA

Department of Alcoholism Studies
Karlovy University
Prague, Czechoslovakia

48

The Organization of Anti-Alcoholic Treatment in Prague

Anti-alcoholic treatment was organized in Czechoslovakia after the end of World War II. The organization of the Prague centre is the model for the organization and co-operation of all forms of anti-alcoholic institutions in this country.

THE DETOXICATION CENTRE

The first link in the chain is the detoxication centre. This is in a ward containing 22 beds to which all persons in an acute state of alcoholic intoxication are taken. The centre was the first of its kind to be set up, not only in Czechoslovakia, but in the whole of Europe. Today there are 40 such centres in Czechoslovakia and their activities are supported by legal statute. The latter states that "Any person who by the consumption of alcohol has promoted in himself a state in which he causes public inconvenience or has fallen into a condition in which he may injure himself, his family, his surroundings or property, is bound to undertake treatment until he reaches full sobriety in the detoxication centre set up for that purpose. The police will assist, if necessary, by accompanying such a person to the centre."

In 95 per cent of the cases it is the police who actually initiate proceedings to take intoxicated persons to one of the centres. The remaining five per cent are persons brought from factories, offices, or health centres, or those who – sporadically – come by themselves. The time spent at the centre varies according to need, but it is never less than eight hours. The fee is CKR 100 (about $15), the cost of ambulance transportation CKR 18.

During the 15 years that the Prague centre has existed, 50,000 persons have sobered up there, or approximately ten every 24 hours. About 20,000, or 40 per cent, were first offenders, the remainder had been one or more times previously. The centre is located in the same building as the anti-alcoholic ward, and is run solely by medically qualified personnel with doctors from the psychiatric clinic on continuous duty. The centre has its own welfare worker who performs the necessary administrative work and organizes the so-called Saturday School, i.e. anti-alcoholic lectures for the patients of the centre. This four-hour lecture for many of them is the first information they have had on the problems of alcoholism as such.

Apart from the medical personnel, patients from the anti-alcoholic ward also serve at the centre. They are usually in the seventh week of their treatment and their tour of duty is also a form of psychotherapeutic exercise. They are on duty at the centre from Sunday evening until Friday both during the day and at night. During this period they meet with from 50 to 100 persons taken to the centre, and watch all phases of their intoxication and sobering. According to the patients their duty at the detoxication centre is one of the most effective weapons in the psychotherapeutic arsenal.

THE ANTI-ALCOHOLIC ADVISORY CENTRE

Each person brought to the detoxication centre is reported to the anti-alcoholic advisory centre in the district in which he lives. There are now ten such centres scattered throughout the districts of Prague, and these form a part of the psychiatric departments of the district health centres. The advisory centre has the same doctor – a psychiatrist – as the psychiatric department, but it has its own welfare worker and visiting hours. At the beginning of 1966 there were 16,000 persons registered in the Prague advisory centres. New admissions each year total about 1,000 persons, of which 50 to 60 per cent, and sometimes more, are sent there from the detoxication centre.

Only a very small percentage of new admissions come spontaneously to the advisory centres, or are invited there on the basis of family reports or reports of employers, courts, or other institutions. In effect, this means that if there were not a detoxication centre there would be far fewer persons registered at the advisory centres as threatened or afflicted with alcoholism. The activity of the detoxication centre also aids in registering such a person sooner, when the prognosis is more favourable. A survey made several years ago concluded that one out of three drunken persons was brought to the detoxication centre through a chance abuse, but the remaining two were alcoholics in the usual sense of the word, the abuse of alcohol constituting a permanent problem in some part of their lives, mainly their family life.

A NEW SYSTEM

The work of the advisory centres is now concentrated on the most pressing, or suitable cases. The patients visit the clinic to obtain their Antabuse, and are invited for individual, and less often, group therapy. At present, family therapy is more of an exception. A negative aspect of the present organization of the advisory centres is that the physician (i.e., the district psychiatrist) is so busy that he has very little time for work in the centre. In addition, he tends to have very little interest in this type of patient.

Not long ago a new system was drawn up which will be put into effect next year. In principle it constitutes the unification of out-patient and hospital treatment of alcoholic cases. The physicians and welfare workers will work primarily in out-patient treatment, but will also participate in the work of the anti-alcoholic ward of the psychiatric clinic. In this way they will be in contact with their patients from registration at the detoxication centre, through out-patient treatment at the advisory centre, and ward treatment, to the post-hospital treatment at the advisory centre and the therapeutic club. Each doctor will be responsible for three district advisory centres. Each centre will continue to have its own welfare worker, be broken down into district health centres, and form a part of the psychiatric departments. The reorganization aims to introduce specialized psychiatrists into the advisory centres as well as forms of group psychotherapy and family therapy, which are now usually undertaken in the hospital ward.

THE ANTI-ALCOHOLIC WARD

In the building housing the detoxication centre there is also the anti-alcoholic ward of the psychiatric clinic. Ward patients come for voluntary treatment from practically all parts of the country. Their stay at the clinic lasts 13 weeks. There are also patients who come for either

TABLE 48–1

WEEKLY PROGRAM OF THE APOLINÁŘ CLINIC

Morning (6:00)	Forenoon (8:30–11:30)	Afternoon (1:00–4:00)	Evening (6:00–8:00)
MONDAY 6:15—exercise 7:30—morning report	examination treatment work therapy	1:00 conference with trustees 2:30 lecture	exercise diary
TUESDAY ditto	ditto	1:00 quiz 1:30 study 2:45 physical exercise	6:00 cultural therapy diary
WEDNESDAY ditto	ditto	1:00 free 4:00 discussion 5:00 film	6:00 exercise therapy diary
THURSDAY ditto and cultural competition	ditto	1:00 groups 2:45 personal tasks	6:00 study 7:00 testing diary
FRIDAY ditto and tests morning report	ditto	1:00 doctor's visit 3:00 evaluation of weekly competition	6:00 running 8:00 exercise diary
SATURDAY leaves		2:00 visits cultural tours	6:00 cultural program 7:30 theatre
SUNDAY	cultural excursion	2:00 visits	diary

voluntary or compulsory repeat treatment as prescribed by the advisory centres. After six weeks these patients are sent to the rehabilitation centre which is located in a beautiful park and has a capacity of 30 patients. Treatment there lasts from four to nine months, or longer in exceptional cases.

Patients convicted of transgressions under the law, who have been sentenced to unconditional or probational terms and also to personal anti-alcoholic treatment, are kept in a special ward of the psychiatric clinic in Prague. To this ward of 70 beds come patients who are not suited for the conditions of treatment in the rehabilitation centre. Treatment here usually continues for several months.

The capacity for hospital treatment in Prague is therefore 150 beds in three wards. Their arrangement and capacity fulfil two very important conditions of hospital treatment: (a) that it be differentiated according to the type of patient and the urgency of his condition; (b) that it be sufficiently long. These two conditions unfortunately do not prevail everywhere in Czechoslovakia. There are only 700 beds in all,

though the need is for two or three times as many, and in some wards the period of treatment is too short.

TREATMENT PROGRAM OF THE PRAGUE CLINIC

Tables 48-1 and 48-2 give some details of the present hospital treatment in the ward of the Apolinář Clinic in Prague. The daily regime maintained in the ward concentrates on treating the main source of the patient's current difficulties, i.e. his alcoholism, which can be defined as a learned response. It is formed primarily by those psychical conditions on which alcohol, as a central psychotropic agent, acts directly and effectively to bring about a change in unpleasant states of tension, anxiety, and frustration, and to produce euphoria. The regime in the Apolinář ward therefore is designed to teach patients to bear conditions of stress and anxiety, to overcome frustrating experiences (and thus increase the threshold of psychic susceptibility to injury), to develop efforts of will and new in-

TABLE 48–2

SURVEY OF THREE MONTH'S TREATMENT IN THE
APOLINÁŘ CLINIC

week	
1	examination, vitamins B_1, B_6, and C (12 ×)
2	
3	Antabuse—alcohol reaction
4	
5	apomorphine 5 × 3 daily sittings, life history
6 x	
7 o	duty at the detoxication centre
8 x	stay in the Lovosice Rehabilitation Centre
9	
10	
11 o	stay at the anti-alcoholic centre in Bohnice (criminal alcoholics and asocial psychopaths)
12 x	apomorphine 2 × 3
13 o	day hospital

o—Individual leave to family.
x—Cultural excursions (theatre, historic sites, etc.).

terests and activities which create the necessary conditions for the emergence of euphoria.

It is evident from the foregoing that we consider a soft and tolerant regime for the curing of alcoholics as not only undesirable but contra-indicated. The desired regime is one that is thorough, exacting, and purposeful. The patient is subject to a long period of controlled stress during his stay of several months; he must fulfil a thousand and one duties. For all he does he is rewarded or punished on the basis of a system of positive and negative points leading to pertinent advantages or lack of them (e.g., leaves). Conflicts between the patients and the strict regime, other patients, or members of the therapeutic team are of a greater or lesser intensity, more or less frequent, but, from the psycho-therapeutic aspect, always desired and constructively used. They provide the opportunity to influence, adapt, or even alter the patient's behaviour. The following example shows how certain group therapeutic forms can be used for this purpose.

THE THERAPEUTIC CLUB

All three wards and advisory centres have their common therapeutic club called KLUS, which in Czech means *to run*, and is an abbreviation of the words meaning "the club of those striving for sobriety." This club was founded in February 1948 and up to the present has met more than 850 times. The KLUS meets in the long lecture hall of the anti-alcoholic ward. In the centre of the room is a podium and the table of the head physician. On his left are those undergoing treatment and on his right those who have undergone the treatment; members of the families of both groups are also present. The club meets each Friday at 6 PM. About 200 people have been attending the meetings regularly over the past few years. Apart from these formal meetings, which are directively guided by the head physician of the department, the members of the club meet informally and socially in a non-alcoholic coffee house. The chairman of the KLUS is an ex-alcoholic with twenty years' abstention behind him. The club itself is divided into five groups and patients are admitted to these according to length of abstention. The Alpha group consists of those abstaining for one year, the Beta one to three years, Gamma three to five years, Delta five to ten years, Omega ten years and over. On attaining the necessary number of years of abstention entitling the member to move to a higher group, a special ceremony takes place during a meeting of the club and the new member receives a diploma.

RECENT DEVELOPMENTS

During the past few years we have been trying to
intensify our care of abstaining patients and we
invite them, for example, to attend regular summer camps together with those currently undergoing treatment in the wards. In these camps
treatment takes place in natural surroundings
and each tent houses one current patient and one
ex-patient who has been abstaining for at least
three years. This year for the first time we organized a sort of jamboree for the entire families of
our ex-alcoholics, who attended a fortnight-long
summer camp. In it we mixed both current patients and abstaining patients, and the wives and
children of both groups.

In the immediate future we plan to concentrate on the care of youth afflicted or endangered
by alcoholism. For this purpose a one-storey
house in the gardens of the department has been
adapted as a special centre, the staff of which will
have the following tasks:
1
The care of alcoholics and addicts up to the age
of 20. These will be registered centrally in a special advisory centre in Prague, and in case of
need will be placed in day or night stations.
2
The preventive and therapeutic care of the children of alcoholics (registered in the Prague anti-
alcoholic advisory centres) where the family
situation is threatening. The centre will only be
able to look after a small fraction of these children (from 6 to 14 years of age) who are estimated to number about 6,000.
3
The preventive care of school children, appren-
tices, and other working youth. The new centre
staff will prepare and test forms of anti-alcoholic
education specially designed for use in schools.

H. J. KRAUWEEL

Medical Consultation Bureau for Alcoholism
Amsterdam, Netherlands

49

History and Administration of a National Alcoholism Program in the Netherlands

When we look at the specialized care for alcoholics, and perhaps also programs for those dependent on other agents, we can hardly maintain that such activities have been well planned from the beginning. As with many other types of illness, maladjustment, or aberrant social behaviour, certain observations have been made, a certain significance has been attached to these observations, and an attempt has been made – in the context of a given society at a given time – to take measures expected or hoped to lead to a solution of the problem defined. Not infrequently, advice has been sought from others, sometimes from societies which had an earlier start in attempts to control a given problem. Measures were adopted as they were or in a modified form, and this sometimes led to a distorted view of the problem. In addition, the results of methodologically inadequate investigations were found sometimes to be in less than complete accordance with reality.

In developing the care for alcoholics in a small country such as the Netherlands, we have had to cope with an historical background of this kind. There have been and there are still difficulties, some of which have been overcome – perhaps less through wisdom and skill than through pure necessity; and much certainly remains to be done (4, 6).

Special care for alcoholics in the Netherlands is of relatively long standing. Some of its roots are to be found in the temperance movements which, closely related as they were to the rise of progressive political parties, were powerful initiators of various forms of community care. On the other hand, it also arose in part from the conviction of professionals in the social and medical fields that alcohol problems in the Netherlands required separate attention in view of the multitude of symptoms which were seen to accompany the abuse of alcohol.

The years between 1880 and 1890 witnessed the establishment of the first special sanitarium for alcoholics, where the patients received a mixture of medical and pedagogic attention during a generally protracted period of isolation from society. Data in old publications indicate that, even then, it was difficult to accommodate and manage alcoholics among the disturbed patients in mental hospitals: the alcoholics proved to be either too normal or too abnormal, and re-admissions were observed to be common. It seemed impossible to achieve a lasting cure. Then the Amsterdam professor of psychiatry, Dr. K. Herman Bouman, and a learned temperance leader, Th. W. van der Woude, advocated a new philosophy, maintaining that alcoholics and other toxicomanic patients would benefit from treatment in an out-patient setting. This would prevent them from developing what might be called "hospitalosis," and it would no doubt facilitate the study of their way of life and relationship to the community. The new trend established itself during the years following 1907. The number of hospitalizations was greatly reduced, although of course hospital treatment was not completely eliminated. Exact figures in this respect are not available, so that we can only accept the assurances of competent authorities.

The first attempts at organized out-patient treatment of alcoholics date back to 1909 when an agency especially established for the purpose was opened in Amsterdam as the Medical Consultation Bureau for Alcoholism (1). This designation may be somewhat misleading, for the agency from the outset extended what may be described as sociopedagogic help – perhaps sometimes ethically coloured sociopsychological help – against a good psychiatric background. The art of dossier preparation was understood to perfection in those days, and Bouman and van der Woude formed an ideal medicopedagogic team, blissfully free of hierarchy. An appeal was made to the patients' own resources and, with their assistance, a special abstinence club was founded which confined its membership to ex-drinkers trying to include other ex-drinkers in their club. No special philosophy of the type found in Alcoholics Anonymous supported this fellowship of alcoholics, who at the time were known as "abolishers" to distinguish them from abstainers who had never used alcohol, from those who used it only in moderation, and from the members of temperance societies, who usually refrained from hard liquor but did accept an occasional glass of wine or beer.

During this period various similar societies and clubs arose in the Netherlands, not infrequently with a religious or political overtone. Therapeutic centres later established elsewhere in the country often carried the signature of these beginnings, and a solution to the alcohol problem was sought largely in improved conditions of life and the application of ethical principles. Between 1909 and 1920, four additional therapeutic centres were established. The enormous decrease in the per capita consumption of alcohol – from 5.18 litres of 100 proof alcohol in 1901 to 3.35 litres in 1920 and 2.48 litres by 1930 – must have had causes beyond the fact that alcoholics were being treated (10). Nevertheless, the results of these early efforts must not be underestimated.

Studies made in these years, for example of alcohol consumption and abuse in relation to delinquency (9), demonstrate that already there was some understanding of the effects of small quantities of alcohol on the human functions, and that there was no tendency to regard abuse as the root of all evil in terms of health and behaviour.

We cannot properly comprehend the history of the care of alcoholics and other toxicomanics unless we see it in relation to various social and economic developments, and in relation to the development of other forms of community care for the individual. Thus, for instance, a few years after the establishment of the first therapeutic centre in Amsterdam, the Poverty Act and the statutory rule on resocialization were introduced. The former enabled municipalities to organize social care for indigents of various types; the latter permitted the courts to impose conditional or partly conditional sentences, and to refer convicted persons to institutions willing to undertake their care and attempt to regulate their behaviour.

Understandably, an appeal was made to the still very young therapeutic centres for alcoholics. As a consequence, besides the patients who wended their more or less voluntary way to these centres, there were an increasing number referred under some pressure. The result was a very rapid increase in admissions, but also an over-emphasis on social work, the more so because medical treatment at that time had limited resources and because, in the Netherlands, the abuse of alcohol was and still is accompanied more by social disturbances than by pronounced mental and physical disorders. Thus, in the past

TABLE 49-1

PERCENTAGE OF ALCOHOLICS REFERRED FROM
DIFFERENT SOURCES TO THE OUT-PATIENT CLINICAL
SERVICE IN AMSTERDAM, 1930–65

	1930–39	1940–49	1950–59	1960–65
referred by medical agencies	2	2	6	17
referred by social services	50	15	19	2
referred by the courts	40	80	60	40
referred by employers	1	—	5	10
other referrals	4	2	1	1
own initiative	3	1	9	30
	100	100	100	100

few years, delirium tremens was observed in only 4 per cent of the alcoholics admitted to our clinical departments; alcoholic convulsions occurred in 5 per cent. After consistent use of certain medications in all newly admitted patients in whom these manifestations might be expected, both figures were reduced to 1 per cent. On the other hand, the vast majority of patients were suffering from neurotic conditions manifesting themselves in poor social adjustment.

We are still engaged in research to establish which factors play a role in the relatively low incidence of neuropsychiatric symptoms in comparison with those in other countries. We suspect that it is not only the quantity of alcohol consumed that is of importance, but at least as much the living habits and in particular the eating and drinking habits of a people whose alcohol consumption is generally moderate (1964: 3.6 litres of 100 proof alcohol per capita). Apart from such fundamental factors influencing the incidence of various pathological conditions, there is the steady flow of newly developed and marketed drugs. There is also the important factor of early detection which results from a relatively strong rejection of excessive drinking by the population.

A study of referral of patients during the period 1930–65 discloses distinct changes in source correlated with socioeconomic conditions in the country (7). During the depression years (1930–40), only 3 per cent of patients made their own way to our out-patient clinic; 50 per cent were referred by social services and 40 per cent by the courts, while only a few were referred by physicians, medical agencies, or employers.

The latest figures, for 1960–65, show that some 30 per cent of patients report on their own initiative; referrals by employers have risen to 10 per cent, and there are few referrals from social services; court referrals have declined from 80 per cent during the war years to about 40 per cent, and medical agencies show their growing interest by being responsible for 17 per cent of referrals. Changes in the pattern of referrals over the period are summarized in Table 49-1.

These figures suggest that a given situation in social life drives certain vulnerable individuals in a given direction. During periods of economic depression, drinkers are unpopular employees who, sooner than others, come to be dependent on public assistance. During the boom, the employers try to save personnel for the production process and persuade their employees to have themselves treated. The abnormal stress of war conditions can lead to combined forms of abnormal behaviour; during the war years it was not uncommon to find excessive drinking associated with economic delinquency, resorted to in an attempt to obtain material things which shortage had placed beyond normal reach. Increased aggressivity is another possibility to be borne in mind. The increased number of referrals by medical agencies results from carefully established, ever closer relations with medical organizations and from the addition to the out-patient clinics of in-patient facilities on a limited scale. The increased number of voluntary patients can be attributed to educational efforts via the media of press, radio, and television.

In the context of these facts we may hold that the roads by which patients reach us are

TABLE 49–2

CRIME RELAPSE RATE OF ALCOHOLICS AND
NON-ALCOHOLICS

Relapses	Addicted alcoholics (per cent)	Non-addicted alcoholics (per cent)	Non-alcoholics (per cent)
0	12.8	41.8	41.6
1	21.2 ⎫	22.8 ⎫	21.2 ⎫
2–3	23–2 ⎬ 44.4	19.6 ⎬ 42.4	17.1 ⎬ 38.3
4–8	33.5	10.9	16.0
> 8	9.4	4.9	4.1

influenced by continuing changes in the life of our society. And so we must ask whether this also affects our therapies and the approach of our institutions to the patient. Again a few examples may serve to highlight this point.

Dutch authorities recently decided in favour of the introduction of a new liquor law. The old system, which granted licences in proportion to the population, was abolished in favour of an unlimited number of licences, available to anyone with a certificate of proficiency in the hotel and restaurant trade, sufficient credit, and a record free of any contact with a criminal court during the five years preceding the request for a licence. In addition, the law provides relatively strict requirements concerning room size, appointments, etc., with a view to raising bar and restaurant standards. Those opposing the new law have argued that more licences, that is more selling points for alcoholic beverages, would lead to an increased alcohol consumption. In support of their arguments they mention statistics indicating an increasing number of younger patients in the intake of the out-patient clinics. In fact the age of admission to these centres fell in the course of seven years from an average of 43.4 years to 38.1 years. An analysis of these figures revealed, however, that the courts were systematically referring young offenders (arrested for joy-riding, aggression, etc.) to out-patient clinics, and they were tending to make use of the mental health program (1). This has led to an earlier recognition of alcohol problems than in the past. This is a significant fact, and an indication that the promotion of mental health need not be (in fact must not be) a prerogative of professional workers within the field.

On the occasion of this analysis it was surprising to see that only a relatively small number of patients were referred to therapeutic centres by the churches. Many factors could be cited to explain this fact; they range from the drinker's alienation from the religious environment to the churches' rejection or ignorance of this problem. It is quite evidently necessary to integrate mental health activities in the social structure to an extent which ensures referral before severe social conflicts have occurred.

Another example can be found in a quite different area. A long-term study of the legal records of alcoholics and non-alcoholics led to the conclusion that drinkers show a rather lively relapse pattern (5). They commit a wider variety of offences and crimes than do non-drinkers, who tend to adhere to a given type of delinquency; and their rate of relapse also differs. In researching this point, we used the classification suggested by Jellinek (3), distinguishing the addicted from the non-addicted alcoholic (the former with loss of control, amnesia, etc.), and we collected a control group of normal drinkers, that is, persons whose use of alcohol caused no disturbance. The study covered some 1,000 individuals; some of its results are presented in Table 49-2.

These data raise questions. The criminological literature often mentions the pronounced criminogenic effect of alcohol. Undoubtedly, the deterioration of the excessive drinker's personality readily leads to disinhibition, overestimation or underestimation of possibilities, and therefore to asocial behaviour. On the other hand, the drinker's conspicuous behaviour readily alerts the attention of the police; the drinker himself promotes his detection after committing an offence. The patient's assertion that he had not intended to commit the offence, that he considers it stupid and beneath his dignity, must not be regarded as merely a feeble excuse; it contains a core of truth. The exact relative values of all these aspects require a great deal of discussion. But whatever the results, such questions must be borne in mind in shaping our program of care and our methods of treatment. A few more examples may be cited to elucidate this point.

If alcoholics with a history of delinquency are relatively young, and voluntary patients relatively old, then the former have a shorter "alcohol career" than the latter; they show less destruction caused by alcohol, but their conflicts with society are more severe. Less severe social conflicts are often associated with greater mental and physical damage from intoxication. And the neuroses that may develop as a result of alcohol abuse, or abuse of other narcotic agents, are of widely varying types. These facts indicate the necessity of differentiation in approach and therapeutic methods. One might say that we are dealing with people who have problems resulting from the use or abuse of alcohol, and with those who suffer from alcoholism – either as habituation or as a more addictive condition – or, in other words, people who are in a state of dependence.

Experience has taught us that more profound psychotherapeutic approaches are unnecessary in helping people with alcohol problems. Particularly after an early diagnosis, it is sufficient to give them a mixture of social support, re-arrangements, and educational and explanatory interviews. Such additional therapy as they require should be suuportive, which is more successful than an analytical approach. A pedagogical approach is called for whenever we are dealing with a young individual who has alcohol problems rather than problems associated with alcoholism. We need not discuss the whole range of therapeutic possibilities in medication, various types of group therapy, individual treatment by a physician or case worker in an out-patient or in-patient setting, creative therapy, or various educational approaches. In all cases the guiding principle is that the patient is met by a community of workers who wish to include him in this

community and help him find his specific place in it, and to assist him in bringing order to his often disturbed relations. It may be useful to expound this principle in detail, because we believe it confronts us with a special question.

The diagnosis in a new case cannot be made exclusively on the basis of the patient's behaviour. It must take into account the sum of his behaviour and the behaviour and reactions of his environment in the restricted and in the broader sense. Therefore we consider the patient's psychological and physical appearance, his relations to his immediate environment (family, friends), to his less immediate environment (work), and to his "world" in general (church, politics, hobbies, and so forth). Acceptance or rejection by the environment, the stress tolerance of the family, etc., largely determine the evaluation of the patient's condition, and the approach and treatment. They also determine the criteria to be used later to assess the results of the efforts made on his behalf and his chances of resuming an acceptable place in society.

The field of forces inhabited by the patient, his relatives, and also the physician, social worker, or nurse, are a subject for intensive study. Accordingly, our research institute (which will be briefly discussed later) has begun a study of the efficiency of our efforts (2). This study encompasses the attitudes of the workers as compared with the patients' expectations concerning the help to be received from the therapeutic centre. Since this study has not yet been completed, I can only discuss a few aspects in brief.

Techniques indicated by Osgood and others are being used. The patients are asked questions about their expectations of the clinic, their opinions of the staff, the procedure in the clinic, and the results they expect. The staff members are asked to state how they regard alcoholics. As expected, the patients' opinions about the staff were more favourable than the staff's opinions of the alcoholics. We suspect that, in spite of acquired professional attitudes, the community's general rejection of the alcoholic has not been without effect on the therapists. This raises a number of questions. For example: is the worker's knowledge of the problems sufficient, and is it sufficiently integrated in his thoughts and emotions? And, even if his knowledge is sufficient, can we expect the worker to be capable in general of separating possible feelings of aversion from an attitude acquired in the practice of his profession? Further research is required in an attempt to improve the purposefulness of mental health programs, and to ensure a more spontaneous interaction between the helper and the helped.

In the Netherlands the enterprise undertaken in Amsterdam in 1909 has so far led to the establishment of 19 out-patient clinics throughout the country. The intake of patients in all these clinics is on similar lines. The clinics are generally to be found in provincial capitals or cities which are the natural centre of a given district. Staff members from the centres have consulting hours in nearby towns, and in fact the country is covered in this way by a network of therapeutic centres and auxiliary aid posts. The present intent is eventually to provide limited in-patient facilities (10–20 beds) with every out-patient clinic. Three such facilities for short-term clinical treatment have so far been established. All clinics are independent and private. All are member institutes of a federation which aids them and undertakes representation. The federation has information services and education as autonomous activities; it provides literature and films, and organizes an annual 100-hour course for social workers, public nurses, personnel managers, and other relevant professionals. In addition there is an independent institute called the Foundation for Study and Documentation on Alcohol and Alcoholism (and other addictions), which is still of limited scope. It formulates and prepares questions, raises funds for research, and co-operates with the universities in the design of research projects. In this way, we make use of existing research centres, which in turn become interested in alcohol problems and related subjects. Data for teaching and publishing purposes become available as a result.

The entire set-up is highly pragmatic, aimed at creating a broad background for work in the fields of treatment and prevention. Adequate information and education is an important requirement in this respect. Public media such as press, radio, and television are used incidentally but to a sufficient extent. As pointed out, literature and films are made available by the federation, and a scientific journal will be launched in the near future. Yet we believe that many of these activities are merely "buckshot" efforts. When we address persons or groups who do not specifically work in the mental health field or in the field of addictions, we may successfully accomplish an occasional *oratio pro domo*, but we know very little about the actual impact of the information we extend. This is why we intend to investigate the approach to key persons in the initial contacts with alcoholics and other addicts and their environment. By key persons we mean family doctors, the clergy, lawyers, and magistrates in the smaller communities. Pilot studies have already shown that general practitioners dislike being approached with information on medical aspects but are more interested in sociopsychological data. Evaluation and research on education will be necessary if we are to achieve a compact package of adequate and effective information.

In view of this urgent necessity, investigations are being made in various fields. In addition to studies concerning the efficiency of the clinics and the aspects of information and education, two research projects in the criminological field have been started. One concerns the nature, extent, and frequency of relapses into delinquent behaviour, and the other deals with the attitudes of traffic violators under the influence of alcohol, because there is some doubt as to the useful effect of sentences so far imposed. Another investigation concerns the impact of commercial advertising (an experimental psychological continuation of a content-analytical study). Studies already completed have dealt with referrals of alcoholics with reference to age, and absenteeism and decreased productivity in alcoholics (7, 8). Research projects in preparation concern the effects of beer and hard liquor on the drinker's behaviour, and a study of the motivation of drinking habits in the Netherlands and the role of social relationships (this is to be a continuation of the study by Dr. I. Gadourek on Dutch drinking habits). Other current projects include studies of the drinker's habits of life as compared with general habits of life; ethical aspects of evaluating the use and abuse of alcohol; economic aspects of alcohol consumption; alcohol and alcoholism in literary writing; alcohol consumption in relation to total fluid intake; and alcohol consumption in juveniles (at school and in the occupational setting).

It has been pointed out that the sources of patients have shown certain changes over the years. In view of this, it was decided that research should be kept as flexible as possible. Accordingly, a uniform statistical system was introduced in all clinics; this makes it possible to centralize evidence of changes and differences. On the basis of such evidence it may be necessary to revise opinions, to change approaches and attitudes, and to observe interrelations of phenomena so that further investigation can be adjusted appropriately. As noted above, our research is still highly pragmatic. But as we come to understand the necessity of attempts to evaluate certain findings, basic research will come to the fore. Research will give birth to research-in-research. But, for the time being, our efforts must be to add applicable knowledge to that already available; this is rendered especially necessary by the urgent requirements of information services and education.

To summarize, we have in the Netherlands a network of therapeutic centres which operate on principles evolved from the ideas and opinions accepted as valid by the founders of the Amsterdam Centre in 1909. Of course there have been modifications and variations, such as the addition of small-scale in-patient facilities to the out-patient clinics, to keep the patients in touch with the community rather than hospitalize them elsewhere. But there are also trends which we do not yet adequately understand. To mention one: we do not know what leads to great differences in consumption. We know that periods of poverty can lead to excessive use of alcohol, and that prosperity can do the same. Yet, although the Netherlands has certainly had its share of the ups and downs in world economy, there have been long periods during which the standard of life remained virtually constant, yet the consumption of alcohol showed fluctuations which could not be ascribed to socioeconomic factors, or to certain tensions in the community. There are changes in customs and in eating and drinking habits; there is the influence of advertising; but we know little about the relative effects of such factors. Clearly further research on this topic is an urgent necessity.

In the Netherlands, we approach and treat a cross-section of the population, and the various forms of referral confront us with a variety of problems arising from the use or abuse of alcohol. Thus we cannot escape the need for evaluation of the effect of alcohol on human behaviour, and we must attempt to identify the personalities most vulnerable, and the situations in which this vulnerability becomes manifest. The same applies to the attitudes of the community towards the use and abuse of alcohol and the resulting complications, for here we touch upon the soil from which words such as "alcohol problems" and "alcoholism" grow. Undoubtedly, all of this is equally true for other forms of dependency on toxic agents, but these are not within the scope of the present paper.

One of the questions to be faced in the future, I believe, is whether the control of alcoholism should constitute a separate activity or be integrated in the totality of mental health programs. I would recommend this subject for discussion, and would add by conviction that such a discussion must include among the participants representatives of those who are most directly involved, namely persons who have had to combat alcoholism in themselves.

If we can continue to take a dispassionate look at our work, at our criteria, results, and investigations, then we shall be able to carry on where he, in whose memory this symposium is held, led the way.

REFERENCES

1
BOUMAN, K.H.
Het Medisch Consultatie-Bureau voor Alcoholisme, 1912
2
HENDRIKSEN, A.
Het onderzoek naar attitudes van alcoholisten en personeel in drie klinieken
3
JELLINEK, E.M.
The disease concept of alcoholism
New Haven: Hillhouse Press, 1960

4
KRAUWEEL, H.J.
The public care of alcoholics in the Netherlands
1954
5
KRAUWEEL, H.J.
Alcohol and criminality, 1955
6
KRAUWEEL, H.J.
Incidence and treatment of alcoholism, 1957
7
VAN DER WAL, H.J.
Analyse van leeftijeden en verwijzingen van
alcoholisten naar consultatie-bureaus
8
VAN DER WAL, H.J.
Absenteisme en prestatieverlies bij alcoholisme
9
VAN DER WOUDE, TH.W.
Alcohol en misdaad
Een bewerking der statistische gegevens betreffende
Nederland
Reprinted in Tijdschrift voor de studie van het
alcoholvraagstuk
Leiden: A. W. Sijthoff's Uitg.-mij., 1935
10
VAN DER WOUDE, TH.W.
Statistics on world consumption of alcoholic
beverages for the liquor trade association

JOY MOSER

Mental Health Unit
World Health Organization
Geneva, Switzerland

50

World Health Organization Activities Concerning Alcoholism

I should like to make it quite clear from the out-set that I am very far from being an expert on the subject of alcoholism, although it is a topic with which I have been concerned for some time and which unites my interests in nutrition and in mental health. Perhaps I have more claim to being knowledgeable about at least some aspects of the activities of WHO, since I have been work-ing in the Organization since 1950.

The World Health Organization was set up to advise and assist all its member states in dealing with their manifold public health problems, and has inevitably been able to concern itself in only a very limited way with alcoholism, although this topic is now recognized to be of great signifi-cance in public health programs.

Perhaps I should first say a few words about WHO in general, in order to give you some idea of the possibilities and limitations of its action. The World Health Organization is one of the spe-cialized agencies of the United Nations, estab-lished in 1948 when its constitution was ratified by 26 United Nations member states. It followed in the steps of the League of Nations Health Committee and other international health bodies which fought against the spread of pestilence, but the new organization set itself the broader task of helping to achieve for all peoples the highest possible level of health.

Most of WHO's work is carried out at the re-quest of governments and takes the form of projects designed to improve national health ser-vices, but the Organization also runs interna-tional services such as the Epidemiological Intelligence Service, which provides rapid infor-mation about the occurrence of quarantinable diseases. These international services are di-rected from the headquarters in Geneva, which also comprises a number of technical units, with central advisory responsibilities. The unit mainly responsible for work on alcoholism is Mental Health, one of the eight units in the Division of Health Protection and Promotion. The Pharma-cology and Toxicology Unit,* which was for-merly called the Addiction-Producing Drugs Unit, is concerned more with the biological as-pects of drug problems, including alcoholism,

*In December 1966 this became the Division of Phar-macology and Toxicology comprising several units, including the Drug Dependence Unit.

and educational aspects are dealt with by the Health Education Unit.

The work of WHO is decentralized, so that direct assistance to governments is channelled through the regional offices, of which there are six: in the Regions of Africa, the Americas, Southeast Asia, Europe, the Eastern Mediterranean, and the Western Pacific; but there are close links between their activities and the advisory and stimulatory work as well as the research undertakings of headquarters.

To come back for a moment to the Mental Health Unit, of which I am a staff member: like all the technical units of WHO it has only a small staff. For many years it consisted of one psychiatrist, a scientific assistant, and a secretary, but now we have four psychiatrists, two dealing particularly with the recently expanded research program. Two of the regional offices – in the Americas and in Europe – have mental health advisers on their staffs.

Despite the limited number of technical personnel and the small budget, WHO has many possibilities for action. We are in the fortunate position of being able to convene meetings to which we can invite outstanding experts from various parts of the world. The number of such meetings that can be held annually and the number that can be devoted to one topic are limited, but several have concentrated on alcohol and alcoholism, and the reports appear to have had widespread impact. Participation in the formal Expert Committee meetings is limited to about ten members and consultants, who are selected from different geographical areas and frequently from different disciplines. These meetings are intended to review urgent health topics and draw up recommendations to governments and WHO for future action. In order to disseminate current knowledge on specific health subjects and to give an opportunity for exchange of experience, WHO organizes seminars, either for one region or for participants from several regions.

Another important method used by the Organization to carry out its functions is to engage consultants, either to assist in developing the policy and planning of projects at headquarters, or to advise governments on WHO's behalf. Some 250 teachers and lecturers are provided by WHO each year to schools of medicine, public health, nursing, etc. In these ways the Organization has been able to draw upon the valuable knowledge and experience of a large number of highly qualified persons without uprooting them for too long from their own occupations.

One of the means by which WHO has helped to improve the qualifications of national personnel is to provide fellowships for study. Each year about 3,000 WHO fellowships are granted to doctors and other members of the health team. This has grown into a carefully organized program; great care is taken to choose candidates who will use the experience gained on return to their own country, and the type and place of training are selected as far as possible to suit individual requirements. Fellowships may be awarded to follow established training courses, or may be given to well trained and often highly placed staff who can profit by studying projects under way in another country.

Two further types of WHO activity should be mentioned: the provision of a limited number of grants, especially to initiate specific research projects; and publication in the various WHO series, or the dissemination of public information through a variety of media.

I should like now to outline what the Organization has been able to do and what it plans to do in the near future in relation to alcoholism. About thirty years ago the League of Nations Health Organization suggested that alcoholism should be considered as part of a worldwide health problem. Soon after the birth of WHO, the Mental Health Unit was created, and during the meeting of the first Expert Committee on Mental Health it was recommended that alcoholism should receive early attention. An Alcoholism Sub-Committee was established and held its first meeting in 1950. It was in the preparation for this meeting that the long association with the Organization of the late Professor E. M. Jellinek began. The Committee approached alcoholism as a disease and as a social problem. It pointed out that the public health services could and should make extensive contributions to meeting the problems involved but that legal and social measures related to the distribution and use of alcohol were also of considerable value.

At its second meeting in 1951 the Committee concentrated more on practical aspects of the development of treatment programs and also considered means of classifying types of alcoholism and estimating their frequency. The Addiction-Producing Drugs Unit, which had cooperated in both meetings, convened an Expert Committee on Alcohol in 1953, where the problems involved were considered mainly from a pharmacological point of view.

The two WHO units joined forces in the convening of an Expert Committee on Alcohol and Alcoholism in 1954, which provided a possibility for "the direct exchange of experience among pharmacologists, physiologists and psychiatrists, as well as their agreement on the interpretation of some basic conceptions of alcoholism" (1). At this meeting it was agreed that the term "alcoholism" does not designate a definite nosological entity, but is a collective term for a "family of problems related to alcohol" and the Committee attempted to "determine and define those features of the various alcohol problems which give them a medical and public-health character." Considerable attention was given at this meeting to the problems of physical and psychological *dependence* on alcohol.

Interest in the problems of alcoholism, and particularly in the public health aspects, has been fostered through the holding of four WHO regional seminars: in 1950 and 1954 in the European Region, and in 1953 and 1960 in South American countries. WHO provided faculties of internationally known experts, including members of the Alcoholism Sub-Committee, and gave fellowships for attendance at the Seminars. The Social Affairs Division of the United Nations also sponsored fellowships. Follow-up investigations indicated that a number of activities were initiated as a direct result of participation in these meetings. Subsequently, a number of WHO fellowships were granted for study at centres engaged in the treatment of alcoholics.

Much of the above work was due to the energy and vision of Professor Jellinek during his appointments as WHO consultant at headquarters and in the European and American Regions. In this capacity he also started an extensive collection of information related to problems of alcohol and alcoholism. He made a lecture tour in Scandinavian countries in 1952, and between 1953 and 1955 he advised governments in several European and American countries. He assisted in the preparation of a WHO-sponsored film on alcoholism and arranged for the provision of

WHO grants to enable sets of the Classified Abstract Archive of the Alcohol Literature to be deposited in libraries in several parts of the world.

After Professor Jellinek completed his consultant assignment with WHO, the Organization was able to give very little consideration to problems of alcoholism for several years, partly because of the pressure of other topics to be dealt with in the mental health program. However, as a result of repeated requests for assistance from governments, and in view of the current widespread recognition of alcoholism as a public health problem, it was found essential to turn again to this important topic.

Meanwhile, from 1949 onwards, the Addiction-Producing Drugs Unit of WHO had held a series of Expert Committee meetings which were devoted largely to drugs of addiction other than alcohol, and mainly from the point of view of international narcotics control. In recent years attention has been given at such meetings to the abuse of sedatives and stimulants. It was proposed that such abuses be brought under the common denominator of drug dependence, and the relationships between alcohol and other drugs were examined. A WHO Scientific Group on Evaluation of Dependence-Producing Drugs, which met in 1963, defined drug dependence as "a state arising from repeated administration of a drug on a periodic or continuous basis. Its characteristics will vary with the agent involved but it is a general term selected for its applicability to all types of drug abuse and carries no connotation in regard to degree of risk to public health or need for a particular type of control" (2). Their report goes on to state that "Individuals may become dependent upon a wide variety of chemical substances covering the whole range of pharmacodynamic effects from stimulation to depression. All these drugs have at least one effect in common. They are capable of creating a state of mind in certain individuals which is termed psychic dependence. This is a psychic drive which requires periodic or chronic administration of the drug for pleasure or to avoid discomfort. ... Some drugs also induce physical dependence, an adaptive state characterized by intense physical disturbances when administration of the drug is suspended or its action is counteracted by a specific antagonist." It is pointed out that "the characteristics of drug dependence show wide variations from one generic type to another, which makes it mandatory to establish clearly the pattern for each type." Alcohol is included among the generic types for which "the consistency of the pattern of pharmacodynamic actions is sufficiently uniform to permit at this time accurate delineation."

This trend towards a combined approach to problems of dependence on alcohol and on other drugs has been reflected in the co-operation between the two WHO units, and can be seen in some national and local bodies, such as the Alcoholism and Drug Addiction Research Foundation of Ontario, Canada, and the recently established Alcoholism and Drug Abuse Section of the Community Research and Service Branch of the National Institute of Mental Health in the USA. In the USSR, I understand that the "narcological" departments of psychiatric services deal with both alcoholics and drug addicts, though the latter appear to be few in number. The *British Journal of Addiction* has, for more than 50 years, dealt with problems of drug addiction as well as alcoholism.

When it was proposed in the Organization to convene an Expert Committee for further consideration of alcoholism problems, it became necessary to decide whether the agenda should include attention to other drugs. After a number of individual contacts and informal group discussion, the Mental Health Unit organized an informal meeting on problems of alcoholism and drug dependence in Geneva in 1965, which brought together representatives of some of the interested national and international bodies, including the ICAA. Among the major conclusions regarding future policy reached by the participants were the following:

1 COMBINED APPROACH TO PROBLEMS OF ALCOHOL AND ALCOHOLISM, AND THE USE AND ABUSE OF DRUGS

Attempts should be made to get authorities to look at problems of alcohol and alcoholism, and the use and abuse of drugs together, for the following reasons:

a) There are many similarities in the causa-
tion and treatment of the problems involved and the concepts underlying the educational programs required (although there are divergencies in legal provisions).

b) Drugs are often used in combination, for example, barbiturates together with heroin or with alcohol; transfer from one drug of abuse to another also frequently occurs, among individuals as well as regionally.

c) Many studies have been carried out on alcoholism which might be applicable to drug abuse, of which much less is known.

d) Public and official attitudes to alcoholism have veered towards the therapeutic and away from the condemnatory; this has not happened to the same extent with regard to drug abuse.

2 ALCOHOLISM AND DRUG DEPENDENCE AS PUBLIC HEALTH PROBLEMS

Alcoholism and drug addiction create or contribute to major public health problems and should therefore be of concern to all public health organizations and administrations.

On the basis of these conclusions and other findings of the group, it was therefore decided that a WHO Expert Committee should be convened in 1966 to consider the topic: "Services for the Prevention and Treatment of Dependence on Alcohol and Other Drugs." As I have mentioned, participation in these formal meetings is limited. However, this one includes experts from ten or eleven countries in five of our six Regions, including members holding important positions in public health, psychiatrists, and a sociologist, and covering a wide range of experience with alcoholics and abusers of other drugs, not forgetting the drugs more recently recognized to be dependence-producing, such as certain tranquillizers and stimulants.

REFERENCES

1
WHO Technical report series, **94**: 4, 1955
2
WHO Technical report series, **287**: 4, 1964

Publications on Alcohol and Alcoholism by E. M. Jellinek 1939-1967

This bibliography was compiled by the staff of the Classified Abstract Archive of the Alcohol Literature, Center of Alcohol Studies, Rutgers University, State University of New Jersey, New Brunswick, New Jersey, USA. It includes all hitherto published writings of E. M. Jellinek related to alcohol which have been located. It may be incomplete. The Archive staff will be grateful for additional references to, and for copies of, unlisted publications.

Names of periodicals are abbreviated in the style of the *World List of Scientific Periodicals*.

Meaning of bracketed supplementary references: [QJSA **12**: 345–346, 1951] means that an abstract of the document has appeared in the *Quarterly Journal of Studies on Alcohol*, in the volume, pages, and year cited.

[CAAAL 1234] means that the document is abstracted in the *Classified Abstract Archive of the Alcohol Literature* (CAAAL), the given number being the serial number of the CAAAL abstract.

Photocopies of CAAAL abstracts may be ordered, by serial number, from CAAAL headquarters (at the above address) at 25 cents each. (Minimum order, 4 or fewer abstracts, $1.)

JELLINEK, E.M. ...
[and Jolliffe, N.]
Effects of alcohol on the individual: review of the literature of 1939.
Quart. J. Stud. Alc. 1: 110–181, 1940. [CAAAL 18]

[and McFarland, R. A.]
Analysis of psychological experiments on the effects of alcohol.
Quart. J. Stud. Alc., **1**: 272–371, 1940. [CAAAL 102]

Immanuel Kant on drinking. (Classics of the Alcohol Literature.)
Quart. J. Stud. Alc., **1**: 777–778, 1941. [CAAAL 117]

[and Bowman, K. M.]
Alcohol addiction and its treatment.
In: E. M. Jellinek, ed. Effects of Alcohol on the Individual. Vol I. Alcohol Addiction and Chronic Alcoholism, ch. 1, pp. 3–80. New Haven: Yale University Press, 1942.
Also in: Quart. J. Stud. Alc., **2**: 98–176, 1941. [CAAAL 150]

The Abstract Archive of the Quarterly Journal of Studies on Alcohol.
Quart. J. Stud. Alc., **2**: 216–222, 1941. Reprinted in: Quart. J. Stud. Alc., **2**: 408–414, 1941. [CAAAL 153]

[and Bowman, K. M.]
Alcoholic mental disorders.
In: E. M. Jellinek, ed. Effects of Alcohol on the Individual. Vol. I, Alcohol Addiction and Chronic Alcoholism, ch. 2, pp. 81–169. New Haven: Yale University Press, 1942. Also in: Quart. J. Stud. Alc., **2**: 312–390, 1941. [CAAAL 172]

A document of the reformation period on inebriety: Sebastian Franck's "On the Horrible Vice of Drunkenness," etc.
(Classics of the Alcohol Literature.)
Quart. J. Stud. Alc., **2**: 391–395, 1941. [CAAAL 174]

[and Jolliffe, N.]
Cirrhosis of the liver.
In: E. M. Jellinek, ed. Effects of Alcohol on the Individual: Vol. I. Alcohol Addiction and Chronic Alcoholism, ch. 6, pp. 273–309. New Haven: Yale University Press, 1942. Also as: Vitamin deficiences and liver cirrhosis in alcoholism: Part VII. Cirrhosis of the liver.
Quart J. Stud. Alc., **2**: 544–583, 1941. [CAAAL 258]

An early medical view of alcohol addiction and its treatment: Dr. Thomas Trotter's "Essay, Medical, Philosophical and Chemical, on Drunkenness." (Classics of the Alcohol Literature.)
Quart. J. Stud. Alc., **2**: 584–591, 1941. [CAAAL 309]

The Problems of Alcohol.
(Lay Supplement No. 1.) New Haven: Journal of Studies on Alcohol, Inc., 1941.

Alcohol, Heredity and Germ Damage.
(Lay Supplement No. 5.) New Haven: Journal of Studies on Alcohol, Inc., 1941.

Alcohol and Length of Life.
(Lay Supplement No. 6.) New Haven: Journal of Studies on Alcohol, Inc., 1941.

Effects of Alcohol on the Individual: Vol. I. Alcohol Addiction and Chronic Alcoholism.
New Haven: Yale University Press, 1942.

Scope and method of the study.
In: E. M. Jellinek, ed. Effects of Alcohol on the Individual: Vol I. Alcohol Addiction and Chronic Alcoholism, pp. xv–xxiii. New Haven: Yale University Press, 1942. Reprinted in part as: Jellinek Jubilee Reprints, No. 1: Scope and method of a review of the effects of alcohol on the individual.
Quart. J. Stud. Alc., **21**: 5–12, 1960.

[and Haggard, H. W.]
Alcohol Explored.
New York: Doubleday, 1942.

Scientific views on the spontaneous combustion of inebriates.
(Classics of the Alcohol Literature.)
Quart. J. Stud. Alc., **2**: 804–805, 1942. [CAAAL 305]

An outline of basic policies for a research program on problems of alcohol.
Quart. J. Stud. Alc., **3**: 103–124, 1942. [CAAAL 249]

The interpretation of alcohol consumption rates, with special reference to statistics of wartime consumption.
Quart. J. Stud. Alc., **3**: 267–280, 1942. [CAAAL 3629]

Seneca's Epistle LXXXIII: On Drunkeness.
(Classics of the Alcohol Literature.)
Quart. J. Stud. Alc., **3**: 302–307, 1942. [CAAAL 314]

"Death from alcoholism" in the United States in 1940; a statistical analysis.
Quart. J. Stud. Alc., **3**: 465–494, 1942. [CAAAL 3630]

Erasmus Darwin on the physiology of alcohol.
(Classics of the Alcohol Literature.)
Quart. J. Stud. Alc., **3**: 495–500, 1942. [CAAAL 315]

The Nature of Alcoholic Beverages and the Extent of Their Use.
(Lay Supplement No. 2.) New Haven: Journal of Studies on Alcohol, Inc., 1942.

Alcohol and Industrial Efficiency.
(Lay Supplement No. 3.) New Haven: Journal of Studies on Alcohol, Inc., 1942.

Facts on Delirium Tremens.
(Lay Supplement No. 4.) New Haven: Journal of Studies on Alcohol, Inc., 1942.

What Happens to Alcohol in the Body.
(Lay Supplement No. 7.) New Haven: Journal of Studies on Alcohol, Inc., 1942.

Alcoholic Beverages as a Food and Their Relation to Nutrition.
(Lay Supplement No. 8.) New Haven: Journal of Studies on Alcohol, Inc., 1942.

Facts on Cirrhosis of the Liver.
(Lay Supplement No. 9.) New Haven: Journal of Studies on Alcohol, Inc., 1942.

Old Russian Church views on inebriety.
(Classics of the Alcohol Literature.)
Quart. J. Stud. Alc., **3**: 663–667, 1943. [CAAAL 265]

Magnus Huss' *Alcoholismus Chronicus.*
(Classics of the Alcohol Literature.)
Quart. J. Stud. Alc., **4**: 85–92, 1943.

The first (1943) summer session of the School of Alcohol Studies, Yale University.
Quart. J. Stud. Alc., **4**: 187–194, 1943.

Introductory note. In: S. D. Bacon.
Sociology and the Problems of Alcohol: Foundations for a Sociological Study of Drinking Behavior. (Memoirs of the Section of Studies on Alcohol, Yale University, No. 1.)
New Haven: Hillhouse Press, 1944.
Also in: Quart. J. Stud. Alc., **4**: 399–401, 1943.

The alcohol problem: formulations and attitudes.
Quart. J. Stud. Alc., **4**: 446–461, 1943.
Also in: Relig. Educ., **39**: 9–17, 1944 [CAAAL 3396]

The observations of the Elizabethan writer Thomas Nash on drunkenness.
(Classics of the Alcohol Literature.)
Quart. J .Stud. Alc., **4**: 462–469, 1943.

Establishment of diagnostic and guidance clinics for inebriates in Connecticut (Yale Plan Clinics).
Quart. J. Stud. Alc., **4**: 496–507, 1943.

Science and the alcohol problem.
In: Abridged Lectures of the First (1943) Summer Course on Alcohol Studies at Yale

University, pp. 1–4. New Haven: Quarterly Journal of Studies on Alcohol, 1944.

The alcohol problem: formulations and attitudes.
In: Abridged Lectures of the First (1943) Summer Course on Alcohol Studies at Yale University, pp. 5–12. New Haven: Quarterly Journal of Studies on Alcohol, 1944.

Acute effects of alcohol on the central nervous system.
In: Abridged Lectures of the First (1943) Summer Course on Alcohol Studies at Yale University, pp. 46–48. New Haven: Quarterly Journal of Studies on Alcohol, 1944.

The heredity of the alcoholic.
In: Abridged Lectures of the First (1943) Summer Course on Alcohol Studies at Yale University, pp. 66–68. New Haven: Quarterly Journal of Studies on Alcohol, 1944.

Alcohol research – theoretical and practical.
Publ. Hlth. Nurs., **36**: 223–229, 301, 1944.

Symposium on therapy of alcohol addiction: Introduction.
Quart. J. Stud. Alc., **5**: 185–188, 1944.

Notes on the first half year's experience at the Yale Plan Clinics.
Quart. J. Stud. Alc., **5**: 279–302, 1944.

The Drinker and the Drunkard.
(Lay Supplement No. 10.) New Haven: Journal of Studies on Alcohol, Inc., 1944.

How Alcohol Affects Psychological Behavior.
(Lay Supplement No. 11.) New Haven: Journal of Studies on Alcohol, Inc., 1944.

The Rehabilitation of Inebriates.
(Lay Supplement No. 12.) New Haven: Journal of Studies on Alcohol, Inc., 1944.

Introduction to the curriculum.
In: Alcohol, Science and Society, Lecture 1, pp. 1–12. New Haven: Quarterly Journal of Studies on Alcohol, 1945.

The problems of alcohol.
In: Alcohol, Science and Society, Lecture 2, pp. 13–29. New Haven: Quarterly Journal of Studies on Alcohol, 1945. Reprinted in part as:

Jellinek Jubilee Reprints, No. 2. Quart. J. Stud. Alc., **21**: 187–202, 1960. [CAAAL 9023]

Effects of small amounts of alcohol on psychological functions.
In: Alcohol, Science and Society, Lecture 7, pp. 83–94. New Haven: Quarterly Journal of Studies on Alcohol, 1945.

Heredity of the alcoholic.
In: Alcohol, Science and Society, Lecture 9, pp. 105–114. New Haven: Quarterly Journal of Studies on Alcohol, 1945.

[and Warner, H. S., and McPeek, F. W.,]
Philosophy of the temperance movement; a panel discussion.
In: Alcohol, Science and Society, Lecture 19, pp. 267–286. New Haven: Quarterly Journal of Studies on Alcohol, 1945.

The alcohol problem: its complexities in modern life.
In: Popularizing the Educational Approach to the Problems of Alcohol. [Columbus?]: Ohio Dept. of Education, [1945?].

[and Haggard, H. W.]
Research on alcoholism.
(Correspondence.) J. Amer. Med. Ass., **127**: 1010, 1945.

A specimen of the sixteenth century German drink literature: Obsopoeus' *Art of Drinking*.
(Classics of the Alcohol Literature.)
Quart. J. Stud. Alc., **5**: 647–661, 1945.

A sixteenth century English alewife and her customers: Skelton's "Tunnyng of Elynour Rummyng."
(Classics of the Alcohol Literature.)
Quart. J. Stud. Alc., **6**: 102–110, 1945.

Symposium on problem of alcoholism in postwar planning: Introduction.
Quart. J. Stud. Alc., **6**: 183–187, 1945. [CAAAL 3745]

Alcohol problem dissected: report on the Summer School of Alcohol Studies at Yale University.
Social Action **11** (No. 3): 5–34, 1945. [QJSA **6**: 261, 1945. CAAAL 4192]

Cultural problems analyzed by summer course.
Yale Sci. Mag., **19** (No. 14): 11, 22–24, 1945.

Phases in the Drinking History of Alcoholics: Analysis of a Survey Conducted by the *Grapevine*, Official Organ of Alcoholics Anonymous.
(Memoirs of the Section of Studies on Alcohol, Laboratory of Applied Physiology, Yale University, No. 5.) New Haven: Hillhouse Press, 1946. Also in: Quart. J. Stud. Alc., **7**: 1–88, 1946. [CAAAL 3770]

The ocean cruise of the Viennese: German poem of the thirteenth century.
(Classics of the Alcohol Literature.)
Quart. J. Stud. Alc., **6**: 540–548, 1946.

Montaigne's essay on drunkenness.
(Classics of the Alcohol Literature.)
Quart. J. Stud. Alc., **7**: 297–304, 1946. [CAAAL 3812]

[and Vredevoe, L. E., Mott, J. R., *et al.*]
Informal Chats on Alcohol, Education and Youth. First Annual Conference, Allied Youth of Texas. [No publ., n.p.] (136 pp.), Feb. 1947.

Recent Trends in Alcoholism and in Alcohol Consumption.
New Haven: Hillhouse Press, 1947. Also in: Quart. J. Stud. Alc., **8**: 1–42, 1947. [CAAAL 3898] Reprinted in part as: Jellinek Jubilee Reprints, No. 3: The interpretation of statistics on the consumption of alcohol. Quart. J. Stud. Alc., **21**: 383–393, 1960. Summarized as: Tendences récentes de l'alcoolisme et de la consommation de l'alcool; Trends of alcoholism in the U.S.A., Gegenwärtige Tendenzen des Alkoholismus und des Alkoholverbrauchs in den U.S.A. Int. Rev. Alcsm, No. 4, pp. 180–186, [1948?].

A national problem.
In: You and Alcohol; pp. 1–3. New York: Columbia Broadcasting System, 1947.

What does alcoholism cost?
Health, Mtn. View, **14**: 13, 29–30, Oct. 1947. [QJSA **10**: 365, 1949. CAAAL 5113]

What shall we do about alcoholism?
Vital Speeches ,**13**: 252–253, 1947. [QJSA **8**: 130, 1947. CAAAL 4613]

Dr. Masserman's cats.
Allied Youth, **17** (No. 6): 3, 7, 1948. Reprinted as: Alcohol, Cats and People. New Haven: Yale Center of Alcohol Studies, 1948.

[and Efron, V. and Keller, M.]
Abstract archive of the alcohol literature.
Quart. J. Stud. Alc., **8**: 580–608, 1948. [CAAAL 153]

A review of treatment methods.
In: Proceedings of the First Industrial Conference on Alcoholism, pp. 24–26. Chicago: Industrial Conference on Alcoholism, 1948.

Expert Committee on Mental Health, World Health Organization.
Report of the First Session of the Alcoholism Subcommittee. Annex 1: Estimates of number of alcoholics and rates of alcoholics per 100,000 adult population (20 years and older) for certain countries. Annex 2: Jellinek estimation formula. World Hlth. Org. Techn. Rep. Ser., No. 42, Sept. 1951.

[and Keller, M.]
Rates of alcoholism in the United States of America, 1940–1948.
Quart. J. Stud. Alc., **13**: 49–59, 1952. [CAAAL 5462]

The estimate of the number of alcoholics in the U.S.A. for 1949 in the light of the Sixth Revision of the International Lists of Causes of Death.
Quart. J. Stud. Alc., **13**: 215–218, 1952. [CAAAL 5442]

Phases of alcohol addiction.
Quart. J. Stud. Alc., **13**: 673–684, 1952.
Also as: Expert Committee on Mental Health, Alcoholism Subcommittee, Second Report. Annex 2: The phases of alcohol addiction. World Hlth. Org. Tech. Rep. Ser., No. 48, Aug. 1952. [CAAAL 3219]

Alkoholbruket sasom en folksed.
Alkoholpolitik **15**: 36–40, 1952. Translation: Drinking as a Folkway. (Substudy 2-2 & Y-65.) Toronto: Addiction Research Foundation, 1965.

European Seminar and Lecture Course on Alcoholism; Copenhagen, Denmark, 22 October–3 November 1951; Review of the Proceedings. Geneva: World Health Organization, [1953?]. [QJSA Rev. **16**: 372–373, 1955. CAAAL 6993]

[and Keller, M., and Efron, V.]
Manual of the Classified Abstract Archive of the Alcohol Literature.

New Haven: Quarterly Journal of Studies on Alcohol, 1953. Also in part as: E. M. Jellinek, V. Efron, and M. Keller. The Classified Abstract Archive of the Alcohol Literature: II. The code dictionary. Quart. J. Stud. Alc., **14**: 285–311, 1953. [CAAAL 153]

The Nosological Position of Alcoholism in the Light of Psychiatry.
(Document WHO/APD/ALC/6.) Geneva: World Health Organization, 1953.

Aspectos de la alcoholomania.
Día méd., Buenos Aires, **25**: 861–867, 1953.

[and Keller, M.]
The magnitude of the problem.
(Symposium on Alcoholism, II.) Alcoholism Res., Toronto, **2** (No. 1): 6–11, 1954.

Distribution of alcohol consumption and of calories derived from alcohol in various selected populations.
Proc. Nutr. Soc., **14**: 93–97, 1955. [QJSA **17**: 344–345, 1956. CAAAL 7449]

The "craving" for alcohol,
pp. 35–38. In: E. M. Jellinek, H. Isbell, G. Lundquist, H. M. Tiebout, H. Duchêne, J. Mardones, and L. D. MacLeod.
The "craving" for alcohol: A symposium by members of the WHO Expert Committees on Mental Health and on Alcohol. Quart. J. Stud. Alc., **16**: 34–66, 1955. [CAAAL 7107]

International perspectives of alcoholism; abstract of address at the 6th annual meeting of the World Federation for Mental Health, held in Vienna, August 1953.
Int. J. Alc. Alcsm., **2**: 43, 1957. [QJSA **18**: 690, 1957. CAAAL 7894]

The world and its bottle.
World Hlth., Geneva **10** (No. 4): 4–6, 1957.
Reprinted in part as: An international review of alcoholism programs. In: North American Association of Alcoholism Programs. Selected Papers Presented at the 8th Annual Meeting. Berkeley, Calif., 1957. Reprinted in part as: Cultural differences in the meaning of alcoholism. In: D. J. Pittman and C. R. Snyder, eds. Society, Culture, and Drinking Patterns, pp. 382–388. New York: Wiley, 1962. [QJSA **19**: 528–529, 1958. CAAAL 8174]

The withdrawal syndrome in alcoholism.
Canad. Med. Ass. J., **81**: 536–541, 1959. [QJSA **21**: 520–521, 1960. CAAAL 8893]

Estimating the prevalence of alcoholism: Modified values in the Jellinek formula and an alternative approach.
Quart. J. Stud. Alc., **20**: 261–269, 1959. [CAAAL 8589]

Films about alcohol and alcoholism.
Quart. J. Stud. Alc., **20**: 782, 1959.

[and Seeley, J. R.]
Correlation on a Triangular Universe.
(Substudy 11–1 & J–59.) Toronto: Addiction Research Foundation, 1959.

The Disease Concept of Alcoholism.
New Haven: Hillhouse Press, 1960. Reprinted in part, from chapters II and III, as: Jellinek Jubilee Reprints, No. 4: Social, cultural and economic factors in alcoholism. Quart. J. Stud. Alc., **21**: 565–583, 1960.

Alcoholism, a genus and some of its species.
Canad. Med. Ass. J., **83**: 1341–1345, 1960. [QJSA **23**: 162–163, 1962. CAAAL 9400]

Goals of alcoholism programs.
Progress, Edmonton 2 (No. 1): 3–7, 1960. Reprinted in: Progress, Edmonton 5 (No. 3): 3–7, 1963.

The last word.
Addictions, Toronto 8 (No. 1): 30–32, 1961.

Drinkers and Alcoholics in Ancient Rome.
(Substudy 2–J–61.) Toronto: Addiction Research Foundation, 1961.

Critical review of the week's proceedings.
In: North American Association of Alcoholism Programs. Selected Papers Presented at the 11th Annual Meeting, Banff, Alberta, 1960; pp. 73–78. [Raleigh, N.C.? 1961?]

Government Programs on Alcoholism: A Review of Activities in some Foreign Countries.
Ottawa: Department of National Health and Welfare (Report Series Memorandum No. 6, Mental Health Division), 1963. [QJSA **25**: 785–786, 1964. CAAAL 10511]

[and Keller, M., and Efron, V.]
CAAAL Manual: A Guide to the Use of the Classified Abstract Archive of the Alcohol Literature. New Brunswick: Rutgers Center of Alcohol Studies, 1965.

[Prepared from notes and tape recordings by R. E. Popham and C. Yawney]
The Symbolism of Drinking: A Culture-Historical Approach. (Substudy 3–2 & Y–65.) Toronto: Addiction Research Foundation, 1965.

[R. E. Popham, ed.]
The Distribution of Alcohol Consumption in Relation to the Place of Alcohol Calories in the Total Calorie Balance.
(Substudy 3–J–67.) Toronto: Addiction Research Foundation, 1967.

[*et al.*] [R. E. Popham and C. Yawney, eds.]
Drinking Patterns and Alcohol Problems.
In preparation.

Name Index

listing the contributing authors, as well as all names
cited in the papers either directly or by reference
number

Subject Index